T0319730

NBER Macroeconomics Annual 2015

NBER Macroeconomics Annual 2015

Edited by
Martin Eichenbaum and Jonathan A. Parker

The University of Chicago Press
Chicago and London

NBER Macroeconomics Annual 2015, Number 30

Published annually by The University of Chicago Press.

Standing orders
To place a standing order for this book series, please address your request to The University of Chicago Press, Chicago Distribution Center, Attn. Standing Orders/Customer Service, 11030 S. Langley Avenue, Chicago, IL 60628. Telephone toll free in the U.S. and Canada: 1-800-621-2736; or 1-773-702-7000. Fax toll free in the U.S. and Canada: 1-800-621-8476; or 1-773-702-7212.

Single-copy orders
In the U.K. and Europe: Order from your local bookseller or direct from The University of Chicago Press, c/o John Wiley Ltd. Distribution Center, 1 Oldlands Way, Bognor Regis, West Sussex PO22 9SA, UK. Telephone 01243 779777 or Fax 01243 820250. E-mail: cs-books@wiley.co.uk

In the U.S., Canada, and the rest of the world: Order from your local bookseller or direct from The University of Chicago Press, Chicago Distribution Center, 11030 S. Langley Avenue, Chicago, IL 60628. Telephone toll free in the U.S. and Canada: 1-800-621-2736; or 1-773-702-7000. Fax toll free in the U.S. and Canada: 1-800-621-8476; or 1-773-702-7212.

Special orders
University of Chicago Press books may be purchased at quantity discounts for business or promotional use. For information, please write to Sales Department—Special Sales, The University of Chicago Press, 1427 E. 60th Street, Chicago, IL 60637 USA or telephone 1-773-702-7723.

This book was printed and bound in the United States of America.

ISSN: 0889-3365
ISBN-13: 978-0-226-39560-9 (hc.:alk.paper)
ISBN-13: 978-0-226-39574-6 (e-book)

10 9 8 7 6 5 4 3 2 1

Relation of the Directors to the Work and Publications of the NBER

1. The object of the NBER is to ascertain and present to the economics profession, and to the public more generally, important economic facts and their interpretation in a scientific manner without policy recommendations. The Board of Directors is charged with the responsibility of ensuring that the work of the NBER is carried on in strict conformity with this object.

2. The President shall establish an internal review process to ensure that book manuscripts proposed for publication DO NOT contain policy recommendations. This shall apply both to the proceedings of conferences and to manuscripts by a single author or by one or more co-authors but shall not apply to authors of comments at NBER conferences who are not NBER affiliates.

3. No book manuscript reporting research shall be published by the NBER until the President has sent to each member of the Board a notice that a manuscript is recommended for publication and that in the President's opinion it is suitable for publication in accordance with the above principles of the NBER. Such notification will include a table of contents and an abstract or summary of the manuscript's content, a list of contributors if applicable, and a response form for use by Directors who desire a copy of the manuscript for review. Each manuscript shall contain a summary drawing attention to the nature and treatment of the problem studied and the main conclusions reached.

4. No volume shall be published until forty-five days have elapsed from the above notification of intention to publish it. During this period a copy shall be sent to any Director requesting it, and if any Director objects to publication on the grounds that the manuscript contains policy recommendations, the objection will be presented to the author(s) or editor(s). In case of dispute, all members of the Board shall be notified,

and the President shall appoint an ad hoc committee of the Board to decide the matter; thirty days additional shall be granted for this purpose.

5. The President shall present annually to the Board a report describing the internal manuscript review process, any objections made by Directors before publication or by anyone after publication, any disputes about such matters, and how they were handled.

6. Publications of the NBER issued for informational purposes concerning the work of the Bureau, or issued to inform the public of the activities at the Bureau, including but not limited to the NBER Digest and Reporter, shall be consistent with the object stated in paragraph 1. They shall contain a specific disclaimer noting that they have not passed through the review procedures required in this resolution. The Executive Committee of the Board is charged with the review of all such publications from time to time.

7. NBER working papers and manuscripts distributed on the Bureau's web site are not deemed to be publications for the purpose of this resolution, but they shall be consistent with the object stated in paragraph 1. Working papers shall contain a specific disclaimer noting that they have not passed through the review procedures required in this resolution. The NBER's web site shall contain a similar disclaimer. The President shall establish an internal review process to ensure that the working papers and the web site do not contain policy recommendations, and shall report annually to the Board on this process and any concerns raised in connection with it.

8. Unless otherwise determined by the Board or exempted by the terms of paragraphs 6 and 7, a copy of this resolution shall be printed in each NBER publication as described in paragraph 2 above.

Contents

Editorial

Martin Eichenbaum, *Northwestern University and NBER*
Jonathan A. Parker, *MIT and NBER*

The NBER's Annual Conference on Macroeconomics celebrated its 30th year by bringing together leading scholars to present, discuss, and debate six research papers on central issues in contemporary macroeconomics, as well as to listen to and question Ben Bernanke, former Chairman of the US Federal Reserve, about the recent and future conduct of monetary policy. This conference volume contains the six papers, two written discussions of each paper by leading scholars, and a summary of the debates that followed each paper.

Two of the six papers deal with the development of China's macroeconomy. "Trends and Cycles in China's Macroeconomy" by Chun Chang, Kaiji Chen, Daniel F. Waggoner, and Tao Zha establishes a number of new facts about the Chinese economy by constructing a set of national accounts data for China. The authors characterize the key characteristics of trend growth and business cycles in China. Among other interesting findings, the paper shows that in striking contrast to most of the world, consumption and investment comove negatively in business cycles. The paper interprets these macroeconomic dynamics within a novel model in which financial frictions and credit policy play critical roles. Specifically, the authors argue that the preferential credit policy for promoting heavy industry played a key role in generating the unusual cyclical pattern of consumption and investment. The same policy also played a critical role in explaining the rising investment rate, the declining labor income share, and the growing foreign surplus that characterize the post-1990 Chinese economy.

The second paper on China, "Demystifying the Chinese Housing Boom" by Hanming Fang, Quanlin Gu, Wei Xiong, and Li-An Zhou constructs a new house price index and shows that house prices have grown by 10% a year over the past decade in China. This increase was concentrated in the largest four cities in China, which experienced average annual house price growth of 13% per year. In addition to presenting a range of novel and interesting information about house price appreciation, the paper presents evidence that the house price boom is not driven by lax credit. Mortgage borrowing typically requires a down payment of 30% of the house value. Further, in the vast majority of Chinese cities, rapid house price appreciation has been matched by equally rapid income growth. Only in the very largest cities have house prices risen disproportionately. In the authors' view, house price appreciation is not an obvious source of macroeconomic instability in China.

Our third paper, "External and Public Debt Crises" by Cristina Arellano, Andrew Atkeson, and Mark Wright, starts with a fascinating question: Why, in the case of large and rising public debt are the fiscal and economic outcomes of a Canadian province like Quebec, a US state like California, and a European state like Greece so different? The paper provides theoretical, historical, legal, and quantitative evidence for a deep answer: differences in the ability of governments to raise additional revenue and differences in the ability of governments to interfere in private contracts. This novel answer is a strikingly different explanation than the existing one, in which different outcomes are due to differences in the exposure of the banking sector to government debt and of the government fiscal balance to a banking crisis. And the paper supports its claims nicely, with legal and historical evidence. The novelty of the explanation excited the discussants, and debate at the conference mainly centered on the roles of the "deep structural" factors that the authors emphasize as opposed to deep cultural factors and the more commonly invoked macrofinancial differences.

The fourth paper in this year's volume deals with the active research program that centers on the role of networks in macroeconomic fluctuations. "Networks and the Macroeconomy: An Empirical Exploration" by Daron Acemoglu, Ufuk Akcigit, and William Kerr shows how the network structure of the US economy propagates the effect of gross-output productivity shocks across upstream and downstream sectors. While not implying that previous analysis mismeasures the impact of value-added shocks to aggregate volatility, the paper clarifies and measures the impact of four different secular changes to the US economy. The first two changes impact the demand side of the economy—variation in industry imports from China and changes in federal spending. The latter two changes impact the supply side—productivity shocks and variation in knowledge and ideas coming from foreign patenting. Using industry-level data, the paper argues that network linkages in the economy lead to a severalfold amplification of the effect of these changes on the US economy relative to the initial direct impact on the industries that buy from China, sell to the government, and so forth. The discussions and debate focused on the macroeconomic importance of network effects, clarifying how the model works and when network effects are relevant for macroeconomics and arguing that network analysis may be even more important in economies with sticky prices.

Two final papers investigate the usefulness of surveys of household's beliefs rather than their actual behavior, a relatively new and exciting area of research. First, "Expectations and Investment" by Nicola Gennaioli, Yueran Ma, and Andrei Shleifer, shows that a chief financial officer's expectations of a firm's future earnings growth is highly informative about both the planned and actual future investment of that firm. The power of these survey expectations is much greater than that of traditional measures constructed from implied market beliefs such as q-theory, according to which the ratio of market value to book value predicts future investment. The authors show that the dynamics of survey beliefs about future earning are consistent with CFOs extrapolating the future from past earnings. The paper makes a strong case for using survey expectations in place of rational expectations and for using survey expectation to learn about the expectations formation process, even for experts like CFOs thinking about their own companies. The discussions and comments at the conference largely agreed that the paper presents a convincing case that there is valuable information contained in the data on expectations, and debate focused on the big research question of how best to measure and use this information in modeling economic systems.

The final paper in the volume, "Declining Desire to Work and Downward Trends in Unemployment and Participation" by Regis Barnichon and Andrew Figura, shows that an increasing fraction of prime-age Americans who are not in the labor force—neither employed nor unemployed and looking for work—report no desire to work and that this decline in desire to work accelerated during the second half of the 1990s. The paper argues that welfare reforms in the 1990s moved people who were out of the labor force from welfare programs, which can require job search, to disability programs, which require one to be unable to work. The paper estimates a model of labor force transitions to explain these trends from the changes in the provision of welfare and social insurance. These factors can explain about half of the observed change in labor force participation. Discussion and debate focused on the timing of the changes, their interpretation, and the role of composition of the labor force (relative to the population).

Finally, the authors and the editors would like to take this opportunity to thank Jim Poterba and the National Bureau of Economic Research for their continued support for the NBER Macroeconomics Annual and the associated conference. We would also like to thank the NBER conference staff, particularly Rob Shannon, for his continued excellent organization and support, and Charlie Radin, for his work on the videotaping and publicity for the conference papers. Financial assistance from the National Science Foundation is gratefully acknowledged. Ben Hebert and Arlene Wong were invaluable in preparing the summaries of the discussions. Finally, we are extremely grateful to Helena Fitz-Patrick for her irreplaceable assistance in editing and producing the volume.

Endnote

For acknowledgments, sources of research support, and disclosure of the authors' material financial relationships, if any, please see http://www.nber.org/chapters/c13588.ack.

Abstracts

1 Trends and Cycles in China's Macroeconomy
Chun Chang, Kaiji Chen, Daniel F. Waggoner, and Tao Zha

We make four contributions in this paper. First, we provide a core of macroeconomic time series usable for systematic research on China. Second, we document, through various empirical methods, the robust findings about striking patterns of trend and cycle. Third, we build a theoretical model that accounts for these facts. Fourth, the model's mechanism and assumptions are corroborated by institutional details, disaggregated data, and banking time series, all of which are distinctive Chinese characteristics. We argue that a preferential credit policy for promoting heavy industries accounts for the unusual cyclical patterns, as well as the post-1990s economic transition featured by the persistently rising investment rate, the declining labor income share, and a growing foreign surplus. The departure of our theoretical model from standard ones offers a constructive framework for studying China's modern macroeconomy.

2 Demystifying the Chinese Housing Boom
Hanming Fang, Quanlin Gu, Wei Xiong, and Li-An Zhou

We construct housing price indices for 120 major cities in China in 2003–2013 based on sequential sales of new homes within the same housing developments. By using these indices and detailed information on mortgage borrowers across these cities, we find enormous housing price appreciation during the decade, which was accompanied by equally impressive growth in household income, except in a few first-tier cities. While bottom-income mortgage borrowers endured severe financial burdens by using price-to-income ratios over eight to buy homes, their participation in the housing market remained steady and their mortgage loans were protected by down payments commonly in excess of 35%. As such, the housing market is unlikely to trigger an imminent financial crisis in China, even though it may crash with a sudden stop in the Chinese economy and act as an amplifier of the initial shock.

3   External and Public Debt Crises
Cristina Arellano, Andrew Atkeson, and Mark Wright

The recent debt crises in Europe and the United States feature similar sharp increases in spreads on government debt, but also show important differences. In Europe, the crisis occurred at high government indebtedness levels and had spillovers to the private sector. In the United States, state government indebtedness was low, and the crisis had no spillovers to the private sector. We show theoretically and empirically that these different debt experiences result from the interplay between differences in the ability of governments to interfere in private external debt contracts and differences in the flexibility of state fiscal institutions.

4   Networks and the Macroeconomy: An Empirical Exploration
Daron Acemoglu, Ufuk Akcigit, and William Kerr

The propagation of macroeconomic shocks through input-output and geographic networks can be a powerful driver of macroeconomic fluctuations. We first exposit that in the presence of Cobb-Douglas production functions and consumer preferences, there is a specific pattern of economic transmission whereby demand-side shocks propagate upstream (to input-supplying industries) and supply-side shocks propagate downstream (to customer industries) and that there is a tight relationship between the direct impact of a shock and the magnitudes of the downstream and the upstream indirect effects. We then investigate the short-run propagation of four different types of industry-level shocks: two demand-side ones (the exogenous component of the variation in industry imports from China and changes in federal spending) and two supply-side ones (TFP shocks and variation in knowledge/ideas coming from foreign patenting). In each case, we find substantial propagation of these shocks through the input-output network, with a pattern broadly consistent with theory. Quantitatively, the network-based propagation is larger than the direct effects of the shocks. We also show quantitatively large effects from the geographic network, capturing the fact that the local propagation of a shock to an industry will fall more heavily on other industries that tend to collocate with it across local markets. Our results suggest that the transmission of different types of shocks through economic networks and industry interlinkages could have first-order implications for the macroeconomy.

5 Expectations and Investment
Nicola Gennaioli, Yueran Ma, and Andrei Shleifer

Using microdata from Duke University's quarterly survey of Chief Financial Officers, we show that corporate investment plans as well as actual investment are well explained by CFOs' expectations of earnings growth. The information in expectations data is not subsumed by traditional variables, such as Tobin's q or discount rates. We also show that errors in CFO expectations of earnings growth are predictable from past earnings and other data, pointing to extrapolative structure of expectations and suggesting that expectations may not be rational. This evidence, like earlier findings in finance, points to the usefulness of data on actual expectations for understanding economic behavior.

6 Declining Desire to Work and Downward Trends in Unemployment and Participation
Regis Barnichon and Andrew Figura

This paper argues that a key aspect of the US labor market is the presence of time-varying heterogeneity across nonparticipants. We document a decline in the share of nonparticipants who report wanting to work, and we argue that that decline, which was particularly strong in the second half of the 1990s, is a major aspect of the downward trends in unemployment and participation over the past 20 years. A decline in the share of "want to work" nonparticipants lowers both the participation rate and the unemployment rate, because a nonparticipant who wants to work has (a) a higher probability of entering the labor force (compared to other nonparticipants), and (b) a higher probability of joining unemployment conditional on entering the labor force. We use cross-sectional variation to estimate a model of nonparticipants' propensity to want to work, and we find that changes in the provision of welfare and social insurance, possibly linked to the mid-1990s welfare reforms, explain about 50% of the decline in desire to work among nonparticipants.

1

Trends and Cycles in China's Macroeconomy

Chun Chang, *Shanghai Advanced Institute of Finance, Shanghai Jiao Tong University*
Kaiji Chen, *Emory University and Federal Reserve Bank of Atlanta*
Daniel F. Waggoner, *Federal Reserve Bank of Atlanta*
Tao Zha, *Federal Reserve Bank of Atlanta, Emory University, and NBER*

I. Introduction

Growth has been the hallmark for China. In recent years, however, China's gross domestic product (GDP) growth has slowed down considerably while countercyclical government policy has taken center stage. Never has this change been more true than after the 2008 financial crisis, when the government injected four trillion RMBs into investment to combat the sharp fall of output growth. Issues related to both trend and cycle are now on the minds of policymakers and economists.[1] Yet there is a serious lack of empirical research on (a) the basic facts about the trends and cycles of China's macroeconomy and (b) a theoretical framework that is capable of explaining these facts. This paper serves to fill this important vacuum by tackling both of these issues. The broad goal is to promote, among a wide research community, empirical studies on China's macroeconomy and its government policies.

Over the past two years we have undertaken a task of providing a core of annual and quarterly macroeconomic time series to be as consistent with the definitions of US time series as possible, while at the same time maintaining Chinese data characteristics for understanding China's macroeconomy. We develop an econometric methodology to document China's trend and cyclical patterns. These patterns are carefully cross-verified by studying different frequencies of the data, employing other empirical methods, and delving into disaggregated time series relevant to our paper. We build a theoretical framework to account for the unique patterns of trend and cycle by integrating the disaggregated time series and institutional details with our theoretical model. All three ingredients—data, empirical facts, and theory—constitute a central theme of this paper; none of the ingredients can be understood apart from the whole.

Since March 1996, the government has been actively promoting what is called "heavy industries," which are largely composed of big capital-intensive industries such as telecommunication, energy, and metal products.[2] The other industries, called "light industries," do not receive the same preferential treatment. Our robust empirical findings about China's macroeconomy since the late 1990s consist of two parts. The first concerns trend patterns and the second pertains to cyclical patterns. The key trend facts are:

1. (T1) A simultaneous rise of the investment-to-output ratio (from 26% in 1997 to 36% in 2010) and a fall of the consumption-to-output ratio (from 45% in 1997 to 35% in 2010), as confirmed by figure 1.

2. (T2) A decline of the labor share of income from 53% in 1997 to 47% in 2010.

3. (T3) An increase in the ratio of long-term loans (for financing fixed investment) to short-term loans (for financing working capital) from 0.4 in 1997 to 2.5 in 2010.

4. (T4) A rise in the ratio of capital in heavy industries to capital in light industries from 2.4 in 1997 to 4 in 2010.

5. (T5) An increase in the ratio of total revenues in heavy industries to those in light industries from 1 in 1997 to 2.5 in 2010.

The key cyclical patterns are:

1. (C1) Weak or negative comovement between aggregate investment and consumption, ranging from –0.6 to 0.2 for the sample from the late 1990s on.

2. (C2) Weak or negative comovement between aggregate investment and labor income, ranging from –0.3 to 0.3 for the sample from the late 1990s on.

3. (C3) A negative comovement between long-term loans and short-term loans, around –0.2 for the quarterly sample and –0.4 for the annual sample from the late 1990s on.

To explain both trend and cyclical patterns listed above, we build a theoretical model on Song, Storesletten, and Zilibotti (2011; henceforth, SSZ) but depart from the traditional emphasis on state-owned enterprises (SOEs) versus privately owned enterprises (POEs). Song et al.

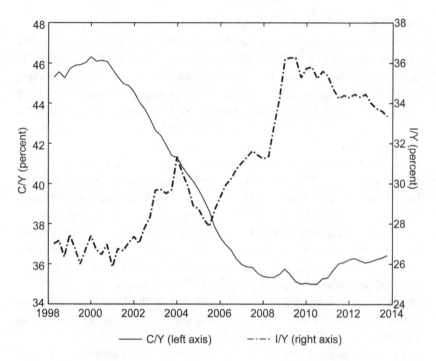

Fig. 1. Trend patterns of household consumption and business investment, estimated from the six-variable regime-switching BVAR model.

construct an economy with heterogeneous firms that differ in both productivity and access to the credit market to explain the observed coexistence of sustained returns to capital and growing foreign surpluses in China in most of the twenty-first century. Their model replicates disinvestment of SOEs in the labor-intensive sector as POEs accumulate capital in the same sector. In this two-sector model, they characterize two transition stages. In the first stage, both SOEs and POEs coexist in the labor-intensive sector, while capital-intensive goods is produced exclusively by SOEs.[3] In the second stage, SOEs disappear from the labor-intensive sector and POEs become the sole producers in that sector. Song et al. present a persuasive story about resource reallocations between SOEs and POEs within the labor-intensive sector and the source of TFP growth since the late 1990s.

Although discussions around SOEs versus POEs have dominated the literature on China, the SOE-POE classification does not help explain the rising investment rate, the decline of labor income share, and the weak or negative cyclical comovement between investment and consumption or between investment and labor income. Since the late 1990s, moreover, the deepening of capital has become the major source of GDP growth in China. To address China's macroeconomic issues in one coherent and tractable framework, we take a different perspective by shifting an emphasis to resource reallocations between the heavy and light sectors. This shift of emphasis is grounded in China's institutional arrangements, which took place in the late 1990s when the Eighth National People's Congress passed a historic long-term plan to adjust the industrial structure for the next 15 years in favor of strengthening heavy industries. The plan was subsequently supported by long-term bank loans giving priority to the heavy sector. As discussed in Sections 5.2 and 8.2.4, heavy industries have been identified as strategically important to China since 1996. Our novel approach is to build a two-sector model with a special emphasis on resource and credit reallocations between the heavy versus light sectors *and* by introducing two new institutional ingredients into our model: a collateral constraint on producers in the heavy sector and a lending friction in the banking sector. We show that with these new ingredients, our model can replicate trend patterns (T1)–(T5) and cyclical patterns (C1)–(C3).

Frictionless neoclassical models rest on certain assumptions that are at odds with the Chinese facts. Models represented by Chang and Hornstein (2013) and Karabarbounis and Neiman (2014) require a fall of the relative price of investment to explain the rise of the investment rate in South Korea or the global decline of labor share across a large number of countries when the elasticity of substitution between capital and labor is greater than one. Evidence in China for such a simultaneous fall of the relative price and the labor income share is weak at best. Frictionless two-sector models of capital deepening à la Acemoglu and Guerrieri (2008) assume that (labor-augmented) total factor productivity (TFP) in the capital-intensive sector grows faster than TFP in the labor-intensive sector when the elasticity of substitution between two sectors is less than one, or that TFP in the capital-intensive sector grows slower than TFP in the labor-intensive sector when the elasticity of substitution between two sectors is greater than one. With this assumption, the investment rate declines over time. For the investment rate to rise and the labor share of income to decline, it must be that the elasticity of substitution between two sectors is greater than one and TFP in the capital-intensive sector grows faster than TFP in the labor-intensive sector. As discussed in section V.B, Chinese evidence is unsupportive of faster TFP growth in the heavy sector. The critical feature of our model is that it *does not rely on any TFP assumption* in explaining the trend patterns of China. What we do rely on is a host of key institutional details that are critical for understanding China's macroeconomy. This paper weaves these institutional details together to formulate our theoretical framework.

Our counterfactual economy shows that the key to generating the trend patterns is the presence of collateral constraint in the heavy sector. With the collateral constraint, the borrowing capacity of heavy firms grows with their net worth. Accordingly, the demand for capital from the heavy sector accelerates during the transition, which leads to an increase in the value share of the heavy sector in aggregate output. This structural change contributes to both an increasing aggregate investment rate and a declining labor-income share along the transition path. By contrast, in the absence of this financial friction as in SSZ, the economy tends to predict a *declining* (aggregate) investment rate during the transition. This result occurs because, under the aggregate production function with the constant elasticity of substitution (CES), the demand for capital from producers in the heavy sector is proportional to output produced by the light sector. As output growth in the light sector slows down over time due to the diminishing returns to capital, the heavy sector experiences a *declining* investment rate. Moreover, the investment rate in the light sector tends to decline during the transition due to either the resource reallocation from SOEs to POEs (in the first stage of transition, which we abstract from our model) or decreasing returns to capital when this kind of reallocation is completed.[4]

The cyclical patterns uncovered in this paper, an issue silent in SSZ, constitute an integral part of our model mechanism. The key to accounting for these important cyclical patterns is the presence of bank lending frictions in our model, which interacts with the aforementioned collateral constraint to deliver a negative externality on the light sector from credit injections into the heavy sector. In response to the government's credit injection, the expansion of credit demand by the heavy sector tends to crowd out the light sector's demand for working capital loans by pushing up the loan rate for working capital. In an economy absent such lending frictions, a credit injection into the heavy sector tends to push up the wage income and therefore household consumption due to the imperfect substitutability between output produced from the heavy sector and output produced by the light sector, a result that is again at odds with what we observe in China (fact [C2]).[5] Specifically, a shock to credit expansion generates the following counterfactual predictions:

- A strong, positive comovement between investment and consumption.
- A strong, positive comovement between investment and labor income.
- A strong, positive comovement between investment loans and working-capital loans.

Standard business-cycle models have a number of shocks that are potentially capable of generating a negative comovement between aggregate investment and household consumption through the negative effect on consumption of rising interest rates in response to demand for investment. Primary examples are preference shocks, investment-specific technology shocks, and credit shocks. In those models, however, an increase of investment raises household income, contradictory to fact (C2). What is most important: most of these standard models are silent about the negative relationships between short-term and long-term loans (fact [C3]) and *are not designed* to address many of the trend facts (T1)–(T5). We view our model's capability of reproducing the cyclical patterns of China's macroeconomy as a further support of our mechanism for the aforementioned trend facts.

More generally, our theory contributes to the emerging literature on the role of financial-market imperfections in economic development (Buera and Shin 2013; Moll 2014). It is a long-standing puzzle from the neoclassical perspective that the investment rate in emerging economies increases over time, since the standard neoclassical model predicts that the investment rate falls along the transition and quickly converges to the steady state due to decreasing returns to capital. The typical explanation in this literature is that in an underdeveloped financial market, productive entrepreneurs, thanks to binding collateral constraints and thus high returns to capital, have a higher saving rate, while unproductive but rich entrepreneurs are financially unconstrained and have a low saving rate. Aggregate investment rate increases during the transition, when productive entrepreneurs account for a larger share of wealth and income in the aggregate economy over time through resource reallocations.

Our model provides a different explanation for an increase in aggregate investment for China. In our model, a persistent increase in aggregate investment is mainly caused by an increasing share of revenues generated by heavy industries in aggregate output as those firms become larger with their expanded borrowing capacity. Such an explanation is consistent with the heavy industrialization experienced in China (facts [T4] and T5). We view our model mechanism as a useful complement to the larger literature.[6]

The rest of the paper is organized as follows. Section II reviews how we construct the annual and quarterly data relevant to this paper. Section III develops an econometric method to uncover the key facts of trend and cycle. Section IV delivers a robustness analysis of these facts using different empirical approaches. Section V provides China's institutional details relevant to this paper. In light of these facts, we build a theoretical framework in Section VI and characterize the equilibrium in Section VII. In Section VIII we discuss the quantitative results from our model, corroborate the model's key assumptions and mechanism with further empirical evidence, and conduct a number of counterfactual exercises to highlight the model's mechanism. We offer some concluding remarks in Section IX. A data appendix is available at http://www .nber.org/data-appendix/c13592.

II. Construction of Macroeconomic Time Series

In this section we discuss how we construct a standard set of annual and quarterly macroeconomic time series usable for this study as well as for future studies on China's macroeconomy.

A. Brief Literature Review and Data Sources

There are earlier works on the Chinese economy, some taking an econometric approach and others employing historical perspectives or narrative approaches (Chow 2011; Lin 2013; Fernald, Spiegel, and Swanson 2013). He, Chong, and Shi (2009) apply standard business-cycle models to the linearly detrended 1978–2006 annual data for conducting business accounting exercises and conclude that productivity best explains the behavior of China's macroeconomic variables. Chakraborty and Otsu (2013) apply a similar model to the linearly detrended 1990–2009 annual data and conclude that investment wedges were increasingly important for China's business cycles late in the first decade of the twenty-first century. But the questions of what explains the dynamics of investment wedges and what are the key cyclical patterns for China's economy are left unanswered. Shi (2009) finds that capital deepening is the major driving force of high investment rates after 2000, consistent with our own evidence presented in Section V.C.

Most of the extensive empirical studies on China, however, take a microeconomic perspective (Hsieh and Klenow 2009; Brandt and Zhu 2010; Yu and Zhu 2013), mainly because there are a variety of survey data that either are publicly available or can be purchased. Annual Surveys of Rural and Urban Households conducted by China's National Bureau of Statistics (NBS) provide detailed information about income and expenditures of thousands of households from at least 1981 through the present time (Fang, Wailes, and Cramer 1998). The survey data on manufacturing firms for studying firms' TFPs come from the Annual Surveys of Industrial Enterprises from 1998 to 2007 conducted by the NBS, which is a census of all nonstate firms with more than five million RMB in revenue as well as all state-owned firms (Hsieh and Klenow 2009; Lu, forthcoming). The longitudinal data from China's Health and Nutrition Surveys provide the distribution of labor incomes over 4,400 households (26,000 individuals) over several years starting in 1989 (Yu and Zhu 2013). There have been recent efforts in constructing more microdata about China. For example, China's Household Finance Survey, conducted by Southwestern University of Finance and Economics, is a survey on 8,438 households (29,324 individuals) in 2011 and 28,141 households (more than 99,000 individuals) in 2013, with a special focus on households' balance sheets and their demographic and labor-market characteristics (Gan 2014).

Macroeconomic time series are based on two databases: the CEIC (China Economic Information Center, now belonging to the Euromoney Institutional Investor Company) database—one of the most comprehensive macroeconomic data sources for China—and the WIND database (the data information system created by the Shanghai-based company called WIND Co. Ltd., the Chinese version of Bloomberg). The major sources of these two databases are the NBS and the People's Bank of China (PBC). For the NBS data, in particular, we consult *China Industrial Economy Statistical Yearbooks* (comprising 20 volumes) and *China Labor Statistical Yearbooks* (comprising 21 volumes).

B. Construction

This paper is not about the quality of publicly available data sources in China. The pros and cons associated with such quality have been extensively discussed in, for example, Holz (2013), Fernald, Malkin, and Spiegel (2013), and Nakamura, Steinsson, and Liu (2014). Notwithstanding possible measurement errors of GDP, as well as other macroeconomic variables, one should *not* abandon the series of GDP in favor of other less comprehensive series, no matter how "accurate" one would claim those alternatives are. After all, the series of GDP is what researchers and policy analysts would pay most attention to when they need to gauge China's aggregate activity.

The most urgent data problem, in our view, is the absence of a standard set of annual and quarterly macroeconomic time series comparable to those commonly used in the macroeconomic literature on Western economies. Our goal is to provide as accurately as possible the series of GDP and other key variables, make them publicly available, and use such a data set as a starting point for promoting both improvement and transparency of China's core macroeconomic series usable for macroeconomic analysis.

Construction of the annual and quarterly time series poses an extremely challenging task because many key macroeconomic series are either unavailable or difficult to obtain. We utilize both annual and quarterly macroeconomic data that are available and interpolate or estimate those that are publicly unavailable.[7] Our construction method emphasizes the consistency across data frequencies and serves as a foundation for improvements in future research.[8]

The difficulty of constructing a standard set of time series lies in several dimensions. The NBS—probably the most authoritative source of macroeconomic data—reports only percentage changes of certain key macroeconomic variables such as real GDP. Many variables, such as investment and consumption, do not even have quarterly data that are publicly available. The Yearbooks published by the NBS have only annual data by the expenditure approach (with annual revisions for the most recent data and benchmark revisions every five years for historical data—benchmark revisions are based on censuses conducted by the NBS). Even for the annual data, the breakdown of the nominal GDP by expenditure is incomplete. The Yearbooks publish the GDP subcomponents such as household consumption, government consumption, inventory changes, gross fixed capital formation (total fixed investment), and net exports. But other categories, such as investment in the state-owned sector and investment in the nonstate-owned sector, are unavailable. These categories are estimated using the detailed breakdown of fixed-asset investment across different data frequencies.

Using the valued-added approach, the NBS publishes some quarterly or monthly series whose definitions are different from the same series by expenditure. For the value-added approach, moreover, the subcomponents of GDP do not add up to the total value of GDP. Many series on quarterly frequency are not available for the early 1990s. For that period, we extrapolate these series. Few macroeconomic time series are seasonally adjusted by the NBS or the PBC. We seasonally adjust all quarterly time series.

The most challenging part of our task is to keep as much consistency of our constructed data as possible by cross-checking different approaches, different data sources, and different data frequencies. One revealing example is construction of the quarterly real GDP series. Based on the value-added approach, the NBS publishes year-over-year changes of real GDP in two forms: a year-to-date (YTD) change and a quarter-to-date (QTD) change. Let t be the first quarter of the base year. The YTD changes for the four quarters within the base year are y_t / y_{t-4} (Q1), $(y_{t+1} + Y_t) / (y_{t-3} + y_{t-4})$ (Q2), $(y_{t+2} + y_{t+1} + Y_t) / (y_{t-2} + y_{t-3} + y_{t-4})$ (Q3), and $(y_{t+3} + y_{t+2} + y_{t+1} + Y_t) / (y_{t-1} + y_{t-2} + y_{t-3} + y_{t-4})$ (Q4). The QTD changes for the same four quarters are y_t / y_{t-4} (Q1), y_{t+1} / y_{t-3} (Q2), y_{t+2} / y_{t-2} (Q3), and y_{t+3} / y_{t-1} (Q4). The published data on QTD changes are available from 1999Q4 on, while the data on YTD changes begin on 1991Q4. Using the time series of both YTD and QTD changes, we are able to construct the level series of quarterly real GDP. There are discrepancies between the real GDP series based on the QTD-change data and the same series based on the YTD-change data. We infer from our numerous communications with the NBS that the discrepancies are likely due to human errors when calculating QTD and YTD changes. The real GDP series is so constructed that the difference between our implied QTD and YTD changes and NSB's reported QTD and YTD changes is minimized. The quarterly real GDP series is also constructed by the CEIC, the Haver Analytics, and the Federal Reserve Board. In comparison to these sources, the method proposed by Higgins and Zha (2015) keeps to the minimal the deviation of the annual real GDP series aggregated by the constructed quarterly real GDP series from the same annual series published by the NBS.

Another example is the monthly series of retail sales of consumer goods, which has been commonly used in the literature as a substitute for household consumption. Constructing the annual and quarterly series from this monthly series would be a mistake because the monthly series covers only large retail establishments with annual sales above five million RMB or with more than 60 employees at the end of the year.[9] The annual series published by the NBS, however, includes smaller retail establishments and thus has a broader and better coverage than the monthly series. A sensible approach is to use the annual series (CEIC ticker CHFB) to interpolate the quarterly series using the monthly series (CEIC ticker CHBA) as an interpolater.

Many series such as M2 and bank loans are published in two forms: year-to-date change and level itself. In our communication with the People's Bank of China, we have learned that when the two forms do not match, it is the year-to-date change that is supposed to be more accurate, especially in early history. We thus adjust the affected series accordingly. Cross-checking various data sources to ensure accuracy is part of our data construction process. For example, the monthly bank loan (outstanding) series from the CEIC exhibits wild month-to-month fluctuations (more than 10%) in certain years (e.g., the first three months in 1999). These unusually large fluctuations may be due to reporting errors, as they are absent in the same series from the WIND Database (arguably more reliable for financial data). Detecting unreasonable outliers in the data is another important dimension of our construction. One prominent example is the extremely low value of fixed-asset investment in 1994Q4. If this reported low value were accurate, we would expect the growth rate of gross fixed capital formation in 1995 to be unusually strong as the 1995Q4 value would be unusually strong relative to the 1994Q4 value. But this is not the case. Growth of gross fixed capital formation in 1995 is more in line with growth of fixed-asset investment in capital construction and innovation than does growth of total fixed-asset investment. Accordingly, we adjust the extreme value of total fixed-asset investment in 1994Q4. The quarterly series of fixed-asset investment is used as one of the interpolators for interpolating the quarterly series of gross fixed-asset capital formation (Higgins and Zha 2015).

C. Core Time Series

We report several key variables that are relevant to this paper. Table 1 reports a long history of GDP by expenditure, household consumption, gross capital formation (gross investment including changes of inventories), government consumption, and net exports. Since 1980, the consumption rate (the ratio of household consumption to GDP) has been trending down and the investment rate (the ratio of gross capital formation to GDP) has been trending up, while the share of government consumption in GDP has been relatively stable. China has undergone many dramatic phases. Table 2 displays major economic reforms from December 1978 onward. Economic reforms toward a market economy were not introduced until December 1978; the period prior to 1979 belongs to Mao's premarket command economy and is not a subject of this paper. The phase between 1980 and the late 1990s is marked by a gradual transition to the implementation of privatiza-

Table 1
Annual GDP Series and Its Subcomponents

Year	GDP	C	I	Govt.	Nex	C	I	Govt.	Nex
			Billion RMB				Percent of GDP		
1980	459.3	233.1	160.0	67.7	−1.5	50.8	34.8	14.7	−0.3
1981	500.9	262.8	163.0	73.4	1.7	52.5	32.5	14.6	0.3
1982	559.0	290.3	178.4	81.2	9.1	51.9	31.9	14.5	1.6
1983	621.6	323.1	203.9	89.5	5.1	52.0	32.8	14.4	0.8
1984	736.3	374.2	251.5	110.4	0.1	50.8	34.2	15.0	0.0
1985	907.7	468.7	345.8	129.9	−36.7	51.6	38.1	14.3	−4.0
1986	1,050.8	530.2	394.2	152.0	−25.5	50.5	37.5	14.5	−2.4
1987	1,227.7	612.6	446.2	167.8	1.1	49.9	36.3	13.7	0.1
1988	1,538.9	786.8	570.0	197.1	−15.1	51.1	37.0	12.8	−1.0
1989	1,731.1	881.3	633.3	235.2	−18.6	50.9	36.6	13.6	−1.1
1990	1,934.8	945.1	674.7	264.0	51.0	48.8	34.9	13.6	2.6
1991	2,257.7	1,073.1	786.8	336.1	61.8	47.5	34.8	14.9	2.7
1992	2,756.5	1,300.0	1,008.6	420.3	27.6	47.2	36.6	15.2	1.0
1993	3,693.8	1,641.2	1,571.8	548.8	−68.0	44.4	42.6	14.9	−1.8
1994	5,021.7	2,184.4	2,034.1	739.8	63.4	43.5	40.5	14.7	1.3
1995	6,321.7	2,837.0	2,547.0	837.9	99.9	44.9	40.3	13.3	1.6
1996	7,416.4	3,395.6	2,878.5	996.4	145.9	45.8	38.8	13.4	2.0
1997	8,165.9	3,692.2	2,996.8	1,121.9	355.0	45.2	36.7	13.7	4.3
1988	8,653.2	3,922.9	3,131.4	1,235.9	362.9	45.3	36.2	14.3	4.2
1999	9,112.5	4,192.0	3,295.2	1,371.7	253.7	46.0	36.2	15.1	2.8
2000	9,874.9	4,585.5	3,484.3	1,566.1	239.0	46.4	35.3	15.9	2.4
2001	10,902.8	4,943.6	3,976.9	1,749.8	232.5	45.3	36.5	16.0	2.1
2002	12,047.6	5,305.7	4,556.5	1,876.0	309.4	44.0	37.8	15.6	2.6
2003	13,661.3	5,765.0	5,596.3	2,003.6	296.5	42.2	41.0	14.7	2.2
2004	16,095.7	6521.8	6,916.8	2,233.4	423.6	40.5	43.0	13.9	2.6
2005	18,742.3	7,295.9	7,785.7	2,639.9	1,020.9	38.9	41.5	14.1	5.4
2006	22,271.3	8,257.5	9,295.4	3,052.8	1,665.5	37.1	41.7	13.7	7.5
2007	26,659.9	9,633.2	11,094.3	3,590.0	2,342.3	36.1	41.6	13.5	8.8
2008	31,597.5	11,167.0	13,832.5	4,175.2	2,422.7	35.3	43.8	13.2	7.7
2009	34,877.5	12,358.5	16,446.3	4,569.0	1,503.7	35.4	47.2	13.1	4.3
2010	40,281.6	14,075.9	19,360.4	5,335.6	1,509.8	34.9	48.1	13.2	3.7
2011	47,261.9	16,895.7	22,834.4	6,315.5	1,216.3	35.7	48.3	13.4	2.6
2012	52,939.9	19,058.5	25,277.3	7,140.9	1,463.2	36.0	47.7	13.5	2.8
2013	58,667.3	21,218.8	28,035.6	7,997.8	1,415.1	36.2	47.8	13.6	2.4

Note: "C" stands for household consumption, "I" for gross capital formation (aggregate investment), "Govt" for government consumption, and "Nex" for net exports.

tion of state-owned firms. Due to the lack of detailed time series prior to 1995, the focus of this paper is on the period since the late 1990s.

As indicated in table 1, net exports as a percent of GDP have become important since the late 1990s. Detailed breakdowns of GDP, as well as other relevant time series, become available from 1995 on, as reported in tables 3 and 4. From these tables one can see that the rapid increase of

Table 2
Chronology of Structural Switches

Dates	Major structural changes
December 1978	Introduction of economic reforms
Early 1990s	Price controls and rationing
Beginning of 1992	Advancing of Deng Xiaoping's economic reforms
January 1994	Ending of the two-tiered foreign exchange system
1994	Major tax reforms and devaluation of RMB
1995–1996	Phased out price controls and rationing
1995	Enacted People's Bank of China law and other banking laws with decentralization of the banking system
March 1996	*Strategic plan to develop infrastructure and other heavy industries*
July 1997	Asian financial crisis started in Thailand
November 1997	Beginning of the privatization
November 2001	Joined the WTO and trade liberalization
July 2005	Ending of the explicit peg to the USD
September 2008	US and world-wide financial crisis
2009–2010	Fiscal stimulus of 4 trillion RMB investment

Table 3
Annual GDP Series and Further Breakdowns (billion RMB)

Year	GDP	C	SOE	POE	HH I	Govt. C	Nex	Invty
1995	6,321.7	2,837.0	926.8	810.7	351.0	837.9	99.9	458.5
1996	7,416.4	3,395.6	1,016.6	963.4	424.8	996.4	145.9	473.7
1997	8,165.9	3,692.2	1,090.9	1,032.8	472.8	1,121.9	355.0	400.3
1998	8,653.2	3,922.9	1,215.7	1,086.8	554.4	1,235.9	362.9	274.5
1999	9,112.5	4,192.0	1,263.5	1,156.5	632.7	1,371.7	253.7	242.4
2000	9,874.9	4,585.5	1,289.2	1,345.9	749.3	1,566.1	239.0	99.8
2001	10,902.8	4,943.6	1,324.2	1,549.7	901.5	1,749.8	232.5	201.5
2002	12,047.6	5,305.7	1,409.3	1,927.4	1,026.4	1,876.0	309.4	193.3
2003	13,661.3	5,765.0	1,525.6	2,504.5	1,318.9	2,003.6	296.5	247.2
2004	16,095.7	6,521.8	1,654.4	3,155.2	1,702.1	2,233.4	423.6	405.1
2005	18,742.3	7,295.9	1,695.7	3,577.1	2,150.5	2,639.9	1,020.9	362.4
2006	22,271.3	8,257.5	2,055.1	4,728.6	2,011.7	3,052.8	1,665.5	500.0
2007	26,659.9	9,633.2	2,327.6	5,839.3	2,228.0	3,590.0	2,342.3	699.5
2008	31,597.5	11,167.0	2,928.3	7,388.3	2,491.8	4,175.2	2,422.7	1,024.1
2009	34,877.5	12,358.5	3,892.9	8,571.1	3,204.0	4,569.0	1,503.7	778.3
2010	40,281.6	14,075.9	4,388.6	10,156.8	3,816.1	5,335.6	1,509.8	998.9
2011	47,261.9	16,895.7	4,323.5	11,855.9	5,388.7	6,315.5	1,216.3	1,266.2
2012	52,939.9	19,058.5	4,708.6	13,460.3	6,006.8	7,140.9	1,463.2	1,101.6
2013	58,667.3	21,218.8	4,991.9	15,111.7	6,803.3	7,997.8	1,415.1	1,128.1

Note: "C" stands for household consumption, "SOE" for the SOE portion of gross fixed capital formation, "POE" for the POE portion of gross fixed capital formation, "HH I" for household investment, "Govt C" for government consumption, "Nex" for net exports, and "Invty" for changes of inventories.

Table 4
Detailed GDP Subcomponents as Percent of GDP

Year	C	SOE	POE	HH I	Govt. C	Nex	Invty
1995	44.9	14.7	12.8	5.6	13.3	1.6	7.3
1996	45.8	13.7	13.0	5.7	13.4	2.0	6.4
1997	45.2	13.4	12.6	5.8	13.7	4.3	4.9
1998	45.3	14.0	12.6	6.4	14.3	4.2	3.2
1999	46.0	13.9	12.7	6.9	15.1	2.8	2.7
2000	46.4	13.1	13.6	7.6	15.9	2.4	1.0
2001	45.3	12.1	14.2	8.3	16.0	2.1	1.8
2002	44.0	11.7	16.0	8.5	15.6	2.6	1.6
2003	42.2	11.2	18.3	9.7	14.7	2.2	1.8
2004	40.5	10.3	19.6	10.6	13.9	2.6	2.5
2005	38.9	9.0	19.1	11.5	14.1	5.4	1.9
2006	37.1	9.2	21.2	9.0	13.7	7.5	2.2
2007	36.1	8.7	21.9	8.4	13.5	8.8	2.6
2008	35.3	9.3	23.4	7.9	13.2	7.7	3.2
2009	35.4	11.2	24.6	9.2	13.1	4.3	2.2
2010	34.9	10.9	25.2	9.5	13.2	3.7	2.5
2011	35.7	9.1	25.1	11.4	13.4	2.6	2.7
2012	36.0	8.9	25.4	11.3	13.5	2.8	2.1
2013	36.2	8.5	25.8	11.6	13.6	2.4	1.9

Note: "C" stands for household consumption, "SOE" for the SOE portion of gross fixed capital formation, "POE" for the POE portion of gross fixed capital formation, "HH I" for household investment, "Govt C" for government consumption, "Nex" for net exports, and "Invty" for changes of inventories.

fixed investment (gross fixed capital formation) is driven by fixed investment of privately owned firms, while fixed investment of state-owned firms as a share of GDP has trended downward steadily. Net exports as a share of GDP reached its peak in 2007 before it gradually descended. Household investment as a share of GDP reached its peak in 2005 and has since hovered around the peak level. Changes of inventories as a share of GDP have fluctuated around a low value since 1997.

Figure 2 displays the annual growth rate of real GDP, the annual change of the GDP deflator (inflation), consumption, gross fixed capital formation (total fixed investment), retail sales of consumer goods, and fixed-asset investment as a percent of GDP. The two measures of real GDP, by expenditure and by value added, have similar growth rates over the time span since 1980. After the economic reforms were introduced in December of 1978, China's growth has been remarkable despite its considerable fluctuations accompanied by the large rise and fall of inflation in the early 1990s. Rapid growth is supported by the steady decline of household consumption and the steady rise of gross

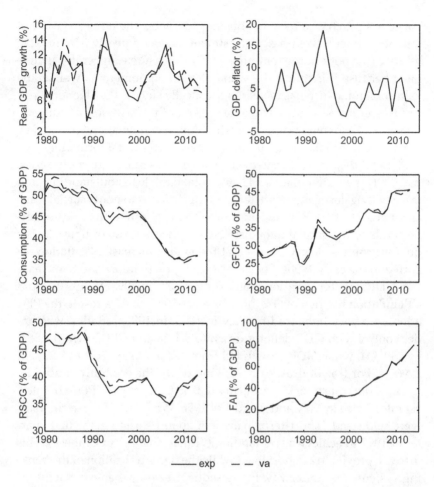

Fig. 2.   Time-series history of trends and cycles in China's macroeconomy: annual data
Note: "Consumption" stands for household consumption, "GFCF" stands for gross fixed capital formation, "RSCG" stands for the retail sales of consumer goods, and "FAI" stands for fixed-asset investment. The legend "exp" means that GDP is measured by expenditure and "va" means that GDP is measured by value added.

fixed capital formation as a percent of GDP (the middle row of figure 2). Consumption as a share of GDP is now below 40% while total fixed investment is at 45% of GDP, prompting the question of how sustainable China's high growth will be in the future. The commonly used measure of consumption, retail sales of consumer goods, shows the same low share of GDP (around 40% by 2012), although this measure includes consumption goods purchased by the government and possibly durable goods purchased by small business owners. The other measure of total investment, fixed-asset investment, takes up nearly 80% of GDP by 2012 (the bottom row of figure 2). This measure exaggerates investment because it includes the value of used equipment as well as the value of land, which has increased drastically since 2000.[10] Nonetheless, fixed-asset investment is available on a monthly basis and its subcomponent "investment in capital construction and innovation" plays a key role in the interpolation of quarterly gross fixed capital formation.

Figure 3 displays (a) year-over-year changes of the quarterly series: real GDP, the GDP deflator, M2, and total bank loans outstanding, and (b) new long-term and short-term quarterly loans to nonfinancial firms as a percent of GDP by expenditure. The first row of this figure corresponds to the annual data displayed in the first row of figure 2. The quarterly series clearly shows that the largest increase of inflation occurred in the early 1990s. Fueled by rapid growth in M2 and bank leading, GDP deflator inflation reached over 20% in 1993Q4–1994Q3 and CPI inflation reached over 20% in 1994Q1–1995Q1. As a result, the PBC adopted a very tight credit policy in 1995. In 1996, inflation was under control with GDP deflator down to 5.45% and CPI down to 6.88% by 1996Q4, while GDP growth fell from 17.80% in 1993Q2 to 9.22% in 1996Q4. For fear of drastically slowing down the economy caused by rising counterparty risks ("Sanjiao Zhai" in Chinese), the PBC cut interest rates twice in May and August of 1996. While new long-term loans were held steady, short-term loans shot up in 1996 and in the first quarter of 1997 to achieve a soft landing ("Ruan Zhaolu" in Chinese). This increase proved to be short lived while the decentralization of the banking system was underway. In subsequent years, whenever medium- and long-term loans increased sharply, short-term loans tended to decline. Another sharp spike of short-term loans (most of which was in the form of bill financing) took place in 2009Q1 right after the 2008 financial crisis. This sharp rise, however, lasted for only one quarter and was followed by sharp reversals for the rest of the year. By contrast, a large increase in medium- and long-term loans lasted for two years after 2008 as part of the government's two-year fiscal stimulus plan. Clearly, long-term and short-term loans tend *not* to move together.

III. Econometric Evidence

In this section we uncover the key facts about trends and cycles. Cyclical facts are as important as trend facts because they help discipline the

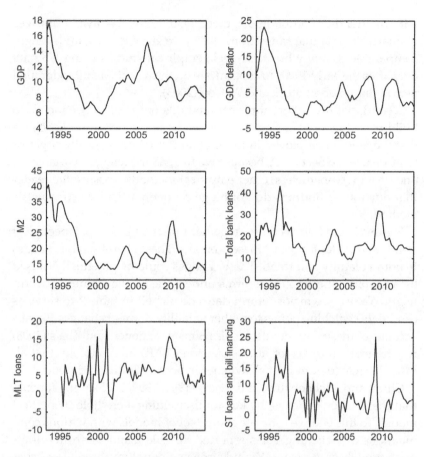

Fig. 3. The top first two rows: year-over-year growth rates (%) of key quarterly time series; the bottom row: quarterly variables as a percent of GDP.

Note: Total bank loans are deflated by the implicit GDP deflator. "MLT loans" stands for medium- and long-term bank loans to nonfinancial firms and "ST loans and bill financing" stands for short-term bank loans and bill financing to nonfinancial firms.

model with stochastic shocks and serve as an identification mechanism to distinguish between theoretical models. To be sure, separating cyclical behavior from trend behavior is inherently a daunting task, especially when the time series are relatively short. We do not view it as an option to abandon this enterprise. Rather, we take a two-pronged approach to safeguard our findings. First, we follow King et al. (1991) and develop a Bayesian reduced-rank time-series method to separate trend and cycle components. The trend component is consistent with the trend definition in our theoretical model. We avail ourselves of quarterly data that range from 1997Q1 to 2013Q4,[11] a sample length comparable to many business-cycle empirical studies using US data only after the early 1990s to concentrate on the recent Great Moderation period discussed in Stock and Watson (2003).

Second, we use other empirical methods outlined in Section IV to build robustness of the findings uncovered in this section. We believe that the method employed in this section is methodologically superior to those used in Section IV because we treat all the relevant variables in one system. Nonetheless, other empirical methods reassure the reader that our robust findings do not hinge on one particular econometric method.

Figures 2 and 3 in Section II together present a broad perspective of trends and cycles for the Chinese economy. These charts exhibit changes in both volatility and trend. These changes could be potentially caused by a number of economic reforms undergone by the Chinese government. We use the major reform dates displayed in table 2 to serve as candidate switching points for either volatility or trend changes. To take account of these date points, we use Sims, Waggoner, and Zha's (2008) regime-switching vector autoregression (VAR) methodology that allows discrete (deterministic) switches in both volatility and trend.

Christiano, Eichenbaum, and Evans (1996, 1999, 2005) argue forcibly that the VAR evidence is the key to disciplining a credible theoretical model. To this end we estimate a large set of models with various combinations of switching dates reported in table 2 and perform a thorough model comparison. We find strong evidence for discrete switches in volatility, but not for any discrete switches in trend. But the steady decline of consumption and the steady rise of investment shown in figure 2 indicate that our VAR model should take into account a possible continuous drift in trend. The model presented below is designed for this purpose.

A.   Econometric Framework

Let Y_t be an $n \times 1$ vector of (level) variables, p the lag length, and T the sample size. The multivariate dynamic model has the following primitive form:

$$A_0 y_t = a_t + \sum_{\ell=1}^{p} A_\ell y_{t-\ell} + D_{s_t} \varepsilon_t, \tag{1}$$

where s_t, taking a discrete value, is a composite index for regime switches in volatility, $\mathcal{D}_{s_t}$ is an $n \times n$ diagonal matrix, and ε_t is an $n \times 1$ vector of independent shocks with the standard normal distribution. By "composite" we mean that the regime-switching index may encode distinct Markov processes for different parameters (Sims and Zha 2006; Sims et al. 2008) or deterministic discrete jumps according to different dates displayed in table 2.

The previous literature on Markov-switching VARs, such as Sims et al. (2008), focuses on business cycles around the trend that is constant across time. Chinese macroeconomic data have a distinctively different characteristic: cyclical variations coexist with trend drifts as shown in figure 2. The time-varying intercept vector a_t, monotone and bounded in t for each element, captures a continuous trend drift. In contrast to the HP filter that deals with each variable in isolation, our methodology is designed to decompose the data into cycles and trends in one multivariate framework. Specifically, unit roots and cointegration are imposed on system (1). These restrictions are made explicit in the error-correction representation as follows

$$F_0 \Delta y_t = c_t + \mathcal{R} y_{t-1} + \sum_{\ell=1}^{p-1} F_\ell \Delta y_{t-\ell} + \mathcal{D}_{s_t} \varepsilon_t, \tag{2}$$

where $\mathcal{R}$ is an $n \times n$ matrix of reduced rank such that $rank(\mathcal{R}) = r$ with $r < n$, implying that there are $n - r$ unit roots and at most r cointegration vectors (i.e., the number of cointegration relationships and the number of stationary relationships sum to r). Long-run relationships are imposed in, for example, Hansen, Heaton, and Li (2008) who measure a long-run risk for the valuation of cash flows exposed to fluctuations in macroeconomic growth. The Bayesian framework developed here helps find the posterior peak by simulating Monte Carlo Markov Chain (MCMC) draws of model parameters.

The relation between (1) and (2) is

$$A_0 = F_0, \ A_1 = \mathcal{R} + F_1 + F_0, \ A_\ell = F_\ell - F_{\ell-1}(\ell = 2, \dots, p - 1),$$

$$A_p = -F_{p-1}, \ c_t = a_t.$$

We consider the following three functional forms of $c_{t,j}$, the jth component of c_t, in a descending order of importance.

- We specify the four-parameter process as

$$c_{t,j} = c_j + (d_j - c_j)(\alpha_j(t - \tau_j) + 1)e^{-\alpha_j(t-\tau_j)},$$

where $\alpha_j > 0$ for $j = 1, \ldots, n$. c_j is the limiting value of $c_{t,j}$ as t increases and d_j is the value of $c_{t,j}$ when $t = \tau_j$. Furthermore, if $d_j < c_j$, then d_j is the minimum value of $c_{t,j}$ and if $d_j > c_j$, then d_j is the maximum value of $c_{t,j}$. The parameter α_j controls how quickly $c_{t,j}$ converges to its limiting value. Our setup is flexible enough for researchers to entertain further restrictions of the form $\alpha_j = \alpha, c_j = c, d_j = d$, or $\tau_j = \tau$ for all or some of j's.

- $c_t = c_{s_t}$, where the discrete process s_t is either Markovian or deterministic.

- The specification, below, is an alternative that is not used for this paper:

$$\underset{n \times 1}{c_t} = \left[\frac{c_1}{1 + \beta_1 \alpha_1^t}, \ldots, \frac{c_n}{1 + \beta_n \alpha_n^t} \right]',$$

where $0 \leq \alpha_j < 1$ for all $i = 1, \ldots, n$. One could consider the restriction $\alpha_j = \alpha$ for all $i = 1, \ldots, n$ or the restriction $\beta_j = \beta$ for all $i = 1, \ldots, n$ or both.

The reduced-form representation of (1) is

$$y_t = b_{s_t} + \sum_{\ell=1}^{p} B_\ell y_{t-\ell} + \mathcal{M}_{s_t} \varepsilon_t, \tag{3}$$

where $b_{s_t} = A_0^{-1} a_{s_t}$, $B_\ell = A_0^{-1} A_\ell$, and $\mathcal{M}_{s_t} = A_0^{-1} \mathcal{D}_{s_t}$. Let $\Sigma_{s_t} = \mathcal{M}_{s_t} \mathcal{M}'_{s_t}$ be the regime-switching covariance matrix.

B.   Design of the Prior

Since the representation (2) is expressed in log difference and of reduced rank, it embodies the prior of Sims and Zha (1998) (with the implication that the Sims and Zha prior become degenerate along the dimension of reduced rank). Therefore we should begin with the prior directly on F_ℓ ($\ell = 0, \ldots, p - 1$), $c_j, d_j, \tau_j, \alpha_j$, and $\mathcal{D}_{s_t}$. The only difficult part is to have a prior that maintains the reduced rank r for $\mathcal{R}$.

Prior on F_ℓ ($\ell = 0, \ldots, p - 1$), $c_j, d_j,$ and τ_j. The prior is Gaussian on each of those elements centered at zero. For F_ℓ ($\ell = 1, \ldots, p - 1$), there is a lag decay factor such that the prior becomes tighter as the lag lengthens.

Prior on α_j and $\mathcal{D}_{s_t}$. The prior on α_j is of Gamma. The prior on each of the diagonal elements of $\mathcal{D}_{s_t}$ is of inverse Gamma.

Prior on $\mathcal{R}$. Because $\mathcal{R}$ is a reduced-rank matrix, the usual decomposition is $\mathcal{R} = \alpha\beta'$, where both α and β are $n \times r$ matrices of rank r. But a more effective decomposition is the singular value decomposition:

$$\mathcal{R} = \mathcal{U}\mathcal{D}\mathcal{V}',$$

where both $\mathcal{U}$ and $\mathcal{V}$ are $n \times r$ matrices with orthonormal columns and $\mathcal{D}$ is an $r \times r$ diagonal matrix. Let the prior on both $\mathcal{U}$ and $\mathcal{V}$ be the uniform distribution and the prior on the diagonal elements of $\mathcal{D}$ be Gaussian.

The set of all $n \times r$ matrices with orthonormal columns is the Stiefel manifold, which is an $[nr - r(r + 1)/2]$-manifold in $\mathbb{R}^{nr}$. Instead of working directly with the elements of the Stiefel manifold, we work with arbitrary $n \times r$ matrices $\tilde{\mathcal{U}}$ and $\tilde{\mathcal{V}}$ and map $\tilde{\mathcal{U}}$ and $\tilde{\mathcal{V}}$ to $\mathcal{U}$ and $\mathcal{V}$ using the QR decomposition. In particular, we map $\tilde{\mathcal{U}}$ to $\mathcal{U}$ and $\tilde{\mathcal{V}}$ to $\mathcal{V}$ via the QR decompositions $\tilde{\mathcal{U}} = \mathcal{U}\mathcal{R}_\mathcal{U}$ and $\tilde{\mathcal{V}} = \mathcal{V}\mathcal{R}_\mathcal{V}$ with the positive diagonals of $\mathcal{R}_\mathcal{U}$ and $\mathcal{R}_\mathcal{V}$. If the prior on each column of $\tilde{\mathcal{U}}$ and $\tilde{\mathcal{V}}$ is any spherical distribution centered at the origin, then the induced prior on $\mathcal{U}$ and $\mathcal{V}$ is uniform as desired. Having the free parameters $\tilde{\mathcal{U}}$, $\tilde{\mathcal{V}}$, and $\mathcal{D}$ defined over Euclidean space, as opposed to a complicated submanifold, makes numerical optimization tractable. While this parameterization is not unique in the sense that different values of $\tilde{\mathcal{U}}$, $\tilde{\mathcal{V}}$, and $\mathcal{D}$ can produce the same $\mathcal{R}$, it is inconsequential because we do not give $\tilde{\mathcal{U}}$, $\tilde{\mathcal{V}}$, and $\mathcal{D}$ any economic interpretation.

We propose a prior on each column of $\tilde{\mathcal{U}}$ and $\tilde{\mathcal{V}}$ to be

$$\frac{\Gamma(n / 2)}{\pi^{n/2} 2^{(n+1)/2} \Gamma[(n + 1) / 2]} \rho e^{-\rho^2/2},$$

where ρ is the norm of a column of $\tilde{\mathcal{U}}$ or $\tilde{\mathcal{V}}$. This prior is spherical and centered at the origin, and thus induces the uniform prior distributions for $\mathcal{U}$ and $\mathcal{V}$. Moreover, it is straightforward to sample independently from this distribution.

Our prior has some similarity to the prior specified by Villani (2005). Working directly with the reduced-form parameters, Villani (2005) uses the $F_0^{-1}\mathcal{R} = \alpha\beta'$ decomposition with normalization such that the upper $r \times r$ block of β is the identity matrix. The prior on β is chosen so that the prior on the Grassmannian manifold is uniform. The Grassmannian manifold is the space of all k-dimensional linear subspaces in $\mathbb{R}^n$ and the columns of β can be interpreted as the basis for an element in this manifold. This is analogous to our use of the uniform distribution on the Stiefel manifold. Villani (2005) does not work directly with α but instead uses

$$\tilde{\alpha} = \alpha(\beta'\beta)^{1/2}.$$

It follows that the prior on the ith column of $\tilde{\alpha}$, conditional on Σ_{s_t}, is normally distributed with mean zero and variance matrix $v\Sigma_{s_t}$, where v is a positive hyperparameter.

Since we work with the primitive error-correction form for the purpose of taking into account time-varying shock variances, our prior is on $\mathcal{R}$ directly, not on $F_0^{-1}\mathcal{R}$. All the reduced-form parameters are derived, through the relations between (2) and (3), as

$$B_1 = F_0^{-1}(\mathcal{R} + F_1 + F_0), \; B_\ell = F_0^{-1}(F_\ell - F_{\ell-1})(\ell = 2,\dots,p-1),$$

$$B_p = -F_0^{-1}F_{p-1}, \; b_{s_t} = F_0^{-1}c_{s_t}, \; \mathcal{M}_{s_t} = F_0^{-1}\mathcal{D}_{s_t}.$$

C.   Decomposing Trends and Cycles

We first estimate system (2) and then convert it to system (3). We express system (3) in companion form:

$$\begin{bmatrix} y_t \\ y_{t-1} \\ \vdots \\ y_{t-p+1} \end{bmatrix} = \begin{bmatrix} b_{s_t} \\ 0 \\ \vdots \\ 0 \end{bmatrix} + \underbrace{\begin{bmatrix} B_1 & \cdots & B_{p-1} & B_p \\ I_n & \cdots & 0_n & n_n \\ \vdots & & & \\ 0_n & \cdots & I_n & 0_n \end{bmatrix}}_{B} \begin{bmatrix} y_{t-1} \\ y_{t-2} \\ \vdots \\ y_{t-p} \end{bmatrix} + \begin{bmatrix} \mathcal{M}_{s_t} \\ 0 \\ \vdots \\ 0 \end{bmatrix} \varepsilon_t, \qquad (4)$$

where the companion matrix B is of $np \times np$ dimension, I_n is the identity matrix of dimension n, and 0_n is the $n \times n$ matrix of zeros. There are $m_2 = n - r$ unit roots and let $m_1 = np - m_2$. We follow the approach of King et al. (1991) by maintaining their assumption that the innovations to permanent shocks are independent of those to transitory shocks. This assumption enables one to obtain a unique block of permanent shocks as well as a unique block of transitory shocks.[12]

To obtain these two blocks of shocks, we first perform a real Schur decomposition of B such that

$$B = \begin{bmatrix} W_1 & W_2 \\ {\scriptstyle np \times m_1} & {\scriptstyle np \times m_2} \end{bmatrix} \begin{bmatrix} \mathcal{T}_{11} & \mathcal{T}_{12} \\ 0 & \mathcal{T}_{22} \\ & {\scriptstyle m_2 \times m_2} \end{bmatrix} [W_1' \; W_2'],$$

where $[W_1 \; W_2]$ is an orthogonal matrix and the diagonal elements of $\mathcal{T}_{22}$ are equal to one.

Our first task is to find the largest column space in which transitory shocks lie. That is, we need to find an $np \times \ell_1$ matrix, V_{1,s_t}, such that the column space of

$$
\begin{bmatrix} \mathcal{M}_{s_t} \\ 0 \\ \vdots \\ 0 \end{bmatrix} V_{1,s_t} \tag{5}
$$

is contained in the column space of W_1, and V_{1,s_t} is of full column rank and has the maximal number of columns. Hence, the transitory shocks lie in the column space represented by (5). This column space must be equal to the intersection of the column space of W_1 and the column space of $[\mathcal{M}'_{s_t}, 0, \dots, 0]'$. In other words, there exists an $m_1 \times \ell_1$ matrix of real values, $\mathcal{A}$, such that

$$
\begin{bmatrix} \mathcal{M}_{s_t} \\ 0 \\ \vdots \\ 0 \end{bmatrix} V_{1,s_t} = W_1 \mathcal{A}.
$$

Since $W_1 \perp W_2$, we have

$$
W_2' \begin{bmatrix} \mathcal{M}_{s_t} \\ 0 \\ \vdots \\ 0 \end{bmatrix} V_{1,s_t} = 0.
$$

It follows that

$$
V_{1,s_t} = \text{Null}\left(W_2' \begin{bmatrix} \mathcal{M}_{s_t} \\ 0 \\ \vdots \\ 0 \end{bmatrix} \right)
$$

and $\ell_1 \geq n - m_1$.

Let

$$
V_{1,s_t} = Q_{s_t} R_{s_t} = \begin{bmatrix} Q_{1,s_t} & Q_{2,s_t} \\ n \times \ell_1 & n \times \ell_2 \end{bmatrix} R_{s_t}
$$

be the QR decomposition of V_{1,s_t}. Since $\ell_1 \geq n - m_1$, it must be that $\ell_2 = n - \ell_1 \leq m_2$. The impact matrix is

$$
\mathcal{M}_{s_t} [Q_{1,s_t} \quad Q_{2,s_t}]
$$

with the first ℓ_1 columns corresponding to contemporaneous responses to the transitory shocks and the second ℓ_2 columns corresponding to those to the permanent shocks.

If we have a different identification represented by $\tilde{\mathcal{M}}_{s_t}$, we can repeat the same procedure to obtain the impact matrix as

$$\tilde{\mathcal{M}}_{s_t} = \left[\tilde{Q}_{1,s_t} \ \ \tilde{Q}_{2,s_t} \right]$$

with $\tilde{\mathcal{M}}_{s_t}\tilde{Q}_{i,s_t} = \mathcal{M}_{s_t}Q_{i,s_t}P_{i,s_t}$ for $i = 1,2$, where $[P_{1,s_t} \ \ P_{2,s_t}]$ is an orthogonal matrix.

D. Results

The sample begins with 1997Q1 because this is the time when China had begun to shift its strategic priority to the development of heavy industries as marked in table 2 (see Section V.B for a detailed discussion).

We estimate a number of six-variable, time-varying quarterly BVAR models with five lags and the sample 1997Q1–2013Q4. Out of these variables, four variables are log values of real household consumption, real total business investment, real GDP, and real labor income (all are deflated by the implicit GDP deflator); two variables are the ratio of new medium- and long-term bank loans to GDP and the ratio of new short-term bank loans and bill financing to GDP. All the variables are seasonally adjusted. The five lags are used to eliminate any residual of possible seasonality. For our benchmark BVAR, the rank of the matrix $\mathcal{R}$ is set to 3, implying one possible cointegration relationship and two stationary variables. We find two stochastic regimes for the shock variances. Finding the posterior mode proves to be a challenging task. The estimation procedure follows the DSMH method proposed by Waggoner, Wu, and Zha (2015). First, we use the DSMH method to obtain the sufficient sample of BVAR coefficients. From these posterior draws, we randomly select 100 starting points independently and use the standard optimization routine to find local peaks. From the 100 local peaks, we select the highest peak as our posterior mode.

We use the model structure and the estimated parameter values to back out a smoothed sequence of shocks, ε_t. Out of the six shocks at each time t, three of them are permanent and the other three are stationary.[13] Conditional on the values of the six variables for the initial five periods, the trend component of each variable is computed recursively by making the predictions from the model by feeding into the model the smoothed permanent shocks at each time t. The stationary component, by construction, is the difference between the data and the trend component.

Across different BVARs, we obtain robust results about cyclical patterns. For the benchmark BVAR, the estimated correlation between stationary components of investment and consumption (the cyclical part) is −0.05, the estimated correlation between investment and labor income is −0.23, and the estimated correlation between short-term loans and long-term loans is −0.51. The results are robust across various BVARs. For example, with the BVAR with all coefficients (including shock variances) being set to be constant across time, the estimated correlation is 0.18 between investment and consumption and −0.44 between investment and labor income; with the BVAR with time-varying intercept terms and regime-switching volatility, the estimated correlation is −0.50 between investment and consumption and 0.14 between investment and labor income. If we set rank($\mathcal{R}$) = 2 (i.e., no cointegration is allowed) and allow for regime-switching volatility, the estimated correlation is 0.01 between investment and consumption and −0.33 between investment an d labor income.

The government's stimulation of investment after the 2008 financial crisis shows up as a rapid run-up of the investment rate in 2009 in the trend movement; the stimulation has a long-lasting impact on sustaining the high investment rate even after the government ceased long-term credit expansions in 2011 (figure 1). The high-volatility regime, characterized by the smoothed posterior probability as displayed in the bottom row of figure 4, reflects the wild fluctuation of banks loans shown in figure 3. After separating these short-lived high volatilities from the general trend, the trend pattern is equally striking with the consumption-to-GDP ratio steadily declining and the investment-to-GDP ratio steadily rising. Both the trend and cycle patterns uncovered here are robust findings, not only from different BVAR models, but also from other empirical studies presented in the next section.

IV.   Robust Empirical Evidence

In this section, we verify robustness of the key facts uncovered in Section III. Given how stark these findings are, it is essential to verify their robustness by other means. We pursue this task in two ways. First, we cross verify the previous findings using the annual data. Second, we apply the HP filter to the relevant variables to verify the cyclical patterns previously obtained.

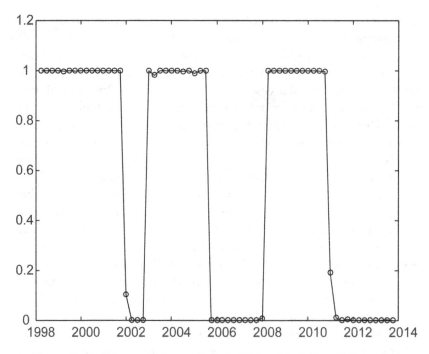

Fig. 4. Estimated smoothed posterior probabilities of the high-volatility regime

The trend patterns, reported in figure 1, are confirmed by the raw annual data displayed in figure 5. Since the late 1990s, household consumption as a share of GDP has steadily declined from 45% in 1997 to 35% in 2010 (the top-left chart), while aggregate investment (total business investment) has risen from 26% in 2000 to 36% in 2010 (the top-right chart).[14] This striking trend pattern is robust when we use the narrow definition of output as the sum of household consumption and business investment (the two charts at the bottom). More telling is the declining pattern of both household disposable income and labor income as a share of GDP since 1997.[15]

With the annual data we are able to study the transition that has a longer period, which covers the early years after the introduction of economic reforms in December 1978. The left column of figure 6 reports the time series of the moving 10-year-window correlations of annual growth rates between household consumption (C) and gross fixed capital formation (GFCF). There is a clear structural break after the early 1990s, when the correlations declined and became extremely low or even negative. Such negative correlations after the mid-1990s are

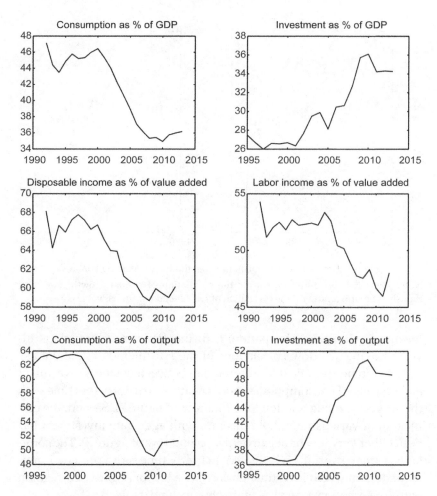

Fig. 5. Annual data: trend patterns for household consumption, investment, GDP, household disposable income, and household labor income.

Note: "Investment" is total business investment, calculated as gross fixed capital formation excluding household investment. "Output" is the sum of household consumption and business investment.

more pronounced for the HP-filtered series, reported in the right-side column of gigure 6. Note that for annual data we follow the analytical formula of Ravn and Uhlig (2002) by setting the smoothing parameter value of the HP filter to 6.25 so that this value is most compatible to the smoothing parameter value (1600) used for quarterly data.

The cyclical pattern uncovered in Section III supports a similar divergence between consumption on the one hand and investment and

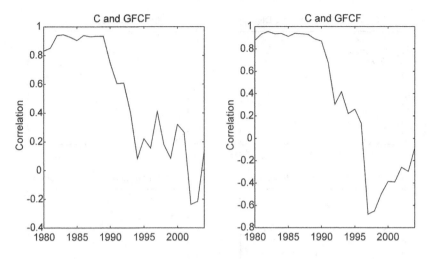

Fig. 6.   Time series of correlations using the 10-year moving window
Note: The left-hand graph represents the correlation of annual growth rates. The right-hand graph represents the correlation of HP-filtered log annual values.

income on the other. This pattern is further confirmed by various 10-year, moving-window correlations of the HP-filtered annual data as reported in figure 7. First, the correlation between business investment and household consumption is more negative than not across time with the 10-year moving window (the first row of figure 7). Second, the correlation of various household incomes with aggregate investment has been either very low or negative (the second row of figure 7). The correlations among various HP-filtered quarterly time series present a similar pattern in which investment has either a low or negative correlation with consumption as well as with labor income (table 5).

Household disposable income is the sum of household before-tax income and net transfers. In China, taxes and transfers play a minor role in explaining the correlation between investment and disposable income because the correlation between investment and household before-tax income shows a similar pattern (the second row of figure 7). For Western economies, household disposable income is different from household labor income because of interest payments and capital gains (household disposable income is the sum of labor income, interest payments, realized capital gains, and net transfers). In China, however, labor income is the main driving force of household disposable income. This fact explains the similar pattern of the correlation of investment with labor income and with disposable income (the second row of figure 7).

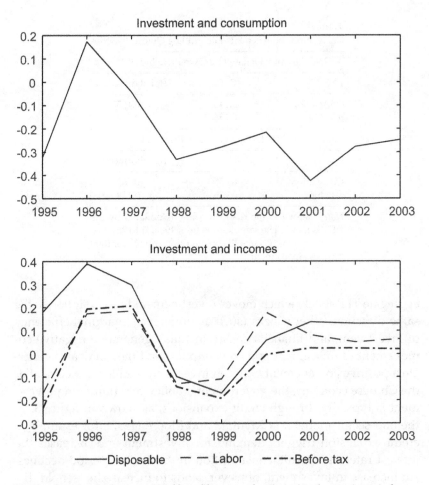

Fig. 7. Correlations between HP-filtered log annual series using the moving window of 10 years

Note: "Consumption" is real household consumption (deflated by the CPI), "Incomes" are various measures of household incomes (deflated by the GDP deflator), "Investment" is real total business investment (deflated by the investment price index), "Disposable" stands for household disposable income, "Labor" stands for household labor income, and "Before tax" stands for household before-tax labor income.

The low or negative correlation between investment and labor income, alongside the negative correlation between investment and consumption, poses a challenging task for macroeconomic modeling. Standard macroeconomic models for explaining the negative correlation of business investment and household consumption rely on an intertemporal substitution of household consumption. Except for an

Table 5
Correlations between HP-Filtered Log Quarterly Series

A. Real Variables Deflated by Own Price Index

	(C, I)	(I, LaborIncome)
Correlation	−0.140	0.165
p-value	0.256	0.179

B. Real Variables Deflated by GDP Price Deflator

	(C, I)	(I, LaborIncome)
Correlation	−0.035	0.165
p-value	0.775	0.178

Note: Labor income (LaborIncome) is deflated by the GDP deflator. The sample runs from 1996Q1 to 2012Q4. "C" stands for household consumption and "I" for total business investment.

aggregate TFP shock, which moves investment and consumption in the same direction, other shocks (such as preference, marginal efficiency of investment, and financial constraint) may generate a negative comovement of investment and consumption, but they may also generate a positive comovement between investment and labor income. For the Chinese economy, the government's policy for stimulating investment is typically through credit expansions, as shown in figure 3. In the one-sector model à la Kiyotaki and Moore (1997), for example, a credit expansion triggers demand for investment and increases the interest rate. As a result, consumption in the current period declines. An increase in investment, however, tends to increase household disposable income as well as savings. Thus one should expect *not just a positive but also a strong* correlation between investment and household income. This is inconsistent with the fact presented in figure 7. The discussion in Section VIII.C at the end of this paper provides examples of how standard models cannot account for the key Chinese facts.

V. China in Transition

Table 2 lists a number of major economic reforms. Out of these reforms we focus on the two most important dimensions of the transition that are relevant to both our empirical findings and our subsequent macroeconomic theory. One dimension, state-owned versus privately owned firms, has been extensively studied in the literature on China. The other dimension, the heavy versus light sectors, is a new and enlightening angle that we argue is most helpful to an understanding of trends and cycles in China's aggregate economy.

A. SOEs versus POEs

The Chinese economy has undergone two kinds of reforms in SOEs simultaneously, the so-called "grasp the large and let go of the small." One transition is privatization that allows many SOEs previously engaged in unproductive labor-intensive industries to be privatized. This reform is the focus of the SSZ work. The other reform is a gradual concentration of SOEs in heavy industries, such as petroleum, commodities, electricity, water, and gas. We use disaggregated data on two-digit industries to quantify this reform. Table 6 lists the 39 two-digit industries. For each industry we obtain the value added, gross output, fixed investment, the capital stock, employment, and the share of SOEs from the NBS data source. We then compute the capital-labor ratio for each industry to measure the capital intensity. We also compute the weight of each industry by value added or by gross output if the value added is unavailable. Table 7 reports the weight and the rank by capital intensity for each of the 39 industries for 1999, 2006, and 2011.[16] Those years give us an informative picture of how the SOE reforms took place from 1999 to 2011; tables 6 and 7 are used in conjunction with figures 8, 9, and 10 to add understanding of the outcome of SOE reforms. In each of these three figures, the left column of each figure displays the SOE share for each industry and the bars are sorted from the most capital-intensive industry (the highest capital-labor ratio) on the top to the least capital-intensive industry (the lowest capital-labor ratio) at the bottom. The right column of each figure plots the SOE share against the capital intensity for each industry.

The rank of industries by capital intensity changes over time (table 7), but this change is not only gradual but also minimal. Indeed, the rank correlations between 1999, 2006, and 2011 are all above 0.93. The SOE share, however, has undergone a significant change. In 1999 many SOEs engaged in labor-intensive industries, in 2006 fewer SOEs engaged in those industries, and in 2011 even fewer SOEs were engaged. Take "Manufacture of General Purpose Machinery" (the industry identifier 29 in table 6) as an example.[17] In 1999 the SOE share was over 60% (the bar chart in figure 8), in 2006 the SOE share dropped to 25% (the bar

Table 6
Industry identifiers

Identifier	Industry
1	Mining and washing of coal
2	Extraction of petroleum and natural gas
3	Mining and processing of ferrous metal ores
4	Mining and processing of nonferrous metal ores
5	Mining and processing of nonmetal ores
6	Mining of other ores
7	Processing of food from agricultural products
8	Food
9	Wine, beverage, and refined tea
10	Tobacco
11	Textile
12	Textile product, garment, shoes, and hat
13	Leather, fur, feather, and its product
14	Wood processing, wood, bamboo, rattan, palm, and grass product
15	Manufacture of furniture
16	Manufacture of paper and paper products
17	Printing, reproduction of recording media
18	Cultural, education, and sport
19	Processing of petroleum, coking, processing of nuclear fuel
20	Chemical material and products
21	Manufacture of medicines (pharmaceutical)
22	Manufacture of chemical fibers
23	Manufacture of rubber
24	Manufacture of plastics
25	Manufacture of nonmetallic mineral products
26	Smelting and pressing of ferrous metals
27	Smelting and pressing of nonferrous metals
28	Manufacture of metal products
29	Manufacture of general purpose machinery
30	Manufacture of special purpose machinery
31	Manufacture of transport equipment
32	Manufacture of electrical machinery and equipment
33	Computer, communication and other electronic equipment
34	Instrument, meter, culture and office machinery
35	Manufacture of artwork and other manufacturing
36	Recycling and disposal of waste
37	Electricity, heat production and supply
38	Gas production and supply
39	Water production and supply

chart in figure 9), and in 2011 the SOE share dropped even further to less than 20% (the bar chart in figure 10). This trend is confirmed by the aggregate data displayed in figure 11. The figure shows that the SOE share of total business investment has declined, while the POE share has increased.

Table 7
Weights and Capital-Intensity Ranks for Various Industries

	1999		2006		2011	
Industry Identifier	Weight (%) by Value added	Capital Intensity Rank	Weight (%) by Value Added	Capital Intensity Rank	Weight (%) by Gross Output	Capital Intensity Rank
1	2.66	23	3.93	22	3.42	16
2	6.77	2	6.57	2	1.52	2
3	0.25	30	0.64	23	0.93	12
4	0.59	24	0.74	24	0.59	15
5	0.55	22	0.41	28	0.45	27
6	n/a	n/a	0.00	16	0.00	8
7	3.59	19	3.83	21	5.22	22
8	1.62	18	1.61	18	1.66	23
9	2.76	11	1.58	12	1.40	17
10	4.20	4	2.61	6	0.80	7
11	5.26	29	4.35	30	3.86	33
12	2.38	35	2.01	38	1.60	37
13	1.33	36	1.28	39	1.05	39
14	0.62	28	0.75	32	1.06	31
15	0.36	33	0.55	35	0.60	35
16	1.67	12	1.52	11	1.43	13
17	0.93	16	0.61	17	0.45	26
18	0.66	34	0.51	37	0.38	38
19	2.78	3	2.54	4	4.36	4
20	5.73	10	5.92	10	7.20	10
21	2.42	13	1.98	13	1.76	21
22	1.19	7	0.66	8	0.79	11
23	0.95	20	0.78	20	0.86	20
24	1.82	21	1.83	26	1.84	30
25	4.73	17	4.01	15	4.75	14
26	5.09	8	7.69	7	7.58	6
27	1.90	9	3.51	9	4.25	9
28	2.54	31	2.44	33	2.76	28
29	3.50	27	4.17	29	4.85	25
30	2.43	25	2.52	27	3.09	24
31	5.62	15	5.41	14	7.49	18
32	4.72	26	5.07	31	6.09	29
33	6.35	14	7.77	19	7.55	32
34	0.85	32	1.06	34	0.90	34
35	n/a	n/a	0.77	36	0.85	36
36	n/a	n/a	0.10	25	0.31	19
37	10.18	1	7.58	1	5.60	1
38	0.17	5	0.21	3	0.37	5
39	0.68	6	0.34	5	0.13	3

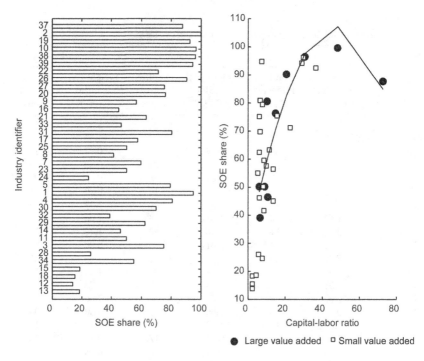

Fig. 8.   The 1999 characteristics of various industries in China

Note: The industries identified by the numerical numbers on the vertical axis of the left-hand graph are listed in table 6. The dark circles in the right-hand graph indicate the top-10 industries by added value to output; the curved line is a fitted quadratic regression of the SEO share on the capital-labor ratio for these top-10 industries.

This pattern of change in SOE reforms is consistent with the fact that the SOE sector has become more productive over time by shedding unproductive small firms through privatization. As documented by Hsieh and Song (2015), the gap between the average TFP in *privatized* firms (i.e., state owned in 1998 and privately owned in 2007) and the average TFP in surviving privately owned firms (i.e., privately owned in 1998 and in 2007) had narrowed from 1998 to 2007. For the same period, the TFP gap between surviving SOEs (i.e., state owned in 1998 and in 2007) or newly entered SOEs and surviving privately owned firms had also narrowed. Of course, the definition of what constitutes a SOE is crucial. Hsieh and Song (2015) provide a careful analysis and argue that simply using the firm's legal registration as state owned is inaccurate. They propose to "define a firm as state owned when the share of registered capital held directly by the state exceeds or equals 50% or when

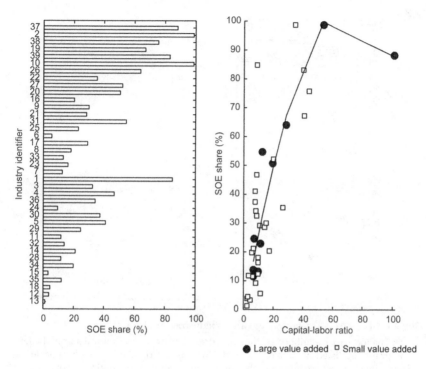

Fig. 9. The 2006 characteristics of various industries in China.

Note: The industries identified by the numerical numbers on the vertical axis of the left-hand graph are listed in table 6. The dark circles in the right-hand graph indicate the top-10 industries by added value to output; the curved line is a fitted quadratic regression of the SEO share on the capital-labor ratio for these top-10 industries.

the state is reported as the controlling shareholder." Even within the SOE sector, there is a degree to which a firm is controlled by the state, depending on the actual share of capital owned by the state. Nonetheless, Hsieh and Song (2015) find that the SOE share of total revenue, calculated according to their definition, is close to the official aggregate data in *China's Statistical Yearbooks* from 1998 to 2007 published by the NBS.[18] Different SOE definitions notwithstanding, a robust finding is that privatization appears to be a critical factor in driving the TFP growth of the SOE sector. As the SOE sector continues to reform,[19] this reallocation from SOEs to POEs through privatization will persist. Despite Hsieh and Song's (2015) finding that the average TFP of surviving SOEs had grown faster than the average TFP of surviving POEs, such a reallocation gain is largely responsible for the continuing decline both in the SOE share of investment (figure 11) and in the state-owned

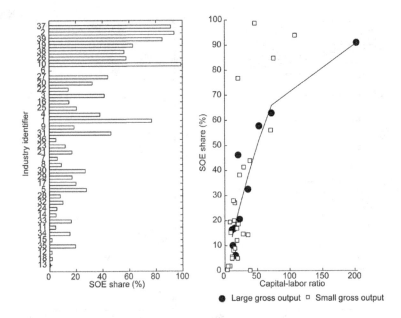

Fig. 10. The 2011 characteristics of various industries in China.

Note: The industries identified by the numerical numbers on the vertical axis of the left-hand graph are listed in table 6. The dark circles in the right-hand graph indicate the top-10 industries by gross output; the curved line is a fitted quadratic regression of the SEO share on the capital-labor ratio for these top-10 industries.

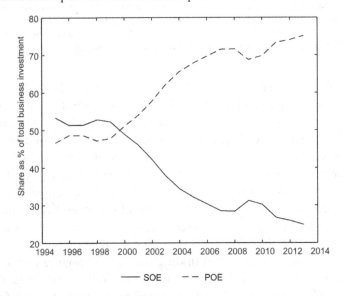

Fig. 11. The share of SOE investment and POE investment as a percent of total business investment, where total business investment equals the sum of SOE investment and POE investment.

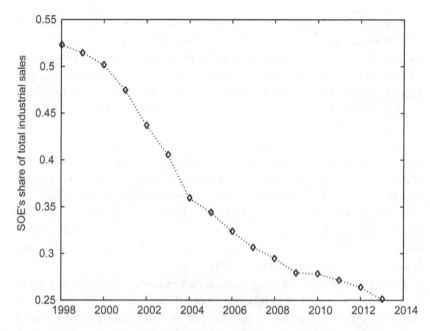

Fig. 12. The ratio of sales revenue in the SOEs to the total sales revenue in all industrial firms.

share of industrial revenues as reported in *China's Statistical Yearbooks* (figure 12).

B. Heavy versus Light Sectors

Although discussions around the role of SOEs have dominated the literature on China's economy, the SOE-POE classification does not naturally lead up to an explanation of the steady rise of investment as a share of total output (fact [T1]). This point is elaborated further in the context of our theoretical model in Section VI.

We place instead an emphasis on studying two distinct sectors: the heavy and light sectors. This shift of focus marks a major departure of our approach from the standard approach in the literature on China and affords a fruitful and tractable way of analyzing the Chinese aggregate economy; it helps avoid the seemingly contradicting fact that the SOE investment share has declined over time, but at the same time the SOE TFP has grown faster than its POE counterpart.

The gradual concentration of large firms or industries in the heavy sector has taken place since the late 1990s. In March 1996, the Eighth

National People's Congress passed the *National Economic and Social Development* and *Ninth Five-Year Program: Vision and Goals for 2010*, prepared by the State Council (see the bold, italicized line in table 2). This program was the first medium- and long-term plan made after China switched to a market economy; it set up a policy goal to adjust the industrial structure for the next 15 years. Specifically, it urged continuation of strengthening the infrastructure (transportation and telecommunication—information transmission) and basic industries (electricity, coal, petroleum processing, natural gas, smelting and pressing of ferrous and nonferrous metals, and chemical industry), boosting pillar industries (electrical machinery, petroleum processing, automobile, and real estate), and invigorating and actively developing the tertiary industry. Most of these industries belong to the heavy sector as illustrated in Section VIII.B. Indeed, the revenue ratio of the heavy sector to the light sector began to increase in 1996.

Our own analysis of disaggregate data reinforces this finding. On the right column of each figure from figure 8 to 10, we mark the top-10 value-weighted industries with dark circles and fit the quadratic curve through these dark circles. In 1999 four of those industries were capital intensive (i.e., the capital-labor ratio is above 20, figure 8); by 2011 not only did more of the top-10 industries became capital intensive, but also the ratio of capital to labor increased for these large industries (figure 10). Large industries became more and more capital intensive during this transition.

Indeed, the reallocation of resources between the heavy and light sectors has a profound effect on the upward trend of the overall investment rate. The NBS provides the time series of gross output, value added, and investment for the heavy and light sectors within the broad secondary industry bar of the construction sector (we compute investment as the first difference of the gross value of fixed assets). The reallocation (between-sector) effect, relative to the sector-specific (within-sector) effect, on the overall investment rate is calculated as

$$\frac{\overline{i^l}P_t^lY_t^l + \overline{i^k}P_t^kY_t^k}{P_t^lY_t^l + P_t^kY_t^k} - \frac{i_t^l\overline{P^lY^l} + i_t^k\overline{P^kY^k}}{\overline{P^lY^l} + \overline{P^kY^k}},$$

where $P_t^lY_t^l$ is value added or gross output for the light sector, $P_t^kY_t^k$ for the heavy sector, i_t^l is the investment rate for the light sector, and i_t^k for the heavy industry. The bar line over each of the variables indicates the sample mean. The series for value added ends in 2007 and there is no published data from the NBS for later years. The relative reallocation effect between 1997 and 2007 is an increase of 16.8 percentage points. For the series of gross output, the relative reallocation effect between 1997 and 2011 is an increase of 11.1 percentage points.[20] These findings provide solid evidence about the importance of a between-sector contribution to the rise of the investment rate discussed in Sections III.D and IV and displayed in figures 1 and 5. In Section VIII.B we discuss further the evolution of heavy versus light sectors in connection with how each sector is financed.

Firms in the heavy sector are a mix of SOEs and POEs (especially large POEs). According to the 2012 report "Survey of Chinese Top 500 Private Enterprises" published by China's National Federation of Economic Ministry, there has been a trend for more large private firms (whose sales are all above 500 million RMB) to engage in heavy industries, partly because these activities are supported by the state. For instance, in 2007 there were only 36 large firms in the ferrous metal and processing industries, and by 2011 there were 65 large firms; in 2007 there were only six large firms in the industries of petroleum processing, coking, and nuclear fuel processing, and by 2011 the number more than doubled. Indeed, out of the 345 largest private firms in 2010, 64 were in the ferrous metal and processing industries (constituting the single-largest fraction of all these large firms) while 54 were in the wholesale and retail trade industries.

As China's economic reforms deepen, the government no longer adheres to the practice of favoring SOEs and bias against POEs. As long as firms help boost growth of the local economy and create tax revenues, the local government would support them. Medium- and long-term bank loans treat large firms symmetrically no matter whether they are SOEs or POEs; labor-intensive firms, most of which tend to be small, have a difficult time obtaining loans, especially in the last ten years. One of the main reasons for heavy-industry firms to gain easy access to bank loans is the firms' ability to use their fixed assets for collateralizing the loans. This feature is built into our theoretical model.

Evidence shows that the labor-intensive sector is more productive than the capital-intensive sector. Using the data set of manufacturing firms by bridging the Annual Surveys of Industrial Enterprises and the Database for Chinese Customs from 2000 to 2006, Ju et al. (2015) calculate the TFP growth rates for the import and export sectors, using both the Olley and Pakes (1996) method and the standard ordinary least squares (OLS) method. In China, the export sector is much more labor intensive than the import sector. Ju et al. (2015) find that TFP growth in the export sector was higher than that in the import sector for the

Table 8
Growth Accounting of China's Economy

Growth Rate (in Percent)	1978–1998	1998–2011	1998–2007
GDP per worker	6.78	9.48	9.42
capital per worker	3.56	7.00	6.13
TFP	3.23	2.48	3.29
Contribution by capital deepening	52.4%	73.9%	65.1%

Note: The computation uses the value of the capital share set at 0.5 as in SSZ and Brandt and Zhu 2010.

period between 2000 and 2006. More direct evidence comes from the careful study by Chen, Jefferson, and Zhang (2011) and Huang, Ju, and Yue (2015). Chen et al. (2011) use the disaggregate data of two-digit industries to document that the TFP in the light sector grew faster than that in the heavy sector.[21] Using the Chinese Annual Industrial Survey between 1999 and 2007, Huang et al. (2015) show that technology improved significantly in favor of more labor-intensive industries. To the extent that estimated TFP growth rates across different sectors are debatable, there is well-established evidence that the TFP level in the light sector is higher than that in the heavy sector. Nonetheless our benchmark model does not rely on *any TFP assumption*.

Despite the fact that the light sector is more productive than the heavy sector, the government has, since 1997, abided by the Strategic Plan passed by the Eighth National People's Congress. Because a significant part of the heavy sector is comprised of large firms that possess a strategic importance to the state, the government assigns lending priorities to this sector. It is this unique institutional arrangement that forms a building block for development of our theoretical model.

C.   Aggregate Economy

Figure 6 shows the sharp break in the correlation between investment and consumption fluctuations since the late 1990s. This stark picture is not an accident. It is a consequence of both banking reforms in 1995 and a new government policy in promoting heavy industries, which began in 1996. Such a preferential credit policy toward heavy industries also generated the sharp trend change in the consumption-output and investment-output ratios (figure 5).

How important is the rise of the investment-output ratio to GDP growth? Table 8 reports the contribution of capital deepening and TFP

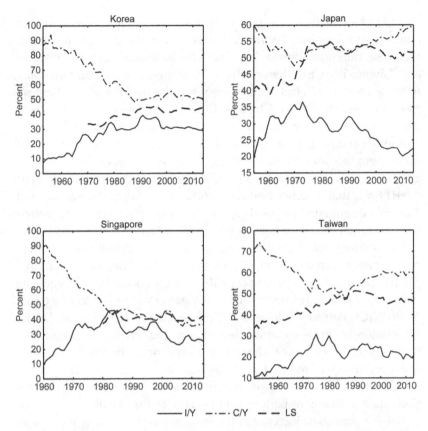

Fig. 13. C: private consumption; I: gross fixed domestic investment (gross fixed capital formation); LS: labor income share; Y: GDP.

Source: The CEIC. The overall correlation between LS and I/Y: 0.718 (Korea), −0.174 (Japan), 0.353 (Singapore), and 0.740 (Taiwan).

growth to the GDP growth rate for various periods, where GDP is measured by value added. Capital deepening accounts for a majority of GDP growth, especially since 1998.[22] Clearly, this investment-driven growth has negative consequences on consumption and labor income, which has caused concern for the Chinese government.

China's capital deepening has its own unique characteristics when compared to other East Asian newly industrializing countries (NICs) studied by Young (1995) and Fernald and Neiman (2011). Figure 13 displays the consumption-output ratio, the investment-output ratio, and the labor share of income for the four NICs: Korea, Japan, Singapore, and Taiwan. The overall correlation between the labor-income share and the investment rate is positive for Korea, Singapore, and Taiwan and negative for Japan. For the early years when the investment-output ratio rose, the correlation is almost zero for Japan and positive for Korea and Taiwan. The CEIC does not have the labor-share data for Singapore in those early years, but Young (1995) reports that the labor-share series were essentially flat. China is different: the labor share of income declined when the investment-output ratio rose as shown in figure 5.

Another unique feature of China is the divergence between the rising investment rate and the diminishing ability to export capital-intensive goods as China moves toward a stage of heavy industrialization. Romalis (2004) finds that as other East Asian NICs (e.g., Korea, Singapore, and Taiwan) accumulated physical capital, their export structure also moved toward capital-intensive goods (the so-called "quasi-Rybczynski" effect in the international trade literature). Ventura (1997) shows how a small open economy can sustain rapid growth without a diminishing marginal product of capital by exporting capital-intensive goods. The disaggregate evidence of China, however, suggests a pattern opposite to other East Asian NICs. Between 1999 and 2007, according to Huang et al. (2015), labor-intensive firms increased their export shares and capital-intensive firms reduced their export share; at the same time, the capital intensity of export firms was reduced. All these reallocations occurred despite the fact that the aggregate investment rate increased steadily during that period. Such a divergent pattern is at odds with the existing theory that explains a persistent increase in the investment rate among East Asian NICs based on the country's ability to export capital-intensive goods (e.g., Ventura 1997). But the pattern, as we have argued, is rooted in the macropolicy of China via the special credit channel under which firms in the heavy sector, instead of those in the light sector (constituting the bulk of the export sector), enjoy preferential access to bank credits.

VI. The Theoretical Framework

In this section we build a theoretical model that is tractable for understanding its mechanism, but rich enough to capture the salient facts presented in the preceding sections.

A. Environment

The economy is populated by two-period lived agents with overlapping generations (OLGs).[23] Agents work when young and consume their savings when old. Agents have heterogeneous skills. In each cohort, half of the population consists of workers without entrepreneurial skills and the other half is composed of entrepreneurs. Entrepreneurial skills are inherited from parents. Without loss of generality we do not allow switching between social classes.

B. Technology

There are two production sectors of intermediate goods, and hence two types of firms. The key feature of our model is that these two production sectors differ in capital intensity and *especially their access to bank loans*. The first sector is composed of firms that are endowed with capital-intensive technology. We call these firms "K-firms," which stands for capital-intensive. Remember that the heavy sector is more capital intensive than the light sector.

The second sector is a newly emerging private sector composed of productive firms. We call these firms "L-firms" that are labor intensive. The firms are managed and operated by entrepreneurs. Specifically, L-firms are owned by old entrepreneurs, who hire their own children as managers, are residual claimants on profits, and consume all the profits.

Technologies for both types of firms have constant returns to scale:

$$Y_t^k = K_t^k, \quad Y_t^l = (K_t^l)^\alpha (\chi L_t)^{1-\alpha},$$

where Y_t^j and K_t^j denote per capita output and the capital stock for the type-j firm, $j \in \{k, l\}$. The superscript k stands for "capital intensive" and l for "labor intensive." The L_t denotes the labor demand by labor-intensive firms. The parameter $\chi > 1$ captures the assumption that L-firms are more productive than K-firms, as supported by the analysis in Section V.B. The results implied by our benchmark model, however, do not rely on this assumption. This assumption is used only for the purpose of measuring the effects of misallocation of resources between the two sectors.

The production of final goods is a CES aggregator of the above two intermediate goods:

$$Y_t = [\varphi(Y_t^k)^{(\sigma-1)/\sigma} + (Y_t^l)^{(\sigma-1)/\sigma}]^{\sigma/(\sigma-1)}.$$

The perfect competition in the final goods market implies the following first-order condition

$$\frac{Y_t^k}{Y_t^l} = \left(\varphi \frac{P_t^l}{P_t^k} \right)^\sigma, \tag{6}$$

where P_t^k is the price of the intermediate goods Y_t^k, and P_t^l is the price of the intermediate goods Y_t^l. Normalizing the final-goods price to one and using the zero-profit condition for final goods, we have

$$[\varphi^\sigma (P_t^k)^{1-\sigma} + (P_t^l)^{1-\sigma}]^{1/(1-\sigma)} = 1. \tag{7}$$

C. K-Firms' Problem

Each K-firm lives for one period only, an assumption that can be relaxed. At the beginning of each period, newborn K-firms receive net worth N_t from the government. K-firms can borrow from the representative financial intermediary at a fixed interest rate (R) to finance investment in capital. K-firms, however, could default on loan payments and receive a fraction of output, $(1 - \theta_t)P_t^k Y_t^k$. The time-varying parameter θ_t reflects the changing loan quota targeted by the government. A higher value of θ_t implies an increase of the targeted loan quota whose payment is implicitly guaranteed by the government. The incentive-compatibility constraint for the K-firm is

$$P_t^k K_t^k - R(K_t^k - N_t) \geq (1 - \theta_t)P_t^k K_t^k. \tag{8}$$

The problem of the K-firm is

$$\Pi_t^k \equiv \max_{K_t^k} P_t^k K_t^k - R(K_t^k - N_t) + (1 - \delta)K_t^k$$

subject to (8). Denote the investment loan to the K-firm by $B_t^k = K_t^k - N_t$. At the end of the period, the K-firm turns in its gross profit (which includes $(1 - \delta)K_t^k$) to the government and dies.[24]

It is straightforward to show that for the financial constraint to bind, the following inequality must hold:

$$\theta_t P_t^k < R < P_t^k.$$

The first inequality is necessary; otherwise, the incentive-compatibility constraint for the K-firm never binds in equilibrium, even when $N_t = 0$. The second inequality holds because it is always profitable for K-firms to expand the production until the financial constraint binds. If the financial constraint is not binding, (8) implies that the demand for capital satisfies the condition $K_t^k \leq N_t / (1 - \theta_t)$ with $R = P_t^k$. If, on the other hand, $K_t^k > N_t / (1 - \theta_t)$, the financial constraint must bind. With the binding constraint, we obtain from (8)

$$K_t^k = \frac{R}{R - \theta_t P_t^k} N_t. \tag{9}$$

Accordingly, the amount borrowed by the K-firm is

$$B_t^k = \frac{\theta_t P_t^k}{R - \theta_t P_t^k} N_t. \tag{10}$$

D. L-Firms' Problem

Before production takes place, L-firms must finance their working capital from intratemporal (short-term) bank loans. For simplicity, we assume that L-firms can borrow working-capital loans freely from the bank. L-firms, however, have no access to intertemporal (long-term) bank loans to fund their fixed investment and must self-finance it through their own savings. We leave to Section VIII.B the discussion of how these assumptions are consistent with China's disaggregated banking data.

Following SSZ, we assume that the old entrepreneur pays the young entrepreneur a management fee as a fixed fraction of output produced, $m_t = \psi P_t^l (K_t^l)^\alpha (\chi L_t)^{1-\alpha}$, where $\psi < 1$.[25] Therefore the old entrepreneur's problem becomes

$$\Pi_t^l \equiv \max_{L_t} P_t^l (1 - \psi)(K_t^l)^\alpha (\chi L_t)^{1-\alpha} - R_t^l w_t L_t + (1 - \delta) K_t^l, \tag{11}$$

where R_t^l is the loan rate on the working capital $w_t L_t$. Note that old entrepreneurs do not choose K_t^l because, as shown below, it is determined when they are young.

The first-order condition gives

$$(1 - \psi)(1 - \alpha) P_t^l (K_t^l / L_t)^\alpha (\chi)^{1-\alpha} = R_t^l w_t. \tag{12}$$

The gross return to the L-firm's capital is

$$\rho_t^l \equiv \Pi_t^l / K_t^l = (1 - \psi)\alpha P_t^l (K_t^l / L_t)^{\alpha-1} (\chi)^{1-\alpha} + 1 - \delta. \tag{13}$$

The young entrepreneur's problem is to decide on consumption and a portfolio allocation between bank deposits and physical capital investment. Since the rate of return to capital investment is ρ_{t+1}^l and $\rho^l > R$ in steady state, the young entrepreneur always prefers investing in capital to depositing in the bank. Specifically, the young entrepreneur's consumption-saving problem is

$$\max_{s_t^E} \frac{(m_t - s_t^E)^{1-(1/\gamma)}}{1 - (1 / \gamma)} + \beta E_t \frac{(\rho_{t+1}^l s_t^E)^{1-(1/\gamma)}}{1 - (1 / \gamma)}.$$

First-order conditions determine the optimal saving of young entrepreneurs:

$$s_t^E = m_t \ / \ (1 + \beta^{-\gamma} E_t(\rho_{t+1}^l)^{1-\gamma}).$$

Since $s_t^E = K_{t+1}^l$, the law of motion for the L-firm's capital becomes

$$K_{t+1}^l = \frac{\psi}{1 + \beta^{-\gamma} E_t(\rho_{t+1}^l)^{1-\gamma}} \ P_t^l(K_t^l)^\alpha (\chi L_t)^{1-\alpha}. \tag{14}$$

E. Workers' Problem

Workers deposit their savings into the representative bank and earn the fixed interest rate R. Workers cannot lend directly to K-firms or L-firms. This assumption is consistent with the fact that the banking sector in China plays a key role in intermediating business loans.

The worker's consumption-saving problem is

$$\max_{c_{1t}^w, c_{2t+1}^w} \frac{(c_{1t}^w)^{1-(1-\gamma)}}{1 - (1 \ / \ \gamma)} + \beta \frac{(c_{2t+1}^w)^{1-(1/\gamma)}}{1 - (1 \ / \ \gamma)}$$

subject to

$$c_{1t}^w + s_t^w = w_t,$$

$$c_{2t+1}^w = s_t^w R,$$

where w_t is the market wage rate; c_{1t}^w, c_{2t+1}^w, and s_t^w denote consumption when young, consumption when old, and the worker's savings.

F. The Bank's Problem

Each period the bank receives deposits D_t from young workers and uses these deposits for intertemporal (long-term) loans to K-firms' investment and intratemporal (short-term) loans to L-firms' working capital. The bank's interest rate for investment loans is simply R, but the loan rate for working capital is R_t^l. The bank is subject to a convex cost of loan processing, $C(B_t)$, which increases with the total amount of loans, denoted as $B_t \equiv B_t^l + B_t^k$. Specifically, $C(B_t) = B_t^\eta$ for $\eta > 1$. Remaining deposits, invested in foreign bonds, earn the interest rate R.

The convex cost of loan processing is discussed in Cúrdia and Woodford (2010). For China, this assumption is more pertinent because various legislative or implicit restrictions on bank loans to small but productive firms become more severe as the loan-to-deposit ratio approaches to the official limit, making loans to productive firms exceedingly expensive (Zhou and Ren 2010).[26] Since bank loans to enterprises with large asset values are always given priority in China, we assume that the bank always meets K-firms' demand for investment loans prior to lending to L-firms. The bank's problem is therefore

$$\Pi_t^b = \underset{B_t^l}{\text{Max}} R_t^l B_t^l + RB_t^k + R(D_t - B_t^k) - RD_t - C(B_t) - B_t^l.$$

In equilibrium, $D_t = s_t^w L_t$ and $B_t^l = w_t L_t$. The first-order condition

$$R_t^l = 1 + C'(B_t) \tag{15}$$

reveals that the loan rate for working capital increases with the total amount of loans.

G. The Government's Problem

The government lasts forever. At the end of each period, the government decides on how much of its revenues to be advanced to newborn K-firms as net worth in the beginning of the next period. For simplicity we assume that N_{t+1} advanced to newborn K-firms is a fraction of K-firms' capital stock at the end of the current period, that is,

$$N_{t+1} = \xi K_t^k, \tag{16}$$

where $0 \leq \xi \leq 1$. A combination of (9) and (16) gives the law of motion for the K-firm's net worth

$$N_{t+1} = \frac{R\xi}{R - \theta_t P_t^k} N_t. \tag{17}$$

The government's budget constraint is

$$B_{t+1}^G + N_{t+1} = \Pi_t^k + \Pi_t^b + RB_t^G, \tag{18}$$

where B_t^G is the beginning-of-period government assets invested in foreign bonds, with the fixed interest rate R.

H. Equilibrium Conditions

The equilibrium conditions are listed as follows.

$$1 = L_t = \left[\frac{(1 - \psi)(1 - \alpha) P_t^l \chi}{R_t^l w_t} \right]^{1/\alpha} K_t^l / \chi,$$

$$\Pi_t^l = \rho_t^l K_t^l,$$

$$\rho_t^l = (1 - \psi)\alpha P_t^l (K_t^l)^{\alpha-1}\chi^{1-\alpha} + 1 - \delta,$$

$$R_t^l = 1 + C'(B_t),$$

$$\Pi_t^k = P_t^k K_t^k - R(K_t^k - N_t) + (1 - \delta)K_t^k,$$

$$\Pi_t^B = (R_t^l - 1)B_t^l - C(B_t),$$

$$m_t = \psi P_t^l (K_t^l)^{\alpha}(\chi L_t)^{1-\alpha},$$

$$s_t^E = m_t \, / \, (1 + \beta^{-\gamma}(E_t\rho_{t+1}^l)^{1-\gamma}),$$

$$c_{1t}^E = m_t - s_t^E, c_{2t}^E = \rho_t^l s_{t-1}^E,$$

$$B_t^k = K_t^k - N_t,$$

$$B_t^l = w_t L_t,$$

$$N_{t+1} = \xi K_t^k,$$

$$Y_t = [\varphi \, (Y_t^k)^{(\sigma-1)/\sigma} + (Y_t^l)^{(\sigma-1)/\sigma}]^{\sigma/(\sigma-1)},$$

$$Y_t^k = K_t^k,$$

$$Y_t^l = (K_t^l)^{\alpha}(\chi L_t)^{1-\alpha},$$

$$1 = [\varphi^{\sigma}(P_t^k)^{1-\sigma} + (P_t^l)^{1-\sigma}]^{1/(1-\sigma)},$$

$$K_t^k = \frac{R}{R - \theta_t P_t^k} N_t,$$

$$B_{t+1}^G = \Pi_t^k + \Pi_t^b + RB_t^G - N_{t+1},$$

$$P_t^l = \frac{P_t^k}{\varphi}\left(\frac{Y_t^l}{Y_t^k}\right)^{1/\sigma},$$

$$s_t^w = w_t \, / \, (1 + \beta^{-\gamma}R^{1-\gamma}),$$

$$c_{1t}^w = w_t - s_t^w, c_{2t}^w = s_t^w R,$$

$$B_t^w = s_t^w - B_t^k.$$

Combining the budget constraints of households, entrepreneurs, and the government, we obtain the following resource constraints

$$C_t + I_t + S_t^f = \text{GNP}_t = Y_t - C(B_t) + (R - 1)(B_t^w + B_t^G), \quad (19)$$

where S_t^f stands for a current account or foreign surplus and

$$C_t = c_{1t}^w + c_{2t}^w + c_{1t}^E + c_{2t}^E,$$

$$I_t = K_{t+1} - (1 - \delta)K_t,$$

$$K_t = K_t^k + K_t^l,$$

$$S_t^f = B_{t+1}^w + B_{t+1}^G - (B_t^w + B_t^G).$$

VII. Characterizing the Equilibrium

In this section we characterize the equilibrium. We first discuss the parameter restrictions for the capital-intensive sector's collateral constraint to bind at steady state. We then discuss the model's implication on a foreign surplus. We end the section by analyzing the determinants of the investment rate and the share of labor income during the transition.

A. Steady State

In steady state, all aggregate variables are constant. We consider the case that the borrowing constraint for the K-firm is binding at steady state. Note that

$$P^k = \frac{R}{\bar{\theta}}(1 - \xi)$$

$$P^k\bar{\theta} < R.$$

For the collateral constraint to bind, that is, $R < P^k$, it must be

$$1 - \xi > \bar{\theta}. \quad (20)$$

Intuitively, the smaller $\bar{\theta}$ is, the stronger the firm's default incentive is, and thus the more binding the collateral constraint is. Similarly, the smaller ξ is, the slower the net worth accumulates, and the more binding the collateral constraint becomes. Condition (20) implies that the collateral constraint always binds along the transition path. It is, therefore, always profitable for K-firms to borrow up to the maximum to expand their production.

B. A Growing Foreign Surplus

Tables 3 and 4 show that net exports since 1997 have grown large in comparison to earlier periods. A large current account surplus, part of the emphasis in SSZ, is a byproduct of our model but with a different mechanism. To see this result, we begin with workers' purchases of foreign bonds denoted as

$$B_t^w = s_t^w - (K_t^k - N_t),$$

where $K_t^k - N_t$ is workers' savings used for domestic capital investment. The net foreign surplus as a fraction of GDP is

$$\frac{B_{t+1}^w + B_{t+1}^G - (B_t^w + B_t^G)}{Y_t - C(B_t)}.$$

Two forces drive up the net foreign surplus: households' savings in foreign bonds ($B_{t+1}^w - B_t^w$) and the government's savings in foreign reserves ($B_{t+1}^G - B_t^G$). In China, the difference between savings and investment (GFCF) as a percent of GDP by expenditure reached its peak at 9.48% in 2007 and declined to .069% in 2012. Although household savings is still the main component of national savings, its growth is much slower than that of the government's savings between 2000 and 2012. According to our calculation based on the NBS annual data, government savings as a percent of GDP increased by 7 percentage points between 2000 and 2012, contributing to 63.90% of an increase of 11 percentage points in the national saving rate during this period (from 37.47% to 48.43%). In our model, the worker's saving rate is constant and all entrepreneurial savings is used to finance investment in the labor-intensive sector. As a result, most of the *increase* in the national saving rate and thus the net foreign surplus are driven by an increase in government savings, consistent with the aforementioned fact for China.

C. Key Transition Paths

We are interested in the dynamic paths of (a) the investment rate, measured as the ratio of aggregate investment to aggregate output, and (b) the share of labor income, measured as the ratio of wage income to aggregate output. For tractability we set $\theta_t = \bar{\theta}$ and assume the complete capital depreciation (i.e., $\delta = 1$) such that $I_t^j = K_{t+1}^j$ for $j \in \{k, l\}$. In our two-sector model, the investment rate can be decomposed as[27]

$$\frac{I_t}{Y_t} = \frac{I_t^k}{P_t^k Y_t^k} \frac{P_t^k Y_t^k}{Y_t} + \frac{I_t^l}{P_t^l Y_t^l} \frac{P_t^l Y_t^l}{Y_t}. \tag{21}$$

In our model, the dynamic paths of the investment rate depend on two channels: the reallocation (between-sector) effect and the sector-specific (within-sector) effect. If the investment rate in the capital-intensive sector is higher than the investment rate in the labor-intensive sector, reallocation of resources from the labor-intensive sector to the capital-intensive sector tends to increase the investment rate (the reallocation effect). Given the ratio of revenue in the capital-intensive sector to that in the labor-intensive sector, a change in the investment rate in the capital-intensive sector tends to move the aggregate investment rate in the same direction (the sector-specific effect).[28]

The other key object is the share of labor income in total output:

$$\frac{w_t L_t}{Y_t} = \frac{(1 - \psi)(1 - \alpha)}{1 + P_t^k Y_t^k / (P_t^l Y_t^l)}. \tag{22}$$

Equation (22) indicates that an increase in the ratio of revenue in the capital-intensive sector to that in the labor-intensive sector reduces the share of labor income.[29]

In summary, an increase in the ratio of revenue in the capital-intensive sector to that in the labor-intensive sector tends to raise the investment rate and reduce the share of labor income simultaneously, as we observe in the data discussed in Sections V.B and VIII.B. Such a trend pattern, as argued below, is driven by the increasing borrowing capacity of the capital-intensive sector.

We now establish the following proportion about the ratio of revenue in the capital-intensive sector to that in the labor-intensive sector during the transition.

Proposition 1. *Given that $\sigma > 1$, during the transition the ratio of revenue in the capital-intensive sector to that in the labor-intensive sector increases monotonically toward the steady state.*

Proof. The growth rate of the ratio of revenues in the two sectors can be expressed as

$$\Delta \log \frac{P_t^k Y_t^k}{P_t^l Y_t^l} = \left(1 - \frac{1}{\sigma}\right) \Delta \log \frac{Y_t^k}{Y_t^l}. \tag{23}$$

Along the transition path, the output ratio of the two sectors is

$$\frac{Y_t^k}{Y_t^l} = \left(\frac{\varphi(1 - \varphi^\sigma (P_t^k)^{1-\sigma})^{1/(1-\sigma)}}{P_t^k} \right)^\sigma. \tag{24}$$

Therefore, the ratio of output in the capital-intensive sector to that in the labor-intensive sector moves in an opposite direction to the relative price of capital-intensive goods. As net worth of the capital-intensive sector increases, the collateral constraint becomes less binding, which reduces the price of capital-intensive goods toward the first-best level R. Therefore, the ratio Y_t^k / Y_t^l increases monotonically during the transition path. Given that $\sigma > 1$, the ratio $P_t^k Y_t^k / (P_t^l Y_t^l)$ increases along the transition path.

The intuition for the above proposition is as follows. Accumulation of net worth in the capital-intensive sector expands the borrowing capacity and henceforth causes output in the capital-intensive sector to grow faster than output in the labor-intensive sector. With the elasticity of substitution greater than one, the ratio of revenue in the capital-intensive sector to that in the labor-intensive sector increases along the transition.

Equation (23) is reminiscent of the finding of Acemoglu and Guerrieri (2008). In a frictionless two-sector model with different capital intensities, their paper explores the impact of capital deepening on the capital income share, and the *efficient* resource reallocation between the two sectors. The focus of their paper, however, is on the US economy, characterized by a roughly constant labor income share and an increasing share of the labor-intensive sector's value in the long run as capital deepens. As a result, the elasticity of substitution of less than one is needed to reconcile these facts. The observation on China's two sectors (elaborated in Sections V.B and VIII.B) clearly indicates that the ratios of both revenues and capital stocks in the capital-intensive and labor-intensive sectors increase while the share of labor income declines with capital deepening, suggesting that the elasticity of substitution greater than one is consistent with the transition pattern of China's macroeconomy.

More important is our finding that the dynamics of the aggregate investment rate along the transition path depend on the source of capital deepening. In our benchmark model, the source of capital deepening is endogenous and the extent to which capital deepens increases with the borrowing capacity of the capital-intensive sector. Consequently, resources are reallocated from the labor-intensive sector to the capital-intensive sector. If the labor-intensive sector is more productive than the capital-intensive sector, the reallocation is *inefficient*. Such a mechanism, as we show in Section VIII, is crucial to explaining not only

Table 9
Parameter Values

Parameter	Definition	Value
α	Capital income share in L-sector	0.40
β	Utility discount factor	$(0.96)^{30}$
ξ	Speed of net worth accumulation for K-sector	0.56
θ	Leverage ratio for K-sector	0.30
ψ	Fraction of L-sector revenue to young entrepreneurs	0.20
δ	Capital depreciation rate	1
χ	Relative TFP of L-sector	4.98
σ	Elasticity of substitution between K- and L-sectors	2
R	Interest rate for K-sector investment loan	1.04
φ	Share of K-sector output in final output production	0.85
η	Curvature parameter in banking cost of borrowing	20
γ	Intertemporal elasticity of substitution	1

the trend patterns but also the cyclical patterns of China. Without the borrowing constraint, our economy would imply a declining aggregate investment rate and an increasing consumption output ratio along the transition path, due to diminishing returns to capital in the labor-intensive sector; the economy would imply a positive comovement between investment and labor income under various shocks, as well as a positive comovement between long-term and short-term loans.

VIII. Quantitative Results and the Mechanism

In this section we report quantitative results for both transition paths, holding θ constant and impulse responses following an expansionary shock to θ. We then discuss the mechanism in our model in the context of disaggregated data and further empirical findings. We conclude this section with counterfactual exercises to illustrate how the mechanism works.

A. Trend and Cyclical Patterns

We set both the initial capital stock in the labor-intensive sector and the initial net worth of the capital-intensive sector to values smaller than the corresponding steady-state values. Moreover, the initial net worth of capital-intensive firms is such that the capital-intensive sector's collateral constraint binds in the initial period. The specific configuration of parameter values is set in table 9.

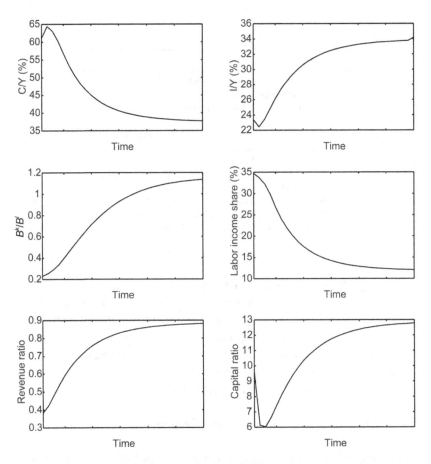

Fig. 14. The trend patterns for the benchmark theoretical model.

Note: "C" stands for aggregate consumption, "I" for aggregate investment, "Y" for aggregate output, "$B^{k'}$" for long-term loans, "$B^{l'}$" for short-term loans, "Revenue ratio" means the ratio of the capital-intensive sector's revenue to that of the labor-intensive sector, and "Capital ratio" means the ratio of capital stock in the capital-intensive sector to that in the labor-intensive sector.

Figure 14 shows the simulated results. Along the transition path, we see that the consumption-output ratio experiences a secular decline, while the investment-output ratio increases steadily after an initial fall.[30] An increase in the investment rate is puzzling from the perspective of neoclassical models. As equation (21) suggests, the main channel for an increase in the investment rate is the increase in the value of the capital-intensive sector relative to that of the labor-intensive sector. In our model economy, the investment rate in the capital-intensive sector is higher than its counterpart in the labor-intensive sector because of capital-intensive firms' ability to leverage against their net worth. When capital-intensive goods producers' net worth increases, resources are reallocated toward the capital-intensive sector, measured by an increasing share of revenues of capital-intensive firms in total output. As a result, the aggregate investment rate tends to increase toward the steady state. The middle row of figure 14 shows that the ratio of investment loans to working-capital loans increases steadily while the share of labor income declines, as we observe in the data. The last row of the figure shows that the ratios of revenue and capital stock in the capital-intensive sector to those in the labor-intensive sector increase steadily. These results are corroborated by the evidence from the disaggregated data presented in Section VIII.B.

We now explore the impulse responses to an increase in the credit quota, that is, an unexpected increase in θ_t. Figure 15 presents a set of impulse responses that are consistent with the empirical findings discussed in previous and later sections. One can see that loans to the capital-intensive sector (long-term loans) increase sharply on impact and the response is persistent. The increase of long-term loans crowds out working-capital loans due to the banking friction (the bottom row of figure 15). As a result, aggregate investment increases, while aggregate consumption decreases moderately (the first row of figure 15). This outcome leads to a hump-shaped increase in aggregate output. The decline of the wage rate and thus labor income is caused by the crowding effect on the labor-intensive sector (the second row of figure 15).

B. Key Mechanism and Data Corroboration

Along the transition path, as capital-intensive firms' net worth increases, their borrowing capacity increases as well. With the elasticity of substitution between the two sectors greater than one, the share of the capital-intensive sector's revenue in total output increases along the transition path. Given that the capital-intensive sector's investment rate is higher than that of the labor-intensive sector, such a resource reallocation leads to a higher aggregate investment rate. Meanwhile, the share of labor income declines and the ratio of the capital stock in the capital-intensive sector to that in the labor-intensive sector rises.

Over the business cycle, if the government decides to increase the loan quota à la an increase of θ_t, long-term credits to capital-intensive

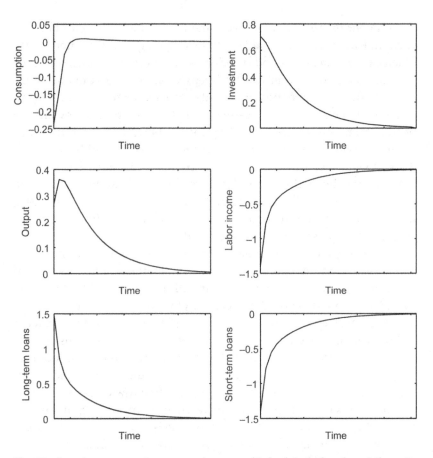

Fig. 15.   Impulse responses to an expansionary credit shock in the benchmark theoretical model.

firms expand. Equations (10) and (15) then imply that an increase in the capital-intensive firm's borrowing capacity exerts a positive externality on the cost of working-capital loans for labor-intensive firms. According to (12), an increase in R_t^l reduces labor demand, thereby crowding out working-capital loans and reducing wage income (the crowding-out effect). Thus, our theoretical model is able to generate a negative correlation between investment and labor income, a negative comovement of investment and consumption, and most importantly a negative comovement of long-term and short-term loans. For similar reasons, such comovement patterns hold during the economic transition (even without credit shocks) because capital-intensive firms' net worth continues to rise.

Estimating the Elasticity of Substitution

The fall of the labor income share generated by our model economy depends crucially on the magnitude of the elasticity of substitution in the aggregate production function being greater than 1. The value greater than one accords with (a) the observed ratio of revenue in the capital-intensive sector to that in the labor-intensive sector and (b) the observed comovement between the ratio of revenues in the heavy and light sectors and the corresponding quantity ratio. Of course, one can directly estimate this important parameter by deriving from (6) the following relationship between the value ratio and the quantity ratio in the two sectors:

$$\log \frac{P_t^k Y_t^k}{P_t^l Y_t^l} = \log \varphi + \frac{\sigma - 1}{\sigma} \log \frac{Y_t^k}{Y_t^l}. \tag{25}$$

The annual data for the value and quantity ratios in the heavy and light sectors are available from 1996 to 2011. Following Acemoglu and Guerrieri (2008), we first HP filter both variables in (25) with the smooth parameter value of 6.25 and then regress the left-hand variable on the right-hand variable. The regression estimate of $(\sigma - 1) / \sigma$ is 0.78 with the t-statistic 5.32, implying that the estimate of σ is 4.53 and significantly greater than 1. To examine the extent to which this estimate is affected by the HP filter, we also regress $\Delta \log(P_t^k Y_t^k / P_t^l Y_t^l)$ on $\Delta \log(Y_t^k / Y_t^l)$ by taking advantage of the relationship

$$\Delta \log \frac{P_t^k Y_t^k}{P_t^l Y_t^l} = \frac{\sigma - 1}{\sigma} \Delta \log \frac{Y_t^k}{Y_t^l}. \tag{26}$$

The regression estimate of $(\sigma - 1) / \sigma$ is 0.74 with the t-statistic 5.65. This implies that the estimate of σ is 3.86, significantly greater than 1.

There are two criticisms for this simple regression exercise. One is that the number of data points is only 16. To address this criticism, we employ the monthly data for P_t^k, P_t^l, Y_t^k, and Y_t^l that are available from 2003:1 to 2012:5 (a total of 113 data points) when Y_t^k and Y_t^l are measured by gross output and from 1996:10 to 2012:12 (a total of 195 data points) when these variables are measured by sales. Running simple regressions on the HP-filtered, seasonally adjusted series (with the smooth parameter being 129600) according to equation (25) yields the estimate of σ being 1.38 for gross output and 1.92 for sales.

The second criticism, which is more serious, is that both variables in (25) or (26) are endogenously determined. Thus, simple-regression results may be biased. To take into account these criticisms and further establish the robustness of the result $\sigma > 1$, we model such a simultaneous relationship explicitly with the following two-variable restricted VAR:

$$A_0 y_t = a + \sum_{\ell=1}^{p} A_\ell y_{t-\ell} + \varepsilon_t,$$

where A_0 is an unrestricted 2×2 matrix allowing for full endogeneity, a is a 2×1 vector of intercept terms, ε_t is a 2×1 vector of independent standard-normal random shocks, and

$$A_0 = \begin{bmatrix} a_{0,11} & a_{0,12} \\ a_{0,21} & a_{0,22} \end{bmatrix}, \ A_\ell = \begin{bmatrix} a_{\ell,11} & a_{\ell,12} \\ 0 & 0 \end{bmatrix}, \ y_t = \begin{bmatrix} \log \dfrac{P_t^k Y_t^k}{P_t^l Y_t^l} & \log \dfrac{Y_t^k}{Y_t^l} \end{bmatrix}'. \quad (27)$$

It follows from (25) and (27) that $\sigma = a_{0,21} / (a_{0,21} + a_{0,22})$. By Theorems 1 and 3 of Rubio-Ramrez, Waggoner, and Zha (2010), the simultaneous system (27) is globally identified almost everywhere. We estimate this model with $p = 13$.[31] Likelihood-based estimation of system (27) is analogous to utilizing a large number of lagged variables as instrumental variables (Sims 2000).

The monthly data for gross output gives us 100 data points (excluding all the lagged variables)—a respectable degree of freedom for estimation. We use the MCMC method of Zha (1999) and Sims and Zha (1999) to obtain maximum-likelihood estimation of the VAR parameters as well as the 68% and 95% posterior probability intervals of the estimated parameter σ, as reported in table 10. Estimation results are robust to whether we first seasonally adjust the four monthly data P_t^k, P_t^l, Y_t^k, and Y_t^l or we do not adjust these series seasonally. Because the estimation applies to the value and quantity *ratios*, the seasonality is largely eliminated. The estimate of σ is 2.32 for seasonally adjusted monthly data and 2.15 for original monthly data. The probability intervals are very tight around these estimates. None of the million MCMC simulations we have generated gives a value of σ that comes even close to being less than or equal to 1.[32]

The robustness of our advanced estimation method is further tested by applying the method to the alternative relationship

$$\log \frac{P_t^k Y_t^k}{P_t^l Y_t^l} = \sigma \log \varphi + (1 - \sigma) \log \frac{P_t^k}{P_t^l}. \quad (28)$$

Table 10
Estimate and Probability Intervals of σ Using System (27) or (29)

Seasonally Adjusted Monthly Data		
Point Estimate	68% Interval	95% Interval
2.32	(2.11, 2.54)	(1.94, 2.79)
Original (Not Seasonally Adjusted) Monthly Data		
Point Estimate	68% Interval	95% Interval
2.15	(1.96, 2.35)	(1.80, 2.57)

Note: The simulated results are based on one million MCMC posterior probability draws.

Thus, the system represented by (27) becomes

$$A_0 = \begin{bmatrix} a_{0,11} & a_{0,12} \\ a_{0,21} & a_{0,22} \end{bmatrix}, \ A_\ell = \begin{bmatrix} a_{\ell,11} & a_{\ell,12} \\ 0 & 0 \end{bmatrix}, \ y_t = \begin{bmatrix} \log \dfrac{P_t^k Y_t^k}{P_t^l Y_t^l} & \log \dfrac{P_t^k}{P_t^l} \end{bmatrix}'. \quad (29)$$

One can show that the estimation result for σ is invariant to whether system (27) or (29) is used. The invariance is confirmed by our MCMC simulations. This robust result is critical because the invariance property breaks down when one estimates this alternative relationship via simple regressions or swaps the left-hand variable and the right-hand variable in the regression. We recommend that the estimated results reported in table 10 be used.

Relative Prices of Investment

In a recent paper, Karabarbounis and Neiman (2014) argue for the elasticity of substitution between capital and labor to be greater than 1 to explain the decline of labor income share. Their model requires that the relative price of investment declines simultaneously. Our model economy for China does not rest on the decline of the relative price of investment to explain the decline of labor income share. Specifically, the relative price is assumed to be flat so that it does not play a dominant role in explaining either trend or cyclical facts.[33] This feature marks a major departure of our model from the standard model so as to account explicitly for Chinese unique characteristics in which we establish, below, a robust finding that there is a weak or little relationship between the labor income share and the relative price of investment in China.

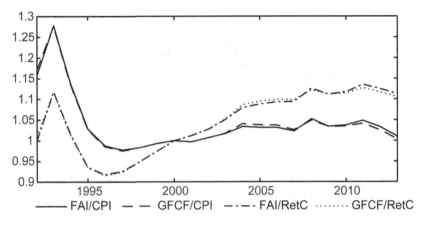

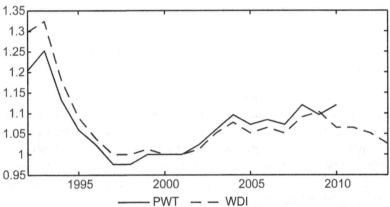

Fig. 16. Various relative prices of investment goods to consumption goods, normalized to 1 for 2000.

Note: "FAI" stands for the price of fixed-asset investment, "GFCF" for the price of gross fixed-asset capital formation, and "RetC" for the price of retail sales of consumer goods. The data on relative prices of investment goods to consumption goods from the PWT and WDI are suggested by Karabarbounis and Neiman (2014), where "PWD" stands for the Penn World Tables and "WDI" the World Bank's World Development Indices. For the PWT data source, the price of investment goods is the price of GFCF, and the price of consumption goods is CPI; for the WDI data source, the price of investment goods is the same as in the PWT data source, but the price of consumption goods is the price of retail sales of consumer goods.

Figure 16 displays various measures of relative prices of investment goods to consumption goods following Karabarbounis and Neiman (2014). In the top chart of the figure, we use two investment price series and two consumption price series. The investment price series are the price indices for fixed-asset investment (FAI) and gross fixed-asset capital formation (GFCF); the consumption price series are CPI and the price index for the retail sales of consumer goods. As one can see from these various measures, the relative price of investment since 1997 has either increased or stayed flat. This pattern is robust to other measures of the relative price of investment. In the bottom chart of figure 16, we report the two other data sources used by Karabarbounis and Neiman (2014): the PWT measure (Penn World Tables) and the WDI measure (World Bank's World Development Indices). Both measures use the price of GFCF. The PWT price index of consumption is the purchasing-power-parity (PPP) price of consumption that is suitably adjusted by the exchange rate. The PWT price index of investment is adjusted by the PPP in the same way. The WDI price index of consumption is the retail sales price of consumer goods. As evident in this chart, the relative price of investment has increased or remained flat since 1997.[34]

Between-Sector Contribution to the Labor Share Decline

The assumption of two sectors in our model accords with the fact that the between-sector contribution to the aggregate labor-share decline is empirically significant for the Chinese economy. The disaggregated data we use are the surveys from 1995 to 2010 of the 17 disaggregated sectors (subsectors) published by the NBS in years ending with 0, 2, 5, and 7. This data set contains four variables: labor income (remuneration of employees), net production tax, profits (operational surplus), and depreciation of fixed assets. The value added of each disaggregated sector is calculated as the sum of these four variables.[35] Table 11 ranks the 17 detailed sectors according to the average labor share between 1995 and 2010. Although the ranking within each broad sector differs between China and the United States, a comparison of our table 11 and Acemoglu and Guerrieri's (2008) table 1 shows the broad consistency of separating the capital-intensive sector from the labor-intensive sector across the two countries.[36] We then group the 17 sectors into two aggregate sectors: the heavy sector and the light sector according to the strategic plan of the Eighth National People's Congress to develop infrastructure, real estate, basic industries (metal products, autos, and high-tech machinery), and other heavy industries (petroleum and telecommunication).

Figure 17 plots the labor shares in the heavy and light sectors, along with the labor share at the aggregate level. The aggregate labor share

Table 11
Labor Shares across 17 Sectors

Labor Share	Detailed Sector	Broad Sector
.199	Real estate, leasing and commercial service	H
.238	Electricity, heating and water production and supply	H
.243	Coking, coal gas and petroleum processing	H
.266	Food, beverage, and tobacco	L
.316	Wholesale, retail, accommodation and catering	H
.330	Banking and insurance	H
.335	Chemical	H
.336	Other manufacturing	L
.365	Mining	H
.370	Transportation, information transmission, computer services and software	H
.375	Metal product	H
.399	Machinery equipment	H
.414	Construction material and nonmetallic mineral product	L
.448	Textile, garment, and leather	L
.580	Construction	L
.738	Other services	L
.886	Farming, forestry, animal husbandry, and fishery	L

Note: "H" stands for the heavy sector and "L" for the light sector. The labor share in each disaggregated sector is calculated as labor compensation from the survey data, divided by value added from the NBS input-output tables. The reported labor-share value is the average value between 1995 and 2010.

from the survey data and input-output tables shows a pattern similar to the trend pattern displayed in the middle row of figure 5 in which the *Flow of Funds* aggregate data are utilized; its decline over time is attributed to a combination of within-sector and between-sector effects. The within-sector effect concerns the decline of the labor share in each of the heavy and light sectors and the between-sector effect reflects the difference between the two sectors. To calculate these two effects, note that

$$LS_t \equiv \frac{w_t L_t}{Y_t} = \frac{w_t L_t^k + w_t L_t^l}{P_t^k Y_t^k + P_t^l Y_t^l} = \alpha_t^l \frac{1 + \beta_t (P_t^k Y_t^k / P_t^l Y_t^l)}{1 + (P_t^k Y_t^k / P_t^l Y_t^l)},$$

where $\alpha_t^l = w_t L_t^l / P_t^l Y_t^l$, $\alpha_t^k = w_t L_t^k / P_t^k Y_t^k$, and $\beta_t = \alpha_t^k / \alpha_t^l < 1$. The between-sector effect is measured by

$$B_t^{effect} = \bar{\alpha}^l \frac{1 + \bar{\beta}(P_t^k Y_t^k / P_t^l Y_t^l)}{1 + (P_t^k Y_t^k / P_t^l Y_t^l)},$$

where $\bar{\alpha}^i$ is the average of α_t^i over t for $i = l,k$ and $\bar{\beta} = \bar{\alpha}^k / \bar{\alpha}^l$, while the within-sector effect is measured by $W_t^{effect} = LS_t - B_t^{effect}$. A change in

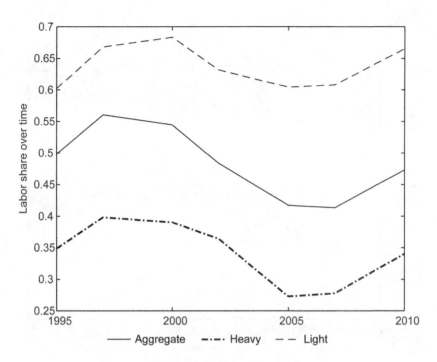

Fig. 17. Labor shares in the heavy and light sectors
Note: The calculation is based on the NBS input-output data for the 17 sectors in China.

the labor share, denoted by $\Delta LS \equiv LS_{t=t_1} - LS_{t=t_0}$ where t_0 is the beginning year and t_1 is the end year in consideration, is decomposed into

$$\Delta LS = \Delta B^{\text{effect}} + \Delta W^{\text{effect}}, \tag{30}$$

where $\Delta B^{\text{effect}} = B^{\text{effect}}_{t=t_1} - B^{\text{effect}}_{t=t_0}$ and $\Delta W^{\text{effect}} = W^{\text{effect}}_{t=t_1} - W^{\text{effect}}_{t=t_0}$. It is straightforward to prove that (30) is equivalent to the decomposition formula proposed by Karabarbounis and Neiman (2014) such that

$$\Delta B^{\text{effect}} = \sum_{i=k,l} \bar{\alpha}^i \Delta \omega^i, \quad \Delta W^{\text{effect}} = \sum_{i=k,l} \Delta \alpha^i \bar{\omega}^i,$$

where $\omega^i_t = P^i_t Y^i_t / (P^k_t Y^k_t + P^l_t Y^l_t)$ and $\bar{\omega}^i$ is the average of ω^i_t over t.

A necessary condition for the between-sector effect on the declining labor share is for the ratio of value added in the heavy sector to value added in the light sector to rise over time. Figure 18 plots this ratio, which shows a strong upward trend since 1990. As shown in figure 17, the labor share α^i_t for both $i = k$ (the heavy sector) and $i = l$ (the light sector) did not change much between 1995 and 2010, while the overall

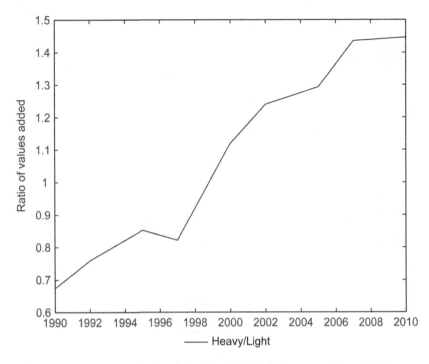

Fig. 18. Ratio of values added in the heavy and light sectors grouped from the 17 sectors in the NBS input-output data.

(aggregate) labor share declined from 0.5 in 1995 to 0.47 in 2010. This presents a very informative case—it illustrates that even when the labor share *changes little* in the heavy sector and *even rises* in the light sector, the aggregate labor share may still decline entirely due to the between-sector effect. If we use 1997 instead as an initial year, the labor share did experience a decline over time for each of the two sectors and the question becomes whether the between-sector effect is still empirically significant.[37] Table 12 reports that with 1997 as an initial year for comparison, the between-sector effect continues to be significant in explaining the decline of the overall labor income share.[38] The table documents the results with and without the agricultural sector for 1995 as an initial year, 1997 as an initial year, 2007 as an ending year, and 2010 as an ending year. The reason for excluding agriculture is to eliminate the potential bias introduced by the extremely high value of labor share in that sector. Our findings are very robust. For a majority of cases, the between-sector effect contributes at least 40% of the decline to the aggregate labor share. In the cases when the initial year is 1995 and the

Table 12
Between-Sector and Within-Sector Decompositions of Changes in the Labor Share

Year	ΔLS	Between	Within	Between (%)	Within (%)
All 17 Sectors, ΔLS Relative to the 1995 Labor Share					
2000	−0.085	−0.052	−0.032	61.84 (−)	38.15 (−)
2010	−0.025	−0.052	0.027	65.81 (−)	34.19 (+)
All 17 Sectors, ΔLS Relative to the 1997 Labor Share					
2000	−0.147	−0.057	−0.089	39.00 (−)	61.00 (−)
2010	−0.088	−0.057	−0.030	65.59 (−)	34.40 (−)
Excluding Agriculture, ΔLS Relative to the 1995 labor Share					
2000	−0.043	−0.019	−0.024	43.30 (−)	56.69 (−)
2010	0.028	−0.019	0.047	29.01 (−)	70.99 (+)
Excluding Agriculture, ΔLS Relative to the 1997 Labor Share					
2000	−0.119	−0.026	−0.093	21.76 (−)	78.23 (−)
2010	−0.048	−0.027	−0.021	55.84 (−)	44.16 (−)

Note: "ΔLS" stands for the change of the labor share relative to the value in the initial year (1995 or 1997). The "−" sign in parentheses indicates a contribution to a decline in the labor share and the "+" sign indicates a contribution to an increase in the labor share. "Excluding agriculture" means all 17 sectors excluding the sector of farming, forestry, animal husbandry, and fishery.

ending year is 2010, the between-sector effect is the only effect that contributes to the labor share decline because the within-sector effect has a *wrong sign* (i.e., it causes the labor share to increase rather than decrease). These robust results reinforce the overriding importance of modeling the heavy and light sectors as two separate sectors for the Chinese economy.

Short-Term versus Long-Term Loans

Figure 19 summarizes the key loan structure in China. Heavy industries, given the priority by the "Five-Year Program" of the Eighth National People's Congress, have enjoyed easy access to bank loans for medium- and long-term investment. One main reason for rapid increases of bank loans toward heavy industries is the persistent monopoly held by large banks (most of them are state owned) in the credit market. According to Yu and Ju (1999), the share of the four largest national banks ("the Big Four") in total bank loans was 70.0% in 1997. This monopolistic power has hardly changed ever since. According to our calculation using the monthly data from 2010:1 to 2014:12 published by the PBC, the share of large national banks in total bank loans was on average 67.4% (with a share of 51.2% for the Big Four). This monopoly is more severe for

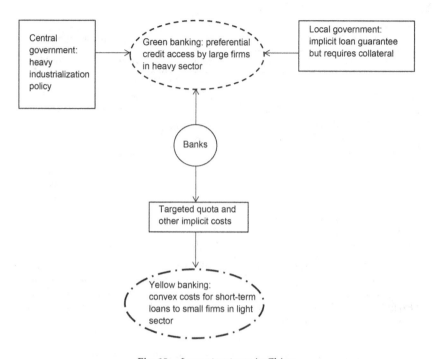

Fig. 19. Loan structures in China

medium- and long-term loans, with an average share of 75.7% between 2010 and 2014 (55.2% for the Big Four).

When assessing loan applications, these large national banks favor loans to large firms and are biased against small firms. This practice is not only because of the asymmetric information problem for small firms when banks assess loan applications, but also because large firms gain implicit government guarantees from local governments (Jiang, Luo, and Huang 2006). In figure 19 we call this type of banking "green banking." As a result, banks favor lending to large firms in heavy industries targeted by the state (e.g., steel and petroleum). Compared to small firms, large firms produce more sales, provide more tax revenues, and help boost the GDP of the local economy, an important criterion for the promotion of local government officials.

Most small firms are concentrated in labor-intensive industries (Lin and Li 2001). Given the monopoly of large banks in the credit market, their preferential loan advances to large firms in the heavy sector, often in the form of "medium- and long-term loans," take priority over other loans to small firms in the light industry, often in the form of

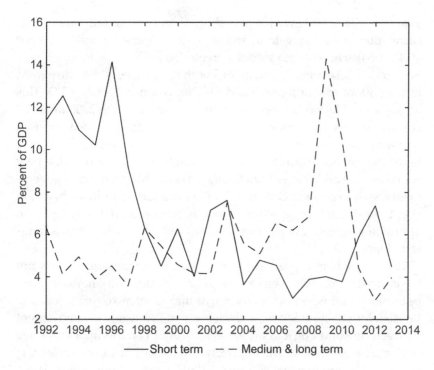

Fig. 20. New bank loans to nonfinancial enterprises as percent of GDP

Note: The correlation between the two types of loans is –0.403 for 1992–2012 and –0.405 for 2000–2012.

"short-term loans and bill financing." A reading of various *China Monetary Policy Reports* prepared by the Monetary Policy Analysis Group of the People's Bank of China (the CMP reports hereafter) reveals that the government often increases medium- and long-term loans at the sacrifice of short-term loans. The purpose of short-term loans is to finance working capital. In fact, the CMP reports sometimes interexchange the terms "short-term loans" and "working capital loans." The costs of short-term loans are much higher than those of long-term loans. We call this type of banking "yellow banking" in figure 19.

Figure 20 presents evidence that is consistent with the CMP reports and with the divergence between green banking and yellow banking. Two series are plotted in the figure: one is the short-term loan series as a percent of GDP and the other is the medium- and long-term loan series as a percent of GDP. Given the fact that the total loan volume is targeted by the government, whenever there is a rise in new long-term loans there is a tendency for new short-term loans to fall. The overall correlation of new long-term and short-term loans is negative (about −0.4), consistent with our model's prediction in response to a credit expansion.[39] These annual data accord with the quarterly data displayed in the bottom row of figure 3 and the discussion in Section III.D. This negative correlation is most conspicuous right after the 2008 financial crisis, when the government injected massive credits into medium- and long-term investment projects with a spike of new long-term loans to blunt the impact on China of the severe global recession, while new short-term loans were left unchanged. When this prodigious government credit expansion ceased in 2010, new short-term loans began to rise. Indeed, the loan structure in our theoretical model is designed to approximate these unique characteristics of short-term versus long-term loans.

These new loan series have one potential shortcoming: it does not have the data on *new* loans made to households. An alternative hypothesis is that when the government makes loans to firms, loans to households get crowded out, which leads to the negative comovement between consumption and investment. To entertain this hypothesis, we obtain a breakdown of the quarterly time series of loans *outstanding* into loans to nonfinancial enterprises (NFE) and to households. These disaggregated series are available from 2007Q1 to 2014Q3. Figure 21 plots the year-over-year growth rates of these quarterly series. The left column of the figure displays the growth rates of short-term and long-term loans to NFEs. This plot confirms the negative correlation pattern displayed in figure 20, with the correlation being −0.744. The right-side column of figure 21 reports the growth rates of short-term and long-term loans to household consumption, alongside the growth rates of long-term loans to NFEs. As one can clearly see, an increase of long-term loans to nonfinancial firms does not crowd out long-term loans to household consumption nor does it crowd out short-term loans to household consumption. To the contrary, all three series comove together with the correlation being 0.725 between short-term and long-term household consumption loans and 0.769 between long-term loans to NFEs and those to household consumption.

The negative correlation between short-term and long-term loans in China is in sharp contrast to the positive one for the US economy. Table 13 reports the correlation between short-term and long-term loans in terms of both the year-over-year growth rate of outstanding loans and the ratio of new loans to GDP by expenditure. All these loans

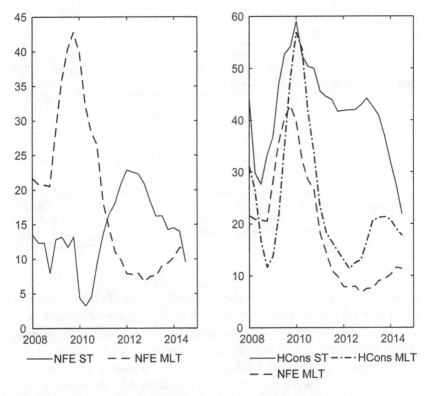

Fig. 21. Year-over-year growth rates of short-term (ST) and medium- and long-term (MLT) bank loans (outstanding) to household consumption (Hcons) and nonfinancial enterprises (NFE) from 2008Q1 to 2014Q3.

Note: The correlation is −0.744 between short-term and medium- and long-term NFE loans, 0.725 between short-term and medium- and long-term household consumption loans, and 0.769 between medium- and long-term NFE and household consumption loans.

are for nonfinancial institutions. The quarterly US series of short-term and long-term outstanding loans extends back all the way to the first quarter of 1960, while the corresponding Chinese series go back to only the first month of 1994, according to the WIND data set.[40] We consider three subsamples relevant to our study: the whole sample period for the Unites States, but unavailable (N/A) in early periods for China (1961:1–2014:3), the sample period for most of our empirical analysis (1997:1–2014:3 or 1997:1–2014:4), and the sample period in which a host of monthly data are available for China (2000:1–2013:4 or 2000:1–2014:3). For the United States, the correlation is highly positive and stable (around 0.60) across all the three subsamples; for China, the

Table 13
Correlation between Short-Term and Long-Term Loans (Quarterly Data)

Start of the Sample	Loan Growth (yoy) United States	Loan Growth (yoy) China	New Loans as Percent of GDP China
1961:1-	0.63 (2014:3)	n/a	n/a
1997:1-	0.60 (2014:3)	−0.26 (2014:4)	−0.27 (2013:4)
2000:1-	0.59 (2014:3)	−0.40 (2014:4)	−0.27 (2013:4)

Note: "Loan growth (yoy)" means the year-over-year growth rate of loans outstanding. "New loans as percent of GDP" means the ratio of new loans to GDP. For the Chinese data, the term "long-term loans" means medium-term and long-term loans. The date in parentheses indicates the end period of the sample. These end-of-sample dates are different for different series, depending on when the latest data of each series is released to the public.

correlation is significantly negative for both the growth of outstanding loans and the ratio of new loans to GDP (above −0.26) for the two subsamples. These negative correlations for the Chinese economy reflects the government's policy priority that supports heavy industries at the cost of crowding out short-term loans to labor-intensive industries.

The link between the government's investment in the heavy sector and its priority in injecting long-term bank loans into this sector is an unusual institutional arrangement central to our storyline. It is this link that constitutes the key architecture of our theoretic framework. From our calculation based on the 2010:1–2014:4 quarterly series of loan classifications reported by the PBC, 89% of medium- and long-term loans is allocated on average to heavy industries and this number has been stable over the years. Figure 22 presents further facts along this dimension, but over a longer span of periods. The top chart shows the ratio of gross output in the heavy sector to gross output in light sector based on the NBS's own classification of heavy versus light sectors within the broad secondary industry bar the construction sector. This ratio fluctuated around one until the mid-1990s and since then has steadily increased to the factor of 2.5 in recent years, consistent with the upward trend displayed in figure 18 based on all the 17 sectors covering the entire economy. The next chart reports the ratio of the capital stock in the heavy sector over that in the light sector within the broad secondary industry bar the construction sector. This chart shows a pattern similar to the top chart. The increasing importance of heavy industries is

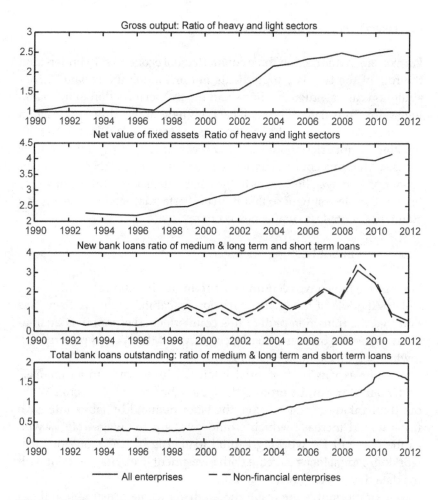

Fig. 22. Secular patterns for heavy versus light sectors and for medium- and long-term bank loans versus short-term bank loans.

Note: The top two charts are based on the NBS data and the 39 industries. The third chart (counting from the top) is based on the *Flow of Funds* annual data and the bottom chart is based on the monthly WIND data (the source of both data sets is the People's Bank of China).

supported by the rising long-term loans relative to short-term loans until 2010, both in the form of new loans and by the outstanding measure (the third and bottom charts). The upward trend has been reversed since 2010 because the government ceased to inject long-term credits that year.[41] The results from our theoretical model are consistent with the facts presented by figure 22.

C. Understanding the Mechanism Further

We explore in this section three counterfactual economies to understand the role of the two key ingredients in our model: the collateral constraint on capital-intensive firms and the financial friction in the banking sector. To isolate the role of each ingredient, we drop one friction at a time. We first drop the banking-sector friction. We then drop both banking-sector friction and collateral constraint on capital-intensive firms so that this counterfactual economy mimics the SSZ two-sector economy. Last, we allow firms in the labor-intensive sector to borrow to finance their investment so that this counterfactual economy becomes a standard frictionless small-open economy.

Economy without Lending Frictions

We remove the convex lending cost from our benchmark model. This isolates the role of the financial friction on capital-intensive firms. We find that the transition path of this counterfactual economy is qualitatively similar to our benchmark economy, but the cyclical patterns following a credit expansion differs.

A credit expansion to capital-intensive firms leads to an increase in demand for output produced by the labor-intensive sector. Without the banking-sector friction, the labor demand by labor-intensive firms would increase, which would push up the wage rate as well as the demand for working capital loans (figure 23). Consequently, working-capital loans increase with investment loans, inconsistent with the data discussed in Section VIII.B.

More important is the result that both aggregate consumption (both entrepreneur's and worker's) and aggregate investment increase (figure 23), which again is inconsistent with the empirical facts. This exercise suggests that the banking-sector friction holds the key to explaining the cyclical patterns we observe in China.

Economy without Lending and Collateral Frictions

We now remove the collateral constraint faced by capital-intensive firms as well. With these two types of frictions removed, our economy is reduced to the SSZ two-sector economy. We explore the transition paths of this counterfactual economy to quantify the role of the collateral constraint.

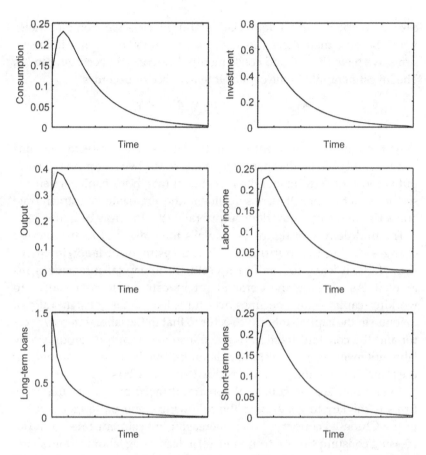

Fig. 23. Impulse responses to an expansionary credit shock in an economy without the bank-lending friction.

Let the starting point be the low initial capital stock below the steady state for labor-intensive firms. Similar to a neoclassical model, the investment-output ratio declines over time while the consumption-output ratio increases. This is opposite of the transition pattern of the economy with collateral constraints. The intuition is simple. Without the collateral constraint on capital-intensive firms, the economy behaves essentially as a neoclassical economy. As the economy grows, output growth in the labor-intensive sector slows down due to the diminishing marginal return to capital. The fall of output growth in the labor-intensive sector in turn reduces the investment rate in the capital-intensive sector because of the imperfect substitutability of outputs between the two sectors. To illustrate this point, we consider the case of complete capital depreciation and the risk-aversion parameter $\gamma = 1$. Because there there is no collateral constraint on capital-intensive firms, we have $P_t^k = R$ and consequently P_t^l is constant according to (7). The investment rate in the capital-intensive sector becomes

$$\frac{K_{t+1}^k}{P_t^k Y_t^k} = \frac{K_{t+1}^k}{P_{t+1}^k Y_{t+1}^k} \frac{P_{t+1}^k Y_{t+1}^k}{P_t^k Y_t^k} = \frac{1}{R} \frac{Y_{t+1}^l}{Y_t^l}.$$

Even though the investment rate in the labor-intensive sector remains constant and because the share of revenues in the two sectors in total output is constant, a decline of the investment rate in the capital-intensive sector leads to a simultaneous decline in the aggregate investment rate and a rise in the consumption-output ratio (the first row of figure 24).[42]

The middle row of figure 24 displays the pattern of loan-structure changes during this transition. When investment in labor-intensive firms falls, it leads to a fall of investment in capital-intensive firms as well. As a result, the demand for investment loans (relative to working-capital loans) declines over time. Due to the constant ratio of revenue in the capital-intensive sector to that in the labor-intensive sector and the constant fraction of wage incomes in output produced by labor-intensive firms, the share of labor income is constant throughout the transition (the middle and last rows of figure 24).

To summarize, the collateral constraint faced by capital-intensive firms is the key to generating the following trend patterns observed in the Chinese economy: (a) an increasing investment rate, (b) a decreasing consumption-output ratio, (c) a decreasing labor income share, (d) an increasing ratio of the capital-intensive sector's revenue to the labor-intensive sector's revenue, and (e) an increasing ratio of long-term loans to short-term loans. Without such a friction (in addition to the absence of the bank-lending friction), the economy essentially becomes neoclassical, which predicts (a) a declining investment rate, (b) an increasing consumption-output ratio, (c) a constant labor income share, (d) a constant ratio of the capital-intensive sector's revenue to the labor-intensive sector's revenue, and (e) a secular decline of long-term loans relative to short-term loans. All these counterfactual trend patterns are at odds with the Chinese data.

Frictionless Economy

In addition to removing both lending and collateral constraints from the benchmark model, we allow the labor-intensive sector to have free

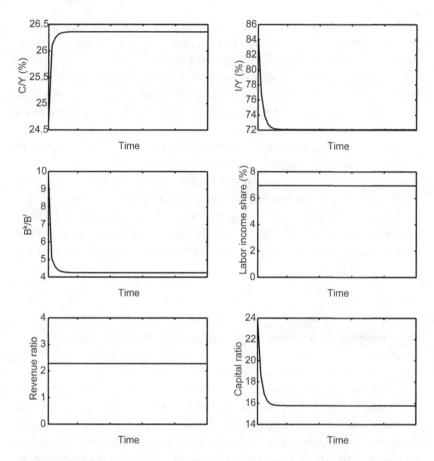

Fig. 24. The trend patterns for an economy without lending frictions and collateral constraints.

Note: "C" stands for aggregate consumption, "I" for aggregate investment, "Y" for aggregate output, "B^k" for long-term loans, and "B^l" for short-term loans. "Revenue ratio" means the ratio of the capital-intensive sector's revenue to that of the labor-intensive sector, and "Capital ratio" means the ratio of capital stock in the capital-intensive sector to that in the labor-intensive sector.

access to the financial market. This is essentially a standard frictionless small-open economy with an exogenous interest rate. Assume, without loss of generality, that the old entrepreneur owns the L-firm that is able to borrow from the bank at the fixed interest rate R for capital input. Note that the interest rate for short-term loans to finance wage bills is $R^l = 1$. Similar to our benchmark model, the young entrepreneur is the manager of the L-firm, and the managerial compensation is a fraction ψ

of the L-firm's total output. At the end of the period, the young entrepreneur decides on how much to consume and how much to save or
deposit in the bank at the fixed interest rate R.

Solving this frictionless economy is straightforward. Because the
labor-intensive sector can borrow freely to finance its production with
the constant interest rate R, this economy is at the steady state in all
periods. In particular, both the consumption rate and the investment
rate are constant across time, which implies that the ratio of long-term
loans to short-term loans is constant. Similar to the economy without
lending and collateral frictions, the labor income share and the ratio
of the capital-intensive sector's revenue to the labor-intensive sector's
revenue is constant. Thus, all the financial frictions introduced in our
benchmark model as a way to encapsulate China's unique financing
arrangements play an indispensable role in accounting for the key facts
laid out in this paper.

IX. Conclusion

We have provided a core set of annual and quarterly time series to
promote transparency and consistency of the data usable for studying
China's macroeconomy. We have styled the key facts that are robust to
disparate empirical analyses. These facts represent the core aspects of
trend and cycle in the Chinese economy. Macroeconomic models for
China should aim to account for all these facts. We have developed
a theoretical framework capable of explaining the stylized facts documented in this paper. This framework does not rest on declining prices
of investment or a particular assumption about the TFPs between the
heavy and light sectors.

There are a host of important dimensions we have not considered,
in which one might consider to extend our model for future studies.
One important extension is to collect the relevant microbanking data to
see how a particular loan is made to a firm, including the information
on the type of loan, the type of firm, and the terms of new loans. This
extension would allow us to study the aggregate impact of current financial reforms. Another extension is to refine and enrich the model for
day-to-day policy analysis, an analysis much needed by the People's
Bank of China.

Perhaps the most relevant extension is to explore policy implications
and banking reforms. The Eighteenth National People's Congress in
2012, when discussing various policy goals, explicitly expressed con-

cerns about low consumption growth and low labor share of income in China.[43] Our theoretical framework sheds light on a potential cause of the twin first-order problems facing China's macroeconomy today: (a) low consumption and income growth and (b) overcapacity of heavy industries with rising debt risks. How to resolve these problems might have profound policy implications. Our paper suggests that both problems have stemmed from a preferential credit policy for promoting the heavy industrialization since the late 1990s. Going forward, financial reforms geared for eliminating such a distortion would go a long way toward making both short-term and long-term loans function efficiently *and* putting the economy on a sustained growth path. We hope that this paper will stimulate further research on China's macroeconomy.

Endnotes

Prepared for the 30th Annual NBER Conference on Macroeconomics. Special thanks go to Marty Eichenbaum, Jonathan Parker, and Chris Sims for critical comments. We thank Toni Braun, Paco Buera, Gregory Chow, Larry Christiano, Xiang Deng, John Fernald, Lars Hansen, Rachel Ngai, Pat Higgins, Loukas Karabarbounis, Sergio Rebelo, Richard Rogerson, Pedro Silos, Aleh Tsyvinski, Harald Uhlig, Mark Watson, Kei-Mu Yi, Vivian Yue, Mei Zhu, Xiaodong Zhu, and seminar participants at People's Bank of China, Princeton University, University of Chicago, Federal Reserve Bank of Chicago, 2014 European Economic Association & Econometric Society Summer Program, Beijing University, 2014 Conference on "Macroeconomic Policies and Business Cycles" hosted by Shanghai Advanced Institute of Finance, 2015 Bank of Canada and University of Toronto Conference on the Chinese Economy, George Washington University, Hong Kong University of Science and Technology, and Hong Kong Monetary Authority for helpful discussions. We also thank Shiyi Chen, Gary Jefferson, Kang Shi, and Jun Zhang for sharing their TFP calculations with us. Last but not least, we are deeply grateful to Pat Higgins, Hongwei Wu, Tong Xu, Jing Yu, and Karen Zhong for extensive research support. This research is also supported in part by the National Science Foundation Grant SES 1127665 and by the National Natural Science Foundation of China Project Numbers 71473168, 71473169, and 71172127. The views expressed herein are those of the authors and do not necessarily reflect the views of the Federal Reserve Bank of Atlanta, the Federal Reserve System, or the National Bureau of Economic Research. For acknowledgments, sources of research support, and disclosure of the authors' material financial relationships, if any, please see http://www.nber.org/chapters/c13592.ack.

1. See various official reports from the research group in China's National Bureau of Statistics (http://www.stats.gov.cn/tjzs/tjsj/tjcb/zggqgl/200506/t20050620_37473.html).

2. Not every capital-intensive industry belongs in the heavy classification. For example, food and beverage industries are capital intensive, but are not strategically important to the government. In this paper we study two aggregate sectors and abstract from the heterogeneity of capital intensity within each sector. Despite the heterogeneity within each sector, the heavy sector is, on average, much more capital intensive than the light sector.

3. To keep our paper transparent and focused, we abstract from their first transition stage, in which the employment share of SOEs keeps declining in the labor-intensive sector. As shown by Chen and Wen (2014), most of the increase in the share of private employment occurred between 1998 and 2004 (from 15% to 50%), while the share increased by only 10% between 2004 and 2011. Nonetheless, our results would hold in a generalized economy that incorporates the first stage of transition.

4. Song et al. (2011) overcome such a deficiency in their quantitative model by feeding in an *exogenous* sequence of interest rate subsidies, which pushes up wages and the capital-labor ratio for both types of firms. This modification, nonetheless, predicts that the growth rates of aggregate investment and labor income tend to comove positively, which is inconsistent with fact (C2).

5. Similar positive comovements between aggregate investment, labor income, and consumption would happen if there is a negative shock to the interest rate subsidy faced by either heavy or light producers, as in SSZ.

6. Our mechanism might potentially explain why the observed fast increase in the ratio of corporate debt to GDP tends to beget a financial crisis, as many East Asian countries experienced in 1997–1998, because unproductive large firms accumulate debts at the cost of loans allocated to productive firms. The pace of rising debts in large firms is a looming issue for China at the present time (see, for example, the article "Digging into China's Debts" published in the February 2, 2015 issue of *Financial Times*).

7. One could in principle interpolate quarterly data using a large state-space-form model for a mixture of frequencies of the data. (A similar argument could be made about seasonal adjustments.) Since computation for such an interpolation is both costly and model dependent, we opt for the approach proposed by Leeper, Sims, and Zha (1996) and Bernanke, Gertler, and Watson (1997).

8. For the detailed description of all the problems we have discovered and of how best to correct them and then construct the time series used in this paper, see Higgins and Zha (2015).

9. See *China's Statistical Yearbook 2001* published by the NBS.

10. See Xu (2010) for more details. The author was deputy director of the NBS when that article was published.

11. *China's Statistical Yearbooks* have not published the subcomponents of GDP by expenditure for 2014. Some quarterly series in 2013 are extrapolated, and the quality of the extrapolation is high. See Higgins and Zha (2015) for details.

12. Shocks within each block are not uniquely determined.

13. While the posterior mode is well estimated with our method, we still have not managed to obtain a convergence of MCMC posterior draws to provide an informative posterior distribution.

14. Total business investment is gross fixed capital formation bar household investment.

15. The series of "labor income" is obtained from the *Flows of Funds*. Alternatively, one could construct the labor share of income by summing up "compensation of labor" across provinces and dividing by sum of "GDP by income" across provinces, which has also declined since the late 1990s. There are, however, serious data problems associated with this alternative measure because of large discrepancies between the national value and the sum of provincial values. For discussions of other data problems, consult Bai and Qian (2009).

16. Since the sixth industry "Mining of Other Ores" receives almost zero weight in value added or gross output, there are effectively 38 active industries.

17. Our evidence indicates that this industry is labor intensive. In table 11, we classify 17 broad sectors according to their respective labor income shares. According to that classification, the sector "Machinery Equipment" belongs to the labor-intensive sector.

18. The SOE definition we use for figure 11 is consistent with the NBS's official definition except for a fraction of limited liability companies (LLCs) excluding "state sole proprietors" that should have been classified as SOE according to the definition of "State Owned & Holding" in *China's Statistical Yearbooks* (Higgins and Zha 2015). Note that LLCs excluding "state sole proprietors" in the series of fixed-asset investment are not further partitioned. For the disaggregate data on the two-digit industries, we use the NBS's official definition of SOE.

19. For informative reading, see the recent article "State-Owned Enterprises: Fixing China, Inc." in the August 30, 2014 issue of the *Economist*.

20. For this calculation we adjust the average investment rate within the secondary sector and bar the construction industry to match the average investment rate for the whole economy for the sample from 1997 to 2011. The investment rate for the whole

economy is measured as the ratio of total business investment to GDP by expenditure. The NBS also provides the input-output tables that contain the series of output and the survey data that contain the series of labor compensation for each of the 17 sectors covering the whole economy, but the investment series is not measured in accordance with our purpose. For each of the 17 sectors, the value of gross fixed capital formation is calculated according to how much of the goods produced by industry A is used for production in industry B. If the output of the food industry is not used for the production of other industries, for example, investment in that industry receives a zero entry.

21. According to their estimates, the result holds for labor-augmented TFP growth rates as well. Such a result does not necessarily contradict the findings of Hsieh and Song (2015) because privatized firms have proven to be very productive and there has been a trend for the largest private firms to engage in heavy industries prioritized by the National People's Congress.

22. We compute the contribution from 1998 and 2007 to compare to a similar finding by Brandt and Zhu (2010). The difference in exact numbers is probably due to different vintage data.

23. While one can extend it to the economy with multiple-period-lived agents, one may lose both tractability and intuition.

24. Alternatively, one can assume that K-firms may exist forever but with a certain surviving rate to prevent the accumulated net worth N_t from growing so large that the collateral constraint (8) is no longer binding.

25. Song et al. (2011) provide a microfoundation for the young entrepreneur's management fee as a fixed fraction of output as follows. There exists an agency problem between the manager and the owner of the business. The manager can divert a positive share of the firm's output for her own use. Such opportunistic behavior can be deterred only by paying managers a compensation that is at least as large as the funds they could steal, which is a share of output. An alternative setup is for parents to leave voluntary bequests to their children, who in turn would invest in the family firm.

26. Reports from various Chinese financial papers confirm these institutional arrangements.

27. For illustrative purposes we use Y_t in the denominator in this section. The correct measurement of GDP in our benchmark model, however, is $Y_t - C(B_t)$, which we adopt in our numerical analysis below. Because B_t increases over time, our results hold when the denominator is replaced by $Y_t - C(B_t)$.

28. Because of the complete capital depreciation, the investment rate in the labor-intensive sector is constant when the risk-aversion parameter γ is set to one. Relaxing the assumption of full depreciation would predict a declining investment rate in the labor-intensive sector due to diminishing marginal returns to capital.

29. Such a prediction holds in a general setup in which the capital-intensive sector also uses labor as an input, as long as the share of labor income in the capital-intensive sector is less than that in the labor-intensive sector.

30. The aggregate investment rate falls initially because the investment rate in the capital-intensive sector falls initially with the initial leverage ratio smaller than the leverage in later periods.

31. The quantity Y_t^k or Y_t^l is measured by gross output. The lag length of 13, instead of 12, is used to take account of any residual seasonality. Estimation results are robust to a choice of lag length.

32. As a robustness check we also apply our estimation method to the monthly data in which the quantity and revenue are measured by sales in each of the heavy and light industries. Again, all of the posterior draws deliver the robust result that $\sigma > 1$.

33. In fact, our results hold both along the transition path and in dynamic responses to a positive credit shock, even if we expand our benchmark model to an economy either with decreasing relative prices of investment to reflect technological advances in the production of investment goods or with endogenously *increasing relative prices* of investment goods due to a fixed input (e.g., land) in the production.

34. Hsieh and Klenow (2007) find that for poor countries, the relative price of investment measured by the domestic price tends to be larger than that measured by the PPP

price. Our finding, however, is not subject to such a measurement issue, since our interest is the time series pattern of the relative price of investment for a given country, that is, China.

35. The sum of values added over the 17 sectors is very close to GDP by value added from 2002 on, although there are some discrepancies between these two measures prior to 2002. Discrepancies also exist between the sum of labor compensations over the 17 sectors and the labor income reported by the NBS's *Flow of Funds* (FOF). The labor income series reported in the *Flow of Funds* contains two components: (a) wage and (b) social insurance payment by company. The discrepancies may be driven mainly by social insurance payments. Despite all these discrepancies, the decline of China's labor income share since the late 1990s is a robust fact, as further confirmed by Bai and Qian (2009) and Qian and Zhu (2012) who have made data adjustments to take into account changes in the statistical coverage of labor compensation over time. To make the definition distinctive, therefore, we use the term "labor income" when the data is from the Flow of Funds and "labor compensation" when it is from the survey data for the 17 disaggregated sectors.

36. To make the grouping of different industries more compatible between China and the United States, one may proceed further by matching sic codes for similar four-digit industries. The results reported in table 11, however, serve our purpose of separating the two general sectors.

37. To keep our model both transparent and focused, we abstract from entering labor in the production function of the heavy sector. For the same reason, we abstract from factors that might potentially explain the changes in the labor income share within the sector. We could, for example, allow for the heterogeneity of technologies and endogenous technology adoption within each sector as in Ngai (2004). Adding these components would *not* change our qualitative results, but may blunt our emphasis on the between-sector contribution to changes in the labor income share.

38. The year 1997 marks the regime switch intended in March 1996 by the "Five-Year Program" of the Eighth National People's Congress to give priority to the heavy industry. All of our results about the importance of the between-sector effect hold if we also choose 2000 as an initial year for comparison.

39. Brandt and Zhu (2007) discuss how bank loans to the SOEs and POEs changed over time (it appears that these breakdown series for loans no longer exist after 2003). The high volume of short-term loans before 1997 reflects the government's loose credit policy for funding small firms (including unproductive SOE firms) in the form of working capital. After the 1995 banking reform, such an easy credit policy ceased. We see from figure 20 a sharp fall of new short-term loans in 1997 and 1998. Since 1997 new short-term loans to small firms, including privatized small firms, have been restrictive and have received lower priority than new medium- and long-term loans to large firms.

40. There is no good comprehensive source of aggregate loan originations (new loans) for the United States. One source we are aware of is the Survey of Terms of Business Lending (STBL) from the Federal Reserve Board, which collects data on commercial and industrial loan originations. It is not a comprehensive count (about 350 banks are surveyed each quarter). To our knowledge, the largest banks are surveyed with certainty and smaller banks are randomly sampled. Consult http://www.federalreserve.gov/apps/reportforms/reportdetail.aspx?sOoYJ+5BzDaSCesXTb1UmHCoyU8rIHWr for details. The aim of the STBL survey is to collect data on terms of new business loans (e.g., lending rates), although the survey collects data on the amount of loan originations (or new loans) as well. Unfortunately, there is no breakdown of short-term versus long-term loan originations.

41. As shown in the third chart, the patterns for new NFE loans and total new loans track each other very closely, suggesting that total new loans can be used to approximate NFE loans when subcategories of the NFE data are unavailable. For these loan data, it is often inquired by the reader as to why a large fall of new short-term loans in 1997 shown in figure 20 is not visible in the third chart of figure 22. This is because the large fluctuations in 1996 and 1997 observed in figure 20 are small in scale when compared to those in 2008 and 2009. Indeed, the ratio of new medium- and long-term loans to new short-term loans in 1996 is $4.53 / 14.14 = 0.32$ and the same ratio in 1997 increases to only $3.58 / 9.18 = 0.39$.

42. With incomplete capital depreciation or the risk-aversion parameter $\gamma > 1$, the investment rate in the labor-intensive sector declines due to diminishing marginal returns to capital.

43. See the third point at http://news.xinhuanet.com/18cpcnc/2012-11/17/c_113711665_5 .htm and http://news.xinhuanet.com/18cpcnc/2012-11/17/c_113711665_8.htm.

References

Acemoglu, D., and V. Guerrieri. 2008. "Capital Deepening and Nonbalanced Economic Growth." *Journal of Political Economy* 116:467–98.

Bai, C., and Z. Qian. 2009. "Factor Income Share in China: The Story Behind the Statistics." *Economic Research Journal* (in Chinese) 3:27–41.

Bernanke, B. S., M. Gertler, and M. W. Watson. 1997. "Systematic Monetary Policy and the Effects of Oil Price Shocks." *Brookings Papers on Economic Activity* 1:91–142.

Brandt, L., and X. Zhu. 2007. "China's Banking Sector and Economic Growth." In *China's Financial Transition at a Crossroads*, ed. C. W. Calomiris. New York: Columbia University Press.

———. 2010. "Accounting for China's Growth." Working Paper no. 394, Department of Economics, University of Toronto.

Buera, F. J., and Y. Shin. 2013. "Financial Frictions and the Persistence of History: A Quantitative Exploration." *Journal of Political Economy* 121:221–72.

Chakraborty, S., and K. Otsu. 2013. "Business Cycle Accounting of the BRIC Economies." *B. E. Journal of Macroeconomics* 13 (1): 1–33.

Chang, Y., and A. Hornstein. 2013. "Transition Dynamics in the Neoclassical Growth Model: The Case of South Korea." FRB Richmond Working Paper no. 11-04R, Federal Reserve Bank of Richmond.

Chen, K., and Y. Wen. 2014. "The Great Housing Boom of China." Unpublished Manuscript, Emory University.

Chen, S., G. H. Jefferson, and J. Zhang. 2011. "Structural Change, Productivity Growth, and Industrial Transformation in China." *China Economic Review* 22:133–50.

Chow, G. C. 2011. *China as a Leader of the World Economy.* Hackensack, New Jersey: World Scientific.

Christiano, L. J., M. S. Eichenbaum, and C. L. Evans. 1996. "The Effects of Monetary Policy Shocks: Some Evidence from the Flow of Funds." *Review of Economics and Statistics* 78:16–34.

———. 1999. "Monetary Policy Shocks: What Have We Learned and To What End?" In *Handbook of Macroeconomics*, vol. 1A, ed. J. B. Taylor and M. Woodford, 65–148. Amsterdam: North-Holland.

———. 2005. "Nominal Rigidities and the Dynamic Effects of a Shock to Monetary Policy." *Journal of Political Economy* 113:1–45.

Cúrdia, V., and M. Woodford. 2010. "Credit Spreads and Monetary Policy." *Journal of Money, Credit and Banking* 42:3–35.

Fang, C., E. Wailes, and G. Cramer. 1998. "China's Rural and Urban Household Survey Data: Collection, Availability, and Problems." CARD Working Paper no. 98-WP 202, Center for Agricultural and Rural Development, Iowa State University.

Fernald, J., I. Malkin, and M. Spiegel. 2013. "On the Reliability of Chinese Output Figures." FRBSF Economic Letter no. 2013-08, Federal Reserve

Bank of San Francisco. http://www.frbsf.org/economic-research/files/el2013-08.pdf.

Fernald, J., and B. Neiman. 2011. "Growth Accounting with Misallocation: Or, Doing Less with More in Singapore." *American Economic Journal: Macroeconomics* 3:29–74.

Fernald, J., M. M. Spiegel, and E. Swanson. 2013. "Monetary and Fiscal Policy Effectiveness in China: Evidence from a FAVAR Model." Unpublished manuscript, Federal Reserve Bank of San Francisco.

Gan, L. 2014. "Income Inequality and an Economy in Transition." Presentation Slides, Texas A&M University and Southwestern University of Finance and Economics.

Hansen, L. P., J. C. Heaton, and N. Li. 2008. "Consumption Strikes Back? Measuring Long-Run Risk." *Journal of Political Economy* 116:260–302.

He, Q., T. Chong, and K. Shi. 2009. "What Accounts for Chinese Business Cycles?" *China Economic Review* 20 (4): 650–61.

Higgins, P. C., and T. Zha. 2015. "China's Macroeconomic Time Series: Method and Implications." Unpublished manuscript, Federal Reserve Bank of Atlanta.

Holz, C. 2013. "The Quality of China's GDP Statistics." Working Paper no. 487, Stanford Center for International Development.

Hsieh, C.-T., and P. J. Klenow. 2007. "Relative Prices and Relative Prosperity." *American Economic Review* 97:562–85.

———. 2009. "Misallocation and Manufacturing TFP in China and India." *Quarterly Journal of Economics* CXXIV:1403–48.

Hsieh, C.-T., and Z. M. Song. 2015. "Grasp the Large, Let Go of the Small: The Transformation of the State Sector in China." Unpublished Manuscript.

Huang, H., J. Ju, and V. Z. Yue. 2015. "A Unified Model of Structural Adjustments and International Trade: Theory and Evidence from China." Unpublished manuscript.

Jiang, S., J. Luo, and J. Huang. 2006. "Credit Concentration and Expansion, Soft Budget Constraints, and Systemic Credit Risks of Banks." *Journal of Financial Research* (in Chinese) 4:40–48.

Ju, J., Y. Lin, Q. Liu, and K. Shi. 2015. "A Dynamic Structural Analysis of Real Exchange Rates: Theory and Evidences from China." Unpublished manuscript.

Karabarbounis, L., and B. Neiman. 2014. "The Global Decline of the Labor Share." *Quarterly Journal of Economics* 129:61–103.

King, R. G., C. I. Plosser, J. H. Stock, and M. W. Watson. 1991. "Stochastic Trends and Economic Fluctuations." *American Economic Review* 81:819–40.

Kiyotaki, N., and J. Moore. 1997. "Credit Cycles." *Journal of Political Economy* 105:211–48.

Leeper, E. M., C. A. Sims, and T. Zha. 1996. "What Does Monetary Policy Do?" *Brookings Papers on Economic Activity* 2:1–78.

Lin, J. Y. 2013. *Demystifying the Chinese Economy.* New York: Cambridge University Press.

Lin, J. Y., and Y. Li. 2001. "Promoting the Growth of Medium- and Small-Sized Enterprises through the Development of Medium- and Small-Sized Financial Institutions." *Economic Research Journal* (in Chinese) 1:10–18.

Lu, D. Forthcoming. "Exceptional Exporter Performance? Evidence from Chinese Manufacturing Firms." *Journal of Monetary Economics.*

Moll, B. 2014. "Productivity Losses from Financial Frictions: Can Self-Financing Undo Capital Misallocation?" *American Economic Review* 104:3186–221.

Nakamura, E., J. Steinsson, and M. Liu. 2014. "Are Chinese Growth and Inflation Too Smooth? Evidence from Engel Curves." Unpublished Manuscript, Columbia University.

Ngai, L. R. 2004. "Barriers and the Transition to Modern Growth." *Journal of Monetary Economics* 51:1353–83.

Olley, G. S., and A. Pakes. 1996. "The Dynamics of Productivity in the Telecommunications Equipment Industry." *Econometrica* 64:1263–97.

Qian, Z., and X. Zhu. 2012. "Why is the Labor Income Share so Low in China?" Unpublished presentation slides.

Ravn, M. O., and H. Uhlig. 2002. "Notes on Adjusting the Hodrick-Prescott Filter for the Frequency of Observations." *Review of Economics and Statistics* 84:371–80.

Romalis, J. 2004. "Factor Proportions and the Structure of Commodity Trade." *American Economic Review* 94:67–79.

Rubio-Ramrez, J. F., D. F. Waggoner, and T. Zha. 2010. "Structural Vector Autoregressions: Theory of Identification and Algorithms for Inference." *Review of Economic Studies* 77 665–96.

Shi, H. 2009. "Understanding China's Economy During 1979-2007: A Business Cycle Accounting Approach." Unpublished Manuscript.

Sims, C. A. 2000. "Using a Likelihood Perspective to Sharpen Econometric Discourse: Three Examples." *Journal of Econometrics* 95:443–62.

Sims, C. A., D. F. Waggoner, and T. Zha. 2008. "Methods for Inference in Large Multiple-Equation Markov-Switching Models." *Journal of Econometrics* 146:255–74.

Sims, C. A., and T. Zha. 1998. "Bayesian Methods for Dynamic Multivariate Models." *International Economic Review* 39:949–68.

———. 1999. "Error Bands for Impulse Responses." *Econometrica* 67:1113–55.

———. 2006. "Were There Regime Switches in US Monetary Policy?" *American Economic Review* 96:54–81.

Song, Z., K. Storesletten, and F. Zilibotti. 2011. "Growing Like China." *American Economic Review* 101:196–233.

Stock, J. H., and M. W. Watson. 2003. "Has the Business Cycle Changed? Evidence and Explanations." Prepared for the Federal Reserve Bank of Kansas City symposium "Monetary Policy and Uncertainty," Jackson Hole, Wyoming, August 28–30.

Ventura, J. 1997. "Growth and Independence." *Quarterly Journal of Economics* 112:57–84.

Villani, M. 2005. "Bayesian Reference Analysis of Cointegration." *Econometric Theory* 21:326–57.

Waggoner, D. F., H. Wu, and T. Zha. 2015. "Dynamic Striated Metropolis-Hastings Sampler for High-Dimensional Models." Unpublished Manuscript, Federal Reserve Bank of Atlanta.

Xu, X. 2010. "An Accurate Understanding of China's Economic Statistics." *Economic Research Journal* (in Chinese) 5:21–31.

Young, A. 1995. "The Tyranny of Numbers: Confronting the Statistical Realities of the East Asia Growth Experience." *Quarterly Journal of Economics* 110:641–80.

Yu, J., and G. Zhu. 2013. "How Uncertain Is Household Income in China?" *Economics Letters* 120:74–78.

Yu, L., and Y. Ju. 1999. "Monopoly and Competition: The Reform and Development of China's Banking Industry." *Economic Research Journal* (in Chinese) 8:48–57.

Zha, T. 1999. "Block Recursion and Structural Vector Autoregressions." *Journal of Econometrics* 90:291–316.

Zhou, M., and R. Ren. 2010. "A Time Series Analysis of the Relationship between Banking Interest Rates and Private Lending Interest Rates." *Statistics and Decision* (in Chinese) 1:126–29.

Comment

Mark W. Watson, *Princeton University and NBER*

Chang et al. make three contributions. First, they describe a new annual and quarterly macro data set for China detailed in Higgins and Zha (2015). Second, they use these data to characterize trend and cyclical variation and covariance between important real and financial aggregates. Finally, they construct a dynamic equilibrium model to explain the trend and cycle facts.

The paper begins in Section II with a discussion of the challenges faced by researchers using China's data and then describes the new data set. The work putting the data set together was substantial and faced several challenges: (a) the raw data come from disparate sources and are based on different approaches; (b) much of the data is annual and there is only limited information about quarterly and monthly variation; (c) data series are available over different, and sometimes short, sample periods; (d) several of the important series are available only as growth rates, sometimes computed in nonstandard ways; (e) some series have pronounced seasonality; and (f) there are challenges converting nominal to real quantities. These are familiar measurement challenges faced by national income accountants everywhere, and the hard and careful work described here goes a long way to producing a macro data set for China that many researchers will find useful.

In this brief discussion I will say nothing more about the first (data) and third (model) contributions of the paper and instead focus on the various "trend" and "cycle" constructs used in the paper. This reflects my comparative advantage and not the relative importance of the paper's three contributions.

Trends and Cycles

Section I of the paper begins by listing five key "trend facts" and three key "cyclical patterns." A prerequisite for understanding these facts and patterns is to understand how "trend" and "cycle" are defined and measured by the authors. They do this in two distinct ways.

The first is exemplified in the paper's figure 2, which plots the annual growth rates of real GDP and its price deflator along with the ratios of consumption-to-income and investment-to-income ratios, each from 1980 through 2013. The growth rates show "ups and downs" with periods of 10 years and shorter. To a macroeconomist this looks like a cycle. The ratios exhibit much lower frequency variability: the dominant feature of these sample paths is a monotonic rise or fall over the entire 30-year sample period. This looks like a trend.

These definitions of trend and cycle rely on periodicities. Variations in a macro time series with periodicities of, say, 10 years or less, define cyclical variation. Variations with much longer periodicities, say beyond 20 or 30 years, define the trend. Spectral analysis provides a framework for analyzing cycles and trends defined in this way. Transformations like first differencing or Hodrick-Prescott moving averages are linear "filters" that amplify or attenuate the various periodicities in the data. The authors use these definitions when discussing trend facts and patterns based on figures 2–3 and 5–7 in Section IV.

In Section III, the authors use a very different definition of trend and cycle based on "permanent" and "transitory" shocks in a vector error correction model (VECM), that is a VAR with common $I(1)$ trends. The model is given in their equation (2), which I rewrite here using slightly different notation, as

$$\Delta y_t = c_t + \alpha\beta'y_{t-1} + \Phi(L)\Delta y_{t-1} + He_t,$$

where the vector y_t includes the logarithms of real values of GDP, consumption, investment, labor income, and the ratio of long-term and short-term loans to GDP, and e_t is vector of shocks. In the authors' formulation there are three common $I(1)$ trends. As they show, this implies that e can be partitioned into three permanent and three transitory shocks: $e_t = (e_t^{Permanent\prime} \ e_t^{Transitory\prime})'$, where $e^{Permanent}$ has a permanent effect on y ($\lim_{k\to\infty} \partial y_{t+k} / \partial e_{it}^{Permanent} \neq 0$), and $e^{Transatory}$ has only a transitory effect ($\lim_{k\to\infty} \partial y_{t+k} / \partial e_{it}^{Transitory} = 0$).

Using this decomposition of e, the authors define the trend in y as the process

$$\Delta y_t^{Permanent} = c_t + \alpha\beta'y_{t-1}^{Permanent} + \Phi(L)\Delta y_{t-1}^{Permanent} + H\begin{bmatrix} e_t^{Permanent} \\ 0 \end{bmatrix},$$

which is the implied value of y from the VECM, but with the transitory shocks set to zero. The cyclical component is defined as $y_t^{Transitory} = y_t - y_t^{Permanent}$. Figure 1 in the paper plots the trend values for the consumption-to-income and investment-to-income ratios using these definitions.

This "permanent shock" definition of the trend in y is much different than the definition based on low-frequency variation because, while $e^{Permanent}$ has a permanent effect on the level of y, it may also have important transitory effects on y. Indeed, VECM models are often used in macroeconomics to measure these transitory effects of permanent shocks, with leading examples being the effect of TFP shocks on output, consumption, investment (King, Plosser, Stock, and Watson 1991) and employment (Gali 1999; Christiano, Eichenbaum, and Vigfusson 2006).

My figure 1 below shows an extreme example of this. Panel A plots a realization from a univariate IMA(1,1) model: $\Delta y_t = \varepsilon_t - 0.9\varepsilon_{t-1}$. Because ε_t has a permanent effect of y, it is a permanent shock, and because the model is univariate, it is the only shock. Thus $y_t = y_t^{Permanent}$. However, much of the variation in $y_t^{Permanent}$ is associated with transitory oscillations (because of the negative MA coefficient), so that, arguably, $y_t^{Permanent}$ is a poor measure of the trend in the process. Panel B shows the same series and two trend measures: one computed as the (two-sided) Hodrick-Prescott trend and the other as the (one-sided, long-run forecast) Beveridge-Nelson (1981) trend. Both appear to capture the trend variation in the series better (to my eye) than does $y_t^{Permanent}$ ($= y_t$). Thus, as a general matter, while $y_t^{Permanent}$ captures interesting variation in the data, it can be a poor measure of the trend.

Let me conclude with two remarks about $y_t^{Permanent}$ as computed by the authors using their data. First, comparing their figure 1 (which plots consumption-income and investment-incomes using $y^{Permanent}$) to their figure 6 (which plots the ratios computed from annual data) shows that their VECM measure of $y_t^{Permanent}$ *does* capture trend variability as defined using long periodicities. (My suspicion is that the flexible deterministic trend included in their VECM helps $y^{Permanent}$ achieve this.) Thus, the point made in my figure 1 does not apply to their analysis. Second, and importantly, they use their equilibrium model to study transition paths, that is, changes in key ratios in response to a permanent shock; $y^{Permanent}$ is well-designed for that purpose.

(a) Realization from the IMA(1,1) process: $\Delta y_t = \varepsilon_t - 0.95\,\varepsilon_{t-1}$

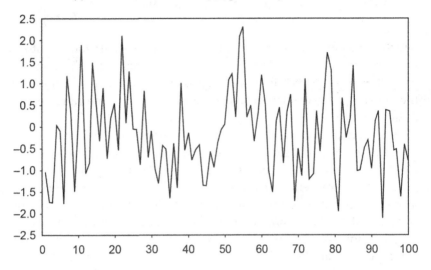

(b) HP Filtered Trend (dashes) and Beveridge-Nelson Trend (dots)

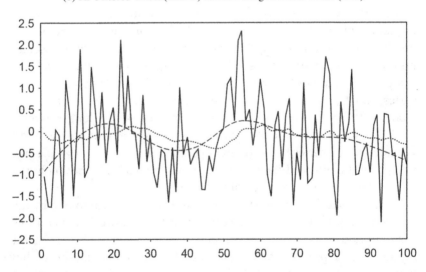

Fig. 1. A: Realization from the IMA(1,1) Process: $\Delta y_t = \varepsilon_t - 0.95\,\varepsilon_{t-1}$; B: HP-Filtered Trend (dashes) and Beveridge-Nelson Trend (dots)

Endnote

For acknowledgments, sources of research support, and disclosure of the author's material financial relationships, if any, please see http://www.nber.org/chapters/c13593.ack.

References

Beveridge, S., and C. R. Nelson. 1981. "A New Approach to Decomposition of Economic Time Series into Permanent and Transitory Components with Particular Attention to Measurement of the Business Cycle." *Journal of Monetary Economics* 7:151–74.

Christiano, L., M. Eichenbaum, and R. Vigfusson. 2006. "Assessing Structural VARs. " *NBER Macroeconomics Annual 2006*, vol. 21, ed. D. Acemoglu, K. Rogoff, and M. Woodford. Cambridge, MA: MIT Press.

Gali, J. 1999. "Technology, Employment, and the Business Cycle: Do Technology Shocks Explain Aggregate Fluctuations?" *American Economic Review* 89 (1): 249–71.

Higgins, P. C., and T. Zha. 2015. "China's Macroeconomic Time Series: Method and Implications." Unpublished Manuscript, Federal Reserve Bank of Atlanta.

King, R. G., C. I. Plosser, J. H. Stock, and M. W. Watson. 1991. "Stochastic Trends and Economic Fluctuations." *American Economic Review* 81:819–40.

Comment

John Fernald, Federal Reserve Bank of San Francisco

The paper by Chang, Chen, Waggoner, and Zha is a rich, big-picture paper about China's recent growth experience. The authors create a new and valuable data set, identify new and perhaps surprising stylized facts about China, and propose a consistent story to explain those facts.

First, the authors create new, internally consistent macro data. It is incredible that this is a contribution for a country of the size and importance of China. But it is. For example, official year-over-year data does not match the official quarter-to-quarter data. It is completely unclear to a researcher which series to use. Making a benchmark series available is a valuable contribution.

Second, the authors identify new stylized facts. A key one is that China does not have the typical comovement patterns between consumption and investment, or between investment and labor income. They also find that labor's share declines over time and that favored industries grow more quickly than less favored ones.

Third, the authors explain the facts with a new model of credit-fueled, investment-led growth.[1] The model is closely related to Song, Storesletten, and Zilibotti (2011). But, rather than emphasize the distinction between state-owned versus privately owned companies, Chang et al. argue that since the late 1990s, China has favored firms in heavy industries. This includes support for large privately owned firms in particular industries.

Before going into the details, let me summarize my takeaways. First, the data still are not very good and need to be treated with caution. The authors have done the best they can, but they cannot escape the problem of "garbage in, garbage out."

Second, the comovement properties of the data are, indeed, surprising in international context. China is a big outlier. The uncertain quality of the data raises a concern about whether we should really take that as a robust fact. Nevertheless, at least for consumption and investment, the data problems mean that the true correlation might even be *more* negative than is measured. Also, I am more impressed by the low labor share than by its downward trend.

Third, in terms of model, the broad story they are telling is plausible and somewhat intuitive. It fits previous Asian experience, where lots of countries have had industrial policies that picked winners (favoring particular firms and industries).

Now take these points in reverse order.

A Model of Favoritism with Chinese Characteristics

The authors present a stylized two-sector model to explain the patterns they see in the data. One sector comprises capital-intensive firms. I will later argue they should be called "favored" firms, but for now I will keep their labels. They produce only with capital and live only one period. Their production function is $Y^K = K^K$.

These favored/capital-intensive firms face a borrowing constraint that comes from incentive compatibility:

$$RB^K = R(K^K - N) \leq \theta P^K K^K.$$

This constraint says that interest payments cannot be too large relative to revenues. The gross interest rate is R. They borrow B^K, which is the difference between the capital they use and their net worth.

The key parameter is θ, which is the maximum the firms can borrow relative to their revenues. One way to interpret θ is as loan guarantees/ loan quota by the government. If the government increases their loan guarantees, then favored firms can borrow and invest more; if the firm's net worth $P^K K^K$ goes up, the firm can also invest more.

Labor-intensive firms produce with both capital and labor: $Y^L = (K^L)^\alpha (\chi L)^{1-\alpha}$. These firms have to fund labor costs before production, so they borrow for working capital purposes. The amount they borrow is $R^L wL = B^L$. So their labor costs—the amount they borrow— depends on their borrowing rate, R^L, as well as their actual wage bill.

In the model, K^L is predetermined by the savings of "old entrepreneurs"—labor-intensive firms cannot borrow this period to increase capital this period, and L is fixed. So in the model, Y^L is also predetermined.

Banks face a convex loan processing cost, $C(.)$. They always meet the capital-intensive firms' demand for investment loans first, then they will make working capital loans. The first-order condition for the bank's problem turns out to be that the working-capital loan rate is rising in total loans: $R^L = 1 + C'(B^K + B^L)$.

What happens if the government raises the loan quota θ? The capital-intensive firm borrows and invests more. Because of the bank's first-order condition, that raises R^L and crowds out working-capital loans B^L. Since $R^L wL = B^L$ goes down, the model implies that the wage and hence labor income has to fall. Lower worker income, in turn, reduces consumption. We thus get negative comovement between consumption and investment.

Of course, the trends are also very important here. In transition, capital-intensive firms are growing faster, which raises the investment rate. So this is a model of a credit-fueled, investment-led growth.

This is a very simple and highly stylized model to summarize a complex and heterogeneous economy. There is a lot one could quibble with or object to. It is missing key features, along various dimensions. But stepping back from any such quibbles, it is telling a particular story of "industrial policy with Chinese characteristics."

In this regard, the paper is implicitly arguing that China is following the example of other Asian economies—picking "winning" industries/firms. Many people have discussed industrial policy in postwar Japan.[2] When I was writing a paper on East Asian productivity puzzle (Fernald and Neiman 2011), we found lots of books and articles where the titles had phrases like, "the Role of Government in East Asian Industrialization" (Wade 1990), or "Korea: A Case of Government-Led Development" (Kihwan and Leipziger 1997). For Singapore, we found that every description of Singapore emphasized favoritism toward particular industries.

These economies have all been incredibly successful growth stories. The successes may have been, in part, because of these policies or, as many studies suggest, in spite of them. Nevertheless, it is not surprising that China might think it is a good idea to emulate that experience.

Stylized Fact on Comovement

A key stylized fact in macroeconomics is the positive comovement of consumption and investment. In contrast, the mechanism in the model

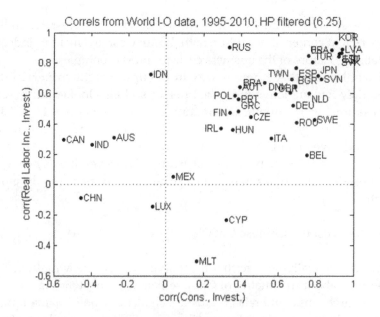

Fig. 1. Business-cycle comovement
Source: World Input-Output Database (Timmer, ed. 2012).

provides a way to generate negative comovement between these variables, as well as between labor income and investment. The model only has one shock, to θ. When θ changes, consumption and investment move in opposite directions. Of course, there could be other factors in the world that they have not modeled, so even finding a positive correlation between these variables would not necessary force us to dismiss the model. But it is, at least, indicative of whether we need such a model.

So how different is China, in fact, in terms of comovement? Figure 1 shows correlations for 40 countries in the World Input-Output database (Timmer, ed. 2012). That database includes real consumption, real investment, and real labor income for the period 1995–2010. Conveniently, that is approximately the period when Chang et al. argue their model applies. As in the paper, I HP-filtered the data before taking correlations, but results were not very sensitive to the filtering parameter or to doing everything in growth rates.

In figure 1, the horizontal axis is the correlation of consumption and investment. The vertical axis is the correlation of real labor income and investment. China is, indeed, an outlier with very low or negative correlations for both of these. Most economies are clustered in the upper-right corner, above 0.5 on both. Positive comovement is, indeed, a defining feature of the business cycle for most economies!

I would note that Korea is way in the upper-right corner. In the past they had an active industrial policy, so I also looked at the Organisation for Economic Co-operation and Development (OECD) data for Korea going back to 1970. The correlation between consumption and investment in Korea is strongly positive in the 1990s and the first decade of the twenty-first century. However, it was negative in the 1970s and 1980s, when industrial policy was arguably more central.

Can We Trust the Chinese Data?

Still, can we really be sure that these stylized facts are actually facts? Concerns about the quality of Chinese data are longstanding. For example, problems could reflect statistical challenges, political manipulation, or a lack of resources to compile appropriate data. The best efforts of the authors of this paper cannot overcome those problems.

One approach is to compare China's national accounts to alternative indicators of Chinese activity, like electricity or rail car shipments or the like. Indeed, in Fernald, Spiegel, and Swanson (2014), we look at Chinese monetary policy without using official gross domestic product (GDP) data at all. Rather, we used an activity factor from other data. In figure 2, I show an activity factor based on the first principal component of nine alternative series.

But of course, even those data are produced in China and could be subject to manipulation or statistical problems. In Fernald, Hsu, and Spiegel (2015), we use exports *to* China and Hong Kong, as reported by trading partners, as an externally verified measure of economic activity in China. There are reasons China's imports might be more or less representative of the overall economy, but I would note that even for a relatively closed economy like the United States, the correlation of year-over-year changes in imports and in GDP is around 0.8. Fernald, Hsu, and Spiegel (2015) find that an activity indicator does, in fact, move quite closely with year-over-year growth in exports to China. In figure 2, I show that measure as well. The correlation with the activity factor is about 0.75.

I would note that figure 2 converts everything into four-quarter growth rates (to avoid seasonal adjustment issues with some of the in-

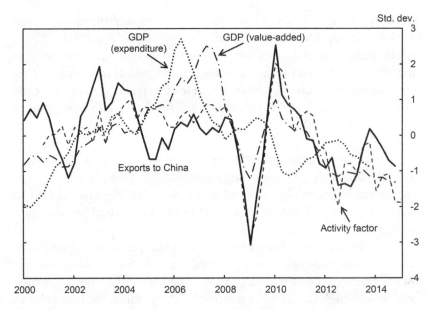

Fig. 2. Indicators of economic activity in China
Source: Fernald, Hsu, and Spiegel (2015) and Chang et al. (2015).
Note: Four-quarter percent changes, normalized (mean zero, unit s.d.).

dicators) before taking principal components. I have also normalized all variables to have mean zero and unit standard deviation.

Chang et al. have two measures of GDP. The first is the "headline" one that usually gets reported in the press, which is from the production side, measuring value added. As figure 2 shows, that value-added GDP measure corresponds much less well to exports to China than the activity factor does. For example, it is much stronger in 2007 than either the activity factor or exports to China. But since 2008, value-added GDP also qualitatively tracks activity and exports to China quite well.

Unfortunately, this is not so true on the expenditure side. The expenditure measure of GDP has a zero or negative correlation with either the activity factor, or with exports to China. In the global financial crisis itself, the figure shows that expenditure GDP rises slightly when everything else collapses. Then, during the recovery, expenditure slumps just as other indicators shoot up. Looking at the components of consumption and investment, those are both negatively correlated with the activity indicators as well.

There is more formal evidence that the official consumption data are not accurate. In particular, Nakamura, Steinsson, and Liu (2014) argue based on Engel curves that true Chinese consumption was much weaker than reported in this period, though especially in 2007–2008.

Still, it is not obvious that the low correlation between consumption and investment is just attenuation bias from classical measurement error. Classical measurement error would tend to raise the variance of the measured data. In contrast, the usual view for China (a view supported by Nakamura et al.) is that measured consumption and output are too smooth.

That said, anecdotally, investment was indeed very strong in the run-up to the financial crisis and, even more so, during the crisis itself. During the crisis, there were clear stimulus efforts by the government to boost investment. If Nakamura et al. are right, then actual consumption *fell* relative to trend during this period.

Thus, the true correlation between consumption and investment could be even more negative than in the data. In other words, measurement error may be attenuating a negative correlation, not a positive one. So although the data are not reliable, the comovement puzzles in the Chinese data that Chung et al. highlight do appear to be ones we want to explain.

Favoritism Not Capital Intensity

Let me now turn to something that initially worried me even more— and that I thought was really damning for their story. That is, relative growth of capital-intensive industries. To do this, I started with the industry data in the World Input-Output database for 1995–2010. I then divided them based on the classifications in table 11 of the paper. When I did so, I could not replicate figure 18 of their paper that showed capital-intensive industries grew faster.

I talked to the people who put together the World Input-Output database. They directed me to Harry Wu at Hitotsubashi University. I also asked Dale Jorgenson about Chinese industry data. Dale told me to talk with Harry Wu.

I called Harry Wu. He is the world's expert on Chinese industry and input-output data, and he sent me his updated data (which are now available online).[3] The dotted line in figure 3 shows the ratio of real (chain weighted) gross output in capital-intensive industries to that in less capital-intensive industries. The capital-intensity classifications come from table 11 of the Chang et al. paper. Unfortunately for the au-

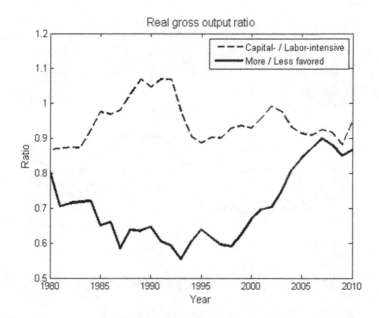

Fig. 3. Gross-output ratios

Source: Wu and Ito (2015). Capital-intensive versus labor-intensive categories are based on table 11 of Chang et al., and favored versus unfavored is also based on the text of Chang et al. Detailed industries are aggregated using chain weights.

thors, it does not show any evidence for their claim that capital-intensive industries grew faster.

More fortunately for the authors, I then read the text of section V.B of Chang et al. more carefully. The Chinese government emphasized infrastructure, basic industries, and various "pillar" industries. This industry classification turns out to be correlated with capital intensity, but not perfectly. Some capital-intensive industries do not show up on this list, and some less capital-intensive industries do—including machinery and motor vehicles.

When I use the specific list of favored industries from the paper, I get the solid line in figure 3. It matches their argument! These industries grew much faster, in both real and nominal terms (the nominal ratio is not shown), and they start growing faster just when the authors say that policies changed to favor this group.

What about labor share? Their story is that the shift toward low labor-share industries explains a decline in labor share. Figure 4 shows that this story still roughly works. The favored industries do

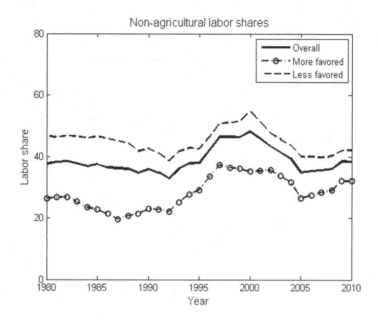

Fig. 4. Nonagricultural labor shares by sector
Source: See notes to figure 3. Vertical axis is percent.

have relatively low labor share, and so a shift toward these industries can contribute toward reducing the aggregate labor share from the late 1990s on.

But what strikes me as being at least as important is that labor's share is always very low. It rose in the 1990s toward almost one-half, then it retreated a bit. One-half is extraordinarily low in cross-country perspective. The usual problem is self-employment/proprietors' income getting counted in gross-operating surplus (see Gollin 2002). However, it turns out China historically put all self-employment income in labor,[4] so these data already control for proprietors' income.

How do we explain the low labor share? Fernald and Neiman (2011) looked at this for Singapore, and argued that the answer was pure economic profits. For example, we found that the state telecom company, the port, and public utilities were all highly efficient, but prices were not low. There are lots and lots of complaints in the press about how these utilities were taking advantage of their monopoly power to earn profits.

So, my presumption is that the model needs to include a role for large markups and pure economic profits.

Conclusions

To conclude, this is a valuable contribution to the ongoing debate regarding China's investment-led growth model. Popular discussions raise concerns about whether the model is sustainable. Still, other Asian economies also relied on policies that favored particular industries, sometimes in ways that also seemed unsustainable, but the policies evolved over time. Despite the occasional bump (such as the Asian financial crisis of the 1990s), their growth experience has by and large been favorable. China certainly hopes to continue that tradition.

Endnotes

The views here are my own and do not necessarily reflect those of others associated with the Federal Reserve Bank of San Francisco or the Federal Reserve System. I thank Bing Wang for excellent research assistance. For acknowledgments, sources of research support, and disclosure of the author's material financial relationships, if any, please see http://www.nber.org/chapters/c13594.ack.
1. As described by the *Financial Times* on April 16, 2015 (p. 5).
2. See, for example, Beason and Weinstein (1995) or, for that matter, Wikipedia (2015).
3. See http://www.rieti.go.jp/en/database/CIP2015/index.html. For a description, see Wu and Ito (2015).
4. I thank Harry Wu for pointing this out to me.

References

Beason, Richard, and David E. Weinstein. 1995. "The MITI Myth: Central Planning Fails in Japan." *American Enterprise* 6 (4): 84–86.
Fernald, John G., Eric Hsu, and Mark M. Spiegel. 2015. "Is China Fudging Its Figures? Evidence from Trading Partner Data." FRBSF Working Paper no. 2015-12. Federal Reserve Bank of San Fransicso. http://www.frbsf.org/economic-research/files/wp2015-12.pdf.
Fernald, John G., and Brent Neiman. 2011. "Growth Accounting with Misallocation: Or, Doing Less with More in Singapore." *American Economic Journal: Macroeconomics* 3 (2): 29–74.
Fernald, John G., Mark M. Spiegel, and Eric T. Swanson. 2014. "Monetary Policy Effectiveness in China: Evidence from a FAVAR Model." *Journal of International Money and Finance* 49 (part A): 83–103.
Gollin, Douglas. 2002. "Getting Income Shares Right." *Journal of Political Economy* 110 (2): 458–74.
Kihwan, Kim, and Danny M. Leipziger. 1997. *Korea: A Case of Government-Led Development (The Lessons from East Asia)*. Ann Arbor: University of Michigan Press.
Nakamura, Emi, Jón Steinsson, and Miao Liu. 2014. "Are Chinese Growth and Inflation too Smooth? Evidence from Engel Curves." NBER Working Paper no. 19893, Cambridge, MA.

Timmer, Marcel P., ed. 2012. "The World Input-Output Database (WIOD): Contents, Sources and Methods." WIOD Working Paper no. 10. http://www.wiod.org/publications/papers/wiod10.pdf.

Song, Zheng, Kjetil Storesletten, and Fabrizio Zilibotti. 2011. "Growing Like China." *American Economic Review* 101 (1): 196–233.

Wade, Robert. 1990. *Economic Theory and the Role of Government in East Asian Industrialization.* Princeton, NJ: Princeton University Press.

Wikipedia. 1995. "Industrial Policy of Japan." Accessed April 17, 2015. https://en.wikipedia.org/wiki/Industrial_policy_of_Japan.

Wu, Harry X., and Keiko Ito. 2015. "Reconstruction of China's National Output and Income Accounts and Supply-Use and Input-Output Accounts in Time Series." RIETI Discussion Paper no. 15-E-004, Research Institute of Economy, Trade and Industry.

Discussion

Tao Zha began by acknowledging the comments from the discussion about the noisiness of the available data on China's macroeconomy. In particular, he noted that it is often difficult to gauge the reliability of the existing data provided by the National Bureau of Statistics in China. Therefore, one of the goals of the project was to collect more reliable and consistent data, which would ultimately be provided to the public through the Federal Reserve Bank of Atlanta.

Rick Mishkin then inquired about the implications of the preferential credit policy for long-term economic growth in China. He asked what the paper's theoretical framework has to say about the ability of China to balance the tension between maintaining high growth and the risk of a financial crisis arising from bad loans. He noted the problem of potential misallocation of capital arising from the preferential credit policy. However, Mishkin also acknowledged that a number of countries, including some countries in Asia, had used similar growth strategies to successfully break through "middle-income" status and become rich.

Tao Zha replied that the model does indeed highlight the serious credit risk associated with the preferential credit policy in China. Specifically, he noted that the policy has the risk of creating very large and unproductive factories in China. This can potentially lead to growth in the number of bad loans, because these factories and the associated buildings are commonly used as loan collateral. Zha gave the example of the construction of a financial center in the city of Tian Xian, despite the close proximity of an existing and popular financial center in Beijing. This resulted in a large number of empty high rises and buildings in Tian Xian. He also noted that the Chinese government has concerns about the credit risk in China and has begun to implement some financial reforms to address these issues. Zha further noted that these financial issues are first order, and the issues of inequality in China are a by-product of the biased policies implemented by the Chinese government.

Kaiji Chen also replied to Mishkin's comment, arguing that capital allocation can be thought of along two dimensions: within sectors and across sectors. Previous papers, such as Song et al. (2011), focus on the within-sector allocation of capital from state-owned enterprises to privately owned enterprises. As these papers have shown, the reallocation within sectors boosted capital efficiency in China between 1998 and 2004/05. However, he argues that after 2007, the reallocation across sectors in China, which is the focus of the authors' paper, is the more important margin affecting capital efficiency. In particular, he spoke about the reallocation from the light to heavy sectors of the economy, which can result in idle capacity.

Daron Acemoglu spoke next, further comparing the current paper and the Song et al. (2011) paper. Specifically, he noted that the two papers share some similar qualitative facts (including the low and stable labor shares in the economy and the fact that labor is priced by the less efficient sector) but come to very different conclusions for the allocation of capital over time. In the Song et al. (2011) paper, capital allocation improves over time as the less efficient firms exit the market, which does not happen in the current paper. He asked whether there is anything in the data that can differentiate between the theories proposed in the two papers.

Tao Zha acknowledged the importance of using data to distinguish between the two papers and conveyed they were in the process of collecting more data to do so. He also referred to anecdotal evidence that supports the authors' conclusion that capital allocation is not likely to continue improving in China. Specifically, he argued that the within-sector reallocation from state-owned to privately owned enterprises is unlikely to result in large productivity improvements. This is because a large number of these privatized firms are reportedly functioning just like state-owned enterprises, despite being reclassified as private firms. He pointed out that these firms specialize in nonferrous metal products and heavy industries, which have low productivity. Kaiji Chen agreed that more detailed microdata will shed further light on the effects of capital reallocation.

Harald Uhlig spoke next, addressing the low consumption share and high savings rates in China. Specifically, he asked whether the consumption and savings patterns reflected private incentives or were a result of government-imposed restrictions to household investment opportunities. He asked about the level of the social rate of return on capital that is needed to generate the observed high levels of household savings and how these rates compare to the interest rates in the data. He noted that one interpretation of the data is that the government is creating distortions by overinvesting in local sectors, using funds that they obtain by taxing households and keeping them from accessing the foreign market.

Tao Zha agreed with Harald Uhlig's interpretation of the distortions to savings created by the government's incentives. He argued that the growing foreign surplus in China is driven by the government surplus. One possible view of this growing surplus is that it is a tax on households, which then shows up in China's rising investment-to-consumption ratio. He pointed out that this also shows up in the authors' model as a by-product of the government's actions.

Kaiji Chen further added the data supports the model's predictions of a growing surplus being driven by rising government savings. Specifically, he noted that the data shows a 10% rise in the current account balance to GDP ratio from 1998 to 2010. This was driven by a 7% rise in government surplus to GDP over the same period. In contrast, the household savings rate did not increase much during that period.

Ricardo Reis spoke next. First, Reis questioned whether the paper's story about the Chinese government's preference for capital could instead be interpreted as favoritism toward exports. He referred to John Fernald's discussion and comments about further splitting the data by tradable versus nontradable sectors and examining the exports and capital intensity of those sectors. Reis hypothesized that the trends could be instead interpreted as the government pushing the tradable sectors. Second, Reis asked about the extent to which data on the current account, trade, and the closed economy can jointly explain the facts in the paper. Specifically, he referred to the fact that both investment- and consumption-to-GDP ratios stabilize somewhat after 2008. The stabilization of these two ratios occurred at the same time as the stabilization of the current account in China. Reis asked whether the trends in investment and consumption after 2008 can be used to distinguish between favoritism versus the alternative story about the supply of savings in China.

Tao Zha responded by noting that it would be difficult to replicate the facts in the data with a standard model with export and import sectors. In these models, the export sectors are more capital intensive than the import sectors. Therefore, opening up the economy leads to growth in the capital-intensive sectors and a decline in the labor share. However, this has not been the case for China, where the exporting sectors consist of labor-intensive sectors, such as textiles. Therefore, growth in exports results in growth for the labor-intensive firms in China, rather than the capital-intensive firms.

Kaiji Chen gave an example that illustrated the growth in the exports of the labor-intensive sectors. Specifically, he referred to China's entry into the World Trade Organization (WTO). Around that time, China's comparative advantage was its labor-intensive technology. Following this event, the export share of labor-intensive firms rose relative to the capital-intensive firms from 1999 to 2007. Chen argues that this implies that the Chinese government has not been favoring the capital-intensive exporting sectors, as was suggested by Ricardo Reis.

Jonathan Parker spoke next, asking three questions. First, he asked to what extent the measured low labor share in China could be reflecting measurement issues related to taxes. In the United States, payroll taxes are added back to post-tax labor income to obtain a true measure of labor share. In contrast, the tax system in China is more informal. He wondered if these informal taxes, not included in the measured labor share, could be a significant issue.

Parker then asked a second question about whether it is possible to distinguish between two stories using data. The first story, which the paper pushes, is that distorted incentives result in high savings that are funneled into the housing market. The second story is that there is a vast supply of labor in nonindustrialized areas, which is now flowing and therefore pushing down wages and potentially the consumption share as well.

Lastly, Parker asked to what extent has credit in China been mismanaged, since there is a large credit boom that has arisen from capital outflows being essentially blocked rather than from a rise in capital inflows.

Tao Zha responded by acknowledging that the paper abstracts from housing and house prices, which could be the motivation behind the high household savings and low consumption ratios. Nonetheless, his view is that the heavy industrialization policies in China were still an important factor driving the trends in China. Specifically, he refers to the fact that in recent years, the consumption-to-income ratio has begun to rise in China, while the consumption-to-investment ratio has begun to decline. He argues that this coincided with various financial reforms in China, which implies that the preexisting policies also played an important role in driving the consumption and investment trends observed in the data.

2

Demystifying the Chinese Housing Boom

Hanming Fang, *University of Pennsylvania and NBER*
Quanlin Gu, *Guanghua, School of Management, Peking University*
Wei Xiong, *Princeton University and NBER*
Li-An Zhou, *Guanghua School of Management, Peking University*

There have been growing concerns across the global economic and policy communities regarding the decade-long housing market boom in China, which has the second largest economy in the world, and has been the major engine for global economic growth during the past decade. News in recent months seems to suggest that the housing boom might be slowing down. A main concern is that a housing market meltdown might severely damage the Chinese economy, which in turn might generate contagious effects across the world and slow down the fragile global economy that has just emerged from a series of crises that originated in the United States and Europe. In particular, critics are concerned that soaring housing prices and the enormous construction boom throughout the country might cause China to follow in the footsteps of Japan, which had an economic lost decade after its housing bubble burst in the early 1990s.

How much have housing prices in different Chinese cities appreciated during the last decade? Did the soaring prices make housing out of the reach for typical households? How much financial burden did households face in buying homes? Addressing these questions is crucial for systematically assessing the risk to the Chinese economy presented by its housing market. We address these questions by taking advantage of a comprehensive data set of mortgage loans issued by a major Chinese commercial bank from 2003 to 2013. Specifically, we construct a set of housing price indices for 120 major cities in China, which allows us to evaluate housing price fluctuations across these cities, in conjunction with the growth of households' purchasing power and stock price fluctuations. The detailed mortgage data also allow us to analyze the participation of low-income households in housing markets and the financial burdens faced by low-income home buyers.

Due to the nascent nature of the Chinese housing market, there are relatively few repeat home sales available for building Case-Shiller type repeated sales housing indices. Instead, we take advantage of the large number of new housing developments in each city and build a housing price index for the city based on sales over time of new homes within the same developments, which share similar characteristics and amenities. Consistent with casual observations made by many commentators, our price indices confirm enormous housing price appreciation across China in 2003–2013. In first-tier cities, which include the four most populated and most economically important metropolitan areas in China—Beijing, Shanghai, Guangzhou, and Shenzhen—housing prices had an average annual real growth rate of 13.1% during this decade. Our sample also covers 31 second-tier cities, which are autonomous municipalities, provincial capitals, or vital industrial/commercial centers, and 85 other third-tier cities, which are important cities in their respective regions. Housing prices in second-tier cities had an average annual real growth rate of 10.5%; third-tier cities had an average annual real growth rate of 7.9%. These growth rates easily surpass the housing price appreciation during the US housing bubble in the first decade of the twenty-first century and are comparable to that during the Japanese housing bubble in the 1980s.

Despite the enormous price appreciation, the Chinese housing boom is different in nature from the housing bubbles in the United States and Japan. Our analysis offers several important observations that are useful for understanding the Chinese housing boom. First, as banks in China imposed down payments of over 30% on all mortgage loans, banks are protected from mortgage borrowers' default risk even in the event of a sizable housing market meltdown of 30%. This makes a US-style subprime credit crisis less likely in China.

Second, while the rapid housing price appreciation has been often highlighted as a concern for the Chinese housing market, the price appreciation was accompanied by equally spectacular growth in households' disposable income—an average annual real growth rate of about 9.0% throughout the country during the decade, with the exception of a lower average growth rate of 6.6% in the first-tier cities. This joint presence of enormous housing price appreciation and income growth contrasts the experiences during the US and Japanese housing bubble. Even during the Japanese housing bubble in late 1980s, the Japanese economy was growing at a more modest rate than that of China. The enormous income growth rate across Chinese cities thus provides some assurance to the housing boom and, together with the aforementioned high mortgage down-payment ratios, renders the housing market an unlikely trigger for an imminent financial crisis in China.

Third, despite the enormous housing price appreciation over the decade, the participation of low-income households in the housing market remained stable. Specifically, we analyze the financial status of mortgage borrowers with incomes in the bottom 10% of all mortgage borrowers in each city for each year. By mapping the incomes of these marginal home buyers into the income distribution of the urban population in the city, we find that they came from the low-income fraction of the population, roughly around the 25th percentile of the distribution in the first-tier cities and around the 30th percentile in the second-tier cities.

Fourth, while these low-income home buyers were not excluded from the housing market, they did endure enormous financial burdens in buying homes at price-to-income ratios of around eight in second- and third-tier cities and, in some years, even over 10 in first-tier cities. In concrete terms, this means that a household paid eight times its annual disposable income to buy a home. In order to obtain a mortgage loan, it had to make a down payment of at least 30%, and more typically 40%, of the home price, which was equivalent to 2.4 times to 3.2 times the household's annual income. Suppose that the household made a down payment of 40% and took a mortgage loan for the other 60% of the home price, which would be 4.8 times its annual income. A modest mortgage rate of 6%, which is low relative to the actual rate observed during the decade, would require the household to use nearly 30% of its annual income to pay for the interest on the mortgage loan. Furthermore, paying the mortgage would consume another 16% of its annual income using a linear amortization, even if the mortgage had a maximum maturity of 30 years. Together, buying the home entailed saving 3.2 times the annual household income to make the down payment and another 45% of its annual income to service the mortgage loan.

To explain the willingness of households to endure such severe financial burdens for a home, it is important to take into account the households' expectations. To the extent that urban household income in China has been rising steadily during the studied period, as well as in the previous two decades, many households may expect their income to continue growing at this rate. At a 10% nominal income growth rate, a household's income in five years would grow to 1.6 times of its initial income and the ratio of current housing price to its future income in five years would drop to five. Thus, a high expected income growth rate renders the aforementioned financial burdens temporary.

Such high income growth expectations might have resulted from extrapolative behavior as emphasized by Barberis, Shleifer, and Vishny (1998) and Shiller (2000), or from contagious social dynamics between households as modeled by Burnside, Eichenbaum, and Rebelo (2013). Recently, Pritchett and Summers (2014) examined historical data on growth rates and demonstrated that regression to the mean is the single-most robust and empirically relevant fact about cross-country growth rates. Thus, they argue that while China might continue to grow for another two decades at a 9, or even a 7 or 6% rate, such continued rapid growth rate would be an extraordinary event, given the powerful force of regression to the mean, which had averaged 2% in the cross-country data with a standard deviation of 2%. If so, the high expectation of future income growth, which might have been a key driver of the observed enormous price-to-income ratios, may not be sustainable and thus presents an important source of risk to the housing market. When China's growth rate eventually regresses to the mean, and especially when China experiences a sudden stop, households' expectations may crash. In such a case, the large price-to-income ratios have substantial room to contract, which in turn could act as an amplifier of the initial shock that triggers the economic slowdown.

Frictions in the Chinese financial system might also have contributed to the high housing prices across Chinese cities, as reflected by the large price-to-income ratios endured by households. It is well known that the spectacular economic growth in China since the 1980s has been accompanied by a high savings rate (e.g., Yang, Zhang, and Zhou 2013). Due to stringent capital controls, savers cannot invest their savings in international capital markets and, instead, have only a few domestic investment vehicles. Bank deposit accounts have remained the predominant investment vehicle, with assets totaling near 100 trillion RMB in 2013, despite the fact that the real one-year deposit rate averaged only 0.01% in 2003–2013. While the Chinese stock market experienced dramatic growth during this decade, it was still relatively small, with a capitalization of slightly less than 20 trillion RMB in 2013. The size of bond markets was even smaller. Facing this largely constrained investment set, it has been common for households to treat housing as an alternative investment vehicle, which also helps explain their willingness to pay dearly for housing.

From an investment perspective, it is interesting to note a tale of two markets at the time of the world economic crisis in 2008–2009. During this period, the Chinese economy faced tremendous pressure. Nevertheless, the housing market in China remained strong. Housing prices in first-tier cities suffered a modest drop of about 10%, and recovered more than the loss shortly after the crisis. Housing prices in second- and third-tier cities continued to rise throughout the period after 2008. This experience was in sharp contrast to the dramatic decline of over 60% in the Chinese stock market in 2008—which has not recovered, even to date. To understand this puzzling contrast, we argue that the frequent policy interventions by the central government and the heavy reliance of local governments on land sales revenue for their fiscal budget might have emboldened many households to believe that the housing market is too important to fall and that the central government would institute policies to support the housing market if necessary.

There are divergent views about the Chinese housing boom. Chow and Niu (2014) use a simultaneous equations framework to analyze the demand and supply of residential housing in urban China in 1987–2012 and find that the rapid housing price growth can be well explained by the force of demand and supply, with income determining demand and construction costs affecting supply. Deng, Gyourko, and Wu (2014a) are far more concerned by the risk in the Chinese housing market. In particular, they present evidence of a rapid increase in housing supply and housing inventory held by developers in various major cities in recent years. Different from these studies, we provide an informed account of the demand side by thoroughly analyzing characteristics of mortgage borrowers. Our analysis leads us to take a more balanced stand between these two contrasting views. On the comforting side, the rapid income growth, which accompanied the enormous housing price appreciation, helped support the steady participation by low-income households in the housing market. On the concerning side, high expectations about future income growth might have motivated low-income households to buy homes by undertaking substantial financial burdens, causing them to be particularly vulnerable to future sudden stops in the Chinese economy.

This paper is organized as follows. Section I briefly describes some institutional background. We introduce the housing price indices in Section II and then discuss the housing price boom across three tiers of cities in Section III. Section IV summarizes characteristics of mortgage borrowers, and Section V discusses housing as an investment vehicle. Section VI provides some conceptual discussion. We summarize the role of government in Section VII and discuss several sources of risk in Section VIII.

I. Institutional Background

The development of housing markets in mainland China is a relatively new phenomenon. From the 1949 founding of the People's Republic of China to 1978, all land was publicly owned and the Chinese constitution prohibited any organization or individual from buying, selling, leasing, or transferring land. Housing was allocated through a working unit-employee linkage as a form of in-kind compensation, with the size and location of homes depending on the length of employment and the size of the household, among other factors. In 1978, per capita residential area in urban areas was 3.6 square meters, which was even lower than that in 1949.

To reform (and to a large extent privatize) the state-owned enterprises in the mid-1980s, it was considered necessary to introduce an alternative housing system that would delink home allocation from employment. An important milestone occurred in 1988 when the Chinese constitution was amended to allow for land transactions, which set the legal stage for the privatization of housing in China.[1]

Comprehensive housing reform was initiated in 1994 when employees in the state sector were allowed to purchase full or partial property rights to their current apartment units at subsidized prices. Nascent markets for homes, known as "commodity houses," emerged in some large cities in the early 1990s, but they grew rapidly only after 1998 when the central government completely abolished the traditional model of housing allocation as an in-kind benefit and privatized housing properties of all urban residents.

Also in 1998, partly as a response to the adverse effects of the 1997 Asian Financial Crisis, the Chinese government established the real estate sector as a new engine of economic growth. As an important impetus to the development of private housing markets, China's central bank, the People's Bank of China (PBC), outlined the procedures for home buyers to obtain residential mortgages at subsidized interest rates in 1998.[2] Moreover, between 1998 and 2002, the PBC lowered the mortgage interest rate five times to encourage home purchases. By 2005, China had become the largest residential mortgage market in Asia. According to a PBC report published in 2013, financial institutions made a total of 8.1 trillion RMB in mortgage loans in 2012, accounting for 16% of all bank loans in that year. At the same time, the PBC also developed policies to encourage housing development, including broadening the scope of development loans and allowing presales by developers.

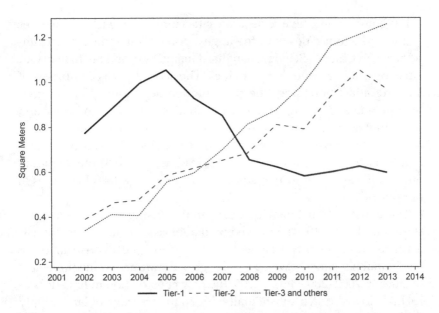

Fig. 1.   Per capita area of newly built residential housing

Note: For each tier of cities, we divide its annual flow of newly constructed residential housing, measured in square meters, by its urban population in 2012. The National Bureau of Statistics provides annual city-level data on space of newly constructed residential housing from 2002 to 2013 and resident population from 2005 to 2012, for 35 large cities only. These cities include all four tier-one cities: Beijing, Shanghai, Guangzhou, and Shenzhen. The other 31 cities all belong to the tier-two cities defined in the paper. We use the aggregate of these 31 cities to compute the per capita area built for tier-two cities. We then subtract these 35 cities from the national aggregates on newly constructed urban housing and urban population to get measures for tier-three (and other) cities. Resident population includes all people residing six months or more in the area governed by the city in the current year (in contrast to the hukou population). We assume all resident populations in tier-one and tier-two cities are urban, which leads to a slight overestimation of urban population in tier-one and tier-two cities and, consequently, a slight underestimation of urban population in tier-three (and other) cities. In 2012, China had a total population of 13.5 billion, out of which 7.2 billion are urban and 6.3 billion are rural. Out of those 7.2 billion who live in cities, 0.7 billion reside in tier-one cities, 2.4 billion in tier-two cities, and 4.1 billion in tier-three cities by our baseline calculation.

These policies were effective in stimulating both the demand and supply of residential housing. During this period, home sales maintained about 15% of annual growth on average, and areas of residential housing under construction grew even faster, reaching about 18% of annual growth. Figure 1 provides a rough estimate of the supply of newly completed residential housing from 2002 to 2013 by city tier, measured by completed areas in each city and each year divided by the city's urban population in 2012.

It is common in China to separate cities into three tiers. The first tier includes the four cities with the largest population and economic importance in China—Beijing, Shanghai, Guangzhou, and Shenzhen. Our data cover all of these first-tier cities. The second tier is comprised of Tianjing and Chongqing (the two autonomous municipalities other than Beijing and Shanghai) and capital cities of the 24 provinces[3] and nine other cities, which are typically vital industrial or commercial centers. Our data cover 31 of these 35 second-tier cities. There is not a commonly used list for third-tier cities. Instead, we group 85 other cities in our sample as the third tier. Appendix B provides a list of all cities in our sample.

The construction boom of residential housing in first-tier cities started in the late 1990s, followed by that of second- and third-tier cities early in the twenty-first century. In figure 1, new construction of residential housing showed a similar growth rate across the three tiers of cities in 2002–2005. From 2005, the new construction in first-tier cities had slowed down substantially due to the shortage of land supply in these cities, while the supply in second- and third-tier cities continued to grow at similar rates as before. The growth rate in third-tier cities was especially strong. Some estimates suggest that investment in residential housing accounted for 25% of total fixed-asset investment and contributed to roughly one-sixth of China's gross domestic product (GDP) growth (Barth, Lea, and Li 2012).

The development of the housing market was also accompanied by an urbanization process throughout China with rural migrants moving into cities, especially into first- and second-tier cities. As shown by figure 2, the total population of the four first-tier cities, the vast majority of which lived inside the city proper, grew from 48 million in 2004 to almost 70 million in 2012. The total population of the second-tier cities, which is distributed roughly half inside the city proper and half outside, grew from 220 million in 2004 to about 260 million in 2012. The total population of third-tier cities remained stable in this period at around 370 million, among which only 100 million lived inside the city proper.

II. Constructing a Chinese Housing Price Index

To systematically examine the housing market boom, it is important to construct an accurate housing price index for major cities in China. The difficulty in constructing a housing price index arises because a

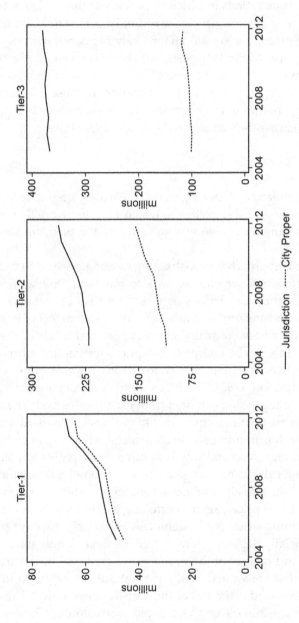

Fig. 2 Population in three tiers of cities

Note: There are two lines in each panel. The solid line depicts the total population within the jurisdiction of each tier of cities, while the dashed line depicts the population within the city proper of each tier.

good price index requires that we compare the prices of the same (or at least comparable) houses over time. To the extent that the set of homes involved in the transactions in different periods of time is likely to be different, a price index constructed by simply comparing the mean or median sale prices per square meter likely measures not only the changes in the prices of similar homes, but also the changes in the composition of transacted homes. This problem is likely to be more severe in emerging housing markets than in mature ones because in emerging housing markets, homes in more central locations are likely to be built and transacted earlier than homes in the outer rings of cities.

A.   Standard Methodologies

There are two standard methodologies that are widely used to construct housing price indices. These methods, which we review briefly below, are aimed at finding a suitable way to compare the prices of similar homes.

One prominent approach for constructing housing prices is to use hedonic price regressions, which goes back to Kain and Quigley (1970). In this approach, the sales price is regressed on a set of variables that characterize the housing unit—number of rooms, square feet of interior space, lot size, quality of construction, condition, and so forth. The regression coefficients can be interpreted as prices for implicit attributes. This hedonic approach can then be used to construct a price index in two ways (Case and Shiller 1987). The first way to construct a price index is to run separate regressions on data from each time period. The estimated equations are then used to predict the value of a standard unit in each period, which is in turn used to construct the housing price index for the standard unit. A second way is to run a single regression on the pooled data from sales in all time periods. Inclusion of a time dummy for the period of the sale allows the constant term to shift over time, reflecting movement in prices, again controlling for characteristics.

Whether hedonic price regressions can accurately capture price movements crucially depends on how well the data capture the actual characteristics and quality of the unit. Unobserved and time-varying characteristics that are valued by the market but not captured in the data can lead to biased estimates of the housing price index. This is a particular issue in China. Due to the rapid expansion of Chinese cities, new housing units have been constructed mostly on land near the urban fringes. According to the *China Urban Statistical Yearbook* (published by Ministry of Housing and Urban-Rural Development), the total size of developed urban area at the national level increased from 19,844 square kilometers in 2003 (Form 3-9, p. 107) to 34,867 square kilometers in 2013 (Form 2-12, p. 90). Such a dramatic expansion of urban residential land parcels implies that unobserved time-varying characteristics as transacted homes move from locations closer to city center to locations in city fringe is likely to lead to biased housing price indices.

Case and Shiller (1987, 1989) popularized another method using repeated sales. This approach originated with Baily, Muth, and Nourse (1963), who initially proposed a method involving a regression where the i-th observation of the dependent variable is the log of the price of the i-th house at its second sale date minus the log of its price on its first sale date. The independent variables consist of only dummy variables, one for each time period in the sample, except for the first (the base period for the index).[4] The estimated coefficients are then taken as the log price index. This initial method builds on a strong assumption that the variance of the error term is constant across houses. As this variance is likely to depend on the time interval between sales, Case and Shiller (1987) proposed a weighted-repeated-sales method with a two-step procedure to relax this assumption.[5]

The repeat sales approach does not require the measurement of quality; it only requires that the quality of individual units in the sample remain constant over time. However, it is well recognized that this repeated sales method wastes a large fraction of transactions data because repeated sales may contribute to only a small fraction of all housing transactions. More important, the set of homes that are sold repeatedly may not be representative of the general population of homes (see Mark and Goldberg 1984).

B. A Hybrid Approach for Chinese Housing Markets

We propose a hybrid approach of constructing housing price indices for a large number of Chinese cities. Our approach takes into account several features of the Chinese housing markets. As a result of the nascent nature of the Chinese housing markets, there are relatively few repeat sales. Many of the observed repeated sales are old-style housing units, which are not representative of the newly developed housing markets. This feature prevents us from directly using the Case-Shiller repeated sales method. On the other hand, there are a large number of new home sales in each city. These new homes are in the form of apartments, and typically, apartments in development projects.[6] As a developer sells apartments in a project over a period of time, and sometimes even completes the development over several phases, we observe sequential sales of apartments in the same development. Within the same development project, the unobserved apartment amenities are similar. This feature allows us to build a hybrid index based on sequential new home sales within housing developments after accounting for hedonic characteristics of individual homes.

We implement the housing price indices from January 2003 to March 2013 by running the following regression *for each city*:

$$\ln P_{i,j,c,t} = \beta_{c,0} + \sum_{s=1}^{T}\beta_{c,s} \cdot 1\{s = t\} + \theta_c X_i + DP_j + \varepsilon_{it},$$

where $P_{i,j,c,t}$ is the price of a new home i sold in month t in city c, $\beta_{c,t}$ is the time dummy for month t, the vector of characteristics X_i includes area, area squared, floor dummies, and dummies for the number of rooms, and DP_j is a set of *development project* fixed effects. The base month ($t = 0$) is January 2003 and the last month is March 2013. The price index $PI_{c,t}$ for month t in city c is simply given by:[7]

$$PI_{c,t} = \begin{cases} 1 & \text{if } t = 0 \\ \exp(\beta_{c,t}) & \text{for } t = 1, 2, \ldots \end{cases}.$$

Figure 3 graphically illustrates our method of constructing the price index. In every month, say month 1, there are many development projects with new apartments for sale in a given city. In figure 3, three units in development project A are sold in month 1 and two units are sold in month 2. We take the sales in our data from development projects that have sales in both month 1 and month 2. In our proposed regression above, we control for the development project and other observable differences in the characteristics of the apartment units (such as area, floor number, etc.), thus the time dummy $\beta_{c,1}$ precisely captures the price difference in city c among otherwise identical units sold between month 1 and month 2. Of course, the *key assumption*, which we believe to be empirically realistic, is that within a development project, differences in the units are fully described by the additional controls we include in the regression. Similarly, as illustrated in figure 3, the price change from month 2 to month 3 is estimated by the price differences of similar units in development project B sold in month 2 versus those sold in month 3; the price change from month 3 to month 4 is estimated by the price dif-

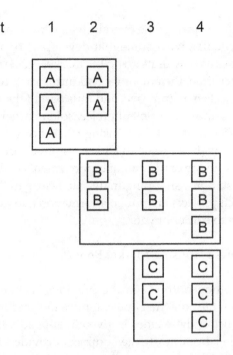

Fig. 3.   An illustration of index construction method

Note: The price change from month 1 to month 2 is estimated by the price differences of similar units in development project A in month 1 versus those sold in month 2. The price change from month 2 to month 3 is estimated by the price differences of similar units in development project B sold in month 2 versus those sold in month 3. The price change from month 3 to month 4 is estimated by the price differences of similar units in development projects B and C that are sold in month 3 versus month 4.

ferences of similar units in development projects B and C that are sold in month 3 versus month 4.[8]

The regression specification we use to construct price indices in a city via time dummies also makes two additional assumptions. First, we assume that the price changes between any two months are *uniform* across development projects that may be located in different parts of the city.[9] To see this, note from figure 3 when we estimate the price change from month 3 to month 4, we pool the units sold in development projects C and D in the two months in the regression; since we restrict the time dummy not to interact with the development projects, we implicitly assume that the price changes in development projects C and D from month 3 to month 4 are the same. Second, we also implicitly assume that the only source of price changes between any two months in a development project is the overall change in the housing market in the city. In particular, we assume that developers do not change their pricing strategies as new units go on the market.[10] One may also be concerned that over time, the amenities and infrastructure around the development projects may improve, and thus part of the price differences for units in the same development project sold in different months may reflect such differences, not the housing market conditions. We believe that this is less likely an issue in China, as buyers of earlier units are almost certainly aware of upcoming improvements in the infrastructure (e.g., subway stations, shopping malls, etc.) close to the development projects, as such projects are public information and developers surely advertise them to earlier buyers.

III.   The Chinese Housing Market Boom

We use the method outlined in the previous section and a detailed mortgage data set to construct housing price indices for 120 major cities in China. The list of these cities is given in appendix B. Our mortgage data is compiled from mortgage contracts provided by a large commercial bank, which accounts for about 15% of the mortgage loan market in China. We restrict the sample to mortgages for new, residential properties and as a result have over one million mortgage loan contracts dating from the first quarter of 2003 to the first quarter of 2013. A typical mortgage contract contains detailed information on the personal characteristics of home buyers (e.g., age, gender, marital status, income, work unit, education, occupation, and region and address of residence), housing price and size, apartment-level characteristics (e.g., complex location, floor level, and room number), as well as loan-level characteristics (e.g., maturity and down payment).

Based on the transacted home prices and characteristics, we build housing price indices for 120 cities in China from 2003 to 2013. As our price indices are nominal, it is useful to keep in mind that inflation was modest during that decade. Figure 4 depicts the national inflation together with bank deposit rate. The national inflation fluctuated substantially from low levels around 2% in 2003–2007 to a peak level of 8% in early 2008, only to quickly drop to below −.5% in the first half of 2009, rising to around 5% in 2011 and eventually returning to a level around 2% in 2013. Inflation had a modest average rate of 2.68% during our sample period. Figure 4 also shows that the bank deposit rate stayed in a narrow range between 2 and 4% during this period.

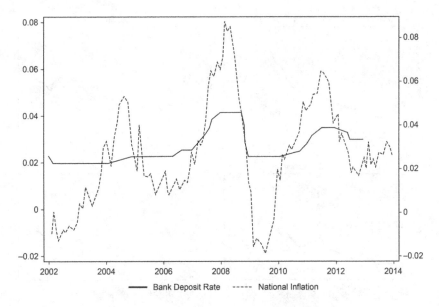

Fig. 4. Bank deposit rate and national inflation

Our housing price indices allow us to precisely characterize the housing market boom in the last decade throughout China. We describe the housing market boom below by tiers of cities.

A. First-Tier Cities

Figure 5 depicts the monthly housing price indices for the four first-tier cities in four separate panels, together with measures of households' purchasing power. In panel A, the housing price index of Beijing experienced an enormous rise from an index level of 1 in January 2003 to 7.6 in March 2013. That is, the housing price level has increased 660% in a short period of 10 years!

During this period, Beijing's housing prices have actually experienced at least two episodes of downward movement. The first episode started in May 2008, when the price index was at 3.50 (relative to January 2003), and continued until March 2009, when the price index slid to 3.05. This represented a 13% price drop and coincided with the global financial crisis. The second episode is more recent. It began in May 2011 and ended in June 2012 when the housing price index fluctuated between the interval of 5.99 and 6.67.

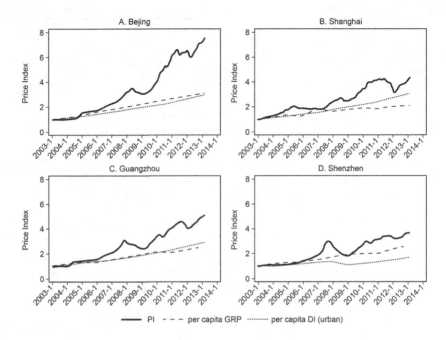

Fig. 5. Housing price indices for first-tier cities

Note: This figure depicts the monthly housing price indices in four separate panels for the four first-tier cities—Beijing, Shanghai, Guangzhou, and Shenzhen—together with two measures of households' purchasing power: per capita GRP and disposable income (urban). Per capita GRP measures the per capita value of output in the whole city and per capita disposable income (urban) measures the per capita income received by urban residents of the city.

As benchmarks for the housing price appreciation, panel A also plots two measures of the households' purchasing power in Beijing: per capita gross regional product (GRP) and disposable income (urban) during the same period. The per capita GRP measures the per capita value of output in the whole city and the per capita disposable income (urban) measures the per capita income received by urban residents of the city. Both of these measures have experienced similar growth from 1 in 2003 to a level around 3 in 2013. While this growth is remarkable by any standard, it is nevertheless substantially smaller than the housing price appreciation in the city.

Panel B plots the monthly housing price index for Shanghai. The index increased from 1 in January 2003 to about 4.43 in March 2013. The overall housing price appreciation in Shanghai was more modest than that in Beijing, even though Shanghai's housing price appreciation actually started faster than Beijing's. Shanghai's housing prices doubled by April 2005 relative to that in January 2003, while Beijing's housing prices did not double until August 2006. However, Shanghai experienced three episodes of price adjustment in the last decade. The first adjustment started in May 2005 when the index was at 2.05, and ended in March 2007 when the index went down to as low as 1.79. This represented a 13% price correction. However, the housing prices picked up again in March 2007 to reach an index level of 2.72 in August 2008. The second episode was a swift and small adjustment with the index dropping from 2.72 in August 2008 to 2.41 in December 2008. The third episode started in June 2011 with the price index dropping from 4.27 to as low as 3.20 in March 2012. This represented a 25% price correction. However, housing prices picked up again in March 2012. By March 2013, the price index reached its peak at 4.43.

The growth of households' disposable income in Shanghai during this period was about the same as that in Beijing, with disposable income of urban residents roughly tripling from January 2003 to March 2013. Thus, the housing price appreciation in Shanghai, while quite substantial, is nonetheless much more closely aligned with the growth of disposable income. The other measure of purchasing power, GRP per capita, exhibits more modest growth in Shanghai, but it still more than doubled in this period.

Panels C and D respectively plot the housing price indices for Guangzhou and Shenzhen. The overall picture of these two cities in Guangdong Province (near Hong Kong) is similar. Guangzhou's price index increased from 1 in January 2003 to 5.1 in March 2013, while it rose from 1 to 3.65 in Shenzhen during the same period. Both cities experienced multiple episodes of price adjustment. The most severe price adjustment occurred in Shenzhen, starting in October 2007 when its price index was at 2.97 and reaching a trough in January 2009 when the index was at 1.82. This represented a 39% price correction. At almost the same time, in November 2007, Guangzhou's housing prices also started dropping from an index level of 3.08 and reached a trough of 2.38 in February 2009. This represented a 23% price correction. Both Guangzhou and Shenzhen are located in the Pearl River delta, the world's largest manufacturing export center. The housing price drops in these two cities were clearly related to the global economic crisis. The fact that our housing price indices for the two cities are able to capture these crisis-induced, price-adjustment episodes lends credence to them.

Panels C and D also reveal that the per capita disposable income in Guangzhou nearly tripled during the same period, while in Shenzhen grew by only 68%. Shenzhen's per capita disposable income growth was much smaller than the growth of the per capita GRP, perhaps because Shenzhen had millions of migrant workers, whose outputs were included in the calculation of the GRP, but not the per capita disposable income for urban residents with *Hukou* (i.e., the official city residence registration).

Table 1 reports, by tiers of city, the summary statistics of the housing return, per capita GRP, and per capita disposable income (DI). We report these statistics for the whole period from January 2003 through March 2013, as well as for subperiods from January 2003 through December 2007 and from January 2009 through March 2013. We exclude 2008 between the two subperiods to isolate the potential crisis effects. Panel A reports these statistics in nominal values, and panel B reports them in real values, after adjusting for the national inflation rate.

To aggregate the price indices for the four first-tier cities, we construct a price index for the tier by setting the initial index level of each city to be 1 at the beginning of a given period and then taking an equal-weighted average of the index levels of these cities for each subsequent month. The resulting index level represents the value of a housing portfolio constructed from investing one RMB into the housing index of each city in the first month and keeping the portfolio composition throughout the subsequent months. We also use the same method to construct indices for second- and third-tier cities.

Among first-tier cities, panel A shows that the nominal housing price index had an average annual return of 21% from January 2003 to December 2007. Housing prices dropped in 2008. After January 2009, the housing price index continued to rise, and on average had another staggering average annual return of 17.7% from January 2009 to March 2013. Over the whole 10-year period from January 2003 to March 2013, the housing price index for the first-tier cities had an average return of 15.9%!

Panel A also reports the nominal growth of two measures of "purchasing power": per capita GRP and disposable income. Both measures have increased significantly in the decade, on average by 9.4% and 9.3% from January 2003 to March 2013. But the housing price appreciation in first-tier cities was nearly twice the magnitudes of the increases in the two measures of purchasing power.

In real values, panel B shows that the housing return for first-tier cities averaged 13.1% per annum, and the two measures of purchasing power grew on average by 6.7% and 6.6% per year.

Table 1
Summary Statistics of Housing Return and Growth of GRP and Disposable Income, by Tier of Cities

Nominal growth	Obs.	January 2003–December 2007				January 2009–March 2013				January 2003–March 2013			
		Mean	Std. Dev.	Min.	Max.	Mean	Std. Dev.	Min.	Max.	Mean	Std. Dev.	Min.	Max.
						A. Nominal Growth							
Tier-1 Cities													
Housing price index	4	.210	.027	.172	.230	.177	.033	.139	.219	.159	.031	.128	.200
Per capita GRP index	4	.114	.020	.097	.144	.066	.020	.038	.081	.094	.016	.074	.112
Per capita DI index (urban)	4	.099	.025	.061	.116	.102	.003	.098	.105	.093	.028	.051	.110
Tier-2 Cities													
Housing price index	31	.168	.056	.021	.290	.116	.034	.043	.216	.132	.022	.082	.189
Per capita GRP index	30	.136	.050	.010	.235	.129	.031	.052	.191	.134	.033	.042	.189
Per capita DI index (urban)	30	.119	.025	.055	.178	.113	.013	.098	.164	.117	.015	.078	.152
Tier-3 Cities													
Housing price index	85	.113	.067	-.099	.250	.114	.036	.041	.242	.106	.036	.007	.178
Per capita GRP index	85	.154	.045	.006	.260	.140	.036	.037	.214	.150	.032	.030	.231
Per capita DI index (urban)	74	.118	.020	.059	.186	.117	.011	.087	.141	.117	.012	.079	.154

(continued)

Table 1
Continued

Real growth	Obs.	January 2003–December 2007				January 2009–March 2013				January 2003–March 2013			
		Mean	Std. Dev.	Min.	Max.	Mean	Std. Dev.	Min.	Max.	Mean	Std. Dev.	Min.	Max.
B. Real Growth													
Tier-1 Cities													
Housing price index	4	.187	.027	.148	.206	.151	.033	.113	.193	.131	.031	.100	.172
Per capita GRP index	4	.090	.020	.074	.120	.040	.020	.012	.055	.067	.016	.046	.085
Per capita DI index (urban)	4	.075	.025	.038	.092	.076	.003	.072	.079	.066	.028	.024	.083
Tier-2 Cities													
Housing price index	31	.145	.056	-.002	.266	.090	.034	.017	.190	.105	.022	.054	.162
Per capita GRP index	30	.113	.050	-.013	.212	.103	.031	.026	.165	.107	.033	.015	.161
Per capita DI index (urban)	30	.095	.025	.031	.154	.087	.013	.072	.138	.090	.015	.050	.125
Tier-3 Cities													
Housing price index	85	.090	.067	-.123	.227	.089	.036	.015	.216	.079	.036	-.021	.150
Per capita GRP index	85	.131	.045	-.018	.236	.114	.036	.011	.188	.123	.032	.003	.204
Per capita DI index (urban)	74	.094	.020	.036	.162	.091	.011	.061	.115	.089	.012	.052	.127

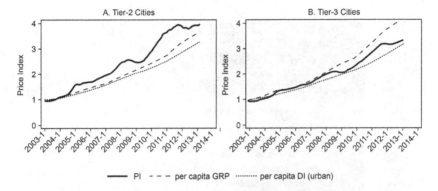

Fig. 6.   Housing price indices for second- and third-tier cities

Note: This figure depicts the monthly housing price indices in two separate panels for second- and third-tier cities, together with two measures of households' purchasing power: per capita GRP and disposable income (urban). Per capita GRP measures the per capita value of output in the whole city and per capita disposable income (urban) measures the per capita income received by urban residents of the city.

B.   Second- and Third-Tier Cities

Due to the large number of cities in second and third tiers, we cannot separately plot the housing price index for each city. Instead, we depict the price index for each of the tiers, together with measures of purchasing power in figure 6.

In panel A of figure 6, the housing price appreciation in second-tier cities is substantial, though not as breathtaking as that in the first-tier cities. Overall, the price index rose from the base of 1 in January 2003 to 3.92 in March 2013. The price fluctuations are also more modest compared to those experienced in the individual first-tier cities, though part of the moderation in price fluctuation is the result of averaging over 31 second-tier cities.

A housing price appreciation of 292% in 10 years is remarkable by any standard. It is larger than the magnitude of housing price appreciation during the US housing bubble in the first decade of the twenty-first century, and is comparable to the price appreciation during the Japanese housing bubble in 1980s. However, what is more surprising in panel A is that the housing price appreciation in second-tier cities is very much in accordance to the growth in measures of purchasing power. To the extent we believe that income growth, or growth in GRP, represents fundamental demand of households for housing, the housing price appreciation in the second-tier cities, though enormous, nonetheless does not appear to have significantly deviated from the increases in households' purchasing power.

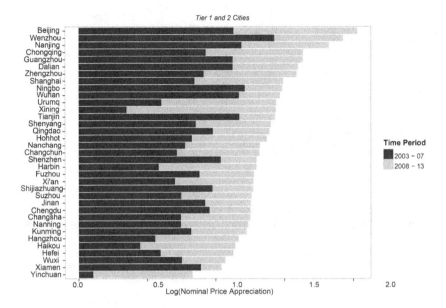

Fig. 7. Housing price appreciation in individual cities

Note: The figure depicts the logarithmic housing price appreciation from January 2003 to March 2013. Each bar represents a city with one part for price appreciation from 2003 to 2007 and the other part for price appreciation from 2008 to 2013. Panel A (above) collects the 35 cities in the first and second tiers in our sample and panel B (facing page) collects the 85 cities in the third tier.

Table 1 reports summary statistics for the 31 second-tier cities in our sample. During the decade from 2003 to 2013, the second-tier cities witnessed an average annual housing return of 13.2% in nominal values and 10.5% in real values. In the same decade, per capita GRP had an average annual growth rate of 13.4% in nominal values, fully comparable to the housing return. The average annual growth rate of per capita disposable income for urban residents was 11.7% in nominal values, which was only slightly smaller than the housing return.

In nominal values, housing prices in the second-tier cities grew on average by 16.8% per year from January 2003 to December 2007, while the increase was 11.6% from January 2009 to March 2013. The increases in housing prices in these two subperiods are again commensurate with the corresponding increases in purchasing power, measured by either per capita GRP or disposable income.

There are substantial variations among the cities. Figure 7 depicts the logarithmic nominal housing price appreciation for each city in our

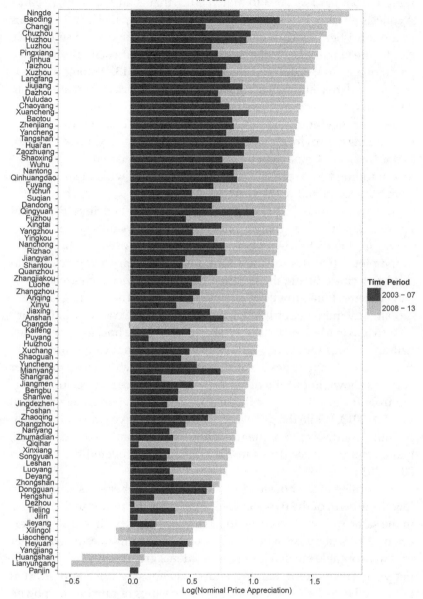

Fig. 7.   (continued)

sample from January 2003 to March 2013, that is, $\ln(P_{2013} / P_{2003})$. Panel A collects all cities in the first and second tiers and panel B collects cities in the third tier. We choose logarithmic price appreciation so that we can further break down the price appreciation of each city into two parts, one in 2003–2007 and the other in 2008–2013. Among the first- and second-tier cities, Beijing had the largest price appreciation in 2003–2013, followed by Wenzhou (a coastal city of Zhejiang Province known for its vibrant manufacturing sector) and Nanjing (the capital city of Jiangsu Province). Yinchuan (the capital city of Ningxia Province in northwestern China) had the lowest price appreciation that neverthe-less amounted to over 120% during this period, which came mostly from the second half of the period.

We now examine the price appreciation in third-tier cities. Panel B of figure 6 depicts the aggregate price index and measures of purchasing power for the 85 third-tier cities in our sample. A remarkable feature of the plot is that despite the enormous housing price appreciation in third-tier cities during the decade, the housing price increase actually lagged behind the growth of disposable income. The housing price in-dex slightly more than tripled, increasing from the base of 1 in January 2003 to 3.13 in March 2013. According to table 1, the housing price index had an average return of 10.6% per year in nominal values or 7.9% in real values. Again, there is substantial heterogeneity across third-tier cities, as shown in panel B of figure 7, with the price appreciation rang-ing from 0.1 to 1.8 in log scale (or 10% to 500% in percentage returns) in 2003–2013. While the price appreciation is positive across all cities in the full period, several of them, such as Lianyungang and Huangshan, had substantial price drops in 2003–2007 and recovered the drops in 2008–2013.

The tripling of the housing index of the third-tier cities is actually be-low the growth of the two measures of purchasing power in these cities in the same period. According to table 1, per capita GRP grew on aver-age by 15.0% per year in nominal values during this decade, while per capita disposable income for urban residents grew on average by 11.7% per year. This pattern, namely, enormous housing price appreciation but nonetheless below the increases in measures of purchasing power, also holds in the two subperiods.

Overall, housing prices across Chinese cities experienced tremendous growth between 2003 and 2013. The housing price appreciation was particularly dramatic in first-tier cities, rising over fivefold in 2003–2013 and substantially outpacing the growth of household purchasing power. The price appreciation in second- and third-tier cities, while remarkable, was matched by equally impressive growth in household purchasing power during the same period.

C. Other Housing Indices for Chinese Cities

Microbased, constant quality housing price indices for Chinese cities are not yet widely available. The National Bureau of Statistics (NBS) of China reports two widely used official housing price series. These two series are commonly known as the "NBS 70-city index" and the "NBS Average Price Index."[11]

NBS 70-City Index. The NBS started to construct quarterly housing price indices for 35 large- and medium-size cities in 1997. Then, it expanded the list to 70 cities and replaced quarterly indices to monthly ones beginning in July 2005. In the construction of the "NBS 70-City Index," technicians from local statistics authorities are sent in each month to sample housing complexes and collect raw information on housing transaction prices. For each housing complex sampled by the local statistics authorities, the average transaction price is calculated in each month and compared with that of the same complex in the previous month. The monthly house price change at city level is then calculated as the average, weighted by transaction volume, of all complexes' price changes in the corresponding months.[12]

NBS Average Price Index. The NBS also publishes the total floor area and revenue of houses sold in 35 major cities, from which average prices can be calculated by simply dividing the total price paid by total floor area of the transacted units in a given month and given city.

As pointed out in Deng, Gyourko, and Wu (2014a), both official series have well-known issues and have been widely criticized: the NBS 70-City Index is remarkably smooth and shows very little real housing price growth in 70 Chinese cities in the last decade, while the NBS Average Price Index fails to control for quality, as it does not account for the fact that the newly transacted units in a given city are gradually moving to the outer rings of the city, an important feature in rapidly expanding Chinese cities.

Figure 8 depicts our housing price index against the two official series for the four first-tier cities. Indeed, the NBS 70-City Index shows little variation in housing prices during the decade and is thus in sharp contrast to common experiences in these cities. Interestingly, the NBS Average Price Index exhibits highly synchronized comovements with

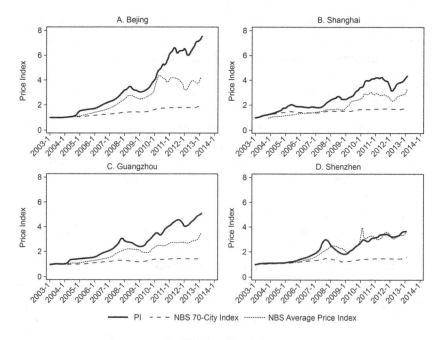

Fig. 8.   Comparing housing price indices

Note: This figure compares the monthly housing price indices for the four first-tier cities constructed by us with the two official series provided by the National Bureau of Statistics (NBS). In each of the panels, the solid line represents our index, the dotted line presents the NBS average price index, and the dashed line the NBS 70-City Index.

our index across all four cities. Such comovements are reassuring as they indicate that our index is capturing similar fluctuations as the straightforward calculation of average transaction prices. It is also useful to note that the NBS Average Price Index shows smaller price appreciation than our index across three of the four cities, which is consistent with the argument that the average price index does not account for the gradual shift in the location of the transacted housing units.

Wu, Deng, and Liu (2014) have made a notable attempt to construct microbased, constant quality housing price indices for 35 Chinese cities by using data from the so-called "Real Estate Market Information System" (REMIS) maintained by municipal housing authorities. This data set contains major attributes of transacted newly built housing units after 2006. They estimated a hedonic model where, for each city, housing transaction prices (log) are regressed on observable characteristics of the unit and its apartment complex and transaction time dummies, which they use to construct housing price indices. Whether Wu et al.'s

(2014) housing price indices represent the constant-quality price indices crucially depends on the extent to which the observed characteristics included in the hedonic price regressions are exhaustive. Nonetheless, the housing price indices of Wu et al. (2014) show that for the 35 major cities there was a dramatic housing price surge from 2006 to 2010, with an average appreciation rate substantially higher than the two official housing price indices.[13]

D.   Experiences in Japan and Singapore

Does the experience of the Chinese housing market differ from that of other Asian countries during the years of their economic miracle? Figure 9 illustrates the experiences in Japan and Singapore.

We cannot find a suitable housing price index for Japan going back to the 1960s and 1970s, which was the period of Japan's rapid economic growth. Instead, panel A of figure 9 depicts an index of urban land price provided by the Japan Real Estate Institute, from 1955 to 2014, together with the per capita GDP of Japan. Both series are in nominal values and are normalized to 1 in 1955. From 1955 to 1990, the per capita GDP grew from a level of 1 to about 40, representing an average growth rate of 10.5% per year. In contrast, the urban land price index grew from 1 to over 80 during the same period, substantially outpacing the per capita GDP. The Japanese economy has staggered since 1990, with the per capita GDP staying flat for the past 25 years. During this period, the urban land price index continued to fall by half and eventually converged back to the same level of the per capita GDP in 2014. The dramatic divergence of the land price index from the per capita GDP before 1990 and the subsequent convergence vividly illustrates the widely recognized Japanese housing bubble. Based on our earlier discussion, the housing price appreciation across Chinese cities during 2003–2013 was rather different from the experience of the Japanese housing bubble. Except for the few first-tier cities, the housing price appreciation in the large number of second- and third-tier cities was largely in line with the growth of household purchasing power.

Panel B of figure 9 depicts the private property resale price index for Singapore, which is provided by the Urban Redevelopment Authority of Singapore, together with the per capita GDP of Singapore, from 1975 to 2010. Both series are in nominal values and are normalized to 1 in 1975. During this period, the per capita GDP grew from a level of 1 to slightly over 10, representing an average growth rate of 6.6% per

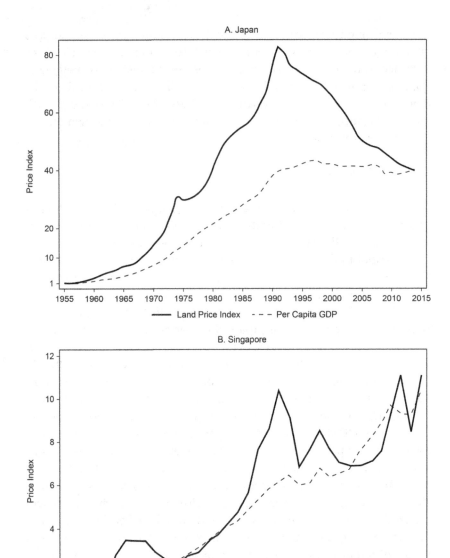

Fig. 9. Housing price and GDP growth in Japan and Singapore

Note: Panel A depicts the Urban Land Price Index for Japan (average assessment value index) provided by the Japan Real Estate Institute, together with the per capita GDP provided by the Japanese Statistics Bureau (Japan Statistical Yearbook), from 1955 to 2014. Panel B depicts the private property resale price index for Singapore (a median sale-price index) provided by the Urban Redevelopment Authority of Singapore, together with the per capita GDP of Singapore provided by the International Monetary Fund (IMF), from 1975 to 2010.

year. Interestingly, the housing price index also grew from 1 to about 11, roughly in line with the GDP growth. While the housing price appreciation was well matched with the GDP growth for the full period from 1975 to 2010, the housing price index did diverge substantially from the GDP in two episodes, one in the early 1980s and the other in 1995–1997, right before the Asian financial crisis. Both episodes happened after a long period of steady economic growth, during which the housing price index rapidly appreciated in a few years, significantly outpacing GDP growth. When the GDP growth slowed, the housing price index collapsed and returned to the level in line with the GDP in a few years. These price corrections appear very relevant for thinking about potential risk in the Chinese housing market, especially in the first-tier cities.

IV. Mortgage Borrowers

The housing price boom across the Chinese cities was ultimately driven by the interplay between supply and demand of housing. Different from the free-market supply of housing in many western countries, it is useful to note that the supply of land for residential developments in Chinese cities is controlled by local municipal governments, which, as we will discuss later, heavily rely on land sale revenues for their fiscal budget. Such fiscal dependence motivates local governments to act as monopolists in strategically releasing land over time in order to maximize their land sales revenue. It remains a challenge to systematically analyze how such strategic behavior affects the supply side of housing in the Chinese cities, which we leave for future studies.

In this section, we further explore our detailed mortgage data to examine the financial burdens faced by home buyers, especially low-income home buyers. This analysis allows us to understand whether housing has been out of the reach of typical households, as many commentators are worried. Specifically, we summarize a set of characteristics of these mortgage borrowers, including household income, down payment, price-to-income ratio, home size, age, and marital status.

Note that households in the most wealthy fraction of the population may purchase homes using cash and thus do not appear in our mortgage data. For this reason, our mortgage data is particularly useful for analyzing the characteristics of relatively low-income home buyers as opposed to those of high-income buyers. We focus on analyzing two sets of borrowers in each tier of cities: The first set has household income in the bottom 10% among all mortgage borrowers in a given city and a given year. We refer to this set as the bottom-income borrower group.

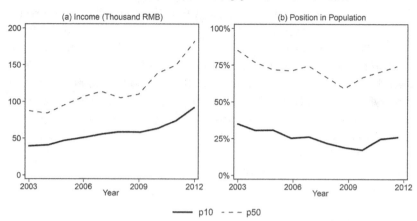

A. Income of Bottom and Median Mortgage Borrowers in Tier-1 Cities

Fig. 10.   Annual income of mortgage borrowers

Note: This figure depicts the time series of the household incomes of p10 and p50 for first-, second-, and third-tier cities in panels A (above), B (facing page, top), and C (facing page, bottom), respectively. In panels A and B, the left plot shows the annual income of p10 and p50 (which is averaged across all cities in the tier) from 2003 to 2012, and the right plot shows the position of p10 and p50 in the income distribution of the city population based on the income distribution reported by the Urban Household Survey (UHS). Panel C shows only the annual income of p10 and p50.

We also denote borrowers with income exactly at the 10 percentile of all borrowers by p10. The second set has household income in the middle range, specifically within the 45th and 55th percentiles of all mortgage borrowers in a given city and a given year. We refer to this set as the middle-income group and denote borrowers with exactly the median income of all borrowers by p50.

A.   Household Income

Figure 10 depicts the time series of the household income of p10 and p50 for first-, second-, and third-tier cities in panels A, B, and C, respectively. In panels A and B, the left plot shows the annual income of p10 and p50 (which is averaged across all cities in the tier) in RMB from 2003 to 2012, and the right plot shows the position of p10 and p50 in the income distribution of the city population based on the income distribution constructed from the Urban Household Survey (UHS). As income distribution is not available for third-tier cities, panel C shows only the annual income of p10 and p50.

B. Income of Bottom and Median Mortgage Borrowers in Tier-2 Cities

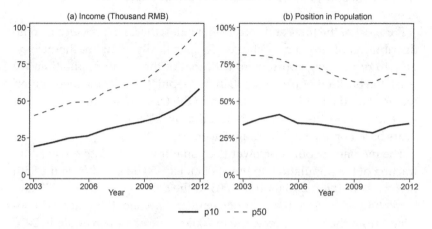

(a) Income (Thousand RMB)

(b) Position in Population

— p10   - - - p50

C. Income of Bottom and Median Mortgage Borrowers in Tier-3 Cities

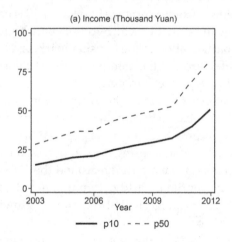

(a) Income (Thousand Yuan)

— p10   - - - p50

Fig. 10.   (continued)

Figure 10 shows steady growth in the household income of both p10 and p50 across the three tiers of cities. In first-tier cities, the annual household income of p10 grew from 39,000 RMB in 2003 to 92,000 in 2012, while the income of p50 grew from 87,000 in 2003 to 184,000 in 2012. In second-tier cities, the annual income of p10 grew from 19,000 RMB in 2003 to 58,000 in 2012, while that of p50 grew from 40,000 in 2003 to 99,000 in 2012. In third-tier cities, the income of p10 grew from 15,000 to 51,000, while that of p50 grew from 28,000 to 83,000. This tremendous income growth of mortgage borrowers is largely consistent with the income growth of the overall urban population we discussed above.

For most of the first- and second-tier cities, the UHS provides income distribution of urban households. To specifically compare the income growth of mortgage borrowers with that of the urban population, we mark the position of p10 and p50 in the population income distribution reported by the UHS. As our data from the UHS cover only 2003–2009, we extrapolate the income distribution in 2009 into the subsequent years based on the city's average income growth.

The median-income borrower p50 came from the relatively wealthy fraction of the population. In first-tier cities, p50 declined from the 85th percentile of the population in 2003 to the 59th percentile in 2009 and then climbed back to the 75th percentile. In second-tier cities, p50 declined from the 81.5th percentile in 2003 to the 62nd percentile in 2010 and then climbed back to the 68th percentile in 2012.

The position of the low-income mortgage borrower p10 is particularly interesting. It indicates the extent to which low-income households in the population were participating in the housing markets. Overall, p10 was located at a position around the 25th percentile of the population in first-tier cities and around the 30th percentile in second-tier cities. These positions indicate that mortgage borrowers were not just coming from the top-income households, and instead were reasonably well represented in the low-income fraction of the population.

Interestingly, despite the rapid housing price appreciation in first-tier cities, p10 steadily declined from a position around the 35th percentile in 2003 to the 17.5th percentile in 2010 before it climbed back to the 26th percentile in 2012. This suggests that the rapidly growing prices in recent years have not prevented households from the low-income fraction of the population from buying homes. In second-tier cities, p10 stayed in a range between the 28th and 40th percentile—it declined from a peak of the 40th percentile in 2005 to the 28.5th percentile in 2010 and then climbed back to the 35th percentile in 2012.

Taken together, figure 10 shows steady increases in the household income of bottom- and middle-income mortgage borrowers across the three tiers of cities. Furthermore, despite the tremendous housing price appreciation in these cities, mortgage borrowers were well represented in the population and the housing market participation of households from the low-income fraction of the population remained stable.

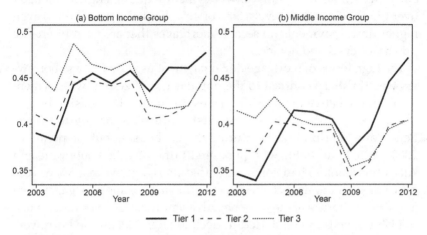

Fig. 11.   Mortgage down payment

Note: The left panel depicts the fraction of mortgage down payment in home value at the time of purchase for bottom-income borrowers in first-, second-, and third-tier cities, and the right panel depicts the fraction of down payment for middle-income borrowers in these three tiers of cities.

B.   *Down Payment*

Mortgage down payment is a key variable that determines the leverage used by mortgage borrowers and serves as an equity buffer to prevent borrowers from defaulting on the loans in the event of a future housing price meltdown. Figure 11 depicts the fraction of down payment in the home value at the time of purchase, separately for the bottom- and middle-income groups.

The right panel shows that for mortgage borrowers in the middle-income group, down payment on average contributed to at least 35% of home value across the three tiers of cities. Interestingly, the left panel shows that for borrowers in the bottom-income group, the fraction of down payment was even higher—it was consistently above 38% across the three tiers of cities.

These high levels of down payment are consistent with the strict mortgage policies imposed by the Chinese government on banks. Specifically, the policies restrict one housing unit from being used as collateral for more than one mortgage loan. The policies also require a minimum down payment of 30% on first mortgages. As detailed in appendix A, this minimum down payment requirement had changed over time between two levels: 30% or 40%. Banks have requested even higher down payments on second mortgages that are used to finance purchases of second homes.

The high levels of mortgage down payment used by Chinese borrowers were in sharp contrast to the popular use of zero down payment loans and negative amortization loans during the US housing bubble of the first decade of the twenty-first century. According to Mayer, Pence, and Sherlund (2009), during the US housing bubble period of 2003–2006, households with poor credit (the so-called subprime and Alt-A households) had commonly used mortgages with a 5% or zero down payment to finance their home purchases. Some mortgages even allowed the borrowers to have negative amortization over time. When the US housing prices started to decline after 2006, these borrowers were more likely to default on their mortgage loans, exacerbating the housing market decline. The high levels of down payments used by households throughout China mitigated the risk of household default in the event of a future housing market meltdown. Unless the housing prices decline by over 30%, the mortgage borrowers are unlikely to default on their loans.[14] Furthermore, mortgage loans in China are all recourse loans, which allow lenders to collect borrowers' other assets in the event of mortgage defaults. These reasons make a US-style subprime credit crisis less of a concern for China.

C. Price-to-Income Ratio

Price-to-income ratio provides a convenient measure of the financial burdens endured by a household in acquiring a home. Figure 12 depicts the price-to-income ratio of mortgage borrowers in the full sample (top panel) and in the subsample of married borrowers (bottom panel). In each panel, there are two plots, the left plot covers the borrowers in the bottom-income group with a separate line for each of the three tiers of cities, while the right plot covers the borrowers in the middle-income group.

The financial burdens faced by the bottom-income group are particularly interesting. In this group, the price-to-income ratio started at a level slightly above 8 across the three tiers of cities in 2003. In first-tier cities, this ratio remained at around 8 before 2008 and then climbed to a peak of 10.7 in 2011 before dropping back to 9.2 in 2012. In second- and third-tier cities, this ratio was very similar and remained in a tight range around 8. It had a modest decline from a level slightly above 8 in

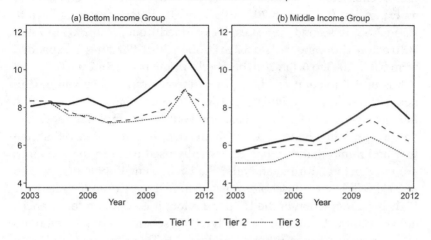

A. Price-to-Income Ratio in Full Sample

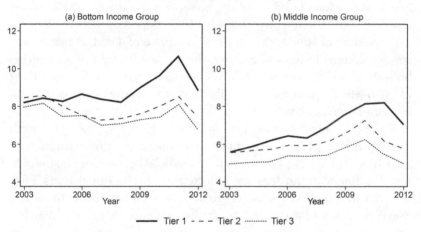

B. Price-to-Income Ratio of Married Sample

Fig. 12. Price-to-income ratio of mortgage borrowers

Note: This figure depicts the price-to-income ratio of mortgage borrowers in the full sample (top panel) and in the subsample of married borrowers (bottom panel). In each panel, there are two plots, the left plot covers the borrowers in the bottom-income group with a separate line for each of the three tiers of cities, while the right plot covers the borrowers in the middle-income group.

2003 to 7.2 in 2007 and then climbed back to a peak slightly below 9 in 2011 before dropping back to around 8 again.

The price-to-income ratio for the middle-income group was consistently lower than that for the bottom-income group. It was highest in the first-tier cities and lowest in the third-tier cities. Across the three tiers of cities, it had a similar pattern over time. In first-tier cities, it had an expansion from 5.6 in 2003 to 8.3 in 2011 before dropping back to 7.5 in 2012. In second-tier cities, it expanded from 5.7 in 2003 to 7.4 in 2010 before dropping back to 6.2 in 2012. In third-tier cities, it expanded from 5.0 in 2003 to 6.4 in 2010 before dropping back to 6.2 in 2012.

It is useful to compare the price-to-income ratios observed in Chinese cities with that in other countries. Cheng, Raina, and Xiong (2014, table 9) examined home purchases by Wall Street employees and lawyers in the United States during the first decade of the twenty-first century and found that they had consistently used price-to-income ratios around 3 before, during, and after the US housing bubble that peaked in 2006. While the households they examined were from the relatively high-income fraction of the US population, it is common for financial advisors in the United States to advise households to purchase homes with price-to-income ratios of around 3.[15] There are few studies of financial burdens faced by mortgage borrowers during the Japanese housing bubble. Indirectly, Noguchi (1991, table 1.3) reported that the average ratio of condominium price (the price of a certain benchmark condominium) to annual income, that is, the income of an average household which may or may not be a home buyer, in Tokyo rose to 8.6 in 1989, which is consistent with the price-to-income ratios used by the bottom-income borrowers in China.

A price-to-income ratio of 8 or higher, which had been commonly used by mortgage borrowers in the bottom-income group throughout the Chinese cities, implies substantial financial burdens on the borrowers. The financial burdens are reflected in several dimensions. First, in order to qualify for a mortgage loan, a borrower needs to make a down payment of about 38% of the home value (figure 12), which is equivalent to about three times the borrower's annual income. This large down payment would require many years of saving. In practice, many home buyers, who are typically in their early thirties (as we will show below), rely on the savings of their parents or other close family members to make the down payment.[16]

Second, monthly mortgage payments also consume a substantial fraction of the household income. To illustrate this burden, consider a household that bought a home at a price that was eight times its annual disposable income. Suppose that it used its savings to make the down payment at three times its annual income and took a mortgage loan that was five times its annual income. As we describe in appendix A, all mortgage loans in China carry floating rate interest payments, with the rate determined by a benchmark lending rate set by the People's Bank of China. If the annual mortgage rate was 6%, a rather low rate relative to the rate observed in recent years, then the annual interest payment would consume 6% × 5 = 30% of the household's annual income. Furthermore, the household also needed to pay back a fraction of the mortgage each year. Suppose that the loan had a maturity of 30 years (maximum maturity allowed in China) and linear amortization. Then, the household had to set aside another 5 / 30 = 16.7% of its annual income to pay the mortgage. Together, servicing the mortgage loan would consume 46.7% of its annual income.

As we will discuss later, a significant fraction of home buyers in the bottom-income group were unmarried. As they would eventually get married, and as it is common in China for a married couple to both work, the household income of a single buyer may soon double upon his/her marriage. Then, the price-to-income ratio of single buyers may not accurately reflect their financial burdens. To isolate this issue, we also compute the price-to-income ratio of married couples in the bottom-income and middle-income groups in each tier of cities. The bottom panel of figure 12 shows that the price-to-income ratio of married borrowers was very similar to that of the full sample with both married and unmarried borrowers across both income groups and different tiers of cities. This lack of difference may reflect the fact that Chinese banks follow a rigid system of using current household income to determine the amount of mortgage loans available to borrowers, regardless of their marital status.

The remarkable income growth of Chinese households during this decade also implies that the large financial burdens endured by mortgage borrowers might be temporary and would subside over time as their income grew. Again, consider the household that purchased a home at an initial price-to-income ratio of 8. Suppose that the household expected its income to grow at an annual rate of 10%, which was roughly the growth rate during this period. Then, it expected its income would rise to 1.6 times of its initial level in five years; the ratio of the current home price to its future income in five years would be 5. Of course, this calculation depends on a crucial assumption that the 10% income growth rate would persist into the future. This assumption is ex ante strong despite that ex post the household income in China has been growing at this impressive rate for three decades.

Nevertheless, this simple calculation shows that the household's expected income growth rate is crucial for determining how much it is willing to pay for a home relative to its current income. If the household expected its income to persistently grow at a high rate, it would expect the large financial burdens brought by buying a home at eight times of its current annual income to be temporary. Furthermore, this expectation might also motivate an expectation about high-income growth of other households, which may in turn lead to an expectation that housing prices will continue to rise. Such an expectation further motivates the household to take on enormous financial burdens to buy the home. In this sense, the households' expectations about their income growth and future housing price appreciation are central for understanding the housing market boom. We will return to this issue in our later discussion.

D.   Home Size

Home size is an important dimension for determining the consumption value of a home. Figure 13 depicts the size of the homes purchased by bottom-income and middle-income mortgage borrowers across the three tiers of cities. Despite the large financial burdens endured by the mortgage borrowers, their homes were rather spacious. The bottom-income borrowers in first-tier cities, which are the most expensive cities in China, bought the smallest homes in our sample. Even for these borrowers, the average size of their home was in a range between 72 and 80 square meters throughout the decade. For a typical family of three (a couple with one child, based on China's birth control policy), this home size implies about 25 square meters per person, which is quite spacious by the standards of most large metropolitan areas in the world such as Hong Kong, New York, Singapore, and Tokyo.

It is also useful to note the evident declining trend in the home size purchased by all groups in the three tiers of cities. The homes purchased by bottom-income borrowers in second-tier cities on average declined from 90 square meters in 2003 to 80 in 2012, while the homes purchased by bottom-income borrowers in third-tier cities declined from 109 square meters in 2004 to slightly above 90 in 2012. The homes purchased by middle-income borrowers tended to be bigger, but also had a similar decline across all three tiers of cities.

E.   Age and Marital Status

Figure 14 shows the age of mortgage borrowers in our sample. Across the three tiers of cities, the mortgage borrowers were on average in their

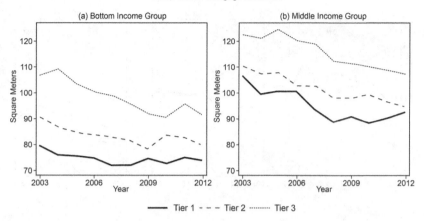

Fig. 13. Home size of mortgage borrowers

Note: The left panel depicts the home size of bottom-income borrowers in first-, second-, and third-tier cities, while the right panel depicts that of middle-income borrowers.

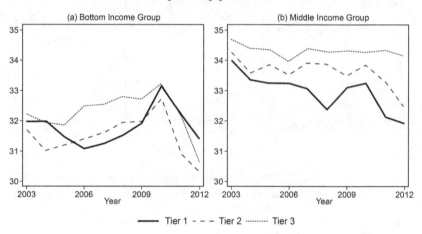

Fig. 14. Age of mortgage borrowers

Note: The left panel depicts the age of bottom-income borrowers in first-, second-, and third-tier cities, while the right panel depicts that of middle-income borrowers.

early thirties. The borrowers in the bottom-income group tended to be slightly younger than those in the middle-income group.

A significant fraction of the borrowers are unmarried. Figure 15 summarizes the fractions of single men and single women among the mortgage borrowers in each income group and each tier of cities. Single men

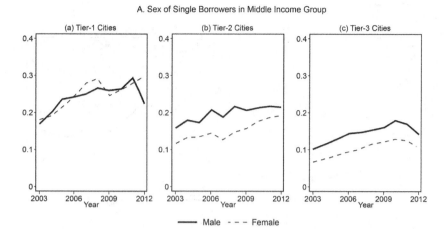

A. Sex of Single Borrowers in Middle Income Group

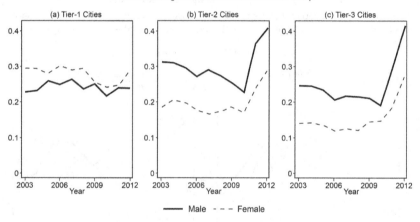

B. Sex of Single Borrowers in Bottom Income Group

Fig. 15.   Marital status of mortgage borrowers

Note: The top panel depicts the fractions of single men and single women among middle-income borrowers in three separate plots for first-, second-, and third-tier cities, while the bottom panel depicts these fractions among bottom-income borrowers in three separate plots for first-, second-, and third-tier cities.

and single women contributed to at least 40% of the bottom-income mortgage borrowers across the three tiers of cities in each of the years from 2003 to 2012. This fraction was lower among the middle-income borrowers, but nevertheless substantial.

Wei, Zhang, and Liu (2014) argue that home ownership is a status that is good for single men to strengthen their competitiveness in the marriage market due to the widespread sex imbalance in China. This argument implies that single men should be more eager to buy homes than single women. Consistent with this argument, the fraction of single men among mortgage borrowers was consistently higher than the fraction of single women in second- and third-tier cities across all years and across the bottom-income and middle-income borrower groups. However, in first-tier cities, the fraction of single men was roughly the same as the fraction of single women among the middle-income borrowers, and the fraction of single men was even lower than the fraction of single women among the bottom-income borrowers throughout the sample period.[17] This suggests that while marriage market competition might be a determinant of home ownership in second- and third-tier cities, it is not as relevant for understanding the particularly high housing prices in first-tier cities.

F. Second Mortgages

An often discussed concern regarding the Chinese housing markets is that many urban households hold multiple homes and leave a significant fraction of homes vacant for prolonged periods of time. Our mortgage data allow us to separate second mortgages (i.e., mortgage loans taken by households to purchase second homes) from first mortgages (i.e., single mortgages taken by households) after 2010.[18]

Table 2 summarizes the fraction of second mortgages among all mortgage loans issued in each tier of cities in each year between 2011 and 2013. This fraction offers a measure of the extent that households took loans to buy investment homes. As wealthy households may simply use cash to buy investment homes, such investment purchases by wealthy households do not appear in our mortgage data. Thus, the fraction of second mortgages underestimates the home purchases driven by investment demands.

In first-tier cities, the fraction of second mortgages was 5.3% and 5.2% in 2011 and 2012, respectively, and this fraction had a dramatic increase to 11.8% in 2013. In second- and third-tier cities, the fraction of second mortgages also had an increasing trend during this period, although the levels were much lower. In second-tier cities, this fraction grew from 2.0% in 2011 to 2.4% in 2012 and 3.3% in 2013. In third-tier cities, it grew from 1.0% in 2011 to 1.3% in 2012 and 1.8% in 2013. Taken together, mortgage-financed investment home purchases were much more pervasive in first-tier cities than in second- and third-tier cities.[19]

Table 2
Fraction of Second Mortgages

	2011 (%)	2012 (%)	2013 (%)
First-tier cities	5.3	5.2	11.8
Second-tier cities	2.0	2.4	3.3
Third-tier cities	1.0	1.3	1.8

In summary, our analysis of the mortgage data shows that despite the enormous housing price appreciation during the last decade, the participation of low-income households in the housing markets remained steady. Nevertheless, the relatively low-income home buyers endured severe financial burdens in order to buy homes at prices commonly over eight times their current income. This behavior reflected expectations of persistently high income growth and further high housing price appreciation.

V. Housing as an Investment Vehicle

The spectacular economic growth of China since the 1980s has been accompanied by a high savings rate. According to Yang et al. (2013), the gross national savings as a percentage of GDP averaged 35% during the 1980s, 41% during the 1990s, and surged to over 50% in the first decade of the twenty-first century. This high saving rate surpassed the rates of all major countries during the same period and was also higher than the prevailing rates in Japan, South Korea, and other East Asian economies during the years of their miraculous growth. Households, firms, and the government have all contributed to the remarkably high savings rate in China. Savings by households and firms had each reached about 20% of the GDP during the early years of the twenty-first century.

Despite the high savings rate, households and firms in China have limited vehicles in which to invest their massive savings. Bank deposit accounts are the predominant investment vehicle in China. Due to China's restrictive capital controls, households and firms cannot freely invest their savings in capital markets outside of China, and although they can invest in the stock market inside China, it is still small by size relative to the pool of savings and has not offered attractive returns in the last two decades.[20] Bond markets in China are even smaller. Given these limited investment choices, Chinese households often use housing as an alternative invest-

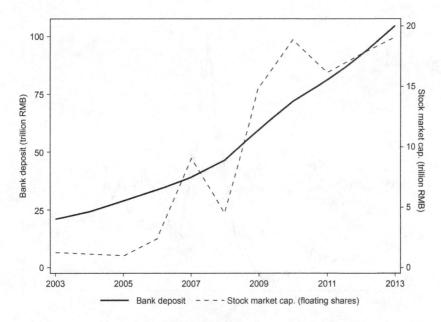

Fig. 16. Bank deposits and stock market capitalization

ment vehicle. In this section, we discuss the performance of housing as an investment vehicle, in comparison to bank deposits and stock market.

A. Bank Deposits

Figure 16 shows that total bank deposits in China rose from slightly above 20 trillion RMB in 2003 to over 100 trillion in 2013. The deposit rate is regulated by the central bank. As shown in figure 4, the nominal bank deposit rate remained in a narrow range, between 2 and 4% in 2003–2013, while the national inflation rate frequently surpassed the nominal deposit rate in 2004, 2008–2009, and 2011–2012, making the real deposit rate negative. The average real deposit rate in 2003–2013 was 0.01%. This low deposit rate makes the huge pool of bank deposits rather striking. Nevertheless, the low deposit rate has motivated Chinese households to search for alternative vehicles to invest their massive savings.

B. Stocks

China established two stock exchanges in the early 1990s, one in Shanghai and the other in Shenzhen. Figure 16 shows that the market capi-

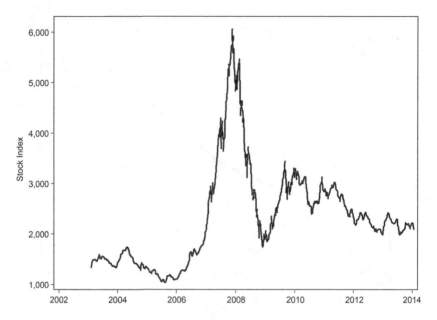

Fig. 17.   Shanghai stock market index

talization of all floating shares in the stock market grew from less than
2 trillion RMB in 2003 to nearly 20 trillion in 2013. Despite this rapid
expansion, the size of the stock market was still substantially smaller
than the total bank deposits.

Figure 17 depicts the Shanghai Stock Market Index, a widely followed
index for the Chinese stock market, for 2003–2013. This period witnessed
a dramatic stock market boom and bust in 2006–2008, when the index
rose from 1,200 at the beginning of 2006 to a peak of 6,092 in October 2007
and then plunged to just below 2,000 in October 2008. This boom and
bust cycle mostly coincided with the rise and fall of stock markets all over
the world in conjunction with the financial crisis in 2008. Since 2008, the
Shanghai Stock Market Index recovered in 2009 to a level slightly above
3,000, but declined again after 2010 to a level around 2,000.

Table 3 summarizes the risk and return from investing in the Shanghai Stock Market Index in 2003–2013. During this period, its annual
return was an average of 7.3% and it had volatility of 51.5%. This high
volatility is not surprising given the dramatic stock market boom and
bust in 2006–2008. To isolate this boom and bust period, table 3 also
splits the sample into two subperiods. In the first half (2003–2008), despite the market crash in 2008, the index return had an average of 8.98%

Table 3
Summary Statistics of Annual Returns of the Shanghai
Stock Market Index (2003–2013)

	Mean	Std. Dev.	Skewness
2003–2013	.073	.515	–.153
2003–2008	.0898	.662	–.337
2009–2013	.053	.339	1.182

Table 4
Summary Statistics of Annual Housing Returns (2003–2013)

	Mean	Std. Dev.	Skewness
Full Sample (2003–2013)			
First-tier index	.157	.154	–.674
Second-tier index	.135	.0989	.564
Third-tier index	.110	.075	.092
Before 2009 (2003–2008)			
First-tier index	.204	.105	–.059
Second-tier index	.173	.099	.852
Third-tier index	.117	.095	–.028
After 2009 (2009–2013)			
First-tier index	.109	.191	–.249
Second-tier index	.097	.094	.474
Third-tier index	.103	.059	–.057

and a staggering volatility of 66.1%. In the second half (2009–2013), the index return had an average of 5.3% and a volatility of 33.9%.

C. Housing

Table 4 summarizes the annual returns of the housing indices of first-, second-, and third-tier cities. During our full sample in 2003–2013, first-tier cities offered the highest average annual return at a staggering level of 15.7% and return volatility of 15.4%, second-tier cities offered an average return of 13.4% and volatility of 9.9%, while third-tier cities offered the lowest average return of 11.0% among the three tiers and also the lowest volatility of 7.5%. Relative to the stock index return in the same period, the housing indices across the three tiers all offered higher average returns and, more impressively, much lower volatility. Despite the economic turmoil after 2008, the volatility of housing returns had been remarkably low.

During the first half of the sample, 2003–2008, the housing returns were particularly high for first- and second-tier cities, with the first-tier housing index offering an average return of 20.4% and the second tier 17.3%. During the second half of the sample, 2009–2013, average returns of both the first and second tier were lower at 10.9% and 9.7%, which are nevertheless attractive relative to the average stock index return during the same period. The index return of third-tier cities was stable across the two subsamples at 11.7% and 10.3%, respectively.

Overall, the housing returns from all three tiers of Chinese cities were surprisingly resilient across the economic crisis period of 2008–2009 and offered returns substantially more attractive than bank deposits and the Chinese stock market.

VI. Discussion

Our analysis provides some basic facts to allow us to understand and interpret the Chinese housing boom. In this section, we offer discussion based on these facts.

Housing booms are often associated with credit expansions, with the recent housing bubble in the United States being a vivid example. As a result, commentators have often been concerned by the potential risk of excessive leverage driving the Chinese housing boom. As we have described earlier, Chinese banks have required down payments of over 30% for all mortgage loans. Such high down-payment ratios substantially alleviate the household default risk faced by banks and make reckless credit expansions to households an unlikely cause of the Chinese housing boom.

A particular concern about the Chinese housing boom is that the enormous housing price appreciation across Chinese cities might constitute a housing bubble that is about to burst. As is well known by economists, it is difficult to reliably identify an asset bubble. There may or may not be a housing bubble in the Chinese housing market. To forcefully determine the presence of a housing bubble, one needs to develop a systematic framework of supply and demand of housing that fully accounts for the growth of the Chinese economy, the frictions in the Chinese financial system, and the strategic behavior of local governments in supplying land. This entails a task substantially more ambitious than the goal of this paper. Nevertheless, our analysis offers some useful observations about the nature of this nationwide housing boom.

On one hand, the enormous price appreciation does not necessarily indicate the presence of a bubble, as the price appreciation has been mostly accompanied by equally impressive household income growth, except in a few first-tier cities. In order to provide a simple conceptual framework in which income growth can act as an anchor for housing price growth, consider a consumer with utility function $u(c, h)$ where c is the numeraire consumption good whose price is normalized to 1, and h is housing consumption. Let R be the rental price for housing. If households' house purchases are only for its consumption value (and not for investment purposes), then they will choose c and h to maximize $u(c, h)$ subject to the budget constraint that $c + Rh \leq y$. If household preferences are homothetic, it can be shown that households will spend a constant share of their income on housing, that is, Rh^* / y will be a constant. In the data, as we discussed earlier, households' choices of h^* remained largely constant, if anything it slightly declined, over the decade (which may also reflect a constraint imposed by government in terms of the size of housing units). Thus, a constant share of housing expenditure will manifest itself in terms of a constant ratio of R / y. Since housing price is simply the discounted present value of rents (in this environment, without investment demand for housing), the growth in the households' willingness to consume housing will track the growth of income. Under an additional assumption of inelastic housing supply, which may ultimately reflect the government's land supply policy, the growth of housing prices may rise in sync with the income growth.

On the other hand, housing prices are indeed expensive relative to the income of many households, in particular, of the low-income mortgage borrowers. While one can justify their willingness, despite the severe financial burdens, to buy homes based on expectations of persistently high income growth, the high price-to-income ratios observed across Chinese cities expose the housing market to substantial risks when households' expectations are subdued in the future, especially in the event of a sudden stop in the Chinese economy.

Our analysis also highlights a few key ingredients for future efforts to develop a systematic framework for analyzing the Chinese housing market:

1. The housing market across first-, second-, and third-tier cities offered high returns, substantially more attractive than bank deposits and the Chinese stock market.

2. Housing price levels were also high across the three tiers of cities with low-income households buying homes at prices that were over eight times their annual income.

3. Concurrent with the housing boom, Chinese households also accumulated a large pool of cash in bank deposits that paid a minimal deposit rate.

It is important to fully account for the distortions brought to the housing market by the imperfections in the Chinese financial system. The low bank deposit rate that had persisted throughout the studied decade is a key factor. To the extent that near 100 trillion RMB has been sitting in bank deposits earning an almost zero real rate, households' investment demand for housing is an important driver of housing prices in China.[21]

Beside the well-known illiquidity of housing, risk is an important dimension in evaluating housing as an investment asset. It is difficult to measure the crash risk of the housing market based on month-to-month price fluctuations. The housing market was rather resilient across the crisis period of 2008–2009. In this regard, the housing market has been more robust to crash risk, relative to the stock market, even though the low risk experienced by the housing market in the past does not necessarily imply low risk going forward. As discussed by Pritchett and Summers (2014), the spectacular growth rate of the Chinese economy during the last three decades is clearly a rare event, and the powerful force of regression to the mean would make a continued high growth rate of 9 or even 7 or 6% an even more unlikely event. This argument implies a substantial risk of an eventual economic slowdown. To the extent that low-income households were buying homes by enduring substantial financial burdens, the risk perceived by them was unlikely to be large. Thus, a systematic framework needs to account for the expectations of households, in particular, their optimistic expectations about persistently high growth rates into the future.[22]

It is also useful to note that housing demand may also be driven by reasons beyond consumption and investment needs. Wei, Zhang, and Liu (2014) emphasize the role of housing as a status good, which strengthens the competitiveness of unmarried men in an unbalanced marriage market where men substantially outnumber women. Indeed, our analysis also confirms relatively larger fractions of unmarried men to unmarried women among mortgage borrowers in second- and third-tier cities, albeit not in first-tier cities.

While our analysis has been largely focused on the demand side of the housing market, the supply side is equally important. There is still a lack of systematic understanding of housing supply in Chinese cities. To the extent that housing prices have been rising at a pace comparable to or even higher than the households' income growth rate during the decade, the housing market equilibrium implies that the growth of housing supply was likely to have stayed either below or comparable to the growth of housing demand, even though Deng, Gyourko, and Wu (2014a) document some evidence of a large housing inventory held by developers in several major cities in recent years. Different from US cities where housing supply is often determined by landscape and local zoning restrictions (e.g., Saiz 2010), housing supply in Chinese cities is determined by land sold by local governments for housing development, as land is legally owned by the state and controlled by local governments. As we will discuss in the next section, land sale revenues have contributed to a substantial fraction of local governments' fiscal budget. As a local monopoly of land supply, local governments' land sales strategy is a key factor in determining housing prices in Chinese cities.

VII.   Roles of Government in the Housing Market

In China, the governments at the central and local levels have been actively engaged in the housing market. The powerful forces induced by government policies not only directly affect physical aspects of the housing market such as supply of land and availability of funds to buyers, but also delicately influence expectations and confidence of households about the housing market. This is an important channel for understanding the drastically divergent performance of the housing and stock markets after 2008. In this section, we briefly discuss the role of government in the housing market, first on the policy interventions of the central government and then on the dependence of local governments on land sales for their fiscal revenues.

A.   Interventions by the Central Government

By 2007, housing prices in most Chinese cities had grown substantially, as discussed in section III. In response, the central government implemented a series of monetary and fiscal policies to curb soaring prices and curtail speculative activities in the housing market. For example, in September 2007, the central government raised the minimum down-payment ratio from 30% to 40%, raised the interest rate on second mortgages to 10% higher than the benchmark rate, and capped the monthly mortgage payment-to-income ratio at 50%. In April 2008, it imposed tax on capital gains from housing sales. The government also started to increase the construction of government-subsidized housing, such as affordable housing, low-cost housing, and public rental housing, to help relieve the pressure on the housing market.

These policies might have had some effect on housing prices, especially in cities in Guangzhou and Shenzhen during this period, though it is hard to distinguish the effects of the policies from that of the emerging global economic crisis. In any event, in October 2008, the central government abruptly reversed these policies and installed a series of measures to support housing market recovery. It reduced the minimum mortgage rates to 70% of the benchmark rate and the down-payment ratio to 30%. As part of its 4 trillion RMB stimulus package, it also designated the real estate sector as one of the primary industries for investment. As a result, the housing market regained momentum in mid-2009 and started a new round of rapid price appreciation.

In early 2010, the government introduced a series of measures, some traditional and some less standard, to cool off what was widely considered a once again overheating housing market. It again raised the down-payment ratio to 40% and the interest rate on second mortgages. More important, starting in April 2010, following the guidelines of the central government, 39 of the 70 major cities in China introduced the *housing purchase restriction policies*.[23] Under these policies, only those with local *Hukou* (household registration), or those who could show proof of employment in the city for a certain number of consecutive years, were eligible for purchasing one or two new homes. Though not covered in our sample period, the slowdown in the Chinese economy has led to a slowdown of the residential housing market since the end of 2013. Many cities loosened the purchase restrictions in mid-2014. Currently, the housing purchase restriction policies are in force only in the four first-tier cities.

The frequent interventions by the central government have created a sense among the households that the housing market is too important to fall, as whenever the market started to fall, the central government would provide supports to sustain it.

B. *Land Sales and Fiscal Revenue of Local Governments*

Land sale revenues have contributed to a substantial fraction of local governments' budgets. This feature was a result of the fiscal reforms enacted in 1994. In the reforms, the central government consolidated provisions for tax revenue collection and sharing in order to redistribute tax revenues to less developed areas. As is well known, local officials in China were evaluated for promotion based to a large extent on regional economic growth (Li and Zhou 2005), which provided strong incentives for investment in infrastructure and capital projects. However, unlike local governments in western countries, local Chinese governments do not have many sources of revenue. In particular, local governments in China are not authorized to levy sales taxes, property taxes, or local income taxes, which are important sources of revenue for local governments in western countries. Moreover, local governments in China are prevented from directly issuing debt to fund capital projects.

As a result of this central/local fiscal arrangement and the restrictions placed on local governments, China has developed a unique source for local governments to obtain capital necessary to fund required large-scale infrastructure investments—they increasingly rely on selling public land. Figure 18 shows the share of land revenues in city fiscal budgets from 2003–2011 averaged across all cities, as well as among the first-tier, second-tier, and all other cities. At the national level, this share started at 68% in 2003 and decreased to 42% in 2008, only to bounce back to even higher than 70% in 2010 and 2011. Across these tiers, the share is relatively low for first-tier cities as their municipal governments have more sources of revenues, but high for second-tier and other cities. For the cities outside the first and second tiers, revenue from land sales was particularly high, contributing over 90% of their fiscal budgets in some years, such as 2003 and 2010.

The central government has also allowed the local governments to create a unique funding mechanism known as Local Government-Backed Investment Units, through which future land-sales revenue can be pledged as collateral.[24] Local governments have used such investment units to access capital markets and issue bonds that would allow more large-scale infrastructure/capital investment, as well as other economic development and social insurance initiatives. This unique mixing of local governmental fiscal policies with local housing markets implies that a substantial drop in housing or land prices might lead to financial distress of local governments or even trigger defaults by Local Government-Backed Investment Units, which would be equivalent to defaults by the local governments. As a result, many households in China have been emboldened to believe that the housing market is "too important to fall," and that the central government will be forced to in-

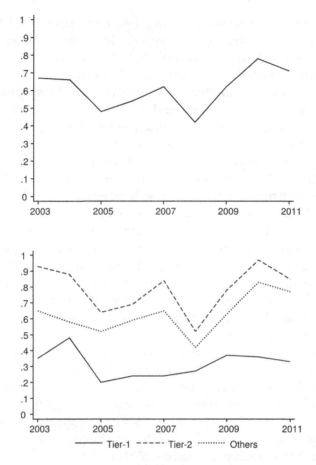

Fig. 18. Share of land revenue in city budget

Source: Data from the China Municipal Statistical Yearbook and China National Land Resource Yearbook.

Note: The top panel depicts the national average of share of land sales revenue in cities' fiscal budgets, while the bottom panel depicts the average among first-tier cities, second-tier cities, and all other cities.

stitute policies to pump up the housing market if it were to deteriorate, just as it had done in the past.

Taken together, the heavy reliance of local governments on land-sales revenue for their fiscal budgets also helped to create a belief among many households that the housing market was too important to fall. This belief might have contributed to the resilient housing prices throughout the last decade.

VIII. Risks for the Chinese Housing Market

In this section, we discuss the key risk factors facing the Chinese housing market. The most important risk factor is no doubt related to the
income growth rate. As the Chinese economy enters a new phase of
growth, the annual GDP growth rate will inevitably drop from its
nearly 10% growth of the last three decades. In 2014, the Chinese economy grew at a rate of 7.4%. As economic growth slows, the growth
of disposable household income will slow as well. As we argued in
section III.C, the high price-to-income ratio among home buyers was
likely sustained by the expectation of sustained high income growth;
as such, a significant decrease in the expectation of income growth will
lead to a commensurate decrease of sustainable price-to-income mul-
tiples for home buyers. As we have shown in section III, housing price
growth in the last decade substantially outpaced that of income growth
in first-tier cities, but not in second- and third-tier cities; thus, a potential income-growth slowdown is likely to have a more dramatic impact
on housing prices in first-tier cities.

Housing supply, however, is much more elastic in second- and
third-tier cities than in first-tier cities. The continued increase in new
construction in second- and third-tier cities, as shown in figure 1, has
kept the housing price growth in these cities in line with their income
growth, but also poses an important source risk to the housing market
in these cities. Note that new construction is constrained by land sold
for housing development and local governments control land sales.
Thus, risks from the glut of new supplies in second- and third-tier cities
can be managed by local governments if they have alternative sources
of fiscal revenue.

Another near-term risk factor for the housing market is demographic
trends. As is well known, 25 years after the initiation of the family planning policy, the Chinese population is rapidly ageing and is expected
to decline beginning in 2030. However, the prime age group for home
buyers, those between 30 and 49, started to decline for China as a whole
in 2005.[25]

Using the 2000 Chinese census microdata, we find that in 2030, the
prime age population of home buyers in China will decline to about
62% of the corresponding level in 2000. Of course, the ongoing urbanization in China is likely to draw a significant share of the rural population to cities (see figure 2), and thus for the urban housing market,
the overall demographic trend may not be as relevant. Ongoing policy

discussions in China regarding the relaxation of the one-child policy, as well as a relaxation or even abolishment of the strict *Hukou* policy, could significantly increase the demand for housing in the cities. Policies that relax the *Hukou* system may become necessary to prevent the meltdown of the housing market if, for example, the economy and income growth slow sharply.

We would also like to discuss the likely effects of some of the pending policy reforms in China that may have more subtle implications on the housing market.

First, we consider the possible imposition of property taxes and new fiscal reform. Property taxes are not presently assessed on home owners in China, with the exceptions of Shanghai and Chongqing, where a small property tax on a certain class of homes was assessed beginning in January 2011. In Shanghai, the property tax is currently at 0.6% of the purchase price of second homes, while in Chongqing, the property tax is 0.5% of the purchase price of second homes, mansions, and luxury apartments. The introduction of property tax in all cities is now on policymakers' agendas. Part of the reason is a desire to increase the cost of speculative purchases of houses, and another part is the desire to have a different source of revenue for local government budgets that have, as we have shown, become increasing reliant on land sales revenue.

An introduction of property taxes will have several effects on the housing market. First, it will make housing speculation less profitable. Speculation would remain profitable only if the expected housing price growth exceeds the opportunity cost of funds used for purchasing the house, plus the property tax assessment. If the property tax rate is chosen properly, it is possible that it could not only deter new speculative demand for housing, but also potentially drive current speculative holdings of homes to the market for sale. Second, the introduction of property taxes, in conjunction with fiscal reform that provides local governments with new revenue sources that are not tied to selling land, is likely to affect households' expectations that the housing market is "too important to fall." Absent such a conviction, the perceived risk associated with housing investment would rise, reducing housing demand. Third, property taxes and other fiscal reform will also put downward pressure on the price that developers are willing to pay for land, which in turn would further lower the cost of housing. All three effects of imposing property taxes are likely to put downward pressure on the housing market.

Another pending reform that may impact the housing market is the unification of the administrative structure of the social insurance system. The current social insurance system in China, particularly the health care and health insurance segments, is poorly designed to facilitate a transition of housing stock from the older generation to the younger generation. Specifically, most of the best hospitals in China are located either in Beijing and Shanghai, or in a few of the provincial capitals, such as Guangzhou and Chengdu. More important, the current health insurance system is mostly based on employment or preretirement employment, and it is implemented under a prefecture- or county-level planning framework, where the planning units have discretion over policy details and are responsible for balancing their own budgets (see Fang [2014] for an overview of the social insurance arrangement in China). Health insurance is not accepted nationwide. This means that if retirees in first-tier cities were to relocate to third-tier cities, they would not only experience more difficulty in accessing the best hospitals, but would also have difficulty in having their medical expenditures covered by their health insurance. This creates strong disincentive for the elderly to relocate as they retire, leading to unnecessary competition between the young and the old for the limited housing resources in the first-tier and some second-tier cities. As China attempts to unify the administrative structure of the social insurance system and equalize medical resources across different areas, it is possible that retirees in first-tier cities will relocate to retirement communities located in cities that have good medical facilities, leaving limited housing resources for the young and creating a healthy life cycle for first-tier city residents. This is likely to be a stabilizing force for the Chinese housing market.

Appendix A

Residential Mortgages in China

Borrowing Requirements

The borrower of a mortgage loan should have a stable source of income and a good credit record, and be between 18 and 65 years of age. Generally, loan-to-value ratio should be lower than 70%, and the loan term should be less than 30 years. According to the requirements announced by the China Banking Regulatory Commission (CBRC) in "Guidelines for the Risk Management of Real Estate Loans of Commercial Banks" in 2004, a borrower's ratio of monthly mortgage payment to income should be lower than 50%, and the ratio of monthly debt payment to income should be lower than 55%.

In China, only houses can act as collateral for mortgage loans. This includes villas, with the down-payment ratio of a villa being higher than that of other types of houses. House age (from its completion date) should be no more than 20 to 30 years, and house age plus the loan term should be no more than 30 to 40 years. Different from other countries, such as the United States, collateral of a mortgage loan has to belong to the borrower.

Loan Application Procedure and Payments

A mortgage applicant should first submit all required documents to a bank. After receiving the application, the bank carries out an eligibility investigation. The most important factor for the investigation is the applicant's income and credit record. The bank can check an individual's credit record through the credit-rating system of the People's Bank of China, which started its trial operation in December 2004 and official operation in January 2006. Upon approval, the borrower signs a mortgage contract with the bank, and then opens a mortgage account with the bank for making mortgage payments. If the loan term is one year or shorter, both principal and interest must be repaid as a lump sum at maturity; if the loan term is longer than one year, the loan may be repaid in equal installments of the principal plus interest, or in equal installments of the principal.

Mortgage Interest Rate

Interest rates for all bank loans, including mortgage loans, are regulated by the central bank of China, known as the People's Bank of China (PBC). All banks need to follow the same lending rules set by the PBC. The PBC regulates interest rates of mortgage loans to be a multiple of the benchmark lending rates it sets for bank loans, which usually depend on loan terms. This multiple has varied over time. It was 0.9 before August 2006, 0.85 from August 2006 to October 2008, and 0.7 from October 2008 to March 2010. After March 2010, the multiple for a first house was 0.85, and for a second house was 1.1. During our studied decade, the benchmark lending rates for different maturities have stayed between 4 and 8%.

An important feature of mortgage loans in China is that all are adjustable-rate mortgages (ARMs); there are no fixed-rate mortgages.[26] When the PBC changes its benchmark lending rates, interest rates of all mortgage loans are adjusted according to the most recent lending rates. Except for a small number of mortgage loans that are adjusted in the next month or next quarter, the majority of mortgage loans are adjusted on the first day of the next year.

Mortgage Termination

Default and full prepayment are two ways to terminate a mortgage contract during its term. The default rate in China has been low. According to the Annual Report of China Banking Regulatory Commission,[27] the ratio of nonperforming loans in residential mortgages declined steadily from 0.59% in 2009 to 0.26% in 2013, and the average during this five-year period was 0.36%.[28] The nonperforming ratio in residential mortgage loans is much lower than that in credit cards, which was on average 1.59% during the same period. One important reason for the low default rate in China is that all mortgage loans are recourse loans. This allows mortgage lenders to recover losses from mortgage loans by collecting the borrowers' other assets. When a default occurs and the value of the home value is lower than the loan balance, the mortgage lender can request courts to sell the home and collect the borrower's other assets. Furthermore, mortgage refinance, that is, the process of paying off an existing loan by taking a new loan, is not allowed in China.[29] This rule prevents borrowers from using homes as ATMs.

Appendix B

List of Cities by Tiers

• First tier includes: Beijing, Shanghai, Guangzhou, and Shenzhen.

• Second tier includes the following 36 cities with brackets denoting cities that are missing from our sample: [Beihai], Changchun, Changsha, Chengdu, Chongqing, Dalian, Fuzhou, [Guiyang], Haikou, Hangzhou, Harbin, Hefei, Hohhot, Jinan, Kunmin, [Lanzhou], Nanchang, Naijin, Nanning, Ningbo, Qingdao, [Sanya], Shenyang, Shijiazhuang, Suzhou, [Taiyuan], Tianjin, Urumqi, Wenzhou, Wuhan, Wuxi, Xi'An, Xiamen, Xining, Yinchuan, and Zhengzhou.

- Third tier includes the following 85 cities: Xuancheng, Fuyang, Chuzhou, Huangshan, Anqing, Bengbu, Wuhu (from Anhui Province); Ningde, Zhangzhou, Quanzhou (from Fujian Province); Jieyang, Zhongshan, Dongguan, Qingyuan, Yangjiang, Heyuan, Shanwei, Huizhou, Zhaoqing, Jiangmen, Foshan, Shantou, Shaoguan (from Guangdong Province); Hengshui, Langfang, Zhangjiakou, Baoding, Xingtai, Qinhuangdao, Tangshan (from Hebei Province); Jiamusi, Qiqihar (from Heilongjiang Province); Zhumadian, Nanyang, Luohe, Xuchang, Puyang, Xinxiang, Luoyang, Kaifeng (from Henan Province); Changde (from Hunan Province); Xilingol, Baotou (from Inner Mongolia Province); Jiangyan, Suqian, Zhenjiang, Yancheng, Huai'an, Lianyungang, Nantong, Changzhou, Xuzhou (from Jiangsu Province); Fuzhou, Shangrao, Yichun, Xinyu, Jiujiang, Pingxiang, Jingdezhen (from Jiangxi Province); Songyuan, Jilin (from Jilin Province); Wuludao, Chaoyang, Tieling, Panjin, Yingkou, Dandong, Anshan (from Liaoning Province); Liaocheng, Dezhou, Rizhao, Zaozhuang (from Shandong Province); Yuncheng (from Shanxi Province); Dazhou, Nanchong, Leshan, Mianyang, Deyang, Luzhou (from Sichuan Province); Changji (from Xinjiang Province); and Taizhou, Jinhua, Shaoxing, Huzhou, Jiaxing (from Zhejiang Province).

Endnotes

This paper is prepared for NBER *Macroeconomics Annual (vol. 30)*. We are grateful to the editors, Marty Eichenbaum and Jonathan Parker, our discussants, Erik Hurst and Martin Schneider, as well as seminar participants at Bank of America, Merrill Lynch, Harvard University, and Princeton University for helpful discussions and constructive comments. We also thank Sean Dong, Qing Gong, Min Wu, and Yu Zhang for excellent research assistance. For acknowledgments, sources of research support, and disclosure of the author's or authors' material financial relationships, if any, please see http://www.nber .org/chapters/c13595.ack.

1. Under current law, land used to build residential properties is leased for a term of 70 years; after the expiration of the lease period, the right to use the land and the property will no longer belong to the current owner. It is commonly presumed that the law will eventually be amended so that property owners will be allowed to renew the leases.

2. See appendix A for detailed information about mortgage loans in China.

3. Lasha, the capital of Tibet, is typically excluded from the list due to its special economic status.

4. Specifically, for each house, the dummy variables are zero except for the dummy corresponding to the second sale (where it is $+1$) and for the dummy corresponding to the first sale (where it is -1). If the first sale was in the first period, there is no dummy variable corresponding to the first sale.

5. In the first stage, they implement the Baily, Muth, and Nourse (1963) procedure and calculate the vector of regression residuals, which is then used to construct the weights to be used in the stage two regression. In the second step, a generalized least squares regression (with weights constructed from the regression residuals in the first stage) is run.

6. *Statistical Yearbook of China*, published by the Chinese National Bureau of Statistics, estimates that the percentage of apartment units in the newly built housing markets was around 94–96% during the past decade at the national level.

7. For several cities in our sample, the mortgage data start later than January 2003. For such cities, $\beta_{c,t}$ only reflects the changes in price beyond the first month in record (which is not January 2003). However, as long as a city has some records in the first quarter of 2003, we still use the above method to construct the price index, assuming that the change in prices from January to March 2003 is likely to be small. If a city has no record in any month in the first quarter of 2003, we do not construct a price index.

8. Our method of constructing housing price indices is related to the pseudo-repeated sales price index recently proposed by Guo, Zheng, Geltner, and Liu (2014). They also recognize that multiple apartments sold by a development project over a period of time can be used to construct matching pairs that are simply pairs of units within a matching space (say, building or a development project) sold at different points in time. They implement their price index using data of new residential transactions in Chengdu. The main difference between their method and ours lies in the regression specifications. In their specification, each unit may appear multiple times in the regression depending on the number of times it is included in matching pairs. This may create a complicated variance-covariance structure for regression noise. In contrast, in our specification, each unit appears exactly once. See also McMillen (2008) and Deng, McMillen, and Sing (2012) for related ideas that similar units, instead of repeated sales of the same unit, may be matched in order to apply the repeated sales approach.

9. This assumption in principle can be relaxed. If each month we have a sufficiently large number of sales located in each district of a city, we can implement our regression at the district level and construct district-specific price indices. As a robustness check, we have divided Beijing into an inner region that is close to the town center and suburban area and constructed separate indices for the two areas. The monthly changes of these two indices are highly correlated with a correlation of 0.93, although the index for the inner region grew slightly faster than that for the suburban area during our sample period.

10. It is not clear how developers would change their pricing strategies during the course of sales of units in a project. Wu, Deng, and Liu (2014) provide some evidence from hedonic regressions that the unit prices tend to lower when the percentage of units in the projects already sold is higher. However, as they admitted, this does not necessarily imply that developers are using different pricing policies for units that go on the market in different months.

11. The full names of the two series are: "Price Indices for Real Estate in 35/70 Large and Medium Sized Cities" and "Average Selling Price of Newly Built Residential Buildings," respectively.

12. The details of the statistical procedure used in the "NBS 70-City Index" can be found at http://finance.sina.com.cn/china/hgjj/20110216/14149383333.shtml (in Chinese). To the best of our understanding, the published procedure for constructing the NBS 70-City Index is conceptually similar to our method, though there are some differences in detail: we include all development projects for sale, while the NBS includes only those sampled housing complexes; we control for a list of unit-level characteristics, while the NBS obtains the complex-level monthly price by dividing total sales revenue in the complex over the total areas.

13. Furthermore, Deng, Gyourko, and Wu (2014b) have constructed a constant-quality, residential land price index, which they refer to as the "Chinese Residential Land Price Index," based on similar hedonic regressions, using sale prices of leasehold estates to private developers for 35 major Chinese cities. Their land price index showed extremely high real land price growth across these cities, much more so and with much more cross-city variations than the "China Urban Land Price Dynamic Monitor" system provided by the Ministry of Land and Resources of China for the same cities.

14. According to annual reports of the China Banking Regulatory Commission (CBRC), the ratio of nonperforming loans in residential mortgages has remained below 0.6% since 2009. Even in Shenzhen, which, as we discussed earlier, experienced a large housing price

drop of 39% in 2008, the ratio of nonperforming loans in our sample remained lower than 1.5% in 2008.

15. The lack of property taxes in China has contributed to the high price-to-income ratio observed in China relative to that in the United States. It is common for homeowners in the United States to pay annual property taxes in the range of 1–2% of home values to local townships, while homeowners in China typically do not pay any property tax.

16. Due to the high savings rates by Chinese households and the Chinese tradition of children supporting parents in their old age, parents are usually able and willing to provide some financial support to their children's home purchases. For this reason, there is typically not another hidden loan (i.e., a loan taken through the shadow-banking system) to pay for the down payment.

17. This pattern is consistent with casual observations that sex imbalance is less severe in first-tier cities as people in these cities have been more open minded about having girls and thus less prone to selecting the sex of their children.

18. As we explain in section VI, in early 2010 the Chinese government raised the down-payment ratio and the interest rate on second mortgages, making them higher than those for first mortgages. Since then, banks need to collect information about whether each mortgage is a first or second.

19. The fraction of second mortgages in our mortgage data may appear substantially lower than the fraction of households owning multiple homes reported by the Chinese Household Finance Survey (2012). According to this survey conducted in 2012, the fraction of urban households owning at least two apartments in China is 15.44%. Note that a significant fraction of the multiple homes owned by the surveyed households was probably old-style housing units that were assigned to the households by their employers as in-kind compensation before the housing reform in late 1990s. These units tended to have undesirable qualities and were different from the newly built homes—the typical homes bought by households in recent years.

20. There is a debate regarding the performance of the Chinese stock market. On one hand, Allen et al. (2014) argue that despite China's spectacular economic growth, the Chinese stock market has performed rather poorly. On the other hand, Carpenter, Lu and Whitelaw (2014) argue that the Chinese stock market has become as informative about future corporate profits as the US stock market.

21. Chen and Wen (2014) derive a theory to explain the persistently faster-than-GDP housing price growth during the Chinese housing boom based on an idea that a self-fulfilling housing bubble can induce productive entrepreneurs to divert capital from profitable investment projects in order to speculate in housing.

22. Zheng, Sun, and Kahn (2014) build a measure of real estate confidence level for 35 Chinese cities by using Internet search data. They show that this index predicts subsequent housing price appreciation and new housing construction.

23. The housing purchase restriction policy was initiated by the central government under the so-called "New National Ten Articles" and "New National Eight Articles" issued in April 2010 and January 2011, respectively, which provided guidelines saying that housing purchase restrictions should be implemented in first-tier cities and could be extended to second- and even third-tier cities on an as-needed basis. In Beijing, for example, the policy requires that only a household with household registration in Beijing can buy a new apartment. Migrants living in Beijing are not allowed to buy any apartment unless they can provide documentation to prove payment of taxes and social security contributions for the previous five consecutive years. Shanghai's policy is similar.

24. According to the latest available statistics published by the National Audit Office, by the end of June 2013, the total volume of outstanding balances on local government debts reached 10.89 trillion RMB, equivalent to 19.15% of China's GDP in 2013, surpassing the 9.81 trillion total volume of central government debt during the same period. Future land sales revenue was used as collateral in 37.23% of the local government debt.

25. In section IV.E, we showed that the average age of mortgage borrowers is the early thirties.

26. From 2007 to 2008, some commercial banks issued a small number of fixed-rate mortgage loans, but stopped the practice.

27. http://www.cbrc.gov.cn/chinese/home/docView/3C28C92AC84242D188E2064
D9098CFD2.html.
28. A loan is defined as nonperforming if it is overdue by more than 90 days.
29. As all mortgage loans in China have floating rates, decreases in interest rates do not
motivate mortgage refinancing.

References

Allen, Franklin, Jun Qian, Susan Chenyu Shan, and Julie Lei Zhu. 2014. "The
  Best Performing Economy with the Worst Performing Market: Explaining the
  Poor Performance of the Chinese Stock Market." Working paper, Imperial
  College London.
Barberis, Nicolas, Andrei Shleifer, and Robert Vishny. 1998. "A Model of Inves-
  tor Sentiment." *Journal of Financial Economics* 49 (3): 307–43.
Bailey, Martin J., Richard F. Muth, and Hugh O. Nourse. 1963. "A Regression
  Method for Real Estate Price Index Construction," *Journal of the American Sta-
  tistical Association*, 58:304: 933-942.
Barth, James R., Michael Lea, and Tong Li. 2012. "China's Housing Market: Is
  a Bubble about to Burst?" Report, Milken Institute, December. http://www
  .milkeninstitute.org/publications/view/543.
Burnside, Craig, Martin Eichenbaum, and Sergio Rebelo. 2013. "Understanding
  Booms and Busts in Housing Markets." Working paper, Duke University and
  Northwestern University.
Carpenter, Jennifer, Fangzhou Lu, and Robert Whitelaw. 2014. "The Real Value
  of China's Stock Market." Working paper, New York University.
Case, Karl, and Robert Shiller. 1987. "Prices of Single Family Homes since 1970:
  New Indexes for Four Cities." *New England Economic Review* 1:45–56.
———. 1989. "The Efficiency of the Market for Single Family Homes." *Ameri-
  can Economic Review* 79:125–37.
Chen, Kaiji, and Yi Wen. 2014. "The Great Housing Boom of China." Working
  paper, Federal Reserve Bank of St. Louis.
Cheng, Ing-Haw, Sahil Raina, and Wei Xiong. 2014. "Wall Street and the Hous-
  ing Bubble." *American Economic Review* 104:2797–829.
Chinese Household Finance Survey. 2012. Southwestern University of Finance
  and Economics, China. http://chfsdata.org/.
Chow, Gregory, and Linlin Niu. 2014. "Housing Price in Urban China as Deter-
  mined by Demand and Supply." Working paper, Princeton University.
Deng, Yongheng, Joe Gyourko, and Jing Wu. 2014a. "Evaluating the Risk of
  Chinese Housing Markets: What We Know and What We Need to Know."
  Working paper, National University of Singapore.
———. 2014b. "The Wharton/NUS/Tsinghua Chinese Residential Land Price In-
  dexes (CRLP) White Paper." Working paper, National University of Singapore.
Deng, Yongheng, Daniel McMillen, and T. F. Sing. 2012. "Private Residential
  Price Indices in Singapore: A Matching Approach." *Regional Science and Ur-
  ban Economics* 42 (3): 485–94.
Fang, Hanming. 2014. "Insurance Markets in China." In *The Oxford Companion
  to the Economics of China*, ed. Shenggen Fan, Ravi Kanbur, Shang-Jin Wei, and
  Xiaobo Zhang, 279–84. Oxford: Oxford University Press.
Guo, Xiaoyang, Siqi Zheng, David Geltner, and Hongyu Liu. 2014. "A New Ap-
  proach for Constructing Home Price Indices: The Pseudo Repeat Sales Model
  and Its Application in China." *Journal of Housing Economics* 25:20–38.

Kain, J., and John Quigley. 1970. "Measuring the Value of Housing Quality." *Journal of the American Statistical Association* 65:532–48.

Li, Hongbin, and Li-An Zhou. 2005. "Political Turnover and Economic Performance: The Incentive Role of Personnel Control in China." *Journal of Public Economics* 89 (9): 1743–62.

Mark, Jonathan H., and Michael A. Goldberg. 1984. "Alternative Housing Price Indices: An Evaluation." *Journal of the American Real Estate and Urban Economics Association* 12 (1): 30–49.

Mayer, Christopher, Karen Pence, and Shane M. Sherlund. 2009. "The Rise of Mortgage Defaults." *Journal of Economic Perspectives* 23 (1): 23–50.

McMillen, Daniel. 2008. "Changes in the Distribution of House Prices over Time: Structural Characteristics, Neighborhood or Coefficients?" *Journal of Urban Economics* 64:573–89.

Noguchi, Yukio. 1991. "Land Prices and House Prices in Japan." In *Housing Markets in the U.S. and Japan*, ed. Yukio Noguchi and James Poterba, 11–28. Chicago: University of Chicago Press.

Pritchett, Lant, and Lawrence Summers. 2014. "Asiaphoria Meets Regression to the Mean." NBER Working Paper no. 20573, Cambridge, MA.

Saiz, Albert. 2010. "The Geographic Determinants of Housing Supply." *Quarterly Journal of Economics* 125:1253–96.

Shiller, Robert. 2000. *Irrational Exuberance*. Princeton, NJ: Princeton University Press.

Wei, Shangjin, Xiaobo Zhang, and Yin Liu. 2014. "Home Ownership as Status Competition: Some Theory and Evidence." Working paper, Columbia University.

Wu, Jing, Yongheng Deng, and Hongyu Liu. 2014. "House Price Index Construction in the Nascent Housing Market: The Case of China." *Journal of Real Estate Finance and Economics* 48 (3): 522–45.

Yang, Dennis, Junsen Zhang, and Shaojie Zhou. 2013. "Why are Saving Rates so High in China?" In *Capitalizing China*, ed. Joseph Fan and Randall Morck, 249–78. Chicago: University of Chicago Press.

Zheng, Siqi, Weizeng Sun, and Matthew Kahn. 2014. "Investor Confidence as a Determinant of China's Urban Housing Market Dynamics." Working paper, Tsinghua University.

Comment

Martin Schneider, *Stanford University and NBER*

Introduction

What drives the spectacular recent movements in Chinese house prices is an important and challenging question. This paper makes progress by providing very interesting new data: it develops new city-level price indices. The key stylized facts that emerge are that (*i*) in large ("first-tier") cities, house price growth outpaces income growth, whereas (*ii*) in smaller cities house prices and income grow together. The paper also provides novel facts on mortgage borrowing by income group. This discussion first comments on the construction and interpretation of the price index and makes some suggestions for future research with transactions data from China. It then considers what relationship between house prices and income we might expect from theory. Finally, it sketches a mechanism for why emerging, urbanizing economies might see particularly dramatic movements in house price-rent ratios.

Measuring City-Level House Price Changes

A major contribution of the paper is to present a novel data set on housing transactions. The data come from mortgage records of a large commercial bank. The authors can see the transaction price, details of the mortgage, characteristics of the house, as well as some demographics. The sample of transactions has two special properties. First, it contains only mortgage purchases (as opposed to cash purchases). Even with this specific focus, the new data represent tremendous progress given the overall lack of microdata on housing in China. Future research could further clarify the relative importance of mortgage borrowers in

China and connect to facts on leverage. In particular, aggregate data show that leverage during the Chinese housing boom was substantially lower than in other countries that recently experienced boom-bust episodes. For example, the ratio of outstanding mortgage debt to GDP in China in 2012 was 15%, whereas the same ratio in the United States in 2006 was 80% (Barth, Lea, and Li 2012). A second feature of the sample is that the data contain relatively few repeat sales of the same property. This is because many transactions are recent sales of new dwellings that were not yet resold within the sample period. Lack of repeat sales generally makes it tricky to control for house quality when developing price indices. However, the structure of urban Chinese housing markets allows the authors to address this issue. Indeed, most sales are apartments in developments that consist of many similar units. It is thus reasonable that we can learn about price movements for a given dwelling by looking at sales prices of very close comparables in the same development. To implement this idea, the authors write down a statistical model of transactions prices in a city. The log price of dwelling i located in development $\delta(i)$ that sells at date t is given by

$$p_t^i = p_t + \beta' X_t^i + q^{\delta(i)} + \varepsilon_t^i \tag{1}$$

where the vector X_t^i consists of a set of property characteristics, $q^{\delta(i)}$ is a development fixed effect, and p_t is a city-time fixed effect. The latter serves as the authors' price index for the city, after appropriate normalization. One way to interpret (1) is that the value of a dwelling reflects both a property-level and a city-level component. The former is described by the characteristics X and the development effect, which, for example, captures the location of the dwelling. The regression removes property-level heterogeneity in prices and what is left is the city-level component, a common force that affects all properties equally. The key assumptions underlying this interpretation are that (i) the relative contribution to dwelling value of living in a particular development is fixed over time, and that (ii) the effects of the individual characteristics are also constant. If these two assumptions do not hold, then the interpretation of the price index becomes more difficult. For example, suppose that the relative contribution to apartment value of living in a particular development increases over time. The measured price index can then grow because more apartments located in that development are traded. Similarly, if both prices and quantities of characteristics like square footage change over time, the index will partly reflect composition effects and not simply a common force that affects all properties equally. The following subsection illustrates these arguments. Future research could show whether they are in fact quantitatively important.

What Does the Price Index Capture?

In order to think about forces that affect the price index p_t, it is helpful to consider a stylized model of housing technology. Suppose that utility from housing is given by an aggregator over attributes that is homogeneous of degree one:

$$F(X_t^1...X_t^{N_x}, Y_t^1...Y_t^{N_y}, Z_t^1...Z_t^{N_z}).$$

Here the Xs are property-level characteristics as above, the Ys are development-level characteristics, and the Zs are city-level characteristics. Under a benchmark assumption of competitive markets for both dwellings and attributes, the value of a dwelling is then a linear combination of the prices of its attributes

$$P_t = \sum_j p_t^{x,j} X_t^j + \sum_j p_t^{y,j} Y_t^j + \sum_j p_t^{Z,j} Z_t^j.$$

A first-order approximation can now deliver the model for log prices (1). For example, assume that the expenditure shares on each property-level characteristic X as well as the overall expenditure share on the development-level characteristics are constant over time, and moreover, that the prices of each property-level characteristic are constant over time. The regression then picks up the relative contribution of each characteristic to dwelling values, as well as the relative contribution of each development. It is not a priori obvious, however, why the relative contributions of attributes X should be constant over time. Suppose the aggregate F is Cobb-Douglas, so expenditure shares on attributes are indeed constant over time. We could now imagine that scarcity of space implies that the characteristic "square footage" becomes relatively more expensive. If, moreover, in response to the shortage of space the average apartment becomes smaller, then this will affect the interpretation of the price index. Indeed, consider an econometrician who estimates the model (1) with a constant coefficient on square footage. Since square footage declines, the econometrician infers a decline in the contribution of square footage to dwelling value. At the same time, transactions prices reflect constant expenditure on square footage. The econometrician will thus further infer an increase in the city-wide price component. The price index he constructs then reflects in part the composition of dwellings that were traded, as opposed to simply a common driver of the prices of all dwellings in the city. The model (1) also imposes a constant value of living in a particular development. To illustrate the implication of this assumption, take differences of equation to represent capital gains on dwellings as

$$\Delta p_{t+1}^i = \beta' \Delta X_{t+1}^i + \varepsilon_{t+1}^i - \varepsilon_t^i.$$

The statistical model thus assumes that differences in capital gains within a city can be explained by changes in dwelling-level characteristics (or noise). In particular, the location of the property does not matter for the capital gain. This implication is in contrast to recent evidence from the US housing boom. For example, Landvoigt, Piazzesi, and Schneider (2015) show that 2000–2005 capital gains were much larger in those census tracts of San Diego County where median house prices were initially low. Moreover, the cross-sectional differences were so large that they cannot plausibly be explained by home improvements (which generate changes in the Xs). There is also evidence for several theoretical mechanisms that generate changes in house prices by location. For example, Guerrieri, Hartley, and Hurst (2013) study a model of gentrification where utility from a dwelling comes in part from the income level of the neighbors. In another example, Landvoigt et al. (2015) study an assignment model in which the quality distribution of houses for sale changes so that richer movers have to be induced to move into lower-quality houses. In both cases, the change in the income of movers into a neighborhood generates a location-specific factor in house prices. Of course, we do not know whether similar patterns are present in the Chinese data. Future research could show, however, whether the location of a development has a systematic impact on capital gains there. This would again help with the interpretation of the price index. If more suburban developments typically grow less in price, then an increase in the share of suburban apartments traded could lower the growth rate of the price index. Thus, the price index would again reflect, in part, the composition of sales.

House Prices and Income

Given the authors' results on house price increases in China, it is interesting to ask whether prices are "too high" or grow "too fast" relative to benchmarks provided by theory. The authors focus on a comparison of price growth and income growth. This section uses a standard neoclassical growth model with a housing sector to provide a benchmark for the relationship of price growth, income growth, and the level of

prices. Consider a small open economy with two goods, housing services and an "other" good. Preferences of an infinitely lived representative agent are assumed to be consistent with balanced growth. For the
purposes of this section, it is enough to specify date t felicity from H_t
units of housing services and C_t units of the other good as $U(C_t^\alpha H_t^{1-\alpha})$.
Population M_t grows at the constant rate g_M. The world interest rate is
constant at r. Housing services are produced one-for-one from housing
capital, which in turn is produced from land and depreciable structures.
While there is a constant supply of land L, structures can be made from
the other good. Housing technology is thus summarized by a production function and a capital accumulation equation. Assuming that all
land is used in housing production they can be written as

$$H_t = L^\lambda (K_t^h)^{1-\lambda},$$

$$K_{t+1}^h = (1 - \delta_h)K_t^h + I_{h,t},$$

where H is housing capital, K^h is structures and I^h is investment in structures.

The other good is produced from fixed capital and labor. There is exogenous labor augmenting technical progress A_t that grows at the rate g_A.
With full employment, the production and capital accumulation imply

$$Y_t = (A_t M_t)^\nu (K_t^y)^{1-\nu},$$

$$K_{t+1}^y = (1 - \delta_y)K_t^y + I_t^y$$

where Y_t is production of other goods, K_t^y is fixed capital, and I_t^y is investment. Consider competitive equilibria in which all variables grow at
a constant rate. Production of the other goods grows at the rate $g_Y = g_M$
$+ g_A$. Consumption of the other good, investment in either technology, as
well as structures and fixed capital, must also grow at g_Y. Housing capital and housing services require the fixed factor land and therefore grow
at the slower rate $(1 - \lambda) g_Y$. With Cobb-Douglas felicity, expenditure on
housing is constant. Rents (the price of housing services) thus grow at
the rate λg_Y, as does the house price per unit of quality H.

The balanced growth model provides a simple benchmark for the
relationship between income and house prices. Indeed, controlling for
house quality captured by H, house prices grow at $\lambda (g_M + g_A)$, whereas
income per capita grows at g_A. It follows that the growth rate of income
matters for prices only if there is a fixed-factor land. Prices grow faster
relative to income if the land share λ is higher or population growth is

higher. It would be interesting to relate this benchmark to the differences between first- and lower-tier cities reported in the paper. It is possible, for example, that prices grow quickly relative to income in first-tier cities in China because those cities experience faster population growth. The balanced growth model also provides a benchmark to judge whether the level of prices at a given point in time is "too high." The price-rent ratio, that is, the value of housing capital divided by the expenditure on housing services, can be written as

$$\text{price rent ratio} = \lambda \frac{1}{r - (g_M + g_A)} + (1 - \lambda) \frac{1}{r + \delta_h}. \tag{2}$$

The price-rent ratio is a weighted average of the present value of rents from land and structures. Both satisfy versions of the Gordon growth formula that relates the price-dividend ratio of an asset to the discount rate and expected dividend growth. For land, dividends (that is, land rents) grow at $g_M + g_A$ and are discounted at r. For structures, rents are constant but are discounted at the higher rate $r + \delta_h$ to account for depreciation. Formula (2) illustrates two familiar points that are useful for thinking about house prices by city. First, to assess whether the level of prices is "too high" requires comparing prices to rents as well as expectations of future rent growth. There is some evidence that Chinese price rent ratios have increased in recent years (Barth et al. 2012). It interesting to ask whether those numbers can be reconciled with reasonable expectations of population and technology growth. Second, the price-rent ratio depends on growth only through the effect on the fixed-factor land. This generates further cross-sectional predictions on land shares, growth, and prices. The previous calculations consider only the balanced growth path of the model and in a strict sense speak only to long-run trends. It is likely, however, that prices in China respond in part to the ongoing process of urbanization, which is inherently a transition phenomenon. A serious quantitative study of prices and rents thus requires studying transition dynamics. Garriga, Tang, and Wang (2014) take on this task and investigate the impact of urbanization in a multisector growth model with endogenous migration choice. They find that urbanization can account for about two-thirds of recent house price movements.

A Learning Model of Housing Bubbles

The previous section considered house price determination in a perfect foresight setup with constant price-rent ratios. This approach ignores the fact that urbanization involves structural change with an uncertain outcome. How fast can cities in China grow and for how long? Which cities will end up growing more? This section uses a learning model of housing bubbles, based on the classic paper by Zeira (1999), to show how growth with an uncertain ending can lead to booms in price-rent ratios. The model describes valuation of houses given subjective expectations about future rent growth. It thus develops a counterpart of (2) with $\lambda = 1$, but with the growth path initially unknown. The rent and learning dynamics are kept simple so as to zero in on the key mechanism. At date 1, rent is equal to one. Thereafter, it increases by one unit every period, until at some date $T \in [2, 10]$ it does not grow anymore and then remains constant forever. At the stopping date, all uncertainty is resolved. Intuitively, as the city grows there is uncertain potential of further growth until convergence occurs. Consider risk-neutral agents who discount the future with factor β and who learn over time about the unknown parameter T. At date 1, they start with a prior probability $\Pr(T = t)$ assumed to be (i) decreasing in t and (ii) convex. The idea here is that (i) converging to very high levels is a priori less likely but also that (ii) once the city has grown for a while, it becomes harder to know what its true potential is. The specific prior used in the calculations below is plotted in the upper panel of figure 1. While it is unlikely that a city manages to grow beyond date 3, once it has done so, "all bets are off" and the posterior over when it will stop becomes much flatter.

Let π_t denote the probability that growth stops at the next date $t + 1$ given agents' knowledge that growth has not stopped by date t. It follows from Bayes' rule starting from the prior probability $\pi_1 = \Pr(T = 2)$. If growth stops at date $t + 1$, the house price settles at the constant level $t / (1 - \beta)$. Let p_t denote the price at date t conditional on growth not having stopped yet. It reflects the current rent t as well as the discounted expected price next period and thus satisfies the recursion

$$p_t = t + \beta \left(\pi_t \frac{\beta t}{1 - \beta} + (1 - \pi_t) p_{t+1} \right). \tag{3}$$

If growth has not stopped by date 9, it is sure to stop at date 10 so that $\pi_9 = 1$ and $p_9 = 9 / (1 - \beta)$. Given the sequence of posteriors and the terminal condition for p_9, the recursion (3) delivers the entire path of p_ts. The bottom panel of figure 1 shows the resulting price dynamics. The solid dark line is the present value of rents $t\beta / (1 - \beta)$ and thus also marks the price that will realize at the next date in case growth stops. The solid light line is the price path p_t that realizes while growth has not

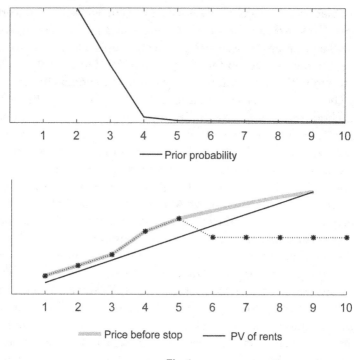

Fig. 1.

stopped. The dotted dark line represents a particular sample path, realized when growth stops at date 6 so the price settles at 5 / (1 − β). Since the dark solid line is proportional to rent, the ratio of the light to dark lines also represents (up to a constant) movements in the price-rent ratio before growth stops. Once growth stops, the price-rent ratio is constant at 1 / (1 − β). The model has several properties that help one think about house prices in emerging urbanizing economies. First, as long as learning is ongoing, the potential of future growth naturally generates prices that are higher than the present value of rents. Second, once growth stops and the true potential of the city is realized, there will typically be a downward price correction. In the example, a "soft landing" where house prices settle at a new plateau without ever falling occurs only along the sample path where the a priori maximum potential of the city is realized (that is, $T = 10$). A final feature of the example is that learning generates increases in the price-rent ratio even as the potential of the city becomes more uncertain. Indeed, along sample paths that reach date 4, the posterior flattens and all bets are off. The increase in expected potential drives up prices relative to rents. This mechanism may be contributing to elevated price-rent ratios in China, as the structural change implied by urbanization forces market participants to assess scenarios for which there is no obvious precedent.

Endnote

Prepared for the NBER *Macroeconomics Annual*. I thank Sean Myers and Monika Piazzesi for helpful comments. For acknowledgments, sources of research support, and disclosure of the author's material financial relationships, if any, please see http://www.nber.org/chapters/c13596.ack.

References

Barth, James, Michael Lea, and Tong Li. 2012. "China's Housing Market: Is a Bubble about to Burst?" Report, Milken Institute, December.
Garriga, Carlos, Yang Tang, and Ping Wang. 2014. "Rural-Urban Migration, Structural Transformation, and Housing Markets in China." Working paper, Federal Reserve Bank of St. Louis.
Guerrieri, Veronica, Daniel Hartley, and Erik Hurst. 2013. "Endogenous Gentrification and Housing Price Dynamics." *Journal of Public Economics* 100:45–60.
Landvoigt, Tim, Monika Piazzesi, and Martin Schneider. 2015. "The Housing Market(s) of San Diego." *American Economic Review* 105 (4): 1371–1407.
Zeira, Joseph. 1999. "Informational Overshooting, Booms and Crashes." *Journal of Monetary Economics* 43:237–57.

Comment

Erik Hurst, *University of Chicago and NBER*

One of the primary goals of this paper is to document house price growth within China at the local level since early in the twenty-first century. The paper shows that for many cities, house price growth outpaced income growth. The paper also discusses potential risks related to Chinese housing markets going forward. Throughout the paper, the authors assume that income growth is a good benchmark for house price growth. In my discussion I will outline the conditions under which income growth is a good benchmark for house price growth. I will then discuss empirically the extent to which house price growth and income growth are linked using data from a large cross section of developed and developing economies.

The models I develop below are relatively standard in the urban literature. The models are based on optimizing households who have preferences over housing, optimizing firms who build housing, and something that makes land special. In these models, land is made special either because it is constrained or because the land offers production or consumption amenities. The production amenities could include factors like the proximity to jobs. The consumption amenities could include factors like climate, a nice view, or the quality of one's neighbors. These amenities, depending on the model, can be either fixed or endogenous.

A Model of Housing Prices: Unbounded City, No Amenities, and Fixed Homogeneous Population

Consider one city with a fixed population of N identical individuals. Suppose the city can be represented on the real line such that each point on the line, i, is a different location. Each location can be thought of as a "neighborhood."[1] Let $n(i)$ be the measure of agents who live in neighborhood i within the city. Let $h(i)$ be the size of the house chosen by agents living in neighborhood i. By definition,

$$\int_{-\infty}^{\infty} n(i)\, di = N.$$

Summing the population across all neighborhoods will equal the total population of the city. For simplicity, the size of each neighborhood is normalized to 1 such that:

$$n(i)h(i) \leq 1.$$

Suppose households maximize their static preferences over nonhousing consumption (c), housing consumption (h), and which neighborhood to live in subject to a static budget constraint:

$$\max_{c,h,i} c(i)^{\alpha} h(i)^{\beta}$$

$$c(i) + R(i)\, h(i) = Y.$$

Preferences are assumed to be Cobb-Douglas over nonhousing and housing consumption with $\alpha > 0$ and $\beta > 0$. The flow rental cost of a unit of housing in location i is defined as $R(i)$. The price of nonhousing consumption is normalized to 1. Households are also endowed with labor income Y that can be used to purchase nonhousing and housing consumption.

On the supply side, there is a continuum of competitive builders who can always build a unit of housing at a constant marginal cost κ. Arbitrage implies a link between flow rental prices and the price of the property, P, such that:

$$P_t(i) = R_t(i) + \frac{1}{1 + r} P_{t+1}(i),$$

where r is the risk-free discount rate. Profit maximization implies that builders will build a unit of housing in neighborhood i anytime $P(i) \geq \kappa$. This restriction will be relaxed in the next subsection when the city size is assumed to be bounded.

Given the above specification, housing demand functions can be computed for each neighborhood such that:

$$h(i) = \frac{\beta}{\alpha + \beta}\left(\frac{1}{R(i)}\right) Y \text{ or}$$

$$\frac{R(i)\, h(i)}{Y} = \frac{\beta}{\alpha + \beta}.$$

With the Cobb-Douglas specification, the share of housing expenditures out of income is held fixed either because the price of housing adjusts ($R(i)$) or because the quantity of housing adjusts ($h(i)$).

Spatial equilibrium implies that households have to be indifferent across all locations such that:

$$c(i)^\alpha h(i)^\beta = c(\tilde{i})^\alpha h(\tilde{i})^\beta$$

for all locations i and $\tilde{i}$. If there is nothing special about any neighborhood relative to any other neighborhood, then $R(i)$ must be constant across all neighborhoods.

Putting all the above together, we can define individual local housing demand curves and a local housing supply curve from this simple model.

$$h(i) = h = \frac{\beta}{\alpha + \beta}\left(\frac{1 + r}{r}\right)\left(\frac{1}{P}\right)Y$$

$$P = \kappa.$$

In a world where no neighborhood is more desirable than any other neighborhood and where supply is unbounded, the supply curve for housing is perfectly elastic. In this model, there is no relationship between housing prices and income growth (if construction costs κ remain fixed). Any shock that increases the demand for housing (increasing income, a reduction in interest rates, increased population, etc.) would be mediated by an increase in the supply of housing. In other words, all the action takes place on the quantity margin. This simple model suggests that income growth would be a poor benchmark for house price growth in cities where the supply of housing is elastic. To go further, the simple model implies that house price growth should be zero in the long run, despite rapid income growth.

By assuming that house price growth is tightly linked to income growth, the authors do not have a model of housing prices in the back of their minds where cities can expand by adjusting the supply of housing and/or there are no within-city amenities that households value that are attached to the land within the city.

Model of Housing Prices: Bounded City, No Amenities, and Fixed Homogeneous Population

The reason that house prices did not respond to unexpected income shocks in the above stylized model was that the supply of housing was unconstrained. Now let us consider a similar model where the city size is constrained. We will formalize the constraint by assuming that neighborhoods within the city must belong to the interval [−I, I] with the center of the city denoted by $i = 0$. Given this, there are only 2I neighborhoods within the city. Suppose that the city size is initially binding such that all land within the city is currently occupied by the N residents. If this was not the case, we would be back in the model outlined above. Finally, assume that all other aspects of the model stayed the same (households have same preferences, the model is static, the marginal cost of building a house is κ, there are no city-specific production or consumption amenities, etc.). In this modified model, housing prices will still be the same within all neighborhoods within the city. However, the fact that the city is bounded implies that the supply curve for housing is perfectly inelastic. Changes in housing demand will show up as increases in housing prices. The increased housing prices will cause individuals within the city to consume smaller quantities of housing (relative to nonhousing consumption). Formally, simple algebra shows that housing prices within each neighborhood can be expressed as the following:

$$P(i) = P = \left(\frac{N}{2I}\right)\left(\frac{\beta}{\alpha + \beta}\right)\left(\frac{1 + r}{r}\right)Y.$$

If city sizes are bounded and if the population is fixed, there is a direct link between income growth and housing price growth such that a 1% increase in income will yield a 1% increase in housing prices. In this case, income growth is a good benchmark for housing price growth. Notice, population growth will also cause house prices to grow in this simple model, even if income does not change. Anything that increases the demand for housing within a city (either because existing residents get richer or because of influx of new residents) will be mediated through higher prices when housing supply is inelastic. If both income and population grows, housing price growth can exceed income growth. The extent to which income price growth is a good proxy for housing price growth depends on (a) whether supply is constrained and (b) whether other factors are also changing the demand for housing.

Discussion of Binding Housing Supply Constraints

While the above models are highly stylized, they are illustrative of the forces necessary to get a tight link between income growth and house price growth within a city. If city size is bounded such that supply is completely constrained, house price growth within a city can track income growth (or population growth). However, in practice, there are many margins in which the city housing supply can adjust. For example:

1. Cities can expand outward. For the most part, this is like the unconstrained supply model developed above. However, there could be additional costs to expand a city outward relative to developing vacant land within a city. For example, new infrastructure may be needed to build on the fringes of cities (electrical grids, plumbing systems, roads, etc.). The costs of such infrastructure can raise the marginal cost of building within a city boundary and across city boundaries.

2. Cities can build up. Our model assumed that each neighborhood was constrained to be a fixed size. However, in practice, each neighborhood can expand its size by building taller buildings. The marginal cost of doing so may be higher than the marginal cost of building on the fringe of the cities or on vacant land within the city. But, if prices rise sufficiently high, there will be an incentive to build upward.

3. People can move to new or existing cities. Factor mobility is a primary way in which housing prices can be kept in check (Blanchard and Katz 1992). As income increases and the demand for housing grows, households may choose to migrate to cheaper locations.

Factor mobility and the ability to expand housing supply by building upward further breaks the link between local income growth and local house price growth. During the first decade of the twenty-first century, most Chinese cities dramatically expanded the supply of housing. Cities like Beijing expanded outward during the early twenty-first century by building "Ring Roads" that were further away from the city center. Deng, Gyourko, and Wu (2015) document that housing supply dramatically increased within most Chinese cities during the 2004–2014 period. These supply changes help limit the growth of housing prices for a given change in income. Deng et al. (2015) further document that there has been a rapid increase in some Chinese cities in the share of unsold inventory held by developers (out of total housing sales volume). For example, in 2014, developers in Shanghai had inventories accounting for over 200% of annual housing sales volume. These excess inventories, they argue, suggest that housing prices in these cities may fall if demand does not sufficiently increase.

Model of Housing Prices: Bounded City, Within-City Amenities, and Fixed Homogeneous Population

Supply constraints are not the only way to generate a relationship between property price growth and income growth. Many urban models can generate such a link, even when housing supply is perfectly elastic. However, in these models, there is some amenity within the city that makes some land within the city more desirable than other land within the city. Early iterations of the literature focused on production amenities within the city. In particular, the work of Alonso (1964), Mills (1967), and Muth (1969) all focused on commuting costs as the production amenity. In these models, individuals value living closer to their jobs so as to forego commuting costs. In recent work, Guerierri, Hartley, and Hurst (2013) and Diamond (2015) emphasize the importance of consumption amenities provided by cities and neighborhoods within cities. For example, Guerierri et al. (2013) assumes individuals get higher utility from living around richer neighbors given the externalities they generate (better schools, lower crime, more restaurants, etc.).

To illustrate that housing prices are related to income changes even in a world where there are no supply housing constraints, we can make one small adjustment to our base model above. To make our point, I highlight the model with a center city where the jobs are located and transportation costs. In particular, assume the household's budget constraint is now represented as:

$$c(i) + R(i)\,h(i) - \tau i = Y$$

where τ is a per unit transportation cost. Again, we will stick with the normalization that the center city (i.e., jobs) is designated by neighborhood $i = 0$. If households live away from the center city, they have to pay τi units in commuting costs. Given the household optimization and the indifference condition needed for spatial equilibrium, the equilibrium housing price in each neighborhood can be expressed as:

$$P(i) = \frac{[Y - \tau i]^{(\alpha+\beta)/\beta}}{[Y - \tau I]^{(\alpha+\beta)/\beta}}\,\kappa$$

where I is the boundary of the city. In this case, the boundary is endogenous. No one would want to live at $I + \varepsilon$ if they could live at I at the same rental price if $I + \varepsilon$ has a higher transportation cost. The transportation cost makes people want to live close to the city center. At $i = I$, the competition among builders implies that housing prices are just equal to the construction cost of housing (κ). At any $i < I$, housing prices are higher than κ because of the amenity of lower commuting costs.

The equilibrium city size is given by:

$$I = Yf(N, \tau, r, \kappa, \alpha, \beta)$$

where $f(.)$ is a function of the other model variables. The function is messy and as a result I did not write it out fully. However, the key is that it is linear in income. As income increases, the size of the city will expand. As seen from the above equations, an increase in income will shift up housing prices in all neighborhoods. The exact amount housing prices will increase by is a function of the model parameters. However, even in a model with perfectly elastic housing supply, house price growth and income growth will be related. The key is that if households value some part of the city more than others (because of small transportation costs or because of other consumption amenities provided by that neighborhood), income growth and house price growth will be related.

Discussion of Paper

The paper provides an excellent set of facts documenting housing price dynamics in Chinese cities. However, after reading the paper I find it hard to interpret (a) why prices have risen and (b) whether the prices reflect fundamentals or whether they represent bubble conditions. By benchmarking house price growth against income growth, the authors are implicitly assuming that income growth is the fundamental driving housing price changes and that housing supply is perfectly inelastic.[2] This is akin to the model outlined above. However, as I read the paper, a bunch of questions entered my mind. In particular, is there any evidence that housing demand is outpacing housing supply within Chinese cities? The paper offers no descriptive data on the supply side of the housing market in Chinese cities. If housing supply is constrained, how is it constrained? Are the constraints due to the fact that land is owned by the public sector and they are releasing it slowly? Are the constraints due to the fact that there are migration restrictions or labor market restrictions that prevent workers (or firms) in high-priced cities from moving to lower-priced cities? What will happen to housing prices when these housing supply constraints are relaxed? As discussed in the paper, the local Chinese governments use land sales to raise revenues. Will a reform of the tax system in China cause a property price collapse because the incentive to hoard land by public officials would be diminished? Is it really income growth that is causing the fundamental increase in housing demand? There is some discussion of property being used as storage device for household saving. If that is true, limited options for other saving channels may be propping up housing demand in China. If there is financial liberalization in China, would that trigger a collapse in the demand for housing in China, which would cause property prices to plummet? Last, how are amenities changing in Chinese cities? Are these amenities the factors that are determining housing price changes? Are the amenities positive (more restaurants, entertainment options, etc.) or negative (more pollution, more congestion)?

As I read the paper, I enjoyed the descriptive facts. However, I am not sure what to make of them given there is no real framework allowing one to evaluate why housing prices are changing. Without such a framework, I am not sure there is a way to tell whether housing prices in China are overvalued, undervalued, or valued just right. This makes many of the claims in the paper—particularly with respect to future house price dynamics—speculative.

Cross-Country Relationship between Income Growth and House Price Growth

Again, the paper asserts that income growth is a good benchmark for house price growth. If that is true, we should be able to see the close relationship between house price growth and income growth within a wide set of countries. To explore this, I used data from the Federal Reserve Bank of Dallas's International House Price Database. The database includes quarterly house price and per capita personal disposable income series for a number of countries. All of the data series begin in the first quarter of 1975. The database includes both real and nominal values where real values are computed using each countries' personal consumption expenditure deflator.[3]

Table 1 shows the cumulative real house price growth and the cumulative real per capita income growth between 1975:Q1 and 2014:Q4 for all countries in the database. Over the 40-year period, is there a systematic relationship between per capita income growth and house price growth for the countries in the Dallas Fed database? The answer is mixed. The countries in table 1 are sorted by their cumulative per capita disposable income growth during the entire period. Countries

Table 1
Real House Price Growth and Real Per Capita Disposable Income Growth, 1975Q1–2014Q4

Country	Cumulative Real Per Capita Disposable Income Growth	Cumulative Real House Price Growth	House Price Growth/ Income Growth
South Africa	0.13	0.19	1.46
Netherlands	0.26	0.79	3.04
Spain	0.27	−0.25	−0.93
Belgium	0.32	0.99	3.09
Denmark	0.37	0.48	1.30
Italy	0.37	−0.01	−0.03
New Zealand	0.38	0.80	2.11
Switzerland	0.47	0.34	0.72
France	0.50	0.89	1.78
Canada	0.52	0.91	1.75
Germany	0.52	−0.01	−0.02
Australia	0.53	1.21	2.28
Sweden	0.56	0.59	1.05
Japan	0.60	−0.20	−0.33
United States	0.63	0.46	0.73
Ireland	0.71	1.19	1.68
Finland	0.75	0.66	0.88
United Kingdom	0.76	1.21	1.59
Norway	0.92	0.94	1.02
Israel	0.99	0.94	0.95
Luxembourg	1.09	1.60	1.47
South Korea	1.53	0.13	0.08
Croatia	2.58	0.08	0.03

Note: Data downloaded from Federal Reserve Bank of Dallas's International House Price Database.

like South Korea and Croatia experienced massive per capita income growth, yet housing prices were roughly constant over the entire 40-year period. Both of these countries, however, experienced large housing price cycles during the 40 years with large house price growth followed by large house price declines. Similar patterns are found in Spain, Italy, and Japan. These patterns are consistent with the elastic supply model developed above. Despite rapid income growth, Germany house prices have been falling consistently since the fall of the Berlin Wall.

Conversely, for many countries, disposable income growth and house price growth tracked each other closely. These countries include the Scandinavian countries (Denmark, Sweden, Finland, and Norway), the United States, Israel, and Switzerland. These patterns could be consistent with either the constrained supply model or the spatial model with within-city urban amenities. For other countries like Canada, Australia, New Zealand, the United Kingdom, Belgium, and France, real house price growth far exceeded disposable income growth.

My reading of the data is that there are very little systematic patterns between house price growth and disposable income growth over long periods of time within countries. Will China—in the long run—resemble South Korea, Japan, or Croatia? Or will China resemble the United Kingdom, Canada, or Luxembourg? These patterns reinforce my main point that without a richer discussion of what is determining housing prices, it is hard to make predictions about whether China's housing price growth is sustainable or not.

References

Alonso, William. 1964. *Location and Land Use.* Cambridge, MA: Harvard University Press.

Blanchard, Olivier, and Larry Katz. 1992. "Regional Evolutions." *Brookings Papers on Economic Activity* 1 (1992): 1–75. http://www.brookings.edu/~/media/projects/bpea/1992-1/1992a_bpea_blanchard_katz_hall_eichengreen.pdf.

Deng, Yongheng, Joe Gyourko, and Jing Wu. 2015. "Evaluating the Risk of Chinese Housing Markets: What We Know and What We Need to Know." Working paper.

Diamond, Rebecca. 2015. "The Determinants and Welfare Implications of US Workers' Diverging Location Choices by Skill: 1980–2000." Working paper.

Guerrieri, Veronica, Daniel Hartley, and Erik Hurst. 2013. "Endogenous Gentrification and House Price Dynamics." *Journal of Public Economics* 100:45–60.

Mills, Edwin. 1967. "An Aggregative Model of Resource Allocation in a Metropolitan Area." *American Economic Review* 57:197–201.

Muth, Richard. 1969. *Cities and Housing.* Chicago: University of Chicago Press.

Endnotes

For acknowledgments, sources of research support, and disclosure of the author's material financial relationships, if any, please see http://www.nber.org/chapters/c13597.ack.

1. For ease of exposition, I will only consider steady states. As a result, time subscripts will be suppressed in all subsequent notations.

2. After my initial comments discussing the paper, the authors have now made this assumption explicit in a paragraph in section VI.

3. The data can be downloaded from http://www.dallasfed.org/institute/houseprice/.

Discussion

Wei Xiong began by acknowledging the need to better understand both the supply and demand factors that are driving house price behavior in China. He argued that the inelastic supply-side dynamics are predominately determined by the Chinese government. He believes that the Chinese government has tried to manage house prices by slowly and strategically releasing land for development. He noted that the policy of government-controlled land supply also exists in a number of Asian countries. He believes that house price dynamics are affected by how much land the government chooses to release. He also gave the example of Singapore, where price appreciation has risen in line with income growth.

Hanming Fang further responded to several points raised by the discussants, Erik Hurst and Martin Schneider. Fang first acknowledged Hurst's suggestion to develop a conceptual framework that provides a link between income growth and housing. He noted that any simple homothetic preference framework will give a condition where housing expenditure will be a constant share of income. In a representative agent model with a fixed-housing supply, income growth will appear as increases in house prices. He noted the unique role that the Chinese local government plays in determining house prices.

Fang also responded to Hurst's discussion about the existence of ownership of multiple homes in China. Hurst suggested that one explanation for the increase in Chinese housing demand, and hence house prices, could be the lack of alternate investment options. Suggestive evidence for this hypothesis comes from data on ownership of multiple homes from China's Urban Household Survey. Fang disagreed about the interpretation of multiple homeownership as evidence of preference for housing as an investment vehicle. He noted that for many people who own more than one apartment, at least one of the apartments was acquired in 1997 or earlier. This fact is significant because prior to 1998, apartment units were typically very poor quality and were provided by work units at a very subsidized price, rather than purchased on the market. It was only after 1998 that the People's Bank of China introduced mortgages and loans, boosting the commercial housing market.

Martin Schneider and Kaiji Chen both raised questions about the heterogeneity in house price dynamics across cities. Schneider, in his discussion of the paper, questioned whether the low volatility in second- and third-tier cities was the result of averaging across cities within the tiers, which downplays the actual volatility of house prices at the city level. Chen also raised a related question about the heterogeneity of house price growth relative to income growth across third-tier cities. He commented that the house price index constructed by the authors showed that house price growth significantly outpaced income growth. This seemed at odds with anecdotal stories about ghost towns in a number of third-tier cities. He wondered if the authors' house price index was averaging out the heterogeneity within the third-tier cities.

Fang responded by acknowledging that they are essentially assuming uniform house price changes across the different parts of the cities when they take an average across all cities within the tier to construct their house price index. This assumption was driven by data considerations, because there were insufficient observations at the subcity level to create a finer district-level price index. They did explore this issue with Beijing, where they had sufficient data for different parts of the city. They found that the subcity level house price indices exhibited similar patterns. Wei Xiong reiterated Fang's comments about the existence of substantial heterogeneity in house price dynamics across cities within a tier but noted that the data quality issues made it difficult to explore this further.

Andrew Atkeson then asked if the authors had any information about land rents and what the patterns in the price-to-rent ratio looked like. He suggested looking at this ratio to distinguish between some of the models proposed in the discussions by Erik Hurst and Martin Schneider. In Hurst's model of land rents, the price-to-rent ratio was constant. This was in contrast to Schneider's model, where the price-to-rent ratio varied over time.

Martin Eichenbaum agreed with Andrew Atkeson's comment about the usefulness of looking at price-to-rent ratios for understanding whether a collapse in the housing market will occur in China. He noted that housing markets in emerging market countries are not stable environments. This can result in heterogeneous beliefs about house price growth, which makes it difficult to predict ex-ante whether a boom-bust or a boom-boom will occur in the future. He suggested that data on price-to-rent ratios could be more informative. If price-to-rent ratios are high, then it can be ex-ante predictive of housing bust episodes.

Robert Hall, on the other hand, commented that it should not be a mystery that price-to-rent ratios are high in rapidly growing countries. It is a direct implication of the Gordon growth formula. He noted that this says that the market believes there is going to be more growth in emerging countries than in the United States, which has been true for quite some time.

Hanming Fang pointed out that there is sparse information about rents in China. There is some limited information on rent from Joseph Gyourko. Fang described an estimate by Gyourko. Gyourko found that the price-to-rent ratio is roughly 50, which is twice as high as what you see in a typical US city. This ratio is even higher than in San Francisco, where the price-to-rent ratio is about 45. He noted that Gyourko was not sure whether the price-to-rent ratio was sustainable in China. Overall, Fang feels that there is a lot of uncertainty surrounding the Chinese housing market, which makes it difficult to know what will happen to it over the next decade.

Harald Uhlig spoke next, commenting on the anecdotal stories of the difficulties of buying a house in China. He gave the example of Chinese parents saving tremendously to give their son resources to buy a house. These stories suggest significant financial fragility for households, despite rising incomes in China, which seems at odds with the conclusions in the paper.

Wei Xiong acknowledged that down payments for housing are large relative to income—typically, about three times the average income in China. He agreed that it is the social norm in China for parents and families to subsidize their children for the down payment, which can create significant financial burden for households. However, he disagreed that this creates financial risk, because the risk is pooled within the household structure between parents and children. The pooling of resources means that children can borrow against expected income growth to buy a house with the help of their parents.

Ricardo Reis then asked the authors to relate their findings to the paper by Chang et al. (2015) that was previously presented. The Chang et al. paper showed that the consumption-to-output ratio has declined significantly over the last few decades. At the same time, rents and house prices have gone up, as the current paper has shown. Reis asked whether this means that the Chinese are consuming much less non-housing-related goods and services. He also asked whether the increased housing consumption is sustainable in the future, given the expectations of income and house price growth. He also highlighted the difference between the housing booms in China and in southern Europe. Specifically, he noted that southern European house price booms were accompanied by declining savings rates, whereas in China the house price boom coincided with increasing savings.

Andrew Atkeson suggested that one way to answer Ricardo Reis's question is to look at a consumer expenditure survey in China. For instance, the survey would tell what fraction of the budget, for renters, goes toward renting a house. Comparing the housing consumption budget share for renters to that of homeowners would be informative about whether homeowners purchased a house because of expected house price appreciation or for rental services.

Jonathan Parker also suggested that the authors disentangle the changes in price-to-rent ratio from changes in the consumption-to-savings ratio. He noted that it is possible, in an accounting sense, for the price-to-rent ratio to rise while real consumption stayed constant. For instance, in a world where the stock of housing and value of land does not change, a doubling of house prices would raise the price-to-rent ratio but leave real consumption of housing unchanged. Savings would then appear to be increasing significantly, and it is saved by buying the capital stock of housing from the government.

Wei Xiong acknowledged the usefulness of examining the expenditure budget allocations of renters and homeowners using China's Urban Household Survey to see whether home buyers are purchasing for investment or consumption. However, Xiong cautioned about the difficulties in measuring consumption, savings rates, and labor income shares. For instance, imputed house services are included in measured consumption in the United States. However, the treatment of house services for consumption varies across surveys in China, which makes consumption difficult to measure consistently. Similarly, there are also issues surrounding the measurement of labor income. For example, he believed that the dramatic reduction in labor income share over the 2003–2004 period was partly due to the fact that the collection of income tax began to be officially enforced in China in 2004. This lead to a large number of firms switching to paying employees "in-kind," which does not show up in the officially measured labor income series. He suspects that this artificially created a drop in measured labor income share, thereby inflating the savings rate.

Finally, Monika Piazzesi commented on the significant political economy questions that could arise in the future in China. She gave the example of housing on the Stanford campus. Whenever Stanford builds more houses on campus, the effects on house prices and the potential adverse implications for existing homeowners are widely discussed by the entire faculty. She imagines that these issues would be even more pronounced for those working in the Chinese government housing office.

3

External and Public Debt Crises

Cristina Arellano, *Federal Reserve Bank of Minneapolis and NBER*
Andrew Atkeson, *UCLA and NBER*
Mark Wright, *Federal Reserve Bank of Chicago and NBER*

I. Introduction

At the end of the first decade of the twenty-first century, the members of two advanced monetary and economic unions, the nations of the euro zone and the US states, experienced debt crises with spreads on government borrowing rising dramatically: in a short period of time, Californian spreads rose sixfold, Italian rose tenfold, Illinois fifteenfold, and Portuguese twenty-fivefold. Despite the similar behavior of spreads on public debt, these crises were fundamentally different in nature. In Europe, the crisis occurred after a period of significant increases in government indebtedness from levels that were already substantial, whereas in the United States, state government borrowing was limited and remained roughly unchanged. Moreover, whereas the most troubled nations of Europe experienced a sudden stop in private capital flows and private-sector borrowers also faced large rises in spreads, there is little evidence that private borrowing in US states was differentially affected by the creditworthiness of state governments. In this sense, we can say that the US states experienced a *public debt crisis*, whereas the nations of Europe experienced an *external debt crisis* affecting both public and private borrowers.

Why did Europe experience an external debt crisis and the US states only a public debt crisis? And why did the members of other economic unions, such as the provinces of Canada, not experience a debt crisis at all despite high and rising provincial public debt levels? In this paper, we argue that these different experiences result from the interplay between the ability of governments to interfere in the private external debt contracts of their citizens and the flexibility of state fiscal institutions.

The governments of US states, for example, are less fiscally flexible than the members of other economic unions as a result of state and federal limitations on their ability to change taxes and borrow, but are prevented by the US Constitution from interfering in private contracts. Together, these factors result in public debt intolerance and yet also limit the likelihood of an external debt crisis affecting private-sector borrowers within the state. Euro zone nations are more fiscally flexible but have a greater ability to interfere with the contracts of their citizens, particularly if one of them exits the euro zone, which together allows for more public borrowing but also raises the likelihood for external debt crises occurring together with public debt crises. Canadian provincial governments are both fiscally flexible and limited in their ability to interfere in private contracts, which both allows for more public borrowing and limits the likelihood that either a public or an external debt crisis will occur.

We establish this argument both empirically and theoretically. Empirically, we document variation in both possibilities for government interference in private contracts and fiscal flexibility across economic unions. We show that interference in private contracts—which can include direct interference such as moratoria on repayments of external debt or the imposition of controls on capital outflows, as well as indirect interference such as deposit freezes that hinder the ability of private borrowers to repay their external debts—is a common occurrence in debt crises. We also show that ratings agencies incorporate the risk of sovereign interference when rating private-sector bonds in both emerging markets and in Europe, but do not consider the risk of state and provincial government interference when rating private borrowers in the United States and Canada. We next show that fiscal flexibility of the governments of members of economic unions—the ability to vary their tax rates and levels of public expenditure in response to economic shocks—also varies across unions.

Theoretically, we model the decisions of a benevolent government to spend, tax, borrow, default on public debts, and interfere in private debt contracts in a world where the private sector can also issue external debt but cannot independently default on its own debts. In our economy, the efficient benchmark under full commitment and full fiscal flexibility has the country borrowing externally to smooth both public and private consumption, and setting public expenditures to equate the marginal utilities of public and private expenditures within each period. We examine how governments with limited commitment to repay public debt and to refrain from interfering in private debts, and facing potential constraints on fiscal flexibility, might find themselves and their citizens unable to borrow enough to smooth consumption over time and across the public and private sectors.

First, we show that if the government is fiscally flexible in the sense that it is unconstrained in its ability to vary taxes and if it can commit to not interfere with private contracts (which we think of as the Canadian case), then neither public debt crises nor external debt constraints can bind. In equilibrium, the citizens of the country and the government can raise the resources they need to smooth consumption, regardless of the government's ability to commit to repay its public debts. The reason no public debt crisis can occur is that, if the government can vary taxes, it prefers to close fiscal gaps with taxes rather than with default on domestically held public debt. As a result, the government can commit to repay its domestically held public debts and hence can implement its optimal borrowing strategy domestically, whereas the private sector does the required borrowing externally. With commitment not to interfere in private external debt contracts, this private external borrowing is unconstrained.

Second, we show that if the government can tax flexibly but cannot commit to refrain from interfering in private debt contracts (the European case), all crises are external debt crises that affect both the private sector and the public sector simultaneously. As in the Canadian case, with tax flexibility, governments can credibly borrow from their own private sector. Hence, the government should not find itself constrained in its borrowing unless the private sector is also constrained from borrowing externally. In contrast to the Canadian case, if the government is tempted to interfere with private external debt contracts, the external borrowing of the country may be constrained. If this occurs, the country is constrained in both its public and external borrowing.

Third, and finally, we show that when taxes are inflexible, but the government can commit to not interfere in private contracts (the American case), it is possible to have a public debt crisis without an external debt crisis. The reason is that, when taxes are inflexible, the government may be tempted to default on domestically held public debts so as to finance the desired level of public expenditure. As a result of this risk of default on all forms of public debt, the public sector may be constrained in its borrowing even when the private sector faces no constraint on its external borrowing.

The spillovers of the public debt crisis in Europe on the private sector have sparked a recent literature focused on the role of the banking system in generating spillovers between private external and public debts.[1] We view such mechanisms as complementary to our theory based on the risk of government interference, and in fact they are closely related, since many examples of government interference with private debt contracts, such as deposit freezes and capital controls, are applied to the banking sector. For example, many observers see the recent drain of deposits from the Greek banking system as being driven by a fear that a deposit freeze and/or capital controls may be imposed. In this context a banking union may be beneficial for Europe, not only to protect banks' balance sheets, but also to remove the temptation of governments to interfere with private debt contracts during times of fiscal distress.

The rest of this paper is organized as follows. Section II documents our claims about the different experiences of euro zone members, the US states, and the members of other economic unions such as Canada. Section III presents our empirical and institutional evidence on the occurrence of sovereign interference, and Section IV discusses fiscal flexibility. Section V presents our model, and Section VI concludes. References to the literature are discussed as they arise throughout the text.

II.   Debt Crises in the Euro Zone and US States

In this section we document the debt crises in the euro zone countries and US states late in the first decade of the twenty-first century. We show that during these crises, the governments faced increases in spreads on their borrowing related to default risk. We document that this increase in spreads occurred even though current public debt levels for US states are quite low relative to those observed in European nations and Canadian provinces. We also show that US states did not increase their public borrowing during the crisis. In contrast, Canadian provinces did not experience debt crises and were able to increase their public borrowing at low spreads. We also show that in the euro zone, the debt crisis was external because these countries experienced reversals in their international private capital inflows and significantly increased spreads on private-sector external borrowing.

A.   Spreads

During late 2008, countries in the euro zone including Greece, Ireland, Italy, Portugal, and Spain experienced increases in the yields and spreads at which they were borrowing, reflecting perceptions of a higher probability of default. Figure 1, panel (a) plots the 10-year spreads for these five countries. The spreads peaked in 2012, reaching, for example, 500 basis points for Spain. Greece actually defaulted in 2012 on its public debt.

The US states and Canadian provinces are similar to euro zone countries in that there is no bankruptcy process for handling state defaults. The US state governments are sovereign in that they can repudiate their debts without recourse for creditors.[2] Historically, in the 1840s many US states did repudiate their debts, but no US states have defaulted on their general obligation debts since the Great Depression.[3]

Several US states, such as California, Illinois, and Michigan, have experienced a debt crisis since 2008 in the sense that they face spreads on the general obligation debt of the state government similar to those faced by several euro zone sovereign borrowers. Figure 1, panel (b) shows the five-year credit default swaps (CDS) spreads on the debts of California, Illinois, Michigan, Virginia, and New York from 2008 to 2014. The CDS spreads on the debts of California, for example, reached about 500 basis points and have been high for much of this period.[4] Although these CDS spreads for California are not as high as the peak sovereign spreads shown for euro zone countries in figure 1, panel (a), these spreads are still sizable.[5]

In contrast to the experiences of the euro zone countries and US states, Canadian provinces did not experience a debt crisis during the Great Recession. Figure 1, panel (c) shows the 10-year bond spreads on the debts of British Columbia, Ontario, and Quebec, which are the three most populous provinces in Canada. These spreads have been quite stable since 2008, with modest rises in 2009 and 2013. As discussed in Bird and Tassonyi (2003) and Wong and Raimes (2013), Canadian provincial governments have a great deal of fiscal autonomy from the Canadian central government, no central restrictions on their borrowing, and broad responsibilities for social services in the province, making them a good comparison group with euro zone countries and US states. Thus, the Canadian provinces appear to serve as examples of relatively independent regional governments in a monetary union that have been able to avoid a public debt crisis.

B.   Debt Levels: US States Are Debt Intolerant

Many US state governments faced high sovereign spreads during the debt crisis despite very low levels of indebtedness. We argue that these US state governments are *public debt intolerant*: the thresholds of public

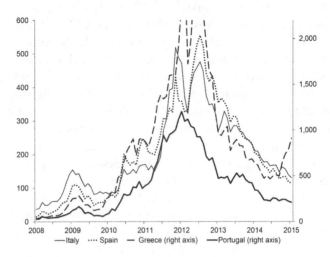

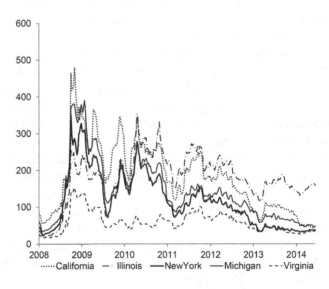

Fig. 1. Government spreads in Europe, US States, and Canadian provinces

Sources: Global Financial Database for Europe, Markit for the United States, and Bank of Canada for Canada.

Notes: Panel (a) (above, top): Spreads for Eurozone countries. Spreads are calculated as the difference between the 10-year government bond yield and each country and the German 10-year yield using monthly data. Panel (b) (above, bottom): Spreads for US states. Spreads are from credit default swaps. Panel (c) (opposite page): Spreads for Canadian provinces. Spreads are calculated as the difference between the 10-year provincial government bond yield and the Canadian 10-year yield using monthly data.

c. Spreads for Canadian Provinces

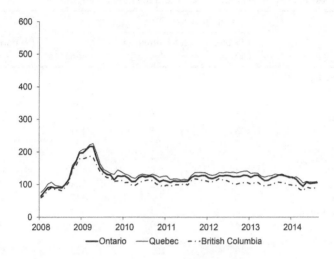

Fig. 1. (continued)

debt to gross domestic product (GDP) at which the public debt is considered safe by the market are extraordinarily low in comparison with public debt levels for the governments of euro zone countries and the regional governments of Canadian provinces, even after including obligations for employee pensions and health care.[6] Moreover, the fiscal response of US states to the Great Recession was strikingly different from the fiscal responses of the provincial governments of the largest Canadian provinces. The US states did not increase their level of borrowing, whereas Canadian provinces increased their level of borrowing substantially.

The first panel of table 1 reports the 2012 ratio of net debt to state GDP for the 10 most populous US states. These public debt-to-GDP ratios lie in a narrow range from a little over 1% for Texas to a little under 5.5% for New York. The second panel of the table reports the net debt for the most populous Canadian provinces. Net debt-to-GDP ratios in Canada are on average eight times larger than in the US states, reaching 48% for Quebec. The third panel reports net debt-to-GDP ratios for countries in the euro zone, and these ratios are 10–20 times larger than is the case for US state governments. As shown in the fourth column of table 1, the debts for Canadian provinces and euro zone countries relative to government revenues are also larger than for US states by a factor of two or more, in many cases.

Table 1
Indebtedness in the United States, Canada, and the Euro Zone (2012)

| | Liabilities to GDP | | | |
	Net Debt (%)	Plus Unfunded (%)	Rating	Revenue/GDP (%)
United States				
California	5	11	A1	9
Texas	1	11	Aaa	7
New York	5	7	Aa2	11
Florida	3	6	Aa1	8
Illinois	5	32	A2	9
Pennsylvania	3	14	Aa2	10
Ohio	3	6	Aa1	10
Georgia	3	5	Aaa	8
Michigan	2	6	Aa2	12
North Carolina	2	5	Aaa	9
Mean	**3**	**10**		**9**
Canada				
Ontario	40	102	Aa2	17
Quebec	48	197	Aa2	19
British Columbia	17	73	Aaa	19
Alberta	2	68	Aaa	19
Mean	**27**	**110**		**19**
Europe				
Greece	170	229	Caa1	44
Italy	111	131	Baa2	52
Ireland	92	147	Baa1	34
Portugal	119	171	Ba1	44
Spain	61	134	Baa2	38
Mean	**110**	**162**		**42**

Sources: United States: Larson (2013, table 5) for net debt; Lombardi and Van Wagner (2014, tables 3 and 7) for pension liabilities and government revenues; and Moody's (2013) for ratings. Europe: IMF (2014) for net debt and government revenues, and Moody's (2014, table 23a) for pensions; Wilson (2014) for ratings, which are for 2014. Canada: Moody's (2013) for net debt and ratings; Palacios, MacIntyre, and Lammam (2014) for pensions liabilities. Government/GDP series from fiscal reference tables (Department of Finance Canada).

The creditworthiness of governments is affected by their total level of indebtedness measured on a comprehensive basis, including explicit and implicit liabilities for employees' pensions and health care. The second column of table 1 reports the total level of debt for US states, Canadian provinces, and euro zone countries, taking into account estimates for unfunded liabilities, including employee pension liabilities and employee health care obligations.

For US states, these unfunded liabilities increase the ratio of debt

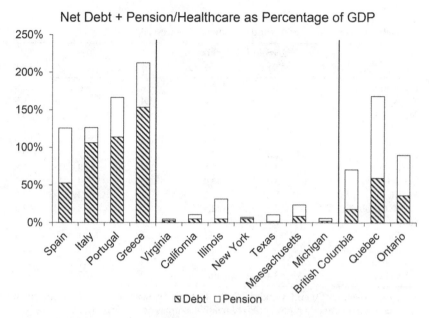

Fig. 2. Net debt and pension/health care liabilities to GDP
Notes: See table 1.

to GDP by a factor of three, on average. Nevertheless, we see that for most states, with the exception of Illinois, the total debt including unfunded liabilities is relatively modest, averaging 10%. The pension and health care liabilities for Canadian provinces and euro zone countries are substantially larger than those for most US state governments. For Canadian provincial governments, estimates indicate that the total liabilities are typically on the order of three times the net indebtedness of the provincial government. In figure 2 we summarize these findings by plotting the net debt-to-GDP ratio (with and without unfunded liabilities) of selected euro zone countries, US states, and Canadian provinces. As is evident in the figure, US states have remarkably low levels of total liabilities when compared with these other regional and national governments.

The Great Recession of 2008 had an important fiscal impact on almost all of the regional and national governments discussed in this paper. The fiscal response of the US state governments was to adjust revenue and expenditures on a year-by-year basis without increasing outstanding debt. In the first panel of table 2, we show the history of the ratio of state net debt to personal income over the period 2008–2012

Table 2
Net Debt to Income in US States and Canadian Provinces, 2008–2012

State	2008 (%)	2009 (%)	2010 (%)	2011 (%)	2012 (%)
California	4.3	4.4	5.6	6.0	6.0
Texas	1.4	1.4	1.4	1.6	1.5
New York	6.3	6.3	6.5	6.7	6.6
Florida	2.8	2.9	2.9	3.0	3.0
Illinois	5.2	4.6	4.4	5.7	6.0
Pennsylvania	2.4	2.5	2.4	2.7	2.8
Ohio	2.9	2.8	2.6	2.8	2.8
Georgia	3.0	3.0	3.3	3.3	3.1
Michigan	2.2	2.2	2.1	2.2	2.2
North Carolina	2.8	2.5	2.3	2.3	2.3
Canada					
Alberta	0.6	2.1	2.1	2.1	2.4
British Columbia	13.4	14.7	14.9	15.6	16.8
Ontario	27.4	34.0	36.1	37.8	40.4
Quebec	43.4	45.	47.2	47.7	48.3

Sources: Larson (2013) and Moody's (2013). Data on US states are relative to personal income. Data on Canadian provinces are relative to gross domestic product.

for US states. As is clear in the table, these indebtedness levels are little changed. By way of contrast, in the second panel of table 2, we show that the provincial governments in Canada responded to the fiscal crisis by issuing substantial additional debt relative to GDP, particularly in the case of Ontario.

The choice by the governments of US states to refrain from issuing more debt in response to their fiscal crisis following the Great Recession was not due solely to their self-imposed legal fiscal constraints on state borrowing.[7] Instead, many US states were charged considerable spreads on their debts once the crisis began.[8]

C. External Debt Crisis in the Euro Zone

The public debt crises in euro zone countries and US states documented above were associated with strikingly different responses in private-sector external borrowing. We document that in several euro zone countries, private capital markets experienced a *sudden stop*, defined as a sharp reversal of private capital inflows.[9] We also document strong comovement in private and sovereign spreads. In sharp contrast to the experience of euro zone countries, we are aware of no evidence linking the borrowing costs of private borrowers domiciled in Califor-

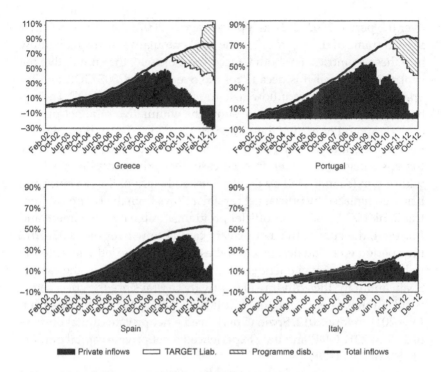

Fig. 3. Private capital flows, program financing, and Euro system financing for Greece, Portugal, Italy, and Spain, 2002–2012 (% of 2007 GDP).

Source: Pisani-Ferry et al. (2013), figure 1.

http://bruegel.org/wp-content/uploads/imported/publications/1869_Blueprint_XIX _-_web__.pdf.

nia (or any other state) to the borrowing costs of the state government. In this sense, we argue that several US state governments have had a public debt crisis without facing an external debt crisis.

As discussed in Lane (2013), the introduction of the euro was associated with a large increase in the volume of cross-border capital flows among the euro zone countries, leading to the accumulation of large gross and net stocks of international indebtedness. With the crisis that started in 2007–2008, there was a dramatic reduction in both the gross and net volume of private capital flows. We now document the disparate impact of this reversal of private capital flows on different euro zone countries.

In figure 3, taken from Pisani-Ferry, Sapir, and Wolff (2013), we show the cumulative net capital flows into Greece, Portugal, Spain, and Italy over the period 2002–2012 as a percentage of 2007 GDP. The solid lines in each frame of the figure show the total cumulative net capital inflow into these countries. For both Greece and Portugal, the cumulative net capital inflow over this decade rose to over 70% of 2007 GDP, and for Spain, this cumulative inflow rose to over 50% of 2007 GDP. The red bars in each frame of the figure show the cumulative total net private capital inflow. For each of these countries, in the earlier part of this time period, the cumulative net capital inflows were primarily private. Since the crisis began, however, in each case, this private capital has been withdrawn (as indicated by the diminished height of the red bars) and has been replaced by official net capital inflows from the European Central Bank (ECB) and other official programs. In the case of Greece and Portugal, the cumulative net private capital flow over the 2002–2012 time period is essentially zero, and these countries are left with external indebtedness to official lenders well over 70% of GDP. In the case of Spain and Italy, the withdrawal of private capital since the crisis began is substantial as well. As noted in IMF (2012), in the 12 months from June 2011 to June 2012, Spain experienced a net private capital outflow of 27% of 2011 GDP, and Italy experienced a net private capital outflow of 15% of 2011 GDP.[10]

We now discuss the comovement of sovereign and private bond spreads. Gilchrist and Mojon (2014) document a strong comovement by constructing indices of nonfinancial corporate spreads in the four largest euro zone countries.[11] These are bonds issued by large nonfinancial corporates in European securities markets. We reproduce these data in figure 4, panel (a). We can see that for the period from mid-2006 to 2009, these bond markets appear to be tightly integrated in that the nationality of the bond issuer does not appear to have an impact on its spread. This was true even though, as shown in figure 1, panel (a), sovereign spreads for these countries began to diverge in 2009. In contrast, however, the heterogeneity in the movement in private nonfinancial spreads is readily evident in the figure after mid-2010. This heterogeneity in private spreads was tightly linked to the heterogeneity in sovereign spreads. For example, the comovement of nonfinancial corporate credit spreads, measured using either bond spreads or CDS spreads, with sovereign CDS spreads in Italy and Spain starting in 2011, can be seen in figure 4, panels (b) and (c), reproduced from Gilchrist and Mojon (2014).[12]

In contrast to the experience of euro zone countries, for the United States, we are aware of no evidence linking the borrowing costs of private borrowers domiciled in a state to the borrowing costs of the state government. We illustrate this disconnect by comparing the ample borrowing possibilities for Los Angeles County in July 2009, at the same time that the state of California experienced very high borrowing costs. As described in Taylor (2009), the state of California regularly engages in substantial short-term borrowing over the course of its fiscal year (July 1–June 30) to deal with the regular seasonal pattern of cash outflows in the first part of the fiscal year and cash inflows due to tax collections late in the fiscal year. Starting in the fall of 2008, the gap between cash inflows and outflows turned out to be much larger than expected due to the dramatic decline in tax revenues for the state. For the 2008–2009 fiscal year, the state's expenditures exceeded revenues by $17.9 billion (roughly 1% of state GDP and 17% of 2007–2008 state revenues). The state faced tremendous difficulty raising the cash necessary to fund this gap. The state controller resorted to a 30-day delay of $4.2 billion in payments in February and issuing registered warrants (IOUs) in lieu of state payments that were not redeemed until September 2009. In July of 2009, the *Los Angeles Times* estimated that California would have had to pay over 5% tax free for further short-term borrowing, while at the same time Los Angeles County was able to borrow short term at 0.8% and short-term Treasury bills paid 0.5%.[13]

In summary, many of the euro zone member countries experienced an external debt crisis with sudden stops of net private capital inflows and rising spreads on both sovereign and private debt. The debt crisis in the US states, and especially California, was distinct because it was restricted to public debt.

III. Government Interference with Private Contracts

We now review evidence that the perceived risk of sovereign interference with domiciled private debt contracts plays an important role in linking private and public borrowing in euro zone countries. We also review the institutional environment that governs protections against government interference, contrasting the strong protections embodied in the United States and Canadian constitutions with the much weaker protections available in Europe.

We start by documenting that the credit ratings agencies cite the risk of sovereign interference as an important factor in rating private borrowers in emerging markets economies and now in euro zone countries as well. They do so because, in practice, episodes of sovereign interfer-

(a) Non-Financial Corporate

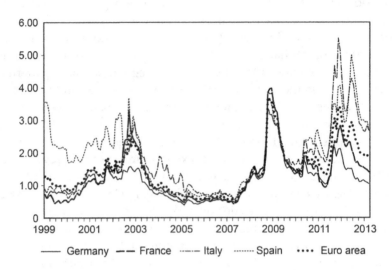

(b) Italy Sovereign and Non-Financial Corporate

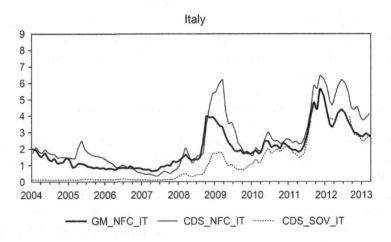

Fig. 4. Euro-area credit spread

Source: Gilchrist and Mojon (2014, figures 2 and 6).

Note: Panel (a) (above, top): nonfinancial corporate; panel (b) (above, bottom): Italy sovereign and nonfinancial corporate; and panel (c) (facing page): Spain sovereign and nonfinancial corporate.

(c) Spain Sovereign and Non-Financial Corporate

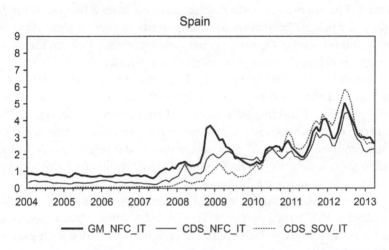

Fig. 4. (continued)

ence with private contracts, which have imposed substantial haircuts for creditors, are correlated with public default. We review this history of episodes and document how these concerns for euro zone countries have risen. We document that the sovereign rating is, in fact, binding as a ceiling on the private credit ratings and has economic impact by affecting the cost and availability of international credit for private borrowers in both emerging market and euro zone economies.

We then review how the contract clause in the US Constitution has insulated private borrowers and creditors in US states from the impact of public debt crises of state governments. We provide a historical account of various rulings that have repeatedly upheld the protection of private creditors against potential cases of sovereign interference, and contrast this experience with the widespread government interference that occurred prior to ratification of the Constitution. We also show how similar protections are available to creditors in the Canadian provinces, while pointing to the weaknesses in European protections.

A. The Sovereign Credit Ceiling

The term "sovereign credit ceiling" refers to the policies of the main credit-rating agencies to restrict the credit ratings that they give to private borrowers to be no greater than the credit rating of the sovereign government of the country in which the private borrower is located. The sovereign credit ceiling has long been a feature of credit ratings for private borrowers in emerging market economies. More recently, it has become a feature of credit-rating agency policies for credit ratings for private borrowers in euro zone countries.[14]

The three credit-rating agencies, Fitch Ratings, Moody's Investors Service, and Standard and Poor's, typically invoke three reasons for their policies of linking sovereign and private credit ratings.[15] The first reason is that both sovereign and private borrowers face common macroeconomic shocks. The second is that a sovereign default would lead to (or coincide with) a financial crisis that would affect the terms of credit available to private borrowers.[16]

The third reason, and the focus of our analysis, is the *risk of sovereign interference with private contracts.* These credit-rating agencies point to a long history of experience with sovereign interference with private debt contracts in emerging-market economies. The interference has typically taken the form of imposition of bank deposit freezes and/or capital or exchange controls in a public or external debt crisis. Because deposit freezes and capital controls directly interfere with a private borrower's ability to transfer the foreign exchange necessary to service his or her external debt, this risk of sovereign interference is often termed "transfer and convertibility risk." This concept captures the risk that a foreign creditor might not get paid on his or her loan to a private borrower because the government of the borrower's country enacts policies that make it difficult for the private borrower to obtain the foreign exchange necessary to repay his or her debts. In the past several years, the credit-rating agencies have pointed to the risk that a euro zone member country would enact such policies upon exiting the euro as a significant risk restricting the ratings offered to private borrowers in several euro zone countries.[17]

The three main ratings agencies make an effort to quantitatively evaluate the impact of sovereign interference in private contracts on the ratings given to private entities separately from the risk of the sovereign's default. Standard and Poor's, for example, provides a Transfer and Convertibility Rating to each country in addition to a sovereign credit rating for both the local currency and foreign currency debt of the sovereign government to attempt to measure the likelihood of sovereign interference with private contracts as distinct from the likelihood of a default on domestic and external public debts. This transfer and convertibility rating is incorporated into the ceiling that Standard and Poor's applies to the credit ratings given to private borrowers in the relevant country. Likewise, Moody's Investors Service and Fitch Ratings provide Country Ceilings, which are similar to Standard and Poor's transfer and convertibility ratings in that they "capture the risk of capital and/or exchange controls being imposed that would prevent or materially impede the private sector's ability to convert local currency into foreign currency and transfer the proceeds to nonresident creditors— transfer and convertibility (T&C) risk. Country Ceilings are not ratings but rather a key analytical input and constraint on the ratings of entities and transactions originating in the sovereign's jurisdiction."[18]

Cavanaugh (2013) provides a history of Standard and Poor's sovereign credit ratings for domestic and foreign currency debt as well as their transfer and convertibility ratings for a large number of countries over the past several decades. In most instances, the transfer and convertibility rating is aligned with the sovereign credit rating. There are, however, several instances in this historical record of countries with a higher transfer and convertibility rating than sovereign foreign currency ratings, indicating that Standard and Poor's assessment of the risk of sovereign interference with private contracts is lower than their assessment of the risk of default on the government's foreign currency debt.[19]

Transfer and Convertibility Risk in Emerging Markets

There is a substantial historical record of sovereign interference with private debt contracts in emerging market economies. In Duggar (2008), Moody's Investors Service surveys the post-1960 history of sovereign bond defaults and the extent to which sovereign defaults have been accompanied by government interference with domiciled borrowers' foreign currency debt service.

This Moody's survey covers 38 episodes of sovereign bond defaults. It finds 27 episodes of deposit freezes, with all but two of these (Korea 1998 and Ukraine 2004) accompanied by a sovereign bond default. It finds that "the most frequent deposit interference measure employed has been the imposition of prolonged deposit freezes, with several freezes lasting one year or longer, followed by outright deposit expropriations, forced deposit conversions into bonds, and forced deposit conversions into local currency." Depositor losses in a freeze have been severe, with haircuts often as high as 70%.

Moody's also finds that since 1960, about 26% of public bond defaults have been accompanied by controls on private-sector debt service payments, with all but one of these also coinciding with a deposit freeze. Of these events of controls on private debt service payments, 44% were full moratoria in which either all external private-sector payments were explicitly banned, or purchases of foreign currency were blocked (e.g., Peru 1985, Venezuela 1994, and Russia 1998). Another 28% of these events included a selective moratorium in which the ability to make private-sector external debt payments was limited to favored sectors or companies, or required a case-by-case authorization by the central bank and/or the ministry of finance (e.g., Costa Rica 1981, the Philippines 1983, Brazil 1990, and Argentina 2001). The other 28% of events included the imposition of exchange controls or regulations that have severely affected external private-sector payments and that have encouraged, implicitly or explicitly, the rescheduling of private foreign debt payments (Mexico 1982 and Argentina 1982).

Transfer and Convertibility Risk in the Euro Zone

Prior to the most recent financial crisis in the euro zone, the three main credit-ratings agencies had essentially eliminated the sovereign credit ceiling for private borrowers in euro zone countries.[20] As described in Cavanaugh and Feinland-Katz (2009) and Fox and Renwick (2014), writing for Standard and Poor's and Fitch Ratings, respectively, prior to this crisis, all countries in the euro zone were assigned either a transfer and convertibility rating or a country ceiling of "AAA," indicating that considerations of transfer and convertibility risk were not relevant in constraining the credit ratings for private entities in the euro zone. The thinking expressed in these documents was that the legal structure of the European Union and the euro zone in particular would make it difficult for a sovereign to interfere with cross-border private debt contracts. In the wake of the recent sovereign debt crisis in the euro zone, and in particular, in the wake of events in Iceland, Greece, and Cyprus, all three of the main credit-ratings agencies have revised their ratings methodology to reflect heightened perceptions of transfer and convertibility risks for euro zone countries.[21]

As discussed in Feinland-Katz (2013), Standard and Poor's has since revised its assessment of the link between sovereign and private credit ratings in the euro zone to recognize that the transfer and convertibility risk for several euro zone countries is higher than they previously thought.[22]

Pitman (2012) indicates that Moody's also reassessed the risk of sovereign interference with private external debt contracts in euro zone countries. Focusing on the potential for transfer and convertibility risk associated with a euro zone exit, Moody's pointed to a number of legal acts that would likely be required of an exiting country, including a deposit freeze, the imposition of capital controls, and the redenomination of financial obligations. As described in Pitman (2012), in June of 2012, Moody's lowered the ceiling for private borrowers in Greece to "Caa2" because of the risk that creditors would not receive payments in the originally contracted currency.[23] Moody's also describes the downgrades of the country ceilings for Spain and Italy in August 2012 for similar reasons (Pitman [2012], 6).

Does the Sovereign Credit Ceiling Bind Ratings?

A large body of empirical work examines the interaction of sovereign credit ratings with private credit ratings and credit terms both in emerging markets and in the euro zone.[24] The first finding in this literature is that the credit-rating agencies' policies of imposing a sovereign credit ceiling does, in fact, constrain the distribution of private credit ratings assigned by the rating agencies. Borensztein, Cowan, and Valenzuela (2013) and Almeida et al. (2014) both examine the empirical distribution of the gap between nonfinancial corporate credit ratings and the associated sovereign credit rating for a large number of emerging market and euro zone foreign bonds.[25] Both papers find a striking spike in the distribution of ratings gaps at zero (i.e., with the private firm and the respective sovereign having the same rating), with very few firms rated higher than the sovereign (that is, with positive ratings gaps) relative to the number of firms rated below the sovereign (negative ratings gaps). This finding is illustrated in our figure 5, which reproduces the distribution of ratings gaps between corporate and sovereign ratings shown in Almeida et al. (2014). More specific to the recent developments in the euro zone, Klein and Stellner (2014) examine a sample of 897 bonds from euro zone countries all denominated in euros covering the period March 2006 through June 2012. Figure 3 in that paper confirms that the vast majority of these private-sector bonds in the euro zone carry ratings that are below the rating of the sovereign.

The second finding in this literature is that changes in sovereign ratings appear to drive changes in the associated private ratings. To evaluate the impact of changes in sovereign ratings on private bond ratings, Borenaztein et al. (2013) run regressions of individual firms' bond rat-

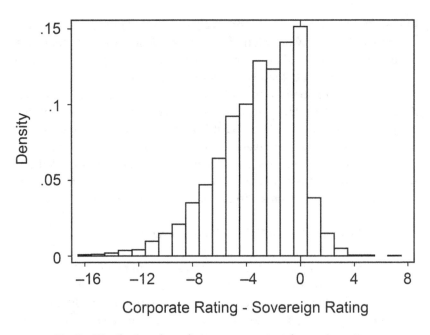

Fig. 5. Distribution of gaps between corporate and sovereign ratings
Source: Almeida et al. (2014).

ings on the country rating, a vector of firm-specific controls using accounting data, a vector of country-specific macroeconomic variables,
and time, country, and industry dummies. They find a significant correlation of sovereign credit-rating changes with changes in the credit
ratings of private borrowers even after controlling for these other factors, particularly for borrowers in emerging-market economies. Klein
and Stellner (2014) find the same result in their sample of euro zone
bonds using a similar methodology. Almeida et al. (2014) take a nonparametric approach to establishing this point. In figure 2 of their paper
(reproduced here in figure 6), these authors show that when a sovereign
downgrade occurs, a large fraction of firms that are initially rated at
or above the sovereign receive a downgrade of the same number of
steps as the sovereign either in the same month as the sovereign or one
month later, whereas only a very small fraction of firms initially rated
below the sovereign experience the same downgrade. They argue that
this asymmetry of responses is indicative of a causal impact of the sovereign downgrade on the highly rated firms in that country.
    The third and fourth findings in this literature are that the price of

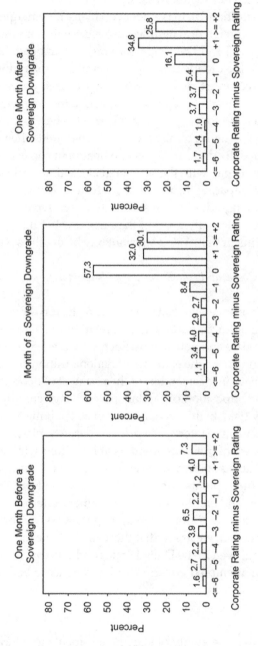

Fig. 6.   Proportion of corporate rating changes around a sovereign downgrade

Source: Almeida et al. (2014).

private external borrowing tends to rise, whereas the quantity of private external borrowing tends to fall, when sovereign credit spreads rise and/ or ratings fall. In addition, there is evidence, chiefly for emerging-market economies, that sovereign downgrades also reduce firm investment (see Areta and Hale [2008] and Das, Papaioannou, and Trebesch [2010]). Almeida et al. (2014) look to identify the impact of sovereign downgrades on private firm investment by taking advantage of their observation that it is those private firms that are rated at or above the sovereign that get downgraded when the sovereign is downgraded, whereas those that are rated below the sovereign typically are not downgraded when the sovereign is downgraded. By dividing firms into treatment and control groups based on their rating gap with the sovereign at the time of the sovereign downgrade and comparing the responses of firm investment, they argue that sovereign downgrades have a substantial negative impact on firm investment for firms initially rated at the same level of the sovereign in comparison to firms initially rated substantially below the sovereign.

B.   Institutional Constraints on Government Interference

The governments of sovereign states have a long history of interfering in private financial contracts, particularly in relation to contracts between the citizens of the state and noncitizens. Such interference can take a variety of forms, ranging from the extremes of nationalization and expropriation through changes in legal tender for the payment of debts (redenomination risk) to the imposition of capital and exchange controls (transfer and convertibility risk). In this section, we review the limits placed on the ability of a government to interfere in private contracts, placing these limits within the context of previous attempts at interference in the histories of the US states, Canadian provinces, and euro zone nations.

We make two main points. First, we show that the legal institutions protecting debtors and creditors from government interference in their contracts is far weaker in Europe than among the US states or the Canadian provinces. Second, we argue that these institutional constraints are frequently binding, even in the United States and Canada, by documenting this history of attempted government interference in both countries.

United States

In the United States, the ability of state governments to interfere in the contracts signed by their citizens is limited by a number of clauses within the US Constitution. The first is the Commerce Clause (Article I, Section 8, Clause 3), which gives Congress the power "to regulate commerce . . . among the several states" and hence prevents state governments from introducing capital controls. The second is the Takings Clause (the last clause in the Fifth Amendment), which limits the power of state governments to expropriate private property without "just compensation."[26]

The third, and arguably the most important set of protections, is contained in the Contract Clause (Article I, Section 10, Clause 1), which reads in full:

No State shall enter into any Treaty, Alliance, or Confederation; grant Letters of Marque and Reprisal; coin Money; emit Bills of Credit; make any Thing but gold and silver Coin a Tender in Payment of Debts; pass any Bill of Attainder, ex post facto Law, or Law impairing the Obligation of Contracts, or grant any Title of Nobility.

This clause serves to limit redenomination risk by preventing the state governments from issuing coins or paper money ("bills of credit") and making them (or anything else) legal tender in the repayment of debts. The clause also limits the risk of a range of other forms of government interference by preventing state governments from impairing the obligations of private debt contracts.

The Contract Clause was explicitly drafted as a counter to the long history of state (and colonial) government interference in private contracts prior to the passage of the US Constitution. Some of the earliest examples arose during the War of Independence and took the form of colonial laws that seized the real property of British loyalists. Following the Revolution, the new state governments widened their interference in private debt contracts by passing debtor relief laws that took one of four basic forms. The first were changes that made paper money, often significantly depreciated, legal tender in the repayment of debts. The colonial governments had experimented with issuing paper money, in the form of bills of credit, since at least 1690 when the Commonwealth of Massachusetts began issuing bills of credit—debts intended to circulate as media of exchange—and made them legal tender in the payment of taxes. New Hampshire, Rhode Island, Connecticut, New York, and New Jersey all quickly followed suit, with South Carolina, Pennsylvania, Maryland, Delaware, Virginia, and Georgia doing likewise at various points over the next half century (Dewey 1902, 21–24).

Following the Revolutionary War, this practice arose again. In one of the best-known cases, Rhode Island issued paper money in 1786 and made it legal tender for the repayment of debts. The money soon traded between 25% to 50% of par and had fallen to one-twelfth of par by 1789. In response, Massachusetts and Connecticut legislated to prevent Rhode Island residents from collecting debts owed by their own residents (Nevins 1924, 539–40, 571). Similar acts occurred in other states: in 1785 North Carolina issued paper money that was used to repay debts in sterling at a 50% discount (Nevins 1924, 524); in 1786, both New Jersey and Georgia issued paper money and made it legal tender for all private and public debts (Nevins, 523–24).[27]

The second form of debtor relief law were changes that made commodities or land legal tender in the repayment of debts, often on terms quite unfavorable to creditors. The most famous of these was South Carolina's Pine Barren Act of 1785, which permitted debtors to tender property to discharge debts. The land was to be appraised and could be used to repay debts at two-thirds of the land's value. However, the lands tendered were often very distant from creditors, making it difficult to challenge their appraised value. South Carolina also allowed payment in kind (such as cattle), with the creditor to pay the costs of driving the animals to market (Ely 2008, 37; Nevins 1924, 404–05, 525–26). Likewise, in 1782 Massachusetts passed a law allowing payment of debt in cattle and other commodities, and in 1785 New Hampshire allowed debtors to repay debts in either real or personal property (Nevins 1924, 537).

The third form of debtor relief laws were stays in the repayments of debts, or alterations in the timing of required repayments. As one example, South Carolina passed a stay law in 1782 that remained in place until 1786 when only one-quarter of the outstanding debt became payable (Nevins 1924, 525). The fourth and final form of debtor relief laws involved the closure of the courts to suits by creditors, or the diminution of the penalties for default. For example, in 1783 North Carolina passed a law suspending suits against debtors (Nevins 1924, 386). Likewise, in 1781, while repealing laws that had made paper money legal tender in the repayment of debts, South Carolina prohibited suits for the recovery of debts until the next general assembly (Nevins 1924, 390). Maryland passed a law in 1787 allowing insolvent debtors to pass through bankruptcy without prison (Nevins 1924, 532).

The history of state interference in debt contracts framed the thinking of delegates to the Constitutional Congress. The Founding Fathers objected to these debtor relief laws not only out of a concern about property rights per se but also, in light of the Rhode Island paper money dispute, because it had the potential to generate interstate conflict. On the former, James Madison wrote in *The Federalist No. 44* that "Bills of attainder, ex post facto laws, and laws impairing the obligation of contracts, are contrary to the first principles of the social compact, and to every principle of sound legislation." On the latter, writing in *The Federalist No. 7*, Alexander Hamilton argued that "Laws in violation of private contracts, as they amount to aggressions on the rights of those States whose citizens are injured by them, may be considered as another probable source of hostility."[28]

Support for the clause was widespread. There was no debate on the contract clause for the first three months of the Congress and, notwithstanding some modifications by the Style Committee, no amendments to the clause were ever proposed (Wright 1938, 9, 12, 15). There was also very little debate on the clause as part of state ratification proceedings. Even in the ratification proceedings for South Carolina, which had frequently interfered in private contracts, most views were positive, with Charles Pinckney trumpeting that "no more shall paper money, no more shall tender-laws, drive their commerce from our shores, and darken the American name in every country where it is known," while David Ramsey argued that the contract clause and the prohibition of state-issued paper money "will doubtless bear hard on debtors who wish to defraud their creditors, but it will be a real service to the honest part of the community" (Ely 2008, 50).

In the years following ratification, state government interference in private contracts was greatly reduced. Debtor relief legislation occasionally arose in response to financial panics, and the courts vigorously applied the contract clause to strike down this legislation.[29] The panic of 1837 led to similar efforts to relieve debtors that were also struck down because of their retrospective application. In both Illinois and Alabama, laws allowing a debtor to redeem previously foreclosed property were struck down (*Bronson v. Kinzie*, 1843; *Howard v. Bugbee*, 1860). A similar fate befell Illinois and Indiana legislation that prohibited the sale of mortgaged property at prices below some fraction of its appraised value (*McCracken v. Hayward*, 1844; *Lessee of Gantley v. Ewing*, 1845; see also Wright [1938], 70).

The largest wave of debtor relief laws was passed during the Great Depression; in an 18-month period between 1933 and 1934, mortgage foreclosure moratorium legislation was enacted in 27 states. Concerned about the constitutionality of these laws, the statutes were designed to be qualitatively different from previous debt relief laws. The most famous example concerned a 1933 Minnesota statute that came before the US Supreme Court in *Home Building and Loan Association v. Blaisdell*, 1934. In this case, a 5-to-4 majority of the Supreme Court ruled that a 1933 Minnesota statute imposing a limited moratorium on the foreclosure of farm mortgages was constitutional. The court described in some detail what made this statute qualitatively different from previous debtor relief legislation that had been ruled unconstitutional. First, it was temporarily enacted in response to an emergency: the law was set to expire once the emergency was over, and in no case later than 1935. Second, it was a conditional moratorium subject to judicial review: debtors in need were allowed to appeal to state courts to have the existing period of redemption from foreclosure sales extended. Finally, it placed limits on the losses imposed on creditors; debtors were required to pay rents to creditors while they remained in possession (see Wright 1938; Olken 1993). The special nature of the statute at issue in the Blaisdell case was emphasized in succeeding cases that struck down debtor relief laws that applied indefinitely and did not discriminate on the basis of the needs of the debtor (*W. B. Worthen Company v. Thomas*, 1934).

Following the recession of the early 1980s, foreclosure moratorium acts were struck down by the Oklahoma Supreme Court (*Federal Land Bank of Wichita v. Story*, 1988), the Kansas Supreme Court (*Federal Land Bank of Wichita v. Bott*, 1987), and the Iowa Supreme Court (*Federal Land Bank of Omaha v. Arnold*, 1988). Only modest debtor relief laws, such as those requiring mediation between debtors and creditors, have been upheld (Walsh 2011). In the recent crisis, legislation was passed in 11 states affecting the mortgage foreclosure process, but in each case the laws served only to require some form of meeting between the borrower and lender before foreclosure. California, Indiana, Massachusetts, Michigan, and Oregon all now require a preforeclosure conference between the debtor and lender aimed at mitigating losses. Connecticut, Maine, Maryland, Nevada, New York, and Vermont now require some form of mediation between the borrower and the lender.

Together, these strong protections from government interference are why, in contrast to the case for private borrowers in emerging markets and in the euro zone, credit-rating agencies impose no linkage between the local sovereign rating and that for private borrowers in US states.[30] Much the same rationale exists for private-sector borrowers in Canada, which, as we will see next, enjoy similar protections from provincial government interference as their US counterparts.

Canada

Protections against provincial government interference in private contracts in Canada are similar to those available in the United States and stem from a similar place: the Canadian Constitution. Paragraph 91 of the Constitution Act, 1982 (formerly the British North America Act, 1867) vests in the Parliament of Canada the exclusive legislative authority over the regulation of trade and commerce, currency and coinage, the issuance of paper money, bills of exchange and promissory notes, legal tender, and bankruptcy and insolvency. That is, like US states, Canadian provinces cannot change legal tender, issue money, nor interfere in interprovincial (and international) trade and commerce.

However, paragraph 92 of the Constitution Act, 1982 does vest the provincial governments with the exclusive legislative authority over property rights within their own province. More than a century of jurisprudence has interpreted this expansively to include laws regarding contracts resulting in some overlap between federal and provincial laws regarding the treatment of debts.[31] As a result, although the provinces have no de jure power over interprovincial debts, they were able to exercise some de facto power over such debts and often used this power to favor local creditors over creditors from other provinces, creating a form of transfer and convertibility risk.

In the early years of the Dominion, the Parliament of Canada attempted to impose a federal insolvency law guaranteeing equal treatment of creditors both within and across provinces.[32] The Insolvency Acts of 1869 and 1875 prohibited an "unjust preference" made in "contemplation of insolvency" with the required proof being an intention to prefer one creditor over another. However, courts interpreted payments made following a creditor's request for repayment as involuntary and hence not an unjust preference (see Telfer 2014). As a result, there existed a de facto, if not de jure, preference in favor of local creditors—often family members and friends—who first observed signals of a debtors distress and could submit early requests for repayment. The rights of creditors from other provinces worsened with the repeal of the federal Insolvency Act in 1880, which led to a period in which a common law "race to courthouse" governed insolvent debtors, a situation that typically favored local creditors who could often initiate and obtain judgments before more distant creditors were informed of the debtor's distress. The provincial governments were slow to legislate to restrict the granting of preferences (New Brunswick only passed legislation in

1895, and Nova Scotia took until 1898) and the resulting legislation was often regarded as ineffectual (e.g., Ontario's law of 1880).

With the passage of the federal Bankruptcy Act of 1919, any de facto or de jure preference in favor of local debtors was eliminated. This situation remains in force today.

European Union

Compared with the legal protections against state and provincial government interference available to private creditors in the United States and Canada, the protections offered among the nations of the European Union are typically substantially weaker. One exception that holds only for those members in the euro zone is in regard to changes in legal tender; Article 128 (1) of the Treaty on the Functioning of the European Union (TFEU) makes euro-denominated banknotes and coins, and only such notes and coins, legal tender.[33] Hence, short of abandoning the euro—a possibility that appears to be explicitly ruled out in the TFEU—the members of the euro zone are unable to change legal tender.[34]

Other protections from government interference in European treaties and conventions are typically weakened by the presence of clauses allowing any such protection to be suspended whenever it is in the public interest. For example, Articles 63 and 65 of the TFEU, although designed to limit the use of capital controls by member states, allow capital controls that are "justified on grounds of public policy or public security," as well as the case law of the European Court of Justice allowing interventions "for overriding reasons of general public interest" (see European Commission 2013).[35]

The only other potential source of protection against government interference comes from Article 1 of Protocol to the Convention for the Protection of Human Rights and Fundamental Freedoms (CPHRFF). However, this clause does not prohibit government interference in private contracts per se; rather, it simply requires that such interference be "in the public interest" and subject to legal principles: "Every . . . person is entitled to the peaceful enjoyment of his possessions. No one shall be deprived of his possessions except in the public interest and subject to the conditions provided for by law and by the general principles of international law." Moreover, Article 15 of CPHRFF allows any government to suspend any human right or fundamental freedom in the event of a public emergency:

In time of war or other public emergency threatening the life of the nation any High Contracting Party may take measures derogating from its obligations under this Convention to the extent strictly required by the exigencies of the situation, provided that such measures are not inconsistent with its other obligations under international law.

In summary, investors in Europe lack the extensive protections against government interference enjoyed by investors in the US states and Canadian provinces today. Moreover, the experience of investors in emerging markets today, as well as in the US states and Canadian provinces throughout history, indicates that governments can be expected to interfere in contracts each time some public emergency, such as a debt crisis, allows them to justify interference "in the public interest."

IV. Fiscal Flexibility

We now briefly review the theoretical and empirical literatures on the link between fiscal flexibility and public debt sustainability. We first discuss the theoretical literature's finding that a government's decision to raise taxes as opposed to default on debt as a way of filling fiscal gaps is determined by the range of tax instruments available to it. We then discuss the empirical literature on debt sustainability, which relies on estimates of a government's ability to vary primary surpluses in response to debt levels and macroeconomic shocks, and the widespread finding that US states are less fiscally flexible than Canadian provinces or European nations. Last, we turn to a discussion of how ratings agencies assess fiscal flexibility when rating the debt of US state and Canadian provincial governments.

Following the theoretical work of Kydland and Prescott (1977) and Lucas and Stokey (1983), we see the sustainability of public debt as being determined by a government's ability to commit to use taxes and spending to generate the primary surpluses needed to repay the public debt rather than choose to default on that debt. In much of the literature, the trade-off the government faces when public debt is due is between the costs of current distortions connected with adjusting tax rates or levels of public expenditure with the reputational and/or resource costs of default on the public debt. This literature has found that whether or not that trade-off leads to a default on public debt depends on the range of tax instruments available to the government. If the government has access to taxes that impose only small distortions on the economy, then it will not be tempted to default on public debt held by domestic agents because closing fiscal gaps through increased taxation will generally be preferable to doing so through costly default on public debt. In contrast, if tax instruments are limited, then default on public debt can become a more attractive option, even if such a default is costly.[36] In this sense, this literature has emphasized a strong connection between fiscal flexibility as measured by the range of tax instruments available and the incentives to default on public debt.

This theoretical literature has led to a large recent literature on the sustainability of public debt that uses empirical estimates of the response of primary surpluses to debt levels and macroeconomic shocks as a reduced form measure of the ability of governments to adjust primary surpluses to repay public debts that can be an input in debt-sustainability calculations.[37] Along this dimension, there is considerable evidence that US states have a strongly procyclical fiscal response to macroeconomic shocks, suggesting fiscal rigidities caused by the nature of fiscal institutions in these states. For example, Poterba (1994), Bohn and Inman (1996), and Aizenman and Gunnarsson (2014) among others examine the impact of fiscal restrictions in US states on their fiscal adjustment to macroeconomic shocks. More relevant for our thesis, Poterba and Rueben (1999, 2001), Lowry and Alt (2001), and Johnson and Kriz (2005) estimate the extent to which legal restrictions on increasing revenue raise the cost of US state borrowing, both in terms of overall levels and in response to fiscal shocks. These modern findings complement the findings of historical studies of public debt in the United States. For example, Sargent (2012) discusses the role of fiscal inflexibility in shaping public debt crises in early US history. Similarly, Wallis (2000) discusses the importance of flexible revenue sources for determining the equilibrium level of public debt at the local, state, and federal levels of US government throughout American history. He shows how changes in institutions restricting the revenue sources available to local, state, and federal levels of US government have had a dramatic impact on these governments' abilities to sustain public debt at different points in history.

In practice, considerations of fiscal flexibility are also an important part of credit-ratings agencies' methodologies for the general obligation bonds issued by US states. When rating US states, Moody's makes an assessment of the role of constitutional constraints in reducing what they call the "financial flexibility" of each state. They argue that "[t]he constitutions of some states include provisions that limit financial flexibility and weaken the institutional governance framework. The initiative and referendum process can particularly constrain flexibility over time. California, Oregon, and Washington are among the states with the most active voter initiative processes, and in all three there have been long-run budgetary effects. Some states are constitutionally blocked from increasing revenues unless they put a referendum to the voters. Those states often can only look to the expenditure side of their budgets to close deficits when a two-pronged approach would offer more flexibility" (Raimes 2013). Similarly, Standard and Poor's provide each US state with a "revenue structure score" that reflects both institutional constraints and the track record of state policymakers with regard to raising revenue, which they use in their ratings.

Considerations of relative fiscal flexibility also play a major role in determining the relative credit ratings of US states relative to Canadian provinces. As Moody's explains, "California's legal and political environment creates obstacles to timely budget management and revenue raising, which restricts its freedom of action relative to other US states and some subsovereigns, including Ontario. Constitutional constraints on budgeting flexibility continue in California, although modest governance changes have helped the state achieve three years of on-time budget passage. California's reliance on highly progressive income taxes creates recurring revenue volatility and financial pressure and constrains California's rating. In comparison, Ontario has relatively stable revenues and like other Canadian provinces, has strong fiscal flexibility, on both the revenue and expenditure sides of the ledger" (Wong and Raimes 2013).

The finding that US states are less fiscally flexible than Canadian provinces and the subnational units of other federal systems is widespread. Rodden and Wibbels (2010) study seven federal systems and conclude that US states engage in far less expenditure smoothing than do the provinces of Canada, as well as the subnational governments of several other countries. Looking at the most recent business cycle, Jonas (2012) also concludes that "[e]ven though a similar procyclical fiscal tightening has been observed at the subnational level during the latest crisis in a number of advanced economies, the US's tightening appears to have been among the most pronounced." In contrast to the United States, Canada is viewed as one of the most decentralized countries in the world in which the provinces "have a virtual free hand in levying taxes" (Bird and Tassonyi 2003). The extent of expenditure smoothing for US states documented by Rodden and Wibbles (2010) also seems low relative to estimates computed for members of the European Union in Hallerberg and Strauch (2002).

V. Model

We now present a theory of external debt constraints and public debt constraints based on the interaction of the risk of sovereign interference with private debt contracts and fiscal flexibility. We use a simple two-period model to illustrate our main points.

A. Environment

Consider a model of a small open economy with two time periods, $t = 1$, 2. This small open economy has access to opportunities to borrow from risk-neutral international creditors. These international creditors have a time discount factor equal to one, and hence the equilibrium (net) international riskless interest rate is equal to zero. This small open economy consists of a representative household, domestic financial intermediaries, and a government that chooses policies to maximize the welfare of the representative household.

The household has utility over private consumption C_t and public expenditure G_t of the form

$$u(C_1) + u(G_1) + u(C_2) + u(G_2).$$

The household is endowed with Y_t units of the consumption good at time $t = 1, 2$, with $Y_1 < Y_2$. This assumption, combined with zero discounting by households and international creditors, ensures that agents in this economy have a motivation to borrow from the international creditors in period $t = 1$ so as to smooth private and public expenditure over time. Specifically, given an international gross interest rate of one, the unconstrained optimal allocation would equate private consumption and public expenditure in all periods such that

$$C_t^* = G_t^* = \frac{1}{4}(Y_1 + Y_2). \tag{1}$$

To implement this unconstrained optimal allocation, this small open economy would incur external debt $D^* = (1 / 2)(Y_2 - Y_1)$ in period $t = 1$ and repay this amount of external debt in period $t = 2$. In the unconstrained optimal allocation, the households' intertemporal marginal rate of substitution for private consumption $u_1'^*) / u_2'^*)$ is equal to the international riskless (gross) interest rate of 1. The same is true of households' intertemporal marginal rate of substitution for public consumption $u_1'^*) / u_2'^*)$.

Borrowing and Default Costs. The government borrows from international creditors D^g and from domestic financial intermediaries B^g. Households borrow from domestic financial intermediaries B^p. Domestic financial intermediaries borrow from international creditors D^p. We refer to the sum of public and private external debt $D^g + D^p$ as the external debt of the country and to the sum of domestic and foreign public debt $B^g + D^g$ as the public debt of the country. In all cases this notation refers to the principal and interest due in period 2. Resources borrowed in period 1 are equal to these amounts times the price of these debts in period 1.

Domestic financial intermediaries and households can commit to repay their debts unless the government interferes with private debt contracts. The government, in contrast, is unable to commit to repay its external and domestic debts and not to interfere with private external debt contracts.

We assume that government default or interference with private external debt contracts imposes a resource cost on the economy in terms of reducing Y_2. The costs of default on external public debt D^g is $\Delta^{dg} \geq 0$; the costs of default on domestic public debt B^g is $\Delta^{bg} \geq 0$; and the costs of government interference with private external debt contracts D^p is $\Delta^p \geq 0$.[38]

Note that we consider the possibility that the government would make separate default decisions on its domestically held and external public debts. In some cases, governments are able to make these separate default decisions because the different types of debt it owes are governed by different laws: domestic and foreign. Alternatively, a government may implement differential default on its externally held public debts and its domestically held public debts (or, at least, those public debts held by domestic financial intermediaries) by defaulting on all of its public debts and then using government funds to bail out domestic financial intermediaries. This is the interpretation that we follow here.

These resource costs of default on public debt and interference with private external debt contracts are potentially stochastic. We denote the realized value of these costs in period 2 by the vector $\Delta = (\Delta^{dg}, \Delta^{bg}, \Delta^p)$. We assume that the cumulative distribution function of these costs is given by $F(\Delta)$. These stochastic costs imply that in equilibrium private and public consumption in period $t = 2$ are also potentially stochastic.

Binding Debt Constraints. In what follows, we will say that the country faces no binding debt constraints, external or public, if it is able to implement the unconstrained optimal allocation (1) in equilibrium. If it is not able to implement the unconstrained optimal allocation in equilibrium, then we say that it faces a binding external or public debt constraint depending on the equilibrium intertemporal marginal rate of substitution of private and public expenditures, respectively.

The commitment problem on the part of the government in our model leads to the households facing a *binding external debt constraint* in equilibrium if $u'(C_1) > Eu'(C_2)$. That is, we say that the country faces a binding external debt constraint if households are constrained from doing the borrowing needed to finance the unconstrained optimal timing of consumption. Taking the household's intertemporal marginal rate of substitution $Eu'(C_2) / u'(C_1) = 1 / R$ as the inverse equilibrium domestic riskless interest rate in this small open economy, we then have, equivalently, that the households face a binding external debt constraint if the equilibrium domestic riskless interest rate in this small open economy exceeds the international riskless interest rate.

In parallel, we say that the commitment problem on the part of the government leads to the government facing a *binding public debt constraint* in equilibrium if, in that equilibrium, $u'(G_1) > Eu'(G_2)$. In this case, household welfare would be increased if the government were able to raise more resources in period $t = 1$ to finance increased government expenditure relative to the government expenditure in period $t = 2$.

Government Policy. We consider two possible regimes restricting the government's choice of taxes in both periods τ_1 and τ_2 to be paid by households. In the first regime, which we term the *flexible tax regime*, we assume that the government can choose taxes freely. In the second regime, which we term the *inflexible tax regime*, we assume that taxes are predetermined as parameters that cannot be altered.

In period 1 the government chooses public expenditure G_1, and domestic and external public indebtedness B^g and D^g due in period 2. The prices paid for these public debts in period 1 are determined endogenously and reflect the risk of government default and interference. In equilibrium, these prices are functions of private external debts and public domestic and external debts $D = (D^p, B^g, D^g)$. The government also chooses taxes τ_1 in the flexible tax regime. Government policies in period 1 must satisfy the budget constraint

$$G_1 = \tau_1 + q^{bg}(D)B^g + q^{dg}(D)D^g, \tag{2}$$

where $q^{bg}(D)$ and $q^{dg}(D)$ are the prices for domestic and external public debt, respectively.

In period $t = 2$, the government chooses whether to repay domestic debt ($I^{bg} = 1$) or not ($I^{bg} = 0$); whether to repay external public debt ($I^{dg} = 1$) or not ($I^{dg} = 0$); and whether to interfere with private external debt contracts ($I^p = 0$) or not ($I^p = 1$), taking the outstanding debts due $D = (D^p, B^g, D^g)$ and the realized costs of default and/or interference Δ as given. For simplicity, we assume that default and interference can be partial by allowing $I^j \in [0, 1]$ for $j = bg, dg, p$. The resource costs of partial default and/or interference are partial and in proportion to the default and/or interference.

The government then chooses public expenditures G_2 and, in the flexible tax regime, taxes τ_2 contingent on these default and interference decisions. We let $I = (I^{bg}, I^{dg}, I^p)$ denote the government's default and interference decisions. We write government policy in period $t = 2$ as functions of private and public debts D and the realized resource costs of default and interference with private external debt contracts Δ as needed. The government's budget constraint in period 2 is given by

$$G_2(D, \Delta) = \tau_2(D, \Delta) - I^{bg}(D, \Delta)B^g - I^{dg}(D, \Delta)D^g. \tag{3}$$

Pricing of External Debts. International creditors take as given government default and interference decisions as functions of the country's aggregate indebtedness D and the default costs Δ and set prices for external borrowing by the government $q^{dg}(D)$ and the domestic private agents $q^p(D)$ to ensure that they receive expected gross return of one on their lending to the public and private sector in this country. Thus, these prices for external borrowing are given by

$$q^{dg}(D) = \int I^{dg}(D, \Delta)dF(\Delta) \tag{4}$$

and

$$q^p(D) = \int I^p(D, \Delta)dF(\Delta). \tag{5}$$

We then define the spread on public external debt as $S^{dg}(D) = 1 / q^{dg}(D) - 1$ and the spread on private external debt as $S^p(D) = 1 / q^p(D) - 1$.

The Decision to Default or Interfere with Debts with Flexible Taxes. In period 2, the government chooses its decisions to default on public debts or interfere with private external debts together with taxes τ_2 to maximize the welfare of the representative household, taking as given outstanding debts due $D = (D^p, B^g, D^g)$ and the realized costs of default and/or interference $\Delta = (\Delta^{dg}, \Delta^{bg}, \Delta^p)$. It is straightforward to show that with flexible taxes, the government's decision to default on its public debts and its decision to interfere with private external debts are made based on a simple comparison of the size of these debts relative to the resource costs of default or interference. In contrast, government will not default on its domestic public debts B^g regardless of how small the costs of such a default might be. Moreover, taxes are set to equate public and private consumption.

Lemma 1. *With flexible taxes, the government will default on its public external debt D^g iff $D^g > \Delta^{dg}$; it will interfere with private external debts if $D^p > \Delta^p$; and it will not default on its domestic public debt B^g for any value of $\Delta^{bg} > 0$.*

Proof. Household welfare in period 2 is given by

$$u(C_2(D, \Delta)) + u(G_2(D, \Delta)).$$

Government provision of the public good $G_2(D, \Delta)$ is given as a function of debt and policies by equation (3).

Private consumption in period 2 is given by the household budget constraint in the second period

$$C_2(D, \Delta) = Y_2 - \sum_{j=bg,dg,p} (1 - I^j(D, \Delta))\Delta^j - \tau_2(D, \Delta) + \Pi(D, \Delta) - B^p, \quad (6)$$

where $\Pi(D, \Delta)$ are the profits that the households receive as owners of the domestic financial intermediaries and $\sum_{j=bg,dg,p}(1 - I^j(D, \Delta))\Delta^j$ are the realized resource costs of the government's default and/or interference decisions.

The aggregate profits of domestic financial intermediaries in period 2 are given by

$$\Pi(D, \Delta) = B^p + I^{bg}(D, \Delta)B^g - I^p(D, \Delta)D^p, \quad (7)$$

since these intermediaries enter the period with assets comprising of loans to the domestic households B^p and loans to the government B^g and liabilities comprising of borrowings from abroad D^p.

By plugging equation (7) for the aggregate profits of domestic financial intermediaries into the period 2 budget constraint of households, we have that private consumption in period 2 is given by

$$C_2(D, \Delta) = Y_2 - \sum_{j=bg,dg,p} (1 - I^j(D, \Delta))\Delta^j - \tau_2(D, \Delta)$$
$$+ I^{bg}(D, \Delta)B^g - I^p(D, \Delta)D^p. \quad (8)$$

Finally, using equation (3) to solve for taxes $\tau_2(D, \Delta)$ and plugging this expression into (8), we get

$$C_2(D, \Delta) + G_2(D, \Delta) = Y_2 - \sum_{j=bg,dg,p} (1 - I^j(D, \Delta))\Delta^j$$

$$- I^{dg}(D, \Delta)D^g - I^p(D, \Delta)D^p. \tag{9}$$

Because the government has full flexibility in setting $\tau_2(D, \Delta)$, it can choose these taxes to implement any combination of private and public second-period consumption that satisfies this joint constraint (9). Thus, with flexible taxes, it is clear that the government maximizes welfare by setting taxes to equate public and private consumption $C_2(D, \Delta) = G_2(D, \Delta)$ and defaulting on external public debt D^g or interfering with private external debt D^p whenever such debts exceed the resource costs of default or interference. In contrast, there is no benefit to default on domestically held public debt because such a default imposes a cost Δ^{bg} reducing resources available for private and public consumption that does not need to be incurred if taxes rather than domestic default is used to finance government expenditures. Hence, the government always chooses to honor domestically held public debts.

We now derive our key results regarding equilibrium in the version of the model in which the government is free to choose taxes fully flexibly.

Canadian Provinces: Neither External nor Public Borrowing Constraints Bind. We first show that with flexible taxes, if the government can commit not to interfere with private external debt contracts, then neither the external nor the public debt constraint can bind in the first period. That is, as long as the costs of sovereign interference with private contracts are large enough, then the country is able to achieve the unconstrained first-best allocation, borrowing abroad privately as necessary. This result holds independently of the resource costs Δ^{bg} and Δ^{dg} of defaulting on domestic and external public debt. We interpret this result as characteristic of Canadian provinces.

Proposition 1. *Assume that $\Delta^p \geq (1 / 2)(Y_2 - Y_1)$ with probability 1 and taxes are fully flexible. Then neither the external nor the public debt constraints binds.*

Proof. We prove this result by showing that the unconstrained optimal allocation in equation (1) can be implemented as an equilibrium. Recall that $D^* = (1 / 2)(Y_2 - Y_1)$ denotes the level of external debt needed to fund the unconstrained optimal allocation for the country. By assumption, we have that $Prob(\Delta^p \geq D^*) = 1$ so that $I^p(D^*, \Delta) = 1$ for all realizations of Δ and hence, from equation (5), the domestic financial intermediaries are able to borrow the unconstrained optimal level of external debt D^* abroad privately at the international riskless interest rate of 1.

To show that the unconstrained socially optimal allocation (1) can actually be implemented as an equilibrium allocation, we must show that the government is able to obtain the resources it needs in each period to pay for the optimal level of public good provision $G_1^* = G_2^* = (1 / 4)(Y_1 + Y_2)$. If we assume that the government has no constraints on its choice of taxes, then this can be accomplished simply by setting taxes $\tau_1 = \tau_2 = (Y_1 + Y_2) / 4$ and having the government run a balanced budget with $G_1 = \tau_1$ and $G_2 = \tau_2$. With a balanced budget, it is clear that both domestic and external public debt are equal to zero ($B^G = D^g = 0$). Thus, we have that the government has no incentive to default on public debts.

Note that with these taxes, the household then has after-tax wealth of $(Y_1 + Y_2) / 2$ and faces a domestic interest rate equal to the international interest rate, so $R = 1$. In equilibrium, the household then consumes the socially optimal levels of private consumption $C_1 = C_2 = (Y_1 + Y_2) / 4$ and borrows internationally through the domestic financial intermediaries $D^p = C_1 + \tau_1 - Y_1 = (Y_2 - Y_1) / 2$. Note since the domestic interest rate $R = 1$ and the price at which the domestic financial intermediaries are able to borrow from abroad is $q^p(D) = 1$, the equilibrium profits of these intermediaries are $\Pi = 0$. Thus this allocation can be implemented as an equilibrium.

Our proof of this proposition uses a particularly strong argument based on the fact that, with flexible taxes, government can change the timing of taxes as needed to balance its budget every period and look to the private sector to do whatever external borrowing is needed to finance the first-best allocation of consumption. Such a strong argument is not, in fact, required. The government does not need to run a balanced budget to implement the unconstrained socially optimal allocation when the government can commit to not interfere with private external debt contracts ($\Delta^p \geq (1 / 2)(Y_2 - Y_1)$ with probability 1) and taxes are fully flexible. Instead, as we have shown above, the government can credibly commit to not default on domestic public debt regardless of the costs of such a default. As a result, as we show in the next proposition, the equilibrium satisfies a particular form of Ricardian equivalence with regard to domestically issued public debt.

Proposition 2.   *Assume that $\Delta^p \geq (1 / 2)(Y_2 - Y_1)$ with probability 1 and that taxes are flexible. Then it is possible to implement the unconstrained so-*

cially optimal allocation as an equilibrium with any values of government borrowing from domestic financial intermediaries $B^g \leq (1 / 4)(Y_1 + Y_2) = G_1^*$ *even if the costs of defaulting on public debt* Δ^{dg} *and* Δ^{bg} *are arbitrarily low.*

Proof. The proof of this proposition relies on the observation from Lemma 1 that, in period 2, default on domestically held public debt has the equivalent impact on the resources available for private and public expenditure as an increase in taxes, except that it entails a reduction in resources available for private and public consumption in period 2 of Δ^{bg}. Thus, as long as the costs of default on public debt $\Delta^{bg} > 0$, the government will strictly prefer to raise taxes to repay domestically held public debt rather than choosing to default on that debt. Even if these costs are zero, the government will weakly prefer to use taxes rather than default on domestic debt in period $t = 2$ to finance government expenditure.

Note that our Ricardian equivalence result applies only to public *domestic* borrowing and not public *external* borrowing. That is, if low realizations of the resource cost Δ^{dg} are possible, then public external borrowing may lead to costly default in equilibrium, which would imply that it would not be possible to implement the unconstrained socially optimal allocation.

We interpret Propositions 1 and 2 as appropriate for Canadian provinces with commitment not to interfere with private debt contracts and flexible taxes. We argue that these provincial governments are able to issue a substantial amount of public debt held by domestic residents with little apparent risk of binding external or public debt constraints.

Euro Zone Countries: Binding External and Public Borrowing Constraints. We now turn to consider the case in which the costs of interfering with private contracts may be low enough such that the government does wish to interfere with these contracts for at least some realizations of Δ^p. We show that if the resource costs of sovereign interference and default Δ are deterministic and taxes are flexible then, if the public constraint is binding, the external debt constraint is binding as well. We interpret this case as characteristic of euro zone countries.

Proposition 3. *Assume that the resource costs of sovereign interference and/ or default Δ are deterministic. If the government has full flexibility in setting taxes then, in any equilibrium, if the public debt constraint is binding in period 1 then the external debt constraint is binding as well.*

Proof. Using the results of Lemma 1, we have that when the costs of default are deterministic, the equilibrium price of private external debt is then $q^p(D) = 1$ if $D^p \leq \Delta^p$ and zero otherwise because default does not occur in equilibrium. Likewise, the equilibrium price of public external debt is $q^{dg}(D) = 1$ if $D^g \leq \Delta^{dg}$ and zero otherwise. Thus, the total combined amount of resources that this country can borrow from abroad in period 1 is $q^p(D)D^p + q^{dg}(D)D^g \leq \Delta^p + \Delta^{dg}$. If this limit on external debt $\Delta^p + \Delta^g > D^*$, then it will be possible to implement the unconstrained socially optimal allocation as an equilibrium outcome, as we discussed for the case of Canadian provinces.

Now consider the case in which the limit on external debt $\Delta^p + \Delta^g < D^*$ so that it is not possible to implement the unconstrained optimal allocation. In this case, we must have that the sum of public and private consumption in period 1, $C_1 + G_1$, is less than the sum of the unconstrained optimal levels of public and private consumption, $C_1^* + G_1^*$. Likewise, because there are no resource costs of default in equilibrium, we also have that private and public consumption in period 2 both exceed their optimal levels $C_2 = G_2 > C_2^* = G_2^*$. Thus, we must have that either the public or the external debt constraint is binding, or they are both binding.

To show that both the public and the external debt constraints must bind at the same time, we must use the assumption that the government chooses fiscal policy in period 1 to maximize welfare subject to its limited power of commitment. What the government would like to do in period 1 to maximize welfare is to choose taxes τ_1 and/or domestic public borrowing B^g to equate private and public consumption $C_1 = G_1$ in period 1 as well as in period 2. Given the constraint on overall external borrowing given by $\Delta^p + \Delta^g < D^*$, this means that in an equilibrium in which financial and fiscal policies are chosen optimally in period 1 as well as in period 2, we have

$$C_1 = G_1 = \frac{1}{2}(Y_1 + \Delta^p + \Delta^{dg}),$$

$$C_2 = G_2 = \frac{1}{2}(Y_2 - \Delta^p - \Delta^{dg}),$$

so that both the external and public debt constraints are binding.

In this case with deterministic costs of sovereign interference and default, it is straightforward to find the constrained optimal equilibrium because no default occurs in equilibrium. In the case with stochastic default costs Δ, the government faces the additional consideration in choosing its fiscal policy in period 1 that its choice of policies impacts both domestic and public external borrowing and hence the equilibrium probability of resource costs in period 2 due to default and/or interference with private external debt. Hence, in this case, the government may wish to constrain its period 1 expenditures (choose $G_1 < C_1$) to reduce the need for private and/or public external borrowing. Such a government might also wish to implement ex ante controls on private external borrowing in period 1 to avoid the temptation to interfere with that borrowing in period 2. Of course, such ex ante capital controls would be inconsistent with the free movement of capital envisioned for countries in the euro zone.

California: Public Debt Constraints with Inflexible Taxes. We now consider a modified version of this economy in which the government has constraints on its ability to set taxes. In particular, assume that τ_1 and τ_2 are fixed at given levels. We now show that when the government is unable to alter taxes in period $t = 2$ to finance its desired level of public expenditures, then it may be tempted to default on outstanding public debts, both external and domestic, as a substitute for taxation for raising revenue. This temptation arises when public expenditure is constrained by rigid low taxes relative to private consumption. This incentive to default on both domestic and external public debts in period 2 can lead to a binding public debt constraint in period 1, with the government unable to raise additional resources through public borrowing either domestically or abroad, even if the private sector is unconstrained in its external borrowing. We interpret this outcome as characteristic of California.

Consider the government's incentives to default on its public debts in period $t = 2$ when taxes are rigid at τ_2. As in the case in the economy with flexible taxes, public and private consumption are given by equations (3) and (8). But now, since taxes τ_2 are inflexible, the choices of public and private expenditure that can be implemented are restricted to those combinations that satisfy equation (9) together with inequalities $G_2(D, \Delta) \leq \tau_2$ and $C_2(D, \Delta) \geq Y_2 - \Sigma_{j=bg,dg,p}(1 - I^j(D, \Delta))\Delta^j - \tau_2$ because the government cannot alter taxes. Because of these restrictions on the choice of public and private consumption in period $t = 2$, now the government may be tempted to default on domestically held public debt even if such a default entails a resource cost that reduces private expenditure over and above the reduction due to the default on the debt itself. This is because, with inflexible taxes, the government has no alternative means of raising revenue other than default on its public debts. Thus, in this environment with fiscal inflexibility, in contradiction to the case with fiscal flexibility, it is possible for the country to face a binding public debt constraint without facing a binding external debt constraint.

We can understand these incentives for the government to default on its domestically public debts as follows. Given realized values of (D, Δ), the government's equilibrium default decisions on domestically and externally held public debt are the choices of I^{bg} and I^{dg} in the interval $[0, 1]$ that maximize welfare $u(C_2) + u(G_2)$ with public and public consumption given by (3) and (8) with taxes τ_2 fixed.

Consider first the government's decision to default on its external public debts. Such a default is optimal if the value of the debt, in utility units, exceeds the value of the default resource cost, also in utility units, or

$$u'(G_2)D^g > u'(C_2)\Delta^{dg}.$$

This result is a simple generalization of the default rule on external public debts with flexible taxes since, with flexible taxes, $G_2 = C_2$, and hence, $I^{dg}(D, \Delta) = 0$ if $D^g > \Delta^{dg}$ and 1 otherwise. Here we see that if taxes are rigid and constrained to be low, so that, in equilibrium, $G_2 < C_2$, then the government will default on external debts D^g even if the costs of such a default Δ^{dg} are somewhat in excess of the amount D^g owed on these debts because, in this case, the marginal social utility of public expenditures strictly exceeds the marginal social utility of private expenditures.

The same logic also can be used to understand the government's decision to default on domestically held public debts. Now the necessary condition for optimality of the default decision requires that default occurs when

$$u'(G_2)B^g > u'(C_2)(B^g + \Delta^{bg}).$$

Note that this condition cannot be satisfied in the economy with flexible taxes because, with flexible taxes, $G_2 = C_2$ and hence $u'(G_2) = u'(C_2)$. This logic delivered us the result that a government with flexible taxes could credibly commit to repay its domestically held public debts in period $t = 2$ regardless of the costs of default on these debts. With rigid taxes, however, it is possible that in equilibrium, we have that $G_2 < C_2$ because τ_2 is set low and hence we may have that in equilibrium, the marginal social utility of public expenditures strictly exceeds the marginal social utility of private expenditures. In this case, we have that government will wish to default on its domestically held public debts whenever those debts are large enough relative to the costs of default.

To develop an example economy in which the government does in fact face a binding public debt constraint in equilibrium with inflexible taxes, assume that default costs Δ are deterministic and satisfy

$$\Delta^{bg} + \Delta^{dg} < Y_2 - 2\tau_2. \tag{10}$$

This inequality (10) implies that $C_2(D) > G_2(D)$ for all values of D even if the government defaults on all of its public debt both domestic and external.

In this case, the government is able to raise up to $\bar{D}^g$ in external public debts in period 1 at price $q^{dg}(D) = 1$ for $D^g \leq \bar{D}^g$ and zero otherwise, where

$$\bar{D}^g = \frac{u'(Y_2 - \tau_2 - \Delta^{bg} - \Delta^{dg})}{u'(\tau_2)} \Delta^{dg}.$$

Furthermore, as long as inequality (10) is satisfied, the government is able to raise domestically held public debts up to $\bar{B}^g$ at price $q^{bg}(D) = 1$ for $B^g \leq \bar{B}^g$ and zero otherwise, where $\bar{B}^g$ solves

$$\frac{\bar{B}^g}{\bar{B}^g + \Delta^{bg}} = \frac{u'(Y_2 - \tau_2 - \Delta^{bg} - \Delta^{dg})}{u'(\tau_2)}.$$

The government then faces a binding public debt constraint in period 1 if the implied public debt limit $\bar{B}^g + \bar{D}^g$ together with the rigid taxes τ_1 in period 1 are not large enough to finance public expenditure $G_1 = G_2$.

Note that if the cost of interference with private external debt contracts Δ^p is high, then it will be possible for the households to borrow abroad as desired to implement optimal private consumption

$$C_1 = C_2 = \frac{1}{2}(Y_1 - \tau_1 + Y_2 - \tau_2)$$

by borrowing abroad privately $D^p = C_1 + \tau_1 - Y_1$ at the international riskless interest rate of 1. We interpret such an equilibrium as corresponding to California.

VI. Conclusions

When the member countries of the euro zone established their monetary union, neither academics nor policymakers anticipated that member states might experience external debt crises.[39] Policymakers' optimism is nicely captured in the European Commission's One Market, One Money report (1990) which posits that "a major effect of EMU is that balance-of-payments constraints will disappear [. . .]. Private markets will finance all viable borrowers, and savings and investment balances will no longer be constraints at the national level." As described in Merler and Pisani-Ferry (2012), policymakers made no explicit provisions for addressing external debt crises among euro zone member states. Rather, policymakers focused on constraining public debt through provisions in the Maastricht Treaty. As a result of this lack of attention to external debt, solutions to the current crisis have had to be improvised.

The academic literature has not provided clear-cut guidance on how to address external debt crises within the euro zone. In part, this is because the literature is typically segmented. Most models of the risk of default on external debt consider the domestic government and private sector as a unified actor, whereas most models of the sustainability of public debt are conducted within closed economies. Our contribution to this literature is to integrate the analysis of default incentives on external and public debt in a simple unified model.

What lessons for addressing debt crises within the euro zone do we draw from our analysis? First, the experiences of Canada and the United States indicate that stronger institutional foundations mitigate the risk of government interference with private contracts. The freedom of private capital flows within the United States and Canada benefits from a strong legal foundation of protection under constitutional law together with federal bankruptcy law and uniform laws governing securities markets. The freedom of these capital flows has also been enhanced over time, particularly in the United States, by the development of stronger federal foundations underpinning the banking system. Although we have not discussed banking explicitly in this paper, the development of an integrated continent-wide banking system in the United States has been a gradual process carried out over two centuries marked by repeated crisis and reform. In contrast, as discussed in Bordo, Redish, and Rockoff (2015), Canada has had a strong nationwide banking system from relatively early on in its history and has been largely free of banking crises. Of course, one often-noted potential benefit of establishing a stronger banking system in the euro zone would be to reduce the risk of member government interference with private contracts in times of crisis.

Second, the institutional features governing fiscal flexibility for state and provincial governments in the United States and Canada also provide lessons for the development of new fiscal institutions in Europe. As described in Sargent (2012) and Henning and Kessler (2012), US states have chosen somewhat distinctive fiscal institutions that result in equilibrium in relatively tight constraints on state government borrowing. In contrast, Canadian provincial governments enjoy much greater fiscal flexibility and as a result are able to sustain substantially higher levels of public debt. These starkly different outcomes suggest that Europe should carefully consider the implications of restrictions on the fiscal flexibility of member states for the future sustainability of public debt.

VII.   Epilogue: An Unfolding Tale of Two Sovereign Defaults

In late June of 2015, after this paper was written, the leaders of the governments of Greece and Puerto Rico nearly simultaneously announced that it was likely that they would default on their respective public debts.[40] These two public debt crises share many aspects in common. In both Greece and Puerto Rico, the governments' fiscal condition has been exacerbated by very large and prolonged recessions.[41] Both governments face high and rising costs of further borrowing, making it infeasible for them to roll over their existing debts. For both governments, the legal structure to support a rescheduling of their debts is fraught with all the uncertainty surrounding a sovereign default.[42]

But there is one dimension in which these two public debt crises differ—the extent to which this public debt crisis has spilled over to the private sector. In the case of Greece, the public debt crisis has been accompanied by a run on Greek banks that has led the government to interfere in private debt contracts by declaring a bank holiday, limiting deposit withdrawals, and imposing controls on capital outflows. On June 29, in response to these measures, Standard and Poor's downgraded the counterparty credit ratings of the four main Greek banks to "SD" (selective default) and the ratings of their senior unsecured debt to "CCC–". Standard and Poor's (2015c) summarizes the outlook for these Greek banks as follows:

We view the banks' liquidity positions as having weakened further after these recent events, which we see as constraining the banks' ability to meet their upcoming financial obligations, when due. We therefore believe the default of the Greek banks is a virtual certainty unless unexpected additional external support materializes.

Standard and Poor's (2015a) has also begun downgrading the credit ratings of Greek nonfinancial corporations.

In contrast, while the recession and public debt crisis in Puerto Rico has implications for the credit ratings of that island's banks, the impact of this public debt crisis on these banks is more limited than in Greece due to the legal certainty that the Commonwealth of Puerto Rico is not able to interfere with private external debt contracts.[43] Specifically, on June 29th, Standard and Poor's (2015b) downgraded the general obligation bonds of Puerto Rico to "CCC–" and wrote "The downgrades are based on our view that a default, distressed exchange, or redemption of the commonwealth's debt appears to be inevitable within the next six months absent unanticipated significantly favorable changes in the issuers' circumstances." The credit rating agencies' views on Puerto Rican banks, however, are more measured, even given the likelihood of a default on the public debt. For example, in February of 2015, Moody's (2015) affirmed its ratings of three of the largest Puerto Rican banks writing

The bank rating affirmations take into account Puerto Rico's current economic conditions, which, although very weak, remain within Moody's expectations for the banks' liquidity and capital profiles. The affirmations were in contrast to the downgrade of Puerto Rico's GO bond rating, which reflected not only the commonwealth's continued economic weakness, but also its reduced liquidity, which has increased the probability of default on central government debt over the next two years. Moody's said the three banks' ratings already incorporate risks stemming from Puerto Rico's broader economic and fiscal challenges, including the high probability of a public-sector default.

It remains to be seen how the macroeconomic implications of the public debt crises in Greece and Puerto Rico will play out. Clearly, in Greece, the public debt crisis has also morphed into an external debt crisis, largely due to sovereign interference with private debt contracts. In Puerto Rico, while there is no risk of such sovereign interference with private contracts, the overall uncertainty surrounding a public debt default is also likely to have an important impact on the private economy. Only time will tell what the resolution of these two public debt crises will look like.

Endnotes

We thank Aaron Kirkman for excellent research assistance. Wright thanks the National Science Foundation for support under grant SES-1059829. The views expressed herein are those of the authors and not necessarily those of the Federal Reserve Bank of Chicago, the Federal Reserve Bank of Minneapolis, or the Federal Reserve System. For acknowledgments, sources of research support, and disclosure of the authors' material financial relationships, if any, please see http://www.nber.org/chapters/c13604.ack. E-mails: arellano.cristina@gmail.com; andy@atkeson.net; mwright@frbchi.org.

1. Bocola (2015) develops a model where public debt crises hurt the balance sheets of banks that hold sovereign debt and lead them to tighten private loans. Farhi and Tirole

(2015) consider a similar mechanism and add government bailouts to banks. They argue that these feedback loops between banks and the government are important for the recent euro zone crisis.

2. The Eleventh Amendment of the US Constitution restricts suits in federal courts against states. In contrast, municipalities, such as Detroit, can undergo a court-supervised bankruptcy process under Chapter 9 of the US bankruptcy code.

3. See Mysak (2010) for a description of Arkansas' default on its debt during the Great Depression.

4. As shown in the case of Virginia, this was not the case for all US states. The spreads shown for Virginia are relatively low and stable.

5. Ang and Longstaff (2013) perform a more systematic comparison of the levels and comovements of the sovereign spreads for US states and euro zone countries. This observation of high credit spreads for US state governments is not unique to the financial crisis of 2008. California, in particular, has had a history of budgetary difficulties reflected in heightened credit spreads in 2003 and 2004, for example.

6. Reinhart, Rogoff, and Savastano (2003) introduced the term "debt intolerance" to describe the combination of high spreads at low external debt to GDP levels observed for many emerging market economies. We borrow this term here to refer to the combination of high spreads at low public debt to GDP levels observed for several US state governments.

7. See, for example, Henning and Kessler (2012). On top of restrictions on debt, many states have restrictions on expenditures and revenues. In the case of California, these are seen as being particularly binding. See, for example, Wong and Raimes (2013).

8. This recent experience is consistent with the earlier findings of Bayoumi, Goldstein, and Woglom (1995). They estimate the spreads charged on debt of US state governments over the period 1981–1990 as a function of various determinants, including the overall debt level. They estimate a Laffer curve for levels of state indebtedness with a peak at indebtedness of 8.7% of state GDP.

9. See Calvo (1998) for a discussion of the genesis of this term.

10. See also IMF (2012) and de Sola Perea and Van Niewenhuyze (2014) for further decomposition of these flows.

11. These authors construct indices of credit spreads in euro zone countries using data on a comprehensive panel of bonds issued by both financial and nonfinancial firms in Germany, France, Italy, and Spain over the period 1999–2013. We focus on bonds issued by nonfinancial firms.

12. Klein and Stellner (2014), Bendendo and Colla (2013), and Bai and Wei (2014) also find similar evidence on the comovement of private and sovereign CDS spreads in both euro zone countries and emerging markets after adding many controls.

13. Tom Petruno, "Wall Street Awaits California's Short-Term Borrowing Plans." *Los Angeles Times*, July 3, 2009.

14. As described in Borensztein, Cowan, and Valenzuela (2013), prior to 1997, this sovereign credit ceiling was applied to all private borrowers in emerging-market countries. During the middle of the first decade of the twenty-first century, this policy was somewhat relaxed, and, in the case of euro zone countries, it was removed altogether in 2005 by both Standard and Poor's and Moody's Investors Service. See, for example, Beers, Cavanaugh, and Feinland-Katz (2005), Truglia (2005), and Cavanaugh and Feinland-Katz (2009), as well as Stendevad (2007). As we discuss in this section, the main credit-rating agencies reconsidered this policy of relaxing the sovereign credit ceiling for private borrowers in euro zone countries following the recent concerns about the possible exit of countries from the euro.

15. See, for example, Fox and Renwick (2014), Gates, Wilson, and Duggar (2012), and Feinland-Katz and Chu (2013). See Loh and Frey (2011) and Chu (2014) for discussions of the impact of the euro zone sovereign credit crisis on the ratings for structured finance transactions.

16. There is a large literature on the linkage between sovereign debt spreads and financing difficulties for banks in both emerging-market economies and the euro zone. See, for example, Reinhart and Rogoff (2013).

17. See, for example, IMF (2012, 39).

18. See Fox and Renwick (2014) and Moody's (2009).

19. For a discussion of this point, see, for example, Cavanaugh and Feinland-Katz (2009) and Heinrichs and Stanoeva (2013).

20. See, for example, Beers et al. (2005) and Truglia (2005).

21. Thinking about the legal basis for sovereign interference with private contracts in the euro zone is rapidly evolving. Slaughter and May (2012) present a summary of the legal issues a company operating in the euro zone would face in the wake of a sovereign default crisis and possible euro exit. Pykett, Harding, and James (2013) provide a discussion of the legal foundations for capital and exchange controls for euro zone countries following the imposition of such controls in Cyprus. In its press release regarding the imposition of capital controls in Cyprus on March 28, 2013, the European Commission noted that "Member States may introduce restrictions on capital movement, including capital controls, in certain circumstances and under strict conditions on grounds of public policy or public security. In accordance with the case law of the European Court of Justice, measures may also be introduced for overriding reasons of general public interest." It noted furthermore that "Such restrictions may include bank holidays, limits on withdrawals, freezing of assets, prohibition of terminating fixed term deposits, prohibition on certain payment orders, restrictions in using credit/debit/prepaid cards, restrictions on other banking operations as well as execution of certain transactions subject to the approval of the Central Bank and other measures." See European Commission (2013).

22. As described in Fox and Renwick (2014), Fitch Ratings has also revised its procedure for setting country ceilings for euro zone countries.

23. To illustrate the application of this country ceiling, on page 5 of Pitman (2012), Moody's reprints its press release describing the impact of this rating change for the Hellenic Telecommunications Organisation, S. A. (OTE plc), a private borrower located in Greece. As indicated in this release, the legal uncertainty surrounding a euro zone exit is considerable.

The terms of the rated instruments issued through OTE plc contain a choice of English law, submission to the courts of England, a clear definition of "euro" as the single currency and payment provisions that were not tied to Greece. However, OTE itself is the borrower under a bank facility governed by Greek law that we consider as being at significant risk of redenomination. The size of the facility relative to the OTE family's total debt outstanding was sufficiently material to justify the risk of a default for redenomination being reflected in OTE's rating. As a consequence, whilst we positioned the corporate family rating one notch above the Greek country ceiling at Caa1(negative)—reflecting (amongst other factors) a lower expected loss for the debt issued by OTE plc—the exposure of the bank facility to a change in currency pushed OTE's probability of default rating to the Greek country ceiling of Caa2 (negative).

24. See, for example, IMF (2012, chapter 2, special feature 8) on page 85 of ECB (2014), and Adelino and Ferreira (2014).

25. Bornensztein et al. (2013) put together a data set of sovereign and private credit ratings as well as accounting data for every publicly traded nonfinancial corporate borrower with a rating from Standard and Poor's as of June 2005. The final sample is an unbalanced panel of 478 nonfinancial corporations from 29 countries, including 14 developed and 15 emerging economies for the time period 1995–2009. Almeida et al. (2014) examines a sample of bonds of nonfinancial firms from 80 countries over the 1990–2012 time period. Their sample has 3,605 unique firms with a credit rating.

26. The Takings Clause was not initially intended to apply to state governments. However, in 1897 the federal court in *Chicago, B. & Q. Railroad Co. v. Chicago* (1897) held that the Fourteenth Amendment extended the effects of that provision to the states.

27. In cases in which the state legislatures refused to issue paper money as legal tender in repaying debts, popular uprisings prevented the execution of judgments against debtors. A prominent example is Shays' Rebellion in western Massachusetts in 1786–1787,

when farmer protests closed courts in the western part of state in order to prevent executions of judgments against debtors, after having unsuccessfully petitioned the state government to issue paper currency for the repayment of debts (Ely 2008, 39).

28. Madison expressed similar sentiments when describing the importance of a strong union in *The Federalist No. 10*: "a rage for paper money, for an abolition of debts, for an equal division of property, or for any other improper and wicked project, will be less apt to pervade the whole body of the union than a particular member of it."

29. State and federal courts struck a 1791 Rhode Island law granting debtors exemptions from attachments for a period of three years (*Champion and Dickason v. Casey*, 1792), a South Carolina law suspending the execution of judgments against debtors (*Jones v. Crittendon*, 1814), and even a modest change to bankruptcy law that applied retroactively (*Sturges v. Crowninshield*, 1819).

30. Moody's rationale for this delinking of private and US state government credit ratings is explained in Wilson (2014, appendix B). We also verified that US state government credit ratings are not a constraint on private credit ratings for US corporates with S&P personnel in private communication.

31. In *Citizen's Insurance Co. v. Parsons*, 1881, a case that involved insurance contracts, the Privy Council ruled that the property and civil rights clause included the power to regulate contracts.

32. Much of our discussion of the history of Canadian insolvency and bankruptcy law is drawn from Telfer (1999, 2014) .

33. Strictly, the TFEU concerns only euro banknotes, whereas Article 11 of Regulation EC/974/98 on the introduction of the euro applies to euro coins.

34. The TFEU refers to the irrevocable fixing of exchange rates in Articles 46(3), 49, and 140(3). However, there is a provision in Article 50 of the TFEU that envisages a member state leaving the European Union altogether.

35. With the imposition of capital and exchange controls in Cyprus, the European Commission proactively issued the opinion that both controls were lawful as a result of the "public policy" exemption.

36. Pouzo and Presno (2014) examine the role of fiscal inflexibility in generating optimal default in a stochastic closed economy in which a government is restricted to proportional taxes and uncontingent debt.

37. See, for example, Bohn (1998) and Ghosh et al. (2013).

38. As discussed in Wright (2006), a conceptual issue arises in modeling competitive equilibria when there is a disconnect between the decentralized decision of individual borrowers and the collective decision to interfere with those debts made by the government. Wright (2006) decentralizes such equilibria with individual specific borrowing constraints; Kehoe and Perri (2004) assume individual borrowers always repay and the government induces the desired allocation with asset taxes; and Kim and Zhang (2012) assume there are no private capital markets. In a previous version of this paper, we introduced oligopolistic domestic financial institutions. In the current version, we do not take a stand on the specific decentralization.

39. See, for example, Blanchard and Giavazzi (2002), who spoke of the end of the Feldstein-Horioka puzzle.

40. The announcement by the Governor of the Commonwealth of Puerto Rico that their public debt is unsustainable was immediately met by announcements from the White House and Congress that there would be no federal bailout of these debts.

41. Puerto Rico's fiscal and economic conditions are analyzed in the report by Krueger, Teja, and Wolfe (2015) recommending the restructuring of Puerto Rico's General Obligation Debts.

42. The Commonwealth of Puerto Rico is specifically exempted from Chapter 9 of the US Bankruptcy Code, so the government does not have access to the same legal structure Detroit and other municipalities have used to reschedule their debts.

43. Of course, the fact that bank deposits in Puerto Rico are insured by the FDIC also plays an important role in insulating the finances from the Commonwealth of Puerto Rico from bank failures. The FDIC closed three banks in Puerto Rico in 2010 and closed Doral Bank, the third-largest bank in Puerto Rico, in the spring of 2015.

References

Adelino, Manuel and Miguel A. Ferreira. 2014. "Bank Ratings and Lending Supply: Evidence from Sovereign Downgrades." Technical Report, Duke University and Nova School of Business and Economics.

Aizenman, Joshua, and Gunnar Gunnarsson. 2014. "Fiscal Challenges in Multilayered Unions: An Overview and Case Study." NBER Working Paper no. 20564, Cambridge, MA.

Almeida, Hector, Igor Cunha, Miguel A. Ferreira, and Felipe Restrepo. 2014. "The Real Effects of Sovereign Rating Downgrades." Technical Report, January. https://www2.bc.edu/felipe-restrepogomez/The%20Real%20Effects%20of%20Sovereign%20Rating%20Downgrades.pdf.

Ang, Andrew and Francis A. Longstaff. 2013. "Systemic Sovereign Credit Risk: Lessons from the US and Europe." *Journal of Monetary Economics* 60: 493–510.

Areta, Carlos, and Galina Hale. 2008. "Sovereign Debt Crises and Credit to the Private Sector." *Journal of International Economics* 74:53–69.

Bai, Jennie, and Shang-Jin Wei. 2014. "When is There a Strong Transfer Risk from the Sovereigns to the Corporates? Property Rights Gaps and CDS Spreads." Staff Report no. 579, Federal Reserve Bank of New York, March. https://www.newyorkfed.org/research/staff_reports/sr579.html.

Bayoumi, Tamim, Morris Goldstein, and Geoffrey Woglom. 1995. "Do Credit Markets Discipline Sovereign Borrowers? Evidence from US States." *Journal of Money, Credit and Banking* 27 (4, part 1):1046–59.

Bedendo, Mascia, and Paolo Colla. 2013. "Sovereign and Corporate Credit Risk: Evidence from the Eurozone." Technical Report, Universita Bocconi, June.

Beers, David T., Marie Cavanaugh, and Laura Feinland-Katz. 2005. "Ratings Associated with Risk of Foreign Exchange Controls Raised in 27 Countries." General Criteria, Standard and Poor's, November.

Bird, Richard M., and Almos Tassonyi. 2003. "Constraining Subnational Fiscal Behavior in Canada: Different Approaches, Similar Results?" In *Fiscal Decentralization and the Challenge of Hard Budget Constraints*, ed. Jonathan Rodden, Gunnar S. Eskeland, and Jennie Ilene Litvack, 85–132. Cambridge, MA: MIT Press.

Blanchard, Olivier, and Francesco Giavazzi. 2002. "Current Account Deficits in the Euro Area: The End of the Feldstein Horioka Puzzle?" *Brookings Papers on Economic Activity* 33 (2):147–86.

Bocola, Luigi. 2015. "The Pass-Through of Sovereign Risk." Working Paper no. 722, Federal Reserve Bank of Minneapolis.

Bohn, Henning. 1998. "The Behavior of US Public Debt and Deficits." *Quarterly Journal of Economics* 113 (3):949–63.

Bohn, Henning, and Robert P. Inman. 1996. "Balanced-Budget Rules and Public Deficits: Evidence from the US states." *Journal of Monetary Economics: Carnegie Rochester Conference Series on Public Policy* 45:13–76.

Bordo, Michael, Angela Redish, and Hugh Rockoff. 2015. "Why Didn't Canada Have a Banking Crisis in 2008 (or in 1930, or 1907, or . . .)?" *Economic History Review* 68 (1):218–43.

Borensztein, Eduardo, Kevin Cowan, and Patricio Valenzuela. 2013. "Sovereign Ceilings 'lite'? The Impact of Sovereign Ratings on Corporate Ratings." *Journal of Banking and Finance* 37:4014–24.

Calvo, Guillermo A. 1998. "Capital Flows and Capital-Market Crises: The Simple Economics of Sudden Stops." *Journal of Applied Economics* 1 (1):35–54.

Cavanaugh, Marie. 2009. "Sovereign Rating and Country Transfer and Convertibility Assessment Histories." Technical Report, Standard and Poor's Ratings Direct.

Cavanaugh, Marie, and Laura J. Feinland-Katz. 2009. "Criteria for Determining Transfer and Convertibility Assessments." General Criteria: Methodology, Standard and Poor's.

Chu, Nancy G. 2014. "Methodology and Assumptions for Ratings above the Sovereign—Single-Jurisdiction Structured Finance." Criteria, Structured Finance, General, Standard and Poor's.

Das, Udaibir S., Michael G. Papaioannou, and Christoph Trebesch. 2010. "Sovereign Default Risk and Private Sector Access to Capital in Emerging Markets." IMF Working Paper no. WP/10/10, International Monetary Fund, January.

Dewey, Davis Rich. 1902. *Financial History of the United States*. London: Longmans, Green and Company.

de Sola Perea, M., and Ch. Van Niewenhuyze. 2014. "Financial Integration and Fragmentation in the Euro Area." *National Bank of Belgium Economic Review* 1:99–125.

Duggar, Elena. 2008. "Sovereign Defaults and Interference: Perspectives on Government Risks." Technical Report no. 110114, Moody's Investors Service.

Ely, James W. 2008. *The Guardian of Every Other Right: A Constitutional History of Property Rights*. Oxford: Oxford University Press.

European Central Bank (ECB). 2014. "Financial Integration in Europe." Annual Report, European Central Bank, April.

European Commission. 2013. "Statement by the European Commission on the Capital Controls Imposed by the Republic of Cyprus." Press Release, March 28.

Farhi, Emmanuel, and Jean Tirole. 2015. "Deadly Embrace: Sovereign and Financial Balance Sheet Doom Loops." Working Paper no. 164191, OpenScholar, Harvard University.

Feinland-Katz, Laura J. 2013. "Ratings above the Sovereign—Corporate and Government Ratings: Methodology and Assumptions." General Criteria, Standard and Poor's, November.

Feinland-Katz, Laura J., and Nancy G. Chu. 2013. "Country Risk Assessment Methodology and Assumptions." General Criteria, Standard and Poor's, November.

Fox, Richard, and Douglas Renwick. 2014. "Country Ceilings." Cross-Sector Criteria Report: Sovereigns, Global, Fitch Ratings.

Gates, Daniel, Alastair Wilson, and Elena Duggar. 2012. "How Sovereign Credit Quality May Affect Other Ratings." Cross-Sector Rating Methodology Report no. 139495, Moody's Investors Service, February.

Ghosh, Atish R., Jun I. Kim, Enrique G. Mendoza, Jonathan D. Ostry, and Mahvash S. Qureshi. 2013. "Fiscal Fatigue, Fiscal Space and Debt Sustainability in Advanced Economies." *Economic Journal* 2013 (2): F4–30.

Gilchrist, Simon, and Benoit Mojon. 2014. "Credit Risk in the Euro Area." NBER Working Paper no. 20041, Cambridge, MA.

Hallerberg, Mark, and Rolf Strauch. 2002. "On the Cyclicality of Public Finances in Europe." *Empirica* 29 (3):183–207.

Heinrichs, Marcel, and Ivelina Stanoeva. 2013. "Country Risk and Sovereign Risk—Building Clearer Borders." Technical Report, Standard and Poor's Capital IQ, February.

Henning, Randall C., and Martin Kessler. 2012. "Fiscal Federalism: US History for Architects of Europe's Fiscal Union." Working Paper no. 12-1, Peterson Institute for International Economics, January.
International Monetary Fund (IMF). 2012. "Global Financial Stability Report." Technical Report, October.
———. 2014. "Fiscal Monitor: Back to Work, How Fiscal Policy Can Help." Technical Report, October.
Johnson, Craig L., and Kenneth A. Kriz. 2005. "Fiscal Institutions, Credit Ratings, and Borrowing Costs." *Public Budgeting and Finance* 25 (1): 84–103.
Jonas, Jari. 2012. "Great Recession and Fiscal Squeeze at US Subnational Government Level." IMF Working Paper no. 12/184, International Monetary Fund, July.
Kehoe, Patrick, and Fabrizio Perri. 2004. "Competitive Equilibria with Limited Enforcement." *Journal of Economic Theory* 119 (1): 184–206.
Kim, Yun Zhung, and Jing Zhang. 2012. "Decentralized Borrowing and Centralized Default." *Journal of International Economics* 88 (1): 121–33.
Klein, Christian, and Christoph Stellner. 2014. "Does Sovereign Risk Matter? New Evidence from Eurozone Corporate Bond Ratings and Zero-Volatility Spreads." *Review of Financial Economics* 23 (2): 64–74.
Krueger, Anne O., Ranjit Teja, and Andrew Wolfe. 2015. "Puerto Rico: A Way Forward." Technical Report, Government Development Bank for Puerto Rico.
Kydland, Finn E., and Edward C. Prescott. 1977. "Rules Rather Than Discretion: The Inconsistency of Optimal Plans." *Journal of Political Economy* 85 (3): 473–91.
Lane, Philip R. 2013. "Capital Flows in the Euro Area." Economic Papers no. 497, European Commission.
Larson, Baye. 2013. "2013 State Debt Medians Report." Median Report, Moody's Investors Service.
Loh, Ning, and Katherine Frey. 2011. "Assessing the Impact of the Eurozone Sovereign Debt Crisis on Structured Finance Transactions." Special Comment, Moody's Investors Service, April.
Lombardi, John, and Marcia Van Wagner. 2014. "US State Pension Medians Increase in Fiscal 2012." Median Report, Moody's Investors Service.
Lowry, Robert C., and James E. Alt. 2001. "A Visible Hand? Bond Markets, Political Parties, Balanced Budget Laws, and State Government Debt." *Economics and Politics* 13 (1): 49–72.
Lucas, Robert E., and Nancy L. Stokey. 1983. "Optimal Fiscal and Monetary Policy in an Economy without Capital." *Journal of Monetary Economics* 12 (1): 55–93.
Merler, Silvia, and Jean Pisani-Ferry. 2012. "Sudden Stops in the Euro Area." Bruegel Policy Contribution no. 6. http://bruegel.org/2012/03/sudden-stops-in-the-euro-area-2/.
Moody's. 2009. "Moody's Ratings Symbols and Definitions." Technical Report, Moody's Investors Service.
———. 2013. "Moody's Statistical Handbook: Non-US Regional and Local Governments." Technical Report, Moody's Investors Service, December.
———. 2015. "Moody's Affirms Ratings on Three Puerto Rican Banks." Moody's Investors Service, February.
Mysak, Joseph. 2010. "Bond Default is About Too Much Debt, Too Little Time." *BloombergBusiness*, July 20. http://www.bloomberg.com/news/articles/2010-07-21/bond-default-means-too-much-debt-too-little-time-commentary-by-joe-mysak.

Nevins, Allan. 1924. *The American States during and after the Revolution, 1775–1789.* New York: Macmillan.

Olken, Samuel R. 1993. "Charles Evans Hughes and the Blaisdell Decision: A Historical Study of Contract Clause Jurisprudence." *Oregon Law Review* 72:513.

Palacios, Milagros, Hugh MacIntyre, and Charles Lammam. 2014. "Canadian Government Debt 2014: A Guide to the Indebtedness of Canada and the Provinces." Technical Report, Fraser Institute, April.

Pisani-Ferry, Jean, Andre Sapir, and Guntram B. Wolff. 2013. "EU-IMF Assistance to Euro-Area Countries: An Early Assessment." Blueprint Series no. 19, Bruegel. http://bruegel.org/2013/06/eu-imf-assistance-to-euro-area-countries-an-early-assessment/.

Pitman, James. 2012. "Credit and Rating Considerations Arising from a 'Euro Exit.'" Special Comment, Moody's Investors Service, October.

Poterba, James M. 1994. "State Responses to Fiscal Crises: The Effects of Budgetary Institutions and Politics." *Journal of Political Economy* 102:799–821.

Poterba, James M., and Kim S. Rueben. 1999. "State Fiscal Institutions and the US Municipal Bond Market." In *Fiscal Institutions and Fiscal Performance*, ed. James M. Poterba and Jurgen von Hagen, 181–208. Chicago: University of Chicago Press.

———. 2001. "Fiscal News, State Budget Rules, and Tax-Exempt Bond Yields." *Journal of Urban Economics* 50 (3): 537–62.

Pouzo, Demian, and Ignacio Presno. 2014. "Optimal Taxation with Endogenous Default under Incomplete Markets." Technical Report, UC Berkeley Economics, July.

Pykett, Benjamin, Matthew Harding, and Benedict James. 2013. "Capital and Exchange Controls." Technical Report, Issue 3, Linklaters, April.

Raimes, Emily. 2013. "US States Rating Methodology." Rating Methodology, Moody's Investors Service, April 17. http://www.mass.gov/anf/docs/anf/fab/debt-management/go-states-method-moodys.pdf.

Reinhart, Carmen M., and Kenneth S. Rogoff. 2013. "Financial and Sovereign Debt Crises: Some Lessons Learned and Those Forgotten." IMF Working Paper no. WP/13/266, International Monetary Fund, December.

Reinhart, Carmen M., Kenneth S. Rogoff, and Miguel A. Savastano. 2003. "Debt Intolerance." *Brookings Papers on Economic Activity* 34 (1): 1–62.

Rodden, Jonathan, and Erik Wibbels. 2010. "Fiscal Decentralization and the Business Cycle: An Empirical Study of Seven Federations." *Economics and Politics* 22 (1): 37–67.

Sargent, Thomas. 2012. "United States Then, Europe Now." *Journal of Political Economy* 120 (1): 1–40.

Slaughter and May. 2012. "Sovereign Default, Bank Default, Eurozone Exit and Related Issues: Is Your Business Prepared? A Practical Guide to Contingency Planning and Legal Risk Management." Memorandum, Slaughter and May, July. http://www.slaughterandmay.com/media/1825223/sovereign-default-bank-default-eurozone-exit-and-related-issues-is-your-business-prepared.pdf.

Standard and Poor's. 2015a. "Greek Corporations Ellaktor, Public Power Corp., and OTE Long-Term Ratings Lowered Following Similar Action on Sovereign." Press Release.

———. 2015b. "Puerto Rico Go Rating Lowered to 'CCC–' from 'CCC+'; Outlook is Negative on Likelihood of Default or Distressed Exchange." Press Release.

———. 2015c. "Ratings on Four Greek Banks Lowered to 'SD' Following Restrictions Imposed on Deposits." Press Release.

Stendevad, Carsten. 2007. "Debating Point: Bosses' Agendas are Converging." *Financial Times*, July 26.

Taylor, Mac. 2009. "California's Cash Flow Crisis: May 2009 Update." Technical Report, Legislative Analysts Office, May.

Telfer, Thomas G. W. 1999. *Reconstructing Bankruptcy Law in Canada 1867 to 1979: From an Evil to a Commercial Necessity*. PhD thesis, University of Toronto.

———. *Ruin and Redemption: The Struggle for a Canadian Bankruptcy Law, 1867– 1919*. Toronto: University of Toronto Press.

Truglia, Vincent. 2005. "Revised Policy with Respect to Country Ceilings." Rating Methodology: Request for Comment, Moody's Investors Service, November.

Wallis, John Joseph. 2000. "American Government Finance in the Long Run: 1790 to 1990." *Journal of Economic Perspectives* 14 (1): 61–82.

Walsh, Geoff. 2011. "The Finger in the Dike: State and Local Laws Combat the Foreclosure Tide." *Suffolk University Law Review* 44:139–91.

Wilson, Alastair. 2014. "Proposed Changes to Local Currency Country Risk Ceilings in Currency Unions." Request for Comment, Moody's Investors Service, November.

Wong, Jennifer A., and Emily Raimes. 2013. "California and Ontario: Peer Comparison." Credit Focus, Moody's Investors Service, October.

Wright, Benjamin F. 1938. *The Contract Clause of the Constitution*. Cambridge, MA: Harvard University Press.

Wright, Mark. 2006. "Private Capital Flows, Capital Controls and Default Risk." *Journal of International Economics* 69 (1): 120–49.

Comment

Ricardo Reis *LSE, Columbia University and NBER*

Introduction

When staring at the US recession of 2008–2010 and at the euro crisis of 2010–2012, it is tempting to look for common features. In both Los Angeles and Madrid, house prices more than doubled between 2000 and 2008, and household debt increased in tandem. Both in the United States and in southern Europe, total public debt reached historical levels and, during the two crises, yields on state debt increased remarkably, as did the price of credit default swaps insuring against default. A story of the crises across the two sides of the Atlantic that is based on leverage and debt is both appealing and superficially correct.

However, a closer look at the data in the two regions leaves too many questions open. The increase in house prices was not uniform across Europe (or the United States), with large movements in Ireland and Spain, but relative stagnation in Portugal and Italy, and only moderate increases in Greece, yet all of these regions went through a sovereign debt crisis. The increase in public debt was at the federal level in the United States (while at the state level in Europe), yet the American sovereign debt problems happened exclusively in a few states, California and Michigan more noticeably. Arellano et al. add a further comparison that makes a simplistic leverage story even harder to take at face value. Look at Canada. House prices also almost doubled in the first decade of the twenty-first century, and private leverage followed suit. But prices have neither fallen (at least yet) nor has there been any sovereign debt crisis. Moreover, as Arellano et al. emphasize, not only was there no public debt crisis, there was also no significant private debt crisis.

How can we make sense of these three data points in their clear commonalities, but also clear differences? At a basic level, one would like that a theory, or even just an account, of the crisis in one of these three regions is not easily dismissed with the events in the other region. Arellano and colleagues deserve credit for bringing this comparison to the frontline of work on the euro crisis, and trying to move the literature to take this comparative analysis into account. At the same time, Arellano et al. emphasize a new mechanism behind these crises, which I will discuss in the next section, and comment on and criticize in the following section, before concluding.

The New Contribution: A Brief Summary

Arellano et al. propose new variables to consider, use them in an insightful model to make new predictions, and then show the potential of this approach by applying it to interpret the data.

Two New Variables

The first fundamental factor that Arellano et al. consider is the *flexibility of fiscal institutions*. In their words, this is the "ability to change taxes and borrow." In their model, it refers to the government's ability to freely choose the level of the primary surplus to pay debts that are coming due. Given their particular assumptions, this translates into the ability to set tax revenues, although since total public spending is taken as given, one could just as well interpret it as the primary surplus. In their discussion of fiscal flexibility in section IV of the paper, they link it to three related, but separate, objects. First, empirical work studying how the primary surpluses of US states respond to macroeconomic shocks. Second, the differences in constitutions across countries imposing limits on the ability to raise taxes. And third, the procedures and views of credit ratings agencies when judging the riskiness of state debts.

In terms of their three data points, the fiscal flexibility of US states is low: their constitutions make it hard to raise new taxes, and past fiscal adjustments have had to rely on often ill-timed spending cuts because the constraint on raising new taxes seems binding. Canadian provinces, instead, can easily raise taxes insofar as they do not have similar legal restrictions and seem to smooth expenditure shocks over time, while European states have successfully and continuously raised taxes in the past few decades to finance the expansion of their welfare states.

The second new factor is *interference in private contracts*. In their words, this is the "perceived risk of sovereign interference with domiciled private debt contracts." In the model, it is the ability of the government to force a default on private debts while incurring a cost. In the data, discussed in section III, this interference is assessed by an institutional analysis of both the legal institutions and the history of their application. Moreover, the authors appeal again to the views of ratings agencies, which discuss this possible interference as a consideration in judging the risk of private bonds. This is perhaps best captured by the "sovereign credit ceiling" whereby ratings agencies stipulate that private creditors cannot be more creditworthy than their sovereign, in great part because the sovereign can (and do) expropriate private assets to pay public debts first.

The authors argue that the United States and Canada have a long tradition of respecting private contracts that the more recently formed European Union still lacks. The authors appeal to several clauses in European treaties that open room for exceptions to free trade and the primacy of private contracts. While they do not mention it, I would also add the differences between Anglo-Saxon and continental European legal traditions, in particular the emphasis that different legal origins put on the protection of investors (La Porta et al. 1998). Moreover, it is important that, unlike the unions of US states and Canadian provinces, the European Union of states is still a very recent work in progress, so there has not been as much time to solidify private rights and to impose limits on the states.

Three New Predictions

Mapping these two new variables into a simple binary classification gives four possibilities, out of which Arellano et al. derive three predictions when focussing on the relevant ranges of parameters.

First, if fiscal flexibility is high and the costs of interference are high, then when a country encounters a fiscal crisis it pays for it by raising taxes. The high costs of interference make private default a bad option, and given the option of raising taxes, in the model this is less costly than public default. In this case, in the authors' model, both public and private interest rates reflect the absence of a risk of default and therefore do not react to a fiscal crisis. Both the government and private agents in the country are able to borrow abroad given the credible commitment to repay, so that there is no sudden stop of financing.

Interference with private contracts

Fiscal flexibility		Low	High
	Low	U.S. states	
	High	Canadian provinces	EU countries

Fig. 1. The data points according to the theory

Second, if fiscal flexibility is still high, but there is little cost of interfering with private contracts, then anytime that the public debt constraint binds, so does the private debt constraint. That is, if the public sector has borrowed all that it can, then it must be that the private sector is also borrowing at the limit. Intuitively, because the public sector can force default by the private sector, it will use this private debt capacity to borrow. Given its fiscal flexibility, it can always tax the private sector to transfer the gains from these private defaults into the public purse. In case of an unexpected need for resources, the public sector can cause a private default instead of the more costly public default.

Third, if fiscal flexibility is instead low, and regardless of the costs of interfering with private contracts, then a default on public debt can occur, even if the costs of doing so are very high. In short, the public authorities may find themselves out of options. They simply cannot raise the resources to pay for the outstanding public debt.

Who Is Where?

The last part in Arellano et al.'s argument is to link these predictions to their three data points, as I illustrate in figure 1. The theory predicts that, unlike US states, Canadian provinces should be able to borrow large amounts from markets that realize that the fiscal flexibility exists to pay these liabilities. Moreover, the theory predicts and the data confirms that during the 2008–2012 period, the interest rates on provincial debt rose by small amounts relative to the federal debt, since default was not a predicted outcome.

The EU states, in turn, have the fiscal flexibility to sustain their observed large public debts. However, when the fiscal crisis hit, default became likely and spreads on public debt rose. The theory predicts that this would only happen if the external debt constraint was also binding, and the evidence again seems to support this prediction. As many have noted (e.g., Mody and Sandri 2012) the premia on credit default spreads on private bonds, and especially the spread on banks were very highly correlated with the premia on public bonds. Moreover, the euro crisis in the periphery was, above all, a sudden stop of the private capital that used to flow from the core to the periphery of Europe, consistent with the tightening of a binding constraint on private indebtedness (e.g., Reis 2013b).

Finally, a few US states may be on the brink of default due to their lack of fiscal flexibility. Yet, as this was known ex ante, their debt levels were always low. Moreover, because they are unable to interfere with private contracts, there is almost no correlation between the interest rate on the state debt and on the private debt of corporates located in that state. During 2008–2010, the public sector may have felt a crunch in its ability to borrow, but there was no contagion toward the private sector.

Comments on Applying the Theory to the Euro-Area Crisis

This comparative approach will hopefully influence the debate, the theory proposes an intriguing new hypothesis, and the arguments behind the new variables should stimulate more research. This article should have a place on reading lists that discuss the euro crisis. To start that discussion, I have five comments on the paper ranging from their variables, to their model, to the application to Europe.

Comment 1: It Is Hard to Measure Fiscal Flexibility

The authors make a compelling case for introducing fiscal flexibility into the analysis of sovereign default. But, to make scientific progress on this important topic, we need to both propose new factors as well as be able to measure them. Only this way can theories be operationalized and predictions be tested. While the concept of fiscal flexibility is tempting, thinking about how it can be measured raises as many questions as it provides answers.

To start, while the institutional evidence put forward by Arellano and colleagues is compelling, most of it pertains to tax *rates*. Yet, what is relevant for the model and for the theory are tax *revenues*. It is the ability of the government to raise resources in a crisis, by whatever means, that is important for whether there will be a sovereign default. The successive

Greek governments of the past few years have found it easy to raise tax rates, but have also found it very hard to raise tax revenues. This experience suggests that Greece may actually have low fiscal flexibility rather than high as argued by Arellano et al. since it is not legal constraints that matter per se, but rather the ability of the state to enforce those laws, prevent tax evasion, and enforce a tax base that is stable and wide.

Perhaps a more accurate way to measure fiscal flexibility would be by the distance between the economy's current position in the Laffer curve and its peak. According to this measure, Trabandt and Uhlig (2011) argue that countries like Greece might indeed have significant room for raising extra revenue using income taxes. However, Laffer-curve calculations typically focus on a single tax and too often neglect the response of tax evasion and enforcement to the level of taxes.

Using the behavior of revenues around fiscal adjustment does not take us very far either. These measure in large part the response of automatic stabilizers, over which governments typically have little discretionary control. Take, for instance, the discussion on moving toward a fiscal union in Europe, replacing national unemployment insurance schemes with a Euro-wide version of this automatic stabilizer. On the one hand, this would lead to more transfers to a country in a recession, automatically adjusting its primary surplus to help it pay for the public debt. On the other hand, this fiscal union would remove some of the ability of the government to raise tax revenues and cut spending in a fiscal crisis, as used for instance by the Portuguese reforms of the past few years that cut the generosity of unemployment benefits. Whether fiscal flexibility would improve or not is far from clear.

Another perspective on fiscal flexibility is that it should not be about the typical business-cycle shocks, thus removing the automatic stabilizers from the discussion, but rather about responding to large crises. This leads to another active discussion in Europe, on whether there should be a joint deposit insurance scheme to complete its proposed banking union so as to respond to large financial crises. This exists today in the United States, but not in Europe. In response to a banking crisis in one state, the US states could benefit today from potentially large transfers from the other states, whereas the European ones do not. From this perspective, it would be the US states that enjoy more fiscal flexibility, the opposite of Arellano et al.'s assumption.

Finally, consider Arellano et al.'s point that one could infer fiscal flexibility from the debt tolerance of private markets. Figure 2 in their paper shows that US states, on average, have less debt outstanding, even in-

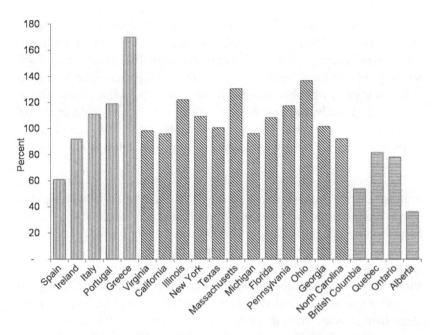

Fig. 2. Net debt including federal obligations as a ratio of GDP

cluding pension and health-care liabilities, than Canadian provinces or European countries. Figure 2 below repeats their calculation, including a few more states and countries. It includes only net debt, but it adds to US states and Canadian provinces their share of the federal debt, apportioned to each state according to its share of gross tax revenues in 2013. Debt tolerance should refer to debt capacity, and the residents of New York or Illinois are responsible not just for the debt of their states, but also for their federal debt. Adding their share of the federal debt, US states no longer stand out from their European counterparts.

Comment 2: The Diabolic Loop Alternative

Public interference in private contracts is a plausible and appealing way to explain the correlation between private and public interest rates in Europe. But there are others, and the literature on the euro crisis has particularly emphasized one: the role of banks.[1]

Brunnermeier et al. (2011) first highlighted that behind the euro crisis was a diabolic loop between banks and sovereigns. When markets feared that Spain or Ireland would not pay their public debt, the price of government bonds fell. But, because banks in those countries hold large amounts of this public debt, this fear leads to immediate losses and contraction in their highly leveraged equity. This in turn feeds back to the public authorities in two ways. Directly, because the increased risk that banks might become insolvent raises the probability of a bank bailout. Indirectly, because banks with lower equity contract credit, causing a recession and worsening public finances. Through either or both of these channels of the diabolic loop, the initial fear would be justified.[2]

This explanation can also account for the difference between Europe and the United States because of the differences in their banking systems.[3] First, Europe lacks a euro-wide safe asset, so while US banks can hold federal securities in their portfolio, European banks hold instead bonds of their sovereigns, creating the diabolic loop. Second, while there is federal deposit insurance and federal regulation of banks so that the costs of bailouts would be shared by all US states, European sovereigns would have to shoulder the full burden of bailing out their large banks, as the Irish government discovered in 2011. Third, banks were crucial in Europe in intermediating capital flows across countries (Brunnermeier and Reis 2015). Therefore, financial problems associated with the structure of modern banks, and global imbalances associated with competitiveness and trade across nations, become intertwined in Europe. In the United States, banks are much less important in channeling capital across state borders. Fourth, when a sudden stop of private capital happened in Europe, banks could look to the central banks for funding, and through the TARGET II system, public capital could flow in from the Eurosystem. Yet, accessing Eurosystem funds required posting as collateral public bonds, therefore worsening the diabolic loop at the height of the crisis.

Comment 3: Bailouts in the Model

In the model, the government must pay a cost to force the private sector to renege on is debt. In the United States, this cost is large, consistent with the contract clause of the constitution that, as Arellano et al. explain, puts a serious limitation on individual states forcing the dissolution of private contracts.

However, US states can bail out local companies. This is not illegal, and in fact happens (perhaps too) often. Consider then the following strategy. The public sector can take over a private company in its state, which includes taking ownership of its assets but also shouldering its liabilities. If the state then defaults on its public debt, it will also default on these new liabilities. Via the bailout, private debt then becomes public debt. Public and private interest rates would be the same, and there would never be a private debt crisis separately from a public debt crisis.

It is not difficult to extend the Arellano et al. model to include bailouts. The government now never interferes with private contracts, but it can bail out the private sector and assume its debt at a new deadweight cost, say Δ^b. After a fiscal crisis, the government now has three options: (a) it can do no bailout and no default, in which case the full private and public debt must be paid costing $D^p + D^g$; (b) it can default, but do no bailout at cost $D^p + \Delta^g$; or (c) it can bailout and default at cost $\Delta^b + \Delta^g$. A similar analysis to the one in Arellano et al. shows what configuration of shocks and debt outstanding leads to each of the equilibria. But it is no longer the case that we can easily distinguish between Europe, Canada, and the United States in terms of their relative costs of bailing companies out.

Comment 4: What Came Before Matters

Greece, Ireland, Portugal, and Spain did not suddenly and unexpectedly find themselves with high debt and an inability to pay for it in 2010–2011. Rather, the crisis was in part the result of a decade of stagnation in productivity growth in their economies mixed with fragility in the banking system, and it was as much due to the resulting low-growth prospects as it was to the size of the debt (Brunnermeier and Reis 2015). Starting with the introduction of the euro, there were large capital flows from the core to the periphery of Europe. These took the form of debt contracts and were intermediated by banks. As this fast financial integration came without an effective financial deepening (Reis 2013b), the capital was misallocated both within and across sectors, flowing toward low-productivity sectors. As a result, total factor productivity stagnated for a decade while nontradables grew, pushing up wages and appreciating the real exchange rate. There was therefore a private-sector crisis, and a long-lasting one, before the public debt crisis hit in 2010. In fact, Ireland and Spain's public debts were small and falling before the crisis, while Portugal's debt increased exclusively via the growth of pensions in spite of cuts in discretionary public spending and increases in taxes.

Compare this account with that of California's public debt crisis. Silicon Valley was the beacon of productivity growth, and the private sector in the state had been thriving. Banks were secondary for many firm's finances, and there was no appreciable increase in capital flows into California or change in wages relative to its neighboring states. Arellano and colleagues contrast the two public debt crises, in Europe and a few US states, and emphasize that they see no spillovers to the private sector in the United States, unlike in Europe. Yet, in Europe, I would argue that the crisis started in the private sector well before the public sector in at least three of the four crisis countries (Ireland, Portugal, and Spain), but was not there in 2000–2008 in California or Illinois.

Comment 5: Canada as a Different Source of Data

The Canadian data illuminates the thesis of Arellano et al.'s paper in more than one way. While the authors focus on the spread between Canadian provinces and the federal government after 2008, going further back in history provides another illuminating episode. On October 30 of 1995, there was a referendum on whether Quebec should leave Canada and become an independent state. This question had been heavily debated for many years, and the turnout of 93.5% was extraordinary. All the way to the day of the vote, polls showed an almost even split of the vote, and the actual result was 50.6% against leaving Canada.

Figure 3 shows the spread on provincial debt around the election. Interest rates clearly declined following the election results. It was not clear, in spite of being heavily discussed during the campaign, how a potential new Quebec government would treat private contracts between its citizens and the rest of Canada. This rudimentary difference-in-difference supports the authors' hypothesis. Once the risk of this interference disappeared, spreads fell.

This example also indicates what may be the more relevant risk of interference in Europe. If a country were to leave the euro, it would likely have to redenominate the debt contracts of its citizens to other Europeans. Otherwise, the expected depreciation of the currency would greatly increase the value of those debts in the new domestic currency, as the "original sin" would hit. During the euro crisis, this seemed to be a concern, at least with respect to Greece. The interest rates on Greek public and private debt rose more than that of any other European country during the crisis.

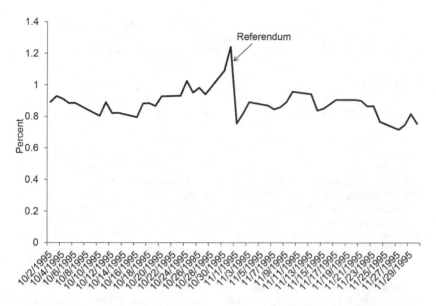

Fig. 3.   Quebec-Canada spread on 10-year bonds around independence referendum

Conclusion

If nothing else, the events of the past few years have reminded us that sovereign debt crises can and do happen everywhere and often, including in the richest areas of the world. There is much to gain from not looking at the euro crisis in isolation, but in comparison with other events across the world and time, as Arellano et al. and a wave of recent work has done (e.g., Reinhart and Rogoff 2009; Taylor 2015). In particular, considering two new factors, fiscal flexibility and government interference with private contracts, will likely be important to understand these crises. In these comments, I raised some challenges both in measuring and applying these factors as well as in applying them to the euro crisis. There remains much to be done in this exciting area, and Arellano and colleagues have taken the important first step in what I hope will be a stimulating literature.

Endnotes

Contact: rreis@columbia.edu. I am grateful to Cynthia Balloch, Keshav Dogra, and Savi Sundaresan for useful discussions. For acknowledgments, sources of research support, and disclosure of the author's material financial relationships, if any, please see http:// www.nber.org/chapters/c13605.ack.

1. See Gennaioli, Martin, and Rossi (2014b) and Bocola (2015), among many others.
2. See Reis (2013a) for a simple model of this at work.
3. See Brunnermeier et al. (2011) and Gennaioli, Martin, and Rossi (2014a).

References

Bocola, L. 2015. "The Pass-Through of Sovereign Risk." Working Paper no. 722, Federal Reserve Bank of Minneapolis. https://www.mpls.frb.org/research/working-papers/the-pass-through-of-sovereign-risk.
Brunnermeier, M., L. Garicano, P. R. Lane, M. Pagano, R. Reis, T. Santos, D. Thesmar, S. van Nieuwerburgh, and D. Vayanos. 2011. "European Safe Bonds (esbies)." The Euro-Nomics Group. www.euro-nomics.com.
Brunnermeier, M. K. and R. Reis. 2015. "A Crash Course on the Euro-Crisis." Unpublished Manuscript, Princeton University and Columbia University. http://scholar.princeton.edu/markus/publications/crash-course-euro-crisis.
Gennaioli, N., A. Martin, and S. Rossi. 2014a. "Banks, Government Bonds, and Default: What do the Data Say?" CEPR Discussion Paper no. 10044, Center for Economic and Policy Research.
———. 2014b. "Sovereign Default, Domestic Banks, and Financial Institutions." *Journal of Finance* 69 (2): 819–66.
La Porta, R., F. L. de Silanes, A. Shleifer, and R. W. Vishny. 1998. "Law and Finance." *Journal of Political Economy* 106 (6): 1113–55.
Mody, A. and D. Sandri. 2012. "The Eurozone Crisis: How Banks and Sovereigns Came to be Joined at the Hip." *Economic Policy* 27 (70): 199–230.
Reinhart, C. M., and K. S. Rogoff. 2009. *This Time is Different: Eight Centuries of Financial Folly*. Princeton, NJ: Princeton University Press.
Reis, R. 2013a. "The Mystique Surrounding the Central Bank's Balance Sheet, Applied to the European Crisis." *American Economic Review* 103 (3): 135–40.
———. 2013b. "The Portuguese Slump and Crash and the Euro-Crisis." *Brookings Papers on Economic Activity* 48: 143–93.
Taylor, A. M. 2015. "Credit, Financial Stability, and the Macroeconomy." NBER Working Paper no. 21039, Cambridge, MA.
Trabandt, M. and H. Uhlig. 2011. "The Laffer Curve Revisited." *Journal of Monetary Economics* 58 (4): 305–27.

Comment

Harald Uhlig, *University of Chicago and NBER*

Introduction

This is a truly wonderful and remarkable paper. It concerns an issue of prime importance: What are the economic consequences of fiscal disruptions and fears of sovereign insolvency? And it also asks: Why do fiscal insolvency issues appear to be so devastating in individual member countries of the European Monetary Union or EMU, while they do not seem to have much of an effect on the private sector, when they arise in individual states of the United States of America? This is a great question, getting right at the heart of the matter.

The paper also throws in a comparison with Canada for good measure. Canada may be interesting, sure, and I can see that it provides yet a different set of possibilities. Its population is smaller than that of South Korea, for example, and it has about as many provinces: so, why Canada and why not South Korea? Or some other country of similar size? With all due respect to the Canadians: my guess is that only a rather limited amount can be learned about the functioning of the world economy and solutions to its various crises by observing Canada. I may be wrong. Nonetheless, I shall stick to the comparison of the EMU to the USA in my discussion.

The authors provide a detailed and remarkably well crafted, insightful, and detailed analysis of key episodes and their facts for the USA and EMU (and Canada, of course), combining it with a rather thorough analysis of the underlying legal issues: thorough and convincing certainly for this discussant, who confesses to a lack of expertise on these matters.

From these case-like studies, they draw the conclusion that the key difference lies in the legal structure. If Illinois or Puerto Rico or California goes bankrupt, they cannot impair private contracts and they cannot introduce their own currency. There is no private-sector fear of redenomination risk or large expropriation risk: taxes may go up a bit, but, in essence, the states are on their own. The situation is different in the EMU, where a Grexit, an exit of Greece from the euro zone, was discussed seriously and openly.

The authors follow up on the wonderful and fact-oriented analysis with a brilliantly simple (but not simplistic!) model-based investigation. The model is not complicated and its mechanics are not particularly surprising, once properly understood: the model simply is the perfect vehicle to clearly and cleanly lay out the issues at hand.

In the model, there is a benevolent government. The government as well as its citizens need to borrow in the first period. The citizens would borrow from some world financial market, while the government can choose to borrow from there or from its own citizens or some mix of the two. The government may face limits to taxation of its citizens in the second period. It may default on its repayment to its own citizens. It may default on its repayment to foreigners, and it may let its citizens default on their foreign debt. The authors consider various combinations of whether such defaults are allowed or limits to taxation exist. Any such default creates a fixed cost, possibly drawn at random from some distribution in the second period. Thus, if the choice is available, the government will compare that fixed cost to the utility pain of repayment in the second period and choose the default option, if that turns out to be more beneficial. All agents understand that in period one already, of course.

The "euro zone countries" case has all choices available to the government. It can freely set taxes in the second period as well as freely choose any of the default options. Given the freedom to set taxes, the government is able to arbitrage away any differential in borrowing costs that might arise between government borrowing from abroad and private borrowing from abroad. For example, if private citizens could borrow more cheaply, the government effectively lets them do that on its behalf, then taxing whatever it needs. If the second-period default costs are known in period one already, for example, there is a fixed limit on how much the government and its citizens can borrow. Due to the arbitrage considerations, the government and its citizens then act as if they were facing one common and overall borrowing constraint, rather than one for the citizens and one for the government. As a result, the citizens face a constraint in borrowing from abroad precisely when the government does. This delivers the result that sovereign default fears in the euro zone countries case impair the private sector at the same time.

The "California" case for US states imposes limits on taxation, while also taking the option of private defaults on foreigners off the table. Now, the constraints are the constraints of the government only: due to its options to default in period two and due to its taxation limits, it now faces constraints on how much it can borrow in period one, while its citizens do not. There are no repercussions from sovereign default fears on the private sector.

This is a fine analysis indeed. It is terrific, insightful, useful, and deserves to be read and studied in many places. Indeed, it is highly accessible. By choice and design, this is not a high-wire act in economic formalism. Anyone with a decent undergraduate degree in economics or anyone with a bit of taste for logical and formal arguments should be able to digest this paper. I sincerely hope that many do so, beyond the narrow group of academics in their ivory towers. It is a transdisciplinary analysis of the best kind, combining economics with a discussion of judicial and historial matters.

In essence the authors argue that if only Europe had adopted a common, centralized legal framework like in the USA, much of the private-sector problems during the euro zone crisis would not have arisen! It would have been so much better, if enforcement of private contracts were enforced from some central euro zone government, and if that central government, moreover, strictly enforced the no-exit-from-the-euro rule.

This discussion would be incomplete if it only heaped praise on these fine authors. Let me then raise the skepticism that dictating common legal rules from a central government in Brussels or, for practical purposes, from Berlin really would be such a great solution for Europe. Anyone with a sense of history of Europe ought to entertain that proposal with considerable trepidation. This trepidation will provide the seed for my comments. But before turning to the details, let me take the liberty afforded to a discussant and get carried away for a bit, by commenting on a side issue in the conclusion of this fine paper.

Did Academics Anticipate the Euro Zone Crisis Ahead of Time?

In their conclusion, the authors remark that "When the member countries of the euro zone established their monetary union, neither academics nor policymakers anticipated that member states might experience external debt crises."

I disagree with that statement. Indeed, the Maastricht rules themselves were very much designed with the fear of an external debt crisis and its potential repercussions for the euro zone as a whole, in mind.

And there certainly have been plenty of academics worrying about the consequences of introducing a common currency and the resulting interplay with fiscal policy. As evidence, let me start with my own contribution here: while perhaps not justified in terms of significance, this is a choice all too tempting to this discussant. In 2002, I participated in a conference organized by a branch of the European Commission in Brussels on the challenges created by a common currency. The explicit aim was the information of and communication with the educated public, and not "just" the usual circle of academics present at our conferences. Put differently, politicians with responsibilities in these matters as well as quality journalists should be able to access these papers, and the hope clearly was that they would. The conference papers were published in a 2003 Cambridge University Press volume edited by Marco Buti, the current director-general for ECFIN. The volume includes Uhlig (2003), my own paper.

That paper devotes an entire section to "fiscal and monetary policy interaction: crisis scenarios." I shall confess that I wrote that "I believe that the European monetary union will enjoy good sailing in pleasant weather for a long time to come." Guilty as charged! But I continued by stating that

it is the task of academics like me to point out what might happen when conditions worsen. The commanding officers on board of the European ship may do well to be prepared for a storm, may do well to be prepared for the worst, even if the worst never takes place. A scenario that is worth thinking through, and in which the potential for dramatic coordination failures between the independent fiscal authorities is great is a scenario of a fiscal crisis or a banking crisis in Europe. This then is the topic to which I shall turn now. . . .Citizens of Europe and the United States look upon banking and exchange rate crises—as, for example, those in Asia, Russia or Latin America in recent years—as they look upon Malaria or starvation: horrible events, to be sure, but certain that they will never take place at home. That complacency may be misguided. Crisis scenarios are hard to imagine in good times such as these: it is the ability of imagination that is now required of the far-sighted reader. Unsustainable fiscal debt build-ups in member countries may not be a concern today, but can one and should one really exclude that they ever will be? If so, what are the consequences? I argue that this scenario merits careful prior analysis. I cannot do more here than raise some of the issues arising.

And with that, I went ahead and tried to analyze the consequences. I shall confess that I did not have sufficient phantasy at the time to truly think through what would happen: for example, I never imagined that the ECB would so liberally interpret the no-bailout clause enshrined in the Maastricht treaty, as it has done.

But still: as far as this discussant is concerned, I certainly felt that I had duly tried to warn the public. And for that, I did not want to be considered a crank either, who constantly claims that the world will end tomorrow. Perhaps now you understand my introduction and, in hindsight, misplaced optimism. It was meant as a piece of analysis for those who, like me, felt it advisable to think through disaster scenarios ahead of time and when everything appears to be calm. The paper was discussed by Vitor Gaspar, then head of research at the ECB, and later finance minister in Portugal: a first-rate thinker and someone who, per officio, might surely have been deeply concerned about this issue. I have only the best things to say about him, but it is a fact that neither was there much echo or interest by the ECB research department for any follow-up on that topic, nor was there any echo by the educated public, that is, politicians in power or journalists of any stripe, for which the whole affair had been arranged. Zero. Nothing. Nada. What is an economist to do? Ram it down their throats?

I was not the only one: I am only reporting about my own case because I happen to know it particularly well. There have been plenty of warners and warnings, and with some effort one could produce a nice list of references, many of them misguided, to be sure, but others not. It was a fascinating mix of Kassandras and Quacks, and one could have spent some effort in sorting it all out. But the euro had been introduced and things seem to be working fine for now. Would the critics please shut up?

But then things did go wrong, in a remarkably short amount of time. With a heavy dose of sadness and cynicism, I have to laugh about the broad masses of utterly uninformed and clueless journalists out there, who, in their ignorance of what is actually going on in our science, proclaim that we economists have not thought about these issues ahead of time or other crises for that matter, and that we had failed to warn and to analyze before they arrive. One really should not take journalists particularly seriously, of course. It is their job to sell newspapers and news journals, nothing more. These are just one more form of entertainment, competing with Hollywood movies, YouTube videos, and the constant bombardment of Twitter messages. Serious investigative journalism is expensive, and, it seems, in low demand by the public, paying for the newspapers that publish them (or, at least, paying for the products advertised in these newspapers). A journalist will much more easily entertain his or her readers by proclaiming a whole profession inept at doing its job. This assertion is assembled by essentially copying from other journalists, who have said exactly the same. This copying method, which appears to be so heavily favored by journalists these days, is cheap and assures that the journalist is in line with popular opinion and common views, since everyone is now saying the same. That does not make it any more true, of course, but it helps to sell the paper. And in a market economy that, really, is all that counts. I cannot complain about this equilibrium: I am merely pointing out its remarkable properties. Reasonably accurate information about the successes and failures of our profession is simply not what one should expect from journalists and their newspapers: that hope would be utterly misplaced.

In any case, we academics should surely not fall in the trap of repeating these journalistic assertions in the conclusion of an otherwise fine paper, as appears to be done here, and thereby giving them the appearance of a backing by serious scientists. They do not deserve it. And with that, let there be enough of this diatribe and digression, and let me return back to the paper. I just had to get this one off my chest.

Is It the Legal Framework?

Let me then examine the central claim of the paper: the difference between the EMU and the USA is the legal framework. The authors conclude that "the experiences of Canada and the United States indicate that stronger institutional foundations are needed to mitigate the risk of government interference with private contracts." What, exactly, is meant and implied by that? Let us think that through.

Let me contrast Greece to Illinois here: Puerto Rico or California may be a more appropriate example, perhaps, but Illinois seems to be reasonably close to bankruptcy, at the moment of writing, to serve well for the illustration. The population of Illinois and Greece is about the same, the GDP of Illinois is more than twice as high, while the debt-to-GDP ratio in Illinois is around 20%, compared to 160% for Greece. So, why is Illinois close to bankruptcy? It is indeed limited in its ability to tax: the bulk of taxation is federal, and too much of an increase in Illinois taxes may lead to an exodus of firms and citizens. For Illinois, its pensions liabilities rather than outright government debt are looming large. The Illinois Supreme Court has decided that the Illinois Constitution thoroughly protects these pensions claims, since these benefits "shall not be diminished or impaired." Greece also faces considerable pension obligations, though they may be of lesser importance there relative to the situation in Illinois. Greek banks were once heavily involved in lending to the Greek government, and some of it is still happening, despite most of the Greek debt now being held by official lenders. In contrast, it does not seem that the issue of Illinois debt is of much concern to banks in Illinois.

According to the authors, Greece may interfere with the obligations of its citizens to foreigners, while Illinois cannot do so. I believe it is fair to interpret this difference to be about renumeration risk. Perhaps Greece exits the euro zone, reintroducing the drachma, and possibly additionally passing laws that all private debt amounts are now in drachma, rather than euros. There appears to be little possibility, on the other hand, for Illinois to leave the dollar zone and introduce its own currency. The difference, the authors argue, lies in the legal framework. Is that really it?

The US Constitution indeed does not permit Illinois to introduce its own currency, but neither does the Maastricht treaty allow this for Greece. There is no exit provision. Moreover, the Maastricht treaty together with the Stability-and-Growth Pact very clearly disallows bailouts of the Greek sovereign by the European Central Bank or other governments in Europe, and imposes a variety of fiscal limits with ensuing deficit procedures, should they be violated. These treaties nearly passed as part of a proposed European Constitution: despite the rejection of passing a constitution outright, they were regarded as constitution-like. As far as I can tell, the Germans actually believed that these treaties were law and would be followed. In actual practice, that turned out to be wrong. So, at the end of the day, I argue, it does not just matter what the Constitution or its European equivalent says: what matters is, how it is interpreted and enforced. The constitution, society, politics, and military options: they all matter.

To illustrate this, let me consider the hypothetical and arguably extreme scenario of an attempt by the government of llinois to exit from the dollar zone, and let me compare that to an attempt by the Greek government to exit from the euro zone.

It would all begin with Illinois declaring its debt and pension obligations as unbearable and "austerity" as nonoption. It might ask the

Federal Reserve Bank to buy Illinois debt and Illinois obligations to reduce its currently high yields. The Federal Reserve Bank would refuse. The Illinois legislature would then meet and introduce the "salamander" as currency (see Peter Greticos, "A Modest Proposal to Fix Illinois Finances," Feb 3, 2015, rebootillinois.com). It devalues, renumerating govermnent contracts, including pension claims. While they are at it, they decide to turn all federal taxes into Illinois taxes. They declare the Chicago Federal Reserve bank to be the new Illinois Central Bank (ICB). There would be a bank holiday and capital controls to prevent initial capital flight.

But that surely would not be the end. The US Supreme Court would declare the action by the Illinois government to be illegal and void. Negotiations between Washington and Springfield would ensue: suppose they fail. The US president would not allow Illinois to secede, however, and threaten military action instead. Imagine that Illinois remains defiant. Civil war breaks out. After many casualties, the union and status quo is restored.

Is that altogether impossible? It happened before. And it was a politician from Illinois, Abraham Lincoln, who eventually succeeded in enforcing the continuation of the union. Civil war is a constitutional crisis. It is not the text of the Constitution alone that matters. The Constitution, society, politics, and military options: they all matter. At the end of the day, it is the threat of civil war and military intervention, as well as the passionate resistance of the rest of the United States population to an Illinois exit, that prevents any serious politician in Illinois from even contemplating the dollar exit option, even if that logic is never laid out explicitly.

Let me compare this to an initially similar scenario in Greece. Suppose that Greece declares its debt as unbearable and "austerity" as a nonoption. It asks the ECB to keep buying its debt: indirectly per emergency liquidity assistance to Greek banks or explicitly, in order to reduce yields. The ECB may actually do so, and, indeed, has done so in the past. But now suppose this is not enough and that the Greek economic problems persist. Greece reintroduces the drachma. It devalues, renumerating government contracts, including in particular debt and pension obligations. There is no need to turn European taxes into Greek taxes: they were always Greek taxes to begin with. Greece already has a national central bank. Greece would declare a bank holiday and capital controls to prevent initial capital flight.

But that surely would not be the end. The European Constitutional Court would declare the ECB actions to be legal, but declare the Greek exit to be illegal. Suppose that European negotiations with the Greek government fail to reach a deal. The European governments threaten to cut off further funding. Suppose Greece remains defiant. European leaders declare that no one wants a war in Europe over this, and, secretly, breathe a sigh of relief. The Maastricht treaty gets rewritten. Greece exits, devalues and defaults on its debt. Impossible? Not at all.

The difference is not the legal rules or the decisions by the Supreme Court. The Constitution, society, politics, and the military option: they all matter. Precisely because everyone would agree that, at the end of the day, it is up to Greece to remain part of the euro zone or not, makes it possible for Greek politicians (or German politicans) to entertain the Grexit option seriously. And surely no serious politician in Europe would entertain the option of an inner-European war. Nobody wants to see German tanks rolling into Greece, enforcing some common legal framework. Europe was there twice already in the last century. These times were not remembered as a "civil war," in a telling contrast to the United States. This part of European history may be more important in explaining the differences in these crisis scenarios than the details in the texts of the constitution and treaties.

One does not have to go to this extreme to see additional differences emerging that have a lot more to do with the structure of the banking system and the role of the central bank, and only indirectly with the legal framework per se (though one might wish to argue that they are connected).

A less extreme, but still severe scenario might look as follows. Suppose the Greek government declares default, leading to disruptions of the Greek economy. The ECB stops its emergency liquidity assistance to Greek banks. The Greek banking system crashes. Capital controls are imposed. The ECB no longer accepts collateral from the Greek central bank. The Greek economy crashes. There will be lots of private defaults.

Contrast this with the initially similar scenario in Illinois. Suppose the Illinois government declares default on bonds and pension obligations. Unionized public employees go on strike over impaired pensions. The Federal Reserve bank, though, never purchased Illinois bonds in the first place. The Illinois banks are not particularly exposed to Illinois debt either. There would be no point in imposing capital controls. There will be few private defaults.

Conclusion

This wonderful paper took up an issue of prime importance: What are the economic consequences of fiscal disruptions and fears of sovereign insolvency, and why is the situation so different between the USA and the EMU? Based on a transdisciplinary investigation of historical and legal facts and economic logic, as well as a model-based analysis, the authors argue that the difference is due to legal matters: in Europe, governments may impair the ability of its citizens to repay foreign debt, in particular in case of an exit from the euro zone, while this is ruled out per the constitution in the United States.

This is an intriguing and insightful comparison: it invites thinking more about these issues, and so I have tried, in my comments. I have argued that one needs to go further than to look at the legal issues alone. The Maastricht treaty may not be so different from the US Constitution, in terms of calling for the common currency as a permanent solution.

However, it is not just the Constitution that matters. The Constitution, society, politics, and the military option: they all matter. As an example, an attempt of Illinois to secede from the union and to introduce its own currency would, in the extreme, lead to civil war in the United States. By contrast, an attempt by Greece to secede from the European Union and introduce its own currency may instead be greeted by a sigh of relief by some, with no serious politician even contemplating a war, civil or otherwise, to prevent this from happening. Legal frameworks matter. So does the societal consensus, the will and the ability to enforce them.

But these remarks are not meant to take anything away from this paper: they are meant to complement and extend the fine analysis there, and to broaden and deepen this important debate. It is a terrific, insightful, and useful paper indeed. It deserves to be read and studied in many places. By choice and design, the authors made it accessible to anyone with a decent undergraduate degree in economics or anyone with a bit of taste for logical and formal arguments. I sincerely hope that many take that option, beyond the confines of the academic ivory towers. The paper and the issues discussed deserve it.

Endnote

Address: Harald Uhlig, Department of Economics, University of Chicago, 1126 East 59th Street, Chicago, IL 60637, U.S.A; e-mail: huhlig@uchicago.edu. This research has been supported by the NSF grant SES-1227280. I have an ongoing consulting relationship with a Federal Reserve Bank, the Bundesbank, and the ECB. For acknowledgments, sources of research support, and disclosure of the author's material financial relationships, if any, please see http://www.nber.org/chapters/c13606.ack.

References

Uhlig, Harald. 2003. "One Money, but Many Fiscal Policies in Europe: What are the Consequences?" In *Monetary and Fiscal Policies in EMU*, ed. M. Buti, 29–56. Cambridge: Cambridge University Press.

Discussion

Andrew Atkeson began by responding to one of the points Ricardo Reis made in his discussion, regarding banking and sovereign debt in Europe. Atkeson noted that in the United States, interest on municipal debt is income-tax deductible at the federal level, and also at the state level for residents of that particular state. He argued that this creates an incentive for individuals, instead of institutions, to hold municipal debt and suggested that Europe could implement a similar policy. He stated that this would not resolve all of Europe's sovereign debt problems but suggested the policy as a starting point.

Francesco Giavazzi summarized the paper as focusing on two dimensions of policy—fiscal flexibility and the ability of the government to interfere in private contracts. He suggested that a third element—whether governments issue their debt in their own currency or in a foreign currency—was central to understanding the current situation in Europe. He characterized European governments, prior to August 2011, as issuing debt in a foreign currency because the European Central Bank (ECB) was not willing to purchase their debt. As a result, multiple equilibria (with low and high interest rates) were possible[1], and the events of the summer of 2011 can be understood as shifts between these equilibria. After August 2011, the ECB declared its willingness to purchase government debt or finance the purchase of government debt by domestic banks. This eliminated the high-interest rate equilibrium, resolving the crisis. Applying these ideas to states in the United States, Giavazzi rhetorically asked whether Illinois and California could issue debt in their own currency. He argued that, formally, the answer is no—they cannot monetize their debt. However, during the crisis, the American Recovery and Reinvestment Act (ARRA) transferred a large amount of money to the states. The federal government was able to do this because its debt was in its own currency, illustrating the importance of the currency issue. What is the impact of governing law? Around the Eurocrisis, Greek sovereign bonds with NYC governing law clauses had lower yields than those with Greece governing law clauses, perhaps because NYC courts offer more favorable terms for creditors in the case of default and/or because Greek courts are less trustworthy. (The two classes of bonds also varied along several other dimensions: time to maturity @ issuance, currency, etc.) Some municipalities must be more attractive than others if their courts help investors extract higher recovery rates in default.

Christopher Sims spoke next, recalling that at one point early in the twenty-first century, Alan Greenspan expressed concern about the possibility that the outstanding stock of treasuries would vanish entirely. At that time, most states were net creditors because of their pension funds. However, those funds are not easy for the states to access and might impact the state's fiscal flexibility. Sims suggested that the authors examine this issue. He also asked about the nature of the fiscal flexibility measure employed by the authors, and in particular whether it was quantitatively important. Sims noted that states differ substantially in their fiscal flexibility, and yet all have low levels of debt (in comparison with European countries). He asked whether the constraints on US states are strong enough for all states to explain this pattern.

Andrew Atkeson responded by acknowledging that the handling of pension systems differs in their data between US states and European countries. He also noted that Ricardo Reis, in his discussion, apportioned federal taxation revenues and debt to the states and also found that US states had low levels of debt relative to their tax revenues and economic activity. Atkeson summarized the existing literature, and in particular the Nobel lecture by Thomas Sargent, as arguing that the states and federal government are fiscally separate and noted that the ARRA seemed to violate this assumption. Nevertheless, transfers from the federal government to the states are based on funding formulas and not directed to specific states. The general result is that state debt levels are very low relative to state revenues. Even with pension liabilities added in, most states' explicit and implicit debts are less than one year's tax revenues, whereas in European countries debt levels are much higher.

Atkeson cited Thomas Sargent as noting that, historically, states have "been on their own" fiscally. As a result, the states have been very conservative about taking on large debt burdens. In the 1840s many states defaulted and subsequently voluntarily adopted constraints on their budgets. These constraints vary from state to state, but it is difficult to determine the consequences of the variation in these policies. What really matters is what the state can do when confronted with financial stress. Recently in California, many of the issues arose from rules that required a two-thirds majority vote to raise tax rates. In contrast, New York was able to change tax rates in response to revenue shortfalls. However, Atkeson noted that it would be difficult to use these differences to explain the observed variation in municipal bond spreads across states.

More broadly, because of limits states have imposed on their debt issuance, Atkeson and coauthors believe the value to the states of being able to access credit markets is low. As a result, states are unable to sustain large debt burdens. The policy consequence of this reasoning for Europe is that, if they were able to implement the Maastricht Treaty and forbid large deficits, they would find their current levels of debt unsustainable. The temptation to default would be too strong, absent a federal system of transfers. Canadian provinces, such as Quebec and Ontario, demonstrate an alternative approach. They responded to the recent recession by issuing large amounts of debt, relative to their GDP, whereas US states followed a more procyclical fiscal policy.

Robert Hall pointed out that, in the past, California had seemingly violated Article 1 of the US Constitution and used a currency other than the dollar. Between the beginning of the Civil War and 1879, Californians continued to use the gold dollar instead of the greenback dollar. At its maximum, the gold dollar was worth $2.50 greenback dollars. Moreover, the legal protections for private contracts permit some interference. In the United States, courts have interpreted the contract clause to rule out the elimination of private debts, but they have permitted legislation that substantially changes those debts' market value. Relatedly, coastal California residents whose property has lost value as a result of regulations have challenged these regulations under the Fifth Amendment's takings clause, but the courts have consistently ruled that, as long as the property retains some value, the takings clause has not been violated.

Martin Eichenbaum noted that issues about interference in private contracts and the takings clause were important during the administration of Franklin Roosevelt. Robert Hall concurred, and mentioned that California issued "IOUs" to many of its suppliers during 2009, effectively forcing them to involuntarily lend money to California. The secondary market in these IOUs suggested that they were worth less than their face value. Hall asked whether the issuance of these IOUs was legal and emphasized the relevance of this kind of legal "leakage" for the authors' work. Mark L. Wright recalled that California banks accepted these IOUs at close to their face value. He suggested that California was legally allowed to issue these IOUs because they were not intended to circulate as a medium of exchange, the way a currency would.

Andrew Atkeson summarized the paper as stating that the US fiscal system was tested twice, once in the Civil War and once in the Great Depression. During the Great Depression, Minnesota interfered with private contracts by passing a moratorium on foreclosures, and the Supreme Court upheld this moratorium, despite Article 1 of the Constitution. As Harald Uhlig noted in his discussion, the Constitution is not a fixed system; the institutions in the United States were developed over time. During the banking panic in 1932, Michigan implemented a banking holiday, even though they did not have authority over nationally chartered banks, which were regulated by the OCC. During the three weeks between Michigan's banking holiday and Roosevelt's inauguration, all forty-eight states put banking holidays or similar restrictions in place. After Roosevelt's inauguration, a national banking holiday was enacted, and the legality of the state banking holidays was never litigated. Based on this precedent, it is hard to answer the question that Harald Uhlig raised in his discussion: What would happen if Illinois did something like that?

Atkeson also noted that in the United States the response to this experience was to create a banking union so that state governments would not be pressured to respond to regional banking crises. He argued that, in the case of Europe, this is an important policy option. However, even if Europe formed a banking union and shrank its banking sector, it would need to develop legal foundations for capital markets, such as a uniform bankruptcy code and securities laws. When the euro was first being considered, many policymakers expressed optimism that balance of payments issues would "sort themselves out," as long as the countries in Europe shared a common currency. This optimism proved unfounded, and Atkeson believes that the current view, that a banking union by itself would resolve many of these problems, will also prove excessively optimistic. Martin Eichenbaum recalled that when the euro was being discussed he asked IMF officials about what would happen if there was a balance of payments problem in Portugal. The officials responded by pointing out that no one would ask what would happen if Detroit has a balance of payments problem. Eichenbaum interpreted this response as exemplifying the excessive optimism Atkeson was referring to.

Mark L. Wright focused on one particular theme that arose in the discussions: to what extent would Europe have had problems even in the absence of any risk of government interference in private contracts because of the connection between European banks and sovereigns? He acknowledged that this is a difficult question to answer but brought up some evidence from the bond market for nonfinancial corporates. For companies headquartered in Germany, France, Italy, and Spain, prior to 2010, average spreads to German sovereign debt moved together, despite differences in the economic performance of those countries. However, as the crisis developed and exit from the euro zone was discussed, Italian and Spanish corporate spreads widened relative to German and French corporates. Wright noted that firms that issue in the corporate bond market are less dependent on bank financing and argued that this evidence suggests the risk of interference in debt contracts was rising.

Harald Uhlig responded to this argument by noting that these firms may have local suppliers and recalled the paper of Acemoglu, Akcigit, and Kerr that was also presented at the 2015 NBER Annual Conference on Macroeconomics. If these large firms' suppliers were dependent on bank financing, network effects may have also harmed firms that issue in the corporate bond market, even though they are not themselves dependent on bank financing. Andrew Atkeson responded by describing the situation of a Greek yogurt company that was headquartered in Greece, but otherwise unconnected to the Greek economy. This firm was facing higher borrowing costs simply because it was headquartered in Greece. Atkeson also noted that credit-rating agencies provide a rating for "transfer and convertibility risk," which is an attempt to separate economic fundamentals from risks related to interference. The authors use this measure in their paper.

Ricardo Reis framed the paper as being concerned with the question, "to what extent are things so different in the United States than in Europe?" He argued that the authors only need a higher risk of interference in private contracts between a Greek and a German than between citizens of different US states and felt that this difference held de facto. The "delta" in the authors' paper represents this difference. Reis discussed the paper with an expert in US insolvency law, who agreed that courts do sometimes cut debt, as Robert Hall argued earlier. However, the courts would not treat cross-state payments differently than within-state payments, which is what is crucial for the authors' model.

Martin Eichenbaum pointed out that the Illinois Constitution explicitly forbids defaulting on pension obligations. Ricardo Reis responded that European constitutions also have this provision.

Endnote

1. As an aside, Giavazzi noted that this story did not apply to Greece.

4

Networks and the Macroeconomy: An Empirical Exploration

Daron Acemoglu, *MIT and NBER*
Ufuk Akcigit, *University of Pennsylvania and NBER*
William Kerr, *Harvard Business School and NBER*

I. Introduction

How small shocks are amplified and propagated through the economy to cause sizable fluctuations is at the heart of much macroeconomic research. Potential mechanisms that have been proposed range from investment and capital accumulation responses in real business-cycle models (e.g., Kydland and Prescott 1982) to Keynesian multipliers (e.g., Diamond 1982; Kiyotaki 1988; Blanchard and Kiyotaki 1987; Hall 2009; Christiano, Eichenbaum, and Rebelo 2011); to credit market frictions facing firms, households, or banks (e.g., Bernanke and Gertler 1989; Kiyotaki and Moore 1997; Guerrieri and Lorenzoni 2012; Mian, Rao, and Sufi 2013); to the role of real and nominal rigidities and their interplay (Ball and Romer 1990); and to the consequences of (potentially inappropriate or constrained) monetary policy (e.g., Friedman and Schwartz 1971; Eggertsson and Woodford 2003; Farhi and Werning 2013).

A class of potentially promising approaches based on the spread of small shocks from firms or disaggregated sectors through their economic and other links to other units in the economy has generally been overlooked, however. The idea is simple. A shock to a single firm (or sector) could have a much larger impact on the macroeconomy if it reduces the output of not only this firm (or sector), but also of others that are connected to it through a network of input-output linkages. The macroeconomic importance of this idea was downplayed by Lucas's (1977) famous essay on business cycles on the basis of the argument that if shocks that hit firms or disaggregated sectors are idiosyncratic, they would then wash out when we aggregate across these units and look at macroeconomic fluctuations—due to a law of large numbers-type argument. Despite this powerful dismissal, this class of approaches has attracted recent theoretical attention. An important paper by Gabaix (2011) showed that when the firm-size distribution has very fat tails, so that shocks hitting the larger firms cannot be balanced out by those affecting smaller firms, the law of large numbers need not apply, opening the way to sizable macroeconomic fluctuations from idiosyncratic firm-level shocks.[1] Carvalho (2008), Acemoglu, Ozdaglar, and Tahbaz-Salehi (2015a, 2015b), Acemoglu et al. (2012), and Baqaee (2015) built on the multisector framework first developed by Long and Plosser (1983) to show how input-output linkages can also neutralize the force of the law of large numbers because shocks hitting sectors that are particularly important as suppliers to other sectors will not wash out and can translate into aggregate fluctuations.

One attractive aspect of these network-based approaches to the amplification and propagation of shocks is that they naturally lend themselves to an empirical analysis that can inform the importance of the proposed mechanisms, and the current paper undertakes such an empirical investigation. We are not the first to empirically study these interactions. One branch of existing research has provided model-based quantitative evaluation of the importance of these interactions (e.g., Horvath 1998, 2000; Carvalho 2008; Foerster, Sarte, and Watson 2011). A number of recent papers have instead focused on observable large shocks to a set of firms or industries and have traced their impact through the input-output network. Acemoglu et al. (2016) do this focusing on the spread of the impact of increased Chinese competition into the US economy through input-output linkages and local labor markets, though focusing on 10-year or 20-year effects. Boehm, Flaaen, and Nayar (2014), Barrot and Sauvagnat (2014), and Carvalho, Nirei, and Saito (2014) focus on the transmission of natural disasters, such as the 2011 Japanese earthquake, over the global input-output network.[2] Our paper contributes to this literature by studying the spread of four different types of shocks through the US input-output network at business-cycle frequencies. We also add to this by evaluating the contribution of the "geographic network" of industries—which measures the collocation patterns of industries across different commuting zones—to the interindustry propagation of macroeconomic shocks.[3]

We begin by developing some theoretical implications of the propagation of shocks through the input-output linkages. Most notably, theory predicts that supply-side (productivity) shocks propagate downstream much more powerfully than upstream—meaning that downstream customers of directly hit industries are affected more strongly than their upstream suppliers. In contrast, demand shocks (e.g., from imports or government spending) propagate upstream—meaning that upstream suppliers of directly hit industries are affected more strongly than their downstream customers. This pattern results from the fact that supply-side shocks change the prices faced by customer industries, creating powerful downstream propagation, while demand-side shocks have much more minor (or no) effects on prices and propagate upstream as affected industries adjust their production levels and thus input demands. In the simplified benchmark model studied in much of the literature, where both production functions and consumer preferences are Cobb-Douglas (so that income and substitution effects cancel out), these effects emerge particularly clearly: there is no upstream effect from supply-side shocks and no downstream effect from demand-side shocks. In addition, we show that there is a restriction on the quantitative magnitudes of the own effect (measuring how a shock to an industry affects that industry) and the network effects.

Our empirical work focuses on four different types of industry-level shocks, all propagating through the input-output linkages at the level of 392 industries as measured by the Bureau of Economic Analysis input-output tables. Our four shocks are: (a) variation from the exogenous component of imports from China, (b) changes in federal government spending (affecting industries differentially on the basis of their dependence on demand from the federal government), (c) total factor productivity (TFP) shocks, and (d) knowledge/productivity stimuli coming from variation in foreign-industry patents. For each one of these shocks, we construct downstream and upstream network effects by using information from the input-output tables—namely by taking the inner product of the corresponding row or column of the input-output matrix with a vector of shocks at the industry level. We then estimate parsimonious models of industry-level value added, employment and productivity growth on their own lags, an industry's own shocks, and downstream and upstream effects from shocks hitting other industries.[4]

A brief summary of our results is as follows. For each one of these four shocks we find propagation through the input-output network to be statistically and economically important and broadly consistent with theory. In particular, for the two demand-side shocks—Chinese imports and federal government spending—we find that upstream propagation is substantially stronger than downstream effects, which are often zero

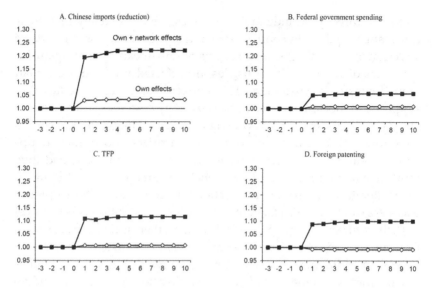

Fig. 1.   Responses to a one standard deviation shock taken in isolation, value added

Notes: Figure plots estimated response to a one standard deviation shock taken in isolation. Trade shocks are presented in positive terms to be visually comparable to the other shocks considered. Network effects focus on upstream contributions for the demand-side shocks of trade and federal spending and downstream contributions for the productivity shocks of TFP and foreign patenting. Responses are measured through log growth rates per the estimating equation and translated into levels off of a base initial level of one. The lag structure for the dependent variables includes three lags.

or of opposite sign. In contrast, for the two supply-side shocks—TFP and foreign patenting—there is strong downstream propagation, and limited or no upstream effects. In addition, the quantitative restrictions between own effects and network effects implied by theory are often verified. We also find the general patterns to be quite robust to different weighting schemes, additional controls, longer time scales, different lag structures, and so on.

The quantitative network effects are sizable and typically larger than the quantitative impact of own shocks. Figure 1 gives an indication of the magnitude of network effects by graphing the impulse response functions that result from a one-time, one standard deviation shock to every manufacturing industry.[5] The different panels show that network effects are more pronounced than own effects. For example, one standard deviation increase in imports from China will have a direct (own) effect of reducing value added growth by 3.46% in 10 years. Factoring in the (upstream) network effects, the total impact of the same shock is a 22.1% decline in value-added growth. This implies a sizable "network multiplier" (defined as the size of the total impact relative to the direct impact of the shock) of 22.1 / 3.46 $\simeq$ 6.4. The implied employment multiplier is similar, approximately 5.9.

We finally consider the effect of geographic collocation ("overlay") of industries. The geographic overlay of industries reflects the importance of localized networks, as industries with substantial exchanges frequently locate near each other to reduce transportation costs and facilitate information transfer (e.g., Fujita, Krugman, and Venables 1999).[6] After deriving a theoretically motivated measure of how industry-level shocks should propagate through the geographic overlay of industries, we show that geographic effects add another dimension of network-based propagation. While our main results are robust to these additional controls for geographic patterns, which demonstrates that input-output networks are operating above and beyond localized factors like regional business cycles, the geographic network also turns out to be a powerful transmitter of shocks from one industry to others. In fact, even though our estimates of the spread of shocks across collocating industries are slightly less robust than our baseline results, the effects appear quantitatively as large or even larger.

Overall, we interpret our results as suggesting that network-based propagation, particularly but not exclusively through the input-output linkages, might be playing a sizable role in macroeconomic fluctuations, and certainly a more important one than typically presumed in modern macroeconomics.

The rest of the paper proceeds as follows. Section II presents the theoretical model on input-output networks and shock propagation. Section III describes our data and provides descriptive statistics. Section IV presents our empirical results, focusing exclusively on national input-output connections, and section V further adds to the geographic overlay. The last section concludes, while appendix A and online appendices B and C contain further results and omitted proofs.[7]

II. Theory

In this section, we develop some simple theoretical implications of input-output linkages, and then turn to a discussion of the macroeconomic consequences of the geographic concentration of industries in certain areas.

A. Input-Output Linkages

We start with a model closely related to Long and Plosser (1983) and Acemoglu et al. (2012), which will clarify the role of input-output linkages.

Consider a static perfectly competitive economy with n industries, and suppose that each industry $i = 1, ..., n$ has a Cobb-Douglas production function of the form:

$$y_i = e^{z_i} l_i^{\alpha_i^l} \prod_{j=1}^{n} x_{ij}^{a_{ij}}. \tag{1}$$

Here x_{ij} is the quantity of goods produced by industry j used as inputs by industry i, l_i is labor, and z_i is a Hicks-neutral productivity shock (representing both technological and other factors affecting productivity). We assume that, for each i, $\alpha_i^l > 0$, and $a_{ij} \geq 0$ for all j (where $a_{ij} = 0$ implies that the output of industry j is not used as an input for industry i), and

$$\alpha_i^l + \sum_{j=1}^{n} a_{ij} = 1,$$

so that the production function of each industry exhibits constant returns to scale.[8]

As equation (1) makes clear, the output of each industry is used as input for other industries or consumed in the final good sector. Incorporating the demand from other industries, the market-clearing condition for industry i can be written as

$$y_i = c_i + \sum_{j=1}^{n} x_{ji} + G_i, \tag{2}$$

where c_i is final consumption of the output of industry i, and G_i denotes government purchases of good i, which are assumed to be wasted or spent on goods households do not directly care about. We introduce government purchases to be able to model demand-side shocks in a simple fashion.

The preference side of this economy is summarized by a representative household with a utility function

$$u(c_1, c_2, ..., c_n, l) = \gamma(l) \prod_{i=1}^{n} c_i^{\beta_i}, \tag{3}$$

where $\beta_i \in (0, 1)$ designates the weight of good i in the representative household's preferences (with the normalization $\sum_{i=1}^{n} \beta_i = 1$), and $\gamma(l)$ is a decreasing (differentiable) function capturing the disutility of labor supply.

The government imposes a lump-sum tax, T, to finance its purchases. Denoting the price of the output of industry i by p_i, this implies $T = \sum_{i=1}^{n} p_i G_i$. Since its income comes only from labor, wl, the representative household's budget constraint can be written as

$$\sum_{i=1}^{n} p_i c_i = wl - T.$$

We focus on the *competitive equilibrium* of this static economy, which is defined in the usual fashion, so that all firms maximize profits and the representative household maximizes its utility, in both cases taking all prices as given, and the market-clearing conditions for each good and labor are satisfied. The amount of government spending and taxes are taken as given in this competitive equilibrium. We also choose the wage as the numeraire (i.e., set $w = 1$).

The Cobb-Douglas production functions in (1), combined with profit maximization, imply

$$\frac{p_j x_{ij}}{p_i y_i} = a_{ij}. \tag{4}$$

In preparation for our main results we will present, let $\mathbf{A}$ denote the matrix of a_{ij}'s,

$$\mathbf{A} = \begin{pmatrix} a_{11} & a_{12} & \cdots & \\ a_{21} & a_{22} & & \\ & & \ddots & \\ & & & a_{nn} \end{pmatrix}.$$

We also define

$$\mathbf{H} \equiv (\mathbf{I} - \mathbf{A})^{-1} \tag{5}$$

as the *Leontief inverse* of the input-output matrix $\mathbf{A}$, and denote its typical entry by h_{ij}.

Proposition 1. *The impact of sectoral productivity (supply-side) shocks on the output of sector i is*

$$d \ln y_i = \underbrace{dz_i}_{\text{own effect}} + \underbrace{\sum_{j=1}^{n} (h_{ij} - \mathbf{1}_{j=i}) \times dz_j,}_{\text{network effect}} \tag{6}$$

where h_{ij} is the ij-th element of $\mathbf{H}$ *(the Leontief inverse of* $\mathbf{A}$*), and* $\mathbf{1}_{j=i}$ *is the indicator function for* $j = i$*. This equation implies that in response to productivity shocks, there are no upstream effects (i.e., no effects on suppliers of affected industries) and only downstream effects (i.e., only effects on customers of affected industries).*

Suppose $\gamma(l) = (1 - l)^{\lambda}$. *Then the impact of government-spending (demand-side) shocks on the output of sector* i *is*

$$
d \ln y_i = \underbrace{\frac{d\tilde{G}_i}{p_i y_i}}_{\text{own effect}} + \underbrace{\sum_{j=1}^{n}(\hat{h}_{ji} - \mathbf{1}_{j=i}) \times \frac{1}{p_j y_j} \times d\tilde{G}_j}_{\text{network effect}}
$$
$$
\underbrace{- \sum_{j=1}^{n}\hat{h}_{ji} \times \frac{1}{p_j y_j} \times \frac{\beta_j}{1 + \lambda} \times \sum_{k=1}^{n}d\tilde{G}_k}_{\text{resource constraint effect}}
$$

(7)

where $\tilde{G}_j = p_j G_j$ *is nominal government spending on sector* j*'s output,* $\hat{h}_{ij}$ *is the ij-th element of the Leontief inverse matrix* $\hat{\mathbf{H}} = (\mathbf{I} - \hat{\mathbf{A}})^{-1}$*, and* $\hat{\mathbf{A}}$ *is the matrix with entries given by* $\hat{a}_{ij} = p_j x_{ij} \, / \, p_j y_j$ *(i.e., sales from industry* j *to industry* i *normalized by sales of industry* j*). This implies that demand-side shocks do not propagate downstream (i.e., to customers of affected industries), only upstream (i.e., only to suppliers of affected industries).*

This proposition is proved in appendix A. Equations (6) and (7) form the basis of our empirical strategy, and link the output of sector i to its own "shock," dz_i, and to "shocks" hitting all other industries working through the input-output linkages of the economy. In particular, in equation (6), dz_i is the own shock, while $\Sigma_{j=1}^{n}(h_{ij} - \mathbf{1}_{j=i})dz_j$ is the *network effect*. Notice that this expression includes the propagation of the own shock through the input-output linkages, $h_{ii} - 1$, together with the network effect, and then subtracts the own effect (via the indicator function $\mathbf{1}_{j=i}$, which takes the value 1 when $j = i$ and the value 0 otherwise), so as not to double count this direct effect.[9] Similarly, in equation (7), $d\tilde{G}_i \, / \, p_i y_i$ is the own shock and $\Sigma_{j=1}^{n}(\hat{h}_{ji} - \mathbf{1}_{j=i})(1 \, / \, p_j y_j)d\tilde{G}_j$ is the network effect.[10] These equations have several important implications.

First, what matters for the network effects is not directly the entries of the input-output matrix, $\mathbf{A}$ or $\hat{\mathbf{A}}$, but its Leontief inverse. The intuition is instructive about the workings of the model. For example, a negative productivity shock to industry j will reduce its production and increase its price. This will adversely impact all of the industries that purchase inputs from industry j. But this direct impact will be further augmented in the competitive equilibrium because these first-round-affected industries will change their production and prices, creating indirect negative effects on other customer industries ("downstream effects"). The Leontief inverse captures these indirect effects.

Second, the network effects in response to the demand-side and supply-side shocks are rather different. For supply-side shocks, the network effect, $\Sigma_{j=1}^{n}(h_{ij} - 1_{j=i})dz_j$, implies that the impact goes downstream (and *not at all* upstream). For demand-side shocks, the network effect is given by the term $\Sigma_{j=1}^{n}(\hat{h}_{ji} - 1_{j=i})(1 / p_j y_j)d\tilde{G}_j$, indicating upstream propagation—the $\hat{h}_{ji}$ term signifies the spread of a shock to industries that are suppliers of the affected industries. Equation (7), in addition, includes the resource-constraint effect, the term $\Sigma_{j=1}^{n}\hat{h}_{ji}(1 / p_j y_j)[\beta_j / (1 + \lambda)]\Sigma_{k=1}^{n}d\tilde{G}_k$, which reflects the impact of government spending on the representative household's budget constraint—the government spending, financed by taxes, leaves fewer resources for private consumption. The parameter β_j here captures the fact that the impact of the lower net income of the representative household on the consumption of sector j depends on the share of this sector in consumption, given by β_j. When $\gamma' = 0$ so that there is no labor-supply response and thus $\lambda = 0$, this impact is maximized. On the other hand, when there is a positive labor-supply response, this effect is partially offset by increased production across the economy. It is also worth noting that these effects are still propagated through the input-output matrix as shown by the $\hat{h}_{ji}$ terms, because a decline in the consumption of good j causes sector j to cut production and its input purchases from other sectors, leading to the upstream transmission of the direct implications of the resource constraint.

The next two examples illustrate in greater detail why supply-side or productivity shocks propagate downstream, while demand shocks propagate upstream.

Example 1 (Downstream propagation of supply-side shocks). Consider an economy with three sectors, with the input-output network as shown in panel (A) of figure 2. Sector 1 is the sole customer of sector 2, sector 2 is the sole customer of sector 3, and sector 3 is the sole customer of sector 1. The sectoral production functions are therefore given as

$$y_1 = e^{z_1}l_1^{\alpha_1^l}x_{12}^{a_{12}}, \quad y_2 = e^{z_2}l_2^{\alpha_2^l}x_{23}^{a_{23}}, \quad \text{and} \quad y_3 = e^{z_3}l_3^{\alpha_3^l}x_{31}^{a_{31}},$$

and are all assumed to satisfy constant returns to scale. It follows from Proposition 1 that sector 1's output is:[11]

$$d \ln y_1 = \frac{dz_1 + a_{12}dz_2 + a_{12}a_{23}dz_3}{1 - a_{12}a_{23}a_{31}}.$$

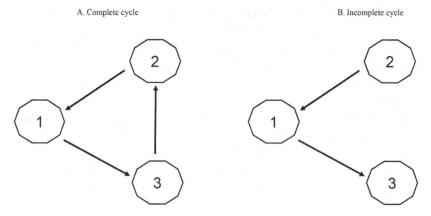

Fig. 2.   Theoretical examples

This expression shows that sector 1's output depends on the shocks to all three sectors. However, this is purely because of the propagation of productivity (supply-side) shocks downstream. For example, sector 3's productivity shock, z_3, affects y_1 not because of upstream propagation, but because of the chain of downstream propagation: sector 1 is a customer of sector 2, and sector 2 is a customer of sector 3. Indeed, the coefficient of z_3 in this expression, $a_{12}a_{23}$, illustrates this indirect effect. To see further that there is no upstream propagation, consider a modification of this input-output network as shown in panel (B) of figure 2, where the link between sector 2 and sector 3 is severed (i.e., $a_{23} = 0$). The output of sector 1 then becomes

$$d \ln y_1 = dz_1 + a_{12}dz_2,$$

with no impact from z_3. This verifies that it was the indirect downstream transmission of sector 3's productivity shock that impacted sector 1. With the link between sectors 2 and 3 severed, this indirect transmission ceases, and there is no longer any impact of z_3 on sector 1. Had it been the upstream propagation of productivity shocks, we would have seen a similar dependence of sector 1's output on z_3 since the input linkage between these two sectors has not changed.

The intuition for why there are no economic effects working upstream through the input-output network—as shown in Proposition 1 and Example 1—is related to the Cobb-Douglas nature of the production functions and preferences. Any impact on upstream industries will depend on the balance of a quantity effect (less is produced in industry *j* after an adverse productivity shock) and price effect (each unit produced in industry *j* is now more expensive). With Cobb-Douglas technologies and preferences from households, these two effects exactly cancel out.[12] Downstream propagation, on the other hand, is a consequence of the fact that an adverse productivity shock to a sector leads to an increase in the price of that sector's output, encouraging its customer industries to use this input less intensively and thus reduce their own production. This downstream propagation is also the reason why the impact of a shock depends only on input-output linkages, and not on the consumption shares, the β_j's. The consumption shares influence the level of production in different sectors, but not the proportional responses to productivity shocks; productivity shocks translate into proportional declines in prices and thus proportional downstream transmission, regardless of consumption shares.

The next example illustrates the propagation of demand-side shocks.

Example 2 (Upstream propagation of demand-side shocks). Consider again the economy depicted in panel (A) of figure 2, but now with government-spending shocks, expressed in nominal terms as $d\tilde{G}_1$, $d\tilde{G}_2$, and $d\tilde{G}_3$, rather than productivity shocks (and thus setting $dz_1 = dz_2 = dz_3 = 0$). We also set $\beta_1 = \beta_2 = \beta_3 = 1/3$. In this case, the change in the nominal output of sector 1 (with tildes again denoting nominal variables) can be derived as

$$d\tilde{y}_1 = \frac{1}{1 - a_{12}a_{23}a_{31}} \left\{ \begin{array}{c} d\tilde{G}_1 + a_{23}a_{31}d\tilde{G}_2 + a_{31}d\tilde{G}_3 \\ -\dfrac{(1 + a_{31} + a_{23}a_{31})}{3(1 + \lambda)}[d\tilde{G}_1 + d\tilde{G}_2 + d\tilde{G}_3] \end{array} \right\}.$$

Once again, shocks to all three sectors influence the nominal output of sector 1, but this time it is because of the cumulative indirect effects working upstream. In particular, the effect of the shock to sector 2, $d\tilde{G}_2$, on sector 1 is working upstream through its impact on sector 3 and then sector 3's impact on sector 1, as can be seen from the fact that this term is multiplied by $a_{23}a_{31}$ in the first line. The resource constraint effect is shown in the second line. Similar to our analysis in the previous example, we can verify that the network effects shown in the first line are not working through downstream propagation by considering panel (B) of figure 2. When the link between sectors 2 and 3 is severed (or equivalently when $a_{23} = 0$), the change in the nominal output of sector 1 becomes

$$d\tilde{y}_1 = d\tilde{G}_1 + a_{31}d\tilde{G}_3 - \frac{(1 + a_{31})}{3(1 + \lambda)}[d\tilde{G}_1 + d\tilde{G}_2 + d\tilde{G}_3],$$

where the second term is again the indirect effect working through the household budget constraint. The absence of an impact from the government-spending shock to sector 2 now confirms that all propagation of demand-side shocks is upstream.

The intuition for why demand-side shocks propagate only upstream, as demonstrated in Proposition 1 and Example 2, is also instructive. With government-spending shocks, affected industries have to increase their production to meet the increased demand from the government. But given that they are using inputs from other supplier industries, this is only possible if industries supplying inputs to them also expand their inputs (proportionately to the role of these inputs in the production function of the affected industries). This is the logic for upstream propagation of demand-side shocks. Why is there no downstream propagation? Since all sectors have constant returns to scale, prices in this economy are entirely independent of the demand side. Government-spending shocks change quantities, but not prices (see appendix A). But this implies that the channel through which downstream propagation took place in response to productivity shocks—changing relative prices—is entirely absent, accounting for the lack of downstream propagation in response to demand-side shocks.

A *third* implication of equations (6) and (7) concerns the magnitudes of the coefficients of the own and network effects. The simplest way of seeing this is to reorganize these equations so that equation (6) becomes

$$d \ln y_i = h_{ii} \times dz_i + \sum_{j \neq i} h_{ij} \times dz_j,$$

which implies that if the indirect impacts of the own shock are included with the direct effect (and excluded from the network effect), then the coefficients of the own and the network effects, when properly scaled by the entries of the Leontief inverse, should be equal.[13] The same is true for the demand-side shocks in equation (7), which can be rearranged as

$$d \ln y_i = \hat{h}_{ii} \frac{d\tilde{G}_i}{p_i y_i} + \sum_{j \neq i} \hat{h}_{ji} \frac{d\tilde{G}_j}{p_j y_j} - \sum_{j=1}^{n} \hat{h}_{ji} \frac{\beta_j}{1 + \lambda} \sum_{k=1}^{n} d\tilde{G}_k,$$

again showing the equality of the coefficients of the properly scaled own and network effects (the first two terms). These results readily extend to the employment equation by observing that the employment effects are derived from the output effects, and are thus proportional to them.

Fourth, equations (6) and (7) also imply that what matters in our theoretical framework are the contemporaneous shocks (e.g., dz_i), not some future anticipated shocks.[14] This motivates our use of current (or one-period lagged) shocks on the right-hand side of our estimating equations.

Finally, we further note that the implications of import shocks are also very similar to government-spending shocks, since a decline in imports (without imposing trade balance) is analogous to an increase in government spending on the same sectors, and for this reason we have not separately introduced these shocks in our theoretical model.

B.   The Effects of the Geographic Network

Another important set of interlinkages, which could be represented as network effects, relates to geographic overlay over industries (corresponding to how industries collocate in various local labor markets, for example, as measured by commuting zones). Thinking through these geographic interactions is important to ensure that our empirical work can distinguish input-output network effects from these geographic interlinkages; moreover, these local linkages are also of direct interest as another transmitter of industry-level shocks.

Let us start with a simple reduced-form model capturing local demand effects

$$d \ln y_{r,i} = \eta \sum_{j \neq i} \frac{y_{r,j}}{y_r} d \ln y_{r,j} + dz_i, \tag{8}$$

where $y_{r,i}$ is the output of industry i in region r, and dz_i is an industry shock normalized to have a unit impact on the industry's output (in a region). In what follows, take η to be small (and in particular less than 1).

This equation captures the idea that if industries in a given region (local labor market) are hit by negative shocks, this will reduce economic activity and adversely affect output and employment in other industries, which is consistent with empirical evidence reported in Autor, Dorn, and Hanson (2013) and Mian and Sufi (2014). For example, if a large employer in a given local labor market shuts down, this will reduce the demand and thus employment and output of other local employers. The most obvious channel for this is through some local demand effects, though other local linkages would also lead to a relationship similar to (8).

The functional form in this equation is intuitive and implies that the impact of a proportional decline in industry j on industry i in the same region will be scaled by the importance of industry j in the region's output ($y_{r,j} / y_r$). Note also that, for simplicity's sake, we ignore the network effects coming from input-output linkages in this subsection.

The next step is to solve the within-region equilibrium implied by (8). Doing this with matrix algebra, we can write

$$d \ln \mathbf{y}_{r,i} = (\mathbf{I} - \mathbf{B})^{-1} d\mathbf{z}_i, \tag{9}$$

where

$$\mathbf{B} = \begin{pmatrix} 0 & \eta(y_{r,2} / y_r) & \eta(y_{r,3} / y_r) & \cdots \\ & 0 & & \\ & & 0 & \\ & & & 0 \\ & & & & 0 \end{pmatrix}.$$

Given our analysis of input-output models, it is not surprising that a Leontief inverse-type matrix is playing a central role here. But in this instance, it is useful for us to go beyond this matrix representation. In particular, when η is small as we have assumed, second- and higher-order terms in η can be ignored, and the within-region equilibrium can be expressed in the following form:[15]

$$d \ln y_{r,i} \approx dz_i + \eta \sum_{j \neq i} \frac{y_{r,j}}{y_r} dz_j.$$

Intuitively, this equation describes the within-region equilibrium as a function of shocks to all industries (solving out all "endogenous" terms from the right-hand side). Now using the fact that $d \ln y_{r,i} = dy_{r,i} / y_{r,i}$, and summing across regions, we obtain

$$dy_i = \sum_r dy_{r,i} \approx y_i dz_i + \eta \sum_r \sum_{j \neq i} \frac{y_{r,i} y_{r,j}}{y_r} dz_j,$$

which then enables us to obtain a simple representation of the geographic effects:

$$d \ln y_i \approx dz_i + \eta \sum_{j \neq i} \text{geographic\_overlay}_{i,j} dz_j, \tag{10}$$

where

$$\text{geographic\_overlay}_{i,j} \equiv \sum_r \frac{y_{r,i} y_{r,j}}{y_i y_r}$$

is the noncentered cross-region correlation coefficient of industries i and j, normalized by their national levels of production, and represents their tendency to collocate.

Intuitively, this equation captures the fact that industries will be impacted not only by their direct shocks but also by the shocks of other industries that tend to collocate with them. For example, if coal and steel industries are always in the same few regions, the steel industry will be negatively affected nationally not only when there is a negative shock to itself but also when there is a negative shock to the coal industry, because when the coal industry is producing less in the region, other industries in that region are also adversely affected, and steel is overrepresented among these industries that happen to be in the same region as coal.

Though the term we have for geographic overlay is simple and intuitive, it is based on an approximation that involves ignoring all terms that are second or higher order in η, thus posing the natural question of whether including some of these additional terms would lead to additional insights. To provide a partial answer to this question, we now include second-order terms (thus ignoring only third- or higher-order terms in η), which leads to a natural generalization of (10). In particular, the within-region equilibrium can now be expressed as

$$d \ln y_{r,i} \approx dz_i + \eta \sum_{j \neq i} \frac{y_{r,j}}{y_r} dz_j + \eta^2 \sum_{j \neq i} \frac{y_{r,j}}{y_r} \sum_{k \neq j} \frac{y_{r,k}}{y_r} dz_k.$$

Now summing across regions and repeating the same steps as above, we obtain

$$d \ln y_i = dz_i + \eta \Sigma_{j \neq i} \text{ geographic\_overlay}_{i,j} dz_j$$

$$+ \eta^2 \Sigma_{j \neq i} \Sigma_{k \neq j,i} \overline{\text{geographic\_overlay}}_{i,j,k} dz_j$$

where the additional geographic overlay term, which includes triple collocation patterns, is

$$\overline{\text{geographic\_overlay}}_{i,j,k} \equiv \sum_r \frac{y_{r,i} y_{r,j} y_{r,k}}{y_i y_r^2}. \tag{11}$$

III. Data and Descriptive Statistics

This section describes our various data sources and the construction of the key measures of downstream and upstream effects and the geographic network.

A. Data Sources

Our core industry-level data for manufacturing come from the NBER-CES Manufacturing Industry Database (Becker, Gray, and Marvakov

2013). We utilize data for the years 1991–2009. Using the first change as a baseline, our estimations cover 17 changes from 1992–1993 to 2008–2009. In the first four changes, we have 392 four-digit industries; thereafter, we have 384 industries for 6,560 total observations. Though the theoretical predictions derived in the previous section are in terms of total industry output (shipments), our baseline analysis focuses on (real) value added due to its adjustment for energy costs, nonmanufacturing inputs, and inventory changes, which are all outside of our model. We show similar results using real and nominal shipments in appendix B.[16]

To construct our linkages between industries, we use the Bureau of Economic Analysis' 1992 Input-Output Matrix and the 1991 County Business Patterns database as described further below. In the next section, we describe the data used for each shock when introducing it.

B.   Upstream and Downstream Networks

The construction of downstream and upstream effects follows Acemoglu et al. (2016). We construct the matrix $\mathbf{A}$ introduced in section II from the 1992 "Make" and "Use" Tables of the Bureau of Economic Analysis. This matrix has input share entries corresponding to

$$a_{ij} \equiv \frac{Sales_{j \to i}}{Sales_i}.$$

As emphasized in section II, this quantity measures the total sales of inputs from industry j to industry i, normalized by the total sales (or equivalently the total costs) of industry i. Intuitively, it corresponds to how many dollars worth of the output of sector j (say tires) sector i (say the car industry) needs to purchase to produce one dollar's worth of its own output. When production functions are Cobb-Douglas, as we have assumed in our theoretical analysis, these input shares are constant regardless of prices. Equation (6) shows that network effects from supply-side shocks directly depend on these input shares. The Leontief inverse of the input-output matrix is then computed from the matrix of these input-output shares as $(\mathbf{I} - \mathbf{A})^{-1}$ to give our downstream network measure. In what follows, we use the notation $Input\%_{j \to i}$ to represent the elements of the Leontief inverse of the input-output matrix.[17]

For constructing the network effects from demand-side shocks, we again follow equation (7), which decomposes the response of a sector into an own effect, a network effect, and the resource-constraint effect.

We first ignore the last one and focus on the network effect. The presence of the $\hat{h}_{ji}$ (or $\hat{a}_{ji}$) terms in this equation underscores the different aspects of input-output linkages involved in upstream propagation. The empirical counterparts of the $\hat{a}_{ij}$ terms are

$$\frac{Sales_{i \to j}}{Sales_i} \equiv a_{ji} \frac{Sales_j}{Sales_i},$$

which we use to compute the upstream network measures. We use $Output\%_{i \to j}$ to represent these Leontief inverse terms. We return to the resource-constraint effect later.

C.   Geographic Overlay

We also measure the geographic overlay of two industries using the metric developed in the theory section,

$$\text{geographic\_overlay}_{i,j} \equiv \sum_r \frac{y_{r,i} y_{r,j}}{y_i y_r}.$$

We define regions through BEA commuting zones and utilize 1991 County Business Patterns data to measure the overlay. We also calculate the higher-order geographic overlay term (11). In practice, however, we observe very little additional explanatory power with the second metric and thus focus simply on the direct collocation case.

D.   Correlation Matrices

Table 1A shows the correlation matrix of these interconnections, excluding own-industry interconnections (i.e., network diagonals). Upstream and downstream material flows are moderately correlated at 0.4 and somewhat less strongly correlated with geographic overlay, indicating that input-output linkages operate, for the most part, beyond common geographies.

Table 1B depicts the correlation of our four measures of shocks with each other and shows that our different shocks are only weakly correlated, assuaging concerns that we may be tracing the effects of omitted shocks when modeling the effect of each shock one at a time. Column (5) of table 1B reports the average between-industry correlation for each shock (e.g., how correlated is, say, the federal spending shock of an industry with the federal spending shocks of other industries). This is relevant in part because a high between-industry correla-

Table 1A
Correlation Matrix of Network Interconnections

	Downstream Leontief (1)	Upstream Leontief (2)	Geographic Overlay (3)
Downstream Leontief	1		
Upstream Leontief	0.400	1	
Geographic overlay	0.108	0.275	1

Notes: Downstream networks represent inputs from supplier industries into the focal industry's production, expressed as a share of the focal industry's sales (e.g., rubber inputs into the tire industry as a share of the tire industry's sales). Upstream networks represent sales from the focal industry to industrial customers, expressed as a share of the focal industry's sales (e.g., sales of tires to car manufacturers as a share of the tire industry's sales). Both networks are measured from the 1991 BEA Input-Output Matrix. Shares allow for flows to nonmanufacturing industries and customers and thus do not sum to 100% within manufacturing. Leontief connections provide the full chain of interconnections in the network matrix. Geographic overlay is measured as the sum across regions of the interaction of a focal industry's employment share in the region times the share of regional activity for other industries. Regions are defined through commuting zones and use 1991 industrial activity from the County Business Patterns database. Correlations are statistically significant at the 1% level.

Table 1B
Correlation Matrix of Shocks

	China Trade Shock (1)	Federal Spending Shock (2)	TFP Shock (3)	Foreign Patenting Shock (4)	Correlation Coefficient (5)
China trade shock	1				0.200
Federal spending shock	0.031	1			0.452
TFP shock	−0.021	0.017	1		−0.002
Foreign patenting shock	−0.023	0.030	0.003	1	0.003

Notes: Baseline trade shocks for manufacturing industries are the lagged change in imports from China relative to 1991 US market volume, following Autor et al. (2013). A negative value is taken such that positive coefficients correspond to likely beneficial outcomes, similar to other shocks. All trade analyses instrument US imports with the rise in Chinese imports in eight other advanced countries, and this table reports the correlation of the IV component. Baseline federal spending shocks for manufacturing industries are the lagged log change in national federal spending interacted with the 1992 share of sales from industries that went to the federal government. Baseline TFP shocks for manufacturing industries are the lagged log change in four-factor TFP taken from the NBER Productivity Database. Baseline patent shocks for manufacturing industries are the lagged log change in USPTO patents filed by overseas inventors associated with the industry. These correlations are presented after year fixed effects are removed from each shock. The Correlation Coefficient column presents the average pairwise correlation of the given shock series between any two industries.

tion of shocks might create spurious network effects in the presence of an omitted higher-order impact of own shocks. The relatively low between-industry correlations, except for the federal spending shock, are comforting in this regard. The higher between-industry correlation for the federal spending shock is unsurprising since it is constructed from the interaction of aggregate time-series variation in federal spending with a time-invariant measure of federal spending dependency of each industry (as detailed further below).

IV. Results: The Input-Output Network

This section provides our primary empirical results that quantify shock propagation through the input-output networks, leaving the analysis of the geographic network to the next section. We focus on four shocks: (a) import penetration, (b) federal spending changes, (c) TFP growth, and (d) foreign-patenting growth. The first two correspond to demand-side shocks, while the latter two are supply side, approximating productivity shocks. We first consider each shock by itself, describing how we measure it, and studying its empirical properties in isolation. After cycling through all four shocks independently, we jointly model them and provide an extended discussion of economic magnitudes.

A. Empirical Approach

Throughout, our main estimating equations are direct analogs of equations (6) and (7) in the theory section, and take the following form:

$$\Delta \ln Y_{i,t} = \delta_t + \psi \Delta \ln Y_{i,t-1} + \beta^{\text{own}} Shock_{i,t-1} \\ + \beta^{\text{upstream}} Upstream_{i,t-1} + \beta^{\text{downstream}} Downstream_{i,t-1} + \varepsilon_{i,t} \quad (12)$$

where i indexes industries, δ_t denotes a full set of time effects, $\varepsilon_{i,t}$ is an error term, and $Y_{i,t}$ stands for one of three industry-level variables from the NBER manufacturing database: real value added (using the industry's shipments deflator), employment, and real labor productivity (real value added divided by employment).

In our baseline results, time periods correspond to years. We start with a model that only considers the core regressors outlined in equation (12), and then we show robustness checks that add extra controls. We allow only a single lag of the dependent variable on the right-hand side for parsimony. The role of additional lags is taken up in robustness checks.

The key regressors are $Shock_{i,t-1}$, the industry's own direct shock (taken from one of the four shocks introduced above), and $Upstream_{i,t-1}$ and $Downstream_{i,t-1}$, which stand for the shocks working through the network. These network shocks are always computed from the interaction of the vector of shocks hitting other industries and a vector representing the interlinkages between the focal industry and the rest (e.g., the row or the column of the input-output matrix); we provide exact details below.

The upstream and downstream terminology in network analyses has some ambiguity. In the remainder, we follow our usage in section II and label "upstream effects" as those arising from shocks to customers of an industry that flow up the input-output chain; in parallel, we describe "downstream effects" as those arising from shocks to suppliers of an industry that flow down the input-output chain. Henceforth, for clarity, we use "upstream" and "downstream" terms to describe exclusively the effects. When there is a need to describe where the shock originates, we will use the terms "customer" and "supplier" to avoid confusion.

Thus, we measure downstream effects (due to supplier shocks) and upstream effects (due to customer shocks) closely mimicking the theoretical equations, (6) and (7). In particular, these are given by the weighted averages of shocks hitting all industries using entries of the Leontief inverse matrices as weights:

$$Downstream_{i,t} = \Sigma_j (Input\%_{j \to i}^{1991} - \mathbf{1}_{j=i}) \cdot Shock_{j,t}, \qquad (13)$$

and

$$Upstream_{i,t} = \Sigma_j (Output\%_{i \to j}^{1991} - \mathbf{1}_{j=i}) \cdot Shock_{j,t}, \qquad (14)$$

where $\mathbf{1}_{j=i}$ is an indicator function for $j = i$, and the summation is over all industries, including industry i itself. Thus as in the equations (6) and (7), when computing the downstream effect for sector i, we take into account the indirect linkages from this industry to itself (e.g., the fact that industry i supplies to industry j, which is also a supplier to i), but we subtract the direct effect of the shock, since in our regressions we will directly control for the shock to sector i.

Several other points are worth noting. First, as already observed, input-output linkages (and thus the Leontief inverse entries) are predetermined and measured in 1991. Thus, downstream and upstream effects are simply a function of shocks in connected industries working through a predetermined input-output network.

Second, we lag both own and network shocks by one period, simply to avoid any concern about contemporaneous measurement issues from our dependent variables to shocks (e.g., in the case of TFP) and about contemporaneous joint determination. It should be stressed, however, that we do not claim that this timing will enable us to estimate causal effects. Rather, we rely on the plausible exogeneity of shocks, especially for imports from China and federal government spending, and caution that this exogeneity is likely to be absent in the case of the TFP and foreign-patenting shocks.

Third, equation (12) is formulated in changes, and shocks are always specified in changes as detailed below. The specification could have alternatively been written in levels together with an industry fixed effect. The advantage of the current formulation is that it both follows more directly from and connects to our theoretical model, and imposes that the error term is stationary in differences, which is generally a better description of macro time series.

Finally, in what follows, unless otherwise stated, we standardize the $Shock_{i,t-1}$ variable so that a unit increase corresponds to a one standard deviation change in the positive direction (e.g., decrease in imports or increase in TFP), and the $Upstream_{i,t-1}$ and $Downstream_{i,t-1}$ variables are constructed in the same units. This implies that the coefficient on the $Shock_{i,t-1}$ variable will measure the impact of a one standard deviation increase in the industry's own shock, whereas the coefficients on $Upstream_{i,t-1}$ and $Downstream_{i,t-1}$ will measure the impact of a one standard deviation increase in the shock of all customers and suppliers of an industry. Moreover, all of these coefficients are directly comparable and are expected to be positive where theory predicts a network-based effect.

B.   China Import Shocks

Our first shock relates to the growth of imports from China and follows Autor et al. (2013) and Acemoglu et al. (2016). Acemoglu et al. (2016) show this pattern for decade-long adjustments, and we extend this analysis to shorter frequencies considered in macroeconomics. As highlighted in section II, this demand-side shock should have greater upstream effects than downstream effects, and in the case of Cobb-Douglas, downstream effects should not be present at all.

We first define $ChinaTrade$ to capture this industry exposure to rising Chinese trade,

$$ChinaTrade_{j,t} = -\frac{\text{US Imports from China}_{j,t}}{\text{US market size}_{j,1991}}.$$

This variable, however, is clearly endogenous, as it will tend to be higher when the industry in question has lower productivity growth for other reasons, creating greater room for a rise in imports, and is thus not a good measure of shocks for our analysis. To deal with this endogeneity concern, we follow Autor et al. (2013) and Acemoglu et al. (2016) and instrument this variable with its exogenous component, defined as the change in import penetration from China to eight major non-US countries relative to 1991 US market volume, with the nations being Austria, Denmark, Finland, Germany, Japan, New Zealand, Spain, and Switzerland:

$$ChinaTrade_{j,t}^{IV} = -\frac{\text{Non-US Imports from China}_{j,t}}{\text{US market size}_{j,1991}}.$$

This instrument has the advantage of not being directly affected by changes in productivity or demand in the US economy.[18]

The downstream and upstream effects are calculated from (13) and (14) adapted to this case. For example, for the downstream effects coming from supplier industries, we model the shock:

$$Downstream_{i,t}^{Trade} = \sum_j (Input\%_{j \to i}^{1991} - \mathbf{1}_{j=i}) \cdot \Delta ChinaTrade_{j,t}. \quad (15)$$

We also construct the network instruments using the same reasoning as in (13) and (14). For example, for the downstream effects this simply takes the form of

$$Downstream_{i,t}^{TradeIV} = \sum_j (Input\%_{j \to i}^{1991} - \mathbf{1}_{j=i}) \cdot \Delta ChinaTrade_{j,t}^{IV}.$$

In summary, we have three endogenous variables, $ChinaTrade_{j,t}$, $Downstream_{i,t}^{Trade}$ and $Upstream_{i,t}^{Trade}$, and three instruments, $ChinaTrade_{j,t}^{IV}$, $Downstream_{i,t}^{TradeIV}$ and $Upstream_{i,t}^{TradeIV}$. The first stages for these three variables are shown in appendix table 1 (all appendix tables are included in appendix B).[19]

Table 2A presents our estimates of own and network effects from this exercise, using a table format that we replicate for each subsequent shock. Table 2A presents our baseline results for the three outcome variables, considering one and three lags for the dependent variable, and shows strong upstream effects on supplier industries (similar to Acemoglu et al. 2016).

More specifically, recall that we have standardized (in terms of standard deviation units) and normalized all of our shocks to be positive, so that an increase in imports from China corresponds to a negative value

Table 2A

China Trade Shock Analysis

	Δ Log Real Value Added		Δ Log Employment		Δ Log Real Labor Productivity	
	(1)	(2)	(3)	(4)	(5)	(6)
Δ Dependent variable $t-1$	0.019	0.020	0.149***	0.132***	-0.117***	-0.120***
	(0.025)	(0.025)	(0.020)	(0.019)	(0.028)	(0.033)
Δ Dependent variable $t-2$		0.047**		0.109***		-0.057
		(0.024)		(0.020)		(0.037)
Δ Dependent variable $t-3$		0.033		0.089***		-0.002
		(0.021)		(0.016)		(0.033)
Downstream effects $t-1$	-0.140	-0.124	-0.056	-0.044	-0.100	-0.108
	(0.086)	(0.081)	(0.040)	(0.037)	(0.099)	(0.099)
Upstream effects $t-1$	0.076***	0.076***	0.049***	0.039***	0.021	0.021
	(0.024)	(0.023)	(0.016)	(0.015)	(0.013)	(0.014)
Own effects $t-1$	0.034***	0.031***	0.023***	0.018***	0.007	0.007
	(0.009)	(0.009)	(0.005)	(0.004)	(0.007)	(0.007)
Observations	6,560	5,776	6,560	5,776	6,560	5,776
P-value: Upstream = own	0.071	0.054	0.086	0.139	0.333	0.350

Notes: Estimations consider network structures and the propagation of trade shocks. Baseline trade shocks for manufacturing industries are the lagged change in imports from China relative to 1991 US market volume, following Autor et al. (2013). A negative value is taken such that positive coefficients correspond to likely beneficial outcomes, similar to other shocks. Explanatory variables aggregate these industry-level components by the indicated network connecting industries. These network explanatory variables are expressed as lagged changes in nonlog values. Downstream and upstream flows use the Leontief inverse to provide the full chain of material interconnections within manufacturing. All trade analyses instrument the direct and network effects from US imports with the rise in Chinese imports in eight other advanced countries. Upstream = own test uses the exact formula discussed in the text and is calculated through unreported auxiliary regressions. Variables are winsorized at the 0.1% level and initial shocks are transformed to have unit standard deviation for interpretation. Estimations include year fixed effects, report standard errors clustered by industry, and are unweighted.

***Significant at the 1 percent level.

**Significant at the 5 percent level.

*Significant at the 10 percent level.

of the shocks, and thus positive coefficients imply that rising imports from China reduce value added and employment in the affected industries. In this light, the results in column (1) indicate that a one standard deviation own-industry shock reduces the focal industry's value-added growth by 3.4%.[20] More interestingly given our focus, they also indicate that a similar one standard deviation change in customers of an industry leads to a 7.6% decline in value-added growth through upstream effects. Downstream effects are of opposite sign and statistically insignificant, though they are sometimes quantitatively sizable. Lack of (same-signed) significant downstream effects in response to demand-side shocks is consistent with our main theoretical implications outlined in section II. Finally, the bottom row of the table tests the other implication from the theory highlighted in Proposition 1, that the relevant diagonal entry from the Leontief inverse matrix (i.e., the coefficient on $h_{ii} \cdot \Delta ChinaTrade_{i,t-1}$) should be equal to the upstream effect from other industries. For value added, this restriction is marginally rejected at 10%, though it is not rejected in any of the other columns.[21]

Column (2) shows that the overall pattern is similar when two more lags of the dependent variable are included on the right-hand side, even though these lags show some evidence of additional persistence. In particular, the quantitative implications are very similar, and it is again the upstream effects that are significant while the downstream ones are not.

Our regression specifications follow directly from Proposition 1 (for example, in the case of the China import shocks, equation [7]). The coefficient estimates in these regression equations do not directly translate into quantitative effects for "multipliers," however. This is because the upstream effect (the relevant dimension of the network effects in this case) corresponds to the impact of the shock of all other industries, weighted by their upstream linkages, on the focal industry. Instead, to obtain an economically meaningful multiplier, measuring how large the total impact of a shock is relative to its direct effect, we need to measure its impact on *all other* industries. To achieve this, we convert upstream and downstream effects into a *weighted average* of shocks in other industries using the Leontief inverse elements of weights.[22] We use these adjusted estimates to construct the impulse response functions depicted in figure 1 and for computing the relevant multipliers. Panel (A) of figure 1 depicts the impulse response of value added to a one standard deviation Chinese import shock obtained from this exercise (with a specification corresponding to column [2] of Table 2A). These impulse responses show that the quantitative magnitude of the network effects (in this

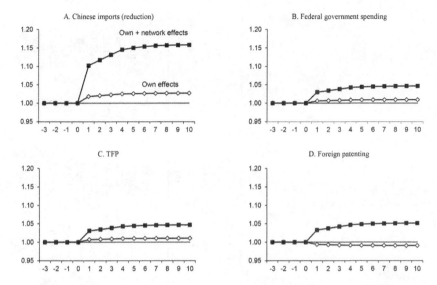

Fig. 3. Responses to a one standard deviation shock taken in isolation, employment
Notes: See figure 1.

case, upstream effects, since we are focusing on demand-side shocks) are considerably larger than the direct effect: the direct effect (from the own shock) after 10 periods is a 3.46% increase in value-added growth, while the total impact is a 22.09% (3.46 + 18.64) increase in value added. This yields a multiplier of 6.4 ($\simeq$ 22.09 / 3.46), and implies that input-output linkages more than double the direct effects of demand-side shocks. It can be seen from the figure that the implied multipliers are very similar at different horizons.

Columns (3) and (4) turn to employment. The overall pattern and even the quantitative magnitudes are very similar, with clear upstream effects and no downstream effects, and the theory-implied restrictions receive support from our estimates. Panel (A) of figure 3 depicts the impulse response of employment to the same shock as in figure 1. The implied multiplier in this case (for employment changes) is 5.86.

Columns (5) and (6) turn to labor productivity. Here we find no robust patterns, which is not surprising since columns (1)–(4) document that the numerator and denominator move in the same direction and by similar amounts.

Table 2B reports multiple robustness checks. Our results are very similar without the own-shock term. Our baseline estimates are un-

Table 2B
Robustness Checks on China Trade Shock Analysis

	Baseline Estimation (1)	Excluding Own Lagged Shock (2)	Weighting by 1991 Log Value Added (3)	Weighting by 1991 Employees (4)	Adding SIC2 Fixed Effects (5)	Adding SIC3 Fixed Effects (6)	Adding SIC4 Fixed Effects (7)	Adding Resource Constraints (8)
			A. Δ Log Real Value Added					
Δ Dependent variable $t-1$	0.019	0.021	0.023	0.114	-0.008	-0.038*	-0.071***	0.018
	(0.025)	(0.025)	(0.026)	(0.071)	(0.025)	(0.023)	(0.020)	(0.025)
Downstream effects $t-1$	-0.140	-0.022	-0.152*	-0.209*	0.000	0.138	0.192	-0.163*
	(0.086)	(0.083)	(0.086)	(0.123)	(0.109)	(0.106)	(0.129)	(0.092)
Upstream effects $t-1$	0.076***	0.068***	0.078***	0.075**	0.051**	0.053*	0.051	0.107**
	(0.024)	(0.023)	(0.023)	(0.034)	(0.023)	(0.032)	(0.042)	(0.042)
Own effects $t-1$	0.034***		0.033***	0.022	0.018**	0.015	0.016	0.032***
	(0.009)		(0.009)	(0.014)	(0.009)	(0.010)	(0.014)	(0.009)
Observations	6,560	6,560	6,560	6,560	6,560	6,560	6,560	6,560
P-value: Upstream = own	0.071		0.053	0.076	0.159	0.266	0.489	0.080

B. *Δ Log Employment*

Δ Dependent variable $t-1$	0.149***	0.156***	0.153***	0.257***	0.097***	0.044**	0.010	0.146***
	(0.020)	(0.021)	(0.020)	(0.034)	(0.020)	(0.019)	(0.020)	(0.020)
Downstream effects $t-1$	−0.056	0.024	−0.055	−0.034	0.009	0.036	0.080	−0.082*
	(0.040)	(0.037)	(0.040)	(0.059)	(0.049)	(0.054)	(0.067)	(0.047)
Upstream effects $t-1$	0.049***	0.044***	0.051***	0.048**	0.029*	0.014	0.012	0.084***
	(0.016)	(0.016)	(0.016)	(0.022)	(0.016)	(0.018)	(0.025)	(0.028)
Own effects $t-1$	0.023***		0.023***	0.020***	0.009**	0.005	0.001	0.021***
	(0.005)		(0.005)	(0.007)	(0.004)	(0.004)	(0.005)	(0.005)
Observations	6,560	6,560	6,560	6,560	6,560	6,560	6,560	6,560
P-value: Upstream = own	0.086		0.069	0.185	0.209	0.616	0.667	0.027

Notes: See table 2A.

***Significant at the 1 percent level.
**Significant at the 5 percent level.
*Significant at the 10 percent level.

weighted, and we obtain similar results when we weight observations by log 1991 value added or by 1991 employment levels. We also consider a series of more demanding specifications where we include a full set of two-, three-, and four-digit Standard Industrial Code (SIC) dummies. Since our specification in equation (12) is in changes, this amounts to including linear time trends for these industry groupings. The results are generally robust, although the downstream effects do move around and sometimes become larger, even if still far from significance.

The final column of table 2B returns to the resource-constraint effect identified in Proposition 1. As noted above, our baseline specifications focusing on demand-side shocks have ignored this resource-constraint effect, corresponding to the third term in equation (7). To the extent that this term is correlated with our network effect, it may lead to biased estimates. We compute the empirical equivalent of this third term following equation (7) closely. We sum nominal manufacturing imports from China to obtain the term $\Sigma_{k=1}^{n}d\tilde{G}_k$, multiply it with an estimate of β_j, computed as the value-added share of industry j, divide it by p_jy_j, and then multiply it with the corresponding entries of the Leontief inverse of the upstream linkages to obtain $\Sigma_{j=1}^{n}\hat{h}_{ji}(1 \ / \ p_jy_j)\beta_j\Sigma_{k=1}^{n}d\tilde{G}_k$ (ignoring the term $1 + \lambda$ in the denominator). We then add this term as an additional regressor instrumented by an additional instrument computed in the same way from Chinese imports by the same eight non-US-advanced economies. The final column of table 2B shows that this specification leads to somewhat larger network effects, but the overall picture remains unchanged.

Appendix table 2A repeats this analysis with log real-shipments growth as the outcome variable, and also shows similar results.[23]

An additional issue is that the presence of the lagged dependent variable on the right-hand side of our estimating equation, (12), introduces the possibility of biased estimates when the time dimension is short due to the challenges of obtaining consistent estimates of the persistence parameter, ψ, with short panels as noted by Nickell (1981). We further investigate this issue in appendix table 2B. In particular, our main concern here is with the network effects, which may inherit the bias of the parameter ψ in short panels. One way of ensuring that this bias is not responsible for our results is to impose different values for the parameter ψ and verify that this has little or no impact on our results (see Acemoglu et al. 2014). Appendix table 2B performs this exercise for the China trade shock and documents that both own and upstream effects are highly significant and similar to our baseline estimates for any value of ψ between our estimate of this parameter in table 2A ($\psi = 0$) and the full unit root limit ($\psi = 1$), becoming only a little weaker at the full unit root case of $\psi = 1$ (while downstream effects remain insignificant except marginally at $\psi = 1$).

Appendix table 2C considers longer time periods, thus linking our results more closely to Acemoglu et al. (2016), who focused on a decadal panel. For two-year periods, we prepare nine time periods from 1991–1993 to 2007–2009. For three-year periods, we consider six time periods from 1991–1994 to 2006–2009. For four-year periods, we consider four time periods from 1991–1995 to 2003–2007. For five-year periods, we consider 1991–1996, 1996–2001, and 2001–2006. In each case, the first period is used to create the network lags. The downstream customer effects and own-industry effects tend to grow with longer time periods.

In addition to these robustness checks, appendix table 6 shows very similar outcomes when we consider nominal value added and shipments growth instead of our baseline real value-added growth and the real shipments shown in appendix table 2A. Appendix table 7 also reports results where we vary the number of lags included for own-industry shocks and network shocks. We report in the table the sums of the coefficients across the deeper lags and their statistical significance. These variants yield quite similar conclusions to our reported estimations.

C. Federal Spending Shocks

The next analysis considers changes in US federal government spending levels, which are anticipated to operate similar to trade shocks by affecting industries through heightened demand from industrial customers. We first calculate from the 1992 BEA Input-Output Matrix the share of sales for each industry that went to the federal government,

$$FedSales\%_i = \frac{Sales_{i \to Fed}}{Sales_i}.$$

This share ranges from zero dependency for about 10% of industries to over 50% for the top percentile of industries in terms of dependency. Some prominent examples and their share of sales include 3731 Ship Building and Repairing (76%), 3761 Guided Missiles and Space Vehicles (74%), 3482 Small Arms Ammunition (65%), and 3812 Search, Detection, Navigation, Guidance, Aeronautical and Nautical Systems and Instruments (51%).

We interact this measure with the log change in federal government expenditures,

$$FederalShock_{i,t} = FedSales\%_i^{1991} \cdot \Delta \ln FederalSpending_{t-1},$$

holding fixed the industry dependency at its 1991 level. Intuitively, the specification anticipates greater shocks from aggregate federal budget changes for industries that have larger initial shares of sales to the federal government. The change in federal spending is lagged one year to reflect the fact that procurement frequently extends into the following year. Once again following (13) and (14), the downstream effects in this case are defined as

$$Downstream_{i,t}^{Federal} = \sum_j (Input\%_{j \to i}^{1991} - \mathbf{1}_{j=i}) \cdot FederalShock_{j,t}.$$

A similar approach is taken for the other network metrics.

Because this variable focuses on federal spending changes in the aggregate (driven by, among other things, swings in political moods, ideology, identity of the government, and wars and budget exigencies), and is then constructed with the interaction of these aggregate changes with the time-invariant and predetermined dependency of each industry on federal spending, we believe that it can be taken as plausibly exogenous to the contemporaneous productivity or supply-side shocks hitting the focal industry.

The structure of table 3A is identical to those examining trade shocks. The results are also similar. For example, in table 3A upstream effects are again significant and quantitatively sizable (about three to five times as large as own effects). Downstream effects are now of the same sign as the upstream effect, but continue to be statistically insignificant. The theory-implied restriction reported in the bottom row is again broadly supported (it is never rejected at 5%). In addition, the own effect is insignificant when we only control for one lag of the dependent variable, but significant both in columns (2) and (4) when we control for three lags.

Table 3B and appendix tables 3A–3C, 6, and 7 perform the same robustness checks as those discussed for trade shocks and show that the above-mentioned patterns are generally quite robust. All in all, the propagation of this very different demand-side shock appears remarkably similar to the propagation of the import shocks, and in both cases in line with the theory we have used to motivate our approach.

The economic magnitudes are once more far from trivial. Panel (B) of figures 1 and 3 depict the impulse response functions for own and upstream effects computed in the same way as for panel (A), and indicate

Table 3A
Federal Spending Shock Analysis

	Δ Log Real Value Added		Δ Log Employment		Δ Log Real Labor Productivity	
	(1)	(2)	(3)	(4)	(5)	(6)
Δ Dependent variable $t-1$	0.019	0.018	0.158***	0.135***	−0.117***	−0.119***
	(0.025)	(0.024)	(0.021)	(0.019)	(0.030)	(0.036)
Δ Dependent variable $t-2$		0.051**		0.116***		−0.057
		(0.023)		(0.019)		(0.038)
Δ Dependent variable $t-3$		0.038*		0.102***		−0.002
		(0.021)		(0.016)		(0.035)
Downstream effects $t-1$	0.017	0.023	0.007	0.013	0.007	0.004
	(0.021)	(0.021)	(0.015)	(0.012)	(0.016)	(0.017)
Upstream effects $t-1$	0.022**	0.020**	0.010*	0.011**	0.012	0.010
	(0.009)	(0.008)	(0.006)	(0.005)	(0.008)	(0.008)
Own effects $t-1$	0.004	0.008**	0.003	0.006***	0.001	0.002
	(0.003)	(0.004)	(0.003)	(0.002)	(0.001)	(0.002)
Observations	6,560	5,776	6,560	5,776	6,560	5,776
P-value: Upstream = own	0.076	0.191	0.321	0.383	0.147	0.330

Notes: See table 2A. Estimations consider network structures and the propagation of federal spending shocks. Baseline federal spending shocks for manufacturing industries are the lagged log change in national federal spending interacted with the 1992 share of sales from industries that went to the federal government.
***Significant at the 1 percent level.
**Significant at the 5 percent level.
*Significant at the 10 percent level.

Table 3B
Robustness Checks on Federal Spending Shock Analysis

	Baseline Estimation (1)	Excluding Own Lagged Shock (2)	Weighting by 1991 Log Value Added (3)	Weighting by 1991 Employees (4)	Adding SIC2 Fixed Effects (5)	Adding SIC3 Fixed Effects (6)	Adding SIC4 Fixed Effects (7)	Adding Resource Constraints (8)
			A. Δ Log Real Value Added					
Δ Dependent variable $t-1$	0.019	0.019	0.023	0.115*	-0.011	-0.042*	-0.076***	0.019
	(0.025)	(0.025)	(0.026)	(0.068)	(0.025)	(0.024)	(0.021)	(0.025)
Downstream effects $t-1$	0.017	0.034*	0.015	0.008	-0.006	0.029	-0.040	0.017
	(0.021)	(0.019)	(0.020)	(0.014)	(0.021)	(0.024)	(0.062)	(0.021)
Upstream effects $t-1$	0.022**	0.022**	0.022**	0.030**	0.012	0.025*	0.069***	0.022*
	(0.009)	(0.009)	(0.010)	(0.014)	(0.008)	(0.015)	(0.023)	(0.012)
Own effects $t-1$	0.004		0.004	0.001	0.002	0.005	0.011	0.004
	(0.003)		(0.003)	(0.002)	(0.003)	(0.005)	(0.011)	(0.003)
Observations	6,560	6,560	6,560	6,560	6,560	6,560	6,560	6,560
P-value: Upstream = own	0.076		0.077	0.027	0.254	0.183	0.031	0.130

B. *Δ Log Employment*

Δ Dependent variable $t-1$	0.158***	0.159***	0.163***	0.269***	0.099***	0.041**	0.006	0.158***
	(0.021)	(0.021)	(0.021)	(0.033)	(0.020)	(0.019)	(0.019)	(0.021)
Downstream effects $t-1$	0.007	0.021**	0.006	0.007	−0.011	0.018	−0.046	0.009
	(0.015)	(0.010)	(0.013)	(0.007)	(0.015)	(0.013)	(0.046)	(0.014)
Upstream effects $t-1$	0.010*	0.010*	0.009	0.009	0.004	0.016***	0.020*	0.006
	(0.006)	(0.006)	(0.006)	(0.005)	(0.005)	(0.006)	(0.011)	(0.007)
Own effects $t-1$	0.003		0.003	0.001	0.002	0.009**	0.022**	0.003
	(0.003)		(0.003)	(0.001)	(0.003)	(0.004)	(0.009)	(0.003)
Observations	6,560	6,560	6,560	6,560	6,560	6,560	6,560	6,560
P-value: Upstream = own	0.321		0.346	0.156	0.747	0.160	0.829	0.717

Notes: See table 3A.

***Significant at the 1 percent level.

**Significant at the 5 percent level.

*Significant at the 10 percent level.

that there are once again sizable network effects. The implied network multipliers for value added and employment at the 10-year horizon are 6.42 and 5.00, respectively.

D.   TFP Shocks

We next turn to supply-side shocks, starting with TFP. Baseline TFP shocks for manufacturing industries are the lagged change in four-factor TFP taken from the NBER Productivity Database. Importantly, these TFP measures control for materials, and thus should not be mechanically a function of downstream effects (changes in prices and quantities in industries supplying inputs to the focal industry).

Similar to our other network-based measures, these are constructed by aggregating these industry-level log components of TFP in connected industries. Continuing our illustration using downstream effects from shocks to supplier industries and again following on (13) and (14), we model

$$Downstream_{i,t}^{TFP} = \sum_j (Input\%_{j \to i}^{1991} - \mathbf{1}_{j=i}) \cdot \Delta \ln TFP_{j,t}.$$

We should caution that the case for the exogeneity of the TFP shocks is weaker, because past TFP may be endogenous to other shocks (e.g., to capacity utilization or labor hoarding), which have a persistent impact on value added and factor demands. With this caveat, we still believe that predetermined TFP shocks are informative about how supply-side shocks spread through the input-output network.

The structure of table 4A is identical to those examining trade and federal spending shocks. Consistent with theory, it is now downstream effects that are more sizable and important, though in this case there are some statistically significant estimates of upstream effects as well. For example, in column (1) of table 4A, downstream effects are estimated to have a coefficient of 0.060 (standard error = 0.020), while upstream effects come in at 0.024 (standard error = 0.011). Interestingly, own effects are small and imprecise for value added, but more precisely estimated (though still about half of the upstream effects) for employment. The theoretical restriction tested in the bottom row is now rejected for value added, where the own effects are small, but is in closer alignment for employment. The robustness checks reported in table 4B and in appendix B confirm this overall pattern.[24]

Economic magnitudes can again be gleaned from panel (C) of figures 1 and 3; the implied multipliers are 15.56 and 4.43 for value-added growth

Table 4A
TFP Shock Analysis

	Δ Log Real Value Added		Δ Log Employment		Δ Log Real Labor Productivity	
	(1)	(2)	(3)	(4)	(5)	(6)
Δ Dependent variable $t-1$	-0.024	-0.031	0.141***	0.118***	-0.194***	-0.211***
	(0.040)	(0.041)	(0.021)	(0.020)	(0.029)	(0.034)
Δ Dependent variable $t-2$		0.049**		0.118***		-0.071**
		(0.023)		(0.019)		(0.034)
Δ Dependent variable $t-3$		0.037*		0.102***		-0.008
		(0.020)		(0.016)		(0.032)
Downstream effects $t-1$	0.060***	0.047**	0.016*	0.011	0.047***	0.043**
	(0.020)	(0.020)	(0.009)	(0.009)	(0.018)	(0.018)
Upstream effects $t-1$	0.024**	0.020*	0.009	0.008	0.015*	0.014
	(0.011)	(0.012)	(0.006)	(0.006)	(0.009)	(0.009)
Own effects $t-1$	0.004	0.007	0.006***	0.007***	0.011**	0.013***
	(0.007)	(0.006)	(0.002)	(0.002)	(0.005)	(0.004)
Observations	6,560	5,776	6,560	5,776	6,560	5,776
P-value: Downstream = own	0.005	0.034	0.041	0.161	0.101	0.276

Notes: See table 2A. Estimations consider network structures and the propagation of TFP shocks. Baseline TFP shocks for manufacturing industries are the lagged log change in four-factor TFP taken from the NBER Productivity Database.
***Significant at the 1 percent level.
**Significant at the 5 percent level.
*Significant at the 10 percent level.

Table 4B
Robustness Checks on TFP Shock Analysis

	Baseline Estimation (1)	Excluding Own Lagged Shock (2)	Weighting by 1991 Log Value Added (3)	Weighting by 1991 Employees (4)	Adding SIC2 Fixed Effects (5)	Adding SIC3 Fixed Effects (6)	Adding SIC4 Fixed Effects (7)
			A. Δ Log Real Value Added				
Δ Dependent variable $t-1$	−0.024	−0.002	−0.024	−0.075	−0.080**	−0.126***	−0.147***
	(0.040)	(0.024)	(0.040)	(0.073)	(0.039)	(0.038)	(0.039)
Downstream effects $t-1$	0.060***	0.062***	0.060***	0.077**	0.039*	0.027	0.027
	(0.020)	(0.021)	(0.020)	(0.034)	(0.020)	(0.018)	(0.019)
Upstream effects $t-1$	0.024**	0.024**	0.025**	0.054***	0.021*	0.017	0.020
	(0.011)	(0.011)	(0.011)	(0.016)	(0.011)	(0.012)	(0.013)
Own effects $t-1$	0.004		0.005	0.025*	0.010	0.014**	0.012**
	(0.007)		(0.007)	(0.014)	(0.006)	(0.006)	(0.005)
Observations	6,560	6,560	6,560	6,560	6,560	6,560	6,560
P-value: Downstream = own	0.005		0.007	0.303	0.198	0.623	0.171

			B. Δ Log Employment			
Δ Dependent variable $t-1$	0.141***	0.154***	0.146***	0.252***	0.081***	0.020	−0.015
	(0.021)	(0.021)	(0.021)	(0.032)	(0.021)	(0.019)	(0.020)
Downstream effects $t-1$	0.016*	0.025***	0.016*	0.024*	0.002	0.011	0.013
	(0.009)	(0.009)	(0.009)	(0.012)	(0.009)	(0.010)	(0.011)
Upstream effects $t-1$	0.009	0.012**	0.009	0.022***	0.007	0.010	0.010
	(0.006)	(0.006)	(0.006)	(0.008)	(0.006)	(0.007)	(0.007)
Own effects $t-1$	0.006***		0.006***	0.003	0.007***	0.008***	0.009***
	(0.002)		(0.002)	(0.002)	(0.002)	(0.002)	(0.002)
Observations	6,560	6,560	6,560	6,560	6,560	6,560	6,560
P-value: Downstream = own	0.041		0.045	0.026	0.712	0.312	0.314

Notes: See table 4A.
***Significant at the 1 percent level.
**Significant at the 5 percent level.
*Significant at the 10 percent level.

and employment growth over 10 years, respectively. The larger multiplier for value added in this case reflects the smaller direct (own) impact.

E. Foreign Patenting Shocks

Our final shock represents changes in patented technology frontiers. Since this shock also captures supply-side changes in productivity, responses to it should be similar to those to TFP shocks.

Baseline patent shocks for manufacturing industries in table 5A are the lagged log change in USPTO-granted patents filed by overseas inventors associated with the industry. We measure foreign patent shocks using United States Patent and Trademark Office (USPTO)-granted patents through 2009. We develop a new concordance of patent classes to four-digit manufacturing industries that extends the earlier work of Silverman (1999), Johnson (1999), and Kerr (2008). Continuing our downstream effects example, we have

$$Downstream_{i,t}^{ForeignPatent} = \sum_j (Input\%_{j \to i}^{1991} - \mathbf{1}_{j=i}) \cdot \Delta \ln Patents_{j,t}^{Foreign}.$$

These foreign patents quantify technology changes in the world technology frontier external to the US economy (e.g., patents filed by car manufacturers in Germany and Japan signal advances in automobile technologies that have not originated in the United States). There are two additional difficulties in this case, however. First, foreign patenting may be correlated with past technological improvements in the US sectors, which might have persistent effects. Second, improved technology abroad may directly impact US firms through fiercer product market competition, not just through technology and productivity spillovers (e.g., Bloom, Schankerman, and Van Reenen 2013).[25] These concerns make us more cautious in interpreting the foreign patenting shocks, especially for own effects, though we believe that this analysis is still informative about network-based propagation.

Table 5A shows strong downstream effects with again no evidence of sizable upstream effects. The theory-implied restrictions in the bottom row of the table are typically rejected, reflecting the very small and sometimes incorrectly signed estimates of own effects. One possible explanation for this pattern of own effects is that, as already noted, an increase in foreign patents in one's own industry likely signals fiercer competition from international competitors. The network effects, which should be less impacted by these considerations, are again quite similar to our theory's predictions. (Robustness checks on foreign patent shock analysis are shown in table 5B.)

Table 5A
Foreign Patent Shock Analysis

	Δ Log Real Value Added		Δ Log Employment		Δ Log Real Labor Productivity	
	(1)	(2)	(3)	(4)	(5)	(6)
Δ Dependent variable $t-1$	0.020	0.020	0.159***	0.138***	-0.117***	-0.120***
	(0.025)	(0.025)	(0.021)	(0.020)	(0.030)	(0.036)
Δ Dependent variable $t-2$		0.051**		0.117***		-0.057
		(0.023)		(0.020)		(0.038)
Δ Dependent variable $t-3$		0.037*		0.100***		-0.003
		(0.021)		(0.016)		(0.035)
Downstream effects $t-1$	0.043***	0.044***	0.018***	0.018***	0.027***	0.028***
	(0.011)	(0.011)	(0.006)	(0.006)	(0.009)	(0.009)
Upstream effects $t-1$	-0.000	0.000	-0.001	-0.000	0.001	0.002
	(0.005)	(0.005)	(0.003)	(0.003)	(0.004)	(0.004)
Own effects $t-1$	-0.006	-0.007*	-0.008***	-0.006**	0.003	0.002
	(0.004)	(0.004)	(0.003)	(0.003)	(0.003)	(0.004)
Observations	6,543	5,761	6,543	5,761	6,543	5,761
P-value: Downstream = own	0.000	0.000	0.001	0.002	0.029	0.026

Notes: See table 2A. Estimations consider network structures and the propagation of foreign patent shocks. Baseline patent shocks for manufacturing industries are the lagged log change in USPTO patents filed by overseas inventors associated with the industry.

***Significant at the 1 percent level.

**Significant at the 5 percent level.

*Significant at the 10 percent level.

Table 5B
Robustness Checks on Foreign Patent Shock Analysis

	Baseline Estimation (1)	Excluding Own Lagged Shock (2)	Weighting by 1991 Log Value Added (3)	Weighting by 1991 Employees (4)	Adding SIC2 Fixed Effects (5)	Adding SIC3 Fixed Effects (6)	Adding SIC4 Fixed Effects (7)
			A. Δ *Log Real Value Added*				
Δ Dependent variable $t-1$	0.020	0.020	0.024	0.120*	-0.012	-0.042*	-0.075***
	(0.025)	(0.025)	(0.026)	(0.070)	(0.025)	(0.024)	(0.021)
Downstream effects $t-1$	0.043***	0.039***	0.042***	0.044**	0.040***	0.038***	0.038***
	(0.011)	(0.011)	(0.011)	(0.021)	(0.011)	(0.011)	(0.011)
Upstream effects $t-1$	-0.000	0.000	0.000	0.007	0.000	0.000	0.000
	(0.005)	(0.005)	(0.004)	(0.007)	(0.005)	(0.004)	(0.005)
Own effects $t-1$	-0.006		-0.006	0.004	-0.003	-0.003	-0.004
	(0.004)		(0.004)	(0.007)	(0.004)	(0.004)	(0.004)
Observations	6,543	6,543	6,543	6,543	6,543	6,543	6,543
P-value: Downstream = own	0.000		0.000	0.354	0.001	0.001	0.000

		B. Δ Log Employment				
Δ Dependent variable $t-1$	0.159***	0.160***	0.163***	0.270***	0.099***	0.044**	0.012
	(0.021)	(0.021)	(0.021)	(0.034)	(0.020)	(0.019)	(0.020)
Downstream effects $t-1$	0.018***	0.013**	0.018***	0.014*	0.015**	0.014**	0.013**
	(0.006)	(0.006)	(0.006)	(0.007)	(0.006)	(0.006)	(0.006)
Upstream effects $t-1$	-0.001	-0.000	-0.001	0.001	-0.001	-0.000	-0.000
	(0.003)	(0.003)	(0.003)	(0.003)	(0.003)	(0.003)	(0.003)
Own effects $t-1$	-0.008***		-0.007***	-0.004	-0.004	-0.003	-0.003
	(0.003)		(0.002)	(0.003)	(0.003)	(0.002)	(0.003)
Observations	6,543	6,543	6,543	6,543	6,543	6,543	6,543
P-value: Downstream = own	0.001		0.001	0.238	0.008	0.016	0.023

Notes: See table 5A.

***Significant at the 1 percent level.
**Significant at the 5 percent level.
*Significant at the 10 percent level.

Panel (D) of figures 1 and 3 again depict the impulse responses of value added and employment. We do not compute multipliers in this case, since the own effects are imprecisely estimated and potentially biased for the reasons explained above, thus making multiplier estimates harder to interpret.

F. VAR Analysis

Our empirical specification, (12), directly builds on our theoretical model (in particular, equations [6] and [7]), and expresses the endogenous response of value added and employment to shocks hitting all industries. An alternative is to follow vector auto regression (VAR) models and express endogenous variables as a function of own shocks and the values of the endogenous variables of linked industries. The analog of equation (12) in this case would be

$$
\begin{aligned}
\Delta \ln Y_{i,t} = \delta_t + \psi \Delta \ln Y_{i,t-1} + \beta^{\text{own}} Shock_{i,t-1} \\
+ \beta^{\text{upstream}} \Delta \ln Y_{i,t-1}^{Upstream} + \beta^{\text{downstream}} \Delta \ln Y_{i,t-1}^{Downstream} + \varepsilon_{i,t}
\end{aligned}
, \quad (16)
$$

which only features the shock hitting sector i, and models upstream and downstream effects from the changes in value added of linked industries—the terms $\Delta \ln Y_{i,t-1}^{Upstream}$ and $\Delta \ln Y_{i,t-1}^{Downstream}$. This equation could also be derived from our theoretical framework. Relative to our baseline empirical model, (12), this specification faces two related problems. First, the terms $\Delta \ln Y_{i,t-1}^{Upstream}$ and $\Delta \ln Y_{i,t-1}^{Downstream}$ generate a version of Manski's well-known reflection problem (Manski 1993), as outcome variables of one industry are being regressed on the contemporaneous (or one-period lagged) outcomes of other industries, creating the possibility of spurious correlation. Second, these terms are also more likely to be correlated with each other, potentially leading to multicollinearity, which will make distinguishing these various effects more difficult.

These problems notwithstanding, we now estimate equation (16) to show that the results from this complementary approach are broadly similar. To avoid the most severe form of the reflection problem, throughout we instrument for the upstream and downstream effects, $\Delta \ln Y_{i,t-1}^{Upstream}$ and $\Delta \ln Y_{i,t-1}^{Downstream}$, using the first and second lags of each shock as experienced in the network (i.e., our instruments are the core regressors in equation [12], $Upstream_{i,t-1}$ and $Downstream_{i,t-1}$). We report two specifications per shock. In the first, we model and instrument the focal part of the network relevant for each shock (e.g., upstream effects for supply-side shocks and downstream effects for demand-side shocks). In the second specification, we include and instrument for both upstream and downstream effects. Also, in the case of China trade shocks, we continue to instrument for the own shock, $Shock_{i,t-1}$, as well.

The results of this exercise are reported in table 6 and are quite consistent with our baseline findings. Even though this empirical specification is more demanding for the reasons explained above, the specifications focusing on China trade and TFP shocks give similar results, and specifications using federal spending shocks also lead to similar results for value added, though not for employment. Foreign patenting results do not hold with this approach, however.[26]

G. Combined Shock Analysis

Table 7 estimates own, upstream, and downstream effects simultaneously from several of the shocks so far analyzed in isolation. This is relevant for two related reasons. First, we would like to verify that our downstream and upstream effects indeed capture network-based propagation of different types of shocks rather than some other omitted characteristics, and attempting to simultaneously estimate these effects provides some information on this concern. Second, it is important to quantify whether the simultaneous operation of all of these networked effects creates attenuation, which is relevant for our quantitative evaluation.

Table 7 shows the estimates of upstream and downstream effects in this joint analysis are remarkably similar to our previous results. Appendix table 8 also shows this similarity when we exclude the foreign patenting shocks due to the concerns about own effects discussed above. These results bolster our confidence in the patterns documented so far and also suggest that the quantitative magnitudes of the propagation through these input-output networks is larger when we consider all four shocks simultaneously.

To quantify impacts from this joint exercise, we now consider one standard deviation changes of the three shocks, imports from China, federal spending and TFP, simultaneously. The impulse response functions from this exercise are shown in figure 2 in appendix B, and the combined multipliers for value added and employment growth in panels (A) and (B) are 11.47 and 8.23, respectively. Thus, the network elements jointly continue to account for more fluctuation than direct components. The lower panels show similar results when including foreign patenting shocks.

Table 6
VAR Estimations for Intermediated Shocks

	China Trade		Federal Spending		TFP		Foreign Patenting	
	(1)	(2)	(3)	(4)	(5)	(6)	(7)	(8)
	A. Δ Log Real Value Added							
Δ Dependent variable $t-1$	-0.045	-0.060	-0.025	-0.011	-0.057	-0.063	0.312***	0.244**
	(0.039)	(0.044)	(0.027)	(0.041)	(0.044)	(0.044)	(0.109)	(0.098)
Δ Downstream real value added $t-1$		0.038		-0.036	0.087***	0.080***	-0.735***	-0.398**
		(0.112)		(0.116)	(0.025)	(0.025)	(0.268)	(0.200)
Δ Upstream real value added $t-1$	0.173***	0.171***	0.113**	0.114**		0.017		-0.162*
	(0.059)	(0.061)	(0.045)	(0.052)		(0.011)		(0.086)
Own shock $t-1$	0.030***	0.030***	0.006**	0.007*	0.009	0.009	-0.012*	-0.006
	(0.008)	(0.008)	(0.003)	(0.004)	(0.007)	(0.007)	(0.007)	(0.006)
Observations	6,168	6,168	6,560	6,560	6,560	6,560	6,543	6,543

316

B. Δ Log Employment

Δ Dependent variable $t-1$	0.132***	0.084	0.185***	0.079	0.089***	0.081***	0.310***	0.268***
	(0.023)	(0.146)	(0.025)	(0.080)	(0.028)	(0.026)	(0.059)	(0.058)
Δ Downstream employment $t-1$		0.097		0.158	0.095**	0.091**	-0.264***	-0.278***
		(0.295)		(0.115)	(0.041)	(0.044)	(0.098)	(0.099)
Δ Upstream employment $t-1$	0.053***	0.035	-0.045*	-0.018		0.017		0.085**
	(0.014)	(0.054)	(0.024)	(0.031)		(0.025)		(0.038)
Own shock $t-1$	0.026***	0.022*	0.005**	0.003	0.007***	0.007***	-0.012***	-0.013***
	(0.004)	(0.011)	(0.002)	(0.003)	(0.002)	(0.002)	(0.004)	(0.004)
Observations	6,168	6,168	6,560	6,560	6,560	6,560	6,543	6,543

Notes: See tables 2A–5A. Rather than model network shocks directly, estimations consider intermediated approaches where the shock indicated by the column header instruments for changes in upstream and downstream economic activity in terms of real value added or employment. Estimations control for own shock and use two lags of upstream and downstream components. In each estimation pair, the first specification considers the focal network element for the shock in question. The second specification adds in the nonfocal element where the first stage fit can be weak.

***Significant at the 1 percent level.
**Significant at the 5 percent level.
*Significant at the 10 percent level.

Table 7
Joint Analysis of Shocks

		Δ Log Real Value Added		Δ Log Employment	
		(1)	(2)	(3)	(4)
Δ Dependent variable $t-1$		−0.043	−0.050	0.125***	0.105***
		(0.041)	(0.041)	(0.020)	(0.020)
Δ Dependent variable $t-2$			0.040*		0.108***
			(0.022)		(0.020)
Δ Dependent variable $t-3$			0.032		0.089***
			(0.021)		(0.016)
Trade:	Downstream effects $t-1$	−0.059	−0.042	−0.016	0.008
		(0.082)	(0.080)	(0.044)	(0.040)
	Upstream effects $t-1$	0.106***	0.107***	0.066***	0.054***
		(0.030)	(0.031)	(0.020)	(0.019)
	Own effects $t-1$	0.032***	0.030***	0.022***	0.017***
		(0.009)	(0.009)	(0.005)	(0.004)
Federal:	Downstream effects $t-1$	−0.006	−0.003	−0.008	0.001
		(0.023)	(0.025)	(0.017)	(0.014)
	Upstream effects $t-1$	0.035**	0.040***	0.020**	0.023***
		(0.014)	(0.014)	(0.009)	(0.008)
	Own effects $t-1$	0.001	0.004	0.001	0.005*
		(0.003)	(0.004)	(0.003)	(0.003)
TFP:	Downstream effects $t-1$	0.062***	0.051**	0.019*	0.014
		(0.021)	(0.021)	(0.010)	(0.010)
	Upstream effects $t-1$	0.030**	0.028**	0.013*	0.011
		(0.013)	(0.014)	(0.008)	(0.008)
	Own effects $t-1$	0.007	0.009	0.007***	0.008***
		(0.007)	(0.007)	(0.002)	(0.002)
Patent:	Downstream effects $t-1$	0.043***	0.043***	0.017***	0.016**
		(0.011)	(0.011)	(0.006)	(0.007)
	Upstream effects $t-1$	0.002	0.002	0.000	0.000
		(0.005)	(0.005)	(0.003)	(0.003)
	Own effects $t-1$	−0.007*	−0.007*	−0.007***	−0.006**
		(0.004)	(0.004)	(0.003)	(0.003)
Observations		6,543	5,761	6,543	5,761

Notes: See table 2A.
***Significant at the 1 percent level.
**Significant at the 5 percent level.
*Significant at the 10 percent level.

H. Monte Carlo Verification

Though our empirical strategy so far has closely followed our theoretical model, there are several aspects in which the true data-generating process might be more complicated than the one implied by our model. First, our model abstracted from dynamic interactions between sectors, whereas the original Long and Plosser (1983) paper assumed that an industry could only use as inputs at time t the output produced by other industries at time $t - 1$. This dynamic structure implies that rather than shocks being transmitted through the Leontief inverse of the input-output matrix as in our equations (6) and (7), they would be transmitted from one period to the next directly through the input-output matrix. Over time, this transmission would still lead to a cumulative impact as summarized by the Leontief inverse (as we show in appendix C).[27] Nevertheless, we might be concerned that this type of slow adjustment would lead to significant misspecification in our empirical work, where we impose equations (6) and (7). In appendix C, we conduct a Monte Carlo exercise where data are generated at quarterly frequency using the Long and Plosser (1983) timing (and shocks are serially correlated), and regressions are run at the annual frequency using the specifications we have utilized so far (thus filtering the observed shocks through the Leontief inverse of the input-output matrix). We find that the time averaging of the higher frequency data to annual observations ensures that specifications based on the Leontief inverse do not lead to any major misspecification. In particular, our results, described in detail in appendix figures 4–7, indicate that regressions run on time-averaged data can recover whether upstream or downstream linkages are important.

A second concern is whether measurement error in the input-output matrix might be significantly amplified when we compute the Leontief inverses. Another Monte Carlo exercise we perform in appendix C verifies that even if the input-output matrix is measured with error, regressions of the sort we have used are capable of recovering the correct parameters. We take these two Monte Carlo exercises as useful confirmation of the robustness and informativeness of our empirical strategy.

V.   Additional Results: The Geographic Network

We next turn to an analysis of the geographic network's impact on the propagation of shocks. The theory in section II describes how shocks to an industry can also propagate regionally (e.g., within commuting zones) because they expand or depress economic activity, impacting the decisions of other industries in the area. Though a full analysis of these local interactions is beyond the scope of the present effort (see, for example, the treatment of Acemoglu et al. [2015] for medium-frequency import shocks on local economies), we can nonetheless get a sense of the importance of these channels of propagation by looking at the impact of a shock to a particular industry on other industries that tend to collocate with it. This is essentially the idea of the geographic network introduced above.

Table 8 considers all four geographic effects simultaneously, which is particularly relevant since they are all working through the same local geographic networks. In columns (1) and (3) we only model own-industry effects and geographic spillovers, while columns (2) and (4) add the downstream and upstream network effects as well. Our most important observation from this analysis is the stability of the network effects compared to table 7. The latter continues to adhere to theory and shows that our network effects are not proxying for regional spillovers or similar local conditions. The second observation is that the geographic effects are almost always precisely estimated and are quite substantial in size for demand-side shocks.

Appendix table 9A shows that these joint patterns are robust to the specification checks considered earlier for input-output linkages. Appendix table 9B considers each of the four shocks in isolation rather than jointly modeling them. Similar to the results presented in table 8, the inclusion of geographic effects has little impact on our estimates of downstream and upstream network effects, which continue to adhere to theory. On the other hand, the geographic effects themselves are less stable and often substantially smaller when measured in isolation compared to the joint format. We thus remain cautious about strong interpretations of the size of the geographic effects compared to the overall stability that these specifications show for our network components.

With these caveats, the economic magnitudes of table 8's effects are substantial. Figure 3 in appendix B shows the impulse response functions including own and network effects in response to a one standard deviation shock in specifications that also include geographic effects, further reported in appendix table 9C. The implied magnitudes of some of these geographic effects are quite large and suggest a fruitful and important area for deeper investigation.[28]

VI. Conclusion

Idiosyncratic firm- or industry-level shocks could spread through a network of interconnections in the economy, propagating and amplifying their initial impact. Though their potential import was initially downplayed because of the belief that their aggregation across many units (disaggregated industries or firms) would limit their macro-

Table 8
Geographic and Networks Analysis

		Δ Log Real Value Added		Δ Log Employment	
		(1)	(2)	(3)	(4)
Δ Dependent variable $t-1$		−0.028	−0.047	0.130***	0.124***
		(0.040)	(0.041)	(0.021)	(0.020)
Trade:	Geographic effects $t-1$	0.125***	0.113***	0.055***	0.049***
		(0.035)	(0.034)	(0.018)	(0.017)
	Downstream effects $t-1$		−0.048		−0.014
			(0.078)		(0.045)
	Upstream effects $t-1$		0.095***		0.061***
			(0.029)		(0.019)
	Own effects $t-1$	0.032***	0.033***	0.023***	0.023***
		(0.009)	(0.009)	(0.005)	(0.005)
Federal:	Geographic effects $t-1$	0.112***	0.101***	0.046***	0.040***
		(0.032)	(0.031)	(0.015)	(0.014)
	Downstream effects $t-1$		−0.036		−0.018
			(0.023)		(0.017)
	Upstream effects $t-1$		0.026**		0.017**
			(0.012)		(0.009)
	Own effects $t-1$	0.001	−0.001	0.002	0.001
		(0.004)	(0.004)	(0.003)	(0.003)
TFP:	Geographic effects $t-1$	0.032***	0.027***	0.014***	0.012**
		(0.010)	(0.010)	(0.005)	(0.005)
	Downstream effects $t-1$		0.055***		0.016*
			(0.019)		(0.010)
	Upstream effects $t-1$		0.024*		0.011
			(0.013)		(0.008)
	Own effects $t-1$	0.008	0.007	0.008***	0.007***
		(0.006)	(0.006)	(0.002)	(0.002)
Patent:	Geographic effects $t-1$	0.005***	0.004***	0.001	0.001
		(0.001)	(0.001)	(0.001)	(0.001)
	Downstream effects $t-1$		0.039***		0.016**
			(0.011)		(0.006)
	Upstream effects $t-1$		0.002		0.000
			(0.005)		(0.003)
	Own effects $t-1$	−0.002	−0.006*	−0.005**	−0.007***
		(0.004)	(0.004)	(0.003)	(0.003)
Observations		6,543	6,543	6,543	6,543

Notes: See table 2A. Estimations include additional effects from indicated shocks and the geographic overlay of industries. Geographic overlay is measured as the sum across regions of the interaction of a focal industry's employment share in the region times the share of regional activity for other industries. Regions are defined through commuting zones and use 1991 industrial activity from the County Business Patterns database.
***Significant at the 1 percent level.
**Significant at the 5 percent level.
*Significant at the 10 percent level.

economic impact, there has been a recent revival of interest in such network-based propagation of microeconomic shocks. This paper contributes to an empirical investigation of the role of such propagation, focusing primarily on input-output linkages but also on connections through the geographic collocation patterns of industries.

One feature that makes propagation through the input-output network particularly attractive for empirical study is that theory places fairly tight restrictions on the form of the transmission of these effects. In particular, in response to demand-side shocks, upstream propagation (to the suppliers of the directly affected industries) should be more pronounced than downstream propagation (to the customers of the directly affected industries), whereas in response to supply-side shocks, the reverse ordering should hold. In fact, when production technologies and consumer preferences are Cobb-Douglas, there should only be upstream propagation with demand-side shocks and only downstream propagation with supply-side shocks. Moreover, the quantitative magnitudes of the direct effects and the downstream/upstream effects are pinned down by theory.

After reviewing these theoretical basics, we turn to an empirical investigation of the propagation of four different types of shocks—China import shocks and federal government spending shocks on the demand side, and TFP and foreign patenting shocks on the supply side. In each case, we study these shocks first in isolation and then in combination with the other shocks, and separately estimate own (direct) effects as well as downstream and upstream effects. Throughout, our focus is on annual variation, which appears more relevant for the question of macroeconomic fluctuations, though we verify the robustness of our results to lower-frequency analysis.

Our empirical results paint a fairly uniform pattern across the different types of shocks. In each case, the patterns are consistent with theory—in the case of demand-side shocks, upstream effects strongly overshadow downstream effects, which are often zero or in the opposite direction, and the converse is true with supply-side shocks. Moreover, the theory-implied quantitative restrictions are often verified, excepting the foreign patenting shocks. Equally important, we also find the network-based propagation of shocks to be quantitatively sizable, and in each case, more important than the direct effect of the shock—sometimes more than five times as important. These patterns appear to be fairly robust across specifications and different control strategies.

In addition to the propagation of shocks through the input-output network, the geographic spread of economic shocks could potentially be important. For example, many economic transactions, particularly for nontradables, take place within the local economy (e.g., a county or commuting zone). If so, a negative shock to an industry concentrated in an area will impact firms and workers in that area. Though a full analysis of this geographic dimension requires detailed data with geography/industry breakdown, we also undertake a preliminary investigation of these linkages by focusing on the collocation patterns of industries. The idea is simple: if two industries tend to collocate strongly, meaning that wherever one industry plays a major role in the local economy, the other industry is also likely to be overrepresented, then shocks to the first industry will tend to be felt more strongly by this collocating industry than other, geographically less connected industries. We derive a theoretical relationship showing how industry-level shocks spread to other industries depending on collocation patterns and then empirically investigate this linkage.

Our results in this domain are somewhat less robust, but still indicate a fairly sizable impact of the propagation of shocks through the geographic collocation network. In fact, quantitatively this channel appears to be, if anything, somewhat more important than the transmission of shocks to the input-output network. Interestingly, however, controlling for this geographic channel does not attenuate or weaken the evidence we find for the propagation of shocks with the input-output network.

Though ours is not the first paper showing that certain shocks spread through the network of input-output linkages (and also of geographic connections), we still consider our paper as part of the early phase of this emerging literature documenting the empirical power of network-based propagation of shocks. Several areas of future work look promising from our vantage point. First, as already noted, the geographic spread of shocks can be better studied by using data and empirical methods that cover multiple geographic scales and levels of interaction, and even better would be to incorporate measures of the geographic span of the operations and plants of multiunit firms using the Census Bureau's Longitudinal Business Database.

Second, the input-output network we utilize is still fairly aggregated. The theoretical logic applies at any level of disaggregation, and even at the level of firms. Though firm input-output linkages require some care (since many such relations may be noncompetitive due to the presence of relationship-specific investments or holdup problems), the same ideas can also be extended to the firm-level network of input-output linkages. Atalay, Hortacsu and Syverson (2014) and Atalay et al. (2011)

take first steps in constructing such firm-level networks, which can then be used for studying this type of propagation.

Third, the simple but powerful nature of the theory we have already exploited in this paper also suggests that more structural approaches could be quite fruitfully applied in this domain, which will enable more rigorous testing of some of the theoretical predictions of this class of models. For example, the Leontief inverse matrix also puts a considerable amount of discipline about the comovement of value added and employment across industries resulting from shocks spreading through the input-output network, which can be formally investigated.

Fourth, the role of the input-output and the geographic networks in the propagation of industry-level (micro)shocks suggests that these networks may also be playing a role in the amplification of macroshocks—such as aggregate demand, monetary and financial shocks—which appears to be a generally understudied area.

Fifth, the two types of networks we have focused on are by no means the only ones that may matter for macroeconomic outcomes. Two others that have recently been investigated are the financial network, which can lead to the propagation and contagion of shocks hitting some financial institutions to the rest of the financial system (e.g., Allen and Gale 2000; Acemoglu et al. 2015c; Elliott, Golub, and Jackson 2014; Cabrales, Gottardi, and Vega-Redondo 2014), and the idea/innovation network, which can lead to the spread of new knowledge, innovations, and practices (studied, for example, in Acemoglu, Akcigit, and Kerr [2015], as well as indirectly in Bloom et al. [2013]). Our decision to abstract from these was partly because of our empirical frame, which centers on industry-level shocks, and also because of our focus on shorter-run fluctuations (whereas the propagation of new ideas and innovations through the innovation network is likely to be more important at five- or ten-year frequencies or even longer). Nevertheless, combining these various types of network linkages may be a fruitful area for future research.

Finally, in addition to the propagation of shocks to other industries or firms, the network linkages emphasized here can also fundamentally change the nature of macroeconomic outcomes and their volatility. For example, Acemoglu et al. (2015a) show how tail macroeconomic risk can be created from the propagation of microeconomic shocks through the input-output network, while Schennach (2013) suggests that these types of network effects may change the persistence properties of macroeconomic time series. These new areas also constitute fruitful directions for future research.

Appendix A

Proof of Proposition 1

Part 1. Let us set government purchases equal to zero for this part of the proof. Recall that profit maximization implies

$$a_{ij} = \frac{p_j x_{ij}}{p_i y_i}, \text{ and } \alpha_i^l = \frac{wl_i}{p_i y_i}. \tag{A1}$$

Utility maximization in turn yields

$$\frac{p_i c_i}{\beta_i} = \frac{p_j c_j}{\beta_j}. \tag{A2}$$

Since total household income is equal to labor income, and in this part we have no government purchases, we also have

$$\sum_{i=1}^{n} p_i c_i = wl,$$

which yields

$$p_i c_i = \beta_i wl, \; \forall i. \tag{A3}$$

Moreover, the first-order condition for labor supply implies

$$-\frac{\gamma'(l)l}{\gamma(l)} = 1,$$

and thus labor supply is determined independent of the equilibrium wage rate because given the preferences in (3), income and substitutions cancel out.

Let us now take logs in (1) and totally differentiate to obtain

$$d \ln y_i = dz_i + \alpha_i^l d \ln l_i + \sum_{j=1}^{n} a_{ij} d \ln x_{ij}. \tag{A4}$$

Let us next totally differentiate (A1) to obtain

$$d \ln y_i + d \ln p_i = d \ln x_{ij} + d \ln p_j,$$

and

$$d \ln y_i + d \ln p_i = d \ln l_i,$$

where we have made use of the fact that the wages are chosen as the numeraire and thus $d \ln w = 0$. Substituting these two equations into (A4), we have

$$d \ln y_i = dz_i + \alpha_i^l(d \ln y_i + d \ln p_i) + \sum_{j=1}^{n} a_{ij}(d \ln y_i + d \ln p_i - d \ln p_j).$$

Next recalling that l remains constant, differentiating (A2) and (A3), and combining with the previous two equations to eliminate prices, we obtain

$$d \ln y_i = dz_i + \alpha_i^l(d \ln y_i - d \ln c_i) + \sum_{j=1}^{n} a_{ij}(d \ln y_i - d \ln c_i + d \ln c_j).$$

Noting that $\alpha_i^l + \Sigma_{j=1}^n a_{ij} = 1$, this simplifies to

$$d \ln c_i = dz_i + \sum_{j=1}^{n} a_{ij} d \ln c_j,$$

which can be rewritten in matrix form as

$$\mathbf{d \ln c = dz + A d \ln c}$$

where $\mathbf{d \ln c}$ and $\mathbf{dz}$ are the vectors of $d \ln c_i$ and dz_i respectively, which is a unique solution given by

$$\mathbf{d \ln c = (I - A)^{-1} dz},\qquad\qquad (A5)$$

in view of the fact that the largest eigenvalue of $\mathbf{A}$ is less than 1. Next combining (2) and (A1), we have

$$\frac{y_j}{c_j} = 1 + \sum_{i=1}^{n} a_{ij} \frac{\beta_i y_i}{\beta_j c_i},$$

which implies that

$$\mathbf{d \ln y = d \ln c}.\qquad\qquad (A6)$$

Then combining (A5) with (A6) we obtain

$$\mathbf{d \ln y = (I - A)^{-1} dz}.\qquad\qquad (A7)$$

This yields the desired result, (6).

Part 2. Normalize $\mathbf{z = 0}$ for this part of the proof. Consider the unit cost function of sector i, which is

$$C_i(\mathbf{p}, w) = B_i w^{\alpha_i^l} \prod_{j=1}^{n} p_j^{a_{ij}},$$

where

$$B_i = \left[\frac{1}{\alpha_i^l}\right]^{\alpha_i^l} \prod_{j=1}^{n} \left[\frac{1}{a_{ij}}\right]^{a_{ij}}.$$

Zero profit condition for producer i implies

$$\ln p_i = \ln B_i + \alpha_i^l \ln w + \sum_{j=1}^{n} a_{ij} \ln p_j \text{ for all } i \in \{1, .., n\}.$$

Since the wage is the numeraire (i.e., $w = 1$), we have $\alpha_i^l \ln w = 0$ and these equations define an n equation system in n prices (for a given vector of productivities $\mathbf{z}$, in this instance normalized to 1), with solution

$$\ln \mathbf{p} = (\mathbf{I} - \mathbf{A})^{-1} \mathbf{b},$$

where $\mathbf{b}$ is the vector with entries given by $\ln B_i$.

This shows that, for a given vector of productivities, the equilibrium price vector is uniquely determined regardless of the value of the vector of government purchases $\mathbf{G}$. Thus demand-side shocks have no impact on equilibrium prices, which are entirely determined by the supply side. But then from (A3), the consumption vector remains unchanged, and from (2), total net supply of all sectors has to remain constant regardless of the change in $\mathbf{G}$. We can then obtain the change in the total production in the economy using (2) combined with (A1) and (A2), which with unchanged prices simply implies

$$d \ln y_i = d \ln x_{ij} \text{ and } d \ln y_i = d \ln l_i.$$

Household maximization implies that, even though prices are fixed, labor supply will change because of changes in consumption (resulting from government purchases). In particular, the following first-order condition determines the representative household's labor supply

$$\frac{wl}{wl - T} = -\frac{l\gamma'(l)}{\gamma(l)},$$

with $T = \sum_{i=1}^{n} p_i G_i$.

When $\gamma(l) = (1 - l)^\lambda$, using the fact that the wage, w, is chosen as the numeraire, we obtain

$$l = \frac{1 + \lambda \sum_{i=1}^{n} p_i G_i}{1 + \lambda}.$$

Therefore, we have that

$$p_i c_i = \beta_i [lw - T]$$

$$= \frac{\beta_i}{1 + \lambda}\left[1 - \sum_{j=1}^{n} p_j G_j\right]$$

which implies

$$d(p_i c_i) = -\frac{\beta_i}{(1 + \lambda)}\sum_{j=1}^{n} d(p_j G_j).$$

The resource constraint then implies:

$$dy_i = dc_i + \sum_{j=1}^{n} dx_{ji} + dG_i.$$

Combining the previous two equations with (A1),

$$\frac{d(p_i y_i)}{p_i y_i} = \sum_{j=1}^{n} a_{ji}\frac{d(p_j y_j)}{p_i y_i} + \frac{dG_i}{y_i} - \frac{\beta_i}{(1 + \lambda)}\sum_{j=1}^{n}\frac{(dp_j G_j)}{p_i y_i}$$

$$= \sum_{j=1}^{n} \hat{a}_{ji}\frac{d(p_j y_j)}{p_j y_j} + \frac{d\tilde{G}_i}{p_i y_i} - \frac{\beta_i}{(1 + \lambda)}\sum_{j=1}^{n}\frac{d\tilde{G}_j}{p_i y_i},$$

(A8)

where $\tilde{G}_j = p_j G_j$. Writing this in matrix form and noting that, because prices are constant, $d(p_i y_i) / p_i y_i = d \ln y_i$, we have

$$\mathbf{d \ln y} = \hat{\mathbf{A}}^T \mathbf{d \ln y} + \Lambda \mathbf{d\tilde{G}}$$

$$= (\mathbf{I} - \hat{\mathbf{A}}^T)^{-1}\Lambda \mathbf{d\tilde{G}}$$

$$= \hat{\mathbf{H}}^T \Lambda \mathbf{d\tilde{G}}$$

where $\hat{\mathbf{H}} = (\mathbf{I} - \hat{\mathbf{A}})^{-1}$, $\tilde{\mathbf{G}}$ is the vector of nominal government spending levels, the $\tilde{G}$'s,

$$\hat{\mathbf{A}} = \begin{pmatrix} \hat{a}_{11} & \hat{a}_{12} & \cdots & \\ \hat{a}_{21} & \hat{a}_{22} & & \\ & & \ddots & \\ & & & \hat{a}_{nn} \end{pmatrix},$$

with entries $\hat{a}_{ij} = x_{ij} / y_i$, and

$$
\Lambda = \begin{pmatrix}
\left(1 - \dfrac{\beta_1}{(1 + \lambda)}\right)\dfrac{1}{p_1 y_1} & -\dfrac{\beta_1}{(1 + \lambda)}\dfrac{1}{p_1 y_1} & \cdots \\[2ex]
-\dfrac{\beta_2}{(1 + \lambda)}\dfrac{1}{p_2 y_2} & \left(1 - \dfrac{\beta_2}{(1 + \lambda)}\right)\dfrac{1}{p_2 y_2} & \\[2ex]
 & & \ddots \\[2ex]
 & & \left(1 - \dfrac{\beta_n}{(1 + \lambda)}\right)\dfrac{1}{p_n y_n}
\end{pmatrix}. \quad (9)
$$

Carrying out the second matrix multiplication, this can also be written as

$$
\mathbf{d \ln y} = \hat{\mathbf{H}}^T \begin{pmatrix}
\dfrac{d\tilde{G}_1}{p_1 y_1} - \dfrac{\beta_1}{(1 + \lambda)}\dfrac{1}{p_1 y_1}\sum_{j=1}^{n}d\tilde{G}_j \\[3ex]
\dfrac{d\tilde{G}_2}{p_2 y_2} - \dfrac{\beta_2}{(1 + \lambda)}\dfrac{1}{p_2 y_2}\sum_{j=1}^{n}d\tilde{G}_j \\[3ex]
\vdots
\end{pmatrix},
$$

or with one more round of matrix multiplication, as

$$
d \ln y_i = \sum_{j=1}^{n}\hat{h}_{ji}\dfrac{1}{p_j y_j}\left(d\tilde{G}_j - \dfrac{\beta_j}{1 + \lambda}\sum_{k=1}^{n}d\tilde{G}_k\right).
$$

Rearranging this equation yields (7).

We also note that the effects of demand-side shocks can be alternatively expressed (without the division by $p_i y_i$ in equation [A8]) in level, rather than log, changes as

$$
\mathbf{d\tilde{y}} = \mathbf{H}^T \begin{pmatrix}
d\tilde{G}_1 - \dfrac{\beta_1}{(1 + \lambda)}\sum_{j=1}^{n}d\tilde{G}_j \\[3ex]
d\tilde{G}_2 - \dfrac{\beta_2}{(1 + \lambda)}\sum_{j=1}^{n}d\tilde{G}_j \\[3ex]
\vdots
\end{pmatrix}, \quad (10)
$$

which is the general form of the expressions used in Example 2.

Endnotes

Authors' addresses (respectively): Massachusetts Institute of Technology, University of Pennsylvania, and Harvard University. This is a revised paper that was presented at the 30th Annual Conference on Macroeconomics. We are grateful to the organizers/editors, Martin Eichenbaum and Jonathan Parker, and our discussants, Lawrence Christiano and Xavier Gabaix, for their very helpful directions and comments. We also thank seminar participants for their comments and ideas, Brendan Price and Pascual Restrepo for data assistance, and Alexis Brownell for excellent research assistance. The online appendices for this paper are available with our NBER working paper and also at www.people.hbs. edu/wkerr. For acknowledgments, sources of research support, and disclosure of the authors' material financial relationships, if any, please see http://www.nber.org/chapters/ c13598.ack.

1. Earlier contributions on this theme include Jovanovic (1987) and Durlauf (1993) who showed how idiosyncratic shocks can accumulate into aggregate risk in the presence of strong strategic complementarities, and Bak et al. (1993) who proposed a model of macroeconomic "self-organized criticality" capable of generating macroeconomic fluctuations from small shocks due to nonlinear interactions between firms and industries.

2. Acemoglu, Akcigit, and Kerr (2015) look at the medium-run spread of new ideas through the innovation (knowledge-flow) network of the US economy.

3. Though our evidence shows that microeconomic (industry-level) shocks are important and propagate strongly, it does not directly speak to the issues discussed in the previous paragraph, that is, to whether a law of large numbers-type argument will ensure that they wash out at the macrolevel.

4. We should add at this point that despite our use of the term "shocks," we would like to be cautious in claiming that our estimates correspond to causal effects of purely exogenous shocks on endogenous economic outcomes. Even though we specify our regression equations to guard against the most obvious forms of endogeneity (contemporaneous shocks affecting both left- and right-hand-side variables and Manski's [1993] reflection problem that would result from having grouped endogenous variables on the right-hand side), our shocks themselves may be endogenous to economic decisions in the recent past. For imports from China, because we are focusing on the exogenous component of the variation, we are fairly confident that our estimates are informative about causal effects. The same applies, perhaps with some additional caveats, to federal-spending shocks, since we exploit variation across industries in their differential responsiveness to such aggregate changes. For the TFP and foreign-patenting measures, the endogeneity concerns are more severe. Nevertheless, even in these cases we believe that our regressions are informative about the propagation of these "predetermined" shocks through the input-output and geographic networks.

5. Here, consistent with theory, "network effects" refer to downstream effects for supply-side shocks and upstream effects for demand-side shocks. The details of how figure 1 is constructed are provided below.

6. Recent work looking at the local coagglomeration of industries includes Ellison, Glaeser, and Kerr (2010), Greenstone, Hornbeck, and Moretti (2010), and Helsley and Strange (2014).

7. Appendices B and C are available online (http://www.nber.org/data-appendix/ c13598/online-appendix.pdf; http://www.nber.org/data-appendix/c13598/online -appendix.pdf).

8. The main results we emphasize do not depend on the absence of physical capital, for example, with a production function that takes the form

$$y_i = e^{z_i} l_i^{\alpha_i^l} k_i^{\alpha_i^k} \prod_{j=1}^{n} x_{ij}^{a_{ij}}.$$

We suppress capital to simplify the notation and discussion.

More consequential is our assumption that this is a static economy where each industry simultaneously buys inputs from others. Long and Plosser (1983) instead assumed that an industry at time t uses as inputs products produced by other industries at date $t - 1$. We discuss the implications of our timing assumption and the robustness of our results to this structure in appendix C (http://www.nber.org/data-appendix/c13598/online-appendix.pdf, available online).

9. The diagonals of the Leontief inverse matrix, $\mathbf{H}$, are no less than 1, so that $h_{ii} - 1$ is nonnegative.

10. In this case, the functional form assumption $\gamma(l) = (1 - l)^{\lambda}$ is imposed to simplify the expressions.

11. Detailed derivations for this and the next example are provided in appendix C, available online.

12. Clearly Cobb-Douglas is an approximation, though arguably not a bad one since the US input-output matrix appears to be fairly stable over time, as shown, for example, in Acemoglu et al. (2012) (and with non-Cobb-Douglas technologies this would not be the case). Our empirical results also give additional credence to the notion that Cobb-Douglas is a useful approximation for our purposes. In any case, it should be emphasized that the qualitative nature of the results emphasized in the proposition—that supply shocks will have larger downstream effects than upstream effects—holds true with non-Cobb-Douglas technologies and preferences, since even in this case quantity and price effects would at least partially offset each other (and in fact, Acemoglu, Ozdaglar, and Tahbaz-Salehi [2015b] show that similar results to those in Proposition 1 can be obtained as first-order approximations under general production technologies).

13. In fact, this equation implies that the coefficients of the own and network effects should both be equal to one, though this prediction depends on the choice of units of the shocks, the dz's. In practice, the coefficients will be different than one but still equal to each other depending on the specific choices of units for measuring our shocks.

14. This can be seen straightforwardly by considering a dynamic version of the model (without additional intertemporal linkages), in which case equations (6) and (7) would apply with time subscripts, with only dz_{it} being relevant for time t outcomes. In the presence of irreversible investments and/or other intertemporal linkages at the sectoral level, expectations of future shocks would also matter.

15. More formally, when η is small, the inverse $(\mathbf{I} - \mathbf{B})^{-1}$ necessarily exists, and thus has an infinite series expansion of the form:

$$(\mathbf{I} - \mathbf{B})^{-1} = \mathbf{I} + \mathbf{B} + \mathbf{B}^2 + \mathbf{B}^3 + \dots .$$

Moreover, when η is small, we can also approximate this inverse with the first two terms, which leads to the next equation. We describe below calculations and empirical tests with higher-order terms.

16. Available online (http://www.nber.org/data-appendix/c13598/online-appendix.pdf).

17. We use this notation rather than h_{ij} as in section II to emphasize that these are the empirical counterparts of the theoretical notions developed above.

18. First-stage equations also naturally control for all other covariates from the second stage, including the lagged dependent variable, to ensure consistent estimation. But, of course, the only excluded instrument is the exogenous component of the change in import penetration.

19. Http://www.nber.org/data-appendix/c13598/online-appendix.pdf.

20. The unweighted standard deviation in industry growth rates for our sample is 0.15 for log value-added growth and 0.10 for log employment growth.

21. This restriction is not tested directly from the reported regression, but from the related regression described in section II, following Proposition 1, where own effects reflect the diagonal elements of the Leontief inverse matrix. We report specifications in which the own effects are not scaled in this manner to maintain transparency about the direct first-order effects of own-industry shocks. In any case, the coefficient estimates when we undertake this scaling are similar to those reported in the tables in the paper.

22. More specifically, focusing on upstream effects, recall that $Upstream_{i,t} = \Sigma_j (Output\%_{i \to j}^{1991} - \mathbf{1}_{j=i}) \cdot Shock_{j,t}$, whereas for this term to capture the quantitative impact of shocks on supplier industries, we would need it to take the form

$$\sum_j \frac{(Output\%_{i\to j}^{1991} - \mathbf{1}_{j=i})}{\Sigma_k(Output\%_{i\to k}^{1991} - \mathbf{1}_{k=i})} \cdot Shock_{j,t},$$

so that it corresponds to a weighted average of shocks hitting industries. The simplest and most transparent approach to make this adjustment is to divide our coefficient estimates by the average of the $\Sigma_k(Output\%_{i\to k}^{1991} - \mathbf{1}_{k=i})$'s, i.e., by $(1 / n)\Sigma_i\Sigma_k(Output\%_{i\to k}^{1991} - \mathbf{1}_{k=i})$ (where n is the number of industries). The adjustment for the downstream effect is very similar. From the US input-output matrix, this adjustment factor is 2.156.

An alternative method would be to rerun all of our specifications using the adjusted upstream and downstream measures (computed as weighted averages as indicated above). This method yields estimates of network multipliers for value added and employment of 5.9 and 8.0, respectively, which are comparable to the 6.4 and 5.9 multipliers estimated by the direct-adjustment method outlined here and reported below.

23. All appendix tables are included in appendix B (http://www.nber.org/data-appendix/c13598/online-appendix.pdf).

24. However, in this case, appendix table 4B shows that the results are sensitive to the exact value of the persistence parameter, ψ.

25. Bloom et al. (2013) develop a strategy for controlling for this competition effect, but the implementation of their strategy is not feasible given our industry-level data.

26. Appendix figure 1 reports impulse response functions akin to figures 1a and 1b using the results from table 6, where we trace out a one standard deviation upstream or downstream network component in terms of value added or employment, as instrumented by each shock, alongside the direct effect of the shock. For brevity, we only plot the stable and theory-consistent estimates, which are the ones that are meaningful to compare to our baseline results. The resulting magnitudes are comparable to, though somewhat larger than, our main estimates.

27. Available at http://www.nber.org/data-appendix/c13598/online-appendix.pdf.

28. Following Autor et al. (2013), Acemoglu et al. (2015) estimate an aggregate reduction of over 1.5 million manufacturing jobs through direct and network effects from the China trade shocks. In terms of our framework, their estimates correspond to a combination of own effects and geographic spillovers; they also control for changes in the underlying population in regions in their econometric specification.

References

Acemoglu, Daron, Ufuk Akcigit, and William Kerr. 2015. "The Innovation Network." Working Paper, MIT.

Acemoglu, Daron, David Autor, David Dorn, Gordon Hanson, and Brendan Price. 2016. "Import Competition and the Great US Employment Sag of the 2000s." *Journal of Labor Economics* 34 (S1): S141–98.

Acemoglu, Daron, Vasco Carvalho, Asuman Ozdaglar, and Alireza Tahbaz-Salehi. 2012. "The Network Origins of Aggregate Fluctuations." *Econometrica* 80 (5): 1977–2016.

Acemoglu, Daron, Suresh Naidu, Pascual Restrepo, and James A. Robinson. 2014. "Democracy Does Cause Growth." NBER Working Paper no. 20004, Cambridge, MA.

Acemoglu, Daron, Asuman Ozdaglar, and Alireza Tahbaz-Salehi. 2015a. "Microeconomic Origins of Macroeconomic Tail Risks." NBER Working Paper no. 20865, Cambridge, MA.

———. 2015b. "Networks, Shocks and Propagation." Working Paper no. 15-04, Department of Economics, MIT.

———. 2015c. "Systemic Risk and Stability in Financial Networks." *American Economic Review* 105 (2): 564–608.

Allen, Franklin, and Douglas Gale. 2000. "Financial Contagion." *Journal of Political Economy* 108 (1): 1–33.
Atalay, Enghin, Ali Hortacsu, Jimmy Roberts, and Chad Syverson. 2011. "Network Structure of Production." *Proceedings of the National Academy of Sciences* 108 (13): 5199–202.
Atalay, Enghin, Ali Hortacsu, and Chad Syverson. 2014. "Vertical Integration and Input Flows." *American Economic Review* 104 (4): 1120–48.
Autor, David, David Dorn, and Gordon Hanson. 2013. "The China Syndrome: Local Labor Market Effects of Import Competition in the United States." *American Economic Review* 103 (6): 2121–68.
Bak, Per, Kan Chen, Jose Scheinkman, and Michael Woodford. 1993. "Aggregate Fluctuations from Independent Sectoral Shocks: Self-Organized Criticality in a Model of Production and Inventory Dynamics." *Ricerche Economiche* 47 (1): 3–30.
Ball, Laurence, and David Romer. 1990. "Real Rigidities and the Non-Neutrality of Money." *Review of Economic Studies* 57 (2): 183–203.
Baqaee, David. 2015. "Labor Intensity in an Interconnected Economy." Working Paper, Harvard University.
Barrot, Jean-Noel, and Julien Sauvagnat. 2014. "Input Specificity and the Propagation of Idiosyncratic Shocks in Production Networks." Working Paper, MIT.
Becker, Randy, Wayne Gray, and Jordan Marvakov. 2013. "NBER-CES Manufacturing Industry Database: Technical Notes." Cambridge, MA, National Bureau of Economic Research. http://www.nber.org/nberces/nberces5809/nberces_5809_technical_notes.pdf.
Bernanke, Ben, and Mark Gertler. 1989. "Agency Costs, Net Worth, and Business Fluctuations." *American Economic Review* 79 (1): 14–31.
Blanchard, Olivier J., and Nobuhiro Kiyotaki. 1987. "Monopolistic Competition and the Effects of Aggregate Demand." *American Economic Review* 77 (4): 647–66.
Bloom, Nicholas, Mark Schankerman, and John Van Reenen. 2013. "Identifying Technology Spillovers and Product Market Rivalry." *Econometrica* 81: 1347–93.
Boehm, Christoph, Aaron Flaaen, and Nitya Pandalai Nayar. 2014. "Input Linkages and the Transmission of Shocks: Firm Level Evidence from the 2011 Tohoku Earthquake." Working Paper no 383, Society for Economic Dynamics.
Cabrales, Antonio, Piero Gottardi, and Fernando Vega-Redondo. 2014. "Risk-Sharing and Contagion in Networks." CESifo Working Paper no. 4715, Center for Economic Studies and Ifo Institute.
Carvalho, Vasco. 2008. "Aggregate Fluctuations and the Network Structure of Intersectoral Trade." Working Paper, Center for Research, Entrepreneurship & Innovation.
Carvalho, Vasco, Makoto Nirei, and Yukiko Saito. 2014. "Supply Chain Disruptions: Evidence from the Great East Japan Earthquake." RIETI Discussion Paper Series no. 14-E-035, Research Institute of Economy, Trade, and Industry.
Christiano, Lawrence, Martin Eichenbaum, and Sergio Rebelo. 2011. "When Is the Government Spending Multiplier Large?" *Journal of Political Economy* 119 (1): 78–121.
Diamond, Peter. 1982. "Aggregate Demand Management in Search Equilibrium." *Journal of Political Economy* 90:881–94.
Durlauf, Steven. 1993. "Nonergodic Economic Growth." *Review of Economic Studies* 60:349–66.

Eggertsson, Gauti, and Michael Woodford. 2003. "The Zero Bound on Interest Rates and Optimal Monetary Policy." *Brookings Papers on Economic Activity* 34 (1): 139–211.

Elliott, Matthew, Benjamin Golub, and Matthew Jackson. 2014. "Financial Networks and Contagion." *American Economic Review* 104 (10): 3115–53.

Ellison, Glenn, Edward Glaeser, and William Kerr. 2010. "What Causes Industry Agglomeration? Evidence from Coagglomeration Patterns." *American Economic Review* 100 (3): 1195–213.

Farhi, Emmanuel, and Ivan Werning. 2013. "A Theory of Macroprudential Policies in the Presence of Nominal Rigidities." NBER Working Paper no. 19313, Cambridge, MA.

Foerster, Andrew, Pierre-Daniel Sarte, and Mark Watson. 2011. "Sectoral versus Aggregate Shocks: A Structural Factor Analysis of Industrial Production." *Journal of Political Economy* 119:1–38.

Friedman, Milton, and Anna J. Schwartz. 1971. *A Monetary History of the United States, 1867–1960.* Princeton, NJ: Princeton University Press.

Fujita, Masahisa, Paul Krugman, and Anthony Venables. 1999. *The Spatial Economy: Cities, Regions and International Trade.* Cambridge, MA: MIT Press.

Gabaix, Xavier. 2011. "The Granular Origins of Aggregate Fluctuations." *Econometrica* 79:733–72.

Greenstone, Michael, Richard Hornbeck, and Enrico Moretti. 2010. "Identifying Agglomeration Spillovers: Evidence from Winners and Losers of Large Plant Openings." *Journal of Political Economy* 118 (3): 536–98.

Guerrieri, Veronica, and Guido Lorenzoni. 2012. "Credit Crises, Precautionary Savings, and the Liquidity Trap." Working Paper, University of Chicago.

Hall, Robert. 2009. "By How Much Does GDP Rise If the Government Buys More Output?" *Brookings Papers on Economic Activity* 40 (2): 183–249.

Helsley, Robert, and William Strange. 2014. "Coagglomeration, Clusters, and the Scale and Composition of Cities." *Journal of Political Economy* 122 (5): 1064–93.

Horvath, Michael. 1998. "Cyclicality and Sectoral Linkages: Aggregate Fluctuations from Sectoral Shocks." *Review of Economic Dynamics* 1:781–808.

———. 2000. "Sectoral Shocks and Aggregate Fluctuations." *Journal of Monetary Economics* 45:69–106.

Johnson, Daniel. 1999. "150 Years of American Invention: Methodology and a First Geographic Application." Economics Working Paper no. 99-01, Wellesley College.

Jovanovic, Boyan. 1987. "Micro Shocks and Aggregate Risk." *Quarterly Journal of Economics* 102:395–409.

Kerr, William. 2008. "Ethnic Scientific Communities and International Technology Diffusion." *Review of Economics and Statistics* 90 (3): 518–37.

Kiyotaki, Nobuhiro. 1988. "Multiple Expectational Equilibria under Monopolistic Competition." *Quarterly Journal of Economics* 103 (4): 695–713.

Kiyotaki, Nobuhiro, and John Moore. 1997. "Credit Cycles." *Journal of Political Economy* 10(2): 211–48.

Kydland, Finn, and Edward Prescott. 1982. "Time to Build and Aggregate Fluctuations." *Econometrica* 50:1345–71.

Long, John, and Charles Plosser. 1983. "Real Business Cycles." *Journal of Political Economy* 9(1): 39–69.

Lucas, Robert. 1977. "Understanding Business Cycles." *Carnegie–Rochester Conference Series on Public Policy* 5:7–29.

Manski, Charles. 1993. "Identification of Endogenous Social Effects: The Reflection Problem." *Review of Economic Studies* 60 (3): 531–42.

Mian, Atif, Kamalesh Rao, and Amir Sufi. 2013. "Household Balance Sheets, Consumption, and the Economic Slump." *Quarterly Journal of Economics* 128 (4): 1687–726.

Mian, Atif, and Amir Sufi. 2014. "What Explains the 2007–2009 Drop in Employment?" *Econometrica* 82 (6): 2197–2223.

Nickell, Stephen. 1981. "Biases in Dynamic Models with Fixed Effects." *Econometrica* 49 (6): 1417–26.

Schennach, Susanne. 2013. "Long Memory via Networking." Working Paper no. CWP13/13, Centre for Microdata Methods and Practice.

Silverman, Brian. 1999 "Technological Resources and the Direction of Corporate Diversification: Toward an Integration of the Resource-Based View and Transaction Cost Economics." *Management Science* 45 (8): 1109–24.

Comment

Xavier Gabaix, *New York University and NBER*

Discussions of published papers are seldom read. Certainly they are almost never cited. So, how to make good use those *Macroeconomics Annual* pages? I thought it might be useful to write a user-friendly introduction to the ideas underlying Acemoglu, Akcigit, and Kerr's very interesting paper: the "macro from microshocks" approach that started with Long and Plosser (1983), which is tightly linked to something I have called the "granular" hypothesis (Gabaix 2011).[1]

In that view, the primitive shocks to the economy are not mysterious aggregate productivity shocks, or aggregate demand shocks, but understandable shocks to Nokia, Microsoft, demand for Boeing planes, and so forth. This may explain the behavior of significant macroaggregates, and in general be a great, fecund source of insight for macro.

I will explain why I think that this approach is promising; as a preview, the main reasons are as follows.

1. Microshocks may be important to understand the business cycle: rather than "there was a [mysterious] productivity shock," we can have more concrete and understandable explanations like "there was a strike at General Motors," "there was large demand for Boeing planes," "Nokia lost market share," and so forth. They may also be quite important quantitatively, with some estimates (reviewed below) attributing to them 30–50% of GDP fluctuations.

2. They allow us to understand the origins of volatility.

3. They are a source of (plausible) instruments for macroeconomics—something very rare and precious.

4. They may allow us to understand the nature of "multipliers."

5. They allow us to trace how a shock propagates in the broad economy:

this is what Acemoglu et al. does particularly well.

6. They ought to be useful for predictions.

7. They have a great promise for international transmission, for example, of Fed shocks to the exchange rate, exports, and so forth.

I like Acemoglu et al.'s paper a lot. It has useful analytics and interesting empirics. I trust that it will be imitated by other teams, with other data sets. Let me show how it integrates in this broader context.

How Microshocks Affect Macro Outcomes

I start with a basic question. What is the impact of a micro TFP shock on the macroeconomy? Perhaps surprisingly, one can obtain a clean definite answer to that.

What Is the Impact of a TFP Shock?

To see this, we need some notations. Suppose a general economy with N goods. The representative consumer's utility is $u(c_1, ..., c_N)$, firm i (or "sector" i—I use the term interchangeably; I think that firms are more concrete, and help the intuition) produces

$$\text{Gross output of firm } i\text{: } Y_i = e^{z_i}F^i(L_i, K_i, (X_{ij})_{j=1...N}) \tag{1}$$

using labor L_i, capital K_i, and inputs $X_{ij} = X_{i\leftarrow j}$ from firm j. The net production of good i goes into consumption:

$$\text{Net output of good } i\text{: } Y_i - \sum_j X_{ji} = c_i \tag{2}$$

and the value added of firm i is:

$$\text{Value added of firm } i\text{: } V_i = p_i Y_i - \sum_j p_j X_{ij} \tag{3}$$

while the sales (value of gross output) of firm i are:

$$\text{Sales of firm } i\text{: } S_i = p_i Y_i \tag{4}$$

In the end, GDP is:

$$\text{GDP: } Y = \sum_i V_i = \sum_i p_i c_i \tag{5}$$

and the resource constraint is: $\Sigma_i K_i = K, \Sigma_i L_i = L$.

Now, suppose that there is a TFP shock dz_i to firm i, what happens to GDP? We will calculate $d \ln TFP$, which is also $d \ln Y$, when there are constant factors K, L.

One plausible answer might be "we need to know the whole input-output structure of the economy to know that." This is indeed the impression one gets from reading Long and Plosser (1983), and the literature building directly on it.

However, this plausible answer is not correct.

Another plausible answer would be that it is the shock times value added of firm i.

$$d \ln TFP \; =^? \; \frac{V^i}{Y} dz_i = \frac{\text{Value added of firm } i}{\text{GDP}} \times (\text{TFP shock to firm } i).$$

That plausible answer is not correct either.

The correct answer is: the impact is the sales of GDP of the firm times the firm's TFP shock.

$$d \ln TFP \; = \; \frac{S_{it}}{Y_t} dz_{it} = \frac{\text{Sales of firm } i}{\text{GDP}} \times (\text{TFP shock to firm } i). \quad (6)$$

Note that you do not need to know the whole input-output matrix for this. It is enough to know the sales of firm i. It summarizes the input-output impacts in one neat, easily observable quantity—the sales of firm i, over GDP. This is Hulten's (1978) result. I give a compact proof in Gabaix (2011). The quick intuition is as follows. Imagine that there is no reallocation of inputs (capital, labor, intermediary inputs)—this is warranted by the envelope theorem. Then, from (1) only, firm i produces $dz_i\%$ more of its output Y_i, which has a price (social value) p_i. So GDP has increased by $p_i Y_i dz_i = S_i dz_i$. In practice, there is also a reallocation of inputs, and so on, but that does not matter for welfare, that is, TFP.

Of course, another important puzzle in macro is the source of comovement.[2] For that, the input-output structure does matter, as the paper illustrates. The point here is solely that it does not matter to predict GDP (in this most basic frictionless model).

Now, if each of the N firms has a shock, we can contrast the direct impact:

$$(d \ln Y_t)^{\text{Direct}} = \sum_{i=1}^{N} \frac{V_{it}}{Y_t} dz_{it} \quad (7)$$

to the total impact keeping factor (K, L) use constant:

$$(d \ln Y_t)^{\text{Constant factors}} = d \ln TFP = \sum_{i=1}^{N} \frac{S_{it}}{Y_t} dz_{it}. \tag{8}$$

Now, if there is flexible factor use, for example, flexible labor supply or capacity utilization, we find:

$$(d \ln Y_t)^{\text{Full}} = \mu \sum_{i=1}^{N} \frac{S_{it}}{Y_t} dz_{it} \tag{9}$$

where $\mu \geq 1$ is a multiplier (e.g., increased labor supply or capital utilization).[3]

In the "granular approach," the shocks to the economy are (9): the underlying economy is not a smooth continuum, but it is made of incompressible "grains" of economic activity (firms, or fine-grained sectors), that affect GDP.

We note another consequence. If shocks are uncorrelated: $\sigma_{Yt}^2 = \mu^2 \Sigma_i (S_{it} / Y_t)^2 var(dz_{it}) = \mu^2 \Sigma_i (S_{it} / Y_t)^2 \sigma_i^2$, then GDP volatility is:

$$\sigma_{Yt} = \mu \sqrt{\sum_{i=1}^{N} \left(\frac{S_{it}}{Y_t} \right)^2 \sigma_i^2}. \tag{10}$$

For instance, if we have equally-sized sectors $S_{it} / Y_t = 1 / N$ and equal volatility,

$$\sigma_{Yt} = \mu \frac{\bar{\sigma}_i}{\sqrt{N}}. \tag{11}$$

We shall use these formulas soon.

What Are "Microeconomic Shocks," Anyway?

This literature started with Long and Plosser (1983), which is a great model. But Long and Plosser had only $N = 6$ sectors, so some might argue that they did not have "microshocks" in their quantification. Indeed, Dupor (1999) and Horvath (2000) ask: What if you had $N = 600$ or six million sectors? Wouldn't volatility go down to 0 very fast? Dupor's answer is that, as in formula (11), then, you would get a very small volatility, about $1 / \sqrt{N}$. Horvath had a proposal to get rid of the difficulty, based on the notion of sparse input-output matrices, but that potential explanation remained conceptually murky.

One solution was to have huge multipliers. For instance, Jovanovic (1987) proposes a model where the multiplier is $\mu \sim \sqrt{N}$. That does generate sizable fluctuations. However, empirical multipliers do not seem nearly that big.

Another possibility has been that of local, nonlinear effects: Bak et al. (1993) was a pioneering paper in that vein, and Nirei (2006) further developed the idea. However, they have yet to be confronted more systematically with the data.

In Gabaix (2011), I propose another take. Even with $N = 10$ million firms/industries, those effects survive. Why? Recall the formula (10) above. With thin-tailed distribution of sizes (e.g., $S_i / Y = 1 / N$, or more generally S_i is drawn from a finite-variance distribution):

$$\sigma_{\hat{Y}_t} \sim \frac{k}{\sqrt{N}}. \tag{12}$$

However, the firm size distribution is fat-tailed, it is closely Zipf distributed: $P(S > x) \sim k / x^\zeta$ with $\zeta' \simeq 1$ (Gabaix 1999, 2009; Axtell 2001). In that case, GDP volatility decays as follows:

$$\sigma_{\hat{Y}_t} \sim \frac{k}{\ln N}. \tag{13}$$

The decay is in $\ln N$ rather than $\sqrt{N}$. So even with 10 million firms/industries, those effects survive. That is because, plainly, there are big firms (and sectors).

There is a plainer way to see that those effects can be big. Take (10). Empirically, a root-Herfindahl is $\sqrt{\Sigma_{i=1}^N (S_{it} / Y_t)^2} \simeq 5.3\%$, and a micro-level TFP volatility $\bar{\sigma}_i \simeq 12\%$ (this is actually quite delicate to measure). More tentatively, take $\mu \simeq 2.6$ (see Gabaix 2011 for justifications). Then, the GDP volatility generated by idiosyncratic shocks is:

$$\sigma_{Yt} = \mu \times \sqrt{\sum_{i=1}^N \left(\frac{S_{it}}{Y_t}\right)^2} \times \bar{\sigma}_i = 2.6 \times 5.3\% \times 0.12 = 1.7\%. \tag{14}$$

This is clearly of the right order of magnitude.

Another implication of granularity is to emphasize the potential importance of networks (Acemoglu et al. 2012; Carvalho 2014). Those large firm-level shocks propagate through networks, which allows to trace interesting effects, as in Acemoglu et al.

A terminological note may be useful. Sometimes, authors contrast the "direct impact" (7) to the "network effects" (8). This is fine. But the whole "granular" impact is still (8) and even (9). From the economics, there is nothing particularly sound about the "direct" impact. To put it differently: *Networks are an expression of granularity, rather than an alternative to it.* If all firms had small sales, the central limit theorem would hold, and idiosyncratic shocks would all wash out—as in (11) and its variants.

Still, the "multipliers" are interesting in themselves. I like the authors' multiplier calculations (e.g., in Section IV.B). Note that as the sales/value added of the economy is about 2, in general we can expect to find the "production" multiplier (i.e., the one coming simply from the production function) to be about 2. When multipliers are larger, one would like to know more about their origins—see below.

Promises for the Granular Approach

I now list major reasons why this approach might be useful, as shown by Acemoglu et al.[4]

Granular Shocks May Be Important for Aggregate Shocks

Microshocks may be important to understand the business cycle, or perhaps even more the behavior of other macroaggregates, such as exports. In Gabaix (2011), I quantify that granular shocks account for about 1/3 of GDP volatility. Foerster, Sarte, and Watson (2011) find: "The role of idiosyncratic shocks increased considerably after the mid-1980s, explaining half of the quarterly variation in Industrial Production." Atalay (2014) finds even bigger effects. Di Giovanni, Levchenko, and Mejean (2014) have great French data. In their finding, "the standard deviation of the firm-specific shocks' contribution to aggregate sales growth amounts to 80% of the standard deviation of aggregate sales growth in the whole economy." Carvalho and Grassi (2015) make conceptual progress on those issues too.

More research has been trying to quantify the importance of microeconomic shocks.

Granular Shocks May Allow Us to Understand the Patterns in
Macroeconomic Volatility

Di Giovanni and Levchenko (2012) want to understand export fluctuations. They find that the preponderance of large firms and their role in aggregate volatility can help explain two empirical regularities: (a) smaller countries are more volatile, and (b) more open countries are more volatile. In Carvalho and Gabaix (2013), we find that the "fundamental" volatility coming from (10) has good predictive power for actual GDP volatility, and indeed explains the great moderation and its undoing, via changes in the sectoral composition of the US economy.

All in all, the evidence is accumulating, made possible by new, disaggregated data (see also Atalay et al. 2011).

Microshocks Are a Source of Instruments for Macroeconomics

One potentially great importance of granular shocks is that they are a plausible source of instruments in macroeconomics. This is very important, as in business-cycle frequency macro, instruments are woefully rare.

One example I like is Amati and Weinstein (2013). They identify idiosyncratic bank-specific shocks, and trace their impact on investment. In their finding, "We show that these [idiosyncratic] bank supply shocks explain 40% of aggregate loan and investment fluctuations." This seems like a good way to make progress in seeing the impact of financial shocks.

In general, in future research, the use of idiosyncratic shocks as instruments for macro seems very fecund.

Microshocks Can Allow Us to Better Understand "Multipliers"
and Propagation

Those shocks need multipliers, like the μ above. The plainest ones are labor supply and capacity utilization of capital. Other candidates might be the relaxation of credit constraints. Otherwise, fancier ones might be via news, expectations, or imitation. Which ones are more important, and when? It would be great to know.

In my view, that is where Acemoglu et al.'s method and findings might be extended most, empirically and conceptually. The authors find repeated evidence for changes in output, rippling through the network, but we do not quite know if they are quantitatively the ones expected from the Cobb-Douglas model, or if there is something more.

We Can Show a Shock Propagates in the Broad Economy

Another payoff is that we can trace back how shocks propagate in the whole economy, both in time, geographically, and in the network. This is something that Acemoglu et al. do particularly well.

Some other recent papers also do this kind of "tracing." Barrot and Sauvagnat (2015) use well-identified shocks coming from natural disasters, with careful controls for causality via other, nonaffected suppliers/customers. Similarly, Carvalho et al. (2015) trace the impact of a Japanese earthquake.

I expect to see many more such papers. It would be great if they took up the challenge of tracing exactly why the shock propagates: which one in the previous list of the multipliers μ matters.

In Principle, Microshocks Ought to Be Useful for Predictions

Are they? This is quite *underexplored* in my opinion. In Gabaix (2011) I find that they (the lagged "granular residuals") are having extra power, but it would be nice to know if that is true more generally.

They Have Great Promise to Think about the International Transmission of Shocks

One would like to trace the impact of trade shocks, policy changes by central banks, and so forth, in the trade network. Little work on that has been done—though Acemoglu et al.'s example with the Chinese import demand shock is quite interesting. More on this would be welcome. This would also impact asset prices. Indeed, in models of imperfect finance (Gabaix and Maggiori 2015 and its online appendix) demand shocks for currencies also have "network" ripple effects on exchange rates—in theory. Investigating that empirically would be very nice.

Conclusion

In conclusion, this is a very exciting line of research, and Acemoglu et al. is a very useful step forward. For the reasons listed above, I am quite hopeful that we will make much progress on macro by continuing along that line.

Appendix

In these economies, there is a danger of double counting. The authors do not make any such mistake, of course. But just for clarity, and because the issue is important for welfare, I take some time to illustrate the issue here. Suppose that there are just two sectors. Sector 1 is final consumption and sector 2 is just an intermediary good. There is 1 unit of labor, and we normalize the wage to 1. Production functions are:

$$y_1 = e^{z_1} \left(\frac{L_1}{b_1}\right)^{b_1} \left(\frac{X_{12}}{b_2}\right)^{b_2}, \qquad y_2 = X_{12} = e^{z_2}L_2,$$

so aggregate production function is:

$$c = y_1 = e^{z_1+b_2z_2} \left(\frac{L_1}{b_1}\right)^{b_1} \left(\frac{L_2}{b_2}\right)^{b_2}.$$

The planner's problem is:

$$\max_{L_1,L_2} c \text{ s.t. } L_1 + L_2 = 1.$$

The first-order condition gives: $b_i c / L_i = w = 1$, so $L_i = b_i$, $Y = y_1 = e^{z_1+bz_2}$, $y_2 = e^{z_2}b_2$.

We start from $z_i = 0$ initially. Hence, a shock dz_2 implies:

$$d \ln y_1 = b_2 dz_2, \qquad d \ln y_2 = dz_2,$$

but GDP shock is:

$$dY = dy_1 = dy_2 = b_2 dz_1.$$

Hence, for GDP, you want to calculate the final output, not the sum of all increases in outputs.

Endnotes

Contact: xgabaix@stern.nyu.edu. I thank Daron Acemoglu for helpful comments and Chenxi Wang for editorial assistance. For acknowledgments, sources of research support, and disclosure of the author's material financial relationships, if any, please see http://www.nber.org/chapters/c13599.ack.
    1. I build on earlier surveys on power laws (Gabaix 2009, 2016).
    2. Simple calibrations indicate that, indeed, a large and realistic amount of comovement between sectors does arise from linkages (as in Carvalho and Gabaix 2013, section IV.B), though understanding the precise nature of comovement remains a fairly open question.
    3. Note also that one may fear some double counting, as $\Sigma_i(S_{it} / Y_t)$ is greater than one (in practice, it is about 2). But there is none here. However, this is exactly what the economics requires.
    4. I leave aside the interesting applications to financial stability already cited in Acemoglu et al. (Allen and Gale 2000; Acemoglu, Ozdaglar, and Tahbaz-Salehi 2015a; Elliott, Golub, and Jackson 2014).

References

Acemoglu, Daron, Vasco M. Carvalho, Asuman Ozdaglar, and Alireza Tahbaz-Salehi. 2012. "The Network Origins of Aggregate Fluctuations." *Econometrica* 80 (5): 1977–2016.
Amiti, Mary, and David Weinstein. 2013. "How Much do Bank Shocks Affect Investment? Evidence from Matched Bank-Firm Data." NBER Working Paper no. 18890, Cambridge, MA.

Atalay, Enghin. 2014. "How Important are Sectoral Shocks?" Working Paper, University of Wisconsin.

Atalay, Enghin, Ali Hortacsu, James Roberts, and Chad Syverson. 2011. "Network Structure of Production." *Proceedings of the National Academy of Sciences* 108 (13): 5199–202.

Axtell, Robert L. 2001. "Zipf Distribution of US Firm Sizes." *Science* 293 (5536): 1818–20.

Bak, P., K. Chen, J. Scheinkman, and M. Woodford. 1993. "Aggregate Fluctuations from Independent Sectoral Shocks: Self-Organized Criticality in a Model of Production and Inventory Dynamics." *Ricerche Economiche* 47:3–30.

Barrot, Jean-Noel, and Julien Sauvagnat. 2015 "Input Specificity and the Propagation of Idiosyncratic Shocks in Production Networks." Working Paper. http://papers.ssrn.com/sol3/papers.cfm?abstract_id=2427421.

Carvalho, Vasco. 2014. "From Micro to Macro via Production Networks." *Journal of Economic Perspectives* 28 (4): 23–48.

Carvalho, Vasco, and Xavier Gabaix. 2013. "The Great Diversification and Its Undoing." *American Economic Review* 103 (5): 1697–727.

Carvalho, Vasco, and Basile Grassi. 2015. "Large Firm Dynamics and the Business Cycle." Economics Working Paper no. 1481, Department of Economics and Business, Universitat Pompeu Fabra.

Carvalho, Vasco, Makoto Nirei, Yukiko Saito, and Tahbaz-Salehi. 2015. "Supply Chain Disruptions: Evidence from the Great East Japan Earthquake." Working Paper. http://www.rieti.go.jp/en/publications/summary/14060011.html.

di Giovanni, Julian, and Andrei A. Levchenko. 2012. "Country Size, International Trade, and Aggregate Fluctuations in Granular Economies." *Journal of Political Economy* 120 (6): 1083–1132.

di Giovanni, Julian, Andrei Levchenko, and Isabelle Mejean. 2014. "Firms, Destinations, and Aggregate Fluctuations." *Econometrica* 82 (4): 1303–40.

Dupor, W. 1999. "Aggregation and Irrelevance in Multi-Sector Models." *Journal of Monetary Economics* 43:391–409.

Foerster, Andrew, Pierre-Daniel Sarte, and Mark Watson. 2011. "Sectoral versus Aggregate Shocks: A Structural Factor Analysis of Industrial Production." *Journal of Political Economy* 119 (1): 1–38.

Gabaix, Xavier. 1999. "Zipf's Law for Cities: An Explanation." *Quarterly Journal of Economics* 114 (3): 739–67.

———. 2009. "Power Laws in Economics and Finance." *Annual Review of Economics* 1 (1): 255–93.

———. 2011. "The Granular Origins of Aggregate Fluctuations." *Econometrica* 79 (3): 733–72.

———. 2016. "Power Laws in Economics: An Introduction." *Journal of Economic Perspectives* 30 (1): 185–206.

Gabaix, Xavier, and Matteo Maggiori. 2015. "International Liquidity and Exchange Rate Dynamics." *Quarterly Journal of Economics* 130 (3): 1369–420.

Horvath, M. 2000. "Sectoral Shocks and Aggregate Fluctuations." *Journal of Monetary Economics* 45:69–106.

Hulten, C. 1978. "Growth Accounting with Intermediary Inputs." *Review of Economic Studies* 45:511–18.

Jovanovic, B. 1987. "Micro Shocks and Aggregate Risk." *Quarterly Journal of Economics* 102:395–409.

Nirei, M. 2006. "Threshold Behavior and Aggregate Critical Fluctuations." *Journal of Economic Theory* 127:309–22.

Comment

Lawrence J. Christiano, *Northwestern University and NBER*

Introduction

A typical firm sells about one-half of its output to other firms and materials purchases from other firms account for roughly half of the firm's input costs. The fact that an individual firm's production occurs within a network of firms is typically ignored by macroeconomists.[1] Acemoglu et al. show that the patterns of amplification and propagation of industry shocks predicted by standard network models are supported by the data. Moreover, they conjecture that incorporating networks into macroeconomic models has first-order implications for macroeconomics. In this comment I describe three examples that support the authors' conjecture. Using a simple model with price-setting frictions, I show that incorporating the network structure of production

- implies quantitatively large costs of inflation,
- cuts the slope of the Phillips curve in half, and
- raises questions about the efficacy of the Taylor principle for stabilizing inflation.

According to conventional wisdom, the social cost of inflation is large.[2] Yet, standard economic models typically imply that the cost of inflation is modest at best.[3] In the words of Paul Krugman, "one of the dirty little secrets of economic analysis is that even though inflation is universally regarded as a terrible scourge, efforts to measure its costs come up with embarrassingly small numbers."[4] I show that mixing networks and price-setting frictions can produce quantitatively large costs of inflation, consistent with the conventional view. The basic idea is that the allocative and other distortions generated by price frictions are amplified by network effects in a way that resembles the familiar mechanism by which networks magnify the effects of firm-level technology shocks (see, e.g., Jones 2013).

I work with a standard New Keynesian (NK) model with Calvo-style price frictions, modified to incorporate production networks in the manner suggested in Basu (1995).[5] The model has the property, well-known in the input-output literature, that network effects magnify a 1% technology shock at the level of the gross output of firms into a 2% shock to aggregate value added. The distortions to the allocation of resources produced by price-setting frictions have effects on gross output that resemble those of a negative technology shock (see Yun 1996). Given the results for technology shocks, it is then not surprising that price distortions large enough to cause a 1% loss to gross output are magnified into a 2% or greater loss to aggregate value added, that is, gross domestic product (GDP).

In the model that I work with, the severity of the allocative distortions in gross output is an increasing function of aggregate inflation.[6] By magnifying these allocative distortions, networks in effect magnify the cost of inflation. I show that these costs can be quite large even relative to the rather modest—by world standards—levels of inflation observed in the United States. For example, the model implies that the high inflation of the 1970s may have had a cost equivalent to a loss of 10% of GDP or more in each year that the inflation was high. Also, there have been proposals to raise the inflation target to perhaps 4 percent, at an annual rate, as a way to reduce the likelihood of the zero lower bound on the nominal interest becoming binding again.[7] According to the calculations below, the cost of such a level of inflation might be a loss of output as high as 1–2% per year. This would be a steep price to pay if, say, zero lower-bound episodes are likely to only occur once every 50 to 75 years.

These cost of inflation numbers are big, perhaps too big. My key point is that introducing networks into macroeconomics—the part with price frictions—matters. The NK model, which is ordinarily thought of as a model that assigns little or no cost to anticipated inflation, actually predicts an abundance of such costs when networks are taken into account.

My calculations involve several assumptions, all presented in detail below. Apart from the assumption that production occurs in networks, the assumptions I make are standard. Still, greater scrutiny will no doubt imply that some of these assumptions deserve adjustment. But, it is quite possible that adjustments would actually imply an even higher cost of inflation. For example, the modeling shortcut that I take to capture networks leaves out much of the richness and detail that Acemoglu et al. describe. A consequence of the simplification is that the number of prices in my framework is substantially less than what would appear in a more empirically realistic analysis. With additional prices there could come additional possibilities for distortions and more reasons for inflation to be costly when there are price setting frictions.[8]

In my analysis, I assume that the frequency of price adjustment is constant. One might suppose that such an assumption implies an overstatement of the cost of a 4% inflation, or of the higher inflation in the 1970s. The idea is that firms would increase the frequency of price adjustment with higher inflation. The empirical results in Golosov and Lucas (2007, figure 3) suggest that this is, in fact, not the case for levels of inflation observed in the United States. They present evidence that the average frequency of price adjustment changes very little for inflation rates in the range of 0 to 16% per year.[9]

Another reason that networks are important has been recognized for a long time, but has not played a significant role in the New Keynesian literature. In particular, networks imply a strategic complementarity among price setters.[10] Consider an individual firm in an environment where the prices of all other firms are inertial (i.e., they respond weakly to shocks). This implies that the firm's price of materials is also inertial, contributing to inertia in its own marginal costs. With inertial marginal costs, the firm has an incentive to be inertial in the setting of its own price.[11] I derive the Phillips curve for this economy and show that the slope of the Phillips curve in terms of marginal cost is cut in half in the presence of networks, as the intuition suggests.

There is a third reason that networks in combination with price-setting frictions may be important. There is a widespread consensus that inflation targeting has valuable macroeconomic stabilizing powers and that the Taylor principle—an interest-rate rule with a large coefficient on inflation—represents a good strategy for implementing inflation targeting. Under this principle, the monetary authority raises the interest rate by more than 1% when inflation rises by 1%. Through a *demand channel*, such an increase in the interest rate induces a fall in GDP and thereby brings inflation back down to target. Suppose now that the funds paid by firms for their variable inputs need to be acquired in advance. These funds will be assigned an interest cost, either because the funds have to be raised in credit markets or because the funds are obtained by suppressing dividends, which have an opportunity cost. That there is an interest component of the cost of variable inputs opens up a second, *working-capital channel*. By raising marginal costs, higher interest rates help to push inflation up. In principle, the working-capital channel could be stronger than the demand channel, with the possibility that the Taylor principle becomes what might better be called the Taylor curse. A sharp rise in the interest rate, rather than being an antidote to inflation, could actually be a trigger for more inflation.

In standard macroeconomic models with price-setting frictions, but no network effects, the working-capital channel is not strong enough to overwhelm the demand channel by enough to destabilize the economy.[12] So, standard models provide support to the Taylor principle. However, I show below that when network effects are taken into account, the possibility that the working-capital channel is stronger than the demand channel is much greater. In that case, an interest-rate rule with a big coefficient on inflation may not work to stabilize inflation and the broader economy.[13] This discussion is relatively brief because it summarizes the findings reported in Christiano, Trabandt, and Walentin (2011).

These examples are why I think Acemoglu et al. are right in their conjecture that network effects have first-order implications for macroeconomics.

The following section provides a rough sketch of the model used in both parts of my analysis. Details about the model and its solution are provided in the appendix. The subsequent two sections focus on the first and second reasons that network effects may be important for macroeconomics, respectively.

A Business-Cycle Model with Networks and Price Frictions

I adopt the usual Dixit-Stiglitz framework, in which there is a homogeneous good, Y_t, that is produced by a representative competitive firm using the following production function:

$$Y_t = \left[\int_0^1 Y_{i,t}^{(\varepsilon-1)/\varepsilon} dj\right]^{\varepsilon/(\varepsilon-1)}, \quad \varepsilon > 1.$$

The representative firm takes output and input prices, P_t and $P_{i,t}$, $i \in (0,1)$, as given and chooses $Y_{i,t}$, $i \in (0,1)$ to maximize profits. The ith input, $Y_{i,t}$, is produced by a monopolist using labor, $N_{i,t}$, and materials, $I_{i,t}$, using the following technology:

$$Y_{i,t} = A_t N_{i,t}^\gamma I_{i,t}^{1-\gamma},$$

$0 < \gamma \leq 1$. The monopolist sets its price, $P_{i,t}$, subject to Calvo price-setting frictions. The monopolist can set $P_{i,t}$ optimally with $1 - \theta$ and with probability θ the ith monopolist must set $P_{i,t} = P_{i,t-1}$ without price indexation. The no-indexation assumption is suggested by the same microeconomic observations that motivate price-setting frictions in the first place. Those observations show that many prices remain unchanged for extended periods of time (see Eichenbaum, Jaimovich, and Rebelo 2011; Bils, Klenow, and Malin 2015). The no-indexation assumption has the implication that the degree of distortion in relative prices is increasing in steady state inflation.

The ith monopolist is competitive in the market for materials and labor. It acquires materials by purchasing the homogeneous good and converting it one-for-one into $I_{i,t}$. Through an analogous mechanism, the ith monopolist sells some of its output to other firms as materials for their use in production. In effect, the ith firm is embedded in a network in which some of its output is sold to other firms for their use as materials and some of its inputs are materials acquired from other firms.

The effective price of labor and materials for intermediate good firms is denoted by $\overline{W}_t$ and $\overline{P}_t$, respectively, where

$$\overline{W}_t = (1 - v)[1 - \psi + \psi R_t]W_t, \overline{P}_t = (1 - v)[1 - \psi + \psi R_t]P_t.$$

Here, W_t denotes the competitively determined price of labor; ψ is the fraction of input costs that must be paid in advance; R_t is the gross nominal rate of interest; and v is a lump sum tax-financed subsidy to costs.

Regarding v, let

$$L_t = \frac{\text{marginal utility cost of labor}_t}{\text{marginal product of labor}_t} = \frac{C_t N_t^\varphi}{F_{N,t}}. \tag{1}$$

The functional form for the marginal utility cost of labor reflects that I work with a standard representation of representative household utility. The denominator will be explained below. In NK literature, v is typically set to ensure that, in the steady state, the cost and benefit of labor are equated, $L = 1$. To achieve this, v must be set to v^*, where

$$1 - v^* = \frac{\varepsilon - 1}{(1 - \psi + \psi R)\varepsilon} \frac{1 - \beta\theta\overline{\pi}^\varepsilon}{1 - \theta\overline{\pi}^\varepsilon} \frac{1 - \theta\overline{\pi}^{(\varepsilon-1)}}{1 - \beta\theta\overline{\pi}^{(\varepsilon-1)}}, R = \frac{\overline{\pi}}{\beta}. \tag{2}$$

Here, R and $\bar{\pi}$ denote the steady state gross nominal rate of interest and gross inflation, respectively. The subsidy is increasing in ψ, to minimize working-capital distortions; it is decreasing in ε to mitigate the effects of monopoly distortions. Inflation impacts on v^* through conflicting channels. The marginal firm that adjusts its price sets it high if inflation is high, and other things the same, this implies a bigger subsidy to reduce the resulting markup. At the same time, firms that do not adjust their price in effect drag the aggregate price level down when inflation is high and this suggests a reduction in the subsidy. Not surprisingly, the effects of $\bar{\pi}$ on v^* turn out to be quantitatively small.

In my analysis, I set $v = v^*$. This allows me to focus on the specific impact of $\bar{\pi}$. The presence of monopoly power does, in fact, amplify the distortionary effects of inflation when $v = 0$. But, I found that this effect is quantitatively small.[14]

In equilibrium, aggregate gross output, Y_t, is related to aggregate employment, N_t, and the aggregate use of materials, I_t, by the following gross output production function:

$$Y_t = p_t^* A_t N_t^\gamma I_t^{1-\gamma} \tag{3}$$

where $0 \le p_t^* \le 1$ is a function of degree of price dispersion. I refer to p_t^* as the Tack Yun distortion because the expression was derived in Yun (1996). The law of motion of the Tack Yun distortion is given by:

$$p_t^* = \left[(1 - \theta) \left(\frac{1 - \theta \bar{\pi}_t^{(\varepsilon-1)}}{1 - \theta} \right)^{\varepsilon/(\varepsilon-1)} + \frac{\theta \bar{\pi}_t^\varepsilon}{p_{t-1}^*} \right]^{-1} . \tag{4}$$

To understand this expression, note that when prices are flexible (i.e., $\theta = 0$), then there is no price dispersion and $p_t^* = 1$. The upper bound on p_t^* is attained when $\theta = 0$ because all firms face the same marginal cost and demand elasticity, so that if they could all flexibly set their prices, then they would all set the same price. Producers of Y_t would in this case demand an equal amount, $Y_{i,t}$, from each of the $i \in (0, 1)$ intermediate good producers. For a given level of aggregate resources, N_t and I_t, the greatest amount of Y_t is produced when labor and materials are distributed in equal amounts across sectors. This is why $p_t^* = 1$ when $\theta = 0$. When there are price setting frictions, $\theta > 0$, then there is price dispersion and homogeneous output is lost because of the resulting unequal allocation of resources across $i \in (0, 1)$. Price dispersion is greater at higher rates of inflation and for this reason the loss of homogeneous output is greater then, too.

Cost minimization by firms leads to the following relationship between aggregate materials and gross output:

$$I_t = \frac{\mu_t}{p_t^*} Y_t,$$ (5)

where μ_t is the cost share of materials at the individual firm level. When prices are flexible ($\theta = 0$) and there is no working-capital channel ($\psi = 0$), then $\mu_t = 1 - \gamma$. In the version of the model with price frictions and a working-capital channel, μ_t fluctuates with changes in the markup of the aggregate price over marginal cost and with changes in the interest rate, R_t.

Using (5) to substitute out for I_t in (3), and solving the latter for Y_t we obtain:

$$Y_t = \left[p_t^* A_t \left(\frac{\mu_t}{p_t^*} \right)^{1-\gamma} \right]^{1/\gamma} N_t.$$ (6)

Gross domestic product (GDP) in this economy is just consumption:

$$C_t = Y_t - I_t = \left(1 - \frac{\mu_t}{p_t^*} \right) Y_t.$$

Making use of (6), we obtain the *value-added production function*:

$$C_t = F_{N,t} N_t,$$

where $F_{N,t}$ is the marginal value-added produced by labor (i.e., the object in the denominator of [1]). In particular,

$$F_{N,t} = \chi_t [A_t \gamma^\gamma (1 - \gamma)^{1-\gamma}]^{1/\gamma},$$ (7)

where

$$\chi_t \equiv (p_t^* \omega_t)^{1/\gamma}, \quad \omega_t \equiv \left(\frac{1 - \mu_t / p_t^*}{\gamma} \right)^\gamma \left(\frac{\mu_t / p_t^*}{1 - \gamma} \right)^{1-\gamma}.$$ (8)

The object, $F_{N,t}$, is total factor productivity (TFP) in this model.[15] In a version of the model with capital, the expression for TFP would also be given by (7) and (8). Numerical experiments suggest that when $v = v^*$, then $\omega_t \simeq 1$. The reason is simple. In the steady state

$$\frac{\mu}{p^*} = 1 - \gamma,$$

in which case ω_t attains its maximal value of unity. It follows that variations in μ_t / p_t^* have no first-order impact on ω_t. That is, to a first-order approximation $\omega_t = 1$.

The percent loss in value added due to inflation, what I call the *allocative cost of inflation*, is:

$$100(1 - \chi_t).$$

This measure of loss takes the aggregate quantity of inputs, N_t, as given. A complete analysis of the cost of inflation would also consider its impact on N_t. An advantage of the more restricted analysis done here is that the allocative cost of inflation is a function of a small subset of model equations. A good approximation for the allocative cost of inflation is:

$$100(1 - \chi_t) \simeq 100(1 - (p_t^*)^{1/\gamma}) \simeq \frac{1}{\gamma}100(1 - p_t^*). \tag{9}$$

The first approximate equality in (9) reflects previous discussion and the second is a first-order Taylor series expansion about $p_t^* = 1$. The last expression in (9), and the fact, $\gamma = 1 / 2$, are the basis for the claim in the introduction that introducing networks doubles the model's implication for the cost of inflation.

The intuition for why networks double the cost of inflation is simple. First, we see from (7) that in the presence of networks, the exogenous disturbance in the value-added production function is a magnified version of the shock, A_t, in the gross output production function. This is the well-known "multiplier effect" in the network literature (see, e.g., Jones 2013). When A_t is treated as an unobserved variable, then this multiplier effect is of limited substantive interest. Given observations on C_t and N_t, TFP and whether we think of the whole of TFP as a shock, or of TFP as a smaller shock that has been magnified, is immaterial. Second, we can see that price dispersion, p_t^*, is also magnified in the value-added production function. This is potentially of substantial significance because, according to (4), p_t^* is a function of inflation, which is observable.

In the version of the model with flexible prices and no working-capital channel, we have enough equilibrium conditions to determine all the equilibrium variables of interest, including C_t, N_t, I_t, p_t^* and χ_t. In the presence of the Calvo price-setting frictions, we are short one equation for determining these variables. I fill this gap in the standard way, with a Taylor rule for setting the nominal rate of interest:

$$R_t / R = (R_{t-1} / R)^\rho \exp[(1 - \rho)1.5(\bar{\pi}_t - \bar{\pi})], \tag{10}$$

where $\bar{\pi}$ represents the monetary authority's inflation target. This is the value of $\bar{\pi}_t$ in steady state.

Networks, Price Frictions, and the Cost of Inflation

According to the NK model described in the previous section, inflation gives rise to a misallocation of resources, which results in a $100(1 - \chi_t)$ percent loss in GDP. This section shows that the loss can be quantitatively large. Networks play an essential role in this result. I will focus in particular on three levels of inflation: the 8% average annual rate during the high inflation of the 1970s in the United States;[16] the level of 4% that has been proposed by some as a way to reduce the risk of hitting the zero lower bound on the nominal rate of interest; and the 2% level that corresponds roughly to the normal inflation rate in recent years before the crisis.

The first subsection examines the distortions using steady-state calculations. The steady state has the advantage in that it is characterized by relatively simple, transparent expressions. The second subsection reports distortions implied by simulating the dynamic formulas, (4) and (8), using actual US inflation data.

Cost of Steady-State Inflation

According to (8), the Tack Yun distortion, p_t^* is a key input into the cost of inflation, χ_t. Its steady-state value, according to (4), is:

$$p^* = \frac{1 - \theta \bar{\pi}^\varepsilon}{1 - \theta} \left(\frac{1 - \theta}{1 - \theta \bar{\pi}^{(\varepsilon - 1)}} \right)^{\varepsilon/(\varepsilon - 1)}. \tag{11}$$

Another input to χ is the cost share of materials, μ, scaled by p^*. In the Appendix, I show that

$$\frac{\mu}{p^*} = (1 - \gamma) \frac{1 - \nu^*}{1 - \nu}, \tag{12}$$

where ν^* is defined in (2). Substituting the last expression into (8), taking into account, $\nu = \nu^*$, we obtain

$$\chi = (p^*)^{1/\gamma}. \tag{13}$$

In my analysis of (13), I consider only $\theta = 3/4$, the case in which prices are held unchanged for one year, on average. I consider three values of ε. I use the value of $\varepsilon = 6$ used by Christiano, Eichenbaum, and Evans (2005), which implies a steady-state price markup of 20% for the intermediate good producers. I also allow for greater amounts of competition by considering price markups of 15 and 10%. The under-

Table 1
Percent of GDP Lost[1] Due to Inflation, $100(1 - \chi_t)$

Without networks ($\gamma = 1$)	With networks ($\gamma = 1/2$)
a: Steady state inflation: 8 percent per year	
2.41[2] (3.92) [10.85]	4.76 (7.68) [20.53]
b: Steady state inflation: 4 percent per year	
0.46 (0.64) [1.13]	0.91 (1.27) [2.25]
c: Steady state inflation: 2 percent per year	
0.10 (0.13) [0.21]	0.20 (0.27) [0.42]

Notes: (1) table reports (13)
(2) number not in parentheses assumes a markup of 20
percent; number in parentheses: 15 percent; number in
square brackets: 10 percent

lying economics suggests that whether χ is increasing or decreasing in ε is ambiguous and depends on other parameters. An increase in ε drives χ up because larger values increase the response of resource allocations to a given distortion in relative prices. At the same time, there is another effect of ε, which goes the other way: an increase in ε raises the elasticity of substitution between goods, making the consequences of a given degree of misallocation less severe.

My quantitative findings are reported in table 1. Panels (a)–(c) report (13) for the three inflation rates of interest. The first and second columns report results for when there are no networks ($\gamma = 1$) and when there are networks ($\gamma = 1/2$), respectively.[17] The results are presented in sets of three numbers. Numbers in parentheses and in braces correspond to markups of 15 and 10%, respectively. The first number in each set of three corresponds to a markup of 20%.

Consider the results in panel (a) first. Even in the absence of networks, the cost of a permanent inflation is high enough to warrant serious concern. In the 10% markup case, for example, 10% of GDP is lost in each period. Still when networks are introduced, then costs are doubled, making the cost of the kind of inflation observed in the 1970s truly alarming.

Consider panel (b), which examines the effects of a permanent 4% annual inflation rate. As discussed in the introduction, this level of inflation has been proposed as a device to reduce the probability of a binding zero lower-bound event. When there are no networks, table 1 suggests that the price of raising the inflation target is already significant. However, the presence of networks doubles the cost to a range of

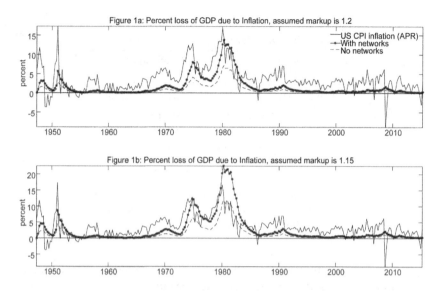

Fig. 1.   Percent loss of GDP due to inflation
Note: Panel (a): assumed markup is 1.2; panel (b): assumed markup is 1.15.

1 to 2% of GDP lost. Costs in such a range may warrant placing greater emphasis on other ways to avoid zero lower-bound problems.[18] Finally, panel (c) is consistent with the conventional view that the cost of inflation in the 2% range are small. Evidently, the table illustrates the general convexity property of the cost of distortions. When inflation doubles, the cost more than doubles.

Dynamic Distortions

Next, we turn to the time-series evidence on $100(1 - \chi_t)$ displayed in figure 1. The objects that determine χ_t are not all observable. In the case of the Tack Yun distortion, p_t^*, I require an initial condition (see [4]). However, I found that the initial condition has a negligible dynamic effect on p_t^*. Figure 1 reports the time series on p_t^* when the initial value of p_t^* (in 1947Q3) is set to unity. The results after 1960 are essentially unchanged if I instead set the initial condition to the much lower value of 0.80.

To compute χ_t I also need time-series data on μ_t / p_t^* in order to construct ω_t (see [8]). For the reasons explained in the second section, I adopt the approximation, $\omega_t = 1$.[19]

Figure 1 has two panels. Panels (a) and (b) display results for the case where the markup is 20% and 15%, respectively. Each panel displays three time series: quarterly observations on quarterly gross inflation in the consumer price index, quarterly observations on $100(1 - p_t^*)$, and quarterly observations on $100(1 - \chi_t) = 100(1 - (p_t^*)^{1/\gamma})$.

Consider panel (a). There are several notable results. First, the percent of GDP lost when it is assumed there are networks is roughly twice as large when the network structure of production is ignored (I set $\gamma = 1 / 2$). Second, the losses due to inflation can be quantitatively large. In normal low-inflation times the average cost is well below 1%, but when inflation rises a bit the costs rise sharply.

In panel (b) the costs are higher. On average, 2.65% of GDP is lost. Also, more than 4% of GDP is lost in 18% of the 273 quarters considered. And, in those quarters the average loss of GDP was 10%. Finally, the losses during the high inflation of the 1970s are quantitatively large. Indeed, they reach a maximum value of over 20% during the high inflation period (see figure 1, panel [b]). The average loss in the high inflation period was 9.73% of GDP per period, according to the results in figure 1, panel (b). This exceeds the 7.68% loss reported in table 1, panel (a) because of the convexity of the loss as a function of inflation. These numbers certainly vindicate the conventional view that the cost of the high inflation in the 1970s was high.

Clearly, the NK model has no trouble rationalizing the view that high inflation imposes a big cost on society. If anything, one is suspicious that the cost suggested by the model is implausibly high.

Networks and the Slope of the Phillips Curve

The standard Phillips curve reported in the literature only holds when there are no price distortions in the steady state. When there are price distortions—as most of the discussion here assumes—then the Phillips curve is more complicated and includes additional variables. Still, to preserve comparability I display the usual Phillips curve for the special case when there is no steady-state inflation. For the same reason, I also drop working capital, so that $\psi = 0$. The appendix shows that the Phillips curve for this model is:

$$\pi_t = \frac{(1 - \theta)(1 - \beta\theta)}{\theta} \gamma(1 + \varphi)x_t + \beta E_t \pi_{t+1}, \tag{14}$$

where $\pi_t \equiv \bar{\pi}_t - 1$ denotes the net inflation rate. Also, x_t represents the output gap, the log of the ratio of GDP (i.e., consumption) to potential GDP. As explained in the appendix, potential GDP can be interpreted either as the level of output that would occur if prices were flexible, or the level of output in the Ramsey equilibrium. The key thing to note in (14) is that the slope of the Phillips curve in terms of the output gap is cut in half by the presence of networks.[20] The underlying intuition, based on strategic complementarities, is explained in the introduction.

Networks and the Taylor Principle

There is a consensus that inflation targeting is a monetary policy with excellent operating characteristics, at least in "normal" times when the zero lower bound on the interest rate is not binding. Inflation targeting can be operationalized by applying a rule like (10) with a coefficient on inflation that is substantially greater than unity, that is, that satisfies the Taylor principle. The idea is that the Taylor principle serves two important objectives. One is the achievement of low average inflation. By raising the interest rate when inflation is above target, the central bank reins in the demand for goods and services. Working through the demand channel, this policy generates a slowdown in economic activity, which brings inflation back down to target by reducing marginal costs.

The second objective of the Taylor principle is to anchor inflation expectations. Unanchored inflation expectations can be a source of instability in inflation as well as in aggregate output and employment. To see this, suppose that for some reason there is a jump in inflation expectations. The resulting lower real rate of interest stimulates spending and output. By producing a rise in marginal cost, the increase in output contributes to a rise in inflation. In this way, the initial jump in inflation expectations is self-fulfilling and so inflation is without an anchor.

The Taylor principle helps to short-circuit this loop from higher inflation expectations to higher actual inflation. This is also accomplished by working through the demand channel. When the monetary authority raises the interest rate vigorously in response to inflation, the demand channel produces a fall in spending that reduces output and hence inflation. As people become aware of the lower actual inflation, the inflation expectations that initiated the loop would evaporate before it could have much of an effect on the macroeconomy. Under rational expectations, the initial rise in inflation expectations would not occur in the first place.

The stabilizing effects of the Taylor principle depend on the demand channel being the primary avenue through which monetary policy operates. When firms have to borrow to pay for their variable inputs, then the interest rate is a part of marginal cost and monetary policy also operates through a working-capital channel. If the working-capital channel is sufficiently important then, instead of curbing inflation, a jump in the nominal rate of interest could actually ignite inflation.

Whether the working-capital or demand channel dominate has been studied extensively in the type of model described in the previous section.[21] The general finding is that when $\gamma = 1$ the demand channel dominates the working-capital channel and the Taylor principle achieves the two objectives described above. This is so, even when the working-capital channel is strongest, with $\psi = 1$. When gross output and value added coincide, there is not enough borrowing for the working-capital channel to overwhelm the demand channel. However, when we take into account the network nature of production (i.e., $\gamma = 2$), then the amount of borrowing for working-capital purposes is potentially much greater. As a result, when $\psi = 1$ and there is no interest rate smoothing in the Taylor rule, that is, $\rho = 0$, the nonstochastic steady-state equilibrium is indeterminate. Even though monetary policy satisfies the Taylor principle, there are many equilibria. These equilibria can be characterized in terms of the loop from higher expected inflation to higher actual inflation discussed above. When there is no working-capital channel, then the Taylor principle short-circuits this loop by raising the interest rate and preventing the rise in expected inflation from occurring. But, when the working-capital channel is sufficiently strong, then the rise in the interest rate simply reinforces the loop from higher expected inflation to higher actual inflation. In this way the Taylor principle could become the "Taylor curse" referred to in the introduction.

It is interesting that the Taylor principle works as hoped for when there is substantial interest-rate smoothing in monetary policy, that is, ρ is large. Presumably, the intuition for this is that demand responds most strongly to long-term interest rates rather than to short-term interest rates. As a result, the strength of the demand channel is increasing in ρ while the working-capital channel, which is only a function of the short-term interest rate, remains unaffected.

The example highlights how the integration of network effects could be important for the design of monetary policy. This is a topic that deserves further study. It is important to know, for example, how pervasive working capital is in the data.[22] It is also important to understand better how the working-capital channel works in network environments that are closer to the more realistic one advocated in the Acemoglu et al. paper, in which firms buy materials directly from other firms.

Conclusion

Acemoglu et al. suggest that the introduction of networks into macroeconomic models could have first-order consequences for the kinds
of questions that interest macroeconomists. I have described three examples in which this is the case. The examples convince me that following the lead of Acemoglu et al. and others by integrating networks into
macroeconomics represents an important priority.

Appendix

Model Used in the Analysis

This comment makes use of a standard NK model, extended to include
network effects following the suggestion of Basu (1995). At the level of
detail, the model corresponds to the one analyzed in Christiano, Trabandt, and Walentin (2011). I include a description of the model in this
appendix for three reasons. First, Christiano et al. do not describe all
the connections between gross output and value added that I use in
my discussion. Second, I explain the properties of the first-best allocations discussed in the text. Third, the text loosely describes some subtle-
ties associated with the Phillips curve in the present context, and the
appendix explains these carefully. Fourth, conclusions from stochastic
simulations of the model are summarized in the third section and the
discussions in the fourth and fifth sections are also based on analyses
that make use of all parts of the model.

Households

There are many identical, competitive households who maximize utility,

$$\max E_0 \sum_{t=0}^{\infty} \beta^t \left(u(C_t) - \frac{N_t^{1+\varphi}}{1 + \varphi} \right), \quad u(C_t) \equiv \log C_t,$$

subject to the following budget constraint:

$$\text{s.t. } P_t C_t + B_{t+1} \leq W_t N_t + R_{t-1} B_t + \text{Profits net of taxes}_t.$$

Here, C_t denotes consumption; W_t denotes the nominal wage rate; N_t
denotes employment; P_t denotes the nominal price of consumption; B_{t+1}
denotes a nominal one-period bond purchased in period t that pays off
a gross, nominal nonstate contingent return, R_t, in period $t + 1$. Also,

the household earns lump-sum profits and pays lump-sum taxes to the government. Optimization by households implies:

$$\frac{1}{C_t} = \beta E_t \frac{1}{C_{t+1}} \frac{R_t}{\pi_{t+1}} \tag{15}$$

$$C_t N_t^\varphi = \frac{W_t}{P_t}. \tag{16}$$

Goods Production

The structure of production has the Dixit-Stiglitz structure that is standard in the NK literature, extended to consider network effects.

Homogeneous Goods

A representative, homogenous good firm produces output, Y_t, using the following technology:

$$Y_t = \left[\int_0^1 Y_{i,t}^{(\varepsilon-1)/\varepsilon} dj \right]^{\varepsilon/(\varepsilon-1)}, \quad \varepsilon > 1. \tag{17}$$

The firm takes the price of homogeneous goods, P_t, and the prices of intermediate goods, $P_{i,t}$, as given and maximizes profits,

$$P_t Y_t - \int_0^1 P_{i,t} Y_{i,t} dj,$$

subject to (17). Optimization leads to the following first-order condition:

$$Y_{i,t} = Y_t \left(\frac{P_t}{P_{i,t}} \right)^\varepsilon, \tag{18}$$

for all $i \in (0, 1)$. Combining the first-order condition with the production function, we obtain the following equilibrium condition:

$$P_t = \left(\int_0^1 P_{i,t}^{(1-\varepsilon)} di \right)^{1/(1-\varepsilon)}. \tag{19}$$

Intermediate Goods

The intermediate good, $i \in (0, 1)$, is produced by a monopolist using the following technology:

$$Y_{i,t} = A_t N_{i,t}^{\gamma} I_{i,t}^{1-\gamma}, \quad 0 < \gamma \le 1.$$

Here, $N_{i,t}$ and $I_{i,t}$ denotes the quantity of labor and materials, respectively, used by the ith producer. The producer obtains $I_{i,t}$ by purchasing the homogenous good, Y_t, and converting it one-for-one into materials. Both $N_{i,t}$ and $I_{i,t}$ are acquired in competitive markets.

Firms experience Calvo-style frictions in setting their price. That is, the ith firm sets its period t price, $P_{i,t}$, as follows:

$$P_{i,t} = \begin{cases} \tilde{P}_t & \text{with probability } 1 - \theta \\ P_{i,t-1} & \text{with probability } \theta \end{cases}, \quad 0 \le \theta < 1. \qquad (20)$$

Here, $\tilde{P}_t$ denotes the price selected in the probability $1 - \theta$ event that it can choose its price. Firms that cannot optimize their price must simply set it to whatever value it took on in the previous period.

Given its current price (however arrived at), the firm must satisfy the Y_{it} that is implied by (18). Linear homogeneity of its technology and our assumption that the ith firm acquires materials and labor in competitive markets implies that marginal cost is independent of $Y_{i,t}$. By studying its cost minimization problem we find that s_t, the ith firm's marginal cost (scaled by P_t) is

$$s_t = \left(\frac{\bar{P}_t / P_t}{1 - \gamma}\right)^{1-\gamma} \left(\frac{\bar{W}_t / P_t}{\gamma}\right)^{\gamma} \frac{1}{A_t}. \qquad (21)$$

Here, $\bar{P}_t$ and $\bar{W}_t$ denote the net price, after taxes and interest-rate costs, of materials and labor, respectively. In particular,

$$\bar{W}_t = (1 - v)(1 - \psi + \psi R_t) W_t$$

$$\bar{P}_t = (1 - v)(1 - \psi + \psi R_t) P_t,$$

where ψ represents the fraction of input costs that must be financed in advance so that, for example, one unit of labor used during period t costs $\psi W_t R_t$ units of currency at the end of the period.[23] Also, v is the subsidy discussed in the text.

Another implication of the ith firm's cost minimization problem is that cost of materials, $\bar{P}_t I_{i,t}$, as a fraction of total cost, is equal to $1 - \gamma$. This implies,

$$I_{i,t} = \mu_t Y_{i,t}, \qquad (22)$$

where μ_t is the share of materials in gross output, and:

$$\mu_t = \frac{(1 - \gamma)s_t}{(1 - v)(1 - \psi + \psi R_t)}. \qquad (23)$$

I now turn to the problem of one of the $1 - \theta$ randomly selected firms that has an opportunity to select its price, $\tilde{P}_t$, in period t. Such a firm is concerned about the value of its cash flow (i.e., revenues net of costs) in period t and in later periods:

$$E_t \sum_{j=0}^{\infty} (\beta\theta)^j v_{t+j} [\tilde{P}_t Y_{i,t+j} - P_{t+j} s_{t+j} Y_{i,t+j}] + \Phi_t. \tag{24}$$

The objects in square brackets are the cash flows in current and future states in which the firm does not have an opportunity to reset its price. The expectation operator in (24) integrates over aggregate uncertainty, while the firm-level idiosyncratic uncertainty is manifest in the presence of θ in the discounting. In (24), cash flows in each period are weighed by the associated date- and state-contingent value that the household assigns to cash. The firm takes these weights as given and

$$v_{t+j} = \frac{u'(C_{t+j})}{P_{t+j}}. \tag{25}$$

The second term in (24), Φ_t, represents the value of cash flow in future states in which the firm is able to reset its price. Given the structure of our environment, Φ_t is not affected by the choice of $\tilde{P}_t$. The problem of a firm that is able to choose its price is to select a value of $\tilde{P}_t$ that maximizes (24) subject to (18), taking $\bar{P}_t$, $\bar{W}_t$, P_t and W_t as given.

To solve the firm problem I first substitute out for $Y_{i,t}$ and v_t using (18) and (25), respectively. I then differentiate (24) taking into account that Φ_t is independent of $\tilde{P}_t$. The solution to this problem is obtained by a standard set of manipulations. In particular, let

$$\tilde{p}_t \equiv \frac{\tilde{P}_t}{P_t}, \bar{\pi}_t \equiv \frac{P_t}{P_{t-1}}, X_{t,j} = \begin{cases} \dfrac{1}{\bar{\pi}_{t+j}\bar{\pi}_{t+j-1}\cdots\bar{\pi}_{t+1}}, & j \geq 1, \\ 1, & j = 0. \end{cases}$$

$$X_{t,j} = X_{t+1,j-1}\frac{1}{\bar{\pi}_{t+1}}, \quad j > 0$$

Then, the (scaled by P_t) solution to the firm problem is:

$$\tilde{p}_t = \frac{E_t \sum_{j=0}^{\infty} (\beta\theta)^j (X_{t,j})^{-\varepsilon}(Y_{t+j} / C_{t+j})(\varepsilon / \varepsilon - 1)s_{t+j}}{E_t \sum_{j=0}^{\infty} (\beta\theta)^j (X_{t,j})^{1-\varepsilon}(Y_{t+j} / C_{t+j})} = \frac{K_t}{F_t}, \tag{26}$$

where

$$K_t = \frac{\varepsilon}{\varepsilon - 1} \frac{Y_t}{C_t} s_t + \beta \theta E_t \left(\frac{1}{\overline{\pi}_{t+1}} \right)^{-\varepsilon} K_{t+1} \tag{27}$$

$$F_t = \frac{Y_t}{C_t} + \beta \theta E_t \left(\frac{1}{\overline{\pi}_{t+1}} \right)^{1-\varepsilon} F_{t+1}. \tag{28}$$

Economy-Wide Variables and Equilibrium

By the usual result associated with Calvo-sticky prices, we have the following cross-price restriction:

$$P_t = \left(\int_0^1 P_{i,t}^{(1-\varepsilon)} di \right)^{1/(1-\varepsilon)} = [(1 - \theta)\tilde{P}_t^{(1-\varepsilon)} + \theta P_{t-1}^{(1-\varepsilon)}]^{1/(1-\varepsilon)}. \tag{29}$$

Dividing by P_t and rearranging,

$$\tilde{p}_t = \left[\frac{1 - \theta \overline{\pi}_t^{(\varepsilon-1)}}{1 - \theta} \right]^{1/(1-\varepsilon)} \tag{30}$$

Combining this expression with (26), we obtain a useful equilibrium condition:

$$\frac{K_t}{F_t} = \left[\frac{1 - \theta \overline{\pi}_t^{(\varepsilon-1)}}{1 - \theta} \right]^{1/(1-\varepsilon)}. \tag{31}$$

It is convenient to express real marginal cost, (21), in terms that do not involve prices:

$$s_t = (1 - v)(1 - \psi + \psi R_t) \left(\frac{1}{1 - \gamma} \right)^{1-\gamma} \left(\frac{1}{\gamma} C_t N_t^\varphi \right)^\gamma \frac{1}{A_t}, \tag{32}$$

where (16) has been used to substitute out for W_t / P_t.

I now derive the value-added production function. To this end, we first compute the equilibrium relationship between aggregate inputs, I_t and N_t, and gross output, Y_t. I do this by adapting the argument in Yun (1996). I then adapt a version of the argument in Jones (2013) to obtain the mapping from aggregate employment to GDP.

Let Y_t^* denote the unweighted sum of $Y_{i,t}$ and then substitute out for $Y_{i,t}$ in terms of prices using (18):

$$Y_t^* \equiv \int_0^1 Y_{i,t} di = Y_t \int_0^1 \left(\frac{P_{i,t}}{P_t} \right)^{-\varepsilon} di = Y_t \left(\frac{P_t}{P_t^*} \right)^\varepsilon,$$

where

$$P_t^* \equiv \left[\int_0^1 P_{i,t}^{-\varepsilon} di \right]^{-1/\varepsilon} = [(1 - \theta)\tilde{P}_t^{-\varepsilon} + \theta(P_{t-1}^*)^{-\varepsilon}]^{-1/\varepsilon}, \tag{33}$$

using the analog of the result in (29). In this way, we obtain the following expression for Y_t:

$$Y_t = p_t^* Y_t^*, \quad p_t^* \equiv \left(\frac{P_t^*}{P_t} \right)^{\varepsilon},$$

$$p_t^* = \begin{cases} \leq 1 & \text{not } P_{i,t} = P_{j,t}, \text{ all } i, j \\ = 1 & P_{i,t} = P_{j,t}, \text{ all } i, j' \end{cases}$$

where p_t^* is the Tack Yun distortion discussed in the text.

By a standard calculation, I obtain the law of motion for p_t^* by dividing (33) by P_t^*, using (30) and rearranging,

$$p_t^* = \left[(1 - \theta) \left(\frac{1 - \theta \bar{\pi}_t^{(\varepsilon-1)}}{1 - \theta} \right)^{\varepsilon/(\varepsilon-1)} + \frac{\theta \bar{\pi}_t^{\varepsilon}}{p_{t-1}^*} \right]^{-1}. \tag{34}$$

Then,

$$Y_t = p_t^* Y_t^* = p_t^* \int_0^1 Y_{i,t} di = p_t^* A_t \int_0^1 N_{i,t}^{\gamma} I_{i,t}^{1-\gamma} di$$

$$= p_t^* A_t \left(\frac{N_t}{I_t} \right)^{\gamma} I_t,$$

where I have used the fact that all firms have the same materials to labor ratio. In this way, we obtain

$$Y_t = p_t^* A_t N_t^{\gamma} I_t^{1-\gamma}. \tag{35}$$

I substitute out for I_t in (35) by noting from (22) that

$$I_t \equiv \int_0^1 I_{i,t} di = \mu_t \int_0^1 Y_{i,t} di = \mu_t Y_t^* = \frac{\mu_t}{p_t^*} Y_t. \tag{36}$$

Use this to solve out for I_t in (35):

$$Y_t = \left(p_t^* A_t \left(\frac{\mu_t}{p_t^*} \right)^{1-\gamma} \right)^{1/\gamma} N_t. \tag{37}$$

GDP for this economy is simply

$$C_t = Y_t - I_t. \tag{38}$$

I conclude,

$$GDP_t = Y_t - I_t = \left(1 - \frac{\mu_t}{p_t^*}\right)Y_t = F_{N,t} \times N_t, \tag{39}$$

after some rearranging. Here, *TFP* denotes total factor productivity and is given by:

$$F_{N,t} = \left(p_t^* A_t \left(1 - \frac{\mu_t}{p_t^*}\right)^{\gamma} \left(\frac{\mu_t}{p_t^*}\right)^{1-\gamma}\right)^{1/\gamma}, \tag{40}$$

or,

$$F_{N,t} = \chi_t (A_t \gamma^{\gamma} (1 - \gamma)^{1-\gamma})^{1/\gamma},$$

where

$$\chi_t \equiv \left(p_t^* \left(\frac{1 - (\mu_t / p_t^*)}{\gamma}\right)^{\gamma} \left(\frac{\mu_t / p_t^*}{1 - \gamma}\right)^{1-\gamma}\right)^{1/\gamma}. \tag{41}$$

There are 12 variables to be determined for the model:

$$K_t, F_t, \bar{\pi}_t, p_t^*, s_t, C_t, Y_t, N_t, I_t, \mu_t, R_t, \chi_t.$$

There are 11 equilibrium conditions implied by private-sector decisions: (27), (28), (31), (34), (15), (35), (38), (37), (32), (23), and (41). In the special case of flexible prices ($\theta = 0$) and no working capital ($\psi = 0$) then the classical dichotomy obtains. That is, equilibrium consumption and employment can be solved and, given the subsidy in (2), we obtain:

$$N_t = 1, C_t = [A_t(\gamma)^{\gamma}(1 - \gamma)^{1-\gamma}]^{1/\gamma}.$$

In the case that is of interest in this discussion, we need an additional equation to solve the model variables. To this end, I adopt the specification of monetary policy, (10). It can be verified that the steady state of the model is determinate when the smoothing parameter is 0.8 but indeterminate when the smoothing parameter is zero. The economic reasons for this are discussed in the fifth section.

To compute the dynamic properties of the model I solve the model using second-order perturbation (with pruning), using Dynare.[24] For this, I require the model steady state in which the shocks, a_t, are held at their steady-state values of zero. The steady state is discussed in the next section.

The parameter values I assign to the model are as follows:

$$\bar{\pi} = 1.025^{1/4}, \quad \psi = 1, \quad \gamma = \frac{1}{2}, \quad \beta = 1.03^{-0.25},$$

$$\theta = 0.75, \quad \varepsilon = 6, \quad \varphi = 1, \quad \nu = \nu^*.$$

The time series representation I use for a_t is that it is roughly a first-order autoregression in its first difference. In particular,

$$a_t = (\rho_1 + \rho_2)a_{t-1} - \rho_1\rho_2 a_{t-2} + \varepsilon_t, \quad E\varepsilon_t^2 = 0.01^2,$$

where $\rho_1 = 0.99$ and $\rho_2 = 0.3$.

Model Steady State

This section displays the steady state of the model. I derive the steady state expressions, (2) and (12), as well as the result that L in (1) is equal to unity when $v = v^*$. In addition, the steady state is required in the next subsection to derive the linearized Phillips curve, which is discussed in the text.

Removing the time subscripts from time-series variables in the model equilibrium conditions, (15), (31), (27), (28), and (34), we find:

$$R = \frac{\overline{\pi}}{\beta}, \quad K_f \equiv \frac{K}{F} = \left[\frac{1-\theta}{1 - \theta\overline{\pi}^{(\varepsilon-1)}}\right]^{1/(\varepsilon-1)},$$

$$s = K_f \frac{\varepsilon - 1}{\varepsilon} \frac{1 - \beta\theta\overline{\pi}^\varepsilon}{1 - \beta\theta\overline{\pi}^{\varepsilon-1}}, \quad p^* = \frac{1 - \theta\overline{\pi}^\varepsilon}{1 - \theta}\left(\frac{1-\theta}{1 - \theta\overline{\pi}^{(\varepsilon-1)}}\right)^{\varepsilon/(\varepsilon-1)}. \quad (42)$$

The steady state share of materials in costs, scaled by p^*, is given by

$$\frac{\mu}{p^*} = \frac{(1 - \gamma)s / p^*}{(1 - v)(1 - \psi + \psi R)}, \quad (43)$$

according to (23). Let v^* be defined by,

$$\frac{\mu}{p^*} = (1 - \gamma)\frac{1 - v^*}{1 - v}. \quad (44)$$

Equating (43) and (44), and using (42), we obtain (2). This establishes (12).
In steady state the marginal product of labor is

$$F_N = \left[p^*\left(1 - (1 - \gamma)\frac{1 - v^*}{1 - v}\right)^\gamma\left((1 - \gamma)\frac{1 - v^*}{1 - v}\right)^{1-\gamma}\right]^{1/\gamma}$$

$$= \left(p^*\left(\frac{1 - (1 - \gamma)(1 - v^*)/(1 - v)}{\gamma}\right)^\gamma\left(\frac{1 - v^*}{1 - v}\right)^{1-\gamma}\right)^{1/\gamma} \quad (45)$$

$$(\gamma^\gamma(1 - \gamma)^{1-\gamma})^{1/\gamma},$$

using (40) and (44).

According to (43) and (44),

$$s = (1 - \psi + \psi R)(1 - v^*)p^*.$$

Using this expression to substitute out for s in the steady state version of (32),

$$\frac{1 - v^*}{1 - v} p^*(1 - \gamma)^{1-\gamma}(\gamma)^\gamma = (CN^\varphi)^\gamma,$$

using the fact, $A_t = 1$, in steady state. Combining the last expression with (45), we obtain

$$\frac{1 - v^*}{1 - v} \frac{F_N^\gamma}{\{[1 - (1 - \gamma)(1 - v^*) / (1 - v)] / \gamma\}^\gamma [(1 - v^*) / (1 - v)]^{1-\gamma}} = (CN^\varphi)^\gamma.$$

After rearranging, the latter expression reduces to

$$\frac{\gamma}{\gamma + (v^* - v) / (1 - v^*)} = L. \tag{46}$$

From this we can see the result cited in the text, that $L = 1$ when $v = v^*$. We can solve (46) for N by using $C = F_N N$:

$$N = \left[\frac{\gamma}{\gamma + (v^* - v) / (1 - v^*)} \right]^{1/(1+\varphi)}.$$

Finally,

$$C = F_N N, \quad Y = \frac{C}{\gamma},$$

$$I = (1 - \gamma)Y, \quad F = \frac{1 / \gamma}{1 - \beta\theta\bar{\pi}^{\varepsilon-1}}, \quad K = K_f \times F,$$

so that all steady-state variables are now available.

Output Gap

The output gap is a key variable in the Phillips curve and I discuss that variable here. The output gap is the log deviation of equilibrium output from a benchmark level of output. Three possible benchmarks include: (a) output in the Ramsey equilibrium, (b) the equilibrium when prices are flexible, and (c) the first-best equilibrium, when output is chosen by a benevolent planner. In the latter case this corresponds to maximizing[25]

$$u(C_t) - \frac{N_t^{1+\varphi}}{1 + \varphi}$$

subject to the maximal level of consumption that can be produced by allocating resources efficiently across sectors:

$$C_t = (A_t\gamma^\gamma(1 - \gamma)^{1-\gamma})^{1/\gamma}N_t.$$

Optimization implies:

$$C_t^* = (A_t\gamma^\gamma(1 - \gamma)^{1-\gamma})^{1/\gamma}, \quad N_t^* = 1. \tag{47}$$

It is easily verified that when there is no working-capital channel, $\psi = 0$, then (a), (b), and (c) coincide (that the equilibrium allocations under flexible prices are given by (47) was discussed in appendix section C). With $\psi > 0$ the three benchmarks differ. In this case expressions (a) and (b) are relatively complicated, while (c) stands out for its analytic simplicity. This is why I work with (c) as my benchmark. This leads me to the following definition of the output gap, X_t:

$$X_t = \frac{C_t}{C_t^*}.$$

The log deviation from the steady state is:

$$
\begin{aligned}
x_t \equiv \hat{X}_t &= \hat{C}_t - \hat{C}_t^* \\
&= \hat{C}_t - \frac{1}{\gamma}\hat{A}_t,
\end{aligned}
\tag{48}
$$

where x_t is also $\log(X_t / X)$ for X_t sufficiently close to its steady-state value, X.

Phillips Curve

Linearizing (27), (28), and (31), about steady state,

$$\hat{K}_t = (1 - \beta\theta\bar{\pi}^\varepsilon)[\hat{Y}_t + \hat{s}_t - \hat{C}_t] + \beta\theta\bar{\pi}^\varepsilon E_t(\varepsilon\hat{\bar{\pi}}_{t+1} + \hat{K}_{t+1}) \tag{49}$$

$$\hat{F}_t = (1 - \beta\theta\bar{\pi}^{\varepsilon-1})(\hat{Y}_t - \hat{C}_t) + \beta\theta\bar{\pi}^{\varepsilon-1}E_t((\varepsilon - 1)\hat{\bar{\pi}}_{t+1} + \hat{F}_{t+1}) \tag{50}$$

$$\hat{K}_t = \hat{F}_t + \frac{\theta\bar{\pi}^{(\varepsilon-1)}}{1 - \theta\bar{\pi}^{(\varepsilon-1)}}\hat{\bar{\pi}}_t. \tag{51}$$

Here, $\hat{x}_t = (x_t - x) / x$ and x denotes the steady-state value of x_t. Substitute out for $\hat{K}_t$ in (49) using (51) and then substituting out for $\hat{F}_t$ using (50), we obtain,

$$(1 - \beta\theta\bar{\pi}^{\varepsilon-1})(\hat{Y}_t - \hat{C}_t) + \beta\theta\bar{\pi}^{\varepsilon-1}E_t((\varepsilon - 1)\hat{\bar{\pi}}_{t+1} + \hat{F}_{t+1}) + \frac{\theta\bar{\pi}^{(\varepsilon-1)}}{1 - \theta\bar{\pi}^{(\varepsilon-1)}}\hat{\bar{\pi}}_t$$

$$= (1 - \beta\theta\bar{\pi}^{\varepsilon})[\hat{Y}_t + \hat{s}_t - \hat{C}_t] + \beta\theta\bar{\pi}^{\varepsilon}E_t\left(\varepsilon\hat{\bar{\pi}}_{t+1} + \hat{F}_{t+1} + \frac{\theta\bar{\pi}^{(\varepsilon-1)}}{1 - \theta\bar{\pi}^{(\varepsilon-1)}}\hat{\bar{\pi}}_{t+1}\right)$$

Collecting terms,

$$\hat{\bar{\pi}}_t = \frac{(1 - \theta\bar{\pi}^{(\varepsilon-1)})(1 - \beta\theta\bar{\pi}^{\varepsilon})}{\theta\bar{\pi}^{(\varepsilon-1)}}\hat{s}_t + \beta E_t\hat{\bar{\pi}}_{t+1}$$

$$+ (1 - \bar{\pi})(1 - \theta\bar{\pi}^{(\varepsilon-1)})\beta\left[\hat{Y}_t - \hat{C}_t + E_t\left(\hat{F}_{t+1} + \left(\varepsilon + \frac{\theta\bar{\pi}^{(\varepsilon-1)}}{1 - \theta\bar{\pi}^{(\varepsilon-1)}}\right)\hat{\bar{\pi}}_{t+1}\right)\right] \tag{52}$$

This expression reduces to the usual Phillips curve in the special case, $\bar{\pi} = 1$.

We require $\hat{s}_t$. Combining (16), (39), and (21),

$$s_t = (1 - \nu)(1 - \psi + \psi R_t)\left(\frac{1}{1 - \gamma}\right)^{1-\gamma}\left(\frac{1}{\gamma}C_t^{1+\varphi}\right)^{\gamma}\frac{TFP_t^{-\varphi\gamma}}{A_t}.$$

Totally differentiating,

$$\hat{s}_t = \frac{\psi R}{(1 - \psi + \psi R)}\hat{R}_t + (1 + \varphi)\gamma\hat{C}_t - \varphi\gamma\widehat{TFP}_t - \hat{A}_t.$$

We obtain $\widehat{TFP}_t$ by totally differentiating (40):

$$\widehat{TFP}_t = \frac{1}{\gamma}\hat{A}_t,$$

where terms in $\hat{p}_t^*$ and $\hat{\mu}_t$ disappear because we set $\bar{\pi} = 1$. Then,

$$\hat{s}_t = \frac{\psi R}{(1 - \psi + \psi R)}\hat{R}_t + \gamma(1 + \varphi)\left[\hat{C}_t - \frac{1}{\gamma}\hat{A}_t\right].$$

Using (48), this establishes:

$$\hat{s}_t = \frac{\psi R}{(1 - \psi + \psi R)}\hat{R}_t + \gamma(1 + \varphi)x_t.$$

Substituting this expression for marginal cost into (52) with $\bar{\pi} = 1$, we obtain the representation of the Phillips curve displayed in the text. The object, x_t, is a conventional measure of the output gap when $\psi = 0$.

When $\psi > 0$ it must be interpreted as the percent deviation between actual and first best output (see appendix section E).

Endnotes

I am grateful for discussions with the authors and with Susanto Basu, V. V. Chari, Martin Eichenbaum, Etienne Gagnon, Shalva Mkhatrishvili, and Yuta Takahashi. For acknowledgments, sources of research support, and disclosure of the author's material financial relationships, if any, please see http://www.nber.org/chapters/c13600.ack.

Northwestern University, Department of Economics, 2001 Sheridan Road, Evanston, Illinois 60208, USA. Phone: +1-847-491-8231. E-mail: l-christiano@northwestern.edu.

1. For a recent exception, see Ascari, Phaneuf, and Sims (2015). This work (done independently from the work described in this comment) makes observations about the cost of inflation that are similar to mine. Early work on the significance of networks can be found in Basu (1995) and Rotemberg and Woodford (1993), among others. As Rotemberg and Woodford point out, when there are no market frictions such as monopoly power or rigidities in pricing, then the standard assumption that output is a function only of capital and labor, and not materials, involves no loss of generality. Thus, the practice in the real business-cycle literature of implicitly ignoring materials is defensible. Much of the New Keynesian literature—which stresses the importance of frictions—has imported the real business-cycle approach to materials. However, as stressed by Basu and Rotemberg and Woodford, when there are frictions then the real business-cycle approach can be highly misleading.

2. A simple revealed-preference argument suggests that the American public thinks the economic costs of inflation are high. It is widely believed that the severe recession of the early 1980s was brought about by Federal Reserve Chairman Paul Volcker as a side effect of his strategy for ending the high inflation of the 1970s. Despite the perceived high cost of Volcker's antiinflation policy, his public reputation is very high. I infer that the public believes that the benefit of Volcker's strategy (ridding the economy of high inflation) is preferred to the cost—the punishing recession of the early 1980s. That is, the public assigns a high cost to inflation.

3. By "standard economic models" I also mean the standard practice of linearizing models about a steady state in which prices are not distorted. See Ascari (2004) for an early discussion of the dangers of this practice.

4. See Krugman (1997).

5. At the level of detail, the model corresponds to the one in Christiano, Trabandt, and Walentin (2011). For a model that uses a similar production structure, but a different specification of price-adjustment frictions, see Nakamura and Steinsson (2010). For other work that emphasizes the importance of materials in production, see Huang and Liu (2001, 2005).

6. For an extensive discussion of the implications of the allocative distortions resulting from inflation—in a setting that ignores networks—see Ascari and Sbordone (2014).

7. For a review, see Ball (2013).

8. Consistent with these observations, Ascari, Phaneuf, and Sims (2015) find bigger costs of inflation than I do. They work with a standard medium-sized NK model, one that includes, among other things, frictions in the setting of wages.

9. See also Alvarez et al. (2011, figure 10). They report empirical evidence that suggests that the frequency of price adjustment is insensitive to inflation rates in the range of 0 to 10%, at an annual rate.

10. Recent papers that have recognized this fact include Basu (1995), Christiano, Trabandt, and Walentin (2011), Nakamura and Steinsson (2010), and Huang and Liu (2001, 2005).

11. This strategic complementarity argument goes back at least to Blanchard (1987) and Gordon (1981).

12. Christiano, Eichenbaum, and Evans (2005) show that the working-capital channel is large enough that a monetary policy-induced rise in the interest rate drives inflation up. But, this effect is only transitory and not enough to wipe out the basic stabilizing effects of the Taylor principle.

13. For another example in which the Taylor principle does not stabilize inflation or the broader economy, see Christiano et al. (2010).

14. Consistent with the observations in Rotemberg and Woodford (1993), networks also amplify the distortionary effects of monopoly power. This can be seen in the expression for the steady state value of $F_{N,t}$ that appears in (45) in the appendix. For example, when $\gamma = 1$, so that there are no networks, then monopoly power has no impact on F_N. But, when $\gamma = 1 / 2$ then the degree of monopoly power potentially has a very large impact on F_N. The impact of monopoly power on F_N is set to zero with my assumption, $\nu = \nu^*$. This assumption does not distract from my central point, which has to do with the effect of inflation on F_N.

15. The expression in (8) is consistent with a central theme in Basu (1995), that networks in conjunction with price-setting frictions and monopoly power in effect provide a theory of endogenous TFP.

16. Here and below, I use data on the consumer price index, CPIAUCSL, taken from the FRED database, maintained by the Federal Reserve Bank of St. Louis. The 8% annual average reported in the text is based on data for the period, 1972Q1–1983Q4.

17. The numerical results in the first column of table 1 are consistent with the findings reported in Ascari and Sbordone (2014), especially their figure 7.

18. See, for example, Rogoff (2014).

19. See the first approximate equality in (9). The approximation depends crucially on $\nu = \nu^*$. In practice, this greatly exaggerates the role of the tax system in undoing monopoly distortions. (Indeed, actually the tax systems provide their own distortions.) However, some preliminary calculations suggest that allowing monopoly power to also reduce χ_t by setting $\nu = 0$ has only a small impact on the contribution of inflation to χ_t.

20. Here, and throughout, I assume that the empirically plausible value of γ is $1/2$.

21. See Christiano, Trabandt, and Walentin (2011).

22. For one revelant study, see Barth and Ramey (2002).

23. We assume that banks create credits that they provide in the amount, $(\psi W_t N_t + \psi P_t I_t)$, to firms at the beginning of the period. At the end of the period they receive $R_t (\psi W_t N_t + \psi P_t I_t)$ back from firms and the profits, $(R_t - 1)(\psi W_t N_t + \psi P_t I_t)$, are transferred to households in lump-sum form.

24. The code is available on my website.

25. I assume the planner has the capacity to avoid the frictions associated with working capital, when $\psi > 0$.

References

Alvarez, Fernando, Martin Gonzalez-Rozada, Andy Neumeyer, and Martin Beraja. 2011. "From Hyperinflation to Stable Prices: Argentina's Evidence on Menu Cost Models." Unpublished manuscript. http://home.uchicago .edu/~falvare/prices_argentina_October2011.pdf.

Ascari, Guido. 2004. "Staggered Prices and Trend Inflation: Some Nuisances." *Review of Economic Dynamics* 7:642–67.

Ascari, Guido, Louis Phaneuf, and Eric Sims. 2015. "On the Welfare and Cyclical Implications of Moderate Trend Inflation." NBER Working Paper no. 21392, Cambridge, MA.

Ascari, Guido, and Argia M. Sbordone. 2014. "The Macroeconomics of Trend Inflation." Staff Report no. 628, Federal Reserve Bank of New York.

Ball, Larry. 2013. "The Case for 4% Inflation." VOX, May 24. http://www. voxeu.org/article/case-4-inflation.

Barth III, M. J., and V. A. Ramey. 2002. "The Cost Channel of Monetary Transmission." In *NBER Macroeconomics Annual 2001*, ed. B. Bernanke and K. Rogoff, 199–256. Cambridge, MA: MIT Press.

Basu, Susanto. 1995. "Intermediate Goods and Business Cycles: Implications for Productivity and Welfare." *American Economic Review* 85 (3): 512–31.

Bils, Mark, Peter J. Klenow and Benjamin A. Malin. 2015. "Resurrecting the Role of the Product Market Wedge in Recessions," Staff Report 516, Federal Reserve Bank of Minneapolis.

Blanchard, Olivier. 1987. "Aggregate and Individual Price Adjustment." *Brookings Papers on Economic Activity* 1 (1987): 57–122.

Calvo, Guillermo A. 1983. "Staggered Prices in a Utility-Maximizing Framework." *Journal of Monetary Economics* 12 (3): 383–98.

Christiano, Lawrence J., Martin Eichenbaum, and Charles Evans. 2005. "Nominal Rigidities and the Dynamic Effects of a Shock to Monetary Policy." *Journal of Political Economy* 113 (1): 1–45.

Christiano, Lawrence J., Cosmin Ilut, Roberto Motto, and Massimo Rostagno. 2010. "Monetary Policy and Stock Market Booms." NBER Working Paper no. 16402, Cambridge, MA.

Christiano, Lawrence J., Mathias Trabandt, and Karl Walentin. 2011. "DSGE Models for Monetary Policy Analysis." In *Handbook of Monetary Economics*, vol. 3A, ed. Benjamin M. Friedman and Michael Woodford, 285–367. Amsterdam: North-Holland.

Eichenbaum, Martin, Nir Jaimovich, and Sergio Rebelo. 2011. "Reference Prices and Nominal Rigidities." *American Economic Review* 101 (1): 234–62.

Golosov, Mikhail, and Robert E. Lucas, Jr. 2007. "Menu Costs and Phillips Curves." *Journal of Political Economy* 115 (2): 171–99.

Gordon, Robert J. 1981. "Output Fluctuations and Gradual Price Adjustment." *Journal of Economic Literature* 19 (June): 525.

Huang, Kevin X. D., and Zheng Liu. 2001. "Production Chains and General Equilibrium Aggregate Dynamics." *Journal of Monetary Economics* 48:437–62.

———. 2005. "Inflation Targeting: What Inflation Rate to Target?" *Journal of Monetary Economics* 52:1435–62.

Jones, Chad. 2013. "Misallocation, Economic Growth, and Input-Output Economics." In *Advances in Economics and Econometrics*, Tenth World Congress, vol. II, ed. D. Acemoglu, M. Arellano, and E. Dekel. Cambridge: Cambridge University Press.

Krugman, Paul R. 1997. *The Age of Diminished Expectations: US Economic Policy in the 1990s*. Cambridge, MA: MIT Press.

Nakamura, Emi, and Jon Steinsson. 2010. "Monetary Non-Neutrality in a Multisector Menu Cost Model." *Quarterly Journal of Economics* 125 (3): 961–1013.

Rogoff, Kenneth. 2014. "Costs and Benefits to Phasing Out Paper Currency." In *NBER Macroeconomics Annual 2014*, vol. 29, ed. Jonathan Parker and Michael Woodford, 445–56. Chicago: University of Chicago Press.

Rotemberg, Julio, and Michael Woodford. 1993. "Dynamic General Equilibrium Models with Imperfectly Competitive Product Markets." NBER Working Paper no. 4502, Cambridge, MA.

Yun, Tack. 1996. "Nominal Price Rigidity, Money Supply Endogeneity, and Business Cycles." *Journal of Monetary Economics* 37 (2): 345–70.

Discussion

Daron Acemoglu began by responding to several points raised by the discussants, Xavier Gabaix and Lawrence Christiano. He agreed with Gabaix that this paper fits into the larger literature about the microeconomic origins of macroeconomic fluctuations. Acemoglu described the Cobb-Douglas production and utility functions in the paper as a natural starting point, because under those assumptions the input-output tables reveal preference and production function parameters. Under other production functions and preferences, relative prices can change dramatically, resulting in input-output tables that are unstable. Acemoglu argued that input-output analysis in some sense forces one to assume preferences and production close to Cobb-Douglas and mentioned that in a recent paper with Asuman Ozdaglar and Alireza Tahbaz-Salehi, he showed that the equations derived under the Cobb-Douglas assumption can be viewed as a first-order approximation under more general production functions (Acemoglu et al. 2015).

Acemoglu next acknowledged Xavier Gabaix's suggestions regarding the discussion of multipliers in the paper. In the paper, the most natural object to analyze is the Leontief cumulative effect. However, this effect is not exactly the same as a multiplier. To capture the notion of a multiplier, the authors study shocks to a particular firm and then trace out the impulse response that this shock causes to other firms throughout the network. Relatedly, the Hulten (1978) formula summarizes the manner in which firm-level shocks sum up to form an aggregate shock, but it does not help determine which other firms are most affected by a shock to one particular firm. Acemoglu also acknowledged that issues about double counting complicate the interpretation of their regression results. He also mentioned another project (Acemoglu et al. 2014) that looks at plant-level shocks relating to import competition and how those shocks propagate through both input-output channels and other channels.

Finally, Acemoglu commented on the discussion by Lawrence Christiano. He emphasized that the precise meaning of the terms "upstream" and "downstream" come from the notion of the input-output table as representing a directed graph. Imagine that the arrows in this graph point from suppliers to their customers. Supply shocks travel "downstream," meaning that they follow the direction of the arrows in this graph, whereas demand shocks travel "upstream," meaning that they move in the opposite direction as do the arrows in this graph. In his discussion Lawrence Christiano pointed out that, over time, the production of all the firms in the economy would comove together. Acemoglu noted that the US input-output matrix forms a strongly connected network, meaning that a shock hitting one sector will ultimately affect all other firms in the economy. As a result, the production of all firms would comove over time, but the extent to which any particular subset of firms is affected by a specific shock, which is what the authors sought to test in their empirical work, would be determined by the network structure.

Next, Robert Hall expressed concern about the authors' interpretation of their regression results. In their results on exposure to Chinese import competition, which the authors argue is a demand shock for firms, the regression results show a large, negative point estimate and large standard errors for the downstream effects. This coefficient is not significantly different from zero, in a statistical sense. Hall characterized the authors' position as claiming that, because the coefficient was not statistically significantly different from zero, it was consistent with their theory. He argued that the right interpretation is that the regressions are uninformative and that this issue arose in several of the regressions run by the authors. Acemoglu responded by arguing that the authors did not find statistically significant effects (for downstream coefficients in response to demand shocks) in any of their specifications. Hall pointed out that this was also consistent with large standard errors, but Acemoglu argued that this issue was not critical for the paper.

Pierre-Olivier Gourinchas noted that shocks such as China opening up to trade should have effects on relative prices. Daron Acemoglu responded by agreeing that relative price impacts could be important. He mentioned a paper on the Japanese earthquake (Carvalho et al. 2014) as an example of downstream effects arising from a demand shock and also mentioned work by Yu Shi, a graduate student at MIT. In general, with CES (as opposed to Cobb-Douglas) production, there are downstream effects from a demand shock, arising because income and substitution effects, which go in opposite directions, do not exactly cancel. However, the prediction that demand shocks cause upstream effects is robust and does not depend on the assumption of Cobb-Douglas preferences.

Christopher Sims recalled a paper by Olivier Blanchard (Blanchard 1988) that used input-output dynamics to discuss the propagation of effects from nominal price changes. Sims suggested that the author consider the dynamics of prices in their framework, and Daron Acemoglu agreed, mentioning that Chad Jones had a series of papers that considered network models with wedges.

Ben Bernanke spoke next, suggesting that inventory dynamics, arising for issues like time to order, delivery times, and the like might help connect the model to an older literature on business cycles and identify whether particular shocks were upstream or downstream of a particular firm. Daron Acemoglu agreed and recalled the work of Long and Plosser (1983). In their model, output depends on inputs purchased in the previous period. Acemoglu pointed out that these types of delays would vary substantially across industries. However, in these models, the second-round effects occur in the second period after the shocks, the third-round effects in the third period, and so on. Acemoglu suggested that there is potentially interesting research to be done using these models but stated that the authors chose to focus on static models initially because they lead to empirically testable regressions.

John Fernald mentioned that Susanto Basu wrote a paper about intermediate inputs and sticky prices (Basu 1995). In the present paper, Acemoglu, Akcigit, and Kerr find no upstream effects of a technology shock because that shock immediately changes prices. In his work with coauthors (Basu et al. 2013), Fernald finds that one-third of the technology shocks passes through into relative prices within one year. Daron Acemoglu agreed that this was an interesting point and that in more realistic models both quantities and prices would adjust slowly. Yuriy Gorodnichenko pointed out that the authors' model makes a strong prediction about how prices should respond to demand shocks and that the authors' data set would allow them to test this. Daron Acemoglu expressed his skepticism about the quality of the price data and pointed out that under the Cobb-Douglas assumptions, the results would be the same regardless of whether one used real value added, nominal value added, real shipments, or nominal shipments.

Finally, Harald Uhlig asked about the stability (over time) of the input-output matrices, and in particular about how this was affected by the ongoing process of firm creation and destruction. Daron Acemoglu replied that they are very stable, with the correlation of entries across five-year periods of above 0.9. He referenced a paper of his (Acemoglu et al 2013) that documented this. However, there is some change over time, and Acemoglu speculated that it would be interesting to combine these changes with high-quality data on prices.

5

Expectations and Investment

Nicola Gennaioli, *Universita' Bocconi*
Yueran Ma, *Harvard University*
Andrei Shleifer, *Harvard University and NBER*

Abstract

Using micro data from Duke University quarterly survey of Chief Financial Officers, we show that corporate investment plans as well as actual investment are well explained by CFOs' expectations of earnings growth. The information in expectations data is not subsumed by traditional variables, such as Tobin's Q or discount rates. We also show that errors in CFO expectations of earnings growth are predictable from past earnings and other data, pointing to extrapolative structure of expectations and suggesting that expectations may not be rational. This evidence, like earlier findings in finance, points to the usefulness of data on actual expectations for understanding economic behavior.

I. Introduction

One of the basic principles of economics in general, and macroeconomics in particular, is that expectations influence decisions. In line with this principle, the use of survey-based expectations data has been the mainstay of macroeconomic analysis since the 1940s, analyzing variables such as railroad shippers' forecasts. The NBER published several volumes on data of this kind, such as *The Quality and Economic Significance of Anticipations Data* (1960), showing that forecasts help to explain real decisions by firms, including investment and production.

The use of expectations data took a nosedive following the Rational Expectations Revolution. Under rational expectations, the model itself dictates what expectations rational agents should hold to be consistent with the model (Muth 1961), so anticipations data are redundant.

Economists also became skeptical about the quality of expectations data; in fact, this skepticism predates rational expectations (Manski 2004). According to Prescott (1977, 30), "Like utility, expectations are not observed, and *surveys cannot be used to test the rational expectations hypothesis*" (emphasis his). In finance, as in macroeconomics, the Efficient Markets Hypothesis implies that expectations of asset returns are predicted by the model (Campbell and Cochrane 1999; Lettau and Ludvigson 2001), so expectations data are not commonly used.

In our view, the marginalization of research on survey expectations deprives economists of extremely valuable information. Whether or not survey expectations predict behavior is an empirical question. The rational expectations assumption should not be taken for granted, but rather confronted with actual expectations data, imperfect as they are. Today, we have theoretical models that do not rely on the rational expectations assumption and make testable predictions, as well as expectations data to compare alternative models. Indeed, Manski (2004) argues forcefully and convincingly that expectations data are necessary to distinguish alternative models in economics.

As an illustration, take the case of finance, where data on expectations of asset returns have been rejected as uninformative (Cochrane 2011). Yet there is mounting evidence that expectations are highly consistent across different surveys of different types of investors, that they have a fairly clear extrapolative structure, that they predict investor behavior, and that they are useful in predicting returns (Greenwood and Shleifer 2014). Most important, expectations of returns obtained from surveys are negatively correlated with measures of expected returns obtained from rational expectations models. The trouble seems to be with conventional rational expectations models of asset prices, not with expectations data.

The message we take from this discussion is that expectations data can be used to address two questions: (a) Do expectations affect behavior? and (b) Are expectations rational? The questions are related. If expectations do not affect behavior, it matters little whether they are rational or not. If, however, expectations do affect behavior, the question of their rationality becomes quite relevant, since it allows us to consider alternative models of belief formation underlying economic decisions.

In this paper, we try to answer these questions for the case of corporate investment. We use new data assembled by John Graham and Campbell Harvey at Duke University to examine expectations formed by Chief Financial Officers (CFOs) of large US corporations and their relationship to investment plans and actual investment of these firms. The Duke data are based on quarterly surveys of CFOs which, among other things, collect information on earnings growth expectations and investment plans. We match these data with Compustat to get information on actual investment and other accounting variables. We also consider earnings forecasts made by Wall Street financial analysts regarding individual firms, which happen to be highly correlated with CFO forecasts.

To organize our discussion, we present a simple q-theory-based model of investment, but one relying on actual expectations rather than stock market data. We then conduct a number of empirical tests suggested by the model of the relationship between earnings growth expectations and investment growth, both in the aggregate and firm-level data. The results suggest that expectations are statistically and substantively important predictors of both planned and actual investment, and have explanatory power beyond traditional variables such as market-based proxies of Tobin's q, discount rates, measures of financial constraints, or uncertainty. We then conduct a number of empirical tests on the rationality of expectations. In our data, expectations do not appear to be rational in the sense that—both in the aggregate and at the level of individual firms—expectational errors are consistently predictable from highly relevant publicly available information, such as past profitability. Some evidence points to the extrapolative structure of earnings expectations, similar to the evidence from finance.

Our paper is related to several very large strands of research. Most clearly, it is related to a large literature on determinants of investment, such as Barro (1990), Hayashi (1982), Fazzari, Hubbard, and Petersen (1988), Morck et al. (1990), Lamont (2000), and many others. Eisner (1978) is the classic study of the effects of sales anticipations on investment, with results broadly similar to ours. Four further papers are closely related to our work. Cummins, Hassett, and Oliner (2006) replace the traditional market-based Tobin's q used in investment equations by q computed using analyst expectations data, and find that the fit of the equation is much better. Guiso, Pistaferri, and Suryanarayanan (2006) use direct expectations data on Italian firms to study the relationship between expectations, investment plans, and actual investment. Arif and Lee (2014) use accounting data to show that high aggregate investment precedes earnings disappointments, and argue that fluctuations in investor sentiment account for the evidence. Greenwood and Hanson (2015) specifically study the shipping industry, and find evidence of boom-bust cycles driven by volatile (and incorrect) expectations and investment that follows them.

Our paper is also related to research on expectations in macroeconomics. A large literature studies inflation expectations and their rationality (e.g., Figlewski and Wachtel 1981; Zarnowitz 1985; Keane and Runkle 1990; Ang,

Bakaert, and Wei 2007; Monti 2010; Del Negro and Eusepi 2011; Coibion and Gorodnichenko 2012, 2015; Smets, Warne, and Wouters 2014). Souleles (2004) finds that consumer expectations are biased and inefficient, yet are strong predictors of household spending. Burnside, Eichenbaum, and Rebelo (2015) present a model of "social dynamics" in beliefs about home prices and match the model to survey expectations data. Fuhrer (2015) shows that survey expectations improve the performance of dynamic stochastic general equilibrium (DSGE) models. Some research suggests that analyst expectations of corporate profits are rational at very short horizons (Keane and Runkle 1998), although the overwhelming majority of studies reject rationality of analyst forecasts (De Bondt and Thaler 1990; Abarbanell 1991; La Porta 1996; Liu and Su 2005; Hribar and McInnis 2012). There is also a literature on expectations shocks in macroeconomics, which generally maintains the assumption of rational expectations (Lorenzoni 2009; Angeletos and La'O 2010; Levchenko and Pandalai-Nayar 2015).

Perhaps most closely related to our work is research in behavioral finance, where biases in expectations have been examined for many years (e.g., Cutler, Poterba, and Summers 1990; De Long et al. 1990). Some of the recent papers include Amromin and Sharpe (2014), Bacchetta, Mertens, and Wincoop (2009), Hirshleifer, Li, and Yu (2015), and Greenwood and Shleifer (2014), to which we return later. Several of these papers find that investor expectations are extrapolative. In the bond market, Piazzesi, Salomao, and Schneider (2015) use data on interest-rate forecasts and also find substantial deviations from rationality. Vissing-Jorgensen (2004) and Fuster, Hebert, and Laibson (2012) are two recent *Macroeconomics Annual* papers that also address expectations formation and rationality.

In the next section, we briefly summarize some of the evidence on the relationship between investor expectations and asset prices, and address some of the criticisms of expectations data. Section III describes our data. Section IV presents a simple q-theory model of expectations and investment that organizes our empirical work. Section V follows with the basic empirical results on expectations and investment. Section VI examines the structure of expectations. Section VII concludes with a brief discussion of implications of the evidence for macroeconomics.

II. Recent Research on Expectations and Asset Prices in Finance

Before turning to our main results on investment, we briefly summarize recent research on expectations and stock market returns, which illustrates the usefulness of expectations data. In recent models with time-varying expected returns (e.g., Campbell and Cochrane 1999; Lettau and Ludvigson 2001), expected returns (ER) are given by required returns, which in turn depend on consumption: investors require higher returns when consumption is low (relative to some benchmark), and lower returns when consumption is high. This research does not generally use data on expectations. Rather, it adopts a rational expectations approach in which ERs are determined by the model itself, so the ER is inferred from the joint distribution of consumption and realized returns.

As discussed in the introduction, recent work has started to use actual expectations data. For our purposes, the most relevant paper is Greenwood and Shleifer (2014). They use data on expectations of returns from six different surveys of investors, including a Gallup survey, investor newsletters, and the survey of CFOs of large corporations that we use in the current paper. The paper reports four main findings relevant to our analysis, which we summarize in tables 1 and 2.

First, expectations of aggregate stock returns are highly correlated across investor surveys, despite the fact that different data sets survey different investors and ask somewhat different questions (see table 1). These measured expectations are also highly positively correlated with equity mutual fund inflows. Survey expectations are thus hardly misleading or uninformative: Why would they otherwise be strongly correlated across groups, across questions, and with fund flows?

Second, return expectations appear to be extrapolative: they are high after a period of high market returns, and low after a period of low market returns (see table 1 and figure 1).

Third, and critically, expectations of returns are strongly negatively correlated with model-based measures of the ER (see again table 1). Put simply, when investors expect returns to be high, models predict that the ER is low. A plausible interpretation of this finding is that model-based ER does not actually capture expectations.

Fourth, when expectations of returns are high and the ER is low, actual returns going forward are low (see table 2). To us, this piece of evidence points to the interpretation, dating back to Campbell and Shiller (1987, 1988), that high market valuations and consumption reflect overvaluation and excessive investor optimism (as directly measured by expectations), and portend reversion going forward. Model-based ER, in other words, does not measure expectations, but rather proxies for overvaluation.

We draw two lessons from this analysis. At the most basic level, direct survey estimates of expectations are useful: they have a well-defined structure across different surveys, and they predict fund flows

Table 1

Correlations among Different Measures of Investor Expectations of Stock Market Returns and Model-Based Expected Returns

	Gallup	CFO Survey	AAII	Investor Intelligence	Shiller	Michigan
CFO Survey	0.77					
	[0.000]					
AAII	0.64	0.56				
	[0.000]	[0.000]				
Investor	0.60	0.64	0.55			
Intelligence	[0.000]	[0.000]	[0.000]			
Shiller	0.39	0.66	0.51	0.43		
	[0.000]	[0.000]	[0.000]	[0.000]		
Michigan	0.61	−0.12	0.60	0.19	−0.56	
	[0.003]	[0.922]	[0.003]	[0.395]	[0.020]	
Log(D/P)	−0.33	−0.44	−0.31	−0.19	−0.55	−0.57
	[0.000]	[0.003]	[0.000]	[0.000]	[0.000]	[0.006]
Cay	0.02	0.14	−0.02	−0.19	0.37	0.00
	[0.776]	[0.380]	[0.788]	[0.000]	[0.000]	[0.988]
−Surplus	−0.48	−0.53	−0.28	−0.05	−0.67	−0.74
consumption	[0.000]	[0.000]	[0.000]	[0.191]	[0.000]	[0.000]
Past 12m stock	0.78	0.36	0.37	0.43	0.05	0.44
returns	[0.000]	[0.018]	[0.000]	[0.000]	[0.578]	[0.042]
Equity fund	0.70	0.71	0.41	0.20	0.33	0.40
flows	[0.000]	[0.000]	[0.000]	[0.000]	[0.000]	[0.068]

Note: This table shows correlations between different measures of investor expectations about future aggregate stock market returns, as well as correlations between survey expectations and discount rate proxies. Survey expectations variables are described in detail in Greenwood and Shleifer (2014). The CFO Survey refers to the Duke/CFO Magazine Survey, and AAII refers to surveys run by the American Association of Individual Investors. Investor Intelligence aggregates opinions expressed in newsletters published by institutional investors. Shiller denotes the survey led by Robert Shiller, and Michigan is University of Michigan Survey of Consumers. Horizon of survey expectations is mostly the next 12 months (Gallup, CFO Survey, Shiller); the AAII survey asks about next-6-month expectations, and the horizon in Investor Intelligence and the Michigan survey varies. Among the discount rate proxies, log(D/P) denotes log dividend yield, *cay* refers to the consumption-wealth ratio in Lettau and Ludvigson (2001), and surplus consumption is constructed by Campbell and Cochrane (1999). Discount rate proxies are presented in a way so that the value is increasing in model-based expected returns (we use the negative of surplus consumption because high surplus consumption should be associated with low expected returns). Numbers in brackets denote p-values on the hypothesis that the correlation between the two series is zero.

as well as future returns. Second, to the extent that survey estimates actually measure expectations is accepted, the evidence points against rational expectations models of stock market valuation. Actual expectations are strongly negatively related to the measures of expected returns that these models generate. In the remainder of this paper, we consider some related findings for corporate investment.

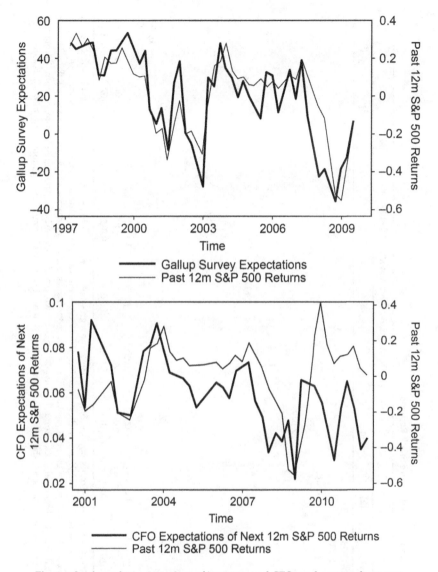

Fig. 1. Stock market expectations of investors and CFOs and past stock returns

Note: The thin line denotes S&P 500 index returns in the past 12 months. In panel (A), the thick line denotes expectations from the Gallup survey (% optimistic − % pessimistic about performance of the stock market in the next 12 months). In panel (B), the thick line denotes the average response in the CFO survey, to the question "Over the next year, I expect the average annual S&P 500 return will be: ___." Frequency is quarterly.

Table 2
Expectations of Stock Returns and Realized Future Stock Returns

				Realized Next 12m Aggregate Stock Market Returns				
	(1)	(2)	(3)	(4)	(5)	(6)	(7)	(8)	(9)
---	---	---	---	---	---	---	---	---	---
Gallup*	-1.985 (-1.370)								
CFO Survey		-0.021 (-0.670)							
AAII*			-1.655 (-0.892)						
Investor Intelligence*				-1.534 (-2.323)					
Shiller*					-0.612 (-0.228)				
Michigan						-0.081 (-3.964)			
Log(D/P)							0.072 (1.424)		
Cay								3.095 (3.031)	
-Surplus consumption									0.958 (4.147)
[p-val, b=1]	[0.040]	[0.000]	[0.154]	[0.000]	[0.550]	[0.000]			
N	132	39	285	579	123	22	579	579	579
R^2	0.057	0.03	0.015	0.036	0.004	0.342	0.03	0.107	0.116

Note: This table presents results from table 6 in Greenwood and Shleifer (2014). The regressions are $R_t^x = a + bX_t + u_t$, where R_t^x denotes next 12-month stock market returns (in excess of the risk-free rate), and X is a predictor variable. The independent variables include measures of expectations from investor surveys and discount rate proxies. Selected investor expectations variables are starred to indicate that they are rescaled versions of the raw data. The rescaled versions can be interpreted in units of nominal stock returns. For details, see Greenwood and Shleifer (2014). The regressions are monthly. In columns (1) to (6), for each measure of survey expectations, we show the p-value on the test that b = 1 (which is the null under rational expectations). t-statistics in parenthesis. Standard errors are Newey-West with 12 lags.

III.   Data for Studying Expectations and Investment

Our empirical analysis of corporate investment draws on two main categories of data: (a) data on expectations, primarily of future profitability; and (b) data on firm financials and investment activities. We focus on nonfinancial firms in the United States. We collect data both at the aggregate and at the firm level, and all data are available at quarterly frequencies. Appendix B provides a list of the main variables, including their construction and the time range for which each variable is available.[1]

A.   Expectations Data

We have data on the expectations of two groups of people: CFOs and equity analysts. We first describe these data and then show that expectations of CFOs and equity analysts are highly correlated.

CFO Expectations

Our data on CFO expectations come from the Duke/CFO Magazine Business Outlook Survey led by John Graham and Campbell Harvey, which was launched in July 1996 and takes place on a quarterly basis. Each quarter, the survey asks CFOs their views about the US economy and corporate policies, as well as their expectations of future firm performance and operational plans.[2] Starting in 1998, the CFO survey consistently asks respondents their expectations of the *future twelve-month growth* of key corporate variables, including earnings, capital spending, and employment, among others. The original question is presented to the CFOs as follows:

Relative to the previous 12 months, what will be your company's PERCENT-AGE CHANGE during the next 12 months? (e.g., +3%, −2%, etc.) [Leave blank if not applicable]
   Earnings: _____; Cash on balance sheet: _____; Capital spending: _____;
   Prices of your product: _____; Number of domestic full-time employees: _____;
   Wage: _____; Dividends: _____.

(Selected items are listed as examples. For a complete listing, please refer to original questionnaires posted on the CFO survey's website.)

   We use CFOs' answers on earnings growth over the next 12 months as the main proxy for CFO expectations of future profitability. As the survey does not ask for expectations beyond the next 12 months, we will explain in Section IV how we interpret and extract information from earnings expectations over the next 12 months.

We then use CFOs' answers on capital spending growth in the next 12 months as a proxy for firms' current investment plans. In the empirical analysis, we investigate how investment plans relate to expectations of future profitability. We adopt this approach in light of well-documented lags between decisions to invest and actual investment spending (Lamont 2000). With lags in investment implementation, current expectations about future profitability may not translate into capital expenditures instantly. Instead, they will affect current investment plans, and show up in actual investment spending with some delay. As a result, it can be more straightforward to detect the impact of earnings expectations by looking at investment plans. We discuss this issue in more detail in sections IV and V.

Our analyses use both aggregate time-series and firm-level panel data. Aggregate variables are revenue-weighted averages of firm-level responses, and they are published on the CFO survey's website. While the survey does not require CFOs to identify themselves, some respondents voluntarily disclose this information. It is then possible to match a fraction of the firm-level responses with data from the Center for Research in Security Prices (CRSP) and Compustat to perform firm-level tests. For example, Ben-David, Graham, and Harvey (2013) use matched firm-level data to study how managerial miscalibration affects corporate financial policies. Because there are privacy restrictions associated with these data, Graham and Harvey helped us implement firm-level analysis using a subsample of their matched data set. The firm-level data we use has 1,133 firm-year observations, spanning from 2005Q1 to 2012Q4.[3] We exclude firms that have negative earnings in the past 12 months because, in that case, earnings growth is not well defined. We also winsorize outliers at the 1% level.

Analyst Expectations

We obtain data on equity analysts' expectations of future firm performance from the Institutional Brokers' Estimate System (IBES) dataset. Beginning in the 1980s, IBES collects analyst forecasts of quarterly earnings per share (EPS) for the next 1 to 12 quarters. We take consensus EPS forecasts (i.e., average forecast for a given firm-quarter in the future) and compute forecasts of total earnings by multiplying by the number of shares outstanding. To compare the results with those using CFO expectations, we compute analyst expectations of future 12-month earnings growth. We calculate aggregate analyst expectations of future 12-month earnings growth by summing up expected future earnings of all firms in the next four quarters, and then divide by the sum of earnings of all firms in the past four quarters. We calculate firm-level analyst expectations of future earnings growth by taking the forecast of total firm earnings in the next four quarters, and then divide by total earnings in the past four quarters. We exclude firms that have negative earnings in the past 12 months when calculating expected future earnings growth.

The sample with analyst expectations covers both a longer time span and a larger set of firms. We set the start date of the aggregate time series and firm panel to be 1985Q1 because some of the quarterly Compustat data items we use only become systematically available around 1985, and because aggregate analyst forecasts have some outliers before 1985. We set the end of the sample to be 2012Q4 so we can match expectations to realized next 12-month earnings growth with accounting data ending in 2013Q4. In total, we have 145,281 firm-level observations of expected earnings growth over the next 12 months, and we winsorize outliers at the 5% level.

Correlation between CFO and Analyst Expectations

The expectations of CFOs and analysts with respect to next 12-month earnings growth are highly correlated. Figure 2 shows aggregate time series of expected next 12-month earnings growth from the CFO survey and from analyst forecasts. The raw correlation between these two series is 0.65. At the firm level, the raw correlation between CFO and analyst expectations of next 12-month earnings growth is 0.4 if we demean by firm, and 0.3 if we demean by both firm and time. The high correlation between expectations of CFOs and analysts indicate that expectations data are consistent and meaningful, and expectations of both groups incorporate information about general business outlook shared by managers and the market.

B. Firm Financials Data

We collect aggregate data on firm assets and investment from the Flow of Funds (table F.102 and table B.102) and the National Income and Product Accounts (NIPA), and firm-level data from Compustat. A key variable in our analysis is realized earnings, which we use to assess the accuracy of earnings expectations of CFOs and analysts. While Compustat mainly records Generally Accepted Accounting Principles (GAAP) earnings, managers and analysts often use so-called "pro forma earnings" (also

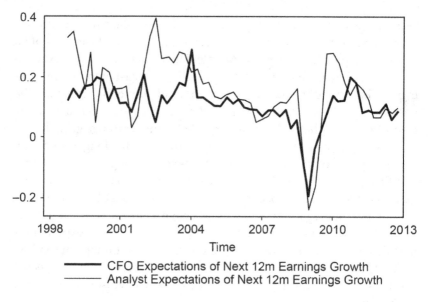

Fig. 2. Expectations of next-12-month earnings growth by CFOs and analysts
Note: The thick line is aggregate CFO expectations of next-12-month earnings growth from the CFO survey. The thin line is aggregate analyst expectations of next-12-month earnings growth computed from analyst EPS forecasts. Frequency is quarterly.

called "street earnings"), which adjust for certain nonrecurring items (Bradshaw and Sloan 2002; Bhattacharya et al. 2003). To make sure we use the same measure of earnings as CFOs and analysts, we collect realized earnings from IBES Actuals files, which closely track earnings as reported by companies in their earnings announcements. These are the numbers that analyst forecasts aim to match and the earnings metric that managers tend to use the most.[4] In the rest of the paper we refer to IBES actual earnings as "earnings," and GAAP earnings as "net income."

Table 3 presents summary statistics of firms for which we have firm-level CFO expectations (panel A) and analyst expectations (panel B), as well as all nonfinancial firms in Compustat (panel C). For comparability, the statistics in panel (B) and panel (C) are generated based on the time period for which we have firm-level CFO expectations (i.e., from 2005 through 2012). We can see that firms with analyst expectations are mostly larger than the median Compustat firm, and firms with CFO expectations are generally even larger. Firms with CFO and analyst expectations also appear to be more profitable than firms in the full Compustat sample in terms of net income, but otherwise very similar in terms of sales, investment, book to market, and q.

IV. Expectations and Firm Investment: Empirical Specifications

We motivate our empirical specification with a basic q-theory model. A firm is run by a risk-neutral owner who discounts the future by factor $\beta < 1$,[5] and the firm's horizon is infinite. In the model, we interpret each period t to be 12 months. The firm's output in period t is obtained by combining capital and labor using a constant returns to scale production function $A_t K_t^\alpha L_t^{1-\alpha}$. At the beginning of period t, the owner hires labor L_t at wage w and makes decisions about investment during this year I_t. Investment takes one year to implement, so $K_{t+1} = (1 - \delta) K_t + I_t$, where δ is capital depreciation rate. The firm's optimal policy in year t maximizes the expected present value of earnings:

$$max_{\{I_s, L_s\}_{s \geq t}} \mathbb{E}_t \left\{ \sum_{s \geq t} \beta^{s-t} [A_s K_s^\alpha L_s^{1-\alpha} - wL_s - C(I_s, K_s)] \right\}$$

subject to $K_{s+1} = (1 - \delta) K_s + I_s$. We assume the commonly used quadratic investment costs:

$$C(I_s, K_s) - I_s = \frac{b}{2} \left(\frac{I_s}{K_s} - a \right)^2 K_s,$$

which allow for convex adjustment costs ($b > 0$) and displays constant returns to scale.

In the optimization problem above, the operator $\mathbb{E}_t (.)$ denotes the owner's expectations conditional on his information at the beginning of year t, computed according to his possibly distorted beliefs. We allow for departures from rational expectations, but restrict to beliefs that preserve the law of iterated expectations. By standard arguments, appendix A[6] shows that the firm's optimal investment chosen at the beginning of year t is described by:

$$\frac{I_t}{K_t} = \left(a - \frac{1}{b} \right) + \frac{\beta}{b} \frac{\mathbb{E}_t [\sum_{s \geq t+1} \beta^{s-(t+1)} \Pi_s]}{K_{t+1}} \tag{1}$$

where $\Pi_s = A_s K_s^\alpha L_s^{1-\alpha} - wL_s - C(I_s, K_s)$ denotes the firm's earnings in year s. Equation (1) corresponds to a generic q-theory equation with quadratic adjustment costs, which takes the form $I_t / K_t = \eta + \gamma Q_t$.

To estimate equation (1), ideally we would like to know expectations of earnings in all future periods. Unfortunately, this is not feasible in practice. For instance, CFOs only report expectations of earnings growth in the next 12 months. Formally, in the CFO survey we only have information about $\mathbb{E}_t (\Pi_t)$, namely expectations at the beginning of year t about earnings Π_t in the following 12 months (which are not yet known,

Table 3
Summary Statistics

Variable	Mean	Std	5%	25%	50%	75%	95%
			A. Sample with CFO Expectations				
CFO expectations of next 12m earnings growth	0.07	0.19	-0.25	0.02	0.10	0.15	0.30
Realized next 12m earnings growth	0.09	0.48	-0.60	-0.11	0.09	0.26	0.85
Realized next 12m earnings/asset	0.06	0.06	-0.02	0.03	0.06	0.10	0.16
CFO expectations of next 12m capital spending growth	0.05	0.23	-0.3	0	0.3	0.1	0.5
Asset	21,808.42	101,176.00	80.48	541.10	1,959.22	6,453.33	44,791.00
Market value	14,326.91	48,370.41	75.81	550.28	1,843.50	6,848.73	45,621.37
Q	1.51	0.73	0.67	0.99	1.35	1.84	2.97
BTM	0.49	0.31	0.16	0.29	0.41	0.60	1.06
Annual net income/asset	0.03	0.17	-0.18	0.02	0.06	0.10	0.18
Annual sales/asset	1.09	0.67	0.27	0.61	0.92	1.38	2.55
Annual capx/asset	0.04	0.03	0.01	0.02	0.03	0.05	0.11
Annual capx growth	0.13	0.53	-0.52	-0.18	0.06	0.33	1.11
			B. Sample with Analyst Forecasts				
Next 12m earnings growth implied by analyst EPS forecasts	0.16	0.34	-0.31	-0.01	0.12	0.28	0.81
Realized next 12m earnings growth	0.09	0.47	-0.65	-0.12	0.09	0.30	0.86
Realized next 12m earnings/asset	0.07	0.05	0.00	0.04	0.06	0.10	0.16
Asset	6,355.03	26,367.43	114.72	401.15	1,178.22	3,835.99	26,735.00
Market value	6,610.21	23,094.48	129.51	473.98	1,287.45	3,887.96	25,692.68
Q	1.53	0.83	0.65	0.93	1.29	1.90	3.27
BTM	0.51	0.32	0.14	0.29	0.45	0.66	1.10

Annual net income/asset	0.06	0.07	-0.03	0.03	0.06	0.10	0.17
Annual sales/asset	1.12	0.63	0.32	0.64	1.00	1.46	2.37
Annual capx/asset	0.05	0.04	0.01	0.02	0.04	0.07	0.15
Annual capx growth	0.17	0.55	-0.54	-0.17	0.08	0.38	1.20
C. All Compustat Firms							
Asset	3,021.22	16,706.02	0.44	25.34	201.06	1,278.93	12,105.00
Market value	3,684.34	16,780.76	17.35	107.49	433.32	1,726.60	14,127.71
Q	1.53	0.91	0.61	0.88	1.24	1.90	3.51
BTM	0.55	0.38	0.11	0.28	0.47	0.73	1.24
Annual net income/asset	-0.11	0.39	-0.87	-0.11	0.02	0.07	0.15
Annual sales/asset	1.01	0.70	0.10	0.47	0.89	1.41	2.40
Annual capx/asset	0.05	0.04	0.00	0.01	0.03	0.06	0.14
Annual capx growth	0.16	0.68	-0.69	-0.28	0.04	0.42	1.53

Note: Summary statistics of firms covered in the CFO Survey sample, analyst forecast sample, and full Compustat sample. Mean, median, standard deviation, and selected percentiles are presented. For comparability, all statistics are based on the sample period for which we have CFO expectations (2005 to 2012).

so expectations are well defined). With respect to investment, we have information on: (a) planned investment over the next 12 months, and (b) actual capital spending in each quarter. We denote investment plans for the next 12 months as I_t^p, which captures the plan made at the beginning of the year about investment in the rest of the year.

Given implementation lags in the investment process, it may be most straightforward to test how expectations at a given point in time affect firms' investment plans.[7] Accordingly, we approximate equation (1) by

$$\frac{I_t^p}{K_t} \approx \theta_0 + \theta_1 \frac{\mathbb{E}_t(\Pi_t)}{K_t}. \tag{2}$$

This approximation is reliable if expectations about the level of future earnings display significant persistence, namely $\mathbb{E}_t(\Pi_t) / K_t$ is not too far from $\mathbb{E}_t(\Pi_{t+1}) / K_{t+1}$ and more generally for earnings further away in the future. We find this assumption to be plausible based on information in the data. Empirically, earnings over assets are relatively persistent, and moreover, are perceived to be very persistent based on analyst forecasts. The IBES data set provides analysts' forecasts of future earnings for up to 12 quarters. With firm-level forecasts, we find $\mathbb{E}_t(\Pi_{i,t+1}) / K_{i,t+1} = 0.83\mathbb{E}_t(\Pi_{i,t}) / K_{i,t} + \eta_i + \varepsilon_{i,t}$ and $\mathbb{E}_t(\Pi_{i,t+2}) / K_{i,t+1} = 0.73\mathbb{E}_t(\Pi_{i,t}) / K_{i,t} + \eta_i + \varepsilon_{i,t}$. Aggregate persistence implied by analyst forecasts is similar. In addition, lagged profitability is not significant if included in these regressions and neither does it affect coefficients on $\mathbb{E}_t(\Pi_{i,t}) / K_{i,t}$. These results suggest that next one-year expectations incorporate a significant amount of information about medium- to long-term expectations. We showed in Section III that CFO and analyst expectations are highly correlated, and it is probable that their beliefs share common structures.

Given this corroborating evidence, it appears that within the limitations of our data, equation (2) is a reasonable approximation of equation (1). For the purpose of our empirical analysis, it is convenient to log-linearize equation (2) and express it in growth rates, since all variables in the CFO survey are in terms of percentage change in the next 12 months relative to the past 12 months. By expressing equation (2) in growth rates, we can directly employ these variables without using them to reconstruct levels. If we denote logs by lowercase variables, then derivations in appendix A[8] show that our equation for investment plans can be approximated as:

$$\underbrace{i_t^p - i_{t-1}}_{\substack{\text{planned investment growth} \\ \text{in the next 12m}}} \approx \mu_1 \underbrace{[\mathbb{E}_t(\pi_t) - \pi_{t-1}]}_{\substack{\text{expectations of earnings growth} \\ \text{in the next 12m}}} + (1 - \mu_1)(k_t - k_{t-1}) \tag{3}$$

where μ_1 is a log-linearization constant ($\mu_1 > 0$). The left-hand-side term is planned investment growth in the next 12 months, which is available from the CFO survey. The first term on the right-hand side of equation (3) is expectations of earnings growth in the next 12 months, which we also observe directly in the data. This specification is very similar to previous studies of investment growth such as Barro (1990), Lamont (2000), and many others.

The intuition of equation (3) is as follows: When firms think that earnings will increase by a lot in the next 12 months, they also tend to believe that future earnings will be higher for a sustained period of time. As a result, they want to invest more, which leads to an immediate increase in planned investment. In equation (3) we need to control for the change in capital stock because both investment and profitability are affected by the size of capital stock. We can also arrive at a specification very similar to equation (3) in a simpler setting with time to build but without adjustment costs.[9] Empirically we use equation (3) to map a basic investment model to testable predictions in our data set. We refrain from testing the parameter restrictions implied by a strict adherence to the approximated q equation.

While investment plans are a convenient starting point to detect the impact of expectations, for equation (2) to be informative about how expectations influence investment, it must also be the case that plans are closely related to realizations. In Section V.C, we show that investment plans are highly correlated with actual capital spending over the planned period. In other words, a significant fraction of capital spending over the next few quarters appears to be determined by ex ante investment plans, consistent with previous findings by Lamont (2000). To the extent that there is a close correspondence between investment plans and realized investment over the planned period, it would also be of interest to test how current expectations translate into actual capital spending in the next 12 months. This additional test allows us to further assess whether expectations have a substantial impact on actual investment activities. We present results from these tests in Section V.C.

V. Expectations and Investment

In this section, we test the relationship between investment decisions and earnings expectations. We focus on CFO expectations, and provide supplementary results using expectations of equity analysts. We begin by studying investment plans. In Section V.A we consider the role of expectations at the aggregate level, and in Section V.B we consider the role of expectations at the firm level. Then, in Section V.C we evaluate the relationship between plans and realized investment, and document the link between expectations and actual capital spending.

A. Expectations and Investment Plans: Aggregate Evidence

Figure 3 visually represents the association between aggregate CFO expectations and aggregate investment. Panel (A) plots CFOs' expectations of next 12-month earnings growth, along with planned investment growth in the next 12 months. Panel (B) adds to panel (A) actual aggregate investment growth in the next 12 months. We see that there is a strong comovement between earnings expectations and investment plans, and between investment plans and actual capital spending. At the very least, expectations data do not appear to be uninformative noise.

We then estimate versions of equation (3) using quarterly regressions:

$$\Delta \widehat{CAPX}_{q_t} = \alpha + \beta E^*_{q_t}[\Delta \text{ Earnings}] + \lambda X_{q_t} + \epsilon_{q_t}$$

where $\Delta \widehat{CAPX}_{q_t}$ is planned investment growth in the next 12 months reported in quarter q_t, and $E^*_{q_t}[\Delta \text{ Earnings}]$ is CFO expectations of next 12-month earnings growth reported in quarter q_t; X_{q_t} includes past change in capital stock as shown in equation (3), as well as a set of additional controls we discuss below. We use Newey-West standard errors with twelve lags.[10]

Table 4, columns (1) and (2), report our baseline results. We find that CFOs' earnings expectations have significant explanatory power for firms' investment plans, both statistically and economically. A one standard deviation increase in earnings growth expectations is associated with a 0.8 standard deviation increase in planned investment growth.[11] Put differently, a 1 percentage point increase in CFO expectations is accompanied by a 0.6 percentage point increase in planned investment growth.[12] Quantitatively, CFO expectations have major explanatory power for aggregate investment.

In interpreting these results, three issues arise. First, how do CFO expectations relate to traditional proxies of Tobin's q? Do data on managers' expectations contain information beyond market-price-based measures of q? Second, is the role of expectations robust to controlling for alternative theories of corporate investment? Third, could the correlation between expectations and investment reflect a reverse causality problem, whereby investment affects expectations of future earnings rather than the other way around? In the following, we address these issues by augmenting our baseline regressions.

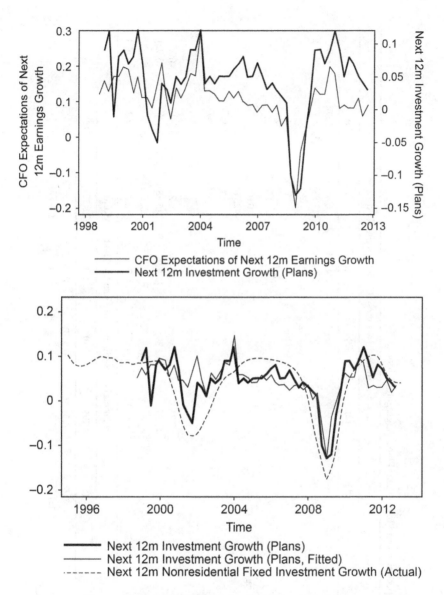

Fig. 3. CFO earnings growth expectations and investment

Note: The plots above present aggregate CFO expectations of future earnings growth, aggregate planned investment growth, and aggregate actual investment growth. In panel (A), the thin line is aggregate CFO expectations of next-12-month earnings growth. The thick line is aggregate planned investment growth in the next 12 months. In panel (B), the thin line is planned investment growth in the next 12 months fitted on contemporaneous CFO earnings growth expectations. The thick line is aggregate planned investment growth in the next 12 months. The dashed line is actual growth of private nonresidential fixed investment in the next 12 months. Frequency is quarterly.

Table 4

CFO Earnings Growth Expectations and Investment Plans: Aggregate Evidence

	Planned Investment Growth in the Next 12 Months						
	(1)	(2)	(3)	(4)	(5)	(6)	(7)
CFO expectations of next 12m earnings growth	0.6313 (9.39)	0.5959 (11.65)	0.5869 (11.40)	0.4235 (7.21)	0.4853 (12.83)	0.5997 (11.79)	0.5435 (9.78)
Q			0.0532 (1.68)				
Past 12m agg. stock returns				0.1082 (3.64)			
Past 12m credit spread change					−0.0352 (−2.26)		
Log(D/P)						0.0271 (0.62)	
Cay							−0.9700 (−1.86)
Past 12m asset growth		0.2181 (3.97)	0.1461 (2.39)	0.0784 (1.89)	0.2643 (5.88)	0.2481 (2.97)	0.2536 (3.92)
Observations	56	56	56	56	56	56	56
R-squared	0.616	0.660	0.672	0.741	0.685	0.663	0.674

	Planned Investment Growth in the Next 12 Months					
	(8)	(9)	(10)	(11)	(12)	(13)
CFO expectations of next 12m earnings growth	0.5969 (11.37)	0.5429 (8.20)	0.5301 (14.03)	0.5882 (8.55)	0.5573 (16.72)	0.4315 (8.21)
Past 12m credit spread change						−0.0447 (−1.49)

	(1)	(2)	(3)	(4)	(5)	(6)
Surplus consumption	0.0154					
	(0.30)					
Past 12m change of net income/asset		0.0433				-0.0433
		(1.70)				(-1.03)
Past 12m agg. stock vol. change			-0.0044			0.0421
			(-0.37)			(2.51)
Bloom policy uncertainty index (past 12m change)			-0.0328			-0.0303
			(-2.11)			(-2.23)
Past 12m GDP growth				0.6118		2.3154
				(0.77)		(1.89)
Past 12m investment growth					-0.1300	-0.5391
					(-2.26)	(-2.69)
Past 12m asset growth	0.2114	0.1716	0.2376	0.0547	0.3859	0.4349
	(3.40)	(3.25)	(4.22)	(0.29)	(6.21)	(3.59)
Observations	56	56	56	56	56	56
R-squared	0.660	0.672	0.694	0.666	0.667	0.739

Note: This table presents aggregate quarterly regression $\Delta \overline{CAPX}_t = \alpha + \beta E_t'[\Delta \text{Earnings}] + \lambda X_t + \varsigma_t.$ $E_t'[\Delta \text{Earnings}]$ is aggregate CFO expectations of earnings growth in the next 12 months, and $\Delta \overline{CAPX}_t$ is aggregate planned investment growth in the next 12 months. All control variables are measured at the end of quarter $t - 1$. Past 12-month stock returns is index returns from the end of quarter $t - 5$ to the end of quarter $t - 1$. Past 12-month aggregate credit spread change is log change in credit spread from the end of quarter $t - 5$ to the end of quarter $t - 1$. Past 12-month changes in stock volatility and Bloom policy uncertainty index, as well as past 12-month asset growth, are calculated in the same way (i.e., as the log difference between values at the end of quarters $t - 5$ and $t - 1$). Past 12-month change of net income/asset is net income from $t - 4$ to $t - 1$ normalized by asset at the end of quarter $t - 5$ minus normalized net income in the previous four quarters. Past 12-month GDP (investment) growth is the log difference between GDP (investment) in quarters $t - 4$ through $t - 1$ and GDP (investment) in the previous four quarters. A constant is included but not reported, and a linear time trend is included. t-statistics in parentheses. Standard errors are Newey-West with 12 lags.

Some variables may affect investment but are likely to do so only through their influence on expectations, such as information relevant for predicting future product demand. In principle, a large part of expectations are formed, perfectly or imperfectly, based on observable information, instead of being exogenous innovations. Thus a flexible enough function of observable information should be able to approximate expectations. The focus of our present analysis is to test the extent to which expectations as a whole, as measured in our data, affect firms' investment decisions. It is not specifically about the impact of variations in expectations that are not explained by observables (so-called "expectational shocks"). Accordingly, we do not explore whether our expectations variables can or cannot be driven out by a full set of factors that are primarily used to explain expectations. Instead, we emphasize controls that represent alternative determinants of investment (such as discount rates, financial constraints, etc.).[13]

CFO Expectations and Market-Based Proxies for Tobin's q

We begin with a comparison of CFO expectations and traditional proxies of Tobin's q. This exercise helps us assess whether expectations data contain additional information relative to standard market-based q measures. In table 4, column (3), we include the empirical proxy of q. In line with previous research, the explanatory power of equity q is very weak. It is well known that equity q is highly persistent and does not line up well with fluctuations in investment activities. In our context, to explain investment growth, the direct theoretical counterpart is not q in levels, but the log change in q. Barro (1990) shows changes in q are almost equivalent to stock returns. He finds that changes in q from the beginning of year $t - 1$ to the beginning of year t is highly correlated with investment growth in year t, and stock returns from the beginning of year $t - 1$ to the beginning of year t perform incrementally better. In column (4), we include past 12-month stock returns. The coefficient on this variable is positive and statistically significant, as predicted by theory. The coefficient on CFO expectations remains large and highly significant.[14] The views of CFOs appear to contain a substantial amount of additional information for investment plans not captured by equity q.

Philippon (2009) finds that a proxy of q obtained from bond yields is also highly correlated with investment activities. Philippon's bond q series end in 2007, which is five years before the end of our sample. However, bond q is highly correlated with credit spread. For example, the correlation between changes in bond q and changes in credit spread over four quarters is 0.84. In column (5), we include changes in credit spread in the past four quarters in lieu of bond q. In addition, credit spread can be relevant as a control also because it may reflect credit availability and financial constraints. The coefficient on this variable is negative and significant—consistent with theory—but CFO expectations retain significant explanatory power.

Overall, CFO expectations explain investment plans beyond market-based q proxies, statistically and economically. Indeed, CFOs may possess information that markets participants either do not possess or process imperfectly. To the extent that managers' and markets' views differ, it is natural that managers' beliefs have a major impact on investment decisions. As we show in Section V.C, this result also extends to actual capital spending.

CFO Expectations and Alternative Theories of Investment

We now test the role of expectations against alternative theories of investment. We introduce a set of variables motivated by these theories, which are the key controls in our analysis.

Time-Varying Discount Rates. A prominent idea in traditional finance holds that variations in required returns, or discount rates, are central to explaining investment in both financial and real assets (e.g., Cochrane 1991, 2011). Lamont (2000) postulates that firm investments rise and fall in response to changes in discount rates so that high investment growth is associated with low future stock returns. Lettau and Ludvigson (2002) argue that time-varying risk premia, as proxied for by the consumption-wealth ratio (known as *cay*), can forecast future investment growth. In table 4, columns (6) to (8), we control for three common measures of discount rates: log dividend yield, cay, and the surplus consumption ratio as constructed by Campbell and Cochrane (1999). *Cay* is somewhat significant, surplus consumption is not, and dividend yield tends to enter with the wrong sign. The explanatory power of CFO expectations is unaffected. We get similar results if we include these variables in past 12-month changes instead of in levels.

We can also control for risk premia implied by long-run risks models, as constructed by Bansal et al. (2014). Unfortunately their series is annual, which leaves us with few observations. We interpolate the series to quarterly frequencies in multiple ways and find it tends to enter with the wrong sign. Taken together, none of these variables compare in their explanatory power to CFO expectations, and their inclusion does not have much of an influence on the coefficient on expectations.[15]

Because proxies for discount rates are generally quite persistent, their coefficients can suffer from Stambaugh (1999) biases. In our case, Stambaugh bias will tend to attenuate the coefficients on discount rates toward zero or make them have the wrong sign.[16] In appendix C, table C6,[17] we report Stambaugh bias-adjusted results, using a multivariate version of the bootstrap method in Baker, Taliaferro, and Wurgler (2006). The bias adjusted results are very similar.

Financing Constraints.   A well-known empirical result, dating back to Fazzari, Hubbard, and Petersen (1988), is that investment is positively correlated with recent firm cash flows. The leading interpretation is that financially constrained firms invest more when high cash flows increase internal resources. In column (9), we control for cash flows in the past 12 months.[18] We can include cash flow variables either in levels or in changes, and results are similar: the coefficient on expectations barely changes, and the coefficient on past cash flows tends to be insignificant. This result confirms earlier findings by Cummins et al. (2006) that unveil the fragility of financial constraint variables once earnings expectations are taken into account.

Economic Uncertainty.   A blooming literature studies the impact of uncertainty on economic activities when investment is irreversible or has fixed adjustment costs (Leahy and Whited 1996; Guiso and Parigi 1999; Bloom, Bond, and Van Reenen 2007; Bloom 2009, among others). During periods of high uncertainty, the theory goes, managers do not want to exercise the option of investing: they prefer to wait for better times and information. It is legitimate to ask whether our measure of CFO expectations still matters when we include proxies for uncertainty in our regression.

In table 4, column (10), we include stock price volatility as a standard uncertainty proxy following Leahy and Whited (1996) and Bloom, Bond, and Van Reenen (2007), together with economic policy uncertainty as measured by Baker, Bloom, and Davis (2015). We can use these variables in levels or in past 12-month changes. In either case, these uncertainty proxies have only weak explanatory power, and the coefficient on CFO earnings expectations remains highly significant.

In table 4, columns (11) and (12), we additionally control for past GDP growth and past investment growth. In the last column, we include multiple controls together. The statistical and economic significance of CFO expectations remains largely intact.

Overall, these tests illustrate that CFO earnings expectations have significant explanatory power that is not accounted for by variables capturing alternative theories, such as time-varying discount rates, financial constraints, and uncertainty. As we show below, similar results hold when we connect expectations to actual capital spending. Our results suggest that expectations data provide substantive information about fluctuations in aggregate investment, and changes in expectations can be central to understanding investment activities.

Reverse Causality

One possible concern is our baseline results could be affected by reverse causality. Specifically, if a firm plans to invest a lot in the next 12 months, managers might also expect earnings to increase as investment leads to more output and sales. This mechanism seems unlikely to be driving our results. First, investment in the next 12 months generally does not translate into output and sales immediately. Second, even if it does, investment is an incremental addition to the capital stock. It is unlikely that a 1% increase in investment (which increases the firm's capital stock by much less than 1%) can instantly lead to a 1% or more increase in firm earnings, as would be required to match the magnitude of coefficients in the data.

We further address the reverse causality concern in supplementary tests, drawing on another question in the CFO survey, which asks respondents to rate their optimism about the US economy on a scale from 0 to 100 (with 0 being the least optimistic and 100 the most optimistic). In appendix C, table C1, we show that CFOs' optimism about the US economy is significantly positively correlated with investment. It is hard to argue that firms' investment plans will mechanically cause CFOs to be more optimistic about *the US economy*. Instead, this result is very much in line with previous findings that firms' expectations and sentiments appear to be a key driver of investment activities.

In appendix C, table C2, we present the same set of tests using analyst expectations. We find analyst expectations are also significantly correlated with investment plans, although not surprisingly, the magnitude of the relationship is smaller; the coefficients on analyst expectations are

generally about one-half of the size of the coefficients on CFO expectations. The evidence suggests that expectations elicited from different
sources are consistent, and there are general views shared by managers
and the market that play an important role in shaping aggregate investment dynamics.

B. Expectations and Investment Plans: Firm-Level Evidence

In table 5, we repeat our analysis at the firm level. As before, we start
with CFO data. We estimate

$$\Delta \widehat{CAPX}_{i,\, q_t} = \alpha + \zeta_i + \beta E^*_{i,q_t}[\Delta \text{ Earnings}_i] + \lambda X_{i,q_t} + \epsilon_{i,q_t}.$$

We report baseline results with firm fixed effects. Results are very similar without fixed effects, or with dynamic panel estimators.[19] Table 5
shows that at the firm level, CFO expectations continue to have substantial explanatory power for investment decisions. The response of
a firm's investment plans to CFO expectations is similar in magnitude
to the relationship unveiled in the aggregate analysis of table 4: when
CFOs expect earnings growth to increase by 1 percentage point, planned
investment growth increases by 0.4 percentage points on average. We
then compare CFO expectations with firm-level q and past 12-month
firm stock returns. We use the book-to-market ratio as a proxy for firm-
level required returns, and all other firm-level controls directly correspond to their aggregate counterparts in table 4. After including these
controls, alone or together, CFO expectations remain statistically and
economically significant. We also examine results adding time fixed effects and the findings are similar.

In appendix C, table C3, we replicate the firm-level analysis with
analyst expectations. The results show that analyst expectations about
a firm's earnings growth can also explain investment plans. As before,
the size of the coefficients on analyst expectations is about one-half of
that on CFO expectations. While CFO expectations play a more dominant role, business outlook shared by managers and specialist analysts
is nonetheless informative about investment decisions.

C. From Plans to Realized Investment

A premise for our analysis in Sections V.A and V.B is that investment
plans are key determinants of actual capital spending. With lags in investment implementation, expectations in a given quarter may not trans-

late into realized investment instantly, so changes in plans can help us pinpoint the impact of expectations, and plans will turn into capital expenditures over a period of time. In this section, we evaluate this proposition empirically. In figure 3, panel (B), it is evident that, at the aggregate level, plans and realized investment over the planned period are closely related. The raw correlation between the two series is 0.78.[20] Figure 3, panel (B), also shows that realized investment is highly correlated with investment plans fitted on CFO expectations. Expectations are a key driver not only of investment plans, but also of actual capital spending.

In table 6 and table 7, we present a full set of results using CFO earnings expectations in a given quarter to forecast actual investment growth in the next 12 months, both in the aggregate and at the firm level. We find that expectations, and CFO expectations in particular, have substantial forecasting power for realized next 12-month investment. Both in the aggregate and at the firm level, a 1 percentage point increase in CFO earnings growth expectations predicts a 0.6 percentage point increase in actual investment growth in the next 12 months. The performance of past stock returns and changes in credit spread has some improvements, but expectations data retain significant power; they are very informative about realized capital spending both alone and in the presence of a list of important controls.

Taken together, evidence in this section shows that expectations data are highly relevant for understanding corporate investment. They are not simply noise, but contain considerable information for explaining investment activities beyond a host of traditional variables.

VI. Are Expectations Rational?

Since expectations shape investment, it is critical to understand their determinants. We now take a first step in analyzing the structure of CFO and analyst expectations about future earnings growth. In particular, we check whether expectations of managers and market participants are consistent with rational benchmarks, or are systematically biased in predictable ways.

The simplest test of rational expectations is to run a regression with realized future earnings growth on the left-hand side and ex ante expectations on the right-hand side. In our context, such tests take the form:

$$\underbrace{\Delta \text{ Earnings}_i}_{\substack{\text{realized next 12m} \\ \text{earnings growth}}} = \alpha + \beta \underbrace{E^*_{i,q_t}[\Delta \text{ Earnings}_i]}_{\substack{\text{expected next 12m} \\ \text{earnings growth}}} + \omega_{i,t+1}$$

Table 5
CFO Earnings Growth Expectations and Investment Plans: Firm-Level Evidence

	Planned Investment Growth in the Next 12 Months										
	(1)	(2)	(3)	(4)	(5)	(6)	(7)	(8)	(9)	(10)	(11)
CFO expectations of next 12m earnings growth	0.4200 (4.44)	0.4259 (4.50)	0.4639 (4.40)	0.3487 (3.25)	0.3887 (3.94)	0.3713 (3.99)	0.4172 (4.25)	0.3420 (3.16)	0.4139 (4.35)	0.4233 (4.28)	0.3149 (2.80)
Q			0.0384 (1.53)								
Book-to-market				−0.2303 (−4.32)							
Past 12m firm stock returns					0.0833 (3.49)						
Past 12m credit spread change						−0.1130 (−4.39)					−0.1391 (−2.99)
Past 12m change of net income/asset							0.0025 (2.23)				0.0025 (1.16)
Past 12m firm stock vol. change								−0.0905 (−2.87)			−0.0148 (−0.33)
Bloom policy uncertainty index (Past 12m change)								−0.0764 (−2.35)			0.0385 (0.96)
Past 12m GDP growth									1.0087 (1.86)		0.6293 (0.95)
Past 12m investment growth										0.0010 (0.05)	0.0048 (0.19)

406

Past 12m asset growth		0.1163	0.1089	0.0529	0.0626	0.0964	0.0929	0.0393	0.0800	0.1276	0.0008
		(1.37)	(1.15)	(0.63)	(0.69)	(1.17)	(0.97)	(0.40)	(1.00)	(1.39)	(0.01)
Observations	850	834	740	761	764	834	809	719	834	790	692
R-squared	0.095	0.104	0.125	0.139	0.132	0.132	0.114	0.115	0.109	0.105	0.132
Number of firms	194	190	171	172	176	190	187	168	190	187	164

Note: This table presents firm-level quarterly regression $\Delta \widehat{CAPX}_{i,t} = \alpha + \eta_{li} + \beta E^*_{i,t} [\Delta \text{Earnings}] + \lambda X_{i,t} + \epsilon_{i,t}$; $E^*_{i,t} [\Delta \text{Earnings}]$ is firm-level CFO expectations of earnings growth in the next 12 months, and $\Delta \widehat{CAPX}_{i,t}$ is firm-level planned investment growth in the next 12 months. All control variables are measured at the end of quarter t – 1. Past 12-month firm stock returns, change of net income/asset, change of stock volatility, investment growth, and asset growth are firm-level counterparts of variables defined in table 4. A constant is included but not reported, and firm fixed effects are included. R-squared excludes firm fixed effects. t-statistics in parentheses. Standard errors are clustered by firm.

Table 6
CFO Earnings Growth Expectations and Realized Investment Growth: Aggregate Evidence

	Realized Investment Growth in the Next 12 Months						
	(1)	(2)	(3)	(4)	(5)	(6)	(7)
CFO expectations of next 12m earnings growth	0.7041 (5.40)	0.5903 (8.14)	0.5853 (8.41)	0.2799 (3.52)	0.2611 (3.20)	0.6278 (7.38)	0.4569 (5.74)
Q			0.0278 (0.37)				
Past 12m agg. stock returns				0.1975 (4.20)			
Past 12m credit spread change					−0.1035 (−3.82)		
Log(D/P)						0.2202 (2.68)	
Cay							−2.4272 (−2.27)
Past 12m asset growth		0.7021 (6.48)	0.6645 (3.53)	0.4473 (3.43)	0.8382 (11.72)	0.9458 (10.36)	0.7909 (8.32)
Observations	57	57	57	57	57	57	57
R-squared	0.380	0.610	0.611	0.748	0.719	0.721	0.655

Realized Investment Growth in the Next 12 Months

	(8)	(9)	(10)	(11)	(12)	(13)
CFO Expectations of next 12m earnings growth	0.5899 (8.43)	0.3727 (3.42)	0.3725 (6.22)	0.5563 (3.94)	0.5913 (6.57)	0.2168 (2.08)
Past 12m credit spread change						-0.0995 (-2.43)
Surplus consumption	-0.0097 (-0.06)					
Past 12m change of net income/asset		0.1779 (3.06)				0.0487 (0.88)
Past 12m agg. stock vol. change			-0.0362 (-3.15)			0.0405 (2.40)
Bloom policy uncertainty index (Past 12m change)			-0.0501 (-2.48)			-0.0154 (-1.12)
Past 12m GDP growth				2.8443 (1.68)		3.2147 (1.88)
Past 12m CAPX growth					0.0032 (0.02)	-0.2927 (-1.21)
Past 12m asset growth	0.7063 (7.22)	0.5112 (5.00)	0.7221 (9.00)	-0.0570 (-0.12)	0.6980 (2.40)	0.3239 (0.67)
Observations	57	57	57	57	57	57
R-squared	0.610	0.717	0.695	0.675	0.610	0.795

Note: This table presents aggregate quarterly regression $\Delta CAPX_t = \alpha + \beta E_t^i[\Delta \text{Earnings}] + \lambda X_t + \epsilon_t; E_t^i[\Delta \text{Earnings}]$ is aggregate CFO expectations of earnings growth in the next twelve months, and $\Delta CAPX_t$ is next 12-month growth in private nonresidential fixed investment. All control variables are the same as those in table 4. t-statistics in parentheses. Standard errors are Newey-West with 12 lags.

Table 7
CFO Earnings Growth Expectations and Realized Investment Growth: Firm-Level Evidence

	Realized Investment Growth in the Next 12 Months										
	(1)	(2)	(3)	(4)	(5)	(6)	(7)	(8)	(9)	(10)	(11)
CFO Expectations of next 12m earnings growth	0.5970 (5.13)	0.5930 (5.04)	0.5482 (3.94)	0.4069 (3.23)	0.3787 (3.08)	0.4118 (3.47)	0.6137 (4.99)	0.3243 (2.53)	0.5622 (4.61)	0.6043 (4.83)	0.3610 (2.53)
Q			0.1298 (1.88)								
Book-to-market				−0.5246 (−4.51)							
Past 12m firm stock returns					0.3047 (4.32)						
Past 12m credit spread change						−0.3801 (−4.62)					−0.1354 (−1.43)
Past 12m change of net income/asset							−0.0003 (−0.08)				0.0002 (0.05)
Past 12m firm stock vol. change								−0.4806 (−5.76)			−0.3511 (−3.24)

410

Bloom policy uncertainty index (Past 12m change)								−0.0844			0.0493
								(−0.96)			(0.54)
Past 12m GDP growth									2.4608		2.8272
									(1.22)		(1.35)
Past 12m CAPX growth										−0.2917	−0.3074
										(−4.68)	(−4.26)
Past 12m asset growth		0.3565	0.2850	0.1675	0.1914	0.3300	0.3371	0.1248	0.2582	0.6969	0.4428
		(1.83)	(1.36)	(0.78)	(1.00)	(1.69)	(1.69)	(0.65)	(1.36)	(4.59)	(2.48)
Observations	852	845	760	784	788	845	819	741	845	810	717
R-squared	0.043	0.054	0.063	0.086	0.103	0.125	0.057	0.175	0.060	0.152	0.271
Number of firms	193	193	172	176	180	193	189	170	193	187	166

Note: This table presents firm-level quarterly regression $\Delta CAPX_{i,t} = \alpha + \eta_t + \beta E^*_{i,t} [\Delta \text{Earnings}] + \lambda X_{i,t} + \epsilon_{i,t}; E^*_{i,t} [\Delta \text{Earnings}]$ is firm-level CFO expectations of earnings growth in the next 12 months, and $\Delta CAPX_{i,t}$ is firm-level actual capital expenditure growth in the next 12 months. All control variables are the same as those in table 5. A constant is included but not reported, and firm fixed effects are included. R-squared excludes firm fixed effects. t-statistics in parentheses. Standard errors are clustered by firm.

411

where i is a firm index, Δ Earnings$_i$ denotes realized earnings growth in the next 12 months, and $E_{i,q_t}^*[\Delta \text{ Earnings}_i]$ denotes expectations of next 12-month earnings growth reported in quarter q_t. The test can be augmented by including on the right-hand side a set of variables that are within time t information set.

Rational expectations postulate that $\alpha = 0$ and $\beta = 1$ (and a zero coefficient on any other variable in time t information set). Using both CFO and analyst expectations, we find β to be significantly lower than 1, and a list of variables known at time t enter significantly. This finding, however, does not necessarily mean that expectations are excessively volatile relative to outcomes. It could be that expectations are measured with error, which would cause a downward bias in β.

An alternative approach is to study the predictability of ex post expectational errors. If expectations are rational, forecast errors should be orthogonal to all information available at the time when the forecast is made, and forecast errors should be unpredictable. If, on the other hand, expectations are systematically biased, then ex post errors would be predictable using information available ex ante. In this case, the structure of error predictability could help us understand potential sources of excessive optimism and pessimism.

To take a first look, consider figure 4. Panel (A) shows errors in aggregate CFO expectations about next 12-month earnings growth against past year corporate profitability. Panel (B) shows the same series using analysts' expectations data.[21] The figures show a striking pattern: expectational errors appear to be systematic and recurring. In particular, they are consistent with the presence of excessive optimism in good times and excessive pessimism in bad times: future realized earnings growth systematically falls short of expectations when past earnings are high, and exceeds expectations when past earnings are low.[22]

To statistically corroborate the patterns in figure 4, we present regressions of expectational errors on past profitability. Column (1) of table 8, panel (A), reports the results using CFO data. Column (1) of table 9, panel (A), reports the results using analyst data. In both cases, high past-year profitability is correlated with over-optimism, while low past-year profitability is correlated with over-pessimism.[23] The magnitude of the bias is large. A one standard deviation increase in past profitability is associated with a 0.6 standard deviation increase in the magnitude of CFOs' expectational errors.[24] Figure 5 further illustrates these results with scatter plots of expectational errors against past profitability. It shows that the bias is present throughout the sample period, and not driven by a single outlier event.

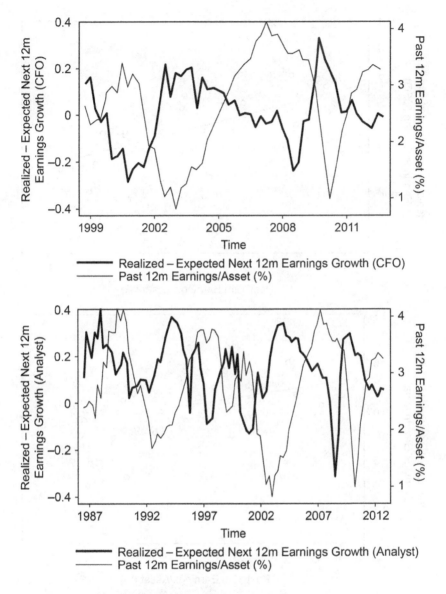

Fig. 4. Errors in earnings expectations and past profitability: Time series plots

Note: The plots above show aggregate errors in earnings expectations and past 12-month corporate profitability. In both panels, the thin line is aggregate earnings over assets in the past 12 months. In panel (A), the thick line is aggregate earnings growth in the next 12 months minus aggregate CFO expectations of earnings growth in the next 12 months. In panel (B), the thick line is aggregate earnings growth in the next 12 months minus aggregate analyst expectations of earnings growth in the next 12 months. Series are linearly detrended. Frequency is quarterly.

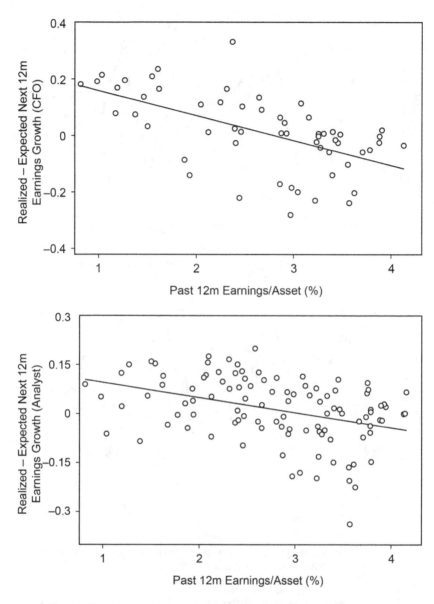

Fig. 5. Errors in earnings expectations and past profitability: Scatter plots

Note: Scatter plots of aggregate errors in earnings expectations against past 12-month corporate profitability. Variables are identical to those in figure 4. Frequency is quarterly.

Table 8

Predicting Errors in CFO Expectations

A. Aggregate Evidence

	Realized – CFO Expected Next 12m Earnings Growth					
	(1)	(2)	(3)	(4)	(5)	(6)
Past 12m earnings/ asset (%)	−0.0881 (−6.48)		−0.0915 (−8.85)		−0.0882 (−7.42)	
Past 12m GDP growth		−3.2999 (−3.06)		−3.6632 (−3.38)		−4.2078 (−3.30)
VIX			−0.2552 (−1.51)	−0.3288 (−1.46)		
Agg. stock index vol.					−0.0089 (−0.02)	−0.4101 (−1.52)
Observations	57	57	57	57	57	57
R-squared	0.335	0.225	0.361	0.266	0.335	0.269

B. Firm-Level Evidence

	Realized – CFO Expected Next 12m Earnings Growth					
	(1)	(2)	(3)	(4)	(5)	(6)
Past 12m firm earnings/asset (%)	−0.0511 (−5.14)		−0.0500 (−5.22)		−0.0324 (−3.40)	−0.0353 (−3.56)
Past 12m GDP growth		−4.1472 (−2.44)		−2.811 (−1.75)		
Firm stock vol.			0.3959 (1.74)	0.2229 (0.94)		0.5299 (1.13)
Firm fixed effects	Y	Y	Y	Y	Y	Y
Time fixed effects	No				Yes	
Observations	606	651	594	638	606	594
R-squared	0.082	0.032	0.103	0.033	0.037	0.050
Number of firms	142	147	139	144	142	139

Note: Quarterly regressions of errors in CFO expectations of next 12-months earnings growth on past profitability and past economic conditions. In panel (A), the dependent variable is aggregate earnings growth in the next 12 months minus aggregate CFO expectations of earnings growth in the next 12 months. Independent variables include aggregate earnings/asset and GDP growth in the four quarters prior to quarter $t − 1$. Controls include VIX by the end of quarter $t − 1$ and aggregate stock volatility as of quarter $t − 1$. In panel (B), the dependent variable is firm-level earnings growth in the next 12 months minus firm CFO expectations of earnings growth in the next 12 months. Independent variables include firm-level earnings/asset in the four quarters prior to quarter $t − 1$, and volatility of firm stock in quarter $t − 1$. A constant is included but not reported. In panel (A), standard errors are Newey-West with twelve lags. In panel (B), standard errors are clustered by firm. R-squared excludes firm and time fixed effects. t-statistics in parentheses.

Table 9
Predicting Errors in Analyst Expectations

A. Aggregate Evidence

	Realized – Analyst Expected Next 12m Earnings Growth					
	(1)	(2)	(3)	(4)	(5)	(6)
Past 12m earnings/ asset (%)	−0.0456 (−3.68)		−0.0550 (−6.16)		−0.0467 (−3.76)	
Past 12m GDP growth		−1.3940 (−1.70)		−1.1277 (−1.67)		−1.6171 (−1.64)
VIX			−0.2904 (−1.73)	−0.3260 (−2.52)		
Agg. stock index vol.					−0.0991 (−0.47)	−0.1116 (−0.51)
Observations	106	112	91	91	106	112
R-squared	0.144	0.057	0.245	0.078	0.150	0.062

B. Firm-Level Evidence

	Realized – Analyst Expected Next 12m Earnings Growth					
	(1)	(2)	(3)	(4)	(5)	(6)
Past 12m firm earnings/asset (%)	−0.0080 (−7.43)		−0.0081 (−7.36)		−0.0061 (−6.71)	−0.0062 (−6.63)
Past 12m GDP growth		−1.6167 (−3.83)		−1.6235 (−3.72)		
Firm stock vol.			0.0158 (0.26)	−0.0256 (−0.50)		−0.0123 (−0.40)
Firm fixed effects	Y	Y	Y	Y	Y	Y
Time fixed effects		No			Yes	
Observations	103,930	123,430	100,451	115,120	103,930	100,451
R-squared	0.005	0.004	0.006	0.004	0.003	0.003
Number of firms	4,432	5,080	4,227	4,606	4,432	4,227

Note: Quarterly regressions of errors in analyst expectations of next 12 months earnings growth on past profitability and past economic conditions. In panel (A), the dependent variable is aggregate earnings growth in the next 12 months minus aggregate analyst expectations of earnings growth in the next 12 months. In panel (B), the dependent variable is firm-level earnings growth in the next 12 months minus analyst expectations of earnings growth in the next 12 months. All control variables are the same as in table 8. A linear time trend is included. A constant is included but not reported. In panel (A), standard errors are Newey-West with 12 lags. In panel (B), standard errors are clustered by firm and time. R-squared excludes firm and time fixed effects. t-statistics in parentheses.

Column (2) in panel (A) of tables 8 and 9 correlate expectational errors with past GDP growth to check whether over-optimism and over-pessimism are predictable by aggregate economic performance. We also find higher past GDP growth is associated with over-optimism, and vice versa (although the statistical significance on past GDP growth is a bit lower).[25]

One way to interpret these results is that expectations depart from rationality in the direction of being extrapolative: when CFOs or analysts observe good or bad earnings realization, they think that similar realization persists into the future and fail to correct for mean reversion. To illustrate, we separately examine, and then compare, how actual future earnings growth and expected future earnings growth correlate with past year profitability. When past year earnings over assets increase by 1 percentage point, actual earnings growth in the next 12 months on average slows down by 0.12. However, CFOs only expect next 12-month earnings growth to slow down by about 0.03. The difference between the true and perceived reversion corresponds to the coefficient of −0.09 in panel (A), column (1).

We find very similar results at the firm level. In table 8, panel (B), we examine expectational errors of individual CFOs. We use past-year firm profitability and GDP growth as main predictors of expectational errors. Consistent with previous evidence at the aggregate level, expectational errors of individual CFOs are also strongly correlated with firm profitability and general economic conditions, in a way that appears to be extrapolative. At the firm level, as past-year earnings over assets increase by 1 percentage point, next 12-month earnings growth tends to slow down by 0.06, whereas CFOs only expect it to slow down by 0.01 on average. This results in a difference of −0.05, as shown by panel (B), column (1).

Note that profitability is likely to be heterogeneous across firms, and the normal level of earnings over assets can be quite different for established firms than for young firms, and for firms in different industries (this can be of particular concern when we turn to the analyst sample, which is much more heterogeneous than the CFO survey sample). To account for firm-specific average profitability, we include firm fixed effects. In the setting of error predictability regressions, strict exogeneity required by traditional fixed effect estimators may not be satisfied. Under the null of rational expectations, only sequential exogeneity will be satisfied. We perform robustness checks using dynamic panel estimators as in Arellano and Bover (1995),[26] and results are very similar. For standard errors in firm-level tests, we always cluster by firm and we double cluster by both firm and time whenever the length of the panel makes it appropriate to do so.

In columns (5) and (6) of table 8, panel (B), we report results adding time fixed effects, which helps us assess the extent to which expectational errors load on the idiosyncratic component of firm profitability. By teasing out aggregate shocks, time fixed effects may also attenuate issues in rational expectations tests when the panel is relatively short (this can be a concern with the CFO panel, which spans seven years and 28 quarters, and is less of a concern with the analyst panel, which covers 28 years and 112 quarters).[27] We find that CFOs seem to significantly extrapolate the idiosyncratic component of past profitability. Together, results in table 8 show that the extrapolative structure of CFO expectations appears pervasive. Past year economic conditions, and both the aggregate and the idiosyncratic component of firm profitability, are all correlated with CFOs' expectational errors.

In table 9, we perform the same set of tests as in table 8 using analyst expectations. The results are similar: analysts also tend to overestimate next 12-month earnings growth when past-year firm profitability is high and when past-year economic conditions are favorable, and underestimate future earnings growth when the past year is rough.

At first glance, the patterns in CFO and analyst expectations are quite consistent with extrapolative biases observed in financial markets. As shown by Greenwood and Shleifer (2014), many market participants—including both individual and institutional investors, as well as CFOs surveyed by Graham and Harvey—tend to extrapolate stock price trends formed in the past year. They generally think that the past year's trend would continue, whereas in reality it tends to revert. As explained in Section II and shown in figure 1, investors tend to become significantly more optimistic about stock market performance in the next 12 months when market returns in the past year are high, and vice versa (figure 1, panel [A]). Corporate CFOs are equally extrapolative in their expectations about next 12-month market returns (figure 1, panel [B]). Piazzesi, Salomao, and Schneider (2015) also find that bond market investors tend to perceive interest rate trends to be more persistent than they are. The extrapolative tendency in expectations formation resonates with the well-known representativeness bias in human judgment (Kahneman and Tversky 1972; Tversky and Kahneman 1974), which can lead people to view events similar to recent experiences as typical and likely, and to discount scenarios that are different from the prevailing situation (Gennaioli, Shleifer, and Vishny 2015).

While our evidence is consistent with extrapolation in earnings expectations, other factors may contribute to apparent deviations from rationality. In the following, we address a set of possible concerns.

Misinterpretation of Survey Question

First, we would like to make sure that the apparent errors in expectations do not simply reflect respondents misinterpreting the survey question. This could be a concern for CFO expectations, as CFOs are directly asked to provide forecasts of earnings growth in the next 12 months, and there could be alternative definitions of next 12-month earnings growth. This is not an issue, however, for analyst expectations, since analysts provide forecasts of total earnings in specific future quarters, and we compute the implied expected next 12-month earnings growth by combining their forecasts with actual past earnings; we then compare this variable to realizations to test forecast accuracy.[28]

To be specific, while the CFO survey asks about earnings growth in the next 12 months defined as the percentage change of earnings in the next 12 months relative to earnings in the past 12 months, respondents could instead provide expectations about earnings 12 months from now relative to current earnings. If this were true, when we compare survey responses to actual earnings growth in the next 12 months—which we follow the survey question to define as earnings in the next 12 months over earnings in the past 12 months—we might get spurious errors. For clarity of exposition, we denote next twelve month earnings growth defined by the survey as

Δ Earnings$_t$ = earnings in the next 12 months / earnings in the past 12 months.

We denote the alternative interpretation as Δ Earnings$_t^{alt}$ = earnings 12 months from now / current earnings, and we denote CFO responses as E_t^{CFO}.

We provide two checks to show that respondents do not appear to misinterpret the question. First, figure 2 shows that CFO responses and analyst expectations are quite consistent with each other when analyst expectations are computed following the survey definition of next 12-month earnings growth. However, if we instead compute analyst expectations of earnings four quarters from now relative to current earnings, the result looks much more different from CFO responses. Second and more importantly, if we compute actual earnings four quarters from now relative to current earnings (namely Δ Earnings^{alt}) and compare it to CFO responses, then CFOs would appear much less accurate in their forecasts. In particular, while aggregate CFO responses are 0.54 correlated with Δ Earnings$_t$, they are only 0.1 correlated with Δ Earnings$_t^{alt}$. In addition, if we construct expectational error as Δ Earnings$_t^{alt} - E_t^{CFO}$, this variable is still predictable by past 12-month profitability.[29] Across all robustness checks, we find actual CFO responses are closest to the survey's intended definition of next 12-month earnings growth, and by comparing CFO responses to Δ Earnings$_t$ we obtain the most conservative results with respect to deviations from rationality.

Asymmetric Loss Functions

A common concern with forecast data is that respondents might have asymmetric loss functions that cause them to report expectations that deviate from their objective views. For instance, analysts may want to please firm management and release upward-biased forecasts (Lim 2001). In the case of CFOs, reputational or other "publicity" considerations are unlikely to be at play, as individual responses in the CFO survey are never published. From this perspective, CFOs should not have much incentive to bias their responses for signaling purposes.

The main challenge for explanations with asymmetric loss functions is to account for the time-varying nature of expectational errors. Commonly used specifications of asymmetric loss functions (such as the LINEX function, and the Lin-Lin function under certain assumptions) generally yield optimal forecasts that are linear in objective expectations and conditional variance of the forecast variable. Given that conditional volatility of earnings tends to be higher in bad times, for asymmetric loss functions to generate more "pessimism" in bad times and more "optimism" in good times, overpredicting must be more costly than underpredicting. In this case, however, we would expect reported expectations to be consistently biased downward (with the magnitude increasing in the size of the conditional variance), which is not the case for either CFOs or analysts.[30]

While we do not find compelling reasons why asymmetric loss functions can drive our results, we nevertheless perform a set of robustness checks. In table 8 and table 9 we control for various proxies of volatility, including the VIX index and recent stock price volatility. We find that the volatility terms do not enter significantly, and our main results are unchanged. This evidence suggests that it is the level of past earnings that affects systematic forecast errors, whereas uncertainty plays a minor role.

Risk-Neutral Probability Weighting

Another possible concern is that CFOs might be reporting expectations not under physical probabilities, but under certain types of risk-neutral probabilities. Reporting expectations of future earnings growth is distinctively different from pricing, or calculation of expected returns of an asset. In the context of pricing, future cash flows may be discounted using a stochastic discount factor, or correspondingly, weighted by risk-neutral probabilities. In the context of forecasting future earnings growth, it is not plausible that any *discounting* is present and that there is an associated stochastic discount factor from optimizing theories.[31] It is possible that certain scenarios might be more salient in people's minds that lead to distorted probability weighting, but this explanation would fall into the category of cognitive biases and nonrational expectations (Bordalo, Gennaioli, and Shleifer 2012).

Conditional Expectations versus other Conditional Moments

Properties of rational expectations tests hold under the assumption that respondents provide conditional expectations of variables of interest. One concern could be that respondents might be reporting conditional medians, conditional modes, or other conditional moments instead of conditional expectations. For medians in particular, we can perform robustness checks with least absolute deviations regressions, which yield similar results to ordinary least squares (OLS). More generally, for this type of problem to affect our results, it has to be that following high past profitability the moment people report is greater than the conditional mean, and vice versa. We check the distribution of future-earnings growth conditioning on past profitability, and do not find any evidence that conditional medians and modes follow this pattern (appendix C, figure C1, plots the distribution of next 12-month earnings growth given a certain level of past profitability). Although we are not able to rule out the possibility that respondents report some other moments that happen to behave this way, it is not obvious what these moments could be and why respondents across different groups all prefer to use them. Certainly, more precise elicitation of expectations will be highly beneficial, as stressed by Manski (2004), but within available data, we do not find compelling evidence that the observed overoptimism and overpessimism could be explained by respondents reporting alternative conditional moments.

Information Rigidities and Rational Inattention

Finally, recent research points to other frictions that can affect expectations formation, including information rigidities (Mankiw and Reis 2002) and inattention (Sims 2003, 2010). While these frictions are important in many economic settings, they may not be natural explanations for the extrapolative errors in CFOs' and analysts' earnings expectations. Although managers and analysts may not pay full attention to information such as GDP growth or inflation, it is not quite plausible that past firm earnings are not in their information set, or that such information just slips their minds. After all, earnings are quite important for firms, as well as for management compensation. Similarly, analysts, who are designated to forecast future earnings and whose performance is judged in part by the accuracy of their forecasts, are also unlikely to be inattentive to earnings.[32]

In sum, our evidence points to systematic extrapolative biases in CFO and analyst expectations. While we cannot definitively rule out that some combinations of limited sample span, measurement error, and more complicated versions of informational frictions and loss functions could account for some these results, extrapolation stands out as the most parsimonious explanation. The findings also echo accumulating evidence in finance that extrapolation arises in many settings, and appears to be a common psychological tendency in expectations formation.

VII. Summary and Implications

Our analysis of data on earnings expectations and investment yields two basic conclusions. First, expectations data appear to be extremely helpful in understanding corporate investment plans and actual investment, more so than some traditional measures of determinants of investment. Second, several empirical tests appear to reject the rational expectations benchmark, pointing to the extrapolative nature of expectations.

At a minimum, the evidence endorses Manski's (2004) call for collecting and using expectations data to evaluate economic theories. Our project would not have been possible without John Graham and Campbell Harvey's CFO data. But as is often the case with a preliminary analysis and with limited data, there are many questions that we cannot address with the data we have.

Yet even our preliminary results suggest some directions for future work. The finding that expectations do so well in accounting for investment plans and actual investment suggests a possible strategy for reviving the q-theory of investment. It is well known that the standard q-theory investment equation does not work well in levels, and requires first differencing to have some explanatory power (Barro 1990). Our findings, along with earlier research by Cummins et al. (2006), suggest that the problem may be not with the q-theory itself, but with the stock market-based measures of Tobin's q. This is not entirely surprising in light of the growing evidence of noisiness and nonfundamental fluctuations of stock prices (Shiller 1981; Morck et al. 1990). A measure of investment opportunities based on actual expectations of corporate managers does much better in explaining investment, regardless of whether the equation is estimated in levels or in changes. A constructive way to revive q-theory is to start with data on expectations, and not on stock market valuations.

The second direction suggested by our evidence, as well as by the previous work, is the need to construct plausible models of expectations. In macroeconomics, in particular, such models have to come to grips with some version of the Lucas critique, which was applied initially precisely to Cagan's and other models of adaptive expectations. In our view, market participants might be backward looking and extrapolative to some extent, but surely they also have some ideas of how the economy evolves that are forward looking. Developing models along these lines is an open problem. Our own approach has been to use psychological models of expectations that incorporate both forward- and backward-looking elements (e.g., Bordalo, Gennaioli, and Shleifer 2013; Gennaioli et al. 2015), but this research is still some way from being ready for a macroeconomic model.

The larger question, of course, is whether expectations have a significant role to play in macroeconomic modeling. A recent literature in macroeconomics considers expectations "shocks," and discusses the extent to which they can contribute to economic fluctuations (Beaudry and Portier 2004; Angeletos and La'O 2010; Lorenzoni 2009; Barsky and

Sims 2012; Angeletos and La'O 2013; Levchenko and Pandalai-Nayar 2015). Our perspective is quite different; the evidence suggests that expectations have a fairly precise extrapolative structure, and do not just vibrate randomly. They are not noise; there is a systematic pattern of errors. Moreover, we believe—and our evidence seems supportive of this belief—that market participants make common expectational errors. Here we show that these errors are common to analysts and CFOs; we suspect the beliefs of policymakers are highly correlated with those of market participants. It seems to us that, as a consequence, plausible models would consider common errors among many economic agents, which therefore would have potential aggregate effects.

The final question is whether such errors can account for some part of macroeconomic fluctuations, such as aggregate overbuilding in important sectors like the housing market, or prolonged recessions with a lack of corporate investment and hiring. Our data have limitations for quantifying how the erroneous component of expectations affects investment, since the rational level of investment is not observable, but has to be inferred from making additional assumptions about the decision makers' environment and information, which requires extra discretion. It is a further step still that a common error translates into aggregate investment distortions. We leave this to future work.

Endnotes

We are deeply grateful to John Graham and Campbell Harvey for providing data from the CFO survey, and to Joy Tianjiao Tong for helping us to access the data. We thank our discussants Monika Piazzesi and Chris Sims, as well as Gary Chamberlain, Martin Eichenbaum, Carlo Favero, Robin Greenwood, Luigi Guiso, Sam Hanson, Chen Lian, Jonathan Parker, Fabiano Schivardi, Jim Stock, and Mirko Wiederholt for useful suggestions. We also thank Yang You for research assistance. For acknowledgments, sources of research support, and disclosure of the authors' material financial relationships, if any, please see http://www.nber.org/chapters/c13589.ack.

1. See the online appendix at http://www.nber.org/data-appendix/c13589/appendix.pdf.

2. Graham and Harvey (2011) provide a detailed description of the survey. Historical questionnaires are available at http://www.cfosurvey.org.

3. The number of observations in our firm-level regressions can be smaller because some respondents do not answer all questions.

4. We performed detailed checks and verified that IBES actual earnings indeed appear to be closest to forecasts by managers and analysts, in terms of accounting treatment, magnitude, variance, and variation over time.

5. The assumption of risk neutrality and constant discount rate is for simplicity of exposition. The framework can be extended to incorporate time-varying discount rates, as derived in Lettau and Ludvigson (2002). In our empirical analysis in Section IV.B and Section IV.C, we will explicitly consider time-varying discount rates.

6. See http://www.nber.org/data-appendix/c13589/appendix.pdf.

7. Plans are particularly helpful in the context of our data, where we observe forward-looking expectations once a quarter rather than once a year. With lags in investment implementation, it is unlikely that expectations in a given quarter will be immediately reflected in capital spending in the same quarter, or even fully incorporated into capital spending in the next quarter. In comparison, investment plans would be more responsive to contemporaneous expectations. When managers become more optimistic, they would revise their plans upward. As plans get implemented over time, the impact on actual capital expenditures can show up with some delay. For this reason, it is more straightforward to start testing the impact of expectations by looking at investment plans.

8. See http://www.nber.org/data-appendix/c13589/appendix.pdf.

9. One might also consider an alternative approximation of equation (1) of the following form $I_{t-1} / K_{t-1} \approx \theta_0 + \theta_1 \mathbb{E}_t (\Pi_t) / K_t$ where I_{t-1} denotes realized investment in the past 12 months, and $\mathbb{E}_t (\Pi_t)$, as before, is current expectations of earnings in the next 12 months. This approximation is reasonable under two conditions. As in the case of equation (2), it should be that expectations over future earnings are stable. Moreover, it has to be that respondents received little information and barely updated their beliefs in the past 12 months, so that current expectations about next-12-month earnings, namely $\mathbb{E}_t (\Pi_t)$, is close to expectations four quarters ago about earnings over the same period, namely $\mathbb{E}_{t-1} (\Pi_t)$. We find this approximation to be less tenable for several reasons. First, from time to time new information arrives over a 12-month period that has a significant impact on people's beliefs. (This can happen even if earnings processes are highly persistent, for example, if it is a random walk.) Second, given implementation lags in real-world investment activities, actual capital spending over a 12-month period tends to be particularly influenced by decisions made at the beginning of the period. As a result, realized capital spending in year $t - 1$, I_{t-1}, may not be well explained by expectations at the end of year $t - 1$. In light of these observations, we use the approximation in equation (2) in the rest of our analysis.

10. We check the autocorrelation structure of the errors: autocorrelations are mostly limited to the first four lags, due to the overlapping structure of our data; autocorrelations after four lags are minimal. Our empirical results are not sensitive to alternative choices of Newey-West lags.

11. At the aggregate level, during the period where we have CFO expectations data, the standard deviation of planned investment growth is about 0.05, and the standard deviation of earnings growth expectations is 0.07. 0.07 * 0.6 / 0.05 = 0.8.

12. Due to lags in investment implementation it is also possible that, at a given quarter, part of the capital spending that firms expect to make in the next 12 months are determined by decisions made, for example, in the last quarter, and therefore affected by expectations then. In aggregate data, we can include lagged expectations, in which case current expectations and past expectations with two lags are significant, and jointly highly significant. Unfortunately, it is difficult to include lagged expectations in firm-level tests, since we do not always observe individual firms continuously. Therefore, in the baseline specifications we include only current expectations.

13. We thank our discussant Chris Sims for the suggestion of a more careful examination of the role of expectational shocks, as well as the feedback among different variables, through VARs. To the extent that expectations experience a meaningful amount of exogenous shocks above and beyond reactions to observable information (so that what appear to be expectational shocks is not simply measurement error), studying expectational shocks may improve identification. It would also be ideal to have a longer time series (we currently only have 57 quarterly observations of CFO expectations and 112 quarterly observations of analyst expectations) to reliably estimate the dynamic relationships. In our first-step analysis, we study the impact of measured expectations as a whole to show the basic core facts. The investigation of expectational shocks is an interesting issue that we leave to future research.

14. As illustrated in Section IV, proxies of q are supposed to represent the q model precisely, whereas survey data can only represent it approximately. Thus it may not be surprising that q proxies remain significant in regressions that include survey expectations.

15. Our results also resonate with recent findings by Sharpe and Suarez (2014) and Kothari, Lewellen, and Warner (2014) that changes in discount rates and user cost of capital have limited impact on investment, and that corporations appear to apply constant hurdle rates in making investment decisions.

16. Stambaugh bias arises when predictor variables are relatively persistent, and innovations in predictor variables and outcome variables are correlated. In theory, investment should be high when discount rates are low. Thus we would expect a negative coefficient on discount rates. To the extent that innovations in investment and discount rates are negatively correlated, Stambaugh bias will be upward, pushing the coefficient on discount rates closer to or above zero.

17. The appendix can be found at http://www.nber.org/data-appendix/c13589/appendix.pdf.

18. Here we use past net income rather than pro forma earnings to be conservative, since the actual internal resources that firms gain from cash flows need to deduct most of the extraordinary items. Results using either form of profit metric to control for past cash flows are very similar.

19. To the extent that strict exogeneity may not be satisfied, fixed effect estimators may be biased in finite sample. In our context, it will bias the coefficient on earnings expectations downwards. Regressions without fixed effects and those using dynamic panel methods show that the bias does not appear to be very important. Given that we do not always continuously observe individual firms in the CFO sample, it is difficult to take first differences and use lagged instruments. Instead, for dynamic panel estimations we apply the forward orthogonal deviations (FOD) transformation as in Arellano and Bover (1995).

20. Figure 2 uses aggregate investment as measured by private nonresidential fixed investment from NIPA. We can alternatively use capital expenditures data from Flow of Funds or Compustat, and results are very similar.

21. The errors are computed as aggregate realized next-12-month earnings growth – aggregate CFO (analyst) expectations of next-12-month earnings growth. As we cannot identify the full set of firms that answer the CFO survey in each quarter, this sample may differ from the full sample with which we use to compute aggregate realized earnings growth. For robustness, to make sure that aggregate earnings growth patterns are representative, we alternatively compute aggregate earnings growth by taking the mean or median earnings growth in each quarter. We find this makes very little difference, and we get similar empirical results in all cases.

22. Note that earnings in quarter t are typically announced several weeks into quarter $t + 1$, thus we use earnings from quarter $t - 5$ through $t - 2$ to compute past-year profitability, so as to ensure that all information in the predictor variable is strictly in the information set of CFOs and analysts when they make forecasts in quarter t.

23. To address concerns that past-year profitability is relatively persistent (though it is much less persistent than variables like discount rate proxies), we present bootstrap bias-adjusted results in appendix C, table C7. We find very similar results. (The appendix is at http://www.nber.org/data-appendix/c13589/appendix.pdf.)

24. During the period where we have CFO expectations, the standard deviation of past-year earnings/asset is 0.88, and the standard deviation of expectational errors is 0.13. $0.88 * 0.09/0.13 = 0.6$.

25. To be conservative, past-12-month GDP growth also ends at quarter t-2 because GDP is reported with a lag.

26. The forward orthogonal deviations (FOD) transformation studied by Arellano and Bover (1995) is most helpful as our CFO panel contains gaps.

27. One possible concern is that time fixed effects may not completely tease out aggregate shocks if different firms are affected differently by an aggregate shock. For this to affect our results, it has to be that firms that happen to have a profitable past year are hit harder by an adverse aggregate shock, and vice versa. We do not find very compelling evidence for this concern.

28. In other words, in the case of analysts, we compute expected next-12-month earnings growth = analyst forecasts of earnings in the next 12 months/actual earnings in the past

12 months, and compare it to realized next-12-month earnings growth = actual earnings in the next 12 months/actual earnings in the past 12 months. We can alternatively normalize analyst forecasts of next-12-month earnings by current assets, and results are very similar.

29. Relatedly, to test the accuracy of earnings expectations, it is highly important that we use the same earnings measure as CFOs and analysts. As mentioned in Section III, we use pro forma actual earnings from IBES instead of GAAP earnings. The earnings measures we use are the ones CFOs report in earnings announcements and the ones analysts generally aim to match. In addition, we check that they are closest to CFO and analyst forecasts in terms of magnitude, variance, and variation over time. When compared to GAAP earnings, CFO and analyst expectations appear to be much less accurate, and error predictability remains.

30. One might also consider alternative scenarios where CFOs and analysts have time-varying loss functions. For this to explain our results, it has to be that people prefer to underpredict in bad times and to overpredict in good times. We do not find compelling reasons why it is optimal to follow this strategy.

31. In addition, to the extent that high earnings are associated with low SDF (i.e., in general, earnings are high in good states), earnings growth under risk-neutral probabilities (which is always a well-defined mathematical object, though its economic interpretation may be unclear) will be consistently lower than earnings growth under physical probabilities. We find no evidence that either CFOs or analysts appear to be persistently pessimistic.

32. We also test the extent to which expectational errors are predictable by the forecast itself or by past forecasts. We find that higher forecasts are associated with less-than-expected actuals, and vice versa. However, this result could be especially susceptible to the influence of measurement errors, as any random measurement error of the forecast would mechanically affect expectational errors. Thus we interpret it with extra caution.

References

Abarbanell, Jeffery S. 1991. "Do Analysts' Earnings Forecasts Incorporate Information in Prior Stock Price Changes?" *Journal of Accounting and Economics* 14:147–65.

Amromin, Gene, and Steven A. Sharpe. 2014. "From the Horse's Mouth: Economic Conditions and Investor Expectations of Risk and Return" *Management Science* 60 (4): 845–866.

Ang, Andrew, Geert Bekaert, and Min Wei. 2007. "Do Macro Variables, Asset Markets, or Surveys Forecast Inflation Better?" *Journal of Monetary Economics* 54 (4): 1163–212.

Angeletos, George-Marios, and Jennifer La'O. 2010. "Noisy Business Cycles." *NBER Macroeconomics Annual 2009*, vol. 24, ed. Daron Acemoglu, Kenneth Rogoff, and Michael Woodford, 319–78. Chicago: University of Chicago Press.

———. 2013. "Sentiments." *Econometrica* 81 (2): 739–79.

Arellano, Manuel, and Olympia Bover. 1995. "Another Look at the Instrumental Variable Estimation of Error-Components Models." *Journal of Econometrics* 68 (1): 29–51.

Arif, Salman, and Charles M.C. Lee. 2014. "Aggregate Investment and Investor Sentiment." *Review of Financial Studies* 27 (11): 3241–79.

Bacchetta, Philippe, Elmar Mertens, and Eric Van Wincoop. 2009. "Predictability in Financial Markets: What Do Survey Expectations Tell Us?" *Journal of International Money and Finance* 28 (3): 406–26.

Baker, Malcolm, Ryan Taliaferro, and Jeffrey Wurgler. 2006. "Predicting Returns with Managerial Decision Variables: Is There a Small-Sample Bias?" *Journal of Finance* 61 (4): 1711–30.

Baker, Scott R., Nicholas Bloom, and Steven J. Davis. 2015. "Measuring Economic Policy Uncertainty." NBER Working Paper no. 21633, Cambridge, MA.

Bansal, Ravi, Dana Kiku, Ivan Shaliastovich, and Amir Yaron. 2014. "Volatility, the Macroeconomy, and Asset Prices." *Journal of Finance* 69 (6): 2471–511.

Barro, Robert J. 1990. "The Stock Market and Investment." *Review of Financial Studies* 3 (1): 115–31.

Barsky, Robert B., and Eric R. Sims. 2012. "Information, Animal Spirits, and the Meaning of Innovations in Consumer Confidence." *American Economic Review* 102 (4): 1343–77.

Beaudry, Paul, and Franck Portier. 2004. "An Exploration into Pigou's Theory of Cycles." *Journal of Monetary Economics* 51 (6): 1183–216.

Ben-David, Itzhak, John R. Graham, and Campbell R. Harvey. 2013. "Managerial Miscalibration." *Quarterly Journal of Economics* 128 (4): 1547–84.

Bhattacharya, Nilabhra, Ervin L. Black, Theodore E. Christensen, and Chad R. Larson. 2003. "Assessing the Relative Informativeness and Permanence of Pro Forma Earnings and GAAP Operating Earnings." *Journal of Accounting and Economics* 36 (1): 285–319.

Bloom, Nicholas. 2009. "The Impact of Uncertainty Shocks." *Econometrica* 77 (3): 623–85.

Bloom, Nick, Stephen Bond, and John Van Reenen. 2007. "Uncertainty and Investment Dynamics." *Review of Economic Studies* 74 (2): 391–415.

Bordalo, Pedro, Nicola Gennaioli, and Andrei Shleifer. 2012. "Salience Theory of Choice under Risk." *Quarterly Journal of Economics* 127 (3): 1243–85.

———. 2013. "Salience and Asset Prices." *American Economic Review* 103 (3): 623–28.

Bradshaw, Mark T., and Richard G. Sloan. 2002. "GAAP versus the Street: An Empirical Assessment of Two Alternative Definitions of Earnings." *Journal of Accounting Research* 40 (1): 41–66.

Burnside, Craig, Martin Eichenbaum, and Sergio Rebelo. 2015. "Understanding Booms and Busts in Housing Markets." Working paper, Northwestern University. http://www.kellogg.northwestern.edu/faculty/rebelo/htm/Booms-busts.pdf.

Campbell, John Y., and John H. Cochrane. 1999. "By Force of Habit: A Consumption-Based Explanation of Aggregate Stock Market Behavior." *Journal of Political Economy* 107 (2): 205–51.

Campbell, John Y., and Robert J. Shiller. 1987. "Cointegration and Tests of Present Value Models." *Journal of Political Economy* 95 (5): 1062–88.

———. 1988. "Stock Prices, Earnings, and Expected Dividends." *Journal of Finance* 43 (3): 661–76.

Cochrane, John H. 1991. "Production-Based Asset Pricing and the Link between Stock Returns and Economic Fluctuations." *Journal of Finance* 46 (1): 209–37.

———. 2011. "Presidential Address: Discount Rates." *Journal of Finance* 66 (4): 1047–108.

Coibion, Olivier, and Yuriy Gorodnichenko. 2012. "What Can Survey Forecasts Tell Us about Information Rigidities?" *Journal of Political Economy* 120 (1): 116–59.

———. 2015. "Information Rigidity and the Expectations Formation Process: A Simple Framework and New Facts." *American Economic Review* 105 (8): 2644–78.

Cummins, Jason G., Kevin A. Hassett, and Stephen D. Oliner. 2006. "Investment

Behavior, Observable Expectations, and Internal Funds." *American Economic Review* 96 (3): 796–810.

Cutler, David M., James M. Poterba, and Lawrence H. Summers. 1990. "Speculative Dynamics and the Role of Feedback Traders." *American Economic Review* 80 (2): 63–68.

De Bondt, Werner, and Richard H. Thaler. 1990. "Do Security Analysts Overreact?" *American Economic Review* 80 (2): 52–57.

De Long, J. Bradford, Andrei Shleifer, Lawrence H. Summers, and Robert J. Waldmann. 1990. "Noise Trader Risk in Financial Markets." *Journal of Political Economy* 98 (4): 703–38.

Del Negro, Marco, and Stefano Eusepi. 2011. "Fitting Observed Inflation Expectations." *Journal of Economic Dynamics and Control* 35 (12): 2105–131.

Eisner, Robert. 1978. *Factors in Business Investment.* National Bureau of Economic Research.

Fazzari, Steven M., R. Glenn Hubbard, and Bruce C. Petersen. 1988. "Financing Constraints and Corporate Investment." *Brookings Papers on Economic Activity* 1988:141–206.

Figlewski, Stephen, and Paul Wachtel. 1981. "The Formation of Inflationary Expectations." *Review of Economics and Statistics* 63 (1): 1–10.

Fuhrer, Jeff. 2015. "Expectations as a Source of Macroeconomic Persistence: Evidence from Survey Expectations in Dynamic Macro Models." Working Paper no. 12-19, Federal Reserve Bank of Boston.

Fuster, Andreas, Benjamin Hebert, and David Laibson. 2012. "Natural Expectations, Macroeconomic Dynamics, and Asset Pricing." *NBER Macroeconomics Annual 2011*, vol. 26, ed. Daron Acemoglu and Michael Woodford, 1–48. Chicago: University of Chicago Press.

Gennaioli, Nicola, Andrei Shleifer, and Robert Vishny. 2015. "Neglected Risks: The Psychology of Financial Crises." *American Economic Review* 105 (5): 310–314.

Greenwood, Robin, and Samuel G. Hanson. 2015. "Waves in Ship Prices and Investment." *Quarterly Journal of Economics* 130 (1): 55–109.

Greenwood, Robin, and Andrei Shleifer. 2014. "Expectations of Returns and Expected Returns." *Review of Financial Studies* 27 (3): 714–46.

Graham, John R., and Campbell R. Harvey. 2011. "The Duke/CFO Business Outlook Survey." Duke CFO Global Business Outlook. http:www.cfosurvey.org.

Guiso, Luigi, and Giuseppe Parigi. 1999. "Investment and Demand Uncertainty." *Quarterly Journal of Economics* 144 (1): 185–227.

Guiso, Luigi, Luigi Pistaferri, and Raghu Suryanarayanan. 2006. "Investment Plans." Working Paper. Einaudi Institute for Economics and Finance.

Hayashi, Fumio. 1982. "Tobin's Marginal *q* and Average *q*: A Neoclassical Interpretation." *Econometrica* 50 (1): 213–24.

Hirshleifer, David, Jun Li, and Jianfeng Yu. 2015. "Asset Pricing in Production Economies with Extrapolative Expectations." *Journal of Monetary Economics* 76 (2015): 87–106.

Hribar, Paul, and John McInnis. 2012. "Investor Sentiment and Analysts' Earnings Forecast Errors." *Management Science* 58 (2): 293–307.

Kahneman, Daniel, and Amos Tversky. 1972. "Subjective Probability: Judgment of Representativeness." *Cognitive Psychology* 3:430–54.

Keane, Michael P., and David E. Runkle. 1990. "Testing the Rationality of Price Forecasts: New Evidence from Panel Data." *American Economic Review* 80 (4): 714–35.

———. 1998. "Are Financial Analysts' Forecasts of Corporate Profits Rational?" *Journal of Political Economy* 106 (4): 768–805.

Kothari, S. P., Jonathan Lewellen, and Jerold B. Warner. 2014. "The Behavior of Aggregate Corporate Investment." MIT Sloan Research Paper no. 5112-14, Sloan School of Management, Massachusetts Institute of Technology.

Lamont, Owen A. 2000. "Investment Plans and Stock Returns." *Journal of Finance* 55 (6): 2719–45.

La Porta, Rafael. 1996. "Expectations and the Cross-Section of Stock Returns." *Journal of Finance* 51 (5): 1715–42.

Leahy, John V., and Toni M. Whited. 1996. "The Effect of Uncertainty on Investment: Some Stylized Facts." *Journal of Money, Credit, and Banking* 28 (1): 64–83.

Lettau, Martin, and Sydney Ludvigson. 2001. "Consumption, Aggregate Wealth, and Expected Stock Returns." *Journal of Finance* 56 (3): 815–49.

———. 2002. "Time-Varying Risk Premia and the Cost of Capital: An Alternative Implication of the Q Theory of Investment." *Journal of Monetary Economics* 49 (1): 31–66.

Levchenko, Andrei A., and Nitya Pandalai-Nayar. 2015. "TFP, News, and 'Sentiments': The International Transmission of Business Cycles." NBER Working Paper no. 21010, Cambridge, MA.

Lim, Terence. 2001. "Rationality and Analysts' Forecast Bias." *Journal of Finance* 56 (1): 369–85.

Liu, Jing, and Wei Su. 2005. "Forecasting Analysts' Forecast Errors." Working paper, University of California, Los Angeles.

Lorenzoni, Guido. 2009. "A Theory of Demand Shocks." *American Economic Review* 99 (5): 2050–84.

Mankiw, N. Gregory, and Ricardo Reis. 2002. "Sticky Information versus Sticky Prices: A Proposal to Replace the New Keynesian Phillips Curve." *Quarterly Journal of Economics* 117 (4): 1295–328.

Manski, Charles F. 2004. "Measuring Expectations." *Econometrica* 72 (5): 1329–76.

Monti, Francesca. 2010. "Combining Judgment and Models." *Journal of Money, Credit and Banking* 42 (8): 1641–62.

Morck, Randall, Andrei Shleifer, Robert W. Vishny, Matthew Shapiro, and James M. Poterba. 1990. "The Stock Market and Investment: Is the Market a Sideshow?" *Brookings Papers on Economic Activity* 1990:157–215.

Muth, John F. 1961. "Rational Expectations and the Theory of Price Movements." *Econometrica* 29 (3): 315–35.

Philippon, Thomas. 2009. "The Bond Market's q." *Quarterly Journal of Economics* 124 (3): 1011–56.

Piazzesi, Monika, Juliana Salomao, and Martin Schneider. 2015. "Trend and Cycle in Bond Premia." Working paper, Stanford University. http://web.stanford .edu/~piazzesi/trendcycle.pdf.

Prescott, Edward. 1977. "Should Control Theory be Used for Economic Stabilization?" *Journal of Monetary Economics* 1977:13–38.

Sharpe, Steven A., and Gustavo A. Suarez. 2014. "The Insensitivity of Investment to Interest Rates: Evidence from a Survey of CFOs." FEDS Working Paper no 2014-02. Federal Reserve Board.

Shiller, Robert J. 1981. "Do Stock Prices Move Too Much to be Justified by Subsequent Changes in Dividends?" *American Economic Review* 71 (3): 421–36.

Sims, Christopher A. 2003. "Implications of Rational Inattention." *Journal of Monetary Economics* 50 (3): 665–90.

———. 2010. "Rational Inattention and Monetary Economics." *Handbook of Monetary Economics* 3:155–81.

Smets, Frank, Anders Warne, and Rafael Wouters. 2014. "Professional Forecasters and Real-Time Forecasting with a DSGE Model." *International Journal of Forecasting* 30 (4): 981–95.

Souleles, Nicholas S. 2004. "Expectations, Heterogeneous Forecast Errors, and Consumption: Micro Evidence from the Michigan Consumer Sentiment Surveys." *Journal of Money, Credit and Banking* 36 (1): 39–72.

Stambaugh, Robert F. 1999. "Predictive Regressions." *Journal of Financial Economics* 54 (3): 375–421.

Tversky, Amos, and Daniel Kahneman. 1974. "Judgment under Uncertainty: Heuristics and Biases." *Science* 185 (4157): 1124–31.

Universities-National Bureau Committee for Economic Research. 1960. *The Quality and Economic Significance of Anticipations Data*. Princeton, NJ: Princeton University Press.

Vissing-Jorgensen, Annette. 2004. "Perspectives on Behavioral Finance: Does 'Irrationality' Disappear with Wealth? Evidence from Expectations and Actions." *NBER Macroeconomics Annual 2003*, vol. 18, ed. Mark Gertler and Kenneth Rogoff, 139–208. Cambridge, MA: MIT Press.

Zarnowitz, Victor. 1985. "Rational Expectations and Macroeconomic Forecasts." *Journal of Business and Economic Statistics* 3 (4): 293–311.

Comment

Christopher A. Sims, Princeton University and NBER

Data sets that combine information on forecasts and actions by economic decision makers are rare, so this paper's analysis of such a data set is interesting. It supports well its conclusions that expectations of earnings growth are related to investment plans and to actual investment at the firm level, and that these relationships do not wash out when aggregated. This suggests, as the paper argues, that expectations, at least by executives in firms, could be a useful measure of aggregate disturbances in the economy and might be an important part of the transmission mechanism by which disturbances to the economy propagate.

Many empirical rational expectations models assume that expectations are not only rational, they are redundant, in the sense that the observable data used to fit the model can fully explain expectations, so that survey data on expectations contribute nothing to fitting the model. This paper would like to convince us that such models can be seriously deficient. To do so, it offers two kinds of evidence. One kind shows that survey data on expectations have predictive value for macroeconomic aggregates, and that their predictive value does not diminish as other macroeconomic variables are added to a predictive regression. The other kind shows that survey expectations are not rational, in the sense that the survey forecasts make systematic and predictable errors. Let's call these two properties of expectations that the paper would like to disprove "redundancy" and "rationality."

The paper recognizes that expectations can be redundant without being rational, and claims that it is most interested in showing us that expectations are not rational. Nonetheless in tables 6 and 7 we are shown that in the presence of 11 other possible variables, alone or in some combinations that might be used to predict investment, CFO expectations of earnings growth retain predictive power. But the coefficients on CFO expectations do change, by more than a factor of two, and by statistically significant amounts, as the other variables are introduced into the equation, and the other variables are in many cases highly statistically significant. The simple static baseline regression in these tables, with next year's investment dependent only on expectations of earnings growth and last period's growth in assets, is derived in the appendix from a simple static investment theory. But that theory has no room for the additional variables introduced in these tables, so the tables might be read as rejection of the theory—along with the fragile assumptions about terms that can be ignored in the derivation.

My own view of these two tables is that they are best read as first-pass assessments of the redundancy issue. If we leave aside the theory, we can read the tables as showing that there is predictive power for investment in the survey expectations data, and this predictive power does not go away in the presence of other variables that people have used in empirical investment models. But from that perspective, one would like to see a more ambitious analysis. The variables considered in these tables are all persistent and all clearly related to one another. These regressions are single equations from a one-lag quarterly VAR system that is never estimated, but ought to be the real focus of interest. Furthermore, with these quarterly data, that a one-lag VAR captures all the dynamics is quite implausible.

To address the rationality issue the paper gives us regressions of the difference between actual earnings growth over the next 12 months and the survey forecasts of earnings growth over the next 12 months on various types of information available at the time the forecasts were made. The regressions seem to show a pattern of extrapolative expectations—forecasts tend to be too high when past earnings growth was above normal. Calling these expectations "extrapolative" might give a misleading impression. As the paper points out, and as its appendix figure C1 shows, actual earnings growth is mean reverting, with actual growth higher when lagged growth was lower and vice versa. So the errors being made are not necessarily "high growth will continue" forecasts, but probably "high growth will decline" forecasts that underestimate the amount of the decline.

The evidence presented here is suggestive, but not completely convincing. The nonzero coefficients on lagged earnings in these regressions are indeed large in table 8, panels (A) and (B), and table 9, panel (A), but the coefficient is estimated, with high precision, to be more than five times smaller in table 9, panel (B). The R^2 of the regression also collapses in table 9, panel (B), to only .003. The t-statistics on the past earnings variable remain about the same in table 9, panel (B), but this is despite the number of observations having risen to on the order of 100,000 from on the order of 100. From table 9, panel (B) alone, one might conclude that there is very strong evidence that the analyst's forecasts at the firm level show negligible tendency to extrapolate. That the table 9, panel (B), results fail to aggregate to the panel (A) results suggests that for analysts, there is very little tendency to extrapolate from a firm's idiosyncratic recent past performance, but some tendency to do so from some measure of aggregate economic conditions not present in the regressions.

The paper discusses in section VI.A the possibility that the CFOs are not forecasting the same object that their forecasts are being compared to. That discussion makes it clear that they are not mostly forecasting month-over-month growth rather than year-over-year growth. But to create bias, it is not necessary that most of the CFOs are misinterpreting the forecast base, or even that all their misinterpretations are the same. There is also an issue about timing. The surveys are handed out with a return deadline early the last month of the quarter. The CFOs therefore cannot possibly know the earnings of the last month of the quarter, and very likely do not have precise current information about the previous month's earnings. If monthly earnings growth were i.i.d., as would be the case if earnings were a random walk with drift, the best forecast of them with no current information would simply be their mean. If CFOs were making their forecasts this way, using only data on the first 10 months of the last year, the best achievable R^2 in explaining their forecast errors (as those are defined in the paper's regressions) would be .167, and the coefficient on lagged earnings would be negative. To be sure, the R^2 in the aggregated CFO table 8, panel (A) are higher than this, and lagged 12-month earnings alone would not achieve the .167 R^2 in this simple example. Nonetheless, the simple example casts doubt on the strength of the evidence in these data for irrationality.

Comment

Monika Piazzesi, Stanford and NBER

Overview

Many empirical studies have documented that stock market proxies of Tobin's q do a poor job in explaining investment. The log-differenced investment equation says that investment growth rates should be explained by contemporaneous stock returns. In the data, however, regressions of investment growth rates on stock returns have low R^2s and the estimated slope coefficient often has a negative sign.

This paper measures q with expected earnings over the next year instead of stock values. The expectations are from quarterly survey data of earnings forecasts by company CFOs and stock analysts. The paper finds that regressions of planned as well as actual investment growth on these survey measures of expected earnings growth have high R^2s and the estimated slope coefficients have positive signs.

This fascinating new evidence on survey forecasts provides important further support to the idea that stock values may not be accurate measures of the value of installed capital. This idea motivated Abel and Blanchard (1986) to construct VAR forecasts of marginal profits from capital in aggregate data. Gilchrist and Himmelberg (1995) construct such VAR forecasts for individual firms. These studies find that VAR proxies of Tobin's q perform better than the more traditional measures based on stock values. Cummins, Hassett, and Oliner (2006) use survey forecasts by stock analysts instead of VAR forecasts and reach similar conclusions.

Interestingly, this paper shows that earnings expectations of CFOs and analysts are highly correlated. Moreover, the paper shows that these expectations are biased; the expectational errors made by these survey forecasts can be predicted with past variables such as lagged

GDP. The positive sign in these predictive regressions suggests that survey expectations are extrapolative: high past GDP numbers predict high errors in earnings expectations.

Below, I will discuss (a) the conventional view in finance about q theory with time-varying discount rates, (b) the recent challenge of this view by survey forecasts to which this paper adds important new facts, and (c) initial thoughts about a quantitative model with heterogeneous expectations that would be consistent with these new facts.

I think it will be crucial for the literature to take the next step and develop such a model. Existing models that feature the conventional view are quantitative and establish clean tensions with the data. To make progress, the finance literature needs to develop models that can compete on the same turf as the existing models. It helps that there is a growing number of surveys that collect microdata and also ask survey respondents to forecast certain variables. These survey data can be used to discipline the specification of beliefs in the new models.

Conventional Finance View

The conventional view in finance is that the high volatility in asset values is driven by time-varying discount rates (e.g., Cochrane's AFA presidential address [2011]). The argument starts from the definition of the return on an asset. The return is defined as the ratio of the payoff tomorrow—which consists of the dividend D_{t+1} and the resale value of the asset P_{t+1}—divided by its current value P_t:

$$R_{t+1} = \frac{P_{t+1} + D_{t+1}}{P_t} = \frac{(P_{t+1} / D_{t+1} + 1)D_{t+1} / D_t}{P_t / D_t} = \frac{(v_{t+1} + 1)g_{t+1}}{v_t}, \quad (1)$$

where v_t is the price-dividend ratio and g_{t+1} is the (gross) growth rate of dividends.

In a large variety of asset markets, we observe that price-dividend ratios v_t are highly persistent but mean reverting: when the value of assets is high relative to their fundamentals, these values are likely to subsequently decline over time, so high v_t predicts low v_{t+1}. The growth rate g_{t+1} of dividends is close to unpredictable. A regression of returns on lagged price-dividend ratios

$$R_{t+1} = \alpha + \beta v_t + \varepsilon_{t+1}$$

recovers the mean-reversion in v_t. The estimated slope coefficient is negative, $\hat{\beta} < 0$, so high asset values relative to fundamentals predict low returns. The conclusion from these regressions is that discount rates vary over time, while expected cash flow growth is roughly constant.

Riskless real rates are roughly constant over time as well. The time variation in discount rates thus has to come from changes in required risk compensation. Any successful mechanism to generate such time variation needs to argue that investors require low compensation for risk in good times. The low discount rates drive up asset values v_t relative to fundamentals. In bad times, investors want to be highly rewarded for holding risky assets, so discount rates are high and asset values v_t are low relative to fundamentals.

By now, we have a variety of models that derive such a mechanism from ambiguity aversion, time-varying aggregate volatility, incomplete markets with time-varying idiosyncratic volatility, habit formation, and other forms of nonseparable utility (for example, with housing). There is an active literature that studies the quantitative predictions of these models and compares them with the data.

When we place q theory in an environment with time-varying discount rates, firms will choose to invest more when discount rates are low. Since low discount rates lead to high stock values relative to fundamentals, q theory predicts investment growth rates to be high when stock returns are high. This is the linear relationship that is tested in regressions of investment growth on contemporaneous stock returns.

Recent Survey Evidence on Return Forecasts

Recent work has studied survey evidence on discount rates from various asset markets. In joint work with Juliana Salomao and Martin Schneider (Piazzesi, Salomao, and Schneider 2015), we studied survey data on interest-rate forecasts. The log returns of bonds do not involve dividends D_t and so equation (1) boils down to changes in log prices:

$$\log R_{t+1} = \log P_{t+1} - \log P_t.$$

The log price is equal to (minus) the interest rate of the bond multiplied by its maturity. For example, for an n-period bond, we have

$$\log P_t = -n i_t^{(n)}.$$

To forecast the log price in $t + 1$, we thus need a measure of interest rate forecasts.

We decompose expected returns as follows. We write the expected value of the log return measured from the predictive regression as an expectational difference—the difference between the OLS predicted log price and a subjective expectation of the log price—plus the subjective expectation of the log return. The subjective expectation is indicated with a star *:

$$E_t(\log R_{t+1}) = E_t(\log P_{t+1}) - E_t^*(\log P_{t+1}) + E_t^*(\log R_{t+1}). \qquad (2)$$

We measure subjective interest-rate forecasts for many maturities using the Bluechip survey. To forecast the log price of a bond with current maturity $n + 1$, we use survey forecasts of the n-period interest rate

$$E_t^*(\log P_{t+1}) = E_t^*(-ni_{t+1}^{(n)}).$$

We measure expected returns on bonds $E_t(\log R_{t+1})$ with predictive regressions on lagged interest rates, following Cochrane and Piazzesi (2005).

Figure 1 shows the left-hand side $E_t(\log R_{t+1})$ of equation (2) as a solid line together with the first term on the right-hand side, the expectational difference $E_t(\log P_{t+1}) - E_t^*(\log P_{t+1})$ as a dashed line. The units are percent returns per year. The figure uses the 11-year bond, so that we are forecasting the 10-year rate $i_{t+1}^{(10)}$ one year from now. The gray bars in figure 1 are NBER recessions.

Two patterns are clear from a look at figure 1. First, predictive regressions recover expected returns on bonds that are strongly countercyclical. The fluctuations are big; the solid line OLS fitted values range from 15% expected bond returns per year to −7% per year. This pattern in OLS-expected returns is well known (see, for example, figure 6 in Cochrane and Piazzesi [2005]). It is precisely the kind of empirical pattern behind the conventional view in finance.

Second, the dashed line forecast differences share the cyclical fluctuations in the solid line OLS-fitted values and are almost comparable in magnitude. This means that subjective expectations of bond returns, $E_t^*(\log R_{t+1})$ on the right-hand side of equation (2), are not as cyclical as OLS-fitted values of return predictions. If survey forecasts provide a measure of expectations, these patterns suggest that discount rates may not fluctuate as much as predictive regressions document. Instead, asset values may be volatile because beliefs systematically differ from these OLS regressions; the difference is cyclical.

Figure 1 is based on Bluechip surveys that started in the mid-1980s. In our paper, we go beyond this short sample using data from previous surveys. Based on these data, we estimate subjective expectations of bond returns during the entire postwar sample. The message from the

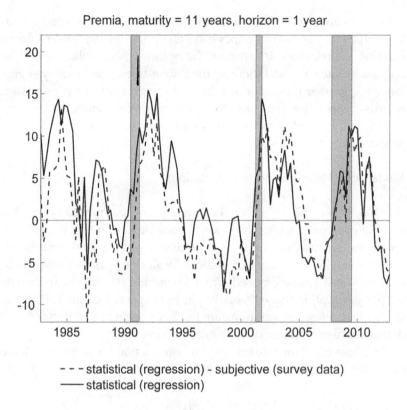

Premia, maturity = 11 years, horizon = 1 year

- - - statistical (regression) - subjective (survey data)
―― statistical (regression)

Fig. 1.

longer sample is that subjective expected returns are not flat, as it may appear from figure 1. The movements in subjective risk compensations are still not cyclical; they move at lower frequencies. Interestingly, subjective expectations of bond returns were particularly high in the late 1970s and early 1980s.

This evidence suggests that quantitative models may not need to generate much cyclical movements in risk compensation or discount rates. The one episode in which subjective bond premia were high was the time during and after the Great Inflation. This suggests that models of bond values need to take a stand on inflation expectations and compensation for inflation risk during a unique episode: a new Fed chairman, Paul Volcker, came into office and was trying hard to get inflation down.

I look at this evidence and conclude that we need more theoretical work about belief formation. This work can be guided as well as disciplined by the survey data. The discipline will be useful to avoid the famous "wilderness" of such models that Chris Sims warned about. The empirical work in this paper takes an important step toward documenting the relationship between the optimal choices that should be implied by such a model (here, optimal investment) and survey expectations. The poor regression results from investment growth on stock returns suggest that the subjective expectations of managers may not be reflected in stock returns. This should further guide the modeling, an issue that I turn to next.

Model with Heterogeneous Expectations

How could we specify a model of investment that would be quantitatively consistent with the evidence documented in this paper? The paper documents that survey expectations by managers—firm insiders—are similar to survey expectations by stock analysts—outsiders to the firm—and both are biased. Thus, I want to first proceed under the simple assumption that q theory holds, but expectations are subjective. In this first setup, expectations are not heterogeneous. The star * will denote these common subjective expectations.

Firms use constant-returns-to-scale production functions and have quadratic adjustment costs. They pay dividends

$$D(K_t, I_t) = A_t K_t^\alpha L(K_t)^{1-\alpha} - w_t L(K_t) - p_t I_t - \frac{a}{2}\left(\frac{I_t}{K_t}\right)^2 K_t$$

where K_t is capital, I_t is investment, $L(K_t)$ is optimal labor demand, w_t is the wage, p_t is the price of investment goods and $a > 0$ is an adjustment cost parameter. The technology A_t is affected by shocks

$$\log A_{t+1} = \rho \log A_t + \varepsilon_{t+1}.$$

Managers of this firm maximize shareholder value. For simplicity, suppose that shareholders are risk neutral. The problem of the managers is to invest

$$\max_{\{I_{t+s}\}} E_t^* \left[\sum_{s>0} \beta^s D(K_{t+s}, I_{t+s})\right]$$

$$\text{s.t.} \quad K_t = (1-\delta)K_{t-1} + I_t$$

$$K_0 \text{ given.}$$

The setup implies the classic equation for optimal investment

$$\frac{I_t}{K_t} = \frac{1}{a}(q_t - p_t)$$

where q_t is the shadow price of installed capital. It involves the following expectation of the present value of future marginal profits

$$q_t = E_t^* \left[\sum_{s>0} (1 - \delta)^{s-1} \beta^s D_K(K_{t+s}, I_{t+s}) \right].$$

Here, managers and shareholders agree; they have the same expectation E^*. In this case, it is fine to measure q_t with stock values. The setup predicts that the regression of investment growth on stock returns works well. This setup with common subjective expectations is thus not consistent with the empirical evidence presented in this paper that stock returns do not explain investment.

The paper documents, however, that the correlation between managerial forecasts and forecasts by stock analysts is not perfect. Thus, there is room for differences in opinion between managers and stock holders. Suppose next that E^* is the subjective expectation by managers, while shareholders have a different expectation E^{**}. There are surveys on both, so we can discipline both E^* and E^{**}. Again, the evidence suggests that both are biased.

How would managers in this model make decisions? Would they maximize shareholder values computed with E^{**}? In this case, we are back to square one. The model again implies an equation that relates investment growth rates to stock returns.

Instead, suppose managers compute their own expected future profits with E^*. In this case, the model predicts that regressions of investment growth on stock returns do not work, because stock values reflect expectations by outside investors E^{**}. However, the model does predict that investment growth should be related to managers' earnings growth forecasts. The data confirm this implication. This setup would predict that expected earnings growth by stock holders should not explain investment growth, or not as well. The findings in the paper confirm this prediction.

In my mind, the key question is whether we can write down a model that makes quantitative sense of both regressions of investment growth on (a) stock returns and (b) analyst forecasts of earnings growth. The first regression should be a disaster with a negative coefficient, while the second regression should work okay (but not as well as managerial forecasts).

In my own work, I found that a tractable way to set up a model with heterogeneous expectations is to apply the temporary equilibrium concept by Grandmont (1982). It allows the researcher to compute optimal decisions based on some beliefs about the future and then to solve for time-t market-clearing prices. With this approach, beliefs can directly be specified to be consistent with data.

An application of this approach is my paper with Martin Schneider (Piazzesi and Schneider 2013) where we study bond, stock, and house valuations during the Great Inflation. During that episode, household inflation forecasts differed across generations in the Michigan Survey. In particular, older households had lower inflation forecasts than younger households. We use these survey data to discipline the beliefs of different generations in an OLG model and study its quantitative implications for asset valuation and household portfolios.

Endnote

Thanks to Sean Myers, Jonathan Parker, and Martin Schneider for helpful discussions. For acknowledgments, sources of research support, and disclosure of the author's material financial relationships, if any, please see http://www.nber.org/chapters/c13591.ack.

References

Abel, Andrew. B., and Olivier J. Blanchard. 1986. "The Present Value of Profits and Cyclical Movements in Investment." *Econometrica* 54:249–73.

Cochrane, John. 2011."Presidential Address: Discount Rates." *Journal of Finance* LXVI (4): 1047–108.

Cochrane, John, and Monika Piazzesi. 2005. "Bond Risk Premia." *American Economic Review* 94 (1): 138–60.

Cummins, Jason G., Kevin A. Hassett, and Stephen D. Oliner. 2006. "Investment Behavior, Observable Expectations, and Internal Funds." *American Economic Review* 96 (3): 796–810.

Gilchrist, S., and C. P. Himmelberg. 1995. "Evidence on the Role of Cash Flow for Investment." *Journal of Monetary Economics* 36:541–72.

Grandmont, Jean-Michel. 1982. "Temporary General Equilibrium Theory." In *Handbook of Mathematical Economics*, ed. K. J. Arrow and M. D. Intriligator, chapter 19. Amsterdam: North-Holland.

Piazzesi, Monika, Juliana Salomao, and Martin Schneider. 2015. "Trend and Cycle in Bond Premia." Working paper, Stanford University.

Piazzesi, Monika, and Martin Schneider. 2013. "Inflation and the Price of Real Assets." Working paper, Stanford University.

Discussion

Yueran Ma began by responding to a number of points made by the discussants. One issue that was raised was the extent of serial correlation in the data. Ma noted that their data is constructed from yearly forecasts and that there was overlap between consecutive forecasts. The authors have used different Newey-West lag lengths in their regressions and found the results were robust to the choice of the number of lags. Next, Ma mentioned an issue from the discussion by Christopher Sims regarding the distinction between expectations and "expectational shocks," which the authors define as the unpredictable component of their survey expectations. The authors chose to focus on survey expectations as a whole, rather than the unpredictable component. Related to this choice, Ma and her coauthors used basic regressions rather than a VAR structure, in part because they have only 60 quarters of survey data. The authors agreed that studying expectational shocks would be useful in future work.

Ma also addressed the issue of the authors' choice of earnings measure. The authors focused on pro forma earnings, in part because they are typically the focus of earnings announcements for CFOs. The authors also reported that, if they used a GAAP earnings measure instead of pro forma earnings, the CFO forecasts appeared to be of lower quality. The authors also tried a variety of alternative specifications, including using median or modal forecasts instead of means and using least-absolute-deviation regressions, all of which yielded similar results. They also found that the level of the forecast predicted forecast errors; however, this would be expected when either the forecast or the outcome is measured with noise. Their results were robust to including additional terms, such as lagged forecasts, but those results were only available at the aggregate (rather than firm) level because the CFOs do not necessarily participate in the survey every quarter.

Finally, Ma responded to some of the points made by Monika Piazzesi in her discussion. Ma and her coauthors agree that their findings are related to a paper by Piazzesi and coauthors (Piazzesi et al. 2013), which documents time variation in forecasts of bond returns. In particular, both sets of authors find that expectations are more persistent over time than known predictors of returns. Piazzesi, in her discussion, mentioned the tension between the authors' finding of extrapolative expectations and firms' ability to time the market. Ma responded by mentioning how mechanical rules might lead to this result and mentioned a finding by Robert Shiller that individuals can simultaneously think that the stock market is overvalued and that it is going to keep rising in value. Ma and coauthors find some suggestive evidence that CFOs hold similar beliefs.

Harald Uhlig spoke next, recalling a conversation he once had with V. V. Chari about investing in the stock market. Chari had complained to Uhlig that he was always losing money and told Uhlig, "My advice to you is to do the exact opposite of what I'm doing. That way, you would make money." Uhlig recalled this advice in the context of the present paper, in which the authors find that CFOs make systematic, predictable errors. Uhlig suggested that, in theory, one could start a consulting firm that asked these CFOs what their plans were and then suggest altering them based on these predictable errors. Uhlig noted that the authors' results suggest this hypothetical consulting firm would help its clients and asked the authors to measure the extra profits the CFOs' firms could make if they didn't have these biases. Uhlig also suggested an alternative interpretation, in which the CFOs' stated expectations cannot be treated as the CFOs' actual expectations but are useful for predicting investment and related quantities. Andrei Shleifer responded by acknowledging that he and his coauthors are unable to estimate the cost of these errors, given their data. He speculated that a more fully developed structural model might be able to answer this question.

Andrew Atkeson spoke next, addressing a question to one of the discussants, Monika Piazzesi. Atkeson summarized a chart Piazzesi presented as showing stable survey expectations of bond returns and volatile statistical estimates of expected bond returns, with expected returns in the statistical model ranging from −10% to +10%. Atkeson argued that, if expected returns moved as much as the statistical model implies,

investment would also be very volatile. Firms, responding to these expected returns, would go through periods in which they slashed investment and periods in which they "go crazy." Atkeson stated that we do
not observe this kind of behavior and suggested that this might indicate
a problem with the statistical model rather than a problem with survey
expectations. If the statistical model happened to work well in-sample
but was overfitted, we would expect the results that Piazzesi documents.

Atkeson also addressed a question to the authors, regarding the time
horizon for CFOs. He used the example of Tesla Motors and argued that
Tesla would make investment plans over a five- or ten-year horizon. If
CFOs were focused on long-term trends, such as whether Tesla could
ever sell as many cars as Volvo, and short-term earnings contained a lot
of noise around these trends, that would rationalize the sort of forecast
errors the authors find. Atkeson asked the authors about the horizon
their CFO survey respondents were using and whether they thought
this type of explanation could make sense of their results.

Andrei Shleifer responded by arguing that growth rates in earnings
are correlated at one-year horizons but not at four- or five-year horizons. Andrew Atkeson disagreed, arguing that there are fast-growing
firms and slow-growing firms, which occasionally switch type. Shleifer
agreed that some firms will exhibit growth dynamics that are different from what their basic model assumes but argued that the authors'
model captures the essential features of the data.

Monika Piazzesi spoke next, agreeing with the points raised by Andrew Atkeson. Piazzesi noted that there is a large literature on the predictability of returns, which she has participated in, and acknowledged
that data mining is a possibility and that papers might find predictability that does not exist. Piazzesi expressed her sympathy with these
concerns while reiterating the point that there is a very large difference between these statistical models and survey data. The survey data
generally exhibit stable risk premia and predict large risk premia only
during the great inflation. Piazzesi pointed out that, under these beliefs,
standard preferences can be consistent with observed asset prices.

Xavier Gabaix praised the authors' use of expectations data and suggested that the authors attempt to "document the expectation formation
function." Gabaix suggested that expectations can be thought of as the
sum of a rational component and an excessively extrapolative component, and then he asked the authors to determine whether investment
responds mostly to the rational component of expectations, the extrapolative component, or expectations as a whole.

Andrei Shleifer replied, claiming that the decomposition Gabaix asked for requires many additional assumptions. In the context of a firm, it is not clear whose expectations—those of CFOs, other managers, board members, shareholders, or activist investors—will actually determine investment. Firms often act as arbitrageurs in their own securities, as documented in Yueran Ma's senior thesis. Additionally, some agents appear to extrapolate past returns rather than past cash flows growth or some other "fundamental." Understanding which combination of these beliefs ultimately determines investment is a challenging problem.

Daron Acemoglu spoke next, making two points. Acemoglu agreed with Andrei Shleifer's point that investment behavior will depend on both the firm manager's beliefs and on market participants' beliefs and argued that there will be some learning, on the part of the market, about the manager's beliefs as a result of her investment decisions. Moreover, the market participants beliefs may constrain the manager, because of the manager's need to finance new investment projects.

Acemoglu also agreed with some of the points made by Harald Uhlig, concerning the treatment of survey expectations as a proxy for actual expectations. Acemoglu cited the work of Nathan Hendren (Hendren 2013) as, in the context of insurance, treating survey expectations as a variable that is not equal to subjective beliefs but has explanatory power above and beyond other observables in predicting those beliefs. Acemoglu pointed out that, in this context, Hendren was able to derive nonparametric restrictions about behavior given prices, conditional on survey beliefs. Acemoglu suggested that the authors might be able to pursue a similar approach in their data.

Andrei Shleifer responding by agreeing that the approach suggested by Acemoglu would be reasonable. However, Shleifer pointed out that the CFOs are being asked about a number that is central to their compensation, job performance, and career concerns. Shleifer agreed that issues regarding whose expectations matter are important but argued that the most sensible way to treat these CFOs forecasts is as their sincere report of their actual beliefs. Acemoglu pointed out that CFOs might be most concerned about some nonlinear function of this growth rate. Shleifer and coauthors responded by noting that they had tried a variety of specifications and found no support for the idea that the CFOs were reporting some other moment of their expectations. Christopher Sims suggested that CFOs might have a "loss function" associated with their expectations that causes them to give biased survey answers. Sims recalled doing a consulting project for the CDC and being told that his forecast of a particular division's revenue growth was useless because his growth forecast was lower than the corporate plan called for. Sims argued that some CFOs might feel obligated to report the corporate plan rather than their actual expectations. Shleifer replied by noting that the CFOs are assured anonymity but agreed that this problem might apply to stock analysts.

Robert Hall raised a more general concern along the lines of what Christopher Sims had suggested, about whether the statistic the CFO survey respondents are forecasting is the same one the authors are using to check their forecasts against. Yueran Ma stated that the question the CFOs are asked is, "Relative to the past 12 months, what is the percentage change over earnings in the next 12 months?" Hall pointed out that there are many ways of describing and measuring earnings growth and asked if the CFOs had really had understood the exact question being asked—the "fine print." Andrei Shleifer objected, arguing that there isn't really any "fine print," and noting that, for a misunderstanding to explain their results, the misunderstanding would have to be correlated with past earnings growth so as to generate the extrapolation that the authors find. Yueran Ma also noted that the results are robust to various transformations and also highly correlated with analysts' forecasts. The authors essentially "do the algebra for the analysts" when they convert the quarterly forecasts into their measure; therefore, this measure is unlikely to be affected by misunderstandings.

Jonathan Parker agreed with the authors' premise that expectations data are informative and worth studying. He noted that the authors take the view that probabilities are observed, but utility is not. Parker pointed out that there is a large literature attempting to measure happiness and well-being, sometimes by using surveys. He then argued that if economists are willing to use surveys to elicit individuals' beliefs, they should also be willing to use surveys to elicit their preferences. Next, he characterized the rational expectations assumption as useful because it determines how expectations change when regimes or policies change. In other words, it allows economists to make forecasts "out of sample." Parker argued that, within sample, it is not necessary to distinguish between beliefs and preferences. Out of sample, this distinction is necessary. Finally, Parker noted that if the CFOs were responding with risk-adjusted beliefs, the authors would be confounding bias expectations with risk premia. Parker stated that there is some evidence in the psychology literature that people do focus on tail events, and in particular worry a lot about these events when prompted to think about them.

Andrei Shleifer responded by arguing that, in some cases, individuals neglect the risk of tail events and don't think about them unless prompted. He argued that there is no unambiguous mapping between the probability of an event and an individual's assessment of that event's probability. In response to Parker's points about measuring happiness, Shleifer reiterated that he felt the CFO's forecasts had a straightforward interpretation, whereas happiness assessments are a lot more complicated. Individuals report significant changes in lifetime happiness in response to small payments and in response to very recent events.

To conclude, Andrei Shleifer reemphasized the importance of considering whose beliefs matter, and how those beliefs are mediated by markets, for the purpose of understanding corporate decision making. He argued that corporations are easier to study than individuals because their goal is to maximize profits, not utility.

6

Declining Desire to Work and Downward Trends in Unemployment and Participation

Regis Barnichon, *CREI, Universitat Pompeu Fabra, and CEPR*
Andrew Figura, *Federal Reserve Board*

I. Introduction

The US labor market has witnessed two remarkable secular trends in the last 30 years. First, the unemployment rate declined secularly after the early 1980s, prompting policymakers to adjust downward their estimate of the natural rate or NAIRU (Non-Accelerating Inflation Rate of Unemployment), as shown in figure 1. Second, a decline in labor force participation has brought down the participation rate to a level not seen in 30 years (figure 2).

However, considerable uncertainty remains about the underlying reasons for these trends. While the aging of the baby boom generation has often been cited as a possible factor,[1] it is not clear that demographics alone are responsible for these trends. This uncertainty is best illustrated with the recent lively debate about the "cyclical" or "structural" nature (i.e., persistence) of the low participation rate observed today.[2]

This paper argues that a key, but so far little studied, aspect of the secular changes witnessed by the US labor market is the presence of time-varying heterogeneity across nonparticipants (individuals outside the labor force), that is, changes in the composition of the nonparticipation pool. We document a strong decline in desire to work among nonparticipants in the second half of the 1990s, and we show that that decline is a major aspect of the downward trends in unemployment and participation over the past 20 years.

The Current Population Survey (CPS) has been measuring individuals' desire for work consistently since 1967, allowing us to construct a measure of nonemployed individuals' desire to work from 1967 to 2014. We find that the share of nonparticipants who want to work has been

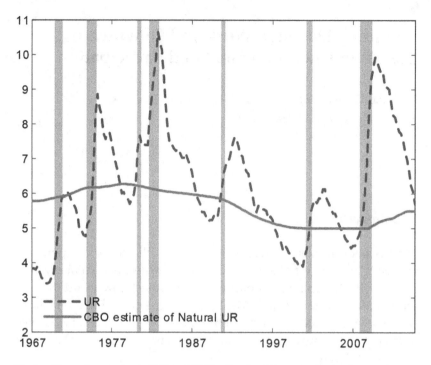

Fig. 1. Unemployment rate (UR) and CBO estimate of the natural rate of unemployment, 1967–2014.

declining secularly over the past 30 years, with a particularly strong decline during the second half of the 1990s.

A downward trend in the share of nonparticipants who want a job has consequences for the aggregate unemployment and participation rates, because people who want a job behave differently from people who do not want a job. Using matched CPS microdata to measure worker transitions between labor market states, we find that a nonparticipant who wants a job enters the labor force (a) often and (b) mostly through unemployment, while a nonparticipant who does not want a job enters the labor force (a) rarely and (b) mostly through employment. Because of this difference in behavior, a decline in the fraction of nonparticipants who want a job lowers *both* the unemployment rate and the participation rate. We develop a stock-flow accounting framework to quantify this effect, and we find that the decline in nonparticipants' desire to work since the mid-1990s lowered the unemployment rate by about 0.5 percentage point (ppt) and the participation rate by 1.75 ppt. This is a large effect: in comparison, the widely studied aging of

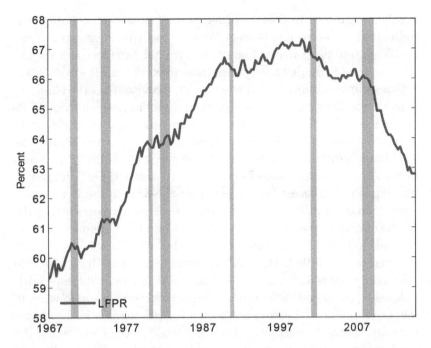

Fig. 2. Labor force participation rate (LFPR) and CBO estimate of the potential LFPR, 1967–2014.

the baby boomers lowered unemployment by 0.7 ppt and participation by 2.5 ppt over the same time period. Taken together, population aging and variations in the share of "want a job" nonparticipants can account for the bulk of the low-frequency movements in unemployment since the late 1960s.

We conclude that a better understanding of the characteristics of individuals outside the labor force is crucial to understand the trends in unemployment and participation, and in the second part of the paper, we explore possible explanations for the decline in nonparticipants' desire to work in the second half of the 1990s.

Looking across different subgroups, the decline in the number of nonparticipants who want to work is due mainly to prime-age females, and, to a lesser extent, young individuals. Moreover, the decline is mainly a low-income and non-single household phenomenon (with virtually no decline in desire to work among single households), and is stronger for families with children than without.

We estimate a model of nonparticipants' propensity to want a job, in which desire to work can depend on individual characteristics, the family structure, as well as the different sources of income, both at the individual and at the family level. We use time fixed effects so that our coefficient estimates depend on cross-sectional variation, and we use our estimates to predict changes in desire to work since the mid-1990s.

Our estimates imply that changes in the provision of (a) welfare insurance and (b) social insurance (mainly disability) explain about 50% of the decline in the share of "want a job" nonparticipants. This finding suggests a possible role for the major welfare reforms of the 1990s —the 1993 Earned Income Tax Credit (EITC) expansion and the 1996 reform of the Aid to Families with Dependent Children (AFDC) program— which precisely affected low-income households with children.

We then use a difference-in-difference strategy to try to identify the causal effects of the EITC expansion and the AFDC reform on low-income mothers. The strategy exploits the fact that households without children receive little EITC or AFDC benefits and were therefore little affected by the reforms. The difference-in-difference estimates attribute between 50 and 70% of the decline in mothers' desire to work to the welfare reforms. In other words, the welfare reforms pushed some nonparticipants further away from the labor force. Thus, while the "welfare-to-work" reform—designed to strengthen the incentives to work and to bring welfare recipients into the labor force—is generally considered to have been successful in bringing many nonparticipants into the labor force (Blank 2002), our results imply that the effect of the reform may have been more subtle than previously thought. For *some* nonparticipants, the reform appears to have had the opposite of the intended effect.

Although the existence of different degrees of desire to work among nonparticipants has been previously documented (Hall 1970; Clark and Summers 1979), the existence of a secular trend in desire to work and its effects on the participation and unemployment rates are, as far as we know, novel. Moreover, the effect of nonparticipants' characteristics on the aggregate unemployment rate measure underscores the difficult issue of the appropriate definition of unemployment and the distinction between the "unemployment" and "out of the labor force" classifications (Clark and Summers 1979; Flinn and Heckman 1983; Jones and Riddell 1999).

To quantify how the decline in desire to work affects unemployment and participation, we build on a large literature, going back at least to Darby, Haltiwanger, and Plant (1986) that studies the flows of workers in and out of unemployment.[3]

Finally, the possibility that changes in the provision of social transfers can affect desire to work and thereby the aggregate unemployment and participation rates echoes Juhn, Murphy, and Topel (2002) and Autor and Dugan (2003) who argue that the growing attractiveness of disability benefits relative to work increased the number of individuals outside the labor force.

Section 2 documents the decline in the fraction of nonparticipants willing to work, section 3 quantifies how the decline in nonparticipants willing to work affects the unemployment and participation rates, section 4 discusses the robustness of our results, section 5 explores the possible reasons for the decline in desire to work, and section 6 concludes.

II. Fewer People Want to Work

In this section, we show that the fraction of nonparticipants who report "wanting to work" has displayed substantial secular movements, with a particularly strong decline during the second half of the 1990s.

A. "Do You Want a Job Now?"

To measure the extent to which nonemployed individuals are interested in working, we use data collected by the Bureau of Labor Statistics (BLS). Since 1967, the Current Population Survey (CPS) has been consistently asking the question "Do you currently want a job now, either full or part time?" to nonemployed individuals outside the labor force, also called "nonparticipants." We use the answer to this question to separate nonparticipants into two groups; nonparticipants who want a job, denoted N^w and nonparticipants who do not want a job, denoted N^n.

Since the phrasing of the CPS question did not change from 1967 to 2014, we can construct a consistent time series of the share of nonparticipants who want to work from 1976 to 2014; that is, the ratio

$$m_t \equiv \frac{N_t^w}{N_t^w + N_t^n}$$

with N_t^w and N_t^n the respective number of "want a job" and "not want a job" nonparticipants. For the period covering 1967–1975, we tabulated the data from successive BLS Employment and Earnings publications, and for the period covering 1976–2014, we used microdata from the CPS.

Figure 3 shows that the fraction of "want a job" nonparticipants (m_t) displays an inverse U-shape pattern over 1967–2014,[4] with a particularly

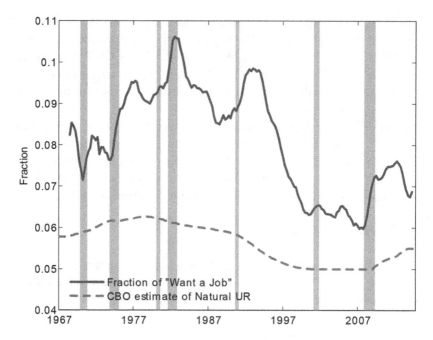

Fig. 3.   Fraction of nonparticipants who report "wanting a job" (solid line, four-quarter moving averages) and CBO estimate of natural unemployment rate (dashed line), 1967–2014.

strong decline in the second half of the 1990s.[5] Interestingly, the behavior of the Congressional Budget Office (CBO)'s estimate of the natural rate—one estimate of the long-run level of unemployment—displays a pattern that is similar to that of m_t, a point to which we will later return.[6]

B.   "Want a Job" versus "Not Want a Job"

While the trend in the share of "want a job" nonparticipants is striking, for it to be of any consequence for the aggregate labor market, people who want to work must behave differently from people who do not want to work.

To evaluate whether this is the case, we match the CPS microdata from 1994 to 2010 to measure and compare the transition rates of nonparticipants who report wanting a job (denoted N^w) with the transition rates of nonparticipants who report wanting a job (denoted N^n).[7]

Figure 4 shows a representation of the labor market with three states—employment (E), unemployment (U), and nonparticipation (N)–, and

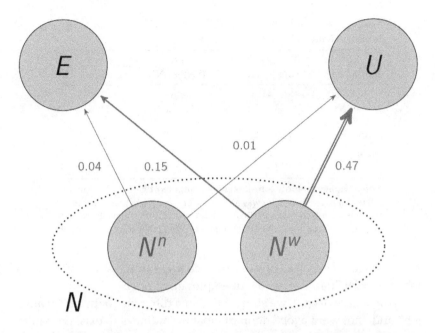

Fig. 4. Average monthly transition probabilities out of nonparticipation for nonparticipants who want a job (N^w) and nonparticipants who do not want a job (N^n), 1994–2010.

reports the average monthly transition rates out of nonparticipation (either to E or U) for "want a job" nonparticipants (N^w) and "not want a job" nonparticipants (N^n).

We can see that someone who wants a job behaves very differently from someone who does not want a job.

First, someone who wants a job (N^w) is very likely to enter the labor force in the near future ($\lambda^{N^w U} + \lambda^{N^w E} = .62$, where λ^{AB} denotes the average transition rate from state $A \in \{E, U, N^w, N^n\}$ to state $B \in \{E, U, N^w, N^n\}$). In other words, someone who wants a job is at the margin of participation. In contrast, someone who does not want a job (N^n) is unlikely to enter the labor force in the near future ($\lambda^{N^n U} + \lambda^{N^n E} = .05$) and is thus "far" from the participation margin and from labor force activity.

Second, a "want a job" nonparticipant is much more likely to enter the labor force through unemployment than through employment ($\lambda^{N^w U} > \lambda^{N^w E}$), but this is the opposite for a "not want a job" nonparticipant: someone who does not want a job is much more likely to enter the labor force through employment ($\lambda^{N^n E} > \lambda^{N^n U}$). These two differences in behavior between "want a job" and "not want a job" nonparticipants—the fact that $\lambda^{N^w U} - \lambda^{N^w E} > 0$ and $\lambda^{N^n E} - \lambda^{N^n U} > 0$—will later

Table 1
Transition Rates of Labor Force Entrants

Transitions	UN $(UN^w + UN^n)$	EN $(EN^w + EN^n)$	UE	EU
Former N^w	.44 (.33 + .11)	.16 (.08 + .09)	.20	.08
Former N^n	.57 (.25 + .32)	.27 (.03 + .24)	.22	.03
Other	.19 (.13 + .06)	.02 (.01 + .01)	.27	.01

Note: Average monthly transition rates computed 1994–2010. Former N^w refers to a participant who was a "want a job" nonparticipant one month ago, former N^n refers to a participant who was a "not want a job" nonparticipant one month ago, and other refers to other labor force participants.

prove crucial when we consider how changes in the share of "want a job" nonparticipants affect the unemployment rate.

To dig a little deeper, we study whether a difference between "want a job" and "not want a job" nonparticipants continues to exist once nonparticipants enter the labor force. Table 1 compares the transition rates of recent (entered a month ago) labor force entrants with the transition rates of other labor force participants (who entered the labor force more than a month ago).[8] We can see that recent labor force entrants have much higher transition rates back to nonparticipation. However, although "want a job" and "not want a job" nonparticipants display very different transition rates into participation (figure 4), the difference is much less marked once these individuals are inside the labor force. Table 1 shows that their job-finding rates are similar and that their labor force exit rates are somewhat comparable. Interestingly, a former "not want a job" (N^n) is more likely to leave the labor force than a former "want a job" (N^w).

C. The Fraction of "Want a Job" across Demographic Groups

Looking at different demographics, a decline in the share of "want a job" nonparticipants can be seen among prime-age females, prime-age males, and young workers. However, in terms of the *number* of individuals affected by the decline, the decline is mainly a prime-age female, and to a lesser extent young worker, phenomenon.

First, similarly to figure 3, figure 5 plots m_{it}, the fraction of "want a job" nonparticipants for four demographic subgroups (denoted with the

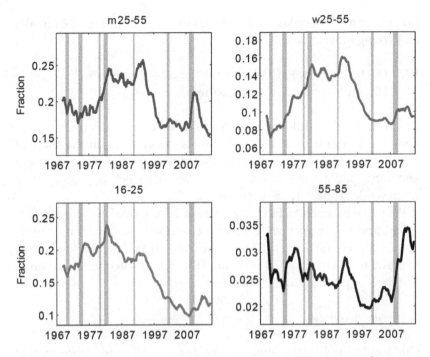

Fig. 5.   Fraction of nonparticipants who report "wanting a job" by demographic group: male 25–55, female 25–55, younger than 25, and older than 55. Four-quarter moving averages, 1969–2014.

subscript i): Prime-age male 25–55, prime-age female 25–55, younger than 25, and over 55. In all groups except for old workers, m_{it} displays an inverted-U shape, rising in the 1970s and declining in the second half of the 1990s.[9]

However these percentage point declines hide large differences in the number of individuals affected by the decline in desire to work. Between 1994 and 2001, the number of prime-age females willing to work declined by 930,000, of young individuals by 680,000, and the number of prime-age males declined by "only" 250,000. Thus, the decline in desire to work is predominantly a (a) prime-age female, and (b) young individuals phenomenon. This difference between groups was not apparent in the behavior of the share of "want a job" nonparticipants because that measure does not capture differences in participation rates across groups. In particular, since prime-age males have a very high participation rate, there are few prime-age male nonparticipants, so that the decline in m_{it} is a phenomenon that affected only a very small share of the prime-age male population. This is not the case for prime-age females and young individuals.

III.   Declining Share of "Want a Job" and Movements in Unemployment and Participation

Given the marked differences in labor market behavior between "want a job" and "not want a job" individuals, movements in the share of "want a job" nonparticipants may affect the aggregate unemployment and participation rates. In this section, we use a stock-flow accounting framework to quantify these effects.

We make two points. First, the share of "want a job" nonparticipants is an important aspect of the inverse U-shape behavior of unemployment between the early 1970s and the early 2000s. Second, the decline in desire to work in the second-half of the 90s is related to the currently low level of participation in the US.

A.   Some Accounting

Our starting point is a labor market described by four labor market states: employment (E), unemployment (U), nonparticipant who wants a job (N^w), and nonparticipant who does not want a job (N^n).

As in the "Ins and Outs" literature (e.g., Shimer 2012), we assume that the labor market can be described by a Markov chain of order 1,[10] so that the number of employed E_t, unemployed U_t, "want a job" nonparticipants N^w_t, and "not want a job" nonparticipants N^n_t satisfies the system

$$
\begin{pmatrix} \dot{E} \\ U \\ N^w \\ N^n \end{pmatrix}_t = \Lambda_t \begin{pmatrix} E \\ U \\ N^w \\ N^n \end{pmatrix}_t
\tag{1}
$$

with

$$
\Lambda_t = \begin{pmatrix}
-\lambda^{EU}-\lambda^{EN^w}-\lambda^{EN^n} & \lambda^{UE} & \lambda^{N^wE} & \lambda^{N^nE} \\
\lambda^{EU} & -\lambda^{UE}-\lambda^{UN^w}-\lambda^{UN^n} & \lambda^{N^wU} & \lambda^{N^nU} \\
\lambda^{EN^w} & \lambda^{UN^w} & -\lambda^{N^wU}-\lambda^{N^wE}-\lambda^{N^wN^n} & \lambda^{N^nN^w} \\
\lambda^{EN^n} & \lambda^{UN^n} & \lambda^{N^wN^n} & -\lambda^{N^nU}-\lambda^{N^nE}-\lambda^{N^nN^w}
\end{pmatrix}_t
$$

and where λ_t^{AB} denotes the hazard rate of transiting from state $A \in \{E, U, N^w, N^n\}$ to state $B \in \{E, U, N^w, N^n\}$.

We can then use (1) to express any stock variable, for instance the unemployment rate $u_t = U_t / (E_t + U_t)$ and the participation rate $l_t = LF_t / Pop_t$ with the population $Pop_t = E_t + U_t + N_t^w + N_t^n$, as functions of the (present and past) worker transition rates $\{\lambda_{t-j}^{AB}, \forall j > 0\}$. For the United States, such functions are particularly simple because the magnitude of the worker flows are so large that, at a quarterly frequency, the labor market is very well described by the steady state of system (1).[11] As detailed in the appendix,[12] the steady state of system (1) then gives us an accounting identity that allows to express the unemployment rate u_t and participation rate l_t as functions $u(.)$ and $l(.)$ of the 12 contemporaneous hazard rates $\{\lambda_t^{AB}\}$.

Then, it is easy to write u_t and l_t as functions of the transition rates out of employment (E), unemployment (U), and nonparticipation (N, including all nonparticipants, N^w or N^n) with

$$
\begin{cases}
u_t = u(\{\lambda_t^{AB}\}) \\
l_t = l(\{\lambda_t^{AB}\})
\end{cases}
, \quad A, B \in \{E, U, N\} \tag{2}
$$

where the N-U and N-E transition rates, denoted λ_t^{NU} and λ_t^{NE}, are weighted averages of the two transition rates out of N^w and N^n

$$
\begin{cases}
\lambda_t^{NU} = m_t \lambda_t^{N^wU} + (1 - m_t)\lambda_t^{N^nU} \\
\lambda_t^{NE} = m_t \lambda_t^{N^wE} + (1 - m_t)\lambda_t^{N^nE}
\end{cases}
\tag{3}
$$

with the weight m_t given by the share of "want a job" nonparticipants.

Since nonparticipants who want a job behave very differently from the nonparticipants who do not want a job (in particular, $\lambda^{N^wU} >> \lambda^{N^nU}$), changes in the fraction of nonparticipants who want a job will affect the transition rates out of nonparticipation through (3) and thus the unemployment and participation rates through (2).

B. Quantifying the Effect of Lower Desire to Work

A Taylor expansion of the accounting identities (2) around the mean of the hazard rates ($\lambda_t^{AB} \simeq \lambda^{AB}$) and a little bit of algebra with (3)[13] gives (see the appendix http://www.nber.org/data-appendix/c13601/appendix.pdf for more details) that the effect of a change in the fraction of "want a job" nonparticipants on the aggregate unemployment rate, denoted du_t^m, is given by

$$du_t^m = \beta^{NU}\left[\left(\lambda^{N^wU} - \lambda^{N^nU}\right) - \frac{\lambda^{NU}}{\lambda^{NE}}\left(\lambda^{N^wE} - \lambda^{N^nE}\right)\right](m_t - m) \qquad (4)$$

with m the average fraction of "want a job" nonparticipants, and $\beta^{NU} > 0$, the coefficient of the first-order Taylor expansion of u_t with respect to λ_t^{NU}.

The effect of a decline in desire to work on the aggregate unemployment rate is a priori ambiguous. On the one hand, as captured by the first term on the right-hand side of (4), a decline in the share of "want a job" nonparticipants lower the average NU transition rate since "want a job" nonparticipants are more likely to join unemployment than "not want a job" nonparticipants ($\lambda^{N^wU} - \lambda^{N^nU} > 0$), and this lowers the unemployment rate. On the other hand, as captured by the second term on the right-hand side of (4), a decline in the share of "want a job" nonparticipants lowers the average N-E transition rate, since "want a job" nonparticipants are more likely to join employment ($\lambda^{N^wE} - \lambda^{N^nE} > 0$), and this increases the unemployment rate. In practice however, a lower share of nonparticipants who want to work unambiguously implies a lower unemployment rate. The two hazard rates out of nonparticipation, λ^{NU} and λ^{NE}, are of similar magnitudes and $\lambda^{NU} / \lambda^{NE} \simeq 1$, so that the sign of the effect of a change in m on the unemployment rate is given by

$$\underbrace{\left(\lambda^{N^wU} - \lambda^{N^wE}\right)}_{>0} + \underbrace{\left(\lambda^{N^nE} - \lambda^{N^nU}\right)}_{>0} > 0$$

which is unambiguously positive for two reasons: (a) a nonparticipant who wants a job enters the labor force mainly through unemployment ($\lambda^{N^wU} - \lambda^{N^wE} > 0$), and (b) a nonparticipant who does not want a job enters the labor force mostly through employment ($\lambda^{N^nE} - \lambda^{N^nU} > 0$).

To quantify the effect of changes in the fraction of "want a job" non-participants on the labor force participation rate, we proceed in the exact same fashion and calculate dl_t^m from a relation similar to (4). Contrary to the unemployment rate, a decline in m_t has an unambiguous effect on the labor force participation rate. Since a lower fraction of "want a job" nonparticipants lowers all transition rates out of nonparticipation, a lower fraction of "want a job" nonparticipants implies a lower labor force participation rate.

C. *Controlling for Demographic Heterogeneity*

Before proceeding with the decomposition results, we generalize our approach to control for changes in demographics.

We do so for two reasons: First, changes in demographics are known to have large effects on the behavior of the unemployment and participation rates, and we want to put the effects of declining desire to work in the context of the contribution of demographics. Second, to the extent that declining average desire to work could be explained by changes in the demographic structure of the nonparticipation pool, we want to control for the demographic composition of the population.

We divide the population into $K = 8$ demographic (age and sex) groups, denoted by subscript $i \in \{1, \dots, K\}$.[14] The approach to identify the effect of lower desire to work is exactly as described in the previous section, except that all variables now have a subscript i. As described in the appendix,[15] we can then aggregate across groups to estimate the effects of (a) demographics, and (b) desire to work among nonparticipants on the aggregate unemployment and participation rates by using the definitions

$$\begin{cases} u_t = \Sigma_{i=1}^{K} \omega_{it} u_{it} \\ l_t = \Sigma_{i=1}^{K} \Omega_{it} l_{it} \end{cases}$$

with ω_{it} the labor force share of group i and Ω_{it} the population share of group i.

D. *Decomposition of the Unemployment Rate*

We start by analyzing the behavior of the unemployment rate.

Figure 6 plots the contributions of (a) demographics (top panel), and (b) the fraction of "want a job" nonparticipants (middle panel) to movements in unemployment. To help put results into perspective, we also plot the CBO estimate of the natural rate (dashed line) as a proxy for trend unemployment.

Demographics and the aging of the baby boom generation first increased unemployment until the late 1970s. Then, between 1979 and 2006 demographics lowered unemployment by about a 0.7 percentage point. However, demographics alone can account for only about half of the trend in unemployment and its inverse U-shape.

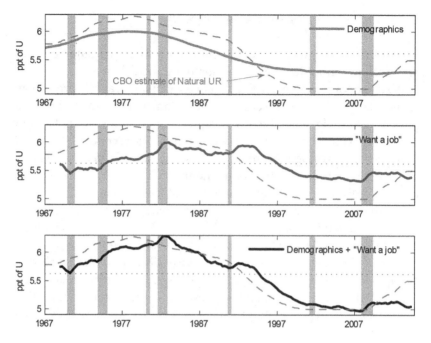

Fig. 6. Effects of composition changes on the aggregate unemployment rate (U). Upper panel: effect of demographics. Middle panel: effect of changes in the share of "want a job" nonparticipants. Bottom panel: effect of changes in demographics and the share of "want a job" nonparticipants. The dashed line is the CBO estimate of the natural unemployment rate. For clarity of exposition, the series are level shifted with their mean set to the mean of the CBO natural rate. The plotted series are four-quarter moving averages, 1967–2014.

The decline in the share of "want a job" nonparticipants lowered the aggregate unemployment rate substantially: Comparing the business-cycle peaks of 1979 and 2006, the decline in desire to work lowered the unemployment rate by about 0.5 ppt over the last 30 years. This contribution is comparable with that of demographics.

Interestingly, taken together, demographics and desire to work among nonparticipants (bottom panel of figure 6) appear to account for most of the low-frequency movements in unemployment, as captured by the CBO estimate of the natural rate.

Another way to make this point is to consider figure 7. In that figure, we plot the result of a decomposition of the unemployment rate into its different flows (stripped of demographic effects). Specifically, we use our stock-flow accounting framework and accounting identity (2) to decompose the movements in the aggregate unemployment rate into

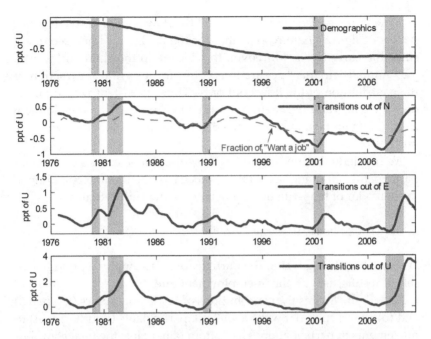

Fig. 7. Decomposition of the unemployment rate into the contributions of (a) demographics (top panel); (b) transition rates out of nonparticipation–NE and N-U flows–(second panel); (c) transition rates out of employment–EN and EU flows–(third panel); and (d) transition rates out of unemployment–UN and UE flows–(bottom panel). Summing up the four components gives the aggregate unemployment rate. The dashed line in the second panel plots the contribution of the share of "want a job" nonparticipants to the unemployment rate. For clarity of exposition, the contribution of each component is set to 0 in 1979Q4. The plotted series are four-quarter moving averages, 1976–2010.

the contributions of, respectively, (a) demographics (first panel); (b) the flows out of nonparticipation (the NU and NE flows, second panel); (c) the flows out of employment (the EU and EN flows, third panel); and (d) the flows out of unemployment (the UE and UN flows, fourth panel). Summing up the four contributions gives the total change in the aggregate unemployment rate. In addition, in the second panel (dashed line) we plot the contribution of the share of "want a job" nonparticipants to movements in unemployment. We plot that contribution in the second panel ("transitions out of N") because the share of "want a job" affects unemployment by modifying the transitions out of N. More details about the decomposition are provided in the appendix.[16]

We can see that the flows out of E or out of U display little trend and thus cannot be responsible for the secular movements in unemployment. Instead, demographics and the flows out of N (the top two panels of figure 7) are responsible for the decline in unemployment since the early 1980s. Moreover, the decline in the share of "want a job" nonparticipants appears to account for a significant fraction of the contribution of the flows out of N. Thus, consistent with figure 6, demographics and the share of "want a job" nonparticipants do seem to be the main factors behind the decline in unemployment since the mid-1980s.

We conclude that understanding how the characteristics of the non-participants can change over time is crucial to a better understanding of the behavior of long-run unemployment in the United States.

E. Decomposition of the Labor Force Participation Rate

We now turn to analyzing the participation rate, and we provide two sets of results, as with the unemployment rate.

First, figure 8 plots the contributions of (a) demographics (top panel) and (b) the fraction of "want a job" nonparticipants (middle panel) to movements in participation. The bottom panel plots the total contribution of (a) and (b). To help put results into perspective, we also plot the actual participation rate.

Second, figure 9 plots the decomposition of the participation rate into its different flows (stripped of demographic effects): (a) demographics (first panel); (b) the flows out of nonparticipation (second panel); (c) the flows out of employment (third panel); and (d) the flows out of unemployment (fourth panel). Summing up the four contributions gives the total change in the aggregate participation rate. In addition, in the second panel (dashed line), we plot the contribution of the share of "want a job" nonparticipants to movements in participation. We plot that contribution in the second panel ("transitions out of N") because the share of "want a job" affects participation by modifying the transitions out of N.

Overall, demographics has had a small effect on participation since the late 1960s, and it is only since the end of the last recession that the aging of the baby boom generation substantially lowered participation.[17] In contrast, movements in the share of "want a job" appear to have substantially affected the participation rate over time. In particular, the decline in the share of "want a job" nonparticipants in the second half of the 1990s lowered the participation rate by about 1 3/4 ppt (second panel of figure 8 or 9).

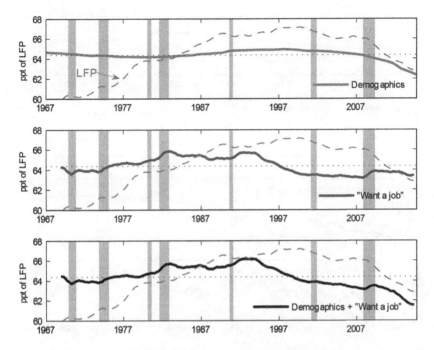

Fig. 8. Effects of composition changes on aggregate labor force participation rate (LFP). Upper panel: effect of demographics. Middle panel: effect of changes in the share of "want a job" nonparticipants. Bottom panel: effect of changes in demographics and the share of "want a job" nonparticipants. The dashed line is the actual LFP. For clarity of exposition, the series are level shifted with their mean set to the mean of aggregate LFP. The plotted series are four-quarter moving averages, 1967–2014.

Putting demographics and desire for work together, the bottom panel of figure 8 shows that demographics and the share of "want a job" account for most of the downward trend in participation since early in the twenty-first century. Currently, there is a large debate on the reasons for the record low level of participation in the United States. Our decomposition suggest that the low share of "want a job" nonparticipants is an important factor behind the current low level of participation.

However, figure 9 also shows that, unlike with the unemployment rate, other flows contributed to the secular movements in participation. In particular, flows out of employment (third panel) are responsible for the strong increase in participation in the 1970s and 1980s. Thus, we do not claim that demographics and "want a job" have always been major forces behind secular movements in participation. We will come back to this point in the next section.

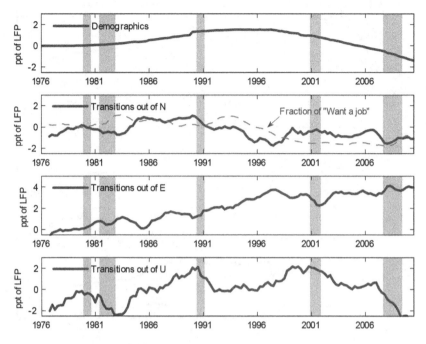

Fig. 9. Decomposition of the participation rate into the contributions of (a) demographics (top panel); (b) transition rates out of nonparticipation–NE and NU flows–(second panel); (c) transition rates out of employment–EN and EU flows–(third panel); and (d) transition rates out of unemployment–UN and UE flows–(bottom panel). Summing up the four components gives the aggregate participation rate. The dashed line in the second panel plots the contribution of the share of "want a job" nonparticipants to the participation rate. For clarity of exposition, the contribution of each component is set to 0 in 1979Q4. The plotted series are four-quarter moving averages, 1976–2010.

IV. Discussion

Our previous results indicate that variation in the characteristics of nonparticipants and specifically changes in the share of "want a job" nonparticipants has been a major factor in the trends in the unemployment and participation rates. In this section, we discuss two possible issues associated with our results.[18] The first issue has to do with timing: the behavior of the participation rate does not line up well with the share of "want a job" nonparticipants, suggesting the absence of any relationship between the two series, and thus apparently contradicting our conclusions. The second issue relates to the way we quantified the effect of a change in the share of "want a job" nonparticipants on unemployment and participation by assigning to any N^w or N^n individual the *average* transition rate out of that state. In this section, we successively discuss these two concerns.

A. Timing

Our previous accounting exercise showed that the decline in the share of "want a job" had a substantial effect on both the unemployment and participation rates. However, while the low-frequency behavior of unemployment lines up reasonably well with the behavior of the share of "want a job" nonparticipants (figure 3), which is consistent with our story, the participation rate shows no apparent correlation with the fraction of "want a job" nonparticipants (figure 8, middle panel). For instance, while participation displayed an inverse U-shaped pattern between 1980 and 2010, the share of "want a job" was roughly flat until the mid-1990s and only then started to decline. This lack of correlation may seem surprising and could suggest some issue with our decomposition exercise.

However, we think that this conclusion would be too hasty. Many different forces have affected the participation rate over the past 45 years, so that the absence of any correlation between participation and one of the factors (in our case, the share of "want a job") is not necessarily a problem.[19]

First, an important factor behind the large increase in participation in the 1970s and 1980s is the increase in the participation rate of women (e.g., Abraham and Shimer 2001). And indeed, going back to our stock-flow decomposition of the participation rate (shown in figure 9), we can see that the most important component behind the secular increase in participation during that time is a secular change in workers' transition rates out of employment (third panel).[20] This effect was very strong and dwarfed the contribution of the other flows.

Another powerful factor behind movements in the participation rate is workers' job-finding rate. In strong labor markets, workers' job-finding rate is high, and this raises the participation rate. This mechanism can be seen in the contribution of two flows: the job-finding rate out of unemployment (UE) and the job-finding rate out of nonparticipation (NE).[21] For instance, in the second half of the 1990s participation increased because both the UE and NE rates reached historically high values.[22]

With these different forces affecting the participation rate through different flows, we conclude that one cannot reject the results of our

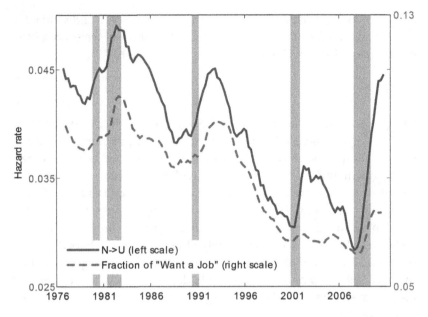

Fig. 10.   The nonparticipation to unemployment transition rate (NU) on the left scale, and the share of "want a job" nonparticipants (right scale). The plotted series are four-quarter moving averages, 1976–2012.

quantitative decomposition from an inspection of the correlation between the participation rate and the share of "want a job" nonparticipants.

However, to evaluate the plausibility of our results, we can focus on the flows directly affected by the share of "want a job" (but little affected by the aforementioned factors). Since we saw in section II that the largest difference between "want a job" and "not want a job" nonparticipants (N) is their transition rate into unemployment (U), we should observe a strong correlation between the share of "want a job" and the N to U transition rate. Figure 10 shows that this is indeed the case: the N to U transition rate displayed a marked decline in the second half of the 1990s that coincides with the decline in the share of "want a job." In other words, the timing is consistent with our story.

B.   Average versus Marginal Change

A more subtle and more difficult issue is the following: when we quantify the effect of a change in the share of "want a job" nonparticipants on the average transition rates out of nonparticipation (N), equation (4) implicitly attributes to any N^w or N^n individual the *average* transition rate out of that state. As a result, as the share of "not want a job" non-participants increased in the late 1990s, we posited that some average N^w individuals (i.e., with very large transition rates out of N) became average N^n individuals (with very small transition rates out of N). Such an assumption is valid if a large event substantially changed the behavior of some nonparticipants. We will refer to this scenario as the "average change" scenario.

However, an alternative scenario could be that the increase in the share of "not want a job" was due to individuals at the *margin* between "want a job" and "not want a job." If this were the case, the true change in behavior would have been marginal, and a change in the share of "want a job" nonparticipants would have had a negligible effect on the transition rates out of nonparticipation, so that our decomposition would strongly overestimate the contribution of the decline in desire to work to unemployment and participation. We will refer to this scenario as the "marginal change" scenario.

Although it is difficult to definitely conclude in favor of either scenario, we will argue that the "average change" scenario is the more likely one.

First, as previously shown in figure 10, the transition rate from non-participation to unemployment displayed a strong downward trend in the 1990s, and that trend does line up well with the decline in the share of "want a job."[23] Moreover, our estimated effect of the decline in the share of "want a job" on transitions out of N matches well with the observed trend in the "transition out of N" component of unemployment (figure 7, second panel), suggesting that we are not attributing an unreasonable weight to that mechanism.

Second, if our story is correct and variations in the share of "want a job" have a sizable effect on unemployment, a group without a decline in the share of "want a job" nonparticipants should have had a markedly smaller downward trend in its unemployment rate.

Figure 11 shows that such a differential behavior did occur in the data: while the fraction of "want a job" nonparticipants declined for individuals not living alone, it was roughly flat for individuals living alone. Thus, if our previous result that a lower share of "want a job" nonparticipants leads to a lower unemployment rate is correct, we should observe diverging trends in the unemployment rates of the two groups.

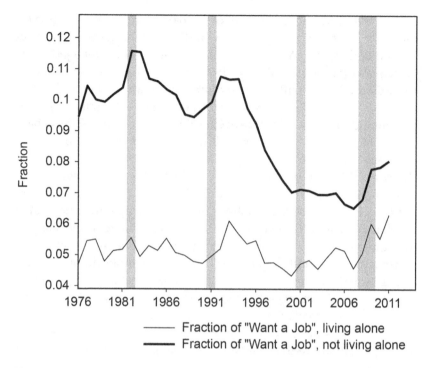

Fig. 11. Fraction of nonparticipants who report wanting a job for nonparticipants living alone (thick line) and nonparticipants not living alone (thin line), 1976–2011.

Figure 12 shows that this is indeed the case. In the top panel, we can see that individuals living alone experienced a smaller secular decline in unemployment than individuals not living alone.[24] To better make this point, the middle panel plots the evolution over time of the difference in (a) unemployment, and (b) the share of "want a job" for individuals, respectively, alone and not alone. That is, we plot $u_t^a - u_t^n$ and $m_t^a - m_t^u$ where u_t^a is the unemployment rate of people living alone, m_t^a the share of "want a job" for people living alone, and with similar definitions for u_t^n and m_t^n for people not living alone. We can see a very high correlation between the two series, which is again consistent with our results that the share of "want a job" affects the behavior of the unemployment rate.

A final, more speculative, element that we think can support our average change scenario is that of a big shock. If a large shock affected nonparticipants, it could have led them to substantially modify their behavior (e.g., by switching from behaving like an average N^w to behaving like an average N^n), and thereby led to large effects on the un-

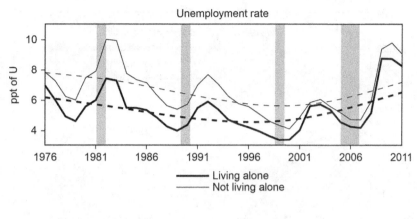

Unemployment rate

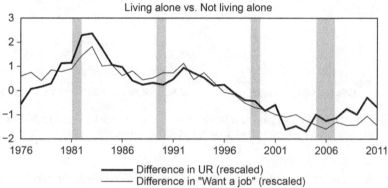

Living alone vs. Not living alone

Fig. 12. Top panel: unemployment rate for individuals living alone (thick line) and individuals not living alone (thin solid line) along with their HP-filter trends (γ = 10⁵, dashed lines). Bottom panel: difference in unemployment rate (thick line) and difference in share of "want a job" nonparticipants (thin line) between individuals alone and not alone. The plotted series are four-quarter moving averages, 1976–2011.

employment and participation rates. In the next section, we explore the reasons for the decline in the share of "want a job" nonparticipants in the second half of the 1990s, and we find that a change in the provision of welfare and social insurance, likely linked to the mid-1990s welfare reforms and thus arguably a large shock, does account for much of the decline in desire to work.

V. Why Do Fewer People Want a Job?

In the second part of the paper, we investigate the reasons for the decline in the share of "want a job" nonparticipants since the mid-1990s.

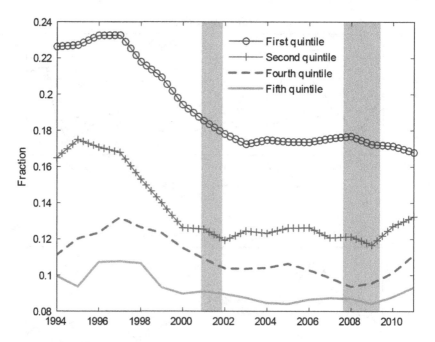

Fig. 13. Fraction of nonparticipants who report wanting a job for individuals with family income in the first, second, fourth, and fifth quintile, 1994–2011.

As a preliminary step, we note that the decline in desire to work is concentrated among (a) nonsingle and (b) low-income households. While we already saw that the fraction of "want a job" nonparticipants did *not* decline for those living alone (figure 11), among nonsingle households the decline in desire to work is concentrated among low-income families (figure 13); among low-income, non-single households, the decline in desire to work is more pronounced for individuals with children than without (figure 14).

Since the family structure seems to play an important role, the next section discusses a very simple model of family labor supply to help frame the discussion and guide the empirical analysis. Then, we estimate an empirical model of nonparticipants' propensity to want a job in which desire to work can depend on individual characteristics, the family structure, as well as the different sources of income. Since the decline in desire to work is a low-income phenomenon, we pay special attention to the role played by welfare income and other social transfer programs.

Our estimates suggest that the mid-1990s welfare reforms may have played an important role, and we try to identify their causal effects on

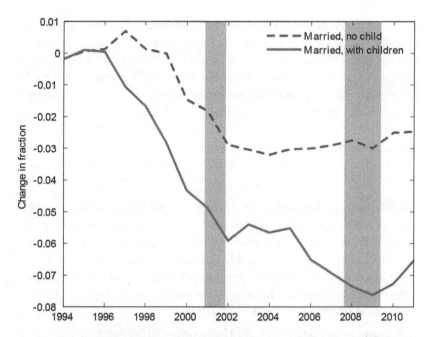

Fig. 14. Changes in the fraction of nonparticipants who report wanting a job for married individuals with children and married individuals without children, 1994–2011.

desire to work by using a difference-in-difference strategy. We conclude by discussing the implications of our results.

A. A Model of Family Labor Supply

We sketch a simple framework of family labor supply.[25] We focus only on family members' decision to search for a job,[26] and we consider a sequential multiple-earner model in which the primary earner makes his/her work decision independently of the secondary earners. The first secondary earner, say the spouse, then makes his/her labor-supply decision by maximizing utility, taking account of the primary earner's income. The next secondary earner, say a teenager living in the household, then makes his/her labor-supply decision in a similar fashion. And so on, for the other family members.

We posit that there exist search frictions, so that each worker must search in order to get a job, and a worker can increase his/her job finding probability by increasing the intensity of the search.[27]

In this framework, we interpret the nonemployment states—nonparticipant who does not want a job (N^n), nonparticipant who wants a job

(N^w), and unemployed (U)—as arbitrary distinctions introduced by the household survey and its imperfect measurement of search intensity. Specifically, while search intensity s is a continuous variable, a survey cannot precisely measure s. Instead, a household survey like the CPS can classify workers into different labor market states—nonparticipant who does not want a job (N^n), nonparticipant who wants a job (N^w), and unemployed (U)—that correspond to increasing intensities of search.

In this framework, it is easy to show that search intensity (or the propensity to report "want a job") is influenced by the following mechanisms:

1. Returns to employment. Higher employment income increases desire to work among primary workers, but has an ambiguous effect on desire to work among secondary workers. The effect is ambiguous because the direct effect is compensated by an added-worker effect (Lundberg 1985; Juhn and Potter 2007): as the family income generated by "higher-order" workers increases through higher employment income, desire to work among secondary workers decline.

2. Returns to nonparticipation. Higher nonparticipation income lowers desire to work among primary workers and has an ambiguous effect on desire to work among secondary workers. The ambiguity occurs again because of the added-worker effect, although this time it is because higher returns to nonparticipation lowers search intensity of higher-order workers, which lowers disposable income.

3. Heterogeneous preferences. If the disutility of search varies with demographic characteristics such as age, gender, or education, search intensity will vary with demographic characteristics and a change in the composition of the population will affect the observed average desire to work.[28]

4. Higher asset income lowers search intensity through a "wealth effect."

B. An Empirical Model of Nonparticipants' Propensity to Want a Job

To quantitatively assess different explanations for the decline in desire to work, we consider a linear model of nonparticipants' propensity to want a job: the probability that a nonparticipant of type i wants a job (i.e., be N^w) at time t is given by

$$P(N^w \mid N)_{it} = \beta X_{it} + \sum_{j=1}^{J} \alpha_j w_{j,it} + \delta_t + \varepsilon_{it} \qquad (5)$$

with X_{it} a vector of characteristics for type i at time t, $w_{j,it}$ an income source of type j, and δ_t a time dummy. Because we use time fixed effects, our coefficient estimates will depend on cross-sectional variation.

To measure worker characteristics as well as income and its different categories, we use matched annual data from the (March) Annual Social and Economic Supplement of the CPS for 1988–2010. In addition to information contained in the basic CPS files, the March supplement includes detailed information on income. Since the March supplement only contains information related to the past year's income, we match the March supplements across successive years, so that we can study the relation between the current year's income and desire to work.[29] Matching March supplements also allows us to instrument for income in year t with income in year $t - 1$. There is likely substantial measurement error in the reported income variables, and instrumenting with lagged income variables allows us to correct for the downward bias imparted by this measurement error (under the assumption that the measurement error is i.i.d.).

An individual of type i is defined by the following demographic characteristics: (a) age group (we classify workers into eight groups spanning 16–85); (b) sex; (c) education level (less than high school, high school or some college, college or more); (d) married or not; (e) school status (in school or not); (f) position in household (head, spouse, child, other); and finally (g) number of children (younger than 19) in the household. The X_{it} is a thus vector of seven dummy variables.

We consider the different income categories: individual social insurance transfers, individual welfare income, other individual income, asset income, total tax payment, earned family income, and family income from social transfers.[30] Social insurance transfers include supplemental security income (SSI), social security disability insurance (SSDI), social security pensions, survivor's insurance, workmen's compensation, and veterans' benefits,[31] but since we are restricting our sample to individuals younger than 55, the "social insurance transfers" category captures mostly disability insurance. Note that we treat separately individual income, which would affect desire to work through changes in the returns to nonparticipation or employment, and the income provided by higher-order family members (labeled "family income"), which would affect desire to work through added-worker effects.[32] We also add asset income to capture a possible wealth effect. Income values are deflated using the BEA deflator for personal consumption expenditures.

Finally, since the impairment associated with the receipt of disability insurance is conditioned on the existence of an impairment that (in theory) precludes any work activity (and thus affects desire to work), we include a dummy for receiving disability insurance (SSI or SSDI). Similarly, since welfare recipients are strongly encouraged or mandated to return to employment, participation in a welfare program may affect search intensity and desire to work, we include a dummy for receiving welfare income.

C. Coefficient Estimates

Table 2 presents our coefficient estimates for the different income categories, and the first column of table 2 reports coefficient estimates for all individuals age 16 to 55.[33]

Most strikingly, receiving welfare and receiving disability insurance have very different implications for desire to work. While receiving disability insurance substantially reduces the probability to want to work by 17 percentage points (ppt), consistent with the fact that an impairment should preclude any work activity and thus lower desire to work, receiving welfare increases the probability to want to work by 17 ppt. This latter result is consistent with the fact that welfare recipients are strongly encouraged (especially since 1988) to return to employment quickly, which should push welfare recipients to exert more search effort.[34]

Increasing the income from social insurance reduces desire to work (a $1,000 increase decreases the probability to want a job by 0.7 ppt), but the effect is small compared to the effect of participation (e.g., being officially recognized as disabled).

Increasing welfare income has no significant effect on desire to work. This small effect is again in contrast with the strong effect of participation (i.e., being on welfare). Thus, most of the effect of the welfare or social insurance programs on desire to work occurs through the program participation margin, as captured by our dummy variables.

Turning to income from higher-order family members, the coefficients for earnings and transfer are highly significant and negative, indicating that an added-worker effect is at play. Specifically, a $1,000 extra annual family income reduces the probability to want a job by 4.5 ppt for earnings and by about 2 ppt for transfer income. Higher-asset income lowers desire to work, consistent with the existence of a wealth effect, although the coefficient is not significant, and lower taxes lowers desire to work, indicating again an added-worker effect.

Finally, for demographic characteristics, individuals with the highest expected lifetime return from work are the most likely to want to work:

Table 2
Coefficient Estimates

		Aggregate	Females 25–55	Young 16–24
Disabled		−17.2***	−13.9***	−6.4
		(11.9)	(7.1)	(1.2)
On welfare		17.5***	22.9***	14.4*
		(4.9)	(5.2)	(1.9)
	Social insurance	−0.7***	−0.6***	−1.5***
Individual income		(9.6)	(5.1)	(2.9)
	Welfare income	0.1	−1.0	1.4
		(0.1)	(1.3)	(0.6)
	Earnings	−4.5***	−4.0***	−3.9***
Family income		(10.7)	(6.6)	(4.8)
	Social transfers	−2.07***	−4.4***	−0.5
		(3.2)	(3.5)	(0.4)
Asset income		−3.8	−0.7	−0.9
		(0.9)	(0.9)	(0.9)
Taxes		8.3***	4.5*	5.9
		(3.7)	(1.9)	(1.1)
Married		−6.3***	−8.3***	−4.2***
		(15.6)	(14.1)	(4.0)
No. of children		−0.1	−0.1	−0.4**
		(0.9)	(0.6)	(2.1)
Demographic controls		Yes	Yes	Yes
Year dummies		Yes	Yes	Yes
No. obs.		65,586	31,960	23,899

Note: The estimation period is 1988–2010. The t-statistics are reported in parentheses. "Disabled" denotes the coefficient on a dummy equal to 1 when the individual receives disability insurance. "On welfare" denotes the coefficient on a dummy equal to 1 when the individual receives welfare income. Demographic controls include age group, age, sex, education level, married or not, school status, position in household, and number of children.

young, highly educated men are the most likely to want to work.[35] Being married lowers desire for work, as well as being in school.

Digging deeper into subgroups, table 2 also presents the coefficient estimates for prime-age females and individuals younger than 25. Overall, the results are similar and consistent with our aggregate regression.

D. The Welfare Reform and Wage Gains of the 1990s

Before discussing the predictions of the model, it is helpful to briefly discuss two changes in the returns to employment and nonparticipation during the 1990s that were of particular relevance for low-income, nonsingle households, the group most affected by the decline in desire to work: (a) the provision of "welfare" was dramatically reorganized in the mid-1990s, and (b) real wages increased strongly across the income distribution, propped up by a booming economy.

The Welfare Reforms of the Mid-1990s

A major reorganization of the provision of welfare took place in the mid 90s in line with Clinton's aim to "end welfare as we know it" and to move welfare recipients into work.

First, traditional welfare was dramatically reorganized by the Personal Responsibility and Work Opportunity Reconciliation Act of 1996. The Aid to Families with Dependent Children (AFDC) program, a federal assistance program that provided financial assistance to low-income families with children (see Moffitt [2003] for a detailed review of the program), was replaced by the stricter (in terms of eligibility and time limits) Temporary Assistance for Needy Families program (TANF). With TANF the duration of benefits is limited to five years and the emphasis on return to work is strengthened with sanctions for noncomplying applicants (Moffitt 2003). Following the reform, the number of welfare caseloads declined massively (Blank 2002) as well as federal spending devoted to AFDC/TANF (figure 15).[36]

Second, the Earned Income Tax Credit (EITC) program, a program aimed at offsetting the social security payroll tax for low-income families with children, was expanded in order to encourage work effort (Rothstein and Nichols 2015). Figure 15 shows the dramatic changes in the organization of "welfare" that took place in the 1990s, as a large increase in federal spending devoted to EITC compensated the decline in AFDC/TANF spending.

Note that both the AFDC/TANF program and the EITC program are targeted at individuals who are (i) low income and (ii) with children, which are precisely the individuals affected by the decline in desire to work.

Strong Wage Growth from 1995 to 2000

The second half of the 1990s also coincides with strong positive growth in real wages for all deciles of the income distribution.[37]

Since higher wage leads to higher search intensity of primary workers, strong wage growth is unlikely to explain the decline in desire

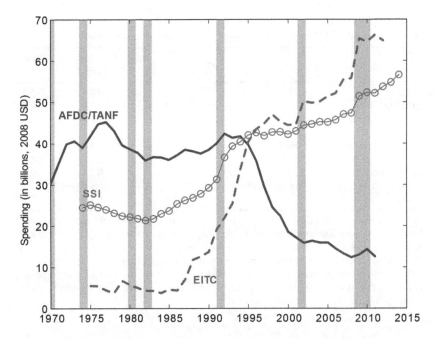

Fig. 15. Welfare spending (in 2008US$) for the Aid to Families with Dependent Children/ Temporary Assistance for Needy Families (AFDC/TANF) program, which provides cash assistance to poor families with dependent children; the Supplemental Security Income program (SSI), which pays cash to low-income people with disabilities or over 65; and the Earned Income Tax Credit (EITC), which provides a tax credit to low-to-middle income families.

to work through its effect on primary earners. However, large gains in wage income imply large gains in real family income, which can, through the added-worker effect, lead to lower desire to work among secondary workers.

A mechanism going through an added-worker effect is consistent with our earlier observation that desire to work only declined among nonsingle households (for which an added-worker effect is active).

E. Predicted Changes in Desire to Work

With the estimated coefficients in hand, we can isolate the contribution of a given characteristic or income variable to the change in the share of "want a job" nonparticipants. Specifically, the contribution of characteristic x_i to the decline in desire to work between 1994 and 2006 is given by:[38]

Table 3
Actual and Predicted Change in the Share of "Want a Job" Nonparticipants

		Aggregate	Females 25–55	Young 16–24
Actual		–4.0	–4.4	–5.7
Predicted, total		–2.2	–2.7	–2.4
Predicted, detail				
Demographics		+0.6	+0.4	0.1
Individual income	Disability	–1.1	–1.4	–0.3
	Welfare	–1.5	–1.8	–1.6
Family income	Earnings	–0.5	–0.4	–0.7
	Social transfers	+0.3	+0.4	+0.2
Other		+0.0	+0.1	–0.1

Note: "Actual" denotes the observed decline in the share of "want a job" nonparticipants between 1994 and 2006, and "predicted" reports the decline in the share of "want a job" nonparticipants as predicted by the model (excluding time fixed effects). In the category "individual income," "disability" combines the effect coming from the disability dummy with the effect coming from changes in the level of social insurance income, and "welfare" combines the effect coming from the welfare participation dummy with the effect coming from changes in the level of welfare income.

$$m_{06} - m_{94} = \beta_i(\bar{x}_{i,06} - \bar{x}_{i,94})$$

with $\bar{x}_{i,t}$ the average value of characteristic i in year t, $\bar{x}_{i,t} = \Sigma_i \varpi_{it} x_{it}$ with ϖ_{it} the share of nonparticipant of type i at time t.

The first column of table 3 shows that, excluding time fixed effects, our model explains about 53% of the decline in the fraction of nonparticipants reporting to want a job.

According to our model, the main factors behind the decline in desire to work are changes in welfare benefits and in insurance transfers (mainly disability insurance). Together, they lowered the share of nonparticipants wanting to work by a total of 2.6 ppt. Most of this effect is driven by the program participation dummies. As the number of individuals on disability increased, aggregate desire to work declined, and as the number of individuals participating in welfare decreased (figure 15), aggregate desire to work declined. We return to this point in our discussion section.

Family income and the added-worker effect had a small effect on desire to work because two forces compensated each other. On the one hand, higher family earnings due to higher wages lowered desire to work by 0.5 ppt, but on the other hand, lower income from social transfers raised desire to work by 0.3 ppt.

Finally, age, sex, education, the fraction of nonparticipants in school, the structure of the household, or the number of children do not explain the decline in desire to work.

Looking into subgroups, the model accounts for, respectively, 62 and 42% of the decline in the share of "want a job" nonparticipants for prime-age women and young workers. The added-worker effect seems to have played the largest role for young workers, as higher family earnings lowered their desire to work by 0.7 ppt.

All in all, our model estimated in the cross section does a good job at accounting for a large share of the decline in desire to work since 1994, particularly among prime-age females, the largest group affected by the decline in desire to work. While we are still short of explaining all of the decline in desire to work, our approach is likely to be downward biased. The income information in the March CPS is self-reported and thus likely plagued with measurement error. In particular, welfare or social security income, which play a large role in our story, are the income categories with the most measurement error (2010 CPS documentation). We have tried to control for measurement error through IV estimation, but some effects may remain. Relatedly, EITC payments may not be reported by respondents, and the previous analysis may miss the effect of the EITC expansion that could have also contributed to the decline in desire to work (through an added-worker effect), a point to which we turn next.[39]

F. Difference-in-Difference Estimates

Our previous results suggest that an important factor behind the decline in desire to work is a change in the provision of social transfers. Since welfare reforms of the mid-1990s are promising candidates for such changes, this section tries to identify the causal effects of (a) the expansion of EITC and (b) the AFDC/TANF reform.

To do so, we build on Eissa and Liebman (1996), Eissa and Hoynes (2004), and Mc Kernan et al. (2000) and we use a difference-in-difference strategy that exploits the facts that households without children receive little EITC or AFDC/TANF benefits and were little affected by the reforms. First, we identify the effects of the EITC expansion on desire to work by focusing on married individuals who are eligible to EITC, but not to AFDC. Then, we focus on single women with the aim of getting a lower bound on the effect of the AFDC-TANF reform.

EITC Expansion and Desire to Work among Married Mothers

Our first empirical implementation follows Eissa and Hoynes (2004) and focuses on married mothers: eligibility to EITC depends on the presence of a qualifying child in the family, and we will estimate the effect of the EITC expansion on desire to work by comparing the outcome of the affected group (married women with children) to the outcome of a comparison group that is little affected by the program (married women without children).[40]

We restrict the sample to married women between ages 25 and 55. To determine EITC eligibility, we treat as a dependent child any member of the tax-filing unit younger than 19. To better select women that are most likely to receive EITC, the sample is limited to individuals with no level of education higher than a high school degree.

We estimate the following formulation

$$P(N^w \mid N)_{it} = \gamma\eta_{gt} + \eta_g + \eta_t + \beta X_{it} + \varepsilon_{it} \qquad (6)$$

where i, g, and t index individual, group, and time, respectively, and with X_{it} a vector of controls (age, sex, education, family income, and number of children), η_g a fixed (group) effect equal to 1 if the woman has a child or more and zero otherwise, η_t a common time effect equal to 1 for any tax year after 1993, and η_{gt} the interaction between fixed group and time effect. Thus, γ measures the relative change in desire to work for single women with children after 1993, the year of the EITC expansion. Our estimation period is again 1988–2010.

Table 4 presents the results. After controlling for characteristics, we find that the EITC explains 71% of the decline in low-educated married mothers' desire to work between 1988–1993 and 1994–2010.

AFDC/TANF Reform and Desire to Work among Single Mothers

Our second empirical implementation follows Eissa and Hoynes (1996) and McKernan et al. (2000) and focuses on single mothers. To identify the effect of the AFDC/TANF reform on single mothers' desire to work, we compare the outcome of the affected group (single women with children) to the outcome of a comparison group that is unaffected by the program (single women without children) after the reform in 1996.

We use the same specification as with married women, except that the time dummy η_t equals 1 after 1996, the year of the AFDC/TANF reform. Table 4 presents the results. After controlling for characteristics,

Table 4
Difference-in-Difference Estimates of Desire to Work for Women with and without Children

	Married Women	Single Women
Policy change	EITC	AFDC/TANF
Source	Eissa and Hoynes (2004)	McKernan et al. (2000) Eissa and Hoynes (1996)
γ	−2.3*** (2.6)	−3.6*** (10.3)
Demographic controls	Yes	Yes
Total decline	−3.2	−6.8
Percent explained	71	52

Note: The estimation period is 1988–2010. The *t*-statistics are reported in parentheses. In the first column ("married women"), γ measures the relative change in desire to work for low-educated married women with children after the EITC 1993 reform. In the second column ("single women"), γ measures the relative change in desire to work for low-educated single women with children after the AFDC/TANF 1996 reform. Controls include age group, the number of children and an "in-school" dummy. "Total decline" depicts the total decline between the post- and prereform sample period. "Percent explained" is the percentage of "total decline" attributed to the policy change.

our coefficient estimate suggests that the AFDC/TANF reform explains 52% of the decline in low-educated single mothers' desire to work between 1988–1995 and 1996–2010.

A caveat is that since single mothers are eligible to both EITC and AFDC/TANF, our difference-in-difference estimate may be contaminated by the EITC expansion, which happened only two years before the AFDC/TANF reform. However, since the EITC expansion should increase desire to work, our estimate can also be seen as a lower bound on the effect of the AFDC/TANF reform on single mothers' desire to work.

G. Discussion: From Welfare to Disability?

Both our cross-sectional estimates (section V.E) as well as our difference-in-difference estimate (section V.F) indicate that the AFDC/TANF reform led to a decline in desire to work among nonparticipants. This set of results is surprising in light of a large literature on the effects of the welfare reforms on the labor market. Indeed, it is well accepted that the reform brought many nonparticipants, in particular single mothers, into the labor force (Blank 2002). However, our findings suggest that the welfare reform lowered desire to work for some nonparticipants, that is, pushed some nonparticipants away from the labor force.

In this section, we argue that these two views are not necessarily incompatible, and we speculate that the strong work requirements introduced by the AFDC/TANF reform could have, through a kind of "sink or swim" experience, pushed the "stronger" welfare recipients into the labor force *and* pushed the "weaker" welfare recipients outside of welfare and further away from the labor force, and possibly into disability insurance.

While employment and participation increased for many nonparticipants following the welfare reform, a significant minority of traditional welfare recipients were left both jobless and without welfare support. The decline in the number of caseloads was substantially larger than the corresponding gains in employment: for instance, while employment among single mothers rose by approximately 820,000 between 1995 and 2001, welfare caseloads fell by approximately twice as much (Blank 2002), suggesting that a number of traditional welfare recipients ended up neither employed nor on welfare. Consistent with this suggestive evidence, welfare leavers' studies (which follow individuals over time after they leave welfare) find that only about 60% of welfare leavers are working at some future point (Cancian et al. 1999; Loprest 2001), and Martinson (2000) finds that 20% of leavers never work in a four-year follow-up of work programs.

The emergence of a minority of traditional welfare recipients both jobless and without welfare support could have been caused by the AFDC/TANF reform. The reform made eligibility for welfare much stricter with (a) time limits and (b) stronger work requirements and the use of sanctions for noncompliant applicants (Blank 2002).[41] This made the receipt of welfare strongly conditional on the recipient's ability to find a job. For individuals with poor job-finding prospects and strong barriers to employment (e.g., mildly disabled, in poor health, emotionally disturbed, mentally slow, or addicted to drugs or alcohol),[42] this requirement can be hard to fulfill, leaving them ultimately out of the welfare system and without financial support.[43]

In turn, the need for financial support could have led a number of these traditional welfare recipients to apply for disability insurance, and in particular nonelderly SSI (which provides income support for low-income disabled individuals). A number of papers have argued that there is some degree of substitutability between AFDC/TANF and nonelderly SSI (e.g., Kubik 1999), and that some of the increase in SSI caseloads can be attributed to the AFDC/TANF reform.[44] Indeed, both programs serve disadvantaged populations that tend to have low levels of education, minimal work history, and high rates of both physical and mental impairments. Schmidt (2012) even suggests that SSI may be partially playing the role of an alternative safety net in the post-welfare-reform era.

However, SSI and AFDC/TANF differ in one important aspect: their emphasis on return to work. While welfare recipients are expected to ultimately return to the labor force, disability recipients are not. In fact, one of the requirements to receive disability benefits is that the "impairment prevents any other work that exists in the national economy" (Daly and Burkhauser 2003). Thus, our conjecture raises an interesting possibility: While the "welfare-to-work" reform was designed to do bring welfare recipients into the labor force, the reform could have had the opposite effect on the weaker nonparticipants by shifting them from a program with some connection to the labor force (welfare) to a program with no connection to the labor force (disability insurance).

H. A Flow Decomposition of the Share of "Want a Job" Nonparticipants

To conclude this paper, we show that the worker flows behind the movements in the share of "want a job" nonparticipants are consistent with our sink or swim conjecture. Importantly, and although the evidence is tantalizing, we caution that these are just correlations, and we leave a proper study of the sink or swim interpretation of the welfare reform for future research.[45] More details about the decomposition are provided in the appendix.[46]

Using our accounting framework, we can proceed as with the unemployment and participation rates and decompose movements in the share of "want a job" nonparticipants into the separate contributions of the worker flows in and out of $\{E, U, N^w, N^n\}$.

We find that two worker flows, the flows between N^w and N^n, account for most of the decline in the fraction of "want a job" nonparticipants (m_t) since the mid-1990s. Figure 16 plots the share of "want a job" nonparticipant, m_t, from 1994 to 2010 along with a counterfactual m_t generated solely by movements in N^wN^n and N^nN^w transitions. We can see that the two flows account for most of the downward trend in m_t since 1994,[47] so that the lower share of "want a job" is due mainly to (a) lower entry of nonparticipants into "want a job" (lower N^nN^w), and (b) higher exit from "want a job" to "not want a job" (higher N^wN^n).[48]

The behavior of the N^nN^w and N^wN^n flows is consistent with the "sink" aspect of the welfare reform, that is, the reform would have pushed the weaker nonparticipants further away from the labor force. The lower

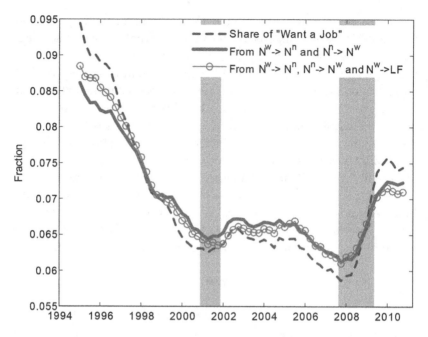

Fig. 16. Share of nonparticipants who report wanting a job (m) along with (a) the movements in m generated solely by changes in the $N^n - N^w$ and $N^w - N^n$ transition rates (thick plain line) and (b) the movements in m generated solely by changes in the $N^n - N^w$, $N^w - N^n$, and $N^w - U$ and $N^w - E$ transition rates, labeled $N^w - LF$ (circled line). Four-quarter moving averages, 1994–2010.

$N^n N^w$ rate could be due to lower entry into welfare (recall that an individual on welfare is much more likely to want a job), and the higher $N^w N^n$ rate could be due to higher exit from welfare (and possibly entry into a disability program).

Interestingly, the flows in and out of "want a job" are also consistent with the "swim" aspect of the welfare, that is, the reform would have pushed the stronger nonparticipants into the labor force. Although most of the decline in the share of "want a job" between 1994 and 2001 is due to flows between N^w and N^n, the next most important factor (figure 16) is an increase in the flows from "want a job" into the labor force (the flows from N^w to U or E).[49]

VI. Conclusion

This paper argues that a key aspect of the US labor market is the presence of time-varying heterogeneity across nonparticipants, that is, changes in the composition of the nonparticipation pool. In particular, we find that the share of nonparticipants who report wanting to work declined over the past 35 years, with a particularly strong decline in the second half of the 1990s. The decline primarily reflected reductions for prime-age females, and to a lesser extent, young people.

A decline in desire to work lowers both participation and unemployment because a nonparticipant who wants to work has both a higher probability of entering the labor force and a higher probability of joining unemployment conditional on entering the labor force. We quantify the effect of the decline in desire to work in the late 1990s on aggregate labor-market variables and find that the unemployment rate was lowered by about 0.5 ppt and the participation rate by about 1.75 ppt. Taken together, population aging and lower desire to work can account for the bulk of low-frequency movements in unemployment since the late 1960s.

We explore possible explanations for the decline in desire to work among nonparticipants using cross-sectional estimates of a model of nonparticipants' propensity to want a job as well as difference-in-difference estimates of the effects of the mid-1990s welfare reforms.

Our findings suggest that the mid-1990s "welfare-to-work" reforms—the 1993 EITC expansion and the 1996 AFDC/TANF reform—played an important role in lowering desire to work among nonparticipants. Our cross-sectional estimates imply that changes in the provision of welfare and social insurance explain about 60% of the decline in desire to work among prime-age females, while the difference-in-difference estimates attribute between 50 and 70% of the decline in mothers' desire to work to the welfare reforms.

We conjecture that two mechanisms could explain these results. First, the EITC expansion raised family income and reduced secondary earners' (typically women) incentives to work. Second, the strong work requirements introduced by the AFDC/TANF reform would have, through a kind of sink or swim experience, left the weaker (i.e., least able to find work) welfare recipients without welfare and pushed them away from the labor force and possibly into disability insurance.

Our conjecture raises an interesting possibility: While the welfare-to-work reform was designed to strengthen the incentives to work and to bring welfare recipients into the labor force, the reform could have had the opposite effect on some nonparticipants, either by giving secondary earners less incentives to work, and/or by shifting the weaker nonparticipants from a program with some connection to the labor force (welfare) to a program with no connection to the labor force (disability insurance). Exploring this possibility is an important task for future research.

We end this paper by speculating about possible future values for the unemployment rate at the next business-cycle peak. As of March 2015, more than five years since the end of the recession (as defined by the NBER), the unemployment rate stands at 5.5%. The "long-run" forces that drove the unemployment rate to a 40-year low of 3.8% in April 2000 (aging and lower desire to work), are still present today (figure 6), but are masked by a low job-finding rate that is still 20% below its pre-recession peak of 2006 and 30% below its 2000 peak. Bringing workers' transition rates back to their 2000 levels and holding the share of "want a job" nonparticipants at its current level imply an unemployment rate at 3.8%. Perhaps more realistically, bringing workers' transition rates back to their 2006 prerecession levels would imply an unemployment rate of 4.5%, suggesting that the unemployment rate still has substantial room for improvement.[50]

Endnotes

We would like to thank Martin Eichenbaum and Jonathan Parker (the editors), Robert Hall and Richard Rogerson (our discussants), as well as Vladimir Asriyan, Vasco Carvalho, Davide Debortoli, Chris Foote, Bart Hobijn, Andreas Hornstein, Chris Nekarda, Kris Nimark, Nicolas Petrosky-Nadeau, Thijs van Rens, Martin Schneider, Justin Wolfers, and Yanos Zylberberg for helpful comments. We also thank Roger Gomis, Erik Larsson, and Sebastien Willis for excellent research assistance. The views expressed here do not necessarily reflect those of the Federal Reserve Board or of the Federal Reserve System. Barnichon acknowledges financial support from the Spanish Ministerio de Economia y Competitividad (grant ECO2011-23188), the Generalitat de Catalunya (grants 2009SGR1157 and 2011BPB00152), and the Barcelona GSE Research Network. Any errors are our own. For acknowledgments, sources of research support, and disclosure of the authors' material financial relationships, if any, please see http://www.nber.org/chapters/c13601.ack.

1. Since older workers have lower unemployment and participation rates than younger workers, an older population will have both lower unemployment and participation rates. The aging of the baby boom generation has been proposed to explain the inverse U-shape movement in unemployment since the early 1970s (Perry 1970; Flaim 1979; Gordon 1982; Summers 1986; Shimer 1998, 2001).

2. See, for example, Aaronson, Davis, and Hu (2012), Elsby and Shapiro (2012), Moffitt (2012), Van Zandweghe (2012), Erceg and Levin (2013), and Hotchkiss, Pitts, and Rios-Avila (2013).

3. See, among others, Blanchard and Diamond (1989, 1990), Bleakley, Ferris, and Fuhrer (1999), Jones and Riddell (1999), Elsby, Michaels, and Solon (2009), Fujita and Ramey (2009), Barnichon (2012), Shimer (2012), and Elsby, Hobijn, and Sahin (2015).

4. There is a subtle difference in the survey before and after 1994. While the "desire for work" question is asked to all rotation groups after 1994, it is only asked to the outgoing rotation groups before 1994, that is, one-quarter of the sample. We verified that this difference did not affect our measurement by calculating the fraction of marginally attached

using only the outgoing rotation groups over the whole sample 1976–2010 and compared it with our main measure. Although this alternative measure is more noisy, the two series behave remarkably similarly after 1994.

5. To assess the robustness of our finding, we use another, little studied, CPS question that has also been consistently asked since 1976: "Do you intend to look for work during the next 12 months?" That measure also displays a marked decline in the second half of the 1990s.

6. Although not the focus of this paper, it is also interesting to note that desire to work among nonparticipants is strongly countercyclical.

7. See the appendix for details on the construction of these series, in particular the time-aggregation bias correction, at http://www.nber.org/data-appendix/c13601/appendix.pdf. Since the question about "desire for work" was only asked to the *outgoing* rotation groups prior to 1994, we cannot measure worker flows in and out of N^w or N^n prior to 1994 because we do not observe the labor force status over two consecutive months.

8. To do so, we match CPS microdata over three consecutive surveys (see Nekarda 2009), and we adjust the transition probabilities for time-aggregation bias as described in the appendix.

9. For young workers the secular decline appears to go back to the early 1980s, pointing to an older phenomenon.

10. Since we found that the most striking difference between N^w and N^n individuals was in their transition rates into the labor force (and not their subsequent transition rates once inside the labor force), we assume that the labor market with four states can be described by a Markov chain of order 1. In other words, once inside the labor force, N^w and N^n individuals behave like the other labor force participants. In the appendix, we consider a richer model that allows N^w and N^n individuals to continue behaving differently once inside the labor force. The quantitative results are similar to what we report in the main text. This is because N^w and N^n individuals do not behave very differently once inside the labor force. Thus, a change in the ratio of N^w and N^n individuals affect the unemployment rate mostly through the differences in their labor force entry rates.

11. In the United States, the magnitudes of the hazard rates are such that the half-life of a deviation of unemployment from its steady-state value is about one month (Shimer 2012).

12. See http://www.nber.org/data-appendix/c13601/appendix.pdf.

13. See the appendix at http://www.nber.org/data-appendix/c13601/appendix.pdf for more details.

14. Specifically, we split the population into the following eight sex/age groups: 16 to 24, male 25–34, male 35–44, male 45–54, female 25–34, female 35–44, female 45–54, and 55 and over.

15. See http://www.nber.org/data-appendix/c13601/appendix.pdf.

16. See http://www.nber.org/data-appendix/c13601/appendix.pdf.

17. The contribution of demographics to the participation rate is mainly driven by the population share of old (65+) workers (who have a much lower participation rate than the other groups), and the population share of 65+ workers has started to increase markedly after 2007.

18. We thank our discussants for pointing out these possible issues.

19. Our point recalls that of Elsby et al. (2015), who show that the apparent acyclicality of the participation rate is in fact the result of off-setting worker flows.

20. Abraham and Shimer (2001) show that this was due to the dramatic decline in women's transition rate from employment to nonparticipation (i.e., to women becoming more attached to the labor force).

21. A higher job-finding rate out of unemployment raises the labor force participation rate because it raises the number of employed workers relative to the number of unemployed workers, and because employed workers are much less likely to leave the labor force than unemployed workers.

22. These effects can be seen in the bottom panel of figure 9 for the UE rate (the high UE rate pushed up the participation rate through the "transitions out of U"), and in the second panel of figure 9 for the NE rate (the high NE rate pushed up the participation rate

through the "transitions out of E" for 1997–1999). See figures 7 and 8 in the appendix for time series of the UE and NE rates.

23. In contrast, the "marginal change" scenario would imply that the change in the share of "want a job" only had a marginal effect on the aggregate transition rate from N to U. Thus, the "marginal change" scenario cannot account for the secular decline in the transition rate from N to U, unless the transition rates from N^w to U and/or from N^n to U themselves displayed strong secular declines. However, there were no such declines (figure 8 in the appendix).

24. Similarly, while the participation of individuals not living alone started declining early in the twenty-first century, the participation rate of individuals living alone kept increasing up until the beginning of the Great Recession. This is again consistent with the smaller decline in desire to work for individuals living alone and consistent with our previous result that a lower desire for work should lead to a lower participation rate.

25. We leave a more formal labor-supply model with intrafamilial choice for the appendix.

26. In particular, the model will not fully capture the complex dynamics associated with the movements in and out of the labor force emphasized in sections III and IV. This aspect of the problem is a very active area of research. See, for instance, Krusell et al. (2012).

27. The model takes the wage- and job-finding rate as given. Such a simple model could be consistent with nonclearing labor-market models, such as search and matching models (Mortensen and Pissarides 1994), efficiency wage models, or search models with job rationing (Michaillat 2011).

28. Another possibility that we will not consider explicitly here is that desire to work changed over time because of a change in preferences. While we do not discard this possibility, we prefer to keep it as a residual explanation.

29. To construct our data set we link individuals and families across consecutive March supplements. The time series and cross-sectional behavior of the "want job" variable in our matched data set is quite similar to that in the unmatched March supplements and to that in the basic monthly CPS. Because unique individual and family-level identifiers comparable to identifiers in other years are missing in the 1995 March supplement, our data set excludes the years 1994 and 1995, but otherwise includes all years from 1988 to 2010. Since some of the detailed income categories we use were not available on a consistent basis prior to 1988, our sample period starts in 1988.

30. Earned labor income includes wages and salaries, self-employed income, and farm income. Welfare income (also called public assistance) includes AFDC/TANF benefits. Asset income includes interest income, dividend income, and rents. The category "other" includes all other individual income sources reported.

31. The SSDI provides income supplements to people who are physically restricted in their ability to be employed because of a notable disability, usually a physical disability. The SSI provides stipends to low-income people who are either aged (65 or older), blind, or disabled. There are two important differences between SSI and SSDI: (a) SSI is means tested, while SSDI is not, and (b) SSDI is only available to individuals with sufficient recent work experience.

32. To "rank" family members, we proceed as follows: We classify as primary earner the family member with the highest earned-labor income, or if none, the household head. The second worker is the spouse (if any) or the individual who is closest in age to the primary earner. We continue by considering family members with increasing distance in age from the primary earner.

33. The coefficients were estimated using cross-sectional variation from 1988 to 2010. Using cross-sectional variation over the pre-1994 period only gives similar results.

34. In 1988, the Job Opportunity program was created and required a much larger number of welfare recipients to engage in work-related activities (Moffitt 2003). The legislation also strongly encouraged states to conduct human capital, education, and training programs meant to facilitate return to employment.

35. The coefficient estimates for demographic characteristics are shown in the appendix.

36. One can note an interesting correlation between federal spending devoted to AFDC/TANF and the share of "want a job" nonparticipants: both increased in the early 1970s and then decreased markedly over the second-half of the 1990s.

37. Figure 4 in the appendix shows the cumulative changes in real wages since 1994 for different percentiles of the wage distribution.

38. We compare 1994 to 2006 in order to avoid cyclical phenomena linked to the Great Recession.

39. In theory, EITC payments are parts of social transfers. However, we fear that they are unlikely to be reported as such by respondents, since the transfer-related survey questions never mention receipts of any tax credit.

40. A caveat of this approach is that, while AFDC/TANF is primarily targeted to non-married individuals, a small fraction (about 7%) of AFDC/TANF caseloads are married couples with children. This is because a program called AFDC-UP provided cash benefits for two-parent families when the primary earner was unemployed. As a result, our estimate of the effect of EITC may be contaminated by the effect of the AFDC/TANF reform.

41. First, adult applicants can only receive benefits for a lifetime maximum of 60 months, and about 20 states chose to impose shorter time limits. Second, according to the federal provision of TANF, states must require recipients to engage in work activities and must impose sanctions (by reducing or terminating benefits) if an individual does not participate. Half of the families receiving TANF assistance must be engaged in a work activity for at least 30 hours a week (20 for single parents with young children). Job search, job readiness activities, or vocation training can only count as a satisfactory work activity for a limited amount of time.

42. For instance, Dworsky and Courtney (2007) find that most of the TANF applicants in Milwaukee face such barriers to employment.

43. Consistent with this idea, Grogger (2000) finds that welfare time limits lowered the number of caseloads by about 200,000 during the second half of the 1990s.

44. Schmidt and Sevak (2004) find that the prereform, state-level welfare waivers—prereform experiments of a welfare system with stronger work requirements—led to a significant increase in the likelihood that single-mother families reported SSI receipt. Schmidt (2012) finds that the TANF sanction policies significantly increased SSI caseloads share for both adults and children. Kubik (2003) also argues that switching from AFDC/TANF to SSI has financial advantages both for the individuals as well as the state.

45. Note that the point of this paper is to show that time variation in the characteristics of nonparticipants—the decline in the share of "want a job"—are a crucial aspect of secular movements in the unemployment and participation rate. We do not claim that the contribution of the late-1990s decline in the share of "want a job" to (a) unemployment (about −.5 ppt) and (b) participation (about −1.75 ppt) *is* the effect of the welfare reform on unemployment and participation. Doing so would require identifying the contribution of the welfare reform to each worker flow (for instance, using a difference-in-difference approach as in the previous section) and then translating the movements in the flows *caused* by the reform into changes in unemployment and participation rates.

46. See http://www.nber.org/data-appendix/c13601/appendix.pdf.

47. Confirming this visual inspection, a variance decomposition exercise as in Fujita and Ramey (2009) shows that $\lambda_t^{N^w N^n}$ and $\lambda_t^{N^n N^w}$ account for, respectively, 50% and 25% of the variance of m_t.

48. The transition rates between N^w and N^n are plotted in figure 9 in the appendix.

49. The transition rates from "want a job" (N^w) to U or E are plotted in figure 8 in the appendix.

50. One can do a similar exercise for the participation rate. Bringing workers' transition rates back to their 2006 levels (but keeping both demographics and the share of "want a job" at their current levels) implies a participation rate of 65.8%, lower than the 2000 peak at 67.3%, but substantially higher than the rate of 62.7% as of March 2015.

References

Aaronson, Daniel, Jonathan Davis, and Luojia Hu. 2012. "Explaining the Decline in the US Labor Force Participation Rate." Chicago FRB Letter no. 296

(March), Federal Reserve Bank of Chicago. https://www.chicagofed.org/publications/chicago-fed-letter/2012/march-296.

Abraham, K. and R. Shimer. 2001. "Changes in Unemployment Duration and Labor-Force Attachment." In *The Roaring Nineties: Can Full Employment Be Sustained?*, ed. Alan B. Krueger and Robert M. Solow, 367–420. New York: Russell Sage Foundation and Century Foundation Press.

Autor D., and M. Duggan. 2003. "The Rise in the Disability Rolls and the Decline in Unemployment." *Quarterly Journal of Economics* 118 (1): 157–205.

Barnichon, R. 2012. "Vacancy Posting, Job Separation, and Unemployment Fluctuations." *Journal of Economic Dynamics and Control* 36 (3): 315–30.

Blanchard, O., and P. Diamond. 1989. "The Beveridge Curve." *Brookings Paper on Economic Activity* 1:1–60.

———. 1990. "The Cyclical Behavior of the Gross Flows of US Workers." *Brookings Papers on Economic Activity* 21 (2): 85–156.

Blank, R. 2002. "Evaluating Welfare Reform in the United States." *Journal of Economic Literature* 40 (4): 1105–66.

Bleakley, H., A. Ferris, and J. Fuhrer. 1999. "New Data on Worker Flows during Business Cycles." *New England Economic Review* 1999 (July): 49–76.

Cancian, M., R. Haveman, T. Kaplan, D. Meyer, and B. Wolfe. 1999. "Work, Earnings and Well-Being after Welfare." In *Economic Conditions and Welfare Reform*, ed. Sheldon H. Danziger, 161–86. Kalamazoo, MI: W. E. Upjohn Institute for Employment Research.

Clark, K., and L. Summers. 1979. "Labor Market Dynamics and Unemployment: A Reconsideration." *Brookings Papers on Economic Activity* 1:13–60.

Daly, M., and R. Burkhauser. 2003. "The Supplemental Security Income Program." In *Means-Tested Transfer Programs in the United States*, ed. Robert Moffitt, 79–140. Chicago: University of Chicago Press.

Darby, M., J. Haltiwanger, and M. Plant. 1986. "The Ins and Outs of Unemployment: The Ins Win." NBER Working Paper no. 1997, Cambridge, MA.

Dworsky, A., and M. Courtney. 2007. "Barriers to Employment among TANF Applicants and Their Consequences for Self-Sufficiency." *Families in Society* 88 (3): 379–89.

Eissa, N., and H. Hoynes. 2004. "Taxes and the Labor Market Participation of Married Couples: The Earned Income Tax Credit." *Journal of Public Economics* 88:1931–58.

Eissa, N., and J. Liebman. 1996. "Labor Supply Response to the Earned Income Tax Credit." *Quarterly Journal of Economics* 111 (2): 605–37.

Elsby, M., B. Hobijn, and A. Sahin. 2015. "On the Importance of the Participation Margin for Labor Market Fluctuations." *Journal of Monetary Economics* 72 (May): 64–82.

Elsby, M., R. Michaels, and G. Solon. 2009. "The Ins and Outs of Cyclical Unemployment." *American Economic Journal: Macroeconomics* 1 (1): 84–110.

Elsby, M., and M. Shapiro. 2012. "Why Does Trend Growth Affect Equilibrium Employment? A New Explanation of an Old Puzzle." *American Economic Review* 102 (4): 1378–413.

Erceg, C., and A. Levin. 2013. "Labor Force Participation and Monetary Policy in the Wake of the Great Recession." CEPR Discussion Paper no. 9668, Center for Economic and Policy Research.

Flaim, P. 1979. "The Effect of Demographic Changes on the Nation's Unemployment Rate." *Monthly Labor Review* 102 (3): 13–19.

Flinn, C., and J. Heckman. 1983. "Are Unemployment and Out of the Labor Force Behaviorally Distinct Labor Force States?" *Journal of Labor Economics* 1 (1): 28–42.

Fujita, S., and G. Ramey. 2009. "The Cyclicality of Separation and Job Finding Rates." *European Economic Review* 76 (May): 60–84.

Gordon, R. 1982. "Inflation, Flexible Exchange Rates, and the Natural Rate of Unemployment." In *Workers, Jobs and Inflation* ed. Martin N. Baily, 89–152. Washington, DC: Brookings Institute.

Grogger, J. 2003. "The Effect of Time Limits, the EITC, and Other Policy Changes on Welfare Use, Work, and Income among Female-Headed Families." *Review of Economics and Statistics* 85 (2): 394–408.

Hall, R. 1970. "Why is the Unemployment Rate so High at Full Employment?" *Brookings Papers on Economic Activity* 33:369–402.

Hotchkiss, J., M. Pitts, and F. Rios-Avila. 2012. "A Closer Look at Non-Participants during and after the Great Recession." Working Paper No.2012-10, Federal Reserve Bank of Atlanta.

Jones, S., and C. Riddell. 1999. "The Measurement of Unemployment: An Empirical Approach." *Econometrica* 67:142–67.

Juhn, C., K. Murphy, and R. Topel. 2002. "Current Unemployment, Historically Contemplated." *Brookings Papers on Economic Activity* 2002 (1): 79–116.

Juhn, C., and S. Potter. 2007. "Is There Still an Added-Worker Effect?" NBER Retirement Research Center Paper no. NB 07-14, Cambridge, MA.

Krusell P., T. Mukoyama, R. Rogerson, and A. Sahin. 2012. "Is Labor Supply Important for Business Cycles?" NBER Working Paper no. 17779, Cambridge, MA.

Kubik, J. 1999. "Incentives for the Identification and Treatment of Children with Disabilities: The Supplemental Security Income Program." *Journal of Public Economics* 73 (2): 187–215.

———. 2003. "Fiscal Federalism and Welfare Policy: The Role of States in the Growth of Child SSI." *National Tax Journal* 56 (1): 61–79.

Loprest, P. 2001. "How Are Families that Left Welfare Doing? A Comparison of Early and Recent Welfare Leavers" *FRBNY Economic Policy Review*. https://www.newyorkfed.org/medialibrary/media/research/epr/01v07n2/0109loprest.pdf.

Lundberg, S. 1985. "The Added Worker Effect." *Journal of Labor Economics* 3 (1): 11–37.

Martinson, K. 2000. "The National Evaluation of Welfare-to-Work Strategies Evaluation: The Experience of Welfare Recipients Who Find Jobs." MDRC for US Dept. Health Human Services, Washington, DC. http://www.mdrc.org/sites/default/files/full_558.pdf.

McKernan, S., R. Lerman, N. Pindus, and J. Valente. 2000. "The Relationship between Metropolitan and Non-metropolitan Locations, Changing Welfare Policies, and the Employment of Single Mothers." JCPR Working Paper no. 192, Northwestern University/University of Chicago Joint Center for Poverty Research.

Michaillat, P. 2011. "Do Matching Frictions Explain Unemployment? Not in Bad Times." *American Economic Review* 102 (4): 1721–50.

Moffitt, R. 2003. "The Temporary Assistance for Needy Families Program." In *Means-Tested Transfer Programs in the United States*, ed. Robert Moffitt, 291–364. Chicago: University of Chicago Press.

———. 2012. "The US Employment-Population Reversal in the 2000s: Facts and Explanations." *Brookings Papers on Economic Activity* Fall:201–64.

Mortensen, D and C. Pissarides. 1994. "Job Creation and Job Destruction in the Theory of Unemployment," *Review of Economic Studies*, 61, 397–415.

Nekarda, C. 2009. "A Longitudinal Analysis of the Current Population Survey: Assessing the Cyclical Bias of Geographic Mobility." Working Paper, Federal

Reserve Board of Governors. https://www.researchgate.net/publication/237587456_A_Longitudinal_Analysis_of_the_Current_Population_Survey_Assessing_the_Cyclical_Bias_of_Geographic_Mobility.

Perry, G. 1970. "Changing Labor Markets and Inflation." *Brookings Papers on Economic Activity* 3:411–41.

Rothstein, J., and A. Nichols. 2015. "The Earned Income Tax Credit." NBER Working Paper no.21211, Cambridge, MA.

Schmidt, Lucie. 2012. "The supplemental Security Income Program and Welfare Reform," Discussion Paper, Federal Reserve Bank of Boston.

Schmidt, L., and P. Sevak. 2004. "AFDC, SSI, and Welfare Reform Aggressiveness: Caseload Reductions vs. Caseload Shifting." *Journal of Human Resources* 39 (3): 792–812.

Shimer, R. 1998. "Why Is the US Unemployment Rate So Much Lower?" *NBER Macroeconomics Annual 1998*, vol. 13, ed. Ben Bernanke and Julio Rotemberg, 11–61. Cambridge, MA: MIT Press.

———. 2001. "The Impact of Young Workers on the Aggregate Labor Market." *Quarterly Journal of Economics* 116:969–1008.

———. 2012. "Reassessing the Ins and Outs of Unemployment." *Review of Economic Dynamics* 15 (2): 127–48.

Summers, L. 1986. "Why Is the Unemployment Rate So Very High near Full Employment?" *Brookings Papers on Economic Activity* 17 (2): 339–96.

Van Zandweghe, W. 2012. "Interpreting the Recent Decline in Labor Force Participation." *Economic Review* 2012 (1): 5–34.

Comment

Richard Rogerson, *Princeton University and NBER*

The stated objective of this paper is to shed light on the forces that have shaped secular trends in the unemployment rate and the participation rate in the United States in recent decades. Due to space limitations, all of my comments will focus on the paper's analysis of the participation rate. Figure 1 in the paper shows that the participation rate has followed a pronounced inverted U-shape since the late 1960s, increasing by more than 7 percentage points between 1970 and the late 1990s, but subsequently decreasing by more than 4 percentage points.

The central message of the paper is that changes in the cross-sectional heterogeneity of *nonparticipants* are key to understanding the recent decline in the participation rate. To support this message, the authors use information from a question in the household survey that asks respondents whether they "want a job." Their key piece of evidence is that the fraction of non-participants who want a job displays a downward trend over the last three decades that accelerated during the later part of the 1990s.

While there are many details in the authors' analysis that merit discussion, my comments will focus on two broad points. First, I argue that the new labor market indicator proposed by the authors as a key (exogenous) driving force—the fraction of nonparticipants who want a job—suffers from serious endogeneity problems that the authors fail to recognize or deal with. Second, I suggest that there is a much simpler and preferable measure that the authors could have examined, namely, the fraction of the *population* that does not want a job. Analysis of this alternative measure yields a very clear negative relationship between it and the participation rate. But this finding—that the participation rate goes down when a greater fraction of the population does not want a job—seems little more than a tautology and does not strike me as a major insight into thinking about the underlying forces that shape secular movements in the participation rate. In summary, while I think the authors' focus on heterogeneity is appropriate and important, I am not convinced that the analysis has delivered new insights into the forces that have shaped the evolution of the participation rate.

To present my arguments, I need to first develop a theoretical framework. For purposes of exposition I develop the simplest framework that allows me to illustrate the key endogeneity problem that the paper ignores. This simple model will not display all of the salient features of transitions found in the data and as documented by the authors. While the key point I make is robust to extensions that would deliver these features, there would be a cost in terms of transparency.

The essence of the model is to provide a rationale for the existence of individuals who say that they want a job, but nonetheless do not engage in search. This sort of conceptual framework is clearly essential to interpret the authors' analysis. Let the population consist of a continuum of individuals, with total mass normalized to 1. These individuals are heterogeneous, with the heterogeneity summarized by a one-dimensional parameter, denoted by z, where z represents the net flow utility value associated with employment. A high positive z individual is someone who sees a very large flow benefit in working, while a very large negative z individual is someone who sees a large flow benefit in not working.[1] An individual's value of z is constant over time, and in what follows I will assume that the distribution of individuals across z has no mass points, so that we do not have to worry about how to assign individuals who are indifferent between two actions.

In a world without any labor market frictions, individuals with z positive would choose to work and individuals with z negative would choose not to work, and a labor market survey would not find any individuals not working who report wanting a job. But adding some basic labor market frictions and costly search can change this. In particular, assume that search is a discrete choice variable with the utility cost of search given by $\bar{u}$. If a nonemployed individual searches, they will receive an employment opportunity with probability ϕ_u. If a nonemployed individual does not incur the search cost, they may still receive an employment opportunity, but the probability is $\phi_n < \phi_u$. Also, assume that individuals who are employed in period t face a probability σ of losing their job at the beginning of the following period, in which case they find themselves nonemployed and need to decide whether to search.

In this frictional labor market, it remains true that anyone with z positive prefers to work, and anyone with z negative prefers not to work. Because individuals with z negative do not desire to work, they would clearly not exert search effort. But in the presence of costly search, individuals with sufficiently small positive values of z will also choose to not search, since the small positive benefit from working is not sufficient to overcome the utility cost associated with search. In fact, there will be a reservation value, denoted by $\hat{z}$, with the property that $\hat{z} > 0$ and only individuals with $z \geq \hat{z}$ choose to search.

At any point in time each individual in this economy is easily assigned to one of the three labor market states of employment (E), unemployment (U), and not in the labor force (N): nonemployed individuals with $z \geq \hat{z}$ will be counted as unemployed, while nonemployed individuals with $z \leq \hat{z}$ will be counted as not in the labor force. Moreover, and central to what follows, the model also delivers a group of nonparticipants that would answer yes to the question of do you want a job, namely those individuals with $0 \leq z \leq \hat{z}$.

Although this model features a continuous distribution of heterogeneity, in terms of labor market dynamics it is sufficient to categorize individuals according to which of the three types they are: those who accept employment when offered and search when not employed (i.e., $z \geq \hat{z}$), those who accept employment when offered but do not search when nonemployed (i.e., $z \in [0, \hat{z}]$), and those who do not accept employment when offered and do not search (i.e., $z \leq 0$). Consistent with the labels that the authors use in their paper I will label those with $z \in [0, \hat{z}]$ as marginal workers (M) and those with $z \leq 0$ as inactive workers (I). Those with $z \geq \hat{z}$ will be referred to as attached workers (A). Denote the shares of each of these three types in the population as μ_j, for $j = A, M,$ or I. These fractions are, of course, functions of the cross-sectional density describing the heterogeneity in the economy. In a steady-state equilibrium, there will be a constant distribution of attached workers across the E and U states (determined by the values of ϕ_u and σ), a constant distribution of the marginal workers across the E and N states (determined by the values of ϕ_n and σ), and all of the inactive workers will be in the N state. For given values of $\phi_u, \phi_n,$ and σ, the aggregate distribution of individuals across the three states $E, U,$ and N will depend on the μ_j.

As noted above, this model is too simple to capture all of the patterns that the authors find in the data and emphasize in their analysis,[2] but it does capture the key mechanism linking participation and heterogeneity that the authors stress: if we move some individuals from the marginal group into the inactive group, then the (steady state) participation rate for this economy will fall. Importantly, the participation rate will also fall if we move some individuals from the attached group into the inactive group, so that the most basic result is simply that an increase in the size of the inactive group will decrease the participation rate. Given the structure that has been assumed, this result is a mathematical proposition and merely serves to establish the logical possibility that changes in composition can lead to changes in the aggregate participation rate. The key objective of this paper is to measure these compositional changes and assess their consequences; this is where I think the authors make a questionable choice about how to proceed.

The authors measure the fraction of *nonparticipants* who say they want a job and take this as a measure of the exogenous change in the composition of types, that is, they interpret a decrease in this ratio as evidence of a shift of individuals from M into I. The problem with this inference is a very basic one: in steady state, marginal individuals are distributed between E and N, with the relative size of the two groups dictated by the parameters ϕ_n and σ. It follows that the fraction of individuals in N who want a job is influenced not only by the μ_j but also by the ϕ_i and σ. Any attempt to isolate movements in composition would have to explicitly decompose the changes in this ratio into changes due to the two different sets of parameters. A basic limitation of the analysis in this paper is that the authors make no effort to do this.[3]

Moreover, it seems apparent that the failure to do so leads to some misguided inference on the part of the authors. It is well known that the 1990s was associated with a booming labor market and, in particular, very high job-finding rates. My simple model predicts that during such a period we will see a decrease in the fraction of nonparticipants who want a job, and as the authors note, this is exactly what is seen in the data. If this decrease were purely the result of a shift of individuals from either A or M into I then we would also have seen a drop in employment, but, of course, the 1990s saw a large increase in the employment-to-population ratio. Does this mean that *all* of the drop in the share of nonparticipants who want a job is due to changes in job-finding rates? Of course not, but the key point is that one cannot assume that all of the drop is driven by exogenous changes in composition, a point that the authors fail to adequately recognize or deal with.

However, while the authors adopt what I see as a seriously flawed empirical strategy, my model suggests a very simple alternative that is

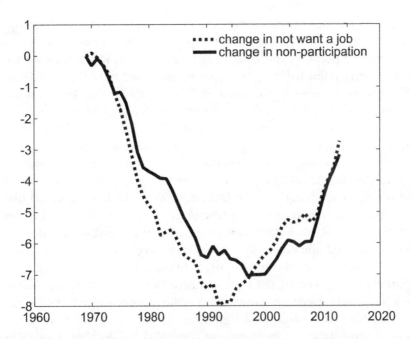

Fig. 1. Changes in share not wanting and job and nonparticipation

relatively immune to the basic endogeneity problem just described. The authors' approach was to look at the ratio of M to I within N to infer something about the overall movement of workers between M and I. The reason this was an unwise strategy is that the ratio of M individuals in N is itself affected by labor market conditions. As I noted earlier, there is nothing special about movements from M into I as opposed to movements from A into I. It follows that our primary concern should be to focus on the size of the I group. In my example one can directly measure the changing size of the I group by simply measuring the number of people in N who do not want a job, relative to the overall population.

What would the authors have found if they had instead focused on the size of the "don't want a job" group relative to overall population (i.e., the noninstitutionalized civilian population age 16 and older)? Using data supplied by the authors on their series for the share of nonparticipants who want a job along with BLS data on the civilian participation rate, I construct two series: the share of the population that does not want a job and the nonparticipation rate (i.e., the percentage of the population that is not in the labor force). Figure 1 plots the two series, normalized so that each is zero in the initial year, 1969.

The two series move almost perfectly in lockstep during both the increasing and decreasing phases of participation. However, whereas the turning point for the share of not want a job is in the early 1990s, the turning point for the participation rate is not until the late 1990s. The earlier discussion provides a likely rationale for this: the booming US economy in the 1990s was characterized by a high job-finding rate, which in turn lead to a greater share of M workers in the labor force, thereby exerting an opposing force on the participation rate.

The main message that comes from figure 1 is simple and mundane: understanding trend changes in participation is tantamount to understanding trend changes in the fraction of individuals who would like to work. This was true when participation was increasing during the 1970s and 1980s, and it remains true during the recent secular decline in the participation rate. Is this observation very powerful? I would say not. To be sure, for those who might think that the recent decline in participation is dominated by discouraged workers—those who want a job but have given up on searching—the answer might be yes, since in this case there could be a significant divergence of the two series. But we already know from numerous existing studies that changes in the size of the discouraged worker group is not driving the decrease in participation. Once this possibility is off the table, it seems to me that saying there is a decrease in the share of the population that wants a job is really just another way of saying that the participation rate is decreasing. That is, I think this observation is effectively tautological in nature and does not provide any powerful new insights into thinking about the forces that are shaping the decline in participation.

In the simple model that I described, changes in the share of the population in I reflect changes in the cross-sectional nature of heterogeneity as summarized by the distribution of z. In this sense I am fully in agreement with the authors that to understand changes in participation it is essential to understand the changes in the nature of cross-sectional heterogeneity. However, I see no basis for suggesting that the key changes in heterogeneity took place within the group of nonparticipants. It is entirely plausible that some individuals have moved from A into I, as would happen, for example, if some change caused an individual working full time to retire sooner than previously planned, or some change led a working mother to leave the labor force and care for her children.

But this distinction aside, the real issue is to isolate the underlying source of the changes in heterogeneity. In my simple model, the heterogeneity was summarized by the variable z. But this variable represents an aggregate of several underlying variables, including market conditions (e.g., the wage, or the price of child care), preferences toward work and/or nonmarket opportunities (e.g., attitudes toward market-provided childcare), and the policy environment (e.g., social insurance programs). It follows that the task is to find the dominant changes underlying the implied changes in the distribution of z. For example, if one looks at the literature on the rise of female labor force participation, it is understood that the proximate driving force is the increase in the share of women that want to work, and the whole point of the literature is to isolate the underlying causes of that increase.

The authors do make some attempt to tackle this issue, arguing that one-time changes in policy during the mid-1990s have played a key role. I think this discussion is interesting, and the possibility that some of the reforms had unintended consequences for participation is an intriguing one. But, at least in its current form, I do not yet find this analysis to be very compelling. The first and main reason is that all of their analysis is filtered through their measure of the share of nonparticipants who want a job, and as I have discussed previously, I see this as a very flawed measure for these purposes. Second, if one looks at figure 1, the share of the population in the "not want a job" category seems to display a very steady secular rise starting around 1992 and continuing until around 2005, at which point it levels off for a few years before showing another sharp uptick following the recent recession. At least on the surface, these dynamics would lead me to look for slow-moving driving forces rather than one-time changes, though this is obviously somewhat speculative.

Endnotes

For acknowledgments, sources of research support, and disclosure of the author's material financial relationships, if any, please see http://www.nber.org/chapters/c13602.ack.

1. My analysis will treat z as exogenous. In a model in which individuals can save, the implicit flow value associated with work will be affected by endogenous savings decisions. But the key point I am making is robust to such an extension.

2. In particular, in this model individuals in M are never unemployed. One could either allow individual types to evolve stochastically, or assume that M individuals have a random component to z that causes them to switch between search and no search when nonemployed. Because I focus on implications for participation, I do not believe that these extensions are of first-order importance here.

3. Note that the value of $\hat{z}$ is in principle affected by changes in the ϕ_j and σ, so that my discussion is somewhat oversimplified.

Comment

Robert E. Hall, *Stanford University and NBER*

About one-third of the working-age US population is neither working nor looking for work in any given month, according to the Current Population Survey. A small group of those who are out of the labor force indicate an interest in working. The authors study that group and attribute the downward trends in unemployment and employment to a downward trend in the fraction of people who are out of the labor force, but interested in working. The paper applies ideas from a model of individual dynamics in the labor market, which emphasizes the roles of transition rates among the three basic categories of labor market status: out of the labor market, unemployed, and employed.

The key question in the Current Population Survey that underlies this research is, "Do you want a job now, either full or part time?" The survey asks this question of everybody ages 16 years and older who did not work in the survey week and did not engage in specific job-seeking activities in the past four weeks. The paper diagnoses a secular decline in "desire to work," especially in the boom of the 1990s. It teaches us a lot about how people behave who are not currently working or looking for work, but are interested in working. The proposition that a period of extraordinarily favorable conditions in the labor market and rapid growth of employment coincided with a decline in interest in working is a surprise. But I'm not convinced that there was a decline in the desire to work in the 1990s; rather, such a decline began around the year 2000.

Table 1 gives some basic data about people who were not in the labor force in 2007, a year of normal conditions in the labor market.[1] About 34% of the population 16 years and older was out of the labor force, neither employed nor looking for work, and recorded as unemployed. The great majority responded "no" to the question about wanting a job

Table 1
Responses to the Question about Wanting a Job and to Related Questions, 2007

	Count (1,000s)	Percent of population
Working age population	231,867	100
Not in labor force	78,744	33.96
Not in labor force, do not want a job now	74,041	31.93
Not in labor force, want a job now	4,703	2.03
Not in labor force, want a job now, did not search for work in previous year	2,748	1.19
Not in labor force, want a job now, searched for work in previous year	1,955	0.84
Not in labor force, want a job now, not available to work now	560	0.24

now. Those answering "yes" accounted for 2% of the population. More than half of them, about 1.2% of the population, had not searched for work in the previous year, suggesting that their interest in working had not actually been high enough to take action to get jobs. A small group, accounting for one-quarter of 1% of the population, said they were not available to work now even though they wanted a job now. Overall, in a normal year, 0.6% of the population 16 and older who were out of the labor force wanted jobs, had taken action to find jobs in the prior year, and were currently available to work. By contrast, in that year, 3.0% of the population was not working but had actively looked for work in the past four weeks and were, therefore, counted as unemployed.

The paper is about changes over time in the fraction of the population who were out of the labor force who wanted jobs. Figure 1 shows the fraction over the period from 1994 (when the Current Population Survey was revamped) to 2014. During the vigorous expansion of the 1990s, unemployment fell to a low of 4.0% of the labor force averaged over the year 2000. The fraction of the population not working but desiring work fell dramatically over that period. Unemployment oscillated through 2007 and the fraction desiring work remained roughly constant through 2007. The want-job fraction rose sharply when unemployment skyrocketed in late 2008 and reached its peak in 2010. With the return of unemployment down to close to normal levels, the want-job fraction has fallen only a small amount.

I find it difficult to reconcile figure 1 with the framework and conclusions of the paper. The interpretation that jumps out of the figure to my eye is that the want-job fraction has the same determinants as does

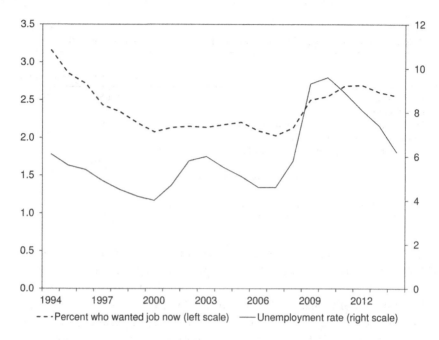

Fig. 1. Percent of population age 16+ who said they wanted a job now

unemployment. In 1994, in this interpretation, the labor market was somewhat soft, with unemployment at 6.1%. Unemployment was high because job-finding rates were abnormally low, according to modern theories of unemployment. The want-job population suffers, in part, from being in a state of concealed unemployment. Job-finding rates in that group are positive but low, and are even lower in a soft market such as in 1994. Higher job-finding rates later in the 1990s resulted in shrinkage of the unemployed population and of the want-job population.

Figure 2 limits the want-job population to those who said they were available now. The positive correlation between the percent of the population in that subgroup and the unemployment rate is even more striking with this limitation. The size of this subgroup seems to be determined by essentially the same forces as is the unemployment rate. On the other hand, figure 3 shows that the other subgroup, who were not available to work, did not track unemployment after 2000, though it did decline along with unemployment in the 1990s. Figure 4 limits the population who wanted to work to those who had searched in the previous year. This limitation also isolates a group whose size appears to be determined by the same forces as unemployment.

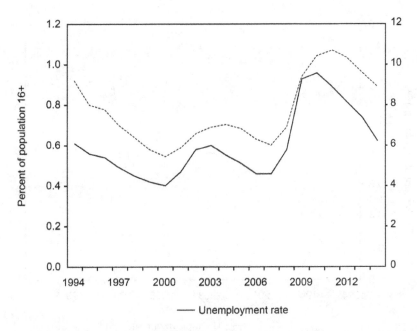

Fig. 2. Percent of population age 16+ who said they wanted a job now and were available to work.

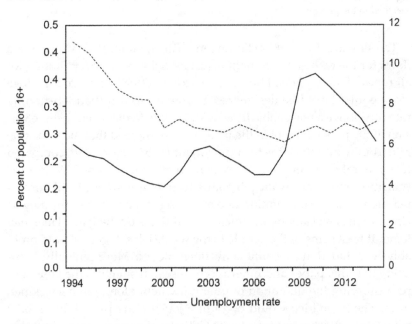

Fig. 3. Percent of population age 16+ who said they wanted a job now but were not available

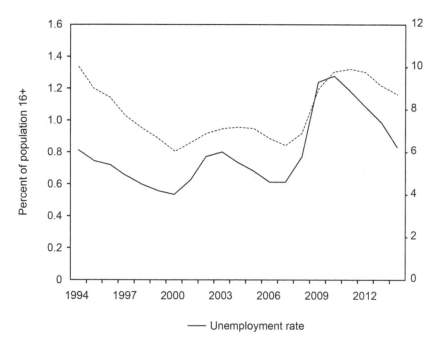

Fig. 4. Percent of population age16+ who said they wanted a job now and had searched in the previous year.

The slowing down of job finding in weak labor markets slows down flows for the want-job population, just as it slows down job finding for all types of job seekers. Flinn and Heckman (1983) advanced the idea that people should be designated as unemployed if their job-finding rates are above a reasonable threshold. Results in the meeting-time version of the paper, but not in the final version, showed that the transition rate from want-job status to employment is 15% per month, compared to a general rate from unemployment to employment of 27%. But the transition rate from want-job status to unemployment is 47 percent per month, so the job-finding rate over longer spans of months may be closer to the level among the unemployed. Thus by the Flinn-Heckman logic, at least some of the people in the want- job category should probably be included in the count of the unemployed. More generally, I conclude that this paper and other recent research suggests the benefit of reconsidering the definition of unemployment along Flinn-Heckman lines. The basic idea would be to fit a job-finding probability model using a wider set of answers to the CPS questions—not just recent job-seeking activities, but answers to questions about wanting a job and

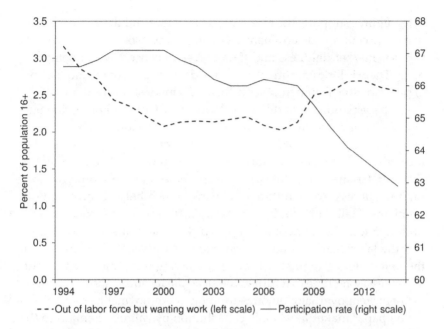

Fig. 5. The labor force participation rate and the fraction of nonparticipants wanting jobs

planning to start a job search. This definition of unemployment would set a threshold value for the estimated probability and classify as unemployed all the nonworking respondents whose fitted job-finding probability met the threshold.

The paper seeks to use the answers to the want-a-job question to measure a concept the authors call the desire to work. To me, the desire to work is the difference between the payoff of working and the payoff of nonwork activities. People who are neither looking for work nor working are those with a negative desire to work. A change in the economic environment that raises the general desire to work will result in an increase in the labor force participation rate, which is the fraction of the population with a positive desire to work. By this logic, the best measure of the desire to work is the participation rate. Figure 5 compares the participation rate to the want-job fraction of the population. The participation rate rose a little during the boom of the 1990s, at the same time that the large decline in the want-job fraction declined sharply. Starting in 2000, participation began to fall. Participation began to fall more rapidly around the time of the Great Recession, and the fall continued at about the same rate as the recovery began in the labor market in 2011. Nothing in the figures supports the idea that participation and the want-job fraction share common determinants. Rather, the want-job fraction responds to labor market tightness and thus moves in concert with unemployment. There is little agreement about the determinants of the movements of participation. Demographics have only a modest contribution.

The paper studies monthly transitions in the Current Population Survey. This approach may give a distorted impression of labor market dynamics because of classification errors in the survey and because of the high incidence of very short jobs (durations of less than one month). Krueger, Cramer, and Cho (2014) were the pioneers in studying job-finding success over multimonth spans, which helps overcome both problems. Hall and Schulhofer-Wohl (2015) pursue the idea for job-finding rates. The claim of the paper (p. 459) that transitions are so fast that the labor market is always close to its steady state is an artifact of the first-order assumption. There is a growing realization that it actually takes a long time to return to the steady state after a shock—witness the persistent overhang of long-duration unemployment.

The paper makes a valuable contribution by calling attention to the neglected want-job questions in the Current Population Survey. Much more research should be done to integrate the answers to those questions into models of labor-market dynamics. However, I'm not sold on the attempt of the paper to link the answers to the want-job question to the concept of the desire to work.

Endnotes

For acknowledgments, sources of research support, and disclosure of the author's material financial relationships, if any, please see http://www.nber.org/chapters/c13603.ack.
1. A spreadsheet with all of the data and calculations in this discussion is available from my website.

References

Flinn, Christopher J., and James J. Heckman. 1983. "Are Unemployment and Out of the Labor Force Behaviorally Distinct Labor Force States?" *Journal of Labor Economics* 1 (1): 28–42.
Hall, Robert E., and Sam Schulhofer-Wohl. 2015. "Measuring Job-Finding Rates and Matching Efficiency with Heterogeneous Jobseekers" NBER Working Paper no. 20939, Cambridge, MA.
Krueger, Alan B., Judd Cramer, and David Cho. 2014. "Are the Long-Term Unemployed on the Margins of the Labor Market?" *Brookings Papers on Economic Activity*, Spring. http://www.brookings.edu/about/projects/bpea/papers/2014/are-longterm-unemployed-margins-labor-market.

Discussion

Regis Barnichon began by responding to several points raised by the discussants, Richard Rogerson and Robert Hall. He agreed with Rogerson's suggestion of developing a structural model to further interpret the trends in the data. The structural model would be useful for determining whether or not the decline in labor participation rates was driven by poor labor market opportunities. He did not believe this to be the case because real wages increased for every single group over the same period as the decline in labor participation.

Barnichon next addressed the comments about the timing of the trends. Both discussants raised the issue that participation and unemployment were almost perfectly negatively correlated over the past three decades. The negative correlation seems at odd with the paper's argument of a single driving force that simultaneously explains decreasing trends in both unemployment and participation. Barnichon acknowledged that the levels of the participation and unemployment rates trended in opposite directions. However, he argued that it is important to look at the flows instead, because the stocks were overwhelmed by the trend toward women joining the labor force prior to 1990.

Barnichon agreed that the authors' employment flow decomposition was an accounting one. It therefore does not take a stance on whether the change in desire-to-work was an exogenous factor, which then caused the trends in participation and unemployment rates, or if it was a response to an alternative driving force.

Barnichon next addressed the comments to expand the number of states of employment status beyond their current eight-state structure. He noted that this is easy to do with their current framework. This will allow the model to capture more subtle differences between "want a job" and "not want a job," which Robert Hall had argued was important for understanding the factors driving trends in employment. Barnichon also acknowledged that the paper's transition matrix for employment dynamics is based on average transition probabilities, rather than the marginal transition probabilities. He saw the paper as a first step toward understanding the importance of changes in the desire to work for driving the trends in employment and unemployment.

Jonathan Parker made a related comment about the assumptions behind the Markov transition matrices. He stated that it is not possible to identify duration dependence from unobserved heterogeneity except by making assumptions about structures of the observed and unobserved heterogeneity. Therefore, while he was sympathetic toward the discussants' push toward using more observables to discipline the transition matrices, he believed that having more states in the transition matrix is just a different way of cutting the data under specific assumptions.

Robert Gordon spoke next, reciting a number of facts. He noted that the labor force participation rate was 66% in 2000. The rate then declined to 60% at the business-cycle peak in 2007, and is now at around 62.8%. Gordon asked whether the paper provides an explanation for the decline in participation rate since 2007. He referred to Robert Hall's work on labor markets, which found that two-thirds of the decline in labor market participation over this period is unexplained.

Regis Barnichon responded by stating that the paper focuses on the trends from around the mid-1990s to 2007, and therefore cannot say anything about the post-2007 period. For the pre-2007 period, the paper's stylized result is that participation declined by 2 percentage points because of welfare reforms and other events in the mid-1990s. Without these reforms, the participation rate would have been higher than it currently is.

Martin Eichenbaum spoke next, noting that there is a significant difference in the labor force participation rate between Canada and the United States. He asked whether there is analogous data in Canada that could shed further light on the paper's hypothesis that declines in desire to work drove the trends in unemployment and participation rates.

Regis Barnichon acknowledged that looking at Canada and comparing it to the United States would be a useful way of examining these trends. He also noted that the European countries provide another striking contrast to the United States. In these countries, the participation rate has been increasing since 2000.

Chris Sims spoke next, in defense of the paper. He argued that the paper's main hypothesis about the decline in desire to work, which came about due to welfare reforms, was a significant change that he would expect to apply to a large number of individuals, not just those at the margin. Therefore, Sims believed that it is still worth considering the hypothesis, even though the analysis in the paper measures transitions based on the average individual rather than at the margin. Sims did not think that the discussants' criticism of the general approach and advocacy of much richer models necessarily subtracted from the main hypothesis of the paper.

Robert Hall, however, argued that the total amount of welfare paid to individuals after the welfare reform may not have significantly changed if the people previously receiving the welfare payments switched to receiving a combination of SSI and food stamps instead.

In response to Robert Hall's comment, Martin Eichenbaum pointed out that even if the welfare reform was dollar neutral, the reforms may still have had an effect on the labor market. The reason is that different types of welfare create different incentives to work. He gave the example of welfare that requires the unemployed person to be actively looking for work in the market. This can create very different behavior, over long horizons, than the behavior that arises from collecting SSI and food stamps.

Ricardo Reis spoke next, asking about the effects of the young on the participation rate. He thought that at the margin, the decline in the desire to work of the young could have an effect on the participation rate that is as large as the effect of the baby boomers retiring. Reis asked if these 20- to 35-year-olds collected disability insurance and about the extent to which welfare affected their desire to work.

Robert Hall followed up on Ricardo Reis' comment about young workers. He expected that welfare reforms may have an impact on the desire to work of the young. The reason for this is that the SSDI provides benefits to families with disabled children. The standards for judging disabilities of a child are much more relaxed than the standards for adults. As a result, families can lose disability insurance once the child becomes 18. Thus, welfare reforms may have an effect on those 16- to 25-year-olds who were on disability insurance as children.

Regis Barnichon replied that it is not clear how the welfare reforms affected the young, and the paper does not say anything about the employment of 16–24-year-olds. Most of the data focuses on prime-age workers. He suspected that the teens may have been less likely to look for work in the second half of the 1990s following huge wage gains for households overall.

Christopher Foote spoke next, asking if there are any relevant questions that the BLS should incorporate into the CPS to help separate out the effects of preference versus disabilities on the participation rate. He gave the example of asking people who are out of the labor force when their last pay occurred, as well as their last occupation.

Regis Barnichon concluded by stating that we need to think more about how we want to define and measure the unemployment rate.